MASS MEDIA
EFFECTS RESEARCH

LEA'S COMMUNICATION SERIES

Jennings Bryant/Dolf Zillmann, General Editors

Selected titles in Communication Theory and Methodology subseries (Jennings Bryant, series advisor) include:

Berger • Planning Strategic Interaction: Attaining Goals Through Communicative Action

Dennis/Wartella • American Communication Research: The Remembered History

Greene • Message Production: Advances in Communication Theory

Harris • A Cognitive Psychology of Mass Communication, Fourth Edition

Hayes • Statistical Methods for Communication Science

Heath/Bryant • Human Communication Theory and Research: Concepts, Contexts, and Challenges, Second Edition

Riffe/Lacy/Fico • Analyzing Media Messages: Using Quantitative Content Analysis in Research, Second Edition

Salwen/Stacks • An Integrated Approach to Communication Theory and Research

Vorderer/Bryant • Playing Video Games: Motives, Responses, and Consequences

For a complete list of titles in LEA's Communication Series, please contact Lawrence Erlbaum Associates, Publishers, at www.erlbaum.com.

MASS MEDIA EFFECTS RESEARCH

Advances Through Meta-Analysis

Edited by

**Raymond W. Preiss
Barbara Mae Gayle
Nancy Burrell
Mike Allen
Jennings Bryant**

LEA LAWRENCE ERLBAUM ASSOCIATES, PUBLISHERS
2007 Mahwah, New Jersey   London

Senior Acquisitions Editor: Linda Bathgate
Assistant Editor: Karin Wittig Bates
Cover Design: Kathryn Houghtaling Lacey
Full-Service Compositor: MidAtlantic Books & Journals, Inc.

This book was typeset in 10/12 pt. Times.
The heads were typeset in Americana, Americana Bold, and Americana Italic.

Lawrence Erlbaum Associates, Inc., Publishers
10 Industrial Avenue
Mahwah, New Jersey 07430
www.erlbaum.com

Library of Congress Cataloging-in-Publication Data

Mass media effects research : advances through meta-analysis /
edited by Raymond W. Preiss . . . [et al.].
    p. cm.
    Includes bibliographical references and index.
    ISBN 0-8058-4998-X (cloth : alk. paper) —
    ISBN 0-8058-4999-8 (pbk. : alk. paper)
    1. Mass media—Social aspects. 2. Mass media—
Psychological aspects. 3. Mass media—Political
aspects. 4. Meta-analysis. I. Preiss, Raymond W.
    HM1206.M374 2006 2007
    302.23—dc22
                               2006019024

Contents

Preface   **ix**

1   Traditions of Mass Media Theory and Research   **1**
Jennings Bryant and R. Glenn Cummins

2   Media, Messages, and Meta-Analysis   **15**
Mike Allen and Raymond W. Preiss

3   Wherefore Art Thou Mass Media Theory?   **31**
Mike Allen and Mary K. Casey

4   Effects of Agenda Setting   **37**
Wayne Wanta and Salma Ghanem

5   Media Priming: A Meta-Analysis   **53**
*David R. Roskos-Ewoldsen, Mark R. Klinger,
and Beverly Roskos-Ewoldsen*

6   The Third-Person Effect: A Meta-Analysis of the
Perceptual Hypothesis   **81**
Bryant Paul, Michael B. Salwen, and Michel Dupagne

7   The Selective Exposure Hypothesis and Media
Choice Processes   **103**
Dave D'Alessio and Mike Allen

8   Meta-Analysis of Television's Impact on
     Special Populations   119
     Robert Abelman, Carolyn A. Lin, and David J. Atkin

9   "And Miles to Go. . . .": Reflections on the Past
     and Future of Mass Media Effects Research   137
     Robin I. Nabi

10   Effects of Media Violence on Viewers' Aggression
     in Unconstrained Social Interaction   145
     P. Niels Christensen and Wendy Wood

11   The Effects of Advertising on Children and Adolescents:
     A Meta-Analysis   169
     Roger Desmond and Rod Carveth

12   Effects of Sexually Explicit Media   181
     *Norbert Mundorf, Mike Allen, David D'Alessio,
     and Tara Emmers-Sommer*

13   Effects of Gender Stereotyping on Socialization   199
     Patricia Oppliger

14   Enjoyment of Mediated Horror and Violence:
     A Meta-Analysis   215
     Cynthia A. Hoffner and Kenneth J. Levine

15   Violent Video Games and Aggression:
     Why Can't We Find Effects?   245
     John L. Sherry

16   Effects of Music   263
     *Mike Allen, Jennifer Herrett-Skjellum, Jill Jorgenson,
     Michael R. Kramer, Daniel J. Ryan, and
     Lindsay Timmerman*

17   Positive Effects of Television on Children's Social
     Interaction: A Meta-Analysis   281
     Marie-Louise Mares and Emory H. Woodard

18   Parasocial Relationships and Television:
     A Meta-Analysis of the Effects   301
     Edward Schiappa, Mike Allen, and Peter B. Gregg

19   Many Faces of Media Effects   315
Tae-Seop Lim and Sang Yeon Kim

20   Meta-Analyses of Mediated Health Campaigns   327
Leslie B. Snyder

21   An Analysis of Media Health Campaigns for
Children and Adolescents: Do They Work?   345
*Lisa Mullikin Parcell, Jae Kwon, Dorina Miron,
and Jennings Bryant*

22   The Impact of Earvin "Magic" Johnson's
HIV-Positive Announcement   363
*Mary K. Casey, Mike Allen, Tara Emmers-Sommer,
Erin Sahlstein, Dan DeGooyer, Alaina M. Winters,
Amy Elisabeth Wagner, and Tim Dun*

23   Media Use and Political Involvement   377
Barry A. Hollander

24   Mass Media and Voter Turnout   391
Dorina Miron and Jennings Bryant

25   The Spiral of Silence: A Meta-Analysis and Its Impact   415
James Shanahan, Carroll Glynn, and Andrew Hayes

26   On the Role of Newspaper Ownership on Bias in
Presidential Campaign Coverage by Newspapers   429
Dave D'Alessio and Mike Allen

27   What's in a Meta-Analysis   455
Michael Pfau

28   Meta-Analysis: Demonstrating the Power
of Mass Communication   467
Elisabeth Perse

29   The Challenge of Media Effects for Teaching and Policy   489
Mike Allen, Raymond G. Preiss, and Nancy Burrell

Author Index   505
Subject Index   525
Author Biographies   527

Preface

Raymond W. Preiss

The nature and outcomes of mediated messages have been the subject of considerable controversy in recent years. Most scholars agree that mass media research is rapidly evolving, and efforts to refine and interpret media theories and processes require both historical and empirical benchmarks. Empirical benchmarks are key topics in upcoming chapters of this book. These issues are summarized by each chapter contributor and by knowledgeable reviewers in the final section of the volume. Of course, the empirical record is actually one type of historical benchmark. The accumulation and progression of research findings provide standards for determining the success of the scientific enterprise over time. In the subsequent chapters, contributors offer meta-analysis as one way to review the empirical historical record and make informed judgments about theoretical progress.

Another way to assess benchmarks involves historical context. Using this standard, the advances in mass media theories and processes have been dramatic. In a manuscript published after his death, Wilbur Schramm Rogers (1997) wrote plainly and forcefully about the "forefathers of the forefathers" who worked in the 1920s and 1930s to establish the foundations of an academic discipline later to be called "communication studies." He traced the intersections of journalism, political science, sociology, and psychology during periods of economic turbulence, war, and technological change. Schramm articulated a vision for a new academic discipline of communication. He also developed a lexicon and supporting models for the new field. His theorizing embraced research on mass media (print, audio, and film), persuasion, propaganda, cognition, and social influence. Schramm believed that understanding human communication was a unifying, not a polarizing, enterprise. He wrote,

> The truth is that there is no frontier. There is only communication research. All parts of it are related to all other parts, and the landscape is marked off only by the fact that some scholars are centrally interested in one part, some in another. (Schramm, 1963, p. 5)

Schramm's essays are optimistic and suggest (perhaps unrealistically) that vital questions will soon be answered and new, more important areas of inquiry will be revealed. He was unabashedly interdisciplinary, exhorting colleagues to "learn to count" (Schramm, 1958, 1963) and extolling the insights to be found in "the broad domain of communication research" (Schramm, 1963, p. 5).

This was the first reference we have been able to find asserting the existence of a "domain" of communication research. Schramm was "certainly interested" in mediated messages, although he was ever cognizant of the interpersonal, group, and cultural contexts framing message production and message interpretation. Studying the forty-seven citations in his 1963 *The challenge to communication research*, the "domain" seems rather thin. But in the fifty years since its publication, this situation has been dramatically reversed. Many scholars were trained to "count" and the rise of quantitative approaches to mass media research has produced a vibrant and rapidly growing body of findings.

As Schramm envisioned, the field has remained interdisciplinary. Political scientists, media psychologists, sociologists, and members of the discipline of communication studies have devoted their shared interests to mediated messages. Lang, Bradley, Chung and Lee (2003) reached this conclusion by tracing the rise of empirical approaches to media processes. Examining five journals specializing in communication issues, they found ten years of consistent productivity in the domain of mediated message processing research. Over 1,200 empirical studies were found to deal with mediated communication and twenty-five percent (308) of those studies addressed the psychological processing of mediated messages. Although Lang et al. (2003) notice some interest in forming a discipline of media psychology, we suspect that Schramm's interdisciplinary vision will prevail. The centrality of the media in our lives will attract scholars from many fields. The domain of findings will continue to proliferate and findings will continue to accumulate.

INTERPRETING THE DOMAIN OF FINDINGS ON MASS MEDIA THEORIES AND PROCESSES

When considering a large and evolving body of empirical findings, reviewers will organize their review around an assumption, theory, or question and explain the available evidence for a specific conclusion. This approach is termed a narrative review, and it involves a verbal description of a body of literature (Pillemer, 1984). In most instances, the narrative reviewer will locate one or more example studies or "classic" experiments that illustrate the question of interest. The researcher often describes these prototype studies as evidence for a conclusion about the larger domain of research. In essence, the narrative reviewer will explicate a basic assumption or question and classify existing research using a vote counting system (Do the studies in the domain of research detect a significant effect? Is the significant effect in the predicted direction? Is the significant effect plausibly attributable to one theory or perspective?). Readers of the narrative review are asked to tally the "votes" (confirming or non-confirming tests) and render a judgment regarding the question of interest.

Interesting and complex questions about mass media theories and processes will rarely produce a clear-cut vote count. Studies may vary in terms of variable selection, sample population, experimental design, or availability (published versus unpublished research). The narrative reviewer is placed in the position of explaining why certain votes should "count" more or less than other votes. As a result, the outcome of a narrative review may range from "strong support" (a uniform, confirming vote count of "quality" studies) for some proposition to "no support" (the failure to detect any confirming votes of "weak" studies). Of course, if 60% or 70% of the votes confirm a proposition, the narrative reviewer may question the generalizability of a relationship or introduce a new variable that explains the non-confirming outcomes. If 30% or 40% of the votes are confirming, the reviewer may disclaim the relationship, express concerns about the larger domain of findings, and call for additional research.

A related difficulty with many narrative reviews involves the probabilistic nature of empirical tests. It is a tautology that the findings of any one study may be the result of sampling error, and narrative reviewers usually do not consider the possibility of Type I (false positive) or Type II (false negative) error as factors influencing trends in the primary research. This means that false positive and false negative outcomes will distort vote counts and prompt reviewers to introduce intervening variables that explain apparent inconsistencies in the experimental record. In instances where sampling error produces discrepancies, the narrative reviewer may assess sample characteristics, research designs, or statistical methods as the source of contradictory findings. If the disagreeing findings come from studies that meet standards for rigor, the narrative reviewer may introduce "confounding variables" as the explanation for unexpected outcomes. This produces a web of issues, theoretical and methodological, that tend to deflect attention away from hypothesized relationships.

We believe that expert narrative reviews are essential components of the scientific enterprise. Informed experts provide a venue for theoretical interpretation, reformulation, and innovation. If the goal is to assess evidence, however, this approach may gain subjective insights by ignoring features of the existing domain of findings. While making the case for an innovative interpretation or conclusion, the reviewer elevates certain studies as exemplars of evidence for a conclusion. The difficulty here is that narrative reviews usually do not report the explicit rules or methods used to locate primary evidence, and the reader may not be aware of other findings that cut against the reviewer's position. The reader is asked to consider the exemplar studies in the context of a theoretical narrative or story that explains what the findings mean, but she or he is often not told why non-confirming exemplars were excluded from the review.

The narrative review offers an important venue for experts to advance their informed conclusions about a domain of literature. This risk is that while making the case for one interpretation, the ballot box for the vote count can be "stuffed" with non-representative example studies. When non-conforming studies are mentioned, new variables may be introduced to explain discrepancies. The intervening variables may have been studied in only a limited number of investigations, and applying them to an entire domain runs the risk of overgeneralization. For these reasons, it is difficult for the vote counting method used by narrative reviews to present a balanced portrayal of a large domain of literature.

THE LOGIC GUIDING THE ORGANIZATION OF THIS VOLUME

Mass media effects research: Advances through meta-analysis represents an effort to expand and consolidate the empirical findings of nearly seventy-five years of empirical media research. In that short time, the notation of "media" has moved from newspapers to telegraphs, from radios to film, and from television to the internet. Media consumers now select from a withering array of choices as they encounter and consider mediated messages. In this volume, we summarize some of those selections and focus on the regularities associated with living in a media-rich society.

While selecting and arranging chapters in this volume, we were mindful of technological changes and of increased sophistication of those using the mediated messages. We sought issues that addressed these changes and selected chapters that attempted to establish significant generalizations about mediated communication. It became clear that meta-analytic methods were gaining acceptance in the mass media literature. We also sought out issues that were fundamental to discussions under way in communication journals and that reflected current (and enduring) controversies. There was no shortage of potential candidates.

We present the issues using five general themes. In the opening sections, we set the stage for the independent meta-analyses reported in later sections. In these sections, one chapter summarizes the traditions of media research and a second chapter makes the case for using meta-analysis to address meaningful issues in the mass communication literature. Next, we present an overview of evidence associated with mass media theories and six meta-analyses reflecting this theme. Contributors discuss media priming, agenda setting, special populations, the third-person effect, and selective exposure. In the third theme, research emphasizing mass media outcomes is considered. In this section, we provide an overview and contributors present meta-analytic summaries on mediated violence, advertising, gender stereotyping, parasocial relationships, mediated horror, sexually explicit media, video gaming, music, and television's effects on children. The fourth section is devoted to mediated campaigns. Meta-analyses in this section address political involvement, voter turnout, perceived media fairness, health communication campaigns, children's health campaigns, HIV campaigns and the spiral of silence. In the fifth section, reviewers assess the contributions (and limitations) of meta-analytic summaries in summarizing and advancing the media theory and processes.

The editors of this volume believe that meta-analysis has the potential to simultaneously synthesize and advance understanding of a domain of empirical findings. The conclusions reached by the contributors to this volume provide direct attention to three vital tasks. First, researchers may opt to replicate controversial average effects in by devising new primary investigations. The results of these studies may be integrated into later, more sophisticated meta-analyses. A second task is for scholars to empirically summarize the variables that are conceptually aligned with the findings presented in this (and other) volume. The goal here is to establish sets of interlocking generalizations that provide breadth of understanding about mediated communication. Finally, readers are invited to replicate and refine the summaries. Meta-analysis is an inherently public enterprise, and the chapters in this book explicitly state search procedures, study inclusion standards, coding rules, and aggregation formulas. Any informed reader of any theoretical or ideological persuasion is welcome to sort through the primary literature and add, recode, reformulate, or reinterpret it. When readers accept the invitations to replicate, interlock, and extend empirical summaries, we believe mass media research and processes will achieve "advances through meta-analysis."

REFERENCES

Lang, A., Bradley, S. D., Chung, Y., & Lee, S. (2003). Where the mind meets the message: Reflections on ten years of measuring psychological responses to media. *Journal of Broadcasting & Electronic Media, 47*, 650–655.

Pillemer, D. (1984). Conceptual issues in research synthesis. *Journal of Special Education, 18*, 27–40.

Rogers, E. M. (1994). *A history of communication study: A bibliographical approach*. New York, NY: The Free Press.

Schramm, W. (1958, 1963). The challenge to communication research. In R. O. Nafziger and D. M. White (Eds.), *Introduction to mass communication research* (pp. 3–31). Baton Rouge, LA: Louisiana State University Press.

Schramm, W. (1963). Communication research in the United States. In W. Schramm (Ed.), *The science of human communication* (pp. 1–16). New York, NY: Basic Books.

Schramm, W. (1997). *The beginnings of communication Studies in America: A personal memoir*. Thousand Oaks, CA: Sage.

MASS MEDIA
EFFECTS RESEARCH

1

Traditions of Mass Media Theory and Research

Jennings Bryant
University of Alabama

R. Glenn Cummins
Kennesaw State University

In examining the use of research methods in mass communication, Lowry (1979) lamented, "For the most part, communication researchers have neglected to conduct systematic studies of their own output" (p. 262). Whether this claim was valid at the time it was published is uncertain, but what is certain is that such a condemnation simply is not true for contemporary communication research. A search through the volumes of the most popular communication journals from recent decades reveals that communication scholars have become quite mindful of where the discipline has been and where it is going. Moreover, attempts to take stock of the state of communication research have been particularly popular in recent years, a trend that may well be an artifact of the hype surrounding the turn of the century and the dawn of a new millennium. Nonetheless, such examinations are useful in understanding the big picture of communication research—past, present, and future.

TRADITIONS OF MASS
COMMUNICATION THEORY

Discerning the dominant, most popular, or most fully developed bodies of theory within mass communication research is a challenge, and any enumeration of these trends is likely to exclude what some would consider significant milestones in the discipline. Moreover, many mass communication "theories" are not true theories in the strictest meaning of the work but rather are a relatively coherent body of research guided by repeated theme and a general framework of ideas and research methods. For example, research into the effects of exposure to media sex or violence frequently is cited as a significant research tradition in our discipline. However, these domains of research subsume numerous research perspectives and theoretical mechanisms, many of which could easily stand as distinct theoretical perspectives.

Still, a review of the scholarly literature within the discipline does reveal a single preeminent theoretical trend that must be addressed first—the absence of theory from the vast majority of our scholarly literature. Numerous content analyses involving various leading communication journals paint a somewhat bleak picture about the use of theory in mass communication research, because they reveal that a mere 27% to 39% of articles within the most widely read communication journals have contained any sort of reference to a specific theory or theoretical orientation (Bryant & Miron, 2004; Cooper, Potter, & Dupagne, 1994; Kamahawi & Weaver, 2003; Riffe & Frietag, 1998). Thus, the dominant theoretical trend in mass communication research is the absence of theory. This absence will be addressed again in the conclusion of this chapter as we explore the future of mass communication theory and research, because a number of trends do give cause for celebration about theory development and testing in mass communication research, and our previous normative disregard for theory needs to be placed in its current context.

Despite this conspicuous absence of theory from communication literature, scholars have identified a number of theoretical perspectives that have dominated the discipline over the last half-century. In trying to identify the dominant trends in mass communication theory, we have the benefit of a number of perspectives, some looking forward and some looking back, to light our path. One of the earliest macroanalytic perspectives on the body of communication research was conducted at the end of a seminal stage of communication research by one of the founding fathers of the field, Wilbur Schramm (1957). Schramm's examination of 20 years of communication research concluded by posing a number of questions about the future of communication study, including the effects of media violence, the functions of the media, their usefulness as a teaching tool, the potential of distance education, and the like. Fortunately, Berelson's (1959) prediction that communication research was "withering away" (p. 1) proved to be false prophecy, and Schramm's approach of raising many fascinating questions became a striking predictor of some of the dominant traditions of mass communication research over the next half-century.

Decades later, at the dawn of the new millennium, a number of other scholars took stock of the most important contributions to mass communication research. DeFleur's (1998) examination of the "milestones" (p. 85) in communication research not only reviewed the brief intellectual history of communication scholarship, but it also provided a provocative condemnation of contemporary communication scholars' failure to contribute any new ideas to the discipline. In his essay, DeFleur cited seven broad theoretical perspectives within mass communication research, including the early "magic bullet" hypothesis, which gave way to more complex selective influence theories. He then cited uses and gratifications research, modeling theories, the adoption of innovations, agenda setting, and research into the effects of television on aggression as the remainder of the milestones in communication research.

Similarly, Rubin and Haridakis (2001) identified what they considered to be the dominant theoretical perspectives at the turn of the century. Although some common ground exists between their perspectives and those of DeFleur (1998), the essayists disagree on a number of significant contributions to communication theory. Like DeFleur, Rubin and Haridakis cited agenda setting, the diffusion of innovations, social cognition, and uses and gratifications research. However, the latter authors also included theoretical perspectives such as cultivation research, critical and cultural studies, and gap hypotheses, as well as relative newcomers such as framing and third-person effects. In addition, Rubin and Haridakis also listed a number of lines of research that are either without a cohesive theoretical perspective or stretch beyond the purview of any single perspective. These dominant lines of research included media portrayals, media constructions, health issues, new technologies, cultural maintenance and change, children and the media, and political communication.

Thus, all three of these reviews aid in identifying the dominant theoretical perspectives in communication research. However, what they lack is any sense of the popularity of these various theoretical perspectives. Although the authors offered numerous citations as evidence of popularity, they shed little light on the relative frequency with which these perspectives were cited or on the waxing or waning of their prominence in mass communication research over time. In one of the most recent examinations of theory and research in mass communication, Bryant and Miron (2004) sought to fill this gap. They conducted an empirical investigation into the use of theory in mass communication literature, in which they not only explored which theories were cited most often but also examined how they were used within the literature and traced the frequency with which they were used across the decades.

Bryant and Miron (2004) conducted a content analysis of articles appearing in three leading communication journals—*Journalism and Mass Communication Quarterly, Journal of Communication*, and *Journal of Broadcasting and Electronic*

Media—that have published mass communication research over a 45-year period. The authors randomly selected one issue per year for coding, and all articles within the issue selected were analyzed, resulting in a total of 1,806 articles coded for analysis. The authors stated three explicit goals: "(1) to identify theories (including models), broad paradigms of scientific investigation and theorizing, and schools of thought that created such paradigms; (2) to locate them in the scientific fields and subfields (areas) that generated them; and (3) to determine what the cited theories were used for in the studies in which we found them" (p. 664).

As previously stated, one of the most alarming findings of a number of content analyses of communication journals is the absence of theory from a majority of articles appearing in these leading communication journals. Bryant and Miron's (2004) findings further validated these findings, as only roughly 32% of the articles they coded included some form of theory. Moreover, this figure could potentially be a mild overestimate of the presence of theory in communication research, given that the random sampling procedure Bryant and Miron utilized resulted in the inclusion of the "Ferment in the Field" issue of *Journal of Communication*.

The big picture for the presence of theory in communication research does not improve when one factors in the data on how these theories were used. Almost half of the articles that contained some theory merely referenced the theory (48.03%), and an additional 26.13% of the articles containing theory used it as a theoretical framework for a study. Other uses included comparison of theories (7.9%) and critiquing a theory (4.31%). Unfortunately, the authors noted that the core elements of theory construction such as proposing a theory (3.16%), testing a new theory (2.58%), integrating theories (2.01%), and expanding a theory (1.87%) were relatively rare. Again, bear in mind that these figures are based only on the articles that contained theory not on the total sample of articles coded in the study. Thus, to some extent these data support the indictment of communication research as being largely atheoretical.

Bryant and Miron's (2004) content analysis also shed light on the dominant trends in mass communication theory. One variable coded was the origin of the various theories cited within communication literature. Although the majority of the theories cited (59.22%) originated from within the communication discipline, the results give partial support to the popular notion of the multidisciplinary nature of communication research (e.g., Rogers, 1994). The content analysis revealed that a number of other disciplines have also contributed theories to mass communication research, including psychology (12.42%), sociology (5.24%), political science (4.74%), and economics (3.30%). Although these figures may belie the oftentimes indirect influence that other social sciences have on communication theory, they nonetheless indicate that communication scholars have made great strides in solidifying communication study as a legitimate and unique domain of scholarly inquiry.

Most beneficial to the present discussion are Bryant and Miron's (2004) findings on the frequency with which scholars have utilized various theories or theoretical perspectives, as well as the distribution of these references over the years. First, it should be noted that not counting references to broad epistemological foundations or general schools of thought, an astonishing 600 theories were cited in their sample. However, only a small fraction of those theories were cited in 10 or more of the articles coded, suggesting that most mass communication theories have a short half-life and a very small loyal following. Based on these normative data, the authors composed a Top 26 list of theories in communication research. Their list reveals that only a handful of these theories—uses and gratifications ($n = 61$; e.g., Katz, Blumler, & Gurevitch, 1974), agenda setting ($n = 61$; e.g., McCombs & Shaw, 1972), and cultivation ($n = 56$; e.g., Gerbner, 1969; Gerbner & Gross, 1976; Gerbner, Gross, Morgan, & Signorielli, 1980)—have truly dominated the mass communication research tradition, and they, the "big 3," were cited almost twice as often as other commonly utilized theories. Other popular theories included Bandura's social learning theory ($n = 34$; e.g., Bandura, 1973), Marxism ($n = 34$; e.g., Marx, 1867; Marx & Engels, 1848), diffusion of innovations ($n = 24$; e.g., Rogers, 1962), and McLuhan's sense-extension theory ($n = 23$; e.g., McLuhan, 1964). To some extent, these findings validate DeFleur's (1998) and Rubin and Haridakis' (2001) enumeration of the dominant trends in mass communication theory and research, as all the theories or thema cited by those authors appeared in Byrant and Miron's list of Top 26 Theories.

TRADITIONS OF MASS COMMUNICATION RESEARCH METHODOLOGIES

Lowry's (1979) critique that communication scholars do not "conduct systematic studies of their own output" (p. 262) also no longer holds true for the research techniques utilized in mass communication research. Examples of scholarly publications examining the varied research techniques and methods used can be found throughout the past five decades of mass communication literature. Moreover, these studies paint a remarkably clear and consistent picture of the dominant trends in research methodology in our discipline, especially on the dominance of quantitative research in mass communication throughout the latter half of the 20th century.

Quantitative Versus Qualitative Methods

A number of scholars have made claims about the increased popularity of qualitative research methods in recent years (e.g., Lindloff, 1991; Pauly, 1991). However, a review of investigations that have systematically examined the use of qualitative versus quantitative methods contests this observation. Again, Schramm (1957) provided one of the earliest examinations of research trends in communication. Of interest to the present discussion was his content analysis of 20 years of *Journalism Quarterly* (now *Journalism & Mass Communication Quarterly*), which charted the rise in the proportion of research articles utilizing quantitative methods from 10% in 1937 to 48% to 1956. In addition to this shift toward quantitative methods, Schramm noted a number of other research trends, including the study of communication process and structures and the study of international communication.

Perloff (1976) renewed this examination of *Journalism Quarterly* by content analyzing and comparing two eras of the journal, 1955 to 1964 and 1965 to 1974. The findings illustrated the fact that Schramm's (1957) predictions on qualitative versus quantitative research were indeed accurate. The proportion of articles using quantitative methods increased from 51% in the first period to 60% in the second period. Perloff's analysis likewise indicated an increase in the proportion of articles that used statistical tests of significance.

Wimmer and Haynes (1978) expanded the scope of this line of self-examination by turning their attention to a different scholarly journal, the *Journal of Broadcasting* (now *Journal of Broadcasting & Electronic Media*). Noting the observed increase in the use of quantitative methods in other journals, the authors content analyzed research in *Journal of Broadcasting* from 1970 to 1976. Much like the aforementioned studies, the analysis showed that quantitative methods were used in 50% of the articles in this period.

Utilizing a more-or-less identical method and coding scheme, Moffett and Dominick (1987) extended the analysis of *Journal of Broadcasting* through 1985. Not only did quantitative methods continue to dominate, the authors found a significant increase in the proportion of articles utilizing quantitative methods to 68% in the 1977 to 1985 sample period.

More recent investigations have noted one of the chief limitations of previous research examining the prevalence of quantitative and qualitative research, namely the difficulty in generalizing the results of those content analyses beyond the sole journals examined. Cooper et al. (1994) examined the research methods used in eight major communication journals from 1965 to 1989. The inclusion of multiple journals in their sample yielded findings that were remarkably similar to those of the single-journal studies; however; 57.8% of the articles Cooper et al. coded utilized quantitative methods. Moreover, the data corroborated previous analyses by indicating an increase in the use of quantitative methods from the beginning of the sample period (42.6% in 1965) to the end (64.1% in 1989).

Kamahawi and Weaver (2003) conducted one of the most recent examinations of the use of quantitative methods, and, like Cooper et al. (1994), they examined a number of scholarly journals. Their sample included the 10 communication journals with the largest circulation from 1980 to 1999. Their data indicated that the increased use of quantitative methods continues (to 70% of the articles coded by the end of the 20th century).

Despite this evidence suggesting the dominance of quantitative methods in mass communication research in the latter half of the 20th century, a number of caveats must be offered. First, most of the aforementioned analyses have acknowledged that the sample selected has the potential to skew the findings. For example, it is possible that the journals analyzed have an editorial scope that lends itself to quantitative methods. As such, scholars conducting qualitative research are likely to find alternative outlets for their work. Indeed, in his early analysis Schramm (1957) noted that communication historians, industry experts, and "insiders" might shun the relatively brief research article and prefer books, with their obvious potential for greater space. Thus, analysis of other journals more qualitative in scope and/or scholarly books in mass communication would probably lead to different results.

In addition, Kamahawi and Weaver (2003) observed that qualitative research reports are generally longer than quantitative reports, and therefore journals would be able to fit more articles using quantitative methods in their pages. This could obviously result in a bias against qualitative research in terms of the sheer number of such articles that could be published annually. Finally, it must be noted (with a touch of irony) that all the analyses discussed utilized quantitative methods and tests of statistical significance to come to their various findings. Although claims regarding the increased popularity of qualitative methods are not supported by an examination of the literature published in the top communication journals, these claims are not without merit. Numerous scholars (e.g., Bryant, 1993; Weaver, 1993) have recognized the potential for a deeper understanding of the communication process through the use of qualitative research methods, and they have called for scholars to utilize multiple methods to address increasingly complex communication theories and models.

Research Methods and Designs

A number of scholars have also examined mass communication journal articles to discern existing trends for the specific research methodologies favored by communication scholars. Again, these findings are remarkably homogeneous, and they suggest that mass communication scholars have become increasingly adroit at utilizing tests of statistical significance to support their hypotheses. Perloff's (1976) content analysis of 20 years of *Journalism Quarterly* showed that among the statistical tests utilized, chi-square tests were used most frequently. The second most popular tests relied upon correlation coefficients, followed by analysis of variance (ANOVA) with their attendant F tests.

Wimmer and Haynes (1978) found similar results in their analysis of the *Journal of Broadcasting* from 1970 to 1976. The authors stated that simple frequencies were the most commonly used form of quantitative analysis, with chi-square test, t tests, and various ANOVA tests also being found in at least 10% of the articles utilizing quantitative methods. In addition, the authors also examined the most popular research approaches as reflected in the pages of *Journal of Broadcasting*. They found that survey research was most popular among mass communication scholars (44.5% of articles using quantitative methods). This was followed by laboratory experiments, content analyses, and the far less frequently employed methods of field studies, interviews, or data-reanalysis.

Moffett and Dominick's (1987) extension of the analysis of *Journal of Broadcasting* showed highly similar results. The tests of statistical significance most frequently employed remained relatively stable. The authors stated that the most notable change was the increase in the use of statistics for economic analyses, such as the Gort coefficient or the Herfindahl-Hirschmann Index. The method of research design also remained stable, with surveys (38% of articles using quantitative methods), content analyses (21%), and experiments (17%) being the most popular research techniques. However, the proportion of articles using secondary analyses of existing data rose dramatically from Wimmer and Haynes' (1978) prior analysis (2% in 1970–1976 to 17% in 1977–1985). The authors attributed this increase to the availability of ratings and other industry data from research firms such as Nielsen Media Research, the now-defunct Arbitron ratings service, and the Federal Communications Commission.

Cooper et al.'s (1994) analysis of eight top communication journals likewise showed that surveys, content analyses, and experiments were the most frequently used research techniques in articles utilizing quantitative methods.

One interesting footnote to this discussion arises from Wimmer and Haynes' (1978) examination of the types of statistical analysis found in the *Journal of Broadcasting*. In addition to coding for the types of tests most frequently used, the authors also considered how well these tests were being conducted and reported. Unfortunately, the authors concluded, "it would appear that literally no study reported in the *Journal of Broadcasting* provided an adequate summary of procedures used or results of the analysis" (p. 247). It remains for other scholars to determine whether that state of affairs has improved.

Media

To say that the mass media landscape has changed since scholars began investigating the media would be an understatement. This dramatic metamorphosis is likewise reflected in the mass communication literature. Schramm's (1957) review of 20 years of journalism research did not even mention electronic media and focused exclusively on print media, such as newspapers and magazines.

Perloff (1976) sought to gauge which media were investigated most frequently in his 20-year analysis of *Journalism Quarterly*. This author found that the majority of articles coded in his analysis focused on print media (56.5%), whereas only 5.5% of the articles examined electronic media. Obviously, these data indicate that scholars were a bit tardy in shifting their focus to the electronic media, which had already become a fixture in society by the time these articles were published.

This early bias in the mass communication research literature toward print media contrasts markedly with the findings of Kamahawi and Weaver (2003).

Those authors found that the print media had lost their stronghold in communication literature, with broadcast media being examined in 42.2% of the literature from 1980 to 1999. Articles examining print media had slipped to 28.7%. Also of note was the increase in the proportion of articles examining the Internet (6.7% in the 1995–1999 time period, the final era coded in their analysis).

FUTURE TRENDS IN MASS COMMUNICATION THEORY AND RESEARCH

The preceding review paints a fairly clear and consistent picture on the dominant theoretical perspectives and research traditions in mass communication study. What then will communication research look like in the coming century? Although it may no longer be true that "communication researchers have neglected to conduct systematic studies of their own output" (Lowry, 1979, p. 262), it may be fair to say that communication scholars have largely failed to follow the advice laid out by countless scholars in our literature. If followed, many of these warnings and recommendations could help unify and advance our understanding of mass communication.

Developing "Communication" Theory

As mass communication research entered into the new millennium, some scholars called for more common ground among the various competing lines of research within our discipline. For example, Bryant (2004) and Bryant and Yang (2004) highlighted a number of these schisms within the discipline, including the conflict between applied and theoretical research, Eastern and Western philosophies of communication, and the competing views of communication as persuasion versus entertainment. Weaver (1993) noted the highly fragmented state of communication research and a conspicuous lack of general theories of communication that could be used by all within the discipline. Moreover, he argued that the most widely utilized theories within communication research originated within the various subfields of the discipline. Sadly, Weaver's comments are highly reminiscent of the state of communication research that Schramm (1957) observed decades earlier, in which communication scholars displayed a "growing anxiety to put the results together into something more general" (p. 106). How little has changed! Thus, despite the significant strides in communication research, much work remains to be done to unify the various lines of research within our discipline into something more universal.

One of the most pressing needs in communication research is the greater development, testing, and synthesis of communication theories. As previously noted, theory is conspicuously absent from a majority of our literature. For example,

Kamahawi and Weaver's (2003) content analysis of theory and research methods in major communication journals concluded with a call for more rigorous theoretical development and integration. In addition, Emmers-Sommer and Allen's (1999) meta-analysis of media effects research likewise called for a deeper understanding of the theoretical mechanisms that shape how media effects occur. A number of scholars (e.g., Riffe & Frietag, 1998; Shoemaker & Reese, 1990) have also called for a greater use of theory in the widely popular research method of content analysis.

Despite these numerous calls for greater theoretical development, the picture regarding the use of theory in communication research is not all bad. Indeed, recent evident suggests that scholars are beginning to advance the cause of theory development and integration. Bryant (1998) analyzed the content of three communication journals over a 20-year span and found that research examining the impact of the media has slowly declined over the decades, whereas research investigating the various reception processes involved in media consumption has increased. Thus, scholars have begun to address the more challenging questions of "how" and "why" media effects occur.

In addition, Bryant and Miron's (2004) content analysis of the use of theory in communication concluded with an examination of theory in the first 4 years of the new millennium. The authors expanded their sample of journals to include newer, more theoretically oriented journals such as *Communication Research, Mass Communication & Society,* and *Media Psychology.* When compared with the content of more established communication journals (*Journalism & Mass Communication Quarterly, Journal of Communication,* and *Journal of Broadcasting & Electronic Media*), articles in these newer journals showed a greater emphasis on theory construction and critique. Thus, the newest generation of communication scholars may be changing the tide with respect to the use of theory in communication research.

Integration of Research Methods

Just as scholars have called for the integration of theoretical perspectives, many have called for the greater use of more diverse research methods. As Lowry (1979) concluded, communication research to date has suffered from a "severe case of tunnel vision" (p. 268), as the vast majority of studies rely on a single method to answer their research questions. With the use of multiple methods, the strengths of one could shore up the deficiencies of another. Thus, what is truly needed is not the greater use of qualitative research methods, but the use of *both* qualitative and quantitative methods and multiple forms of each (i.e., so-called *triangulation*) so that the two research traditions can together provide a fuller understanding of the communication process. Calling the argument between quantitative and qualitative research methods a "pseudo-debate," Weaver (1993, p. 203) argued that what is really needed with the discipline are good theories of communication. He suggested that the method of testing these theories was of secondary importance.

Bryant (1993) likewise called for the use of multiple research methods to investigate the ever-changing nature of media consumption. For example, a decade before the development of TiVo and other "smart" digital video recorders, as well as Microsoft's Media Center edition of their XP operating system, Bryant noted the coming of these technologies and labeled them "intelligent communication networks" (p. 149). To examine media consumption in this new environment, he argued that researchers would have to use an array of methods, including unobtrusive remote observation of research participants, content analysis, pseudo-field experiments, focus groups, and one-on-one participant interviews to record and analyze the way contemporary media consumers use the media.

This more complex view of the nature of media consumption is indicative of the state of communication research in the 21st century. Numerous scholars have noted the inadequacy of the traditional linear stimulus-receiver or transmission model that has guided much mass communication research over the last half-century. As such, scholars continue to develop more complex models of media consumption, recognizing the importance of the reception process in shaping the effects of media consumption. As Weaver stated, "the meaning of a media message lies not only in the text, but also in the reader, viewer, or listener" (p. 212). Moreover, Rogers (1993) argued that with the increased recognition of the value of qualitative research methods, communication research is coming full circle and recreating the diversity in research methods that characterized the field before World War II. Clearly, scholars have made a strong case for the use of both qualitative and quantitative research methods in communication study. However, it remains to be seen whether future communication scholars will heed this advice.

ADVANCES THROUGH META-ANALYSIS

One final critique of the body of communication research to date is that the various theoretical perspectives and research traditions have not been compiled into a coherent whole. DeFleur (1998) cited the lack of programmatic research as one of the reasons that contemporary communication study had failed to yield any new milestones. Moreover, he argued that scholars too often failed to use consistent terminology in their studies, and, thus, their findings were not additive. Likewise, Lowry's (1979) content analysis of empirical research in seven communication journals showed that the overwhelming majority of studies had no longitudinal aspect built into their designs and that most studies were simple one-shot, cross-sectional examinations of a single group of research participants at one point.

Bryant (1998) noted that such cross-sectional research is one of the least regarded forms of social scientific study by lawmakers and those who set public policy, whereas the most highly regarded type of research is longitudinal studies that assess the impact of the mass media over time. However, it is noteworthy that the next most highly regarded form of scholarship is *meta-analysis*. If indeed one of the chief critiques of the communication research to date is that many individual studies fail to build upon the extant body of knowledge, then meta-analysis is a highly valuable method to address this shortcoming. Endeavors such as those collected in this volume demonstrate how communication scholars are addressing the need to gain a more coherent understanding of the vast body of knowledge generated within the discipline, and they serve as significant milestones in communication research in many of the prevailing traditions of mass communication scholarship.

REFERENCES

Bandura, A. (1973). *Aggression: A social learning analysis*. Englewood Cliffs, NJ: Prentice-Hall.

Berelson, B. (1959). The state of communication research. *Public Opinion Quarterly, 23*, 1–6.

Bryant, J. (1993). Will traditional media research paradigms be obsolete in the era of intelligent communication networks? In P. Gaunt (Ed.), *Beyond agendas: New directions in communication research* (pp. 149–167). Westport, CN: Greenwood Press.

Bryant, J. (1998). Trends in mass communication theory and research: Differences that make a difference. In J. S. Trent (Ed.), *Communication: Views from the helm for the 21st century* (pp. 264–269). Boston: Allyn & Bacon.

Bryant, J. (2004). Critical communication challenges for the new century. *Journal of Communication, 54*, 389–401.

Bryant, J., & Miron, D. (2004). Theory and research in mass communication. *Journal of Communication, 54*, 662–704.

Bryant, J., & Yang, M. H. (2004). A blueprint for excellence for the *Asian Communication Research*. *Asian Communication Research, 1*, 133–151.

Cooper, R., Potter, W. J., & Dupagne, M. (1994). A status report on methods used in mass communication research. *Journalism Educator, 48*(4), 54–61.

DeFleur, M. L. (1998). Where have all the milestones gone? The decline of significant research on the process and effects of mass communication. *Mass Communication & Society, 1*, 85–98.

Emmers-Sommer, T. M., & Allen, M. (1999). Surveying the effect of media effects: A meta-analytic summary of the media effects research in *Human Communication Research*. *Human Communication Research, 25*, 478–497.

Gerbner, G. (1969). Toward "cultural indicators": The analysis of mass mediated message systems. *AV Communication Review, 17*(2), 137–148.

Gerbner, G., & Gross, L. P. (1976). Living with television: The violence profile. *Journal of Communication, 26*(2), 172–199.

Gerbner, G., Gross, L. P., Morgan, M., & Signorielli, N. (1980). The "mainstreaming" of America: Violence profile no. 11. *Journal of Communication, 30*(4), 10–29.

Kamahawi, R., & Weaver, D. (2003). Mass communication research trends from 1980 to 1999. *Journalism & Mass Communication Quarterly, 80*, 7–27.

Katz, E., Blumler, J. G., & Gurevitch, M. (1974). Utilization of mass communication by the individual. In J. G. Blumler & M. Gurevitch (Eds.), *The uses of mass communications: Current perspectives on gratifications research* (pp. 19–32). Beverly Hills, CA: Sage.

Lindloff, T. R. (1991). The qualitative study of media audiences. *Journal of Broadcasting and Electronic Media, 35*, 23–42.

Lowry, D. T. (1979). An evaluation of empirical studies reported in seven journals in the '70s. *Journalism Quarterly, 56,* 262–268, 282.

Marx, K. (1867). *Das Kapital* [Capital]. Hamburg: Meissner.

Marx, K., & Engels, F. (1848). *Manifest der Kommunistischen partei veroffentlich in Februar 1848* [Manifest of the Communist Party issued in February 1848]. London: Burghard.

McCombs, M. E., & Shaw, D. L. (1972). The agenda-setting function of mass media. *Public Opinion Quarterly, 36,* 176–187.

McLuhan, M. (1964). *Understanding media: The extensions of man.* New York: McGraw-Hill.

Moffett, E. A., & Dominick, J. R. (1987). Statistical analysis in the *Journal of Broadcasting* 1970–85: An update. *Feedback, 28*(2), 13–16.

Pauly, J. J. (1991). A beginner's guide to doing qualitative research in mass communication. *Journalism Monographs, 125.*

Perloff, R. M. (1976). Journalism research: A 20-year perspective. *Journalism Quarterly, 53,* 123–126.

Riffe, D., & Frietag, A. (1998). A content analysis of content analyses: Twenty-five years of *Journalism Quarterly. Journalism & Mass Communication Quarterly, 74,* 873–882.

Rogers, E. M. (1962). *Diffusion of innovations.* New York: Free Press of Glencoe.

Rogers, E. M. (1994). *A history of communication study: A biographical approach.* New York: Free Press.

Rubin, A.M., & Haridakis, P. M. (2001). Mass communication research at the dawn of the 21st century. *Communication Yearbook, 24,* 73–97.

Schramm, W. (1957). Twenty years of journalism research. *Public Opinion Quarterly, 21,* 91–107.

Shoemaker, P. J., & Reese, S. D. (1990). Exposure to what? Integrating media content and effects studies. *Journalism Quarterly, 67,* 649–652.

Weaver, D. H. (1993). Communication research in the 1990s: New directions and new agendas? In P. Gaunt (Ed.), *Beyond agendas: New directions in communication research* (pp. 199–220). Westport, CN: Greenwood Press.

Wimmer, R. D., & Haynes, R. B. (1978). Statistical analyses in the *Journal of Broadcasting,* 1970–1976. *Journal of Broadcasting, 22,* 241–248.

2

Media, Messages, and Meta-Analysis

Mike Allen
University of Wisconsin–Milwaukee

Raymond W. Preiss
University of Puget Sound

The social sciences continue to undergo transformation as the application of meta-analysis resolves empirical controversies. The most pressing problem plaguing the social sciences remains the inconsistency of findings among empirical investigations. Without the ability to generate consistency across a body of empirical findings there exists no basis for determining facts. Facts serve as grist for the mill of theory. Without an ability to appeal to facts as a yardstick to measure the accuracy of any particular theoretical claim, theories cannot be assessed for predictive validity. When multiple theories offer explanation (some inconsistent with the other), some means of evaluation to determine which theory provides better or more accurate descriptions must exist. The empirical accuracy of a theory, particularly when judged over time against a constantly increasing set of empirical generalizations, provides a basis for preferring of one theory over another. Although other standards for evaluating and preferring a theory exist (parsimony, heuristic value, etc.), one fundamental requirement for any theory remains explanatory consistency with collected data.

The process of science requires a platform of facts (empirical data) that form the basis for accountability of future or current theoretical formulations. The process of establishing a fact both complicates and simplifies the problems of theoretical construction and evaluation. The complication comes from the additional questions that focus on the "why?" of the association and the desire for additional explanation. Questions on why a relationship exists are especially important when the empirical data challenge existing formulations and assumptions about other existing observations. This complication increases when one considers the use of that "fact" in a real-world application. Crafting policies or programs requires boundaries and limitations of any claim based on the fact. The simplifying aspect arises from the potential resolution of a current controversy over the accuracy of an empirical description (something as simple as whether variable X is correlated with variable Y). The demonstration of empirical consistency provides for the generation of a single, accurate empirical description. The problem of the tension between simplification and complication represents the contrasting perspective of a particular scholar at a point in the process of scientific discovery. The resolution of an ongoing controversy (that may be decades old) simplifies a dizzying complex set of findings but at the same moment increases the challenges for explanation and requires additional research.

Meta-analysis provides a snapshot of the current state of empirical research. These pictures generate an image used to clarify and understand the current state of the art. Snapshots are always disappointing because of the limited view, the lack of uniform focus, and the failure to include important details. Thus, research represents a process, and when meta-analyses are strung together and combined across domains, a vast theoretical panorama emerges (much like snapshots when strung together produce a motion picture). The hope of the editors of this book is that the meta-analyses contribute to that panoramic view of empirical findings and theoretical explanation. The snapshots contained in this book should be viewed with the appropriate degree of caution and skepticism, as well as disappointment. We trust that the views will remain useful to scholars studying the effects of media theories and processes.

This chapter addresses how to define the process of meta-analysis. Questions about the parameters of the process and the limitations of the techniques receive consideration. We close the chapter by assessing application of meta-analysis to gain understanding of media effects and the promise meta-analysis offers to future social scientific investigations. Meta-analysis offers no magic bullet solution to many of the theoretical controversies summarized in this book. However, meta-analysis does resolve several problems faced by the scientific community, and the resolution of those problems provides the possibility for realizing the potential of social scientific enterprise.

DESCRIPTION OF META-ANALYSIS

The heart of meta-analysis consists of combining data sets to estimate a parameter. The estimate becomes more accurate because combining samples reduces sampling error. The fundamental assumption is that there exist two sources of variability in the observed set of relationships in any given study: (a) random and (b) systematic. The random factors usually reflect the impact of sampling error. In fact, several authors refer to the process of averaging across studies as "correcting for sampling error."

Random variance remains the single greatest source of an advantage for meta-analysis. When significance tests are used on samples, two types of error can occur: (a) Type I error or false-positives and (b) Type II error or false-negatives. Type I error is usually assessed as the alpha error, and most social scientists use a probability of 5% ($p = .05$). Thus, the Type I error rate across a domain is 5%. However, the level of Type II error is a combination of three factors ($1 -$ Type II error rate, size of the effect, and size of the sample). For an average sample size ($N = 80$) with an average size effect ($d = .40$) and standard alpha level ($p = .05$), the Type II error rate is about 50% (Hunter & Schmidt, 1990). Assuming that the alpha level does not change and that the size of the effect is the object of measurement, the only way to diminish Type II error involves increasing sample size.

By combining data sets, meta-analysis diminishes Type II error by increasing sample size. The averaging process essentially creates an estimate that theoretically possesses the properties of an effect with the combined sample size of the investigations. Averaging effects decrease the size of the confidence interval and provide a more accurate estimate of the population parameter. Hedges (1987) pointed out that the variability in outcomes of experiments in particle physics can be compared with outcomes observed in several areas of social science research. This variability in outcomes is actually greater in particle physics! No one questions the fact that physics is a science, but the solution that physics uses to this variability involves data averaging. In fact, in most of the natural sciences forms of meta-analysis are routinely used to handle divergent empirical findings among investigations. The problem of inconsistent findings hindering the advancement of social science simply reflects the failure to employ a solution for inconsistent data sets. Meta-analysis offers social scientists that solution.

The importance of effects averaging can be seen in early investigations dealing with the problems of literature review. These studies indicate that naïve or untrained persons do a better job than experienced social scientists when summarizing literature (Cooper & Hedges, 1994). For example, untrained persons did a better job of interpreting a set of six studies, three of which find significant associations and three of which do not. The explanation is relatively simple. Trained and experienced faculty would blame the inconsistency on complex methodological differences between investigations. Naïve persons simply looked at the three consistent, significant findings and the three consistent in direction but nonsignificant findings and concluded that an association existed. The reliance on the significance test, without consideration of Type II error, created a situation in which expertise actually hindered correct inference making. Meta-analysis demonstrates statistically what the naïve interpreters instinctively understood—that consistency exists without reliance on the significance test.

The second source of variability among empirical investigations arises from systematic factors. One type of systematic variance involves measurement artifacts (attenuated measurement, regression to the mean, restriction in range, dichotomization of continuous variables, etc.). Measurement artifacts can be corrected for and the estimate of the true parameter made more accurate (Hunter & Schmidt, 1990). Another type of systematic factor involves issues of design in which the choice of a sample (senior citizens versus high school students), the type of measurement (self-report versus physiological), the type of stimulus (written message reading versus active role playing), or others can provide for differences in outcomes between types of studies. Measurement artifacts, when they occur, should be corrected for statistically, but design issues require empirical comparison to determine the impact.

This second type of systematic source of variability (design issues) often comes from theoretical arguments and can be assessed by comparing studies or arranging the quality on a metric for tests of association. The consideration of sources of design variability may reflect a particular theoretical model that posits the reason for variability in the outcome of theoretical interest. What typically happens is that the individual data sets provide an incomplete test of the theory. Only a meta-analysis can, by comparing data sets, provide a test for the model of theoretically meaningful observations.

In summary, we believe that meta-analysis should do more than simply average effects to produce an estimate. Although finding an average statistical effect is critical, meta-analysis can test theoretical models as well as examine various sources of variability. More importantly, systematic correction for statistical artifacts (which may occur differentially across a pool of studies) combined with consideration of design characteristics permits comparisons of apples to apples rather than of apples to oranges.

THE PARAMETERS OF META-ANALYSIS

The parameters of meta-analysis focus on the prerequisites necessary to gain the insights that meta-analysis can provide. Boundary conditions simply set the various expectations of what a meta-analysis can and should accomplish. We have commented on some of these issues previously (Allen, 1998, Allen & Preiss, 1997, 1998, 2002; Preiss & Allen, 1994, 1995, 2002). Questions about the use of meta-analysis deal with the scope of the inquiry and how the particular meta-analysis can or should be used to summarize the existing experimental evidence. The scholar conducting the analysis should provide unambiguous expectations. Any good empirical summary should establish a clear goal for the review and assess whether or not the goal has been achieved. Often, a disappointment or objection to a particular meta-analysis flows from a failure to achieve some outcome sought by the reader. However, the scholar conducting the meta-analysis may not be seeking that outcome or simply may be unable to reach the reader's goal because of deficiencies or limitations in the current database. Explicit expectations and assessments can reduce objections while pointing to limitations that interested scholars can use when designing new primary investigations. Thus, the meta-analysis simultaneously summarizes the domain while stimulating new avenues of research.

A related meta-analytic parameter involves the scope of the empirical summary. Meta-analysis can be either a limited or focused review (based on criteria for the inclusion of investigations) or a comprehensive and more global review of the literature for an entire area. At the same time the review process can be targeted to establishing an empirical association or an entire set of theoretical propositions. Figure 2.1 provides an analysis of these possibilities.

The choice made by the reviewer indicates a commitment to the purpose of the review and reflects no necessary set of objective decisions. The issues set forth in the justification for the meta-analysis establish the purpose and parameters of the scope of the inquiry. Nothing is probably more disappointing than reading a meta-analysis that fails to answer the question that the reader considers important. But that failure only indicates divergence between the reviewer and the reader about the scope of the inquiry. The problem may stem from what persons want out of the process of a meta-analysis. Even when one is attempting to summarize a large domain, individual meta-analyses are likely to provide a narrow, focused set of propositions about a set of theoretical issues. When compared with broader narrative reviews, any meta-analysis may appear quite tiny in scope. However, when the narrative reviewer employs a large number of individual meta-analyses as evidence to support empirical claims, the narrative review begins to capitalize on the advantages of meta-analyses. By summarizing many interlocking meta-analyses, the narrative reviewer can provide thorough, comprehensive, and systematic reviews of the literature about a set of empirical relationships.

The parameters for meta-analysis serve as both a source of euphoria and depression regarding the scientific process. Euphoria is rooted in the ability to generate empirical consistencies when a theoretical relationship is considered. Finding that a relationship exists demonstrates the viability of the theory used to

FIG. 2.1   Meta-analysis outcomes.

	Researcher's Goal	
Historical Record Resolve a Specific Scope of The Review	Test Hypotheses Narrow Descriptive Question	Narrow Inferential
	Summarize A Domain	Comprehensive Descriptive	Comprehensive Inferential

explain the direction and magnitude of the average effect. Each new meta-analysis illustrates the potential of a theory to organize facts, subsume previous positions, and advance new questions. The depression associated with meta-analysis comes from the recognition that establishing single relationships becomes time consuming and provides only a miniscule contribution to what emerges as an enormous theoretical picture. While coding, sorting, and combining effects, the meta-analyst is often struck by the consistency of outcomes over decades of research or dismayed by the number of investigations that must be discarded because of inadequate reporting. The depression associated with uneven theoretical progress and careless reporting is usually outweighed by the euphoria!

THE LIMITATIONS OF META-ANALYSIS

The virtues of meta-analyses are constrained by factors that limit the claims that can be drawn by the reviewer. Principally, we perceive five limitations of meta-analysis as an enterprise: (a) contextual restrictions, (b) unequal value of claims, (c) ethnographic trap, (d) multiplicity of interpretation, and (e) misapplication of the level of analysis. These limitations are not flaws, however. They simply determine the extent to which claims remain possible. It is important to understand that meta-analysis constitutes a literature review (albeit a quantitative and systematic review) and possesses the limitations of the available literature. Even if the implementation of the meta-analysis is perfect, if the literature is thoroughly and exhaustively searched, if the statistical analysis is meticulous, documented, and accurate, and if all potential sources of variability are coded and examined, the same constraints for interpreting the results specified in this section will still apply.

Limitations reflect an understanding of what even a perfect application and implementation of the technique cannot accomplish. For example, the technique cannot answer all potential questions in the quest for knowledge, but in our view no technique can do this. Understanding the limitations of any particular technique permits an assessment of what is known and what still requires consideration.

Contextual Restrictions

Contextual restrictions are a systematic limitation on the issues associated with the conditions under which the investigations were conducted. Even a large database with hundreds of studies may not contain sufficient variability in stimulus, measurements, or samples to warrant universal generalizations. Any empirical investigation involves an examination of some relationship within this context. The limitation of the single investigation is a case in point. Meta-analysis can provide a solution to increased generalizability by demonstrating whether that relationship consistently occurs across a variety of situations or methods, (Hunter, Hamilton, & Allen, 1989). A domain with one investigation or a few will be limited to the contexts used in the primary studies.

For example, a meta-analysis comparing the self-disclosure of males and females (Dindia & Allen, 1992) reported that about 98% of the studies were conducted in either Canada or the United States. Whereas the more than 200 studies (with a combined sample of more than 20,000) represents a large database, the variability across cultures was small. If one considers culture to be a potential factor that might change the relationship between self-disclosure probability and gender, then the data lack generalizability. Because one could easily argue that cultural patterns represent a source of gender differences, the limitation to North America may produce a consistent finding, but not one generalized beyond that geographic/cultural grouping. Similar arguments may apply to outcomes of media investigations using limited geographical samples.

This limitation is problematic because no sample contains sufficient samples of stimuli or persons to generalize across all possible conditions. This is a tautology no matter how large, expansive, or diverse the database appears. The real challenge is identifying and specifying a reasonable set of expectations so that the scientist is permitted to make the inductive leap. The real goal of science is establishing a set of empirical reports that allow the discipline to claim or to expect that the next set of studies should produce the same set of relationships. Because the expectation is usually future oriented, the challenge becomes having a sufficient set of data that reasonably allows the expectation of generalizability. Unfortunately, culture is dynamic, not static, so any finding must address underlying features that would generalize across the range of culture in both space and time. For example, several meta-analyses demonstrate that high-fear appeals are more persuasive then low-fear appeals, and this finding appears to be consistent across both space and time (Boster & Mongeau, 1984; Mongeau, 1998; Sutton, 1982; Witte & Allen, 2000). But even a large database cannot cover the future incarnations or variations of culture. The challenge represents one of finding enough varied data so that the scientist can reasonably expect the finding to generalize to future situations.

In chapter 27 of this volume, Pfau makes a similar assessment about several of the claims made by authors. He questions the reason that various elements are not considered and acknowledged (in terms of data limitations). The answer to this question may be in the eye of the beholder! Reasonable people may differ in terms of what methodological requirements or expectations they think must exist for minimal claim-making. For some persons, a set of five well-conducted studies with consistent findings might be enough to provide sufficient evidence for a claim. For others, the five studies would provide only a mere beginning of establishing the empirical proof necessary to make such a claim.

The problem of methodology for establishing claims is the dynamic nature of the enterprise. Methodological standards change and evolve over time. The gold standard of the year 2005 will not meet the minimal requirements standards in 2025. Similarly, some of the requirements considered essential in 2005 may be deemed unnecessary and not required in 2025. The same logic is true for trying to establish the necessary requirements for generalizing from any body of research because the standard remains dynamic. However, currently there exists no accepted, complete articulation of standards for generalizability. What this lack of standards means is that claims always remain limited, but limited in unknown and perhaps unknowable ways.

Unequal Value of Claims

This limitation addresses the process of meta-analysts use when considering moderator variables. The researcher may start with an enormous set of data, but the domain may dwindle when particular combinations receive consideration. To use a metaphor, the trunk of a gigantic tree may be large, but the outermost branches relatively fragile and thin. The existence of multiple moderator variables dealing with the same relationship makes the problem of dwindling data for particular combinations of moderator levels (classes) a fundamental challenge. In the experience of the authors (with more than 125 published meta-analyses between them), seldom do data exist to support complex systems of moderator variables.

An example of this occurs in the meta-analysis for treatment of communication apprehension (Allen, Hunter, & Donohue, 1989) in which the overall analysis has more than 200 studies considering three basic types of remediation (systematic desensitization, cognitive modification, skills training, and the various combinations). The understanding of the impact of the therapies by themselves or in dual combinations represents significant samples; the impact of the triple combination of the approaches was limited (2 studies with a combined sample of 20). Although an additive mathematical model fit the data, drawing an implication from a cell with such a small number of entries appears unwarranted. Even though the rest of the model fit, a person should consider the fact that particular claims (even in the context of an overall large set of results) may rest on thin or very limited data.

This limitation has led to one particularly useful application of meta-analysis: facilitating future research applications. The existence of a meta-analysis can often lead to a corresponding empirical investigation that tests either moderator conditions or some theoretical model stemming from that finding (see Allen, 1991; Allen et al., 1990, 2002; O'Keefe, 1987). Thus, the limitation was not a dead end. It served to appropriately guide future research into areas that expand the existing data in more productive directions.

Ethnographic Trap

Meta-analysis provides a measure of association between conceptual entities. However, understanding the nature these conceptual entities may require articulation and enactment in everyday living. It would be a mistake for the scientist to believe that the knowledge in the meta-analysis provides the practical equipment for living. Basically, reading about navigation and studying navigation are not the same as actually navigating a ship. A gulf will always exists between the ability to do something and the knowledge about how things are done. In the context of an empirical investigation, it is possible to know that health campaign messages using higher levels of fear are more effective in changing health behaviors and attitudes. This is useful knowledge, but it fails to provide the understanding necessary to actually construct the message. The knowledge necessary for such message construction exists in each investigation (to collect data such a message must exist), but that knowledge remains unarticulated. The trap comes from the representation of information or confidence in the understanding that does not exist because the necessary experience is lacking. There should not be confusion between understanding the relationship and understanding the construct. The problem that the necessary information to permit successful social planning remains unavailable in a meta-analysis must be recognized before an analyst provides advice.

Meta-analysis is only an exercise in reviewing the literature. The analyst understands the issues from the point of view of someone having read many articles and primary data reports on a topic or issue. The hands-on experience or understanding cannot be gained from the meta-analysis. This amounts to a serious limitation of the knowledge. To apply the findings of meta-analysis requires an understanding of the particular communication and context of application, something that is not possible (and may not be desirable) in a meta-analysis.

Multiplicity of Interpretations

One fundamental implication of any set of findings is that interpretation is required for both understanding and application. What must be noted from the outset is that any set of empirical findings provides a potentially infinite set of explanations consistent with the findings. Although theoretical positions may a priori define and describe a set of relationships, other possible explanations and theoretical configurations are possible that would adequately explain the set of findings.

What this should indicate to any scientist is that any representation or interpretation must be understood in the context of other possible competing explanations. As with all sets of empirical or theoretical arguments, the scientist should remain open to other explanations. This openness does not mean that there does not exist a current "best" explanation (or explanations) that provides adequate interpretation. For example, the standard of parsimony provides one basis for preferring a simple, elegant explanation over complex, clumsy alternatives.

Openness to alternatives is important because there is a tendency for some to believe that if the empirical data are consistent with a theoretical explanation, then a theory has been proven to be true. Of course, despite a strong or great consistency with empirical data there will always exist a multitude of explanations that would also explain the empirical facts. Theories serve as organizing rationales to understand and represent what are often complex processes. Empirical tests of that scheme, when consistent, provide a basis for continuing acceptance of that interpretation. Empirical inconsistency begins the process of reevaluation and refor-mulation that ultimately leads to the development of alternative theories.

When applying research to social conditions, society operates or uses scientific knowledge as though it represents facts. At the same time, there always exists some uncertainty about scientific knowledge because the application or under-standing of that knowledge is organized on the basis of some theory. Theories in science emerge and change, not usually because of a rejection of empirical data but instead because of a changed understanding of those very empirical facts. As theoretical perspectives or understandings change, so will the applications or poli-cies assuming the accuracy of those theories.

In summary, meta-analysis provides empirical consistency among observa-tions. Unfortunately, although meta-analysis contributes to theoretical develop-ment and resolves inconsistencies between the empirical predictions of theories, the conclusions of meta-analysis are in one sense equivocal. The conclusion is equivocal in the sense that the explanation for the empirical consistency may take many forms. This means that science is always subject to revision and current explanations represent the best available consensus of the community.

Misapplication of Level of Data

Social science is the analysis of aggregates and the relationship not of individuals but of samples or populations. The counterpart to social science is often referred to as clinical science, which focuses on the individual. Usually, clinical science deals with a particular application targeted to improvement or treatment of that individual. A claim in a meta-analysis offers a guide to what should be the expected value or average association across a number of applications or examples. The intention of meta-analysis is not to predict outcomes for individuals or individual circumstances.

The critical issue should be the distinction between clinical application of infor-mation to an individual versus the understanding of social forces. The clinician is a professional interested in an individual circumstance and that outcome. For example, a psychologist working with a client provides a clinical application that focuses on improving that particular individual. The larger social issues are only relevant to the extent that the scientific information assists in understanding the immediate application to that patient.

Similarly, medicine as practiced by physicians is an art, not a science. How-ever, medical knowledge operates on the basis of scientific understanding gener-ated as a result of empirical data. The doctor uses medical knowledge (the scien-tific theories and knowledge) in application to the individual patient. The general knowledge of science indicates that a particular outcome is likely, and the doctor makes choices using professional judgment guided by the science. The doctor's application to the individual patient represents the art of medicine.

This distinction between art and science represents a real tension for the use of meta-analysis. The meta-analysis reflects group level data operating at the social level across aggregates of individuals. Taking the conclusion of any particular meta-analysis and making statements about a particular individual (as explanation or prediction) represent a serious danger. Knowing that exposure to media violence increases subsequent violent behavior may represent an important social finding for a meta-analysis. However, referring to a particular child's violent behavior and then offering the media consumption pattern of the child as an explanation would be inappropriate. At the same time, the meta-analytic finding may inform the art of parenting! Whereas the meta-analysis permits an explanation for social or population behavior, trying to apply meta-analytic findings to an individual as an explanation violates the assumption of the technique.

In this section we have argued that meta-analysis offers understanding of social phenomenon at the level of the aggregate, not at the level of the individual. The problem, of course, is that violent behavior occurs at the level of the individual. What meta-analysis demonstrates is that changes in the average level of one variable correspond to changes in the average levels in the other variable across a population. Meta-analysis is useful in understanding individual circumstances, but the application to individuals requires a clinical step not found in the meta-analysis. Meta-analysis can and should guide clinical understandings, but meta-analysis does not substitute for the requirements of clinical application.

THE PROMISE OF UNDERSTANDING MEDIA EFFECTS

Any review of the impact of media on society or on individuals in society will find a great deal of controversy. Because there is evidence supporting many theories, examining many studies will reinforce a variety of opinions, even when one considers the same essential set of information. What would appear to one set of scholars as clear evidence for media effects may appear to another group of scholars as inconsistent evidence or provide proof for an alternative theoretical interpretation. Exactly this type of argument is found in the media violence literature. One group reasons that mediated violence provides a catharsis that reduces interpersonal conflict, whereas a second group concludes that modeling aggression is the cause of violent behavior. The controversy produces contradictory and inconsistent recommendations for public action. By estimating the average effect across the domain, meta-analysis provides a format for discussing competing interpretations and assessing empirical evidence.

This collection of summaries does not offer a final word or solution to the problem of establishing or interpreting media effects. However, taken as a body, the various meta-analyses provide the foundation for a dialogue about the existence, as well as the magnitude, of media effects. The question about whether the media has a social impact appears to have an affirmative answer. Finding a meta-analysis reporting a zero association would be difficult. When one considers the implication of experimental versus survey research, the issue of self-selection as an explanation cannot be sustained. Although surveys linking the amount of exposure to various outcomes reflect self-selection, experimental investigations using random assignment cannot be dismissed on that basis. What the combination of methods provides is a stronger argument for the impact of media on the persons exposed to the message.

THE APPLICATION OF META-ANALYSIS IN THIS BOOK

The central question considered by the various reviews is whether exposure to some particular media content is associated with an outcome. One example involves whether consumption of sexually explicit material is associated with attitudes that devalue women or sexually violent behavior. The consideration of these associations provides a basis for understanding the potential social impact of the media. Each meta-analysis considers a particular question by examining the current data pertinent to that question. If one considers the data insufficient to answer the question, then the solution is more data collection and the answer should be held in abeyance until sufficient information is available. On the other hand, if all the various meta-analyses found zero or near-zero associations across the board a different conclusion emerges. The totality of the evidence would be against any conclusion that media content is associated with various outcomes. That outcome carries particular social significance given the blame many ascribe to the media for various events. If the meta-analyses conclude that some type of association exists, then a necessary but not sufficient condition exists for the conclusion that the media cause particular social outcomes.

Attempts to interpret these issues need to make a distinction between the intentional and unintentional impacts of media content. In some cases, media content may intend some outcome, and the audience may be willing participants in generating that event. For example, in debates between two presidential candidates, both the message providers and message receivers intend to affect attitudes. The candidates want the viewers to accept the message conclusion and the viewers watch to try to reinforce or create particular attitudes. Any investigation of this process would be examining a very conscious and purposeful activity on the parts of the media organization and the message consumer (among other stakeholders). Figure 2.2 offers a description of the possible outcomes when considering the intentions of both the media sender and the audience are considered.

It is also possible that the audience may draw meaning from content intended as entertainment. Consider Charles Manson's reaction to the Beatles' song *Helter-Skelter,* which in England refers to what Americans would call a child's slide in a playground. Manson found social commentary from something intended literally to indicate child's play. An audience view a program intended to be social commentary and simply find it entertaining and thus miss the message. Figure 2.2

FIG. 2.2   Intentions and outcomes of media exposure.

Media Message Sender Intention	Message Receiver Intention	Outcome/Example
Active	Active	Attitude change/Political debate/news
Active	Passive	Entertainment/*All in the Family*
Passive	Active	Assignment of Meaning/*Helter-Skelter*
Passive	Passive	Entertainment/*Seinfeld*

shows not only the intentional outcomes, but also references the problem of mis-interpretation or miscommunication by both sides in a mediated environment.

The problem is a bit different when one considers entertainment programming. The intent of the person providing the content of the program may or may not have some underlying social or political message or commentary. Arthur Miller's *The Crucible* has a very clear intentional message on the part of the author. That symbolic message may or may not be perceived correctly by the audience. For example, the program *All in the Family* had a main character who portrayed racial stereotyping, but not all viewers found that portrayal negative (despite the clear intention of the writer). However, *Seinfeld* is a program intentionally about nothing, so meaning might be derived by an audience that was not intentional from the message sender. Entertainment programming serves a function for the audience, but the function may be affected by inner states and gratifications.

Subtle aspects of entertainment programming may shade the issue of audience intention. While intending to be entertained, the audience may not be actively seeking a message. Buller's meta-analyses on distraction (Buller, 1986, Buller & Hall, 1998) indicated that such messages can be very persuasive. Many aspects of the impact of media (horror, violence, music, sexually explicit, or gender stereotypes) may reflect the consideration of messages that intend to entertain but contain information that forms and shapes the attitudes and behaviors of individuals. Whether unintentional outcomes on the part of the message provider exist are the challenge and the concern of this area of media effects. The effects can be either prosocial or antisocial depending on the perception of the audience. An example of a movie that had a prosocial impact was *The Passion of the Christ:* Several criminals confessed to crimes after viewing the picture. The same film, it should also be noted, was interpreted by some Muslim Arabs as revealing the truth about the Jews and the torturing of Christ.

Differential interpretations of the same media content point to the problem of unintended media effects. As the meta-analysis on the response of criminal sexual offenders to sexually explicit material (Allen, D'Alessio, & Emmers-Sommer, 1999) indicates, groups of persons with common characteristics can respond quite differently than other groups. The physiological response of criminal sexual offenders was stronger and the exposure to sexual material was an event more likely to occur before they engaged in sex than for other groups. What the findings indicate is that important responses to material may differ based on some aspect of the individual. Unfortunately, when one considers other entertainment content (music, violence, etc.) the responses may not be known in advance.

Differential interpretations are one of several factors that complicate efforts to craft policy based upon average effects. When one tries to make predictions about the impact of media, a high degree of confidence in the relationship is an essential if policymakers are to adopt new legislation or implement new procedures. This confidence must necessarily involve the direction, magnitude, and stability of the average effect. Even if these qualities are present, the ability to confidently assert a proposition may be difficult. For example, the question about the justification for banning some media content may not exist because the causality stems from probability for a sample, not an immediate and inevitable connection. At the same time, the relationship may be based on movement of the entire curve (each individual moves an average amount), and the result is that some persons are pushed past the threshold of whatever action is predicted. A simultaneous third explanation may exist for the relationship, because some individuals may move a great deal whereas the rest of the sample is unaffected. The policy implications of these forces are difficult to calculate.

Causality in this case is not a one-to-one kind of correspondence. Instead the causality represents a probabilistic view of the connection between cause and outcome. One view of causality has a correspondence between event A inevitably resulting in event B. In the case of social science, the argument is that event A takes place for a population of individuals and then for some portion of the sample event B occurs. The implications for science and application to policy considerations quickly become complex.

THE PROMISE OF SOCIAL SCIENCE

Scholars interested in media processes and effects strive to understand the complexities of mediated messages. The implications of the meta-analytic findings in this volume, when combined with ongoing programs of research and other meta-analyses, begin to establish the impact of media. The results of the various meta-analyses do not support a simple analysis, such as that of hypodermic needle models, in which a passive public is injected and manipulated by the content of media. However, the argument that the impact of media on various social issues is miniscule is without foundation. The meta-analytic results indicate that the various forms of media demonstrate a consistent pattern of effect across a variety of domains, but the explanation for this association remain uncertain.

The problematic exercise of the findings remains the inability to generate simple recommendations that provide the basis for definitive and effective action. For example, the limits of the First Amendment provide a barrier to those wanting some type of across-the-board censorship. The empirical findings support public concern, but the lack of clear theoretical explication supported by data does not provide the assurance that banning or changing content produces the kinds of outcomes sought by the censor. Sanitizing the environment, particularly for children, has great appeal but no certainty of effectiveness. Manufacture and possession of child pornography is illegal, but the passage of a federal law in the 1980s may not have reduced the level of sexual crimes against children. Of course, sensitivity or openness by society may have simply increased the reporting and willingness of victims, both of current abuse and of events that occurred farther in the past, to come forward to make knowledge about the effects of the media ban unclear. In addition, the introduction of the Internet and the corresponding availability of material may make censorship virtually impossible.

The applications of social science to the design of interventions that use media are important. Policymakers understand that knowing a policy "works" justifies continuing the program. Similarly, knowing that some versions of a program are more effective than other versions (or that some types of persons are more affected) represents important knowledge for intervention design. A challenge for social intervention is always continuing to justify the intervention as a means of effectively reducing or eliminating (or promoting and maintaining) a set of conditions. Meta-analysis provides an important tool in providing evidence to those challenging or assessing the justification as well as continuation of such efforts.

Several of the meta-analyses in this book provide evidence about what impact should be expected from media actions related to a problem. Such an analysis can serve as a baseline to compare various future incarnations or versions of any program. The baseline also permits the ongoing assessment and comparison of program variations to the baseline and can affirm improvements or diminished effectiveness.

The overall picture emerging in the literature supports the idea that the media does produce an effect on the audience. However, that impact is probably not universal, and different audiences are affected differently. At the same time, the effect is not always negative. Positive, prosocial outcomes are evident, as well as pernicious ones. Future investigations and applications will need to balance these outcomes by promoting positive effects and minimizing negative effects. Meta-analysis will play a role in designing these policies.

REFERENCES

Allen, M. (1991). Meta-analysis comparing effectiveness of one and two-sided messages. *Western Journal of Speech Communication, 55,* 390–404.

Allen, M. (1998). Methodological considerations when examining a gendered world. In D. Canary and K. Dindia (Eds.), *Handbook of sex differences & similarities in communication: Critical essays and empirical investigations of sex and gender in interaction* (pp. 427–444). Mahwah, NJ: Lawrence Erlbaum Associates.

Allen, M., Adamski, L., Bates, M., Bernhagen, M., Callendar, A., Casey, M., et al. (2002). An examination of timing of communicator identification and level of source credibility on perceptions of credibility and attitude. *Communication Research Reports, 19,* 46–55.

Allen, M., D'Alessio, D., & Emmers-Sommer, T. (1999). Reactions to criminal sexual offenders to pornography: A meta-analytic summary. In M. Roloff (Ed.), *Communication Yearbook 22* (pp. 139–169). Thousand Oaks, CA: Sage.

Allen, M., Hale, J., Mongeau, P., Berkowitz-Stafford, S., Stafford, S., Shanahan, W., et al. (1990). Testing a model of message sidedness: Three replications. *Communication Monographs, 57,* 275–291.

Allen, M., Hunter, J., & Donohue, W. (1989). Meta-analysis of self-report data on the effectiveness of public speaking anxiety treatment techniques. *Communication Education, 38,* 54–76.

Allen, M., & Preiss, R. (1997). Persuasion, public address, and progression in the sciences: Where we are at what we do. In G. Barnett & F. Boster (Eds.), *Progress in Communication Sciences* (Vol. 13, pp. 107–131). Greenwich, CT: Ablex.

Allen, M., & Preiss, R. (1998). Evaluating the advice offered by the tool users. In M. Allen and R. Preiss (Eds.), *Persuasion: Advances through meta-analysis* (pp. 243–256). Cresskill, NJ: Hampton Press .

Allen, M., & Preiss, R. (2002). An analysis of textbooks in interpersonal communication: How accurate are the representations? In M. Allen, R. Preiss, B. Gayle, & N. Burrell (Eds.), *Interpersonal communication research: Advances through meta-analysis* (pp. 371–388). Mahwah, NJ: Lawrence Erlbaum Associates.

Boster, F.J., & Mongeau, P. (1984). Fear-arousing persuasive messages. In R. Bostrom (Ed.), *Communication yearbook 8* (pp. 330–375). Newbury Park, CA: Sage.

Buller, D (1986). Distraction during persuasive communication: A meta-analytic review. *Communication Monographs, 53,* 91–114.

Buller, D., & Hall, J. (1998). The effects of distraction during persuasion. In M. Allen & R. Preiss (Eds.), *Persuasion: Advances through meta-analysis* (pp. 155–174). Cresskill, NJ: Hampton Press.

Cooper, H., & Hedges, L.V. (1994). Research synthesis as a scientific enterprise. In H. Cooper and L. Hedges (Eds.), *Handbook of research synthesis* (pp. 3–14). New York: Russell Sage.

Dindia, K., & Allen, M. (1992). Sex differences in self-disclosure: A meta-analysis. *Psychological Bulletin, 112,* 106–124.

Hedges, L. V. (1987). How hard is hard science, how soft is soft science? The empirical cumulativeness of research. *American Psychologist, 42,* 443–455.

Hunter, J., Hamilton, M., & Allen, M. (1989). The design and analysis of language experiments in communication. *Communication Monographs, 56,* 341–363.

Hunter, J., & Schmidt, F. (1990). *Methods of meta-analysis: Correcting for artifact and bias in research findings.* Thousand Oaks, CA: Sage.

Mongeau, P. (1998). Another look at fear-arousing persuasive appeals. In M. Allen & R. Preiss (Eds.), *Persuasion: Advances through meta-analysis* (pp. 53–68). Cresskill, NJ: Hampton Press.

O'Keefe, D. (1987). The persuasive effects of delaying identification of high- and low-credibility communicators: A meta-analytic review. *Central States Speech Journal, 38,* 63–72.

Preiss, R., & Allen, M. (1994). Prospects and precautions in the use of meta-analysis. In M. Allen and R. Preiss (Eds.), *Prospects and precautions in the use of meta-analysis* (pp. 1–33). Dubuque, IA: Brown and Benchmark Publishing.

Preiss, R., & Allen, M. (1995). Understanding and using meta-analysis. *Evaluation & the Health Professions, 18,* 315–335.

Preiss, R., & Allen, M. (2002). Meta-analysis and interpersonal communication: Function and applicability. In M. Allen, R. Preiss, B. Gayle, & N. Burrell (Eds.), *Interpersonal communication research: Advances through meta-analysis* (pp. 3–12). Mahwah, NJ: Lawrence Erlbaum Associates.

Sutton, S. (1982). Fear arousing communications: A critical examination of theory and research. In J. Eiser (Ed.), *Social psychology and behavioral medicine* (pp. 303–337). New York: Wiley.

Witte, K., & Allen, M. (2000). A meta-analysis of fear appeals: Implications for effective health campaigns. *Health Education & Behavior, 27,* 591–615.

3

Wherefore Art Thou Mass Media Theory?

Mike Allen
Mary K. Casey
University of Wisconsin–Milwaukee

Media effects theories tend to pose simple relationships and often reflect the basic premise, "monkey see, monkey do." Whether one expresses this premise as social learning, excitation transfer, stimulus/response, identification, the theory of reasoned action, or extended parallel processing, the general relationship holds: The audience copies the content of the media. At the core of the theories that explain media effects is the argument that exposure to media content will generate some demonstrable impact on an audience. Obviously, the effect differs on the basis of the various individual characteristics of the viewer, but the theories cast the consumers of mass media as essentially passive persons in the process.

The first empirical question is, does media content produce effects? By that we mean, does media exposure generate various outcomes on persons who consume the material (this is a social not a clinical question so the effect is measured at the level of group mean differences)? If a group of persons consume violent material, sexually explicit material, or certain types of music does this consumption produce a demonstrable impact on the attitudes and behaviors of that group compared with those of a group of persons who did not consume the material or consumed alternative material lacking the important characteristic under study. The overwhelming answer to that simple question is yes. Media consumption is related to a lot of various outcomes, and an examination of almost all meta-analyses, including those in this book, shows that there are demonstrable effects for media content on the group of consumers.

The usual argument against the adequacy of such findings is the presence of some type of self-selection bias in survey research or demand hypothesis in experimental research. However, the problem with such logic is that both sets of investigations are producing the same outcomes. This was illustrated best in Herrett-Skjellum and Allen's (1996) meta-analysis, replicated by Oppliger (chap. 13, this volume), in which both the longitudinal and experimental studies showed the same effects. The longitudinal studies indicate the impact of essentially what happens when persons consume material over a period of time. That research is subject to the self-selection artifact—that persons of a particular type can choose to consume material with particular content. However, the experimental studies indicate that the same effect is observed, and those studies use random assignment to conditions. What this research indicates is that although self-selection may be occurring, it does not by itself account for the observed impact of the viewing of material.

Simple exposure indicates that effects models should have been considered shattered by the nature of the active audience, however. By active audience we mean that the audience is not passive during the consumption of this programming. Audiences attend and reinterpret based on their experiences and uses for the information. Consider two examples: (a) the effects of pornography and (b) the impact of Earvin "Magic" Johnson's announcement that he was HIV positive.

In their meta-analysis, Allen, D'Alessio, and Emmers-Sommer (1999) found that convicted criminal sexual offenders did not report consumption of pornography more often than normal males. However, the function of the material differed, as the offenders more often used the material before engaging in sexual actions with another person. In addition, the physiological reactions (measured by genital blood volume) tripled compared with those of normal males when the content of the material was matched to the crime for which the individual was convicted. Essentially, the conclusion is that it is not exposure to but function of media materials that differentiates the impact on individuals.

Magic Johnson's announcement that he was HIV positive had the impact of improving knowledge for everyone (see Casey et al., chap. 22, this volume, and the full report of Casey et al., 2003). The outcome was that increased knowledge for adults increased anxiety or fear about the disease; however, for children the increased knowledge diminished anxiety. Knowledge about HIV transmission for adults increased the perception of risk, whereas for children it diminished the perception of risk. The conclusion is that media content, even about a health matter, may generate divergent impacts, depending on the perspective of the audience.

What all the preceding information indicates is that the chapters in this book are setting out a context in which future questions about the effect of mass media have to change. The issue of whether or not an effect exists has been largely answered in the current generation of empirical research. However, larger and very important questions remain that the next set of theoretical formulations should consider.

THE NEXT GENERATION OF THEORIZING

The meta-analyses in this book address what could start to be considered the "next generation" of questions or challenges for media effects theories. First, how and why do people select the media to consume? Second, how does television begin to form a sense of relationship or affiliation with the consumer? Finally, what can be done, if anything, to change the outcomes that may exist, particularly the outcomes that are socially undesirable?

Selection of Materials

Why, when given a multitude of choices, do persons select particular content or programs? In several chapters in this section of the book, the authors consider the idea of what motivates a person to select particular media. D'Alessio and Allen start the process of answering this question in their meta-analysis by pointing out that selection of material may or may not be based on prior opinions.

Clearly, expectations about the content of material guide selection. Research and subsequent meta-analyses are needed to start the process of examining why persons prefer some materials over others. How does the initial exposure even transpire? Why do some persons become addicted to programs such as *Survivor* or *24?* What makes the person tune in and then develop some type of affinity for that programming? There is a lack of research on this question; the general focus has been logically on the impact of any such choice for materials but now how that choice is developed.

That media establishes or sets agendas is not surprising. In their meta-analysis, Wanta and Levine -confirm the long-held suspicion that news coverage does not simply reflect but also creates an agenda or issue salience. This finding on media priming is consistent with that of Roskos-Ewoldsen, Klinger, and Roskos-Ewoldsen. As these authors conclude, we would echo the need to "focus on the development of theoretical explanations for the phenomenon." The same can be said for the entire selection issue. Although empirical data about the basis of such choices are slowly emerging, currently little theoretical thinking on this issue has been done. After all, before experiencing an effect for media content, the consumer must choose to select that material.

Relationship With Media

The second question deals with the development of the kind of relationship that persons develop with the media. The question of a relationship with the media is a bit difficult because the person would be anthropomorphizing a process of reception with the media. The problem is that media (and the material broadcast) are not a real person, and therefore the perception of a relationship creates conceptual difficulty for interpersonal communication and other scholars. If one defines a necessary requirement of a relationship as some type of exchange, then the relationship cannot really exist. But, for example, every night many Americans invite a favorite newscaster to deliver information to them about the world.

However, the perception of interaction or the actions that an audience take with respect to the media may create or feel like a relationship. Schiappa and Allen point to the basis for the formation of such interactions and relationships. Persons are more likely to develop this relationship if they are lonely, view television as real, and see the characters as similar to them. This indicates the possibility that the formation of these relationships becomes a kind of surrogate or substitute for other relationships.

The formulation of uses and gratifications focuses on the function of the media. How does the audience achieve goals by using media content and form? What may require examination is how the kind of habits that persons develop in media consumption define and serve as a surrogate relationship. Is the use of television or the movies a kind of fantasy or other relationship similar to what children have with their stuffed animals?

Managing or Controlling the Perception

The last issue deals with the education and the proper perspective or contextualization required for understanding and responding to a media experience. The question of who is the master is an important one for understanding media effects. The mixed results of the media priming meta-analysis (Roskos-Ewoldsen, Klinger, & Roskos-Ewoldsen, chap. 5, this volume) indicate that the argument about whether media priming becomes influential meets with mixed support. The extent to which media information is later utilized in other circumstances or remains context bound is unclear, indicating that the impact of media on the priming for other information does not reach a clear-cut conclusion for all content. The results suggest that although there is cause for attention, the need to develop a more sophisticated view of the media effect is going to require greater attention to the preconditions that exist before the introduction of media content. In addition, priming may be found only in the case of some content and not simply constitute a general effect of media.

A great deal of consideration needs to be placed on examination of how special populations (such as children) use or confront media images. The answer to this question is complex, revealing positive and negative implications. The increased diversity of the media indicates that special populations will all eventually be provided a tailored media outlet (e.g., channels already exist for golf, classic sports, biography, and style). The bad news is that the motives of the broadcaster are commercial. Yet, the potential for education and for reducing the pernicious effects of media represents a real possibility as some research suggests (Allen, D'Alessio, Emmers, & Gebhardt, 1996; Wilson, 1987; Wilson & Weiss, 1991).

Whether the person or event is captured and used by the media remains an open-ended question. The person creating the media image may not generate the interpretation that is formed in the mind of the viewer; indeed, the interpretation will variably diverge from the intended message. Appropriate interventions or education could change the trajectory of undesirable outcomes by providing a frame for the interpretation of the images. A critical eye on the content of the media may be the simplest method of changing the various outcomes.

THE TRAIL INTO THE FUTURE

The fundamental step that needs to be taken is the acceptance that uncensored and unfiltered media images produce effects on audiences. However, in this chapter we use the terms of censorship and filter as applied to individuals making choices and decisions not to governmental or societal bodies trying to regulate or control. The distinction is important because the move from the consideration of how *audiences* are affected by media to how *individuals* are affected begins the move toward recognition that the results of media exposure have an impact on individuals. The term *media effects* is a bit of a misnomer because the study of media effects is usually conducted by scholars in mass media; however, the effect of media is not a media issue per se, but rather an issue of social influence. What is being studied really is how one source of social influence (mass media content) has an impact on the personal lives and choices of the individual. To study the effect of media might more accurately be thought of as an interpersonal/psychological exercise with the aim of simply isolating and connecting exposure to one type of information source. As a result, with the focus on media, researchers often fail to fully consider how the use of media integrates into the entire social influence system that creates the individual. This process of investigation is going to become even more complex in the future.

Future types of media are going to be more diverse and less capable of being regulated than those available currently. The technological genie is out of the bottle, and there is no going back. The concern should then be focused not on changing content or changing the medium but instead changing the audience. Media education, often reflected in calls for media literacy programs of some type, indicate a way of recasting or providing a reinterpretation of media content. Education provides an option that is more effective and represents a positive step in control rather than the negative actions of censorship and restriction.

The move to a more active view of the audience, illustrated in some of the meta-analysis findings, indicates a kind of shift in the thinking about what constitutes an audience and how audience members react to material. This thinking takes the audience from a kind of passive mass of individuals, beginning the process of considering individual difference to ask the question about the audience member. That process is begun by the meta-analyses in this section, which find that various types of persons or situations are associated with various outcomes.

What the future of theoretical thinking projects is division and specialization for niche audiences with higher degrees of homogeneity but smaller in size. Increased specialization results in media content that is more extreme or focused on various gratifications for an audience seeking very particular content to achieve a desirable media experience. The idea of "mass" media becomes increasingly a misnomer, representing a past when there were but three networks and the news came on at 6 P.M. every night. The explosion of channels and diminished size of the audience combined with increased ability to select particular content 24 hours/per day (either broadcast or on demand) means that the control for what is watched or surfed really begins to reside with the viewer.

The current meta-analyses probably underestimate, in a very real sense, the nature of the problem with and impact of the various media. The improved ability to highly select media means increased choice, instant gratification, and selectivity. The arguments made by Eveland (2003) about the need to consider media effects in an era of new technology should receive consideration. Whether the changes in format taking place with web access and on-demand cable will ultimately generate different effect outcomes is unclear. However, the ability of the consumer to make various kinds of selections and the implications of the technology for that part of the process of media consumption are evident.

The study of media effects and the accompanying theories represents an ongoing enterprise of social significance. Every recent presidential election has involved issues of control and access to various media. The arguments about the existence of effects seem clear; the implications of those effects for social policy are far less clear. The attention and exploration of various elements involved in media selection deserve consideration and, more importantly, so does the development of coherent and comprehensive theories that will account for empirical data and offer explanation.

REFERENCES

Allen, M., D'Alessio, D., & Emmers-Sommer, T. (1999). Reactions of criminal sexual offenders to pornography: A meta-analytic summary. In M. Roloff (Ed.), *Communication yearbook 22* (pp. 139–169). Thousand Oaks, CA: Sage.

Allen, M., D'Alessio, D., Emmers, T., & Gebhardt, L. (1996). The role of educational briefings in mitigating effects of experimental exposure to violent sexually explicit material: A meta-analysis. *Journal of Sex Research, 33,* 135–141.

Casey, M., Allen, M., Emmers-Sommer, T., Sahlstein, E., DeGooyer, D., Winters, A., Wagner, A., & Dun, T. (2003). When a celebrity contracts a disease: The example of Earvin "Magic" Johnson's announcement that he was HIV positive. *Journal of Health Communication, 8,* 249–266.

Eveland, W. (2003). A "mix of attributes" approach to the study of media effects and new communication technologies. *Journal of Communication, 53,* 395–410.

Herrett-Skjellum, J., & Allen, M. (1996). Television programming and sexual stereotypes: A meta-analysis. In B. Burleson (Ed.), *Communication yearbook 19* (pp. 157–186). Thousand Oaks, CA: Sage.

Wilson, B. J. (1987). Reducing children's emotional reactions to mass media through rehearsed explanation and exposure to a replica of a fear object. *Human Communication Research, 14,* 3–26.

Wilson, B. J., & Weiss, A. J. (1991). The effects of two reality explanations on children's reactions to a frightening movie scene. *Communication Monographs, 58,* 307–326.

4

Effects of Agenda Setting

Wayne Wanta
University of Missouri

Salma Ghanem
University of Texas–Pan American

Agenda-setting research has now spanned three decades, since the initial investigation by McCombs and Shaw (1972) was conducted during the 1968 election. In the intervening years, the role that the news media play in influencing the perceived importance of issues held by the public has been the focus of hundreds of investigations. The vast majority of these studies have found widespread support for a media influence on issue salience. In other words, the amount of press coverage that issues receive gives individuals salience cues with which they learn the relative importance of these issues.

Agenda-setting researchers have utilized a wide variety of methodologies in their investigations. Some, such as Winter and Eyal (1981), have tracked agenda setting across several years. Others, such as Miller and Wanta (1996), have examined agenda setting through cross-sectional analyses.

Because of the differing methodologies, a meta-analysis of agenda setting seems especially appropriate. Several methodological artifacts could influence the magnitude of agenda-setting effects found by researchers.

We will investigate four potential factors. The first two are factors previously noted by McCombs (1981) and McCombs, Danielian, and Wanta (1995): the number of issues examined (single issue vs. multiple issue studies) and the unit of analysis under investigation (individual vs. aggregate data studies). The third factor involves the independent variable in agenda-setting studies: whether the variable under investigation was media content (issue coverage) or media exposure (the amount of media content consumed). The final factor involves the time frame under examination: whether the analysis utilized a cross-sectional survey or employed a longitudinal examination.

THE AGENDA-SETTING APPROACH

Through the three decades of research investigating the agenda-setting function of the news media, researchers have refined the theory in several ways. Whereas most research has found support for a link between the amount of media coverage devoted to issues and the public's perception regarding the importance of these issues, recent research has moved into several new areas.

Many recent studies, for example, have examined contingent conditions affecting the magnitude of agenda-setting effects. Researchers such as Hill (1985) and Wanta (1997) have examined personal characteristics of individuals most likely to demonstrate agenda-setting effects. Hill (1985) found that agenda-setting influences were most pronounced among highly educated individuals. Other variables, such as respondents' media use patterns, were less important. Wanta (1997), meanwhile, demonstrated an agenda-setting process that was impacted by individuals' demographics, psychological attitudes, and behavior. His study showed an agenda-setting process in which demographics affected individuals' perceived credibility of the news media. Credibility, in turn, influenced respondents' reliance upon the media for political information. Reliance affected media use, which ultimately influenced the magnitude of agenda-setting effects that individuals demonstrated.

A second area of concentration involves examinations of sources of the media agenda. Researchers are interested in the question of who sets the media agenda, moving their investigations earlier in the communication process to examine how the media agenda is constructed. Researchers have examined areas ranging from the president–press relationship (Wanta, Stephenson, Turk, & McCombs, 1989) to city council meetings and subsequent coverage of issues discussed by council members (Weaver & Elliott, 1985). Researchers also have investigated intermedia agenda setting, or how one medium, such as the *New York Times,* influences the coverage patterns of other news media (e.g., see Shoemaker, Wanta, & Leggett, 1989).

Agenda-setting researchers also have conducted several examinations with the purpose of utilizing methodological advancements. Several researchers have employed advanced statistical tools to increase the rigor in agenda-setting studies. Brosius and Kepplinger (1992b), for example, conducted a weekly survey in Germany and thus were able to use time series analysis, a stringent statistical approach that requires many data points with no missing data. Previous researchers attempting to use time series analysis were forced to either violate important data restrictions or extrapolate from existing data, essentially creating data to fit the analysis (e.g., Zhu, 1992).

Finally, researchers have begun to examine a "second-level" of agenda-setting research, or an "agenda of attributes" (see Ghanem, 1997, for a discussion). Studies in this area combine framing research with agenda setting, examining how coverage in the news media influences the salience of attributes. Individuals learn not only the importance of issues but also important attributes of public officials based on how the public officials are portrayed in the media. If President Clinton were to be portrayed as an international leader in news reports, for example, individuals will tend to link positive international leadership attributes to him.

AGENDA-SETTING CATEGORIES

Previous agenda-setting research can be categorized in several ways. One useful typology was introduced by McCombs (1981), who argued that all agenda-setting research can be categorized into four groups based on two factors: the type of data utilized (aggregate or individual) and the type of issue (single issue or issue sets), all of which would be useful to examine in a meta-analysis of agenda setting. McCombs, Danielian, and Wanta (1995) further detailed the resulting categories and labeled them mass persuasion, automaton, natural history, and cognitive portrait.

Mass Persuasion Studies

These studies focus on sets of issues and on aggregated data. Agenda setting is viewed mainly from the societal level—respondents as a group. This was the typology for many of the early studies in agenda setting, including the initial studies of McCombs and Shaw (1972) and Funkhouser (1973).

Weaver (1984) pointed out an important distinction about mass persuasion studies: These studies do not show that the news media influenced individuals' agendas, but instead that the media influenced the *distribution* of the top one or two issues among some populations. As Weaver noted: "Even though this is not as dramatic an effect as some advocates of agenda-setting might hope for, it is still an important phenomenon, for it suggests that the relative amount of emphasis on various issues by the media determines the size of various groups of individuals in a given community or society who are most concerned about these same issues" (p. 683).

Mass persuasion studies have employed a very simple operationalization of the agenda-setting effect. McCombs and Shaw (1972), for example, used a cross-sectional survey in Chapel Hill, North Carolina, asking respondents what they thought were the key issues of the 1968 presidential campaign. The issues were rank ordered based on the percentage of respondents who named the issues as important. This public agenda was then compared with content from television, newspapers, and news magazines. They found a strong correlation between the two issue agendas ($r = .97, p < .001$).

Funkhouser (1973) compared data from the Gallup polls that asked "What is the number one problem facing our country today?" with media coverage in three weekly magazines—*Time, Newsweek,* and *U.S. News.* The number of articles dealing with issues mentioned in all Gallup polls from 1960 to 1970 were highly correlated with Gallup responses to the most important problem question ($r = .78$, $p < .001$). Thus, the amount of coverage issues received in the decade of the 1960s closely matched the issue concerns reported in Gallup polls for the same time period.

Automaton Studies

These studies examine sets of issues and individual agendas—in other words, an agenda unique to each respondent. Very few agenda-setting studies can be classified here. Indeed, McCombs et al. (1995) noted that there would be little reason to expect an individual to mirror perfectly the ranking of issues covered in the news media. The article by McLeod, Becker, and Byrnes (1974) is perhaps the purest example of automaton studies. They found only limited support for the agenda-setting hypothesis when they asked individuals to rank order six or more issues.

A closer look at McLeod et al.'s (1974) operationalization of agenda-setting gives some indication of why few researchers have either attempted studies that would fit into this category of methodology or have found support for the agenda-setting hypothesis. McLeod et al. asked potential voters to rank six issues on their level of relative importance. These rankings were then compared with the coverage these issues received in two competing newspapers.

Issue agendas for the two newspapers varied greatly. In addition, the authors found only limited support for the agenda-setting hypothesis. This support, however, could be attributed to one specific issue. Here, the media gave a great deal of coverage to honesty in government, but the public rated it average. Thus, whereas many issue ranks were relatively consistent across the public and press agendas, one of the six issues—honesty in government—may have minimized the observed agenda-setting effect found here.

Relatively few automaton studies in agenda setting have been undertaken. Moreover, Weaver (1984) concluded that studies of this type, which typically compare the ranking of a set of issues emphasized by the media with the ranking of those same issues by individuals, generally offer much less support for the agenda-setting hypothesis than other types of studies. As Weaver noted: "this is not terribly surprising, given the stringency of the test (media ranking of a set of issues transferred intact to each individual in the study)" (p. 687).

Natural History Studies

These studies examine agenda-setting effects across single issues with aggregate public agenda data. Several studies in this classification have shown powerful agenda-setting effects. Winter and Eyal (1981), for example, found an agenda-setting influence of the news media for the civil rights issue. Other research in this area includes the studies of Lang and Lang (1983) and MacKuen and Coombs (1981).

Winter and Eyal (1981) operationalized the agenda-setting effect by tracking the civil rights issue across an extended time period of 22 years, from 1954 to 1976. They used aggregate data, utilizing 27 Gallup polls that asked the most important problem question. Thus, their measure was not a public "agenda," but public "concern," as determined by the percentage of Gallup poll respondents who named civil rights as the number one problem facing our country today. Again, the analysis here is placed on the issue of civil rights and not on individuals' level of concern with civil rights. They then compared this public concern measure with the number of front page stories in the *New York Times* that were devoted to civil rights. They found strong support for an agenda-setting effect for the civil rights issue.

Natural history studies in agenda setting, as Weaver (1984) noted, have been extremely successful and have provided substantial support for the agenda-setting hypothesis. The success of studies in this area may be attributed to the time frames examined. Agenda-setting effects, then, may be best examined across extensive time frames. In other words, the magnitude of the agenda-setting effect may be cumulative over time, much like the findings dealing with the cultivation research suggest.

Cognitive Portrait Studies

These studies look at single issues and individual agendas. Most cognitive portrait studies have found strong support for agenda setting, in sharp contrast to the automaton studies.

The experimental studies of Iyengar and Kinder (1987) and the quasi-experiments of Protess, Leff, Brooks, and Gordon (1985) are two good examples of research in this category. Because Iyengar and Kinder (1987) utilized an experimental design, their operationalization of the agenda-setting effect was one of the most powerful in this area of research. They essentially constructed an index by combining responses in three areas: the subjects' personal concern for eight national issues—including the experimental treatment issues—the extent to which each issue was deserving of additional government action, and the frequency with which the research participants talked about each issue in everyday conversation. They then compared pretest scores with posttest scores. Their results yielded "striking evidence of agenda-setting" (p. 19).

Cognitive portrait studies, as Weaver (1984) argued, have been extremely successful in supporting the agenda-setting hypothesis, especially if the study employed a rigorous methodology. The experiments of Iyengar and Kinder (1987), for example, provided strong support for agenda setting, whereas the panel studies of Schoenbach (1982) and Schoenbach and Weaver (1983) provided moderate support. The one-shot, cross-sectional study of Erbring, Goldenberg, and Miller (1980) produced the weakest support.

Content Versus Exposure as an Independent Variable

Generally, agenda-setting researchers have utilized two main independent variables in their investigations. Some researchers have ignored how often individuals use the news media and instead have concentrated on the coverage pattern of the news media. Indeed, McCombs (1981) noted that many researchers assume exposure to the news media as a given, because media content is so accessible through both new media channels and through indirect exposure from interpersonal discussion with friends and family members.

As Wanta and Wu (1992) found, interpersonal communication can enhance agenda-setting effects, even for low media users, if the discussions deal with issues covered in the news media. Thus, exposure may not be a prerequisite for agenda-setting influences to occur.

On the other hand, exposure to media messages would appear to be an important factor influencing the magnitude of agenda-setting effects displayed by individuals. The more individuals see the news media's coverage of issues, the more likely they are to think that the issues covered in the media are important. If agenda setting is social learning (see Shaw & McCombs, 1977), learning may be enhanced by repetitious exposure to media messages.

Wanta and Hu (1994), for example, included exposure to the news media as the independent variable. High exposure to news media messages did indeed lead to strong agenda-setting effects. They also examined several factors influencing media use, including demographics and psychological variables. They found education, attitudes toward the media, reliance on the media, and exposure to the media all had some effect on the magnitude of agenda-setting effects demonstrated by individuals.

In their initial study, McCombs and Shaw (1972), on the other hand, correlated media content with issue concerns of respondents in their survey. The media agenda closely matched the public agenda, suggesting that media coverage of issues influences the perceived importance of those issues among the public.

Longitudinal Versus Cross-Sectional Studies

The time periods under investigation in agenda-setting studies can be classified in two broad categories. Some researchers such as Winter and Eyal (1981), for example, have tracked agenda setting over time. Utilizing a number of data point across several years and, indeed, even decades, researchers have used the theoretical framework of agenda setting to track public opinion change over time. In their study, Winter and Eyal (1981) found a strong link between media coverage and public concern with civil rights. Points in time when civil rights was high on the public agenda corresponded with periods of high media coverage of civil rights. Many of the longitudinal studies employed Gallup poll data on the most important problem question ("What is the number one problem facing our country today?"), but several other studies utilized panel studies with several interviewing waves. Brosius and Kepplinger (1992c), for example, interviewed respondents weekly for an entire year.

Cross-sectional studies have also been successful. These studies typically compare media coverage before a set survey period with responses from respondents. Miller and Wanta (1996) utilized a cross-sectional design in their examination of differences between racial groups. They analyzed content of several news media in the 4 weeks before their survey period and compared survey responses to the media coverage.

METHOD

A total of 90 agenda-setting studies were initially identified as potential cases for inclusion in our meta-analysis (Table 4.1). Some studies were eliminated for the following reasons:

The lack of any data analysis. Several studies were discussions or overviews of agenda-setting research and did not involve an actual test of the agenda-setting hypothesis. For example, Downs (1972) discussed the "issue attention cycle" but did not conduct an actual statistical test of agenda setting.

An inappropriate focus. Some agenda-setting studies examined a "policy agenda" of public officials that did not involve a test of the press–public interface. For example, Wanta, Stephenson, Turk, and McCombs (1989) examined the relationship between the issue emphases of three presidents and media coverage of those issues. Thus, the focus was not on the public.

Unusual data analysis strategies. Some agenda-setting studies employed data analysis strategies that were deemed not comparable to the vast majority of agenda-setting studies. Brosius and Kepplinger (1992), for example, utilized a time series analysis in their examination of agenda setting in Germany. Because the majority of agenda-setting studies have used Pearson correlations, eliminating these few time series studies did not substantially reduce the number of studies included in our analysis.

TABLE 4.1
Studies Included in the Meta-Analysis

Author	Date	r	N
Atwater	1985	.64–.46	304
Atwood	1978	.44	150
Behr	1985	.73–.37	MIP*
Benton	1976	.81–.62	111
Brosius	1992a	.62	1000
Brosius	1992b	.12	1000
Demers	1989	.21–.77	MIP
Eaton	1989	.48	MIP
Einsiedel	1984	.45	488
Erbring	1980	.10–.11	MIP
Funkhouser	1973	.78	MIP
Heeter	1989	.96	193
Hill	1985	.19	1204
Hubbard	1975	.24	150
Iyengar	1979	.35–.47	MIP
Iyengar	1993	.85	1500
Jablonski	1996	.19	1324
Kaid	1977	.64	166
Lasorsa	1990	.57	624
McCombs	1972	.967	100
McLeod	1974	.05–.16	389
Miller	1996	.59	577
Palmgreen	1977	.50–.70	400
Salwen	1988	.54–.98	304
Salwen	1992	.56	629
Siune	1975	.91	1302
Smith	1987	.65	400
Smith	1988	.71	471
Sohn	1978	.24	150
Stone	1981	.47–.55	302
Swanson	1978	.45	83
Tipton	1975	.75–.88	42-303
Wanta	1994a	.54	MIP
Wanta	1994b	.29	341
Wanta	1994c	.60–.92	341
Wanta	1992	.31	341
Watt	1981	.35–.69	MIP
Weaver	1980	.27–.31	339
Weaver	1975	.21–.33	421
Williams	1977	.49–.83	350
Williams	1978	.11–.24	503
Williams	1983	.22–.78	356
Winter	1981	.71	MIP
Yagade	1990	.79	MIP
Zhu	1992	.52	MIP

*Note. Because the number of respondents in the "most important problem" polls conducted by the Gallup organization varied over the years, we used 1,000 as the N for these studies.

Several of the remaining studies involved multiple tests of the agenda-setting hypothesis; thus, the analysis here involved comparisons of 90 results. These results were first examined together, then categorized and compared on the basis of the four factors mentioned earlier: (a). studies on single issues versus multiple issues; (b). studies with individual versus aggregate data; (c). studies with media content versus media exposure as the independent variable; and (d). studies with used longitudinal versus cross-sectional designs.

RESULTS

The majority of studies examined here showed statistically significant findings. This comes as no surprise because many previous researchers have noted that the vast majority of studies have found support for a media influence on the perceived importance of issues held by members of the public. The overall mean correlation for the studies was .53.

We then calculated the corrected population standard deviation, which was 2.31, larger than the standard deviation of a normal curve, which is 1.96. Thus, the study correlation is positive in the studies examined here.

Next, we calculated the 95% confidence interval for the studies included. The results show that the 95% confidence level is $.47 \leq .53 \leq .59$. Thus, for a factor to increase agenda-setting results, the mean correlation for studies using this factor would have to meet or exceed .5860. For a factor to decrease agenda-setting results, the mean correlation for studies employing this factor would have to be $\leq .47$.

Surprisingly, none of the factors produced a mean correlation exceeding .59. In fact, the two factors noted by McCombs (1981), multiple versus single issue studies and aggregate versus individual data, produced only slight changes in the mean correlation. Single-issue studies had a mean correlation of .54, compared with a correlation of .53 for multiple-issue studies. Similarly, studies using aggregate data produced a mean correlation of .54, compared with a correlation of .52 for individual-level data studies. Apparently, these factors matter little in agenda-setting research.

The other two variables examined here produced slightly larger differences. Researchers using news content as the independent variable produced a mean correlation of .53, whereas researchers using media exposure as the independent variable produced a mean correlation of .49. Finally, longitudinal studies produced a mean correlation of .56 to .49 for cross-sectional studies.

Chi-square tests were also performed, and the results were as follows. For the multiple versus single issue studies: $\chi^2 = 0.54, p > .05$. For the individual versus aggregate data analysis: $\chi^2 = 1.75, p > .5$. For the exposure versus content studies: $\chi^2 = 17.95, p < .01$. For the longitudinal versus cross-sectional studies: $\chi^2 = 46.14, p < .01$. These tests show that studies examining content have been more successful than studies examining level of exposure, perhaps because the content gets filtered through even to individuals who do not use the news media much. This result might support a two-step flow of agenda-setting influence.

The tests also show that longitudinal studies are more successful than cross-sectional studies. Two reasons are possible: (a) agenda setting is more of a long-term effect that does not always show up in a one-shot survey but does show up over time; and (b) agenda-setting researchers have not been overly precise or consistent in their calculations of the optimal time lag for agenda-setting effects to occur. Cross-sectional studies have looked at time lags as short as 1 week and as long as several months.

DISCUSSION

The meta-analysis here points out several conclusions about agenda-setting research. First, these results show how wide ranging the agenda-setting influence of the news media is. None of the factors examined here were shown to statistically increase or decrease agenda-setting effects. In other words, significant agenda-setting effects were found for studies using a variety of methodologies, for example, whether the analysis involved a single issue or an agenda of issues or whether the unit of analysis was the individual or the issue. Methodological artifacts had little impact on the magnitude of effects found in agenda-setting research.

Second, these results show that the largest differences on agenda-setting influences involved the time period used in the analyses. Longitudinal studies—those involving more than one time point—produced a larger mean correlation (.5629) than that (.4931) for cross-sectional studies—those involving a one-shot survey period. Even though these two mean correlations were within the 95% confidence level limits, the trend here shows that studies across time were more successful in producing stronger agenda-setting findings than were single surveys.

These results again could demonstrate the broad agenda-setting impact of the news media. Studies involving one survey must contend with historical events unique to that specific time period. Wanta (1988), for example, had to contend with news reports of the hijacking of the Achille Lauro in his agenda-setting experiment. Other events may affect findings of other cross-sectional studies.

Historical events are less of a concern with longitudinal studies, however. Because longitudinal studies involve several time points, unique historical events may occur during one time point but not necessarily all time points. Winter and Eyal (1981), for instance, examined 27 Gallup polls across 22 years in their study of the civil rights issue. The impact of key news events, such as a major hijacking or a highly publicized murder investigation, on the agenda-setting process would be less across several years of news content.

Also showing a sizable difference were the two categories of independent variables used in agenda-setting research. Here, research using news content as the independent variable produced a larger mean correlation (.5317) than did research using media exposure (.4889), which was a statistically significant difference. Again, this result could be due to the widespread agenda-setting influence of the news media. Which issues the news media cover appears to be slightly more important than how much content individuals consume.

Although exposure to media messages is indeed a key factor in the agenda-setting process, the messages that the news media transmit apparently are even more important. In other words, the media content may affect individuals in a society even if they are low media users. Thus, two explanations are plausible here: Either low media users receive media messages through interpersonal communication channels or low media users are affected by their limited exposure to mass media channels. In either case, media influences appear to have powerful effects at a societal level. This could be the case particularly with "high threshold" issues. Brosius and Kepplinger (1995), for example, found that high profile, "killer" issues can force many other issues off the news media agenda and thus attract attention for all individuals, regardless of how often they use the news media.

Finally, the two factors first identified by McCombs (1981)—the number of issues examined and the unit of analysis—played a very limited role in influencing the magnitude of agenda-setting effects. Studies utilizing the issue as the unit of analysis were only slightly more successful in demonstrating agenda-setting influences than studies utilizing the individual as the unit of analysis (.5353 to .5217). This small difference is surprising, given the nature of agenda setting. The concept of agenda setting was originally proposed as a societal influence (McCombs & Shaw, 1972). This societal influence would be more likely to be present in analyses that concentrate on society as a whole; that is, studies using aggregate data, in which individuals are grouped together based on issues of concern to them. However, the results here show that agenda-setting effects in studies examining the individual as the unit of analysis were not significantly smaller than studies with issues as the unit of analysis. Thus, whereas agenda setting is a societal effect, it nonetheless takes place within individuals. Researchers have been relatively successful in finding this influence within individuals.

The smallest difference found here dealt with single-issue versus multiple-issue studies—.5425 for single-issue studies to .5349 for multiple-issue studies. Two points should be made here. First, the original agenda-setting hypothesis dealt with an "agenda" of issues. The media's agenda of issues, as determined by the relative amount of coverage issues received, influences the public's agenda of issues, as determined by the rank ordering of issues by survey respondents. Thus, the notion of agenda setting was based on multiple issues—a list or agenda of issues.

On the other hand, it seems more likely that the news media's influence on the public deals with the top issues on the agenda and not the entire agenda. If an issue such as the environment generally receives little coverage from the media but suddenly gets substantial coverage, for whatever reason, media consumers would be likely to notice this change and may raise the environment higher on their issue agendas. However, if the environment receives relatively little coverage but suddenly receives even less coverage, the public would be less likely to drop this issue from a low spot on their agenda to an even lower spot.

The ebb and flow of individual issues at the top of the media agenda, then, logically would have more influence on the public than the ebb and flow of individual issues at the bottom of the media agenda. Thus, studies tracking a single issue would be more likely to find an agenda-setting influence if that issue is given at least some coverage and has some salience.

However, a single issue rising or falling also influences the entire agenda of issues as well. And as the meta-analysis here shows, there is very little difference in the magnitude of agenda-setting effects for studies examining a single issue and those examining an agenda of issues.

This meta-analysis showed significant agenda-setting effects for the four factors examined: single versus multiple issues, individual versus aggregate data, media content versus media exposure, and cross-sectional versus longitudinal data. It focused on the effects of the media on the public. Further meta-analysis studies could investigate the contingent conditions affecting agenda-setting effects, factors influencing the media agenda and the emerging second level of agenda setting. Wanta and Chang (1999), for example, examined media use and the second-level of agenda setting, which is concerned with an agenda of attributes rather than an agenda of issues. Their analysis found that respondents linked different attributes to President Clinton based on the types of media content they used often. Thus, a meta-analysis examining factors mediating this agenda of attributes would be worthwhile.

REFERENCES

*Atwater, T., Salwen, M. B., & Anderson, R. B. (1985). Media agenda-setting with environmental issues. *Journalism Quarterly, 62,* 393–397.
*Atwood, E. L., Sohn, A. B., & Sohn, H. (1978). Daily newspaper contributions to community discussion. *Journalism Quarterly, 55,* 570–576.
*Behr, R. L., & Iyengar, S. (1985). Television news, real-world cues, and changes in the public agenda. *Public Opinion Quarterly, 49,* 38–57.
*Benton, M., & Frazier, P. J. (1976). The agenda setting function of mass media at three levels of information holding. *Communication Research, 3,* 261–274.
*Brosius, H., & Kepplinger, H. (1992a). Beyond agenda-setting: The influence of partisanship and television reporting on the electorate's voting intentions. *Journalism Quarterly, 69,* 893–901.
Brosius, H., & Kepplinger, H. (1992b). Linear and nonlinear models of agenda setting in television. *Journal of Broadcasting and Electronic Media, 36,* 5–23.
*Brosius, H., & Kepplinger, H. (1992c). The agenda setting function of television news: Static and dynamic views. *Communication Research, 17,* 183–211.
Brosius, H., & Kepplinger H., (1995). Killer and victim issues: Competition in the agenda-setting process of German television. *International Journal of Public Opinion Research, 7*(3), 211–231.

*Demers, D. P., Craff, D., Yang-Ho, C., & Pessin, B. M. (1989). Issue obtrusiveness and the agenda-setting effects of national network news. *Communication Research, 16*, 793–812.

Downs, A. (1972). Up and Down with Ecology: The Issue Attention Cycle, *The Public Interest, 28*, 38–50.

*Eaton, H., Jr. (1989). Agenda-setting with bi-weekly data on content of three national media. *Journalism Quarterly, 66*, 942–948 & 959.

*Einsiedel, E. F., Salomone, K. L., & Schneider, F. P. (1984). Crime: Effects of media exposure and personal experience on issue salience. *Journalism Quarterly, 61*, 131–136.

*Erbring, L., Goldenberg, E. N., & Miller, A. H. (1980). Front page news and real-world cues: A new look at agenda-setting by the media. *American Journal of Political Science, 24*, 16–49.

*Funkhouser, G. R. (1973). The issues of the sixties: An exploratory study in the dynamics of public opinion. *Public Opinion Quarterly, 37*, 62–75.

Ghanem, S. (1997). Filling in the tapestry: The second level of agenda setting. In M. E. McCombs, D. L. Shaw & D. H. Weaver (Eds.). *Communication and democracy* (pp. 3–11). Hillsdale, NJ: Lawrence Erlbaum Associates.

*Heeter, C., Brown, N., Soffin, S., Stanley, C., & Salwen, M. (1989). Agenda setting by electronic text news. *Journalism Quarterly, 66*, 101–106.

*Hill, D. B. (1985). Viewer characteristics and agenda setting by television news. *Public Opinion Quarterly, 49*, 340–350.

*Hubbard, J., DeFleur, M., & DeFleur, L. (1975). Mass media influences on public conceptions of social problems. *Social Problems, 23*, 22–34.

*Iyengar, S. (1979). Television news and issue salience: A reexamination of the agenda-setting hypothesis. *American Politics Quarterly, 7*, 395–416.

Iyengar, S., & Kinder, D. R. (1987). *News that matters: Television and American opinion.* Chicago: University of Chicago Press.

*Iyengar, S., & Simon, A. (1993). News coverage of the Gulf crisis and public opinion: A study of agenda-setting, priming and framing. *Communication Research, 20*, 408(28).

*Jablonski, P. M., & Gonzenbach, W. J. (1996). Crime and agenda-setting, 1988–1995: The relationship among the president, the press, and the public. *World Communication, 25*, 157–168

*Kaid, L. L., Hale, K., & Williams, J. (1977). Media agenda setting of a specific political event. *Journalism Quarterly, 54*, 584–587.

Lang, K., & Lang, G. E. (1983). *The battle for public opinion: The president, the press and the polls during Watergate.* New York: Columbia University Press.

*Lasorsa, D. L., & Wanta, W. (1990). The effects of personal, interpersonal and experience on issue salience. *Journalism Quarterly, 67*, 804–813.

MacKuen, M. B., & Coombs, S. L. (1981). *More than news: Media power in public affairs.* Beverly Hills, CA: Sage.

McCombs, M. E. (1981). The agenda-setting approach. In D. D. Nimmo & K. R. Sanders (Eds.), *Handbook of Political Communication* (pp. 121–140). Beverly Hills, CA: Sage Publications.

McCombs, M. E., Danielian, L., & Wanta, W. (1995). Issues in the news and the public agenda: The agenda-setting tradition. In T. L. Glasser & C. T. Salmon (Eds.), *Public opinion and the communication of consent* (pp. 281–300). New York: Guilford.

*McCombs, M. E., & Shaw, D. L. (1972). The agenda-setting function of mass media. *Public Opinion Quarterly, 26*, 176–87.

*McLeod, J. M., Becker, L. B., & Byrnes, J. E. (1974). Another look at the agenda setting function of the press. *Communication Research, 1*, 131–165.

*Miller, R. E., & Wanta, W. (1996). Race as a variable in agenda setting. *Journalism & Mass Communication Quarterly, 73*, 913–925.

*Palmgreen, P., & Clark, P. (1977). Agenda setting with local and national issues. *Communication Research, 4*, 435–452.

Protess, D. L., Leff, D. R., Brooks, S. C., & Gordon, M. T. (1985). Uncovering rape: The watchdog press and the limits of agenda-setting. *Public Opinion Quarterly, 49,* 19–37.

*Salwen, M. B. (1988). Effect of accumulation on issue salience in agenda setting. *Journalism Quarterly, 65,* 100–106 & 130.

*Salwen, M. B., & Matera, F. R. (1992). Public salience of foreign nations. *Journalism Quarterly, 69,* 623–632.

Schoenbach, K. (1982, May). Agenda-setting effects of print and television in West Germany. Paper presented at the International Communication Association Annual Convention, Boston, MA.

Schoenbach, K., & Weaver, D. H., (1983, May). Cognitive bonding and need for orientation during political campaigns. Paper presented at the International Communication Association Annual Convention, Dallas, TX.

Shoemaker, P. J., Wanta, W., & Leggett, D. (1989). Drug coverage and public opinion 1972–1986. In Pamela J. Shoemaker (Ed.),. *Communication campaigns about drugs: Government, media and the public* (pp. 67–80). Hillsdale, NJ: Lawrence Erlbaum Associates.

Shaw, D. L., & McCombs, M. E. (1977). *The emergence of American political issues: The agenda-setting function of the press* (pp. 33–51). St. Paul, MN: West Publishing.

*Siune, K., & Borre, O. (1975). Setting the agenda for a Danish election. *Journal of Communication, 25,* 65–73.

*Smith, K. A. (1987). Newspaper coverage and public concern about community issues. *Journalism Monographs,* 101.

*Smith, K. A. (1988). Effects of coverage on neighborhood and community concerns. *Newspaper Research Journal, 9,* 35–47.

*Sohn, A. B. (1978). A longitudinal analysis of local non-political agenda setting effects. *Journalism Quarterly, 55,* 325–333

*Stone, G. C., & McCombs, M. E. (1981). Tracing the time lag in agenda-setting. *Journalism Quarterly, 58,* 51–55.

*Swanson, L. L., & Swanson, D. L. (1978). The agenda-setting function of the first Ford-Carter debate. *Communication Monographs, 45,* 330–353.

*Tipton, L., Haney, R. D., & Basehart, J. R. (1975). Media agenda-setting in city and state election campaigns. *Journalism Quarterly, 52,* 15–22.

Wanta, W. (1988). The effects of dominant photographs: An agenda-setting experiment. *Journalism Quarterly, 65,* 107–111.

Wanta, W. (1997). *The public and the national agenda: How people learn about important issues.* Mahwah, NJ: Lawrence Erlbaum Associates.

Wanta, W., & Chang, K. (1999, May). *Priming and the second level of agenda-setting.* Paper presented at the Annual Convention of the International Communication Association, San Francisco, CA.

*Wanta, W., & Hu, Y. (1994a). The agenda-setting effects of international news coverage: An examination of differing news frames. *International Journal of Public Opinion Research, 5,* 250–264.

*Wanta, W., & Hu, Y. (1994b). The effects of credibility, reliance, and exposure on media agenda-setting: A path analysis. *Journalism Quarterly, 71,* 9–98.

*Wanta, W., & Hu, Y. (1994c). Time-lag differences in the agenda process: An examination of five news media. *International Journal of Public Opinion Research, 6,* 225–240.

Wanta, W., Stephenson, M. A., Turk, J., & McCombs, M. E. (1989). How president's state of union talk influenced news media agenda. *Journalism Quarterly, 66,* 537–541.

*Wanta, W., & Wu, Y. (1992). Interpersonal communication and the agenda-setting process. *Journalism Quarterly, 69,* 847–55.

*Watt, J. H., Jr., & van den Berg, S. (1981). How time dependency influences media effects in a community controversy. *Journalism Quarterly, 58,* 43–50.

*Weaver, D. H. (1980). Audience need for orientation and media effects. *Communication Research, 7,* 361–376.

Weaver, D. H. (1984). Media agenda-setting and public opinion: Is there a link? in R. N. Bostrom & B. H. Westely (Eds.), *Communication yearbook 8* (pp. 680–691). Beverly Hills, CA: Sage.

Weaver, D. H., & Elliott, S. N. (1985). Who sets the agenda for the media? A study of local agenda-building. *Journalism Quarterly, 62,* 87–94.

*Weaver, D. H., McCombs, M. E., & Spellman, C. (1975). Watergate and the media: A case study of agenda setting. *American Politics Quarterly, 3,* 452–472.

*Williams, W., Jr., & Larsen, D. C. (1977). Agenda-setting in an off-election year. *Journalism Quarterly, 54,* 744–749.

*Williams, W., Jr., & Semlak, W. (1978). Campaign Agenda setting during the New Hampshire Primary. *Journal of Broadcasting, 22,* 531–540.

*Williams, W., Jr., Shapiro, M., & Cutbirth, C. (1983). The impact of campaign agendas on perceptions of issues in 1980 Campaign. *Journalism Quarterly, 60,* 226–232.

*Winter, J. P., & Eyal, C. (1981). Agenda-setting for the civil rights issue. *Public Opinion Quarterly, 45,* 376–83.

*Yagade, A., & Dozier, D. M. (1990). The media agenda-setting effect of concrete versus abstract issues. *Journalism Quarterly, 67,* 3–10.

*Zhu, J. (1992). Issue competition and attention distraction: A zero-sum theory of agenda-setting. *Journalism Quarterly, 69,* 825–26.

5

Media Priming:
A Meta-Analysis

David R. Roskos-Ewoldsen
University of Alabama

Mark R. Klinger
University of Alabama

Beverly Roskos-Ewoldsen
University of Alabama

Throughout most of the twentieth century, study of the mass media has focused on the consequences of the media for various aspects of people's lives (Rogers, 1994; Schramm, 1997). Early research attempted to ascertain whether the media had an influence and, if so, the extent of that influence. In the last 25 years, however, the focus has shifted toward the development of theories that specify the mechanisms by which the media exert whatever influence they have on people. One such theoretical perspective, first used in the early 1980s to explain media effects, involves the potential for the media to *prime* people's thoughts, beliefs, judgments, and behaviors (Berkowitz, 1984; Iyengar, Peters & Kinder, 1982; Roskos-Ewoldsen, Roskos-Ewoldsen, & Carpentier, 2002).

"Priming" refers to the effect of some preceding stimulus or event on how we react, broadly defined, to some subsequent stimulus. At this level, priming is an effect and not a theory. The effect is analogous to what happens when one primes a water well. When a person primes a well, the act of priming the well makes it possible for the well to produce water when it is pumped at a later time. As applied to the media, "priming" refers to the effects of the content of the media (e.g., extensive coverage of certain political stories, depictions of violence, the use of brief "teasers" about an upcoming story on a newscast) on people's later behavior or judgments (e.g., evaluations of the president, aggressive behavior, attention to news stories related to the teaser).

Cognitive and social psychologists have used priming paradigms since the early 1970s to study various aspects of the cognitive system. Given the extensive research on priming within social and cognitive psychology, it is not surprising that priming has been found to be useful as an explanation of a number of the effects of the media on people's thoughts, beliefs, judgments, and behavior. For several reasons, the characteristics of the media make it a likely source of priming. First, the ubiquitous nature of the media in our lives makes them a powerful tool for priming various concepts—often outside of our awareness—that may influence how we interpret later information. In particular, situations in which we have the TV on, but are not paying particular attention to it, create an ideal situation for priming to occur because explicit awareness of a prime often mitigates the influence of the prime (Herr, 1986; Higgins, 1989; Lombardi, Higgins, & Bargh, 1987). Second, particular types of media, most notably the news, are well suited to act as primes. A typical newscast covers a wide variety of topics, which may result in the priming of a correspondingly wide variety of concepts, which increases the likelihood that one of the primed items will influence how we interpret later ambiguous information. In addition, any particular story (e.g., the war in Iraq or President Clinton's sexual liaisons) will receive extensive coverage across time, which may result in related concepts (foreign policy or sexual indiscretion) being primed for an extended period of time (however, as will be discussed, if priming is occurring in this situation, then the degree of activation of the prime will certainly vary within this time period, depending on how long ago the story that acted as a prime was viewed or read). However, as we shall see, the influences of media priming are more complex than these simple examples suggest.

The two most prominent research areas that use priming to explain the effects of the media are media violence (Anderson, 1997; Anderson, Anderson, & Deuser, 1996; Anderson & Morrow, 1995; Beaver, Gold, & Prisco, 1992; Berkowitz, 1984, 1990, 1994; Bushman, 1995, 1998; Bushman & Geen, 1990; Carver, Ganellen, Froming, & Chambers, 1983; Josephson, 1987; Langley, O'Neal, Craig, & Yost, 1992; Malamuth & Check, 1985; Scharrer, 2001; Wann & Branscombe, 1990) and the impact of political news coverage on evaluations of the president (Domke, Shaw, & Wackman, 1998; Goidel, Shields, & Peffley, 1997; Hetherington, 1996; Highton, 2002; Iyengar & Kinder, 1987; Iyengar, Kinder, & Krosnizk, 1984; Iyengar, Peters, & Kinder, 1982; Iyengar & Simon, 1993; Krosnick & Brannon, 1993a, 1993b; Krosnick & Kinder, 1990; McGraw & Ling, 2003; McGraw & Pinney, 1990; Mendelberg, 1997; Miller & Krosnick, 2000; Mutz, 1992, 1994; Pan & Kosicki, 1997; Valentino, 1999; Willnat & Zhu, 1996). These two areas are discussed further below and are the main topics of the meta-analysis described later. Priming also has been used to explain the effects of rock music videos on gender stereotyping (Hansen & Hansen, 1988; Hansen & Krygowski, 1994), the interpretation of ambiguous print advertisements (Yi, 1990a, 1990b), the impact of news teasers on attention to and memory for news stories (Schleuder, White, & Cameron, 1993), stereotyped judgments of blacks and women (Domke, 2001; Domke, McCoy, & Torres, 1999; Forehand & Deshpande, 2001; Power, Murphy, & Coover, 1996), and perceptions of rape (Beaver, Gold, & Prisco, 1992; Wyer, Bodenhausen, & Gorman, 1985).

AN OVERVIEW OF PRIMING

To understand the basic nature of media priming, a brief foray into the study of priming by cognitive and social psychologists is in order. A brief review of some of the basic theories and findings concerning priming will help to identify some of the distinguishing characteristics of priming. This, in turn, should help us ascertain potential similarities and differences between media priming and the priming phenomenon that cognitive and social psychologists have been studying. Any similarities or differences found in the nature of priming phenomena studied by media scholars and cognitive and social psychologists should aid in the development of theories of media priming and identification of future directions for research on media priming.

Priming procedures were first used in cognitive psychology to explore the structure and representation of information within network models of memory (Anderson, 1983).[1] Network models of memory assume that information is stored in memory in the form of nodes and that each node represents a concept (e.g., there is a "doctor" node in memory). Furthermore, these nodes are connected to related nodes in memory by associative pathways (e.g., "doctor" is linked to "nurse" but probably is not directly linked to "butter"). An additional assumption of network models of memory is that each node has an activation threshold. If the node's level of activation exceeds its threshold, the node fires. When a node fires, it can influence the activation levels of other, associatively connected nodes. For example, if the "nurse" node fires, activation spreads from the "nurse" node to related nodes, such as "doctor." One consequence of spreading activation is that the related node now requires less additional activation for it to fire. The additional activation may accrue as a result of spreading activation from other related nodes, or it may result from the other major factor that influences a node's degree of activation: environmental input. Environmental input could be as simple as seeing the word. That is, seeing the word "doctor"

---

[1]The use of network models to explain priming effects should not be taken as evidence that the authors necessarily agree with network models of memory. Most models of memory (e.g., connectionist models) can explain priming effects. We use network models to explain priming because these models provide a convenient and useful way to explain priming.

should produce some level of activation of the "doctor" node. A final assumption of network models of memory is that the activation level of a node will dissipate over time if no additional source of activation is present. Eventually, given no more activation, the activation level of the node returns to its resting state and is no longer considered to be activated. Recall the classic "Joe Isuzu" advertisements where Joe Isuzu makes outlandish claims (which were identified as such by subscripts on the advertisement) about the remarkable characteristics of Isuzu vehicles. The viewing of such an advertisement might activate a "liar" node in memory. If the "liar" node is sufficiently activated, then activation would spread from that node to related nodes in memory, such as "corrupt," "unscrupulous," and "dishonorable."

According to network models of memory, priming works by the spread of activation between related nodes (i.e., concepts) in memory. A priming procedure that has been used extensively in cognitive psychology to test network and related models of memory involves a lexical decision task (Meyers & Schvaneveldt, 1971). In a lexical decision task, research participants are presented with letter strings, and their task is to judge as quickly as they can whether the string is a word or a nonword. The effects of priming are seen when the lexical decision times for a word are analyzed as a function of its relation to the previous word. When the immediately preceding word is semantically related to the current word (e.g., "doctor" is preceded by "nurse"), lexical decision times are quicker than they are when the current word is preceded by an unrelated word (e.g., "doctor" is preceded by "bread"). Network models of memory explain this priming effect easily. The presentation of the first item (the prime) produces enough activation for its node to fire and afford a lexical (i.e., word–nonword) decision. Activation from this node then spreads to connected (i.e., related) nodes, producing a level of activation above their resting states. Of course, the activation level of unrelated nodes would be unchanged by the first node's firing. Presentation of the second item (the target) also produces enough activation to cause its node to fire and permit a lexical decision. However, when the target item is related to the prime item, the target's node already has some activation from the prime and requires less activation for its firing than when the target is unrelated to the prime. One way in which the target node's increased readiness to fire reveals itself behaviorally is in the time it takes the participant to complete the lexical decision. That is, the lexical decision for a target that is related to its prime is faster than that for a target unrelated to its prime.

Returning to the Joe Isuzu example, if an advertisement for a politician were to appear after the Joe Isuzu commercial, people should be more likely and faster to identify the unfortunate politician as a charlatan because of the activation of "corrupt," "unscrupulous," and "dishonorable" nodes in memory by the Joe Isuzu advertisement. However, according to network models of memory, the influence of the Joe Isuzu commercial will be short lived and should not influence the interpretation of the politician's commercial if there are other commercials appearing between the Joe Isuzu advertisement and the politician's advertisement, because the activation of the "corrupt," "unscrupulous," and "dishonorable" nodes will dissipate with time.[2]

Social psychologists began using priming procedures in the late 1970s to study person perception, stereotyping, and attitude activation. The general procedure in social psychological experiments on priming involved participants who were initially exposed to some priming event. For example, Srull and Wyer (1979) gave research participants an unscrambling task in which they had to complete a sentence. In this task, participants are given four words and their task is to use three of the words to construct a sentence. For example, participants might be given the following words: "he," "Sally," "hit," and "kicked." Srull and Wyer (1979) took advantage of the fact that only two sentences can be constructed from these four words: "He hit Sally" and "He kicked Sally." After completing this priming task, participants take part in what they think is a second, unrelated study. In the "unrelated" study, participants are typically asked to make various judgments about an ambiguously described person or event. This research has consistently found that the priming event influences the interpretation of the later ambiguous information. Typically, the ambiguous information is biased toward the primes, so that if the primes are negative, the ambiguously described person will be judged more harshly than if the primes are positive (Higgins, Rholes, & Jones, 1977; Srull & Wyer, 1979, 1980; Todorov & Bargh, 2002).

Research on priming by both cognitive and social psychologists has demonstrated two important characteristics of priming effects. First, the strength of a priming effect is a dual function of the *intensity* and the *recency* of the priming event (see Higgins, Bargh, & Lombardi's synapse model of priming, 1985). Furthermore, a stronger prime will result in higher activation levels in the target item, and its effect on the target will dissipate more slowly than that of a weaker prime (see Higgins et al., 1985). The strength or "intensity" of the prime can refer to the frequency of the prime (e.g., a single exposure to the priming word vs. five exposures to the priming word in quick succession) or the duration of the priming event. "Recency" simply refers to the time lag between the prime and the target. Recent primes are stronger than temporally distant primes.

A second important characteristic of priming is that the effects of a prime fade with time. More specifically, in lexical decision tasks and other related judgment tasks, where reaction time is used as the dependent variable, the effect of the prime usually fades within 700 ms (Fazio, Sanbonmatus, Powell, & Kardes, 1986;

---

[2]Indeed, the first author vividly recalls watching the movie *The Day After,* which is about the survivors of a nuclear war. It seemed strange when President Reagan announced his plans to seek re-election immediately after this movie, because the movie "primed" all of the author's concerns about President Reagan's hawkish foreign policy and the ensuing risk of war. Unfortunately, at least from the author's standpoint, no one else seemed to be so primed by the movie—President Reagan won re-election in 1984 by a landslide.

Neely, 1977). Likewise, in tasks that involve judgments or evaluations of a social stimulus, the effect of the prime fades with time—though the effect appears to fade more slowly (Srull & Wyer, 1979, 1980). In many experiments involving the influence of primes on judgments, the priming effect will last up to 15 to 20 minutes and possibly up to 1 hour (Srull & Wyer, 1979).[3]

MEDIA VIOLENCE AND PRIMING

The impact of media violence on viewers' subsequent behavior and judgments has been the subject of numerous investigations (for reviews, see Geen, 1990; Geen & Thomas, 1986; Gunter, 1994; Huesmann & Miller, 1994). In addition, many theoretical explanations have been advanced to explain the effects of media violence on behavior (Perry, 1996). One of the prominent explanations of the consequences of media violence is Berkowitz's (1984, 1990, 1994, 1997) neo-associationistic model. Berkowitz's model draws heavily from network models of priming that were discussed earlier. Based on this model, Berkowitz hypothesized that depictions of violence in the media activate hostility- and aggression-related concepts in memory and that the activation of these concepts in memory makes it more likely that others' behavior will be interpreted as aggressive or hostile. Likewise, the activation of hostile and aggressive concepts in memory is hypothesized to increase the likelihood that a person will engage in aggressive behaviors. Finally, the activation of hostile and aggressive concepts in memory will fade with time.

Early findings on the effects of the media violence can be reinterpreted as consistent with Berkowitz's priming hypothesis. For example, research has found that the impact of a violent program on judgment and behavior fades across time (Bollen & Phillips, 1982; Buvinic & Berkowitz, 1976; Doob & Climie, 1972).[4] Likewise, as Geen and Thomas (1986) note, the finding that media violence generalizes to other forms of violence is inconsistent with other explanations of the effect of media violence, such as modeling; the generalization effect is perfectly consistent with a priming explanation of media violence.

Interestingly, given the popularity of the priming explanation of media violence, little empirical research has directly tested the effect of *media* priming on

---

[3]Srull and Wyer (1979, 1980) found evidence of priming effects influencing judgments after 24 hours. However, we are aware of no replications of this effect. Most research on the influence of priming on subsequent judgments involves a maximum delay of 15 to 20 minutes.

[4]We should note that the research by Bollen and Phillips (1982) on the time course of imitative suicides after coverage of a suicide is not strictly consistent with a priming explanation. Although Bollen and Phillips find that the effect of the media on suicides fades with time, the effect is more complicated than this. Specifically, and surprisingly, Bollen and Phillips found that the effect peaked 3 days after the coverage and then faded across the next week. The peak on the third day after the coverage is inconsistent with current models of violence priming. A priming explanation would predict a peak immediately after the media coverage of the suicide and then a decay over time.

subsequent aggression. Using a rather loose definition of "media" (including film clips, pictures from magazines, one-page written descriptions), we could find only eighteen published experiments testing the media priming explanation of the effects of media violence on judgments and behavior (Anderson, 1997; Anderson et al., 1996; Anderson & Morrow, 1995; Beaver et al., 1992; Bushman, 1995, 1998; Bushman & Geen, 1990; Carver et al., 1983; Josephson, 1987; Langley et al., 1992; Leyens & Dunand, 1991; Malamuth & Check, 1985; Scharrer, 2001; Wyer et al., 1985). Other than research on the media, there have been tests of the priming explanation of aggressive behavior in other domains, such as the effect of heat on aggression (Anderson, Anderson, & Deuser, 1996; Anderson, Deuser, & DeNeve, 1995; Rule, Taylor, & Dobbs, 1987), the weapon effect (Anderson, Benjamin, & Bartholow, 1998), differences in the aggressive associative networks of high- and low-trait aggressive individuals (Bushman, 1996), and the effects of thinking about aggressive sports (Wann & Branscombe, 1990).

In general, the results of the eighteen published experiments have been consistent with the priming explanation of media violence. However, the research has two important limitations. First, none of the studies tested the time course of priming effects (Roskos-Ewoldsen et al., 2002). As discussed earlier, one characteristic of priming is that the effects of priming fade with time. Josephson (1987) did find that when boys had been primed with aggressive media and then played field hockey, that most of the boys' aggressive behavior occurred within the first 3 minutes of play. This finding has been interpreted as consistent with the time course of priming (Geen, 1990). The important point is that no study has manipulated the time between the media violence prime and aggressive behavior to determine if aggressive behavior decreases at longer intervals from the media prime. Second, none of the studies have tested the effect of prime intensity on later aggression. As discussed earlier, a characteristic of priming is that more intense primes have stronger effects. If priming is to be considered a viable explanation of the effects of media violence on behavior, then both the time course of media priming and the effect of prime intensity need to be tested. In the meta-analysis described below, we tested the effect of both of these variables on the impact of media priming.

POLITICAL NEWS COVERAGE AND PRIMING

The concept of political priming was an outgrowth of research on agenda setting (Iyenger & Otatti, 1994), which has been a major focus for media scholars for the past 25 years (McCombs & Shaw, 1993). The research on agenda setting was an outgrowth of the earlier minimal effects research tradition of the 1950s and 1960s. Whereas the minimal effects tradition insisted that the media had little or no effect on people, the research on agenda setting demonstrated that the media influence what people think *about*. For example, McCombs and Shaw (1972) found a strong relationship between the primary stories in the media leading up to the 1968 presidential election and the judgments of what the important issues were at that time.

The political priming research moved beyond the notion of the media influencing what people think about to the idea that media coverage influences how people judge presidential performance. The research on political priming argues that extensive media coverage of an issue primes the likelihood that people will use the heavily covered issue as a criterion to judge the president's performance. For example, during most of 1991 (i.e., during and immediately after the Gulf War), several studies demonstrated that the American people's beliefs about President Bush's performance on foreign policy matters predicted their overall evaluation of President Bush's performance (Iyengar & Simon, 1993; Krosnick & Brannon, 1993a, 1993b; Pan & Kosicki, 1997). However, in 1992, President Bush's popularity dropped dramatically. According to the political priming perspective, the shift in President Bush's popularity was a result of a shift in the media's coverage from foreign policy issues (the Gulf War) to economic issues (the recession). As hypothesized, in 1992, people's beliefs about President Bush's handling of the economy was a better predictor of their evaluations of President Bush than were their beliefs concerning President Bush's handling of foreign policy (Pan & Kosicki, 1997).

Although both experimental studies and survey research have supported the political priming hypothesis, there are several problems with this area of research. First, the theoretical mechanisms by which the media prime particular judgmental critieria for making evaluations of the president are largely unspecified (Roskos-Ewoldsen et al., 2002). Only one model of political priming has been developed sufficiently (Price & Tewksbury, 1997), and the priming component of that model has not been subjected to empirical test. However, some research has begun testing the idea of spreading activation, which is central to cognitive models of political priming (Domke, 2001; Domke et al., 1998, 1999). Furthermore, the time span involved in political priming makes it unlikely that priming, in the sense used by cognitive and social psychologists (whom they cite to support their conceptualizations) is influencing the evaluations of the president. Priming results in the temporary increase in the accessibility of a node (i.e., concept), and the increased accessibility of the node (concept) dissipates relatively quickly. Rather than calling this phenomenon "priming," it is more likely that the frequent and repeated stories on a particular issue (e.g., the Gulf War) increase the *chronic* accessibility of the information (see Lau, 1989; Roskos-Ewoldsen, 1997; Shrum, 1999; Shrum & O'Guinn, 1993; Todorov & Bargh, 2002). "Chronic accessibility" refers to concepts that are always highly accessible from memory (see research by Bargh, Bond, Lombardi, & Tota, 1986; Fazio et al., 1986; Higgins, King, & Mavin, 1982). In the attitudinal domain, someone's attitude toward cockroaches is probably chronically accessible from memory. On the other hand, someone's attitude toward Tibetan food is probably not chronically accessible. As one would expect, research has demonstrated that chronically accessible concepts have more persistent effects on people's judgments and behavior than do temporarily accessible concepts. For example, Fazio (1995) reports that as few as five attitude judgments can increase the chronic accessibility of an attitude from memory across a 2-week period, an effect that is far longer than the normal priming effect. Research on chronically accessible concepts shows that they can be primed to become temporarily even more accessible from memory (Bargh et al., 1986). In addition, without some form of reinforcement, the accessibility of chronically accessible concepts fades across time (Grant & Logan, 1993). Increasing the chronic accessibility of foreign policy matters could explain the influence of this information on later judgments of the president. In addition, the decrease in chronic accessibility across time could explain the finding that the influence of foreign policy judgments decreased across time with decreased media coverage of foreign issues (Pan & Kosicki, 1997).

QUESTIONS ADDRESSED IN META-ANALYSIS

A number of questions concerning media priming were addressed in this meta-analysis. First, are priming effects of the media across all areas reliable and homogeneous? We anticipate that, given the differences across the various media priming studies, media priming effects will not be homogeneous. This leads to the second question: Are priming effects of political news and media violence reliable? Furthermore, are the magnitudes of the priming effects across these two domains similar?

The third question is whether media priming has the same characteristics as priming in cognitive and social psychology. That is, does the intensity of the prime influence the impact of the prime? If the media are operating as a prime, then the effects should be stronger if the prime is of greater intensity. To test this hypothesis, the intensity of the priming event was coded. Because the majority of studies in this area of research do not provide direct information concerning the intensity of the prime, only one component of prime intensity was coded—the duration of the priming event. For example, Bushman (1995) showed participants 15-minute film clips as the violent prime in experiments 2 and 3. The intensity of this prime would be 15 minutes. When no specific information concerning the length of the prime was provided, we estimated the approximate length of the prime from the information presented in the article.

Fourth, as discussed above, the effects of the media as a prime should dissipate across time. To test this question, the inter-trial interval (ITI) was coded for each study. The ITI refers to the time between the end of the prime and the measurement of the effect of the prime. For example, Iyengar and Kinder (1987) measured participants' evaluations of the president 24 hours after the last newscast, during which the priming news stories were presented. The ITI in this study would be 24 hours. Again, when no specific information concerning the ITI was provided, we estimated the approximate length of the ITI from the information presented in the article.

In addition, several questions specific to the two major research areas in media priming were tested. First, sex of respondent has been hypothesized to be a moderator of media priming. Some prior studies have demonstrated that women respond differently to media violence than do men (for reviews, see Geen, 1990; Lagerspetz & Bjorkqvist, 1994). Generally, men are hypothesized to be more susceptible to violent primes than women. For those studies that included sex of respondent as a factor in the analysis of priming, we coded the prime X sex of respondent interaction. Second, trait aggressiveness has also been hypothesized to be a moderator of the priming effect of media violence (Bushman, 1995; Bushman & Geen, 1990; Josephson, 1987). People who are high in trait aggressiveness are hypothesized to be more influenced by media priming than people who are low in trait aggressiveness. Again, for those studies that included measures of trait aggressiveness, we coded the prime X trait aggressiveness interaction.

Within political priming research, the hypothesis has been advanced that the strength of the priming effects depends on the type of judgments about the president. Specifically, there should be stronger priming effects for judgments of the president's overall performance, a lesser effect for judgments of the president's competence, and the least effect for judgments of the president's integrity (Iyengar & Kinder, 1987; Iyengar et al., 1982, 1984; Krosnick & Kinder, 1990). The reasoning behind this hypothesis is that the media coverage will tend to focus on the president's performance and not his integrity. Thus, the priming effects of the media's coverage should be stronger with judgments that are similar to the information in the priming stimulus.

METHODOLOGY

The Sample of Priming Studies

A total of 48 published articles on priming were found, representing 63 studies and using 21,087 participants. We used several techniques for identifying studies of media priming. First, an "ancestry" approach was used; that is, the reference lists from several recent reviews of this research domain were examined for potential articles (Berkowitz, 1990; Jo & Berkowitz, 1994; Price & Tewksbury, 1997). Second, the PSYCInfo, PSYCLit, CommAbstract, and ERIC data bases were used to identify potential articles. Third, after the articles identified through these first two methods were collected, the reference sections of these articles were checked to identify additional studies of media priming. Finally, we included six experiments from Iyengar and Kinder's (1987) book, because it is the classic work in this area and almost doubled the number of political priming studies in the meta-analysis.

For purposes of setting clear boundaries of what research on media priming the meta-analysis included, we set two limitations on the selection of studies. First, the selection of studies was limited to those studies that directly tested priming effects. For example, studies cited by Berkowitz (1984) that did not specifically test media priming were excluded from the meta-analysis. By Berkowitz's criteria, any study that involves the presentation of a media stimulus and then measures the effect of that media stimulus is a test of media priming. We disagree with this approach for this meta-analysis—one does not test a specific model of media priming by including every study involving the media.

Second, for each of the two priming traditions (violence, political), a standard set of dependent measures exists. We excluded studies if they did not include at least one of the standard dependent variables. For example, in the political priming literature, the standard dependent variable involves judgments of the president's performance or voting behavior. We excluded a study by Demers, Craff, Choi, and Pessin (1989) because the dependent variable involved judgments of issue importance, the standard dependent variable in the agenda setting literature, and did not include any measure of the participants' judgment of the president.

Coding the Studies

The three authors each coded a subset of the studies. The studies were coded for the standard demographic variables, including author(s), journal that published the study, date of publication, and whether the critical comparisons were within or between subjects.

In addition, we coded several other variables to answer the questions posed earlier. First, the research domain of the study (political, violence, other) was coded. Second, we coded the duration of the prime. We assigned each study to one of the following categories: very short (prime lasted up to 2 seconds), short (prime lasted up to 5 minutes), moderate (prime lasted up to 30 minutes), or campaign (the prime was a media campaign across several months). Third, we coded the approximate elapsed time between the time at which the prime ended and the time the dependent measure was taken (i.e., inter-trial interval or ITI). The ITI was included to test whether priming effects in media priming fade across time as they do in social-cognitive research (Fazio et al., 1986; Higgins et al., 1985; Neely, 1977; McKoon & Ratcliff, 1986). Although ITI is typically a continuous variable, we assigned each study's ITI to one of five categories: extremely brief (within 1,000 ms), brief (up to 5 minutes), intermediate (5 to 20 minutes), long (up to 1 day), and extremely long (longer than 1 day).

For the political priming studies, we also noted whether the dependent measure involved global judgments of the president's performance, judgments of the president's competence, or judgments of the president's integrity. Finally, for the violence priming studies, we noted whether the study tested for prime X trait aggression and/or prime X gender interactions.

All three authors coded eleven of the studies (17%) to determine inter-coder reliability. The agreement across the three coders was extremely high (97%).

RESULTS AND DISCUSSION

r was used as the measure of effect size in this meta-analysis. We used Johnson's (1989) d-stat program to compute r and to conduct the major analysis within this meta-analysis. We did not make any corrections that are typical of many meta-analysis for two reasons. First, the number of studies in this meta-analysis is limited, so we were not confident that the corrections would be reliable. In addition, few of the studies provided the necessary information for certain corrections (e.g., reliability estimates for the dependent variables). Second, there is a risk that corrections overestimate the effect size (Rosenthal, 1991), and we were more concerned with obtaining an estimate of the effect sizes across the studies than with obtaining a hypothetical effect size based on ideal conditions (see Rosenthal, 1991, for a similar point).

One question that we addressed was how to handle multiple indices of the effect size from a single study. One solution would be to get an effect size for each of the dependent variables and include all effect sizes in the meta-analysis. However, this procedure would give too much weight to those studies with multiple dependent variables. Instead, we followed one of two procedures to determine which dependent variables to use when studies had more than one principal dependent variable. First, if it was clear from the report that one of the dependent variables was of primary concern, we used only these data for the meta-analysis. For example, in experiment 2, Bushman (1998) reported both reaction times and error rates as measures of priming in the lexical decision task. However, Bushman is clear that reaction time was the primary independent variable in this experiment. Likewise, in the political priming research, several studies measured the effect of media priming on general evaluations of the president, as well as judgments of the president's competence and integrity (Iyengar, et al., 1982, 1984; Krosnick & Kinder, 1990). Again, in these studies, it was hypothesized that the strongest effects of media priming would occur for general evaluations of the president, so that was the data we used in the meta-analysis. Second, in those studies where multiple dependent variables were used and the author(s) did not specify a primary measure, we calculated the effect size for each dependent variable and then averaged the r values, following an r to z transformation.

General Media Priming Effects

We were interested in answering four general questions about media priming. First, does the media act as a prime? Second, does the magnitude of the media priming effect vary across the domains of media violence and political media? Third, does the intensity of the prime influence the extent of the media's influence? Fourth, as with other forms of priming, does the effect of media priming fade across time?

The answer to the first question of whether reliable media priming occurs across the wide variety of studies on media priming is yes. Across the 63 studies on media priming, there was a small but significant effect of media primes on subsequent judgments or behaviors ($r = .10$; 95% conf. interval $= .09 < .10 < .11$). However, as was expected, the effect size across the 63 media priming studies was not homogeneous ($Qw(62) = 487.76, p < .001$). The fact that the effect size was not homogeneous for the full set of studies is not surprising, for several reasons. First, the studies on media priming cover a wide variety of topics (e.g., violence vs. political priming) and use a variety of different priming techniques (e.g., print vs. video), which should increase the variability of the media priming effect. Second, both the interval between the prime and the measurement of the prime's effect (ITI) and the duration of the prime varied widely across the different studies. As argued earlier, the differences in the ITI and duration of the prime should influence the magnitude of the priming effect. Finally, we did not correct for various sources of variance (e.g., measurement error, dichotomization of variables, etc.), which makes it unrealistic to expect the effect size to be homogeneous across studies (Hunter & Schmidt, 1990). We will not be concerned with the homogeneity of the effect for the remaining analyses because our interest concerns the testing of specific hypothesis and not the identification of all possible moderators of media priming effects. To foreshadow, in our opinion, not enough systematic research on media priming effects has occurred to allow us to identify confidently all the meaningful moderators of media priming effects.

The results of this meta-analysis indicate that the media can act as a prime. That is, the content of the media may temporarily influence people's attention, judgment, or behavior. However, the overall result of the media as a prime ($r = .10$) falls in the range of what is generally considered a small effect (Rosenthal, 1991). Of course, at this point, caveats are in order to justify why media priming is still an important phenomenon despite the relatively small effect size. First, the small effect size may reflect the inclusion of the eleven surveys that were used to test political media priming within the meta-analysis. The results from the eleven surveys had a disproportionate influence on the overall effect size that we found because we weighted the effect size for each study by the number of research participants in that study. The surveys had a much larger number of participants than did the experimental studies. When we look only at the effect size for the fifty-two experimental studies, the overall effect size increases substantially ($r =$ .19). The difference in the effect size for the surveys ($r = .08$) and the experimental studies may reflect several factors. Experiments, with the tighter controls they afford, should result in stronger effects. In addition, consistent with a priming explanation, the surveys measured the effect of the prime substantially later than in any of the experimental studies, which means that the prime had more time to dissipate and should have had a smaller effect on subsequent judgments.

A second caveat justifying why media priming is an important phenomenon is that people are constantly exposed to the media. Though the argument can be made that, when an individual is repeatedly exposed to violent media content, the media acts as a repetitive prime that keeps violent concepts activated in memory, we argue that two different but related mechanisms are involved: priming and chronic accessibility. Numerous studies have demonstrated that repeated exposures to the same concept increase the chronic accessibility of the concept from memory (Fazio, 1995; Roskos-Ewoldsen, 1997; Shrum, 1999; Shrum & O'Guinn, 1993). If the same individual repeatedly views coverage of the Persian Gulf War, the initial exposures to the Gulf War may temporarily increase the accessibility of the "Gulf War" through priming, but repeated exposure should increase the chronic accessibility of the "Gulf War" in memory (Shrum, 1999).

There are three points that need to be kept in mind when the media's role in increasing the chronic accessibility of concepts is discussed. First, priming a concept increases the likelihood that the concept will become chronically accessible (Roskos-Ewoldsen, 1997; Roskos-Ewoldsen, Arpan-Ralston, & St. Pierre, 2002). Accessible concepts are more likely to attract attention (Roskos-Ewoldsen & Fazio, 1992), which means that if the media primes violence, violent behaviors are more likely to attract, at least temporarily, that individual's attention, which increases the frequency that violence has been primed. Furthermore, primed concepts bias the interpretation of ambiguous information (Fazio, Roskos-Ewoldsen, & Powell, 1994; Roskos-Ewoldsen, 1997; Roskos-Ewoldsen et al., 2002), which suggests that the same individual will be more likely to interpret ambiguous behaviors as violent, which again increases the frequency that violence has been primed. Second, both theory and research suggest that the chronic accessibility of a concept can fade across extended time periods (Grant & Logan, 1993). When the media stop covering the Persian Gulf War, the chronic accessibility of the Persian Gulf War will begin to fade. Third, chronically accessible concepts can be primed (Bargh et al., 1986). Thus, for a person who already has chronically accessible violence concepts, exposure to media violence could increase to an even higher level the accessibility of the violent concepts.

The second general question concerned whether priming effects from violence priming and political priming were comparable in size. There were twenty-nine political priming studies. The global effect size across these twenty-nine studies was small but significant ($r = .08$; 95% conf. interval $= .07 < .08 < .09$). There was a total of eighteen violence studies. The global effect size across these eighteen studies was of moderate size ($r = .30$; 95% conf. interval $= .26 < .30 < .34$). The effect size for the violence priming studies was significantly stronger than the effect size for the political priming studies ($\chi^2 (1) = 91.33, p < .0001$). However, it is difficult to know whether this difference reflects the actual priming potential of the media across these two domains or reflects some artifact of the way research is conducted across these two domains. First, a simple examination of Table 5.1 reveals that all of the research on media violence had relatively short delays between the presentation of the prime and the measure of priming effects (a short ITI). However, in the political priming studies, nineteen of twenty-nine studies had at least a 24-hour delay between the presentation of the prime and the measurement of the prime's effect on judgments of the president. The priming effects in the political studies may be smaller because of this longer delay between the prime and the measure of the effect of the prime, which allows the prime to fade. Second, all of the research on violence priming was conducted in the lab, whereas eleven of the twenty-nine political priming studies involved survey data from actual political events. The research in the lab, with its corresponding tighter controls, should result in stronger effects.

The third question dealt with the impact of prime intensity on priming effects. Earlier research on priming has demonstrated that priming effects are stronger when the priming event is more intense or of longer duration. Though there are a number of ways to operationalize the intensity of the prime, given the information that was provided in the various studies on media priming, we opted to operationalize prime intensity as the duration of the media prime. All things being equal, longer primes should result in stronger priming effects. The results of the meta-analysis were partially consistent with the finding that intense primes result in stronger priming effects. The very short intensity prime category was discarded from the analysis because there were no studies that fell into this category. The overall effect size for the short intensity priming studies (prime up to 5 minutes) was moderate ($r = .14$; 95% conf. interval $= .11 < .14 < .17$). As predicted, the effect size for the moderate-intensity priming studies (prime up to 20 minutes) was stronger ($r = .27$; 95% conf. interval $= .23 < .27 < .30$). This difference in effect size between the short and moderate-intensity priming studies was significant ($\chi^2 = 27.98, p < .0001$). Surprisingly, the effect size for the campaign studies, arguably the most intense priming experience, was the smallest ($r = .08$; 95% conf. interval $= .07 < .08 < .09$). The effect size for the campaign studies is significantly smaller than either the short priming intensity studies ($\chi^2 = 15.79, p < .0001$) or the moderate priming intensity studies ($\chi^2 = 95.93, p < .0001$). At one level, this finding is somewhat surprising, because one would expect that a media campaign would operate as a much more intense prime than a 15-minute movie clip in the lab. However, the research on media campaigns also had the longest ITI of any of the published research on media priming. As a consequence, although

TABLE 5.1

Summary Information on the Studies included in the Meta-Analysis

Author & Year of Publication (Experiment #)	N	Independent Variable	Dependent Variable	Prime Intensity[1]	ITI[2]
Aggression Studies					
Anderson, 1997 (1)	53	Video Clip	Pronunciation Task (R.T.)	Long	Short
Anderson, 1997 (2)	66	Video Clip	Pronunciation Task (R.T.)	Long	Short
Anderson, et al., 1996 (1)	415	Mag. Pictures	Stroop Interference Task (R.T.)	Long	Short
Anderson & Morrow, 1995 (2)	60	Video game	Creatures Killed	Long	Short
Beaver, et al. 1992	173	Written	Ratings of Rapist	Short	Short
Bushman, 1995 (2)	160	Video Clip	State Hostility	Long	Short
Bushman, 1995 (3)	296	Video Clip	Aggressive Behavior	Long	Short
Bushman, 1998 (1)	200	Video Clip	Aggressive Homonyms	Long	Short
Bushman, 1998 (2)	300	Video Clip	Lexical Decision Task (R.T.)	Long	Short
Bushman & Geen, 1990 (1)	100	Video Clip	Aggressive Thoughts	Long	Short
Bushman & Geen, 1990 (2)	120	Video Clip	Aggressive Thoughts	Long	Short
Carver, et al., 1983	78	Video Clip	Person Perception Task	Short	Short
Josephson, 1987	66	Video Clip	Aggressive Behavior	Long	Short
Langley, et al., 1992	30	Written	Ratings of Interest in Watching Violent Films	Short	Short
Leyens & Dunand, 1991	49	Written	Aggressive Behavior	Short	Short
Malamuth & Check, 1985	145	Audiotape	Ratings of Rape Victim	Short	Short
Scharrer, 2001	60	Video Clip	Self Reported Aggressive Behavior	Long	Short
Wyer, et al.,1985 (1)	30	Pictures	Perceptions of Rape	Short	Short
Political Studies					
Domke, Shah, & Wackman, 1998	373	Written	Judgments of Candidate Integrity	Short	Short
Goidel, Shields, & Peffley, 1997	982	Campaign	Ratings of President	Campaign	Campaign

Study	N	Media Type	Dependent Variable		
Hetherington, 1996	308	Campaign	Voting Behavior	Campaign	Campaign
Highton, 2002	4,065	Campaign	Voting Behavior	Campaign	Campaign
Holbert, et al., 2003	195	Episode of *West Wing*	Ratings of President	Long	Short
Iyengar & Kinder, 1987 (1)	28	T.V. News	Ratings of President	Long	Long
Iyengar & Kinder, 1987 (2)	28	T.V. News	Ratings of President	Long	Long
Iyengar & Kinder, 1987 (3)	73	T.V. News	Ratings of President	Long	Long
Iyengar & Kinder, 1987 (4)	140	T.V. News	Ratings of President	Long	Long
Iyengar & Kinder, 1987 (8)	63	T.V. News	Ratings of President	Long	Long
Iyengar & Kinder, 1987 (9)	34	T.V. News	Ratings of President	Long	Long
Iyengar, et al., 1984 (1)	73	T.V. News	Ratings of President	Long	Short
Iyengar, et al., 1984 (2)	140	T.V. News	Ratings of President	Long	Short
Iyengar, et al., 1982 (1)	28	T.V. News	Ratings of President	Long	Long
Iyengar, et al., 1982 (2)	44	T.V. News	Ratings of President	Long	Long
Iyengar & Simon, 1993	3,425	Campaign	Ratings of President	Campaign	Campaign
Krosnick & Brannon, 1993	1,090	Campaign	Ratings of President	Campaign	Campaign
Krosnick & Kinder, 1990	1,063	Campaign	Ratings of President	Campaign	Campaign
McGraw & Ling, 2003	240	Written	Ratings of President	Short	Short
McGraw & Pinney, 1990	94	Written	Ratings of President	Short	Short
Mendelberg, 1997	77	TV News	Evaluation of Political Policies	Short	Short
Mendelsohn, 1996	1562	Campaign	Voting Intention	Campaign	Campaign
Miller & Krosnick, 2000 (1)	286	T.V. News	Ratings of President	Short	Short
Miller & Krosnick, 2000 (2)	367	T.V. News	Ratings of President	Short	Short
Mutz, 1992	300	Campaign	Ratings of President	Campaign	Campaign
Mutz, 1994	479	Campaign	Ratings of President	Campaign	Campaign
Pan & Kosicki, 1997	935	Campaign	Ratings of President	Campaign	Campaign
Valentino, 1999	289	T.V. News	Ratings of President	Short	Short
Willnat & Zhu, 1996	500	Campaign	Evaluation of Political Policy	Campaign	Campaign

(Continued)

TABLE 5.1 (Continued)

Summary Information on the Studies included in the Meta-Analysis

Author & Year of Publication (Experiment #)	N	Independent Variable		Dependent Variable	Prime Intensity[1]	ITI[2]
Miscellaneous Other						
Domke, 2001	160	Written		Prime (Race) Related Thoughts	Short	Short
Domke, McCoy, & Torres, 1999	172	Written		Prime (Race) Related Thoughts	Short	Short
Forehand & Deshpande, 2001 (1)	109	TV Ads		Judgments of Ethnic Self-Awareness	Short	Short
Forehand & Deshpande, 2001 (2)	175	Print Ads		Judgments of Ethnic Self-Awareness	Short	Short
Hanson & Hanson, 1988	221	Video Clip		Person Perception Task	Long	Short
Hanson & Krygowski, 1994 (1)	86)	Video Clip		Person Perception Task	Short	Short
Hanson & Krygowski, 1994 (2)	163	Video Clip		Person Perception Task	Short	Short
Johnson, et al., 2000	90	Rap Music		Person Perception Task	Short	Short
Potts & Swisher, 1998	60	Video Clip		Judgments of Risk Taking	Long	Short
Power, et al., 1996 (1)	110	Newsletter		Person Perception Task	Short	Short
Power, et al., 1996 (2)	101	Newsletter		Person Perception Task	Short	Short
Schleuder, et al., 1993	46	T.V. News		Recognition, Secondary Task R.T.	Short	Short
Wyer, et al., 1985 (2)	20	Pictures		Perceptions of Rape	Short	Short
Yi, 1990a	72	Magazine Article		Brand Attitude	Short	Short
Yi, 1990b (1)	40	Magazine Article		Brand Attitude	Short	Short
Yi, 1990b (2)`	120	Magazine Article		Brand Attitude	Short	Short

[1]Prime intinsity was categorized into three categories: short (prime duration less than 5 minutes), long (prime duraction between 5 and 20 minutes), and campaign (the prime is a media campaign).

[2]The intertrial interval was categorized into three levels: short (prime and dependent measures during the same experimental session); long (dependent measures occurred the day after the last prime), and campaign (the dependent measures occurred some time after a media campaign).

the media priming studies may have involved the most intense primes of any of the media priming studies, the priming effect in these studies also had the most time to decay. If the effects of the media as prime were measured closer to the campaign, the effect of the prime may have been stronger.

The final general question concerned the effect of time on the effect of the media as a prime. One of the hallmarks of priming effects is that they fade across time (Higgins et al., 1985; Srull & Wyer, 1979, 1980). One measure of the duration of a priming effect is the inter-trial interval (ITI). The ITI is a measure of the time between the end of the priming stimuli and the measure of the effect of the prime. The ITI of each study was coded into one of three categories: 1 hour (prime and dependent variable within the same experimental session, $k = 44$), 24 hours (dependent variable measured the following day, $k = 8$), and campaign (dependent variable measured as part of a survey some time after extensive media coverage of the issue, $k = 11$). The extremely brief (within 1,000 ms) and brief (up to 5 minutes) categories were collapsed with the 1-hour ITI category because there were not enough studies in these two categories to include them in the analysis.

The pattern of effect sizes across the three categories of ITI does not follow the expected pattern of decreasing effect sizes as time increases. The strongest effect was for those studies where the dependent measure was measured 24 hours after the priming event ($r = .22$; 95% conf. interval $= .12 < .22 < .30$). Surprisingly, the effect size was smaller when dependent measure was completed during the same experimental session as the priming event ($r = .19$; 95% conf interval $= .17 < .19 < .22$). However, there was not a significant difference between the effect size when the dependent variable was measured during the same session or 24 hours later ($\chi^2 (1) = .23$, ns). The campaign effect size ($r = .08$) is the same as the campaign effect size for the prime duration analysis because the same eleven studies are used. The intermediate (1 hour) ITI effect size was significantly larger than the campaign effect size ($\chi^2 = 70.70$, $p < .0001$). Likewise, the 24-hour ITI effect size was significantly larger than the effect size for the campaign studies ($\chi^2 (1) = 8.10$, $p < .005$).

Media Violence Priming

The first question we answered specific to priming in media violence concerned the moderating role of sex of respondent on violent media priming effects. Based on the more general research on media violence, one could hypothesize that men and women would respond differently to media depictions of violence (Geen, 1990; Lagerspetz & Bjorkqvist, 1994). Indeed, men have been hypothesized to be more susceptible to violent media primes then women. Ten studies tested the moderating role of sex of respondent on violent media priming. However, in none of the ten studies was sex of respondent a significant moderator of this relationship ($r = 0$). Based on the current data, sex of respondent does not appear to mediate the effect of violent media primes. One limitation of the analysis of the potential role of sex of respondent as a moderator of the violent media priming effect is that all ten studies tested the effect of biological sex as a moderator of violent media priming. None of the studies can address the question of whether gender roles (e.g., feminine vs. masculine) moderate the violent media priming effect.

The second question we addressed concerned whether trait aggressiveness acted as a moderator for the priming effect of media violence. People with high trait aggressiveness are hypothesized to be more influenced by media priming than are people who are low in trait aggressiveness. There were eight studies that looked at the interaction between violent media primes and trait aggressiveness. Across these eight studies, there was a significant interaction between trait aggressiveness and violent media primes ($r = .11$; 95% conf. interval $= .05 < .11 < .17$). People with high trait aggressiveness tended to show stronger media priming effects than did people who were low in trait aggressiveness. Thus, violent media content appears to have a stronger priming effect on people who are already predisposed to be aggressive. This finding provides a hint to an earlier question concerning the effect of media priming on people who already have chronically accessible concepts. It seems likely that people who are high in trait aggressiveness probably have chronically accessible violence concepts. If so, our finding suggests that the media can indeed prime chronically accessible concepts. This interpretation is consistent with the findings of Bargh et al. (1986), which demonstrated that chronically accessible concepts can be temporarily made more accessible through a priming procedure in the lab.

Political Priming

Iyengar et al. (1982) hypothesized that the effects of political media priming would be specific to judgments of the president's overall performance and that media priming would have a smaller effect on judgments of the president's competency and the least effect on judgments of the president's integrity. There were five studies that included measures of all three of these judgments (Iyengar et al., 1982, 1984; Krosnick & Kinder, 1990). We decided to test the hypothesis of Iyengar et al. (1982) with the use of these five studies. For these studies, the effect size for the president's overall performance was higher ($r = .07$; 95% conf. interval $= .01 < .07 < .12$) than for judgments of the president's competence ($r = .04$; 95% conf. interval $= -.02 < .04 < .09$) or judgments of the president's integrity ($r = .03$, 95% conf. interval $= -.03 < .03 < .08$). But while the pattern is in the right direction, none of the effect sizes are significantly different from each other (overall vs. competence, $\chi^2 (1) = .59, p > .70$; overall vs. integrity, $\chi^2 = .96, p > .30$; competence vs. integrity, $\chi^2 (1) = .04, p > .95$). Thus, based on the five studies that have tested this hypothesis, we cannot conclude that the effects of political media priming are any stronger on overall judgments of the president than on judgments of the president's competence or the president's integrity.

However, consistent with the hypothesis of Iyengar et al., only the judgments of the president's overall performance showed a reliable effect size. In addition, the results of the meta-analysis are tenuous because there are only five studies in this analysis.

At one level, the hypothesis of Iyengar et al. (1982) is reasonable; but there is a sense in which the hypothesis seems overly broad. Specifically, the relationship between what the media primes in its political coverage and which judgments of the president are influenced should depend, at least in part, on the issues the media are covering. Given the topics that were manipulated in the five studies (e.g., economic issues, foreign policy issues, unemployment), it makes sense that the media coverage would influence judgments of the president's overall performance, because the criteria used to judge that performance are shifting, depending on the policy crisis the media is covering. However, given the political coverage of President Clinton's sexual indiscretions that led to the impeachment vote in the House of Representatives and the trial in the Senate, one would expect that any political priming that occurred because of media coverage of these events would influence judgments of President Clinton's integrity and not general judgments of his overall performance. Indeed, political polls have shown that the public's evaluation of President Clinton's general performance actually increased after the media coverage of the various scandals that led up to the impeachment vote and subsequent trial (Zaller, 1998).

GENERAL IMPLICATIONS OF THE META-ANALYSIS

The goal of a meta-analysis is not to provide the final answers about the area of study that is the focus of the meta-analysis (Dillard, 1998; Hale & Dillard, 1991). Rather, the goals of a meta-analysis should be twofold. First, a meta-analysis should identify the strength or confidence with which various claims can be made within that research tradition. For example, based on this meta-analysis, we are confident that the media can act as a prime and influence how people react to ensuing stimuli. In addition, the meta-analysis indicates that violent media primes have a more powerful influence on people who have high trait aggressiveness. The finding that people who are high in trait aggression show stronger media violence priming effects is consistent with the idea that chronically accessible concepts can be primed. Future research is needed to explore the impact of media as a prime on the behaviors of people who already have chronically accessible concepts. This discussion of the potential influence of the media on chronic accessibility is not intended to decrease the importance of the media as a prime. Rather, we discuss this to highlight the importance of clearly identifying the impact that the media are having on the cognitive system.

The results of this meta-analysis also suggest that we should be less confident in claiming that media priming shares the characteristics of the priming phenomenon studied by social and cognitive psychologists during the past two decades. The priming phenomenon that cognitive and social psychologists are interested in shares two important characteristics: the prime fades with time and primes of greater intensity have stronger effects. The meta-analysis provides mixed support for the supposition that media primes should become stronger when they are of greater duration. For example, media primes that lasted from 5 to 20 minutes had stronger effects than did media primes that were less than 5 minutes in length. On the other hand, media priming effects that resulted from media campaigns (e.g., coverage of the Gulf War), which were of the longest duration, were significantly smaller than the priming effects from shorter duration media primes. However, these apparently contradictory results are confounded by the lag between the priming event and the measurement of the prime's effect. The lag was substantially longer in the campaign studies than in the other media priming studies.

The results of the meta-analysis were even less encouraging with the second characteristics of priming—that priming effects fade with time. The size of the media priming effect was larger, with a lag of 24 hours between the presentation of the prime and the measurement of the prime's effect, than when the effect of the prime was measured within 30 minutes of the priming event. However, the difference between the effect sizes was not significant. To conclude: while media priming might fade with time and the duration of the media prime might influence the magnitude of the priming effect (except for media campaigns), the results of the meta-analysis indicate that we need to be cautious in advancing the claim that media priming shares important characteristics with the type of priming that cognitive and social psychologists have been studying. Understanding whether media priming has the same characteristics as the priming phenomenon that cognitive and social psychologists have studied is important for determining the extent to which theories of priming from cognitive and social psychology can be commissioned to provide the mechanisms by which media priming works.

Finally, the results of the meta-analysis imply that violent media primes have stronger effects than political primes. However, given the confounding variables in this analysis (e.g., delay between presentation of prime and measurement of the prime's effect), we should be extremely cautious in advancing this finding. Given the current body of research, we are extremely skeptical of this validity of this finding.

A second major goal of a meta-analysis should pertain to some kind of theoretical advancement (Dillard, 1998; Hale & Dillard, 1991). The meta-analysis may provide support (or lack thereof) for a current theory or propose a new theoretical explanation for the domain of study. Unfortunately, we cannot provide any theoretical advancement in this meta-analysis. Given the current state of research on media priming, there is no real theory to test. Berkowitz (1984, 1990, 1994, 1997; Jo & Berkowitz, 1994) has proposed a neo-associationistic model of media priming for explaining the effects of media violence. However, there have been no critical tests of the proposed *mechanisms* of this model within the domain of media priming. Likewise, the availability heuristic has been proposed as a "theoretical" explanation of political priming (Krosnick & Kinder, 1990). But again, there have been no experimental tests of the mechanisms proposed by the availability heuristic (e.g., the recall of exemplars that influence subsequent judgments; see Zillmann, 1999). Likewise, the Price and Tewksbury (1997) model has not been subjected to experimental test.

At this point, research needs to identify the important characteristics of media priming. Do media primes fade with time? To date, no published study of media priming has manipulated ITI to determine if this is the case. Likewise, do more intense media primes result in stronger media priming effects? To date, no published study of media priming has manipulated prime intensity to determine if this is the case. Until research is conducted that identifies the important characteristics of media priming, the development of theories of media priming will be impoverished. In reading the literature on media priming, one gets the impression that scholars who are interested in media priming identified the concept of priming in cognitive and social psychology and used the concept of priming to metaphorically explain the media effects they were interested in explaining. However, media scholars have not appeared to be particularly interested in testing whether media priming is, in fact, a result of priming. This is not to say that priming is not occurring in the research on media priming, because the data are consistent with that interpretation of the results. Rather, the point that we want to conclude with is that the potential for the media to act as a prime is well established. Now research needs to ascertain the characteristics of media priming and focus on the development of theoretical explanations of this phenomenon.

REFERENCES

*Included in the meta-analysis.

*Anderson, C. A. (1997). Effects of violent movies and trait hostility on hostile feelings and aggressive thoughts. *Aggressive Behavior, 23,* 161–178.

*Anderson, C. A., Anderson, K. B., & Deuser, W. E. (1996). Examining an affective aggression framework: Weapon and temperature effects on aggressive thoughts, affect, and attitudes. *Personality and Social Psychology Bulletin, 22,* 366–376.

Anderson, C. A., Benjamin, A. J., & Bartholow, B. D. (1998). Does the gun pull the trigger? Automatic priming effects of weapon pictures and weapon names. *Psychological Science, 9,* 308–314.

Anderson, C. A., Deuser, W. E., & DeNeve, K. M. (1995). Hot temperatures, hostile affect, hostile cognition, and arousal: Tests of a general model of affective aggression. *Personality and Social Psychology Bulletin, 21,* 434–448.

*Anderson, C. A., & Morrow, M. (1995). Competitive aggression without interaction: Effects of competitive versus cooperative instructions on aggressive behavior in video games. *Personality and Social Psychology Bulletin, 21,* 1020–1030.

Anderson, J. (1983). *The Architecture of Cognition.* Cambridge, MA: Harvard University Press.

Bargh, J. A., Bond, R. N., Lombardi, W. J., & Tota, M. E. (1986). The additive nature of chronic and temporary sources of construct accessibility. *Journal of Personality and Social Psychology, 50,* 869–878.

*Beaver, E. D., Gold, S. R., & Prisco, A. G. (1992). Priming macho attitudes and emotions. *Journal of Interpersonal Violence, 7,* 321–333.

Berkowitz, L. (1984). Some effects of thoughts on anti- and prosocial influences of media events: A cognitive-neoassociationistic analysis. *Psychological Bulletin, 95,* 410–427.

Berkowitz, L. (1990). On the formation and regulation of anger and aggression: A cognitive-neoassociationistic analysis. *American Psychologist, 45,* 494–503.

Berkowitz, L. (1994). Is something missing? Some observations prompted by the cognitive-neoassociationist view of anger and emotional aggression. In L. R. Huesmann (Ed.), *Aggressive Behavior: Current perspectives* (pp. 35–57). New York: Plenum Press.

Berkowitz, L. (1997). Some thoughts extending Bargh's argument. In R. S. Wyers (Ed.), *The Automaticity of Everyday Life: Advances in social cognition* (Vol. 10, pp. 83–92). Mahwah, NJ: Lawrence Erlbaum.

Bollin, K. A., & Phillips, D. P. (1982). Imitative suicides: A national study of the effects of television news stories. *American Sociological Review, 47,* 802–809.

*Bushman, B. J. (1995). Moderating role of trait aggressiveness in the effects of violent media on aggression. *Journal of Personality and Social Psychology, 69,* 950–960.

Bushman, B. J. (1996). Individual differences in the extent and development of aggressive cognitive-associative networks. *Personality and Social Psychology Bulletin, 22,* 811–820.

*Bushman, B. J. (1998). Priming effects of media violence on the accessibility of aggressive constructs in memory. *Personality and Social Psychology Bulletin, 24,* 537–545.

*Bushman, B. J., & Geen, R. G. (1990). Role of cognitive_emotional mediators and individual differences in the effects of media violence on aggression. *Journal of Personality and Social Psychology, 58,* 156–163.

Buvinic, M. L., & Berkowitz, L. (1976). Delayed effects of practiced versus unpracticed reponses after observation of movie violence. *Journal of Experimental Social Psychology, 12,* 283–293.

*Carver, C. S., Ganellen, R. J., Froming, W. J., & Chambers, W. (1983). Modeling: An analysis in terms of category accessibility. *Journal of Experimental Social Psychology, 19,* 403–421.

Demers, D. P., Craff, D., Choi, Y. H., & Pessin, B. M. (1989). Issue obtrusiveness and the agenda-setting effects of national network news. *Communication Research, 16,* 793–812.

Dillard, J. P. (1998). Evaluating and using meta-analytic knowledge claims. In M. Allen & R. W. Preiss (Eds.), *Persuasion: Advances through meta-analysis* (pp. 257–270). Cresskill, NJ: Hampton Press.

*Domke, D. (2001). Racial cues and political ideology: An examination of associative priming. *Communication Research, 28,* 772–801.

*Domke, D., McCoy, K., & Torres, M. (1999). News media, racial perceptions, and political cognition. *Communication Research, 26,* 570–607.

*Domke, D., Shaw, D. V., & Wackman, D. B. (1998). Media priming effects: Accessibility, association, and activation. *International Journal of Public Opinion Research, 10,* 51–74.

Doob, A. N., & Climie, R. J. (1972). Delay of measurement and the effects of film violence. *Journal of Experimental Social Psychology, 8,* 136–142.

Fazio, R. H. (1995). Attitudes as object_evaluation associations: Determinants, consequences, and correlates of attitude accessibility. In R. E. Petty & J. A. Krosnick (Eds.), *Attitude Strength: Antecedents and consequences* (pp. 247–282). Mahwah, NJ: Lawrence Erlbaum.

Fazio, R. H., Roskos-Ewoldsen, D. R., & Powell, M. C. (1994). Attitudes, perception, and attention. In P. M. Niedenthal & S. Kitayama (Eds.), *The Heart's Eye: Emotional influences in perception and attention* (pp. 197–216). New York: Academic Press.

Fazio, R. H., Sanbonmatsu, D. M., Powell, M. C., & Kardes, F. R. (1986). On the automatic activation of attitudes. *Journal of Personality and Social Psychology, 50,* 229–238.

*Forehand, M. R., & Deshpande, R. (2001). What we see makes us who we are: Priming ethnic self-awareness and advertising response. *Journal of Marketing Research, 38,* 336–348.

Geen, R. G. (1990). *Human Aggression.* Milton Keynes, England: Open University Press.

Geen, R. G., & Thomas, S. L. (1986). The immediate effects of media violence on behavior. *Journal of Social Issues, 42,* 7–27.

*Goidel, R. K., Shields, T. G., & Peffly, M. (1997). Priming theory and RAS models: Toward an integrated perspective on media influence. *American Politics Quarterly, 25,* 287–318.

Grant, S. C., & Logan, G. D. (1993). The lose of repetition priming and automaticity over time as a function of degree of initial learning. *Memory & Cognition, 21,* 611–618.

Gunter, B. (1994). The question of media violence. In J. Bryant & D. Zillmann (Eds.), *Media Effects: Advances in theory and research* (pp. 163–211). Hillsdale, NJ: Lawrence Erlbaum.

Hale, J. L., & Dillard, J. P. (1991). The uses of meta-analysis: Making knowledge claims and setting research agendas. *Communication Monographs, 58,* 463–471.

*Hansen, C. H., & Hansen, R. D. (1988). How rock music videos can change what is seen when boy meets girl: Priming stereotypic appraisal of social interaction. *Sex Roles, 19,* 287–316.

*Hansen, C. H., & Krygowski, W. (1994). Arousal_augmented priming effects: Rock music videos and sex object schemas. *Communication Research, 21,* 24–47.

Herr, P. M. (1986). Consequences of priming: Judgment and behavior. *Journal of Personality and Social Psychology, 51,* 1106–1115.

*Hetherington, M. J. (1996). The media's role in forming voters' national economic evaluations in 1992. *American Journal of Political Science, 40,* 372–395.

Higgins, E. T. (1989). Knowledge accessibility and activation: Subjectivity and suffering from unconscious sources. In J. S. Uleman and J. A. Bargh (Eds.), *Unintended Thought* (pp. 75–152). New York: Guilford Press.

Higgins, E. T., Bargh, J. A., & Lombardi, W. (1985). Nature of priming effects on categorization. *Journal of Experimental Psychology: Learning, Memory, & Cognition, 11,* 59–69.

Higgins, E. T., King, G. A., & Mavin, G. H. (1982). Individual construct accessibility and subjective impressions and recall. *Journal of Personality and Social Psychology, 43,* 35–47.

Higgins, E. T., Rholes, W. S., & Jones, C. R. (1977). Category accessibility and impression formation. *Journal of Experimental Social Psychology, 13,* 141–154.

*Highton, B. (2002). Bill Clinton, Newt Gingrich, and the 1998 House elections. *Public Opinion Quarterly, 66,* 1–17.

*Holbert, R. L., Pillion, O., Tschida, D. A., Armfield, G. G., Kinder, K., Cherry, K. L., & Daulton, A. R. (2003). *The West Wing* as endorsement of the U.S. presidency: Expanding the bounds of priming in political communication. *Journal of Communication, 53,* 427–443.

Huesmann, L. R., & Miller, L. S. (1994). Long-term effects of repeated exposure to media violence in childhood. In L. R. Huesmann (Ed.), *Aggressive Behavior: Current perspectives* (pp. 153–186). New York: Plenum Press.

Hunter, J. E., & Schmidt, F. L. (1990). *Methods of Meta-analysis: Correcting error and bias in research findings.* Newbury Park, CA: Sage.

*Iyengar, S., & Kinder, D. R. (1987). *News That Matters: Television and American opinion.* Chicago: University of Chicago Press.

*Iyengar, S., Kinder, D. R., Peters, M. D., & Krosnick, J. A. (1984). The evening news and presidential evaluations. *Journal of Personality and Social Psychology, 46,* 778–787.

Iyengar, S., & Ottati, V. (1994). Cognitive perspective in political psychology. In R. S. Wyer & T. K. Srull (Eds.), *Handbook of Social Cognition, Volume 2: Applications* (2nd ed., pp. 143–187). Hillsdale, NJ: Lawrence Erlbaum.

*Iyengar, S., Peters, M. D., & Kinder, D. R. (1982). Experimental demonstrations of the "not-so-minimal" consequences of television news programs. *American Political Science Review, 76,* 848–858.

*Iyengar, S., & Simon, A. (1993). News coverage of the Gulf crisis and public opinion: A study of agenda-setting, priming, and framing. *Communication Research, 20,* 365–383.

Jo, E., & Berkowitz, L. (1994). A priming effect analysis of media influences: An update. In J. Bryant & D. Zillmann (Eds.), *Media Effects: Advances in theory and research* (pp. 43–60). Hillsdale, NJ: Lawrence Erlbaum.

Johnson, B. T. (1989). *Software for the Meta-analytic Review of Research Literatures*. Mahwah, NJ: Lawrence Erlbaum.

*Johnson, J. D., Trawalter, S., & Dovidio, J. F. (2000). Converging interracial consequences of exposure to violent rap music on stereotypical attributions of blacks. *Journal of Experimental Social Psychology, 36,* 233–251.

*Josephson, W. L. (1987). Television violence and children's aggression: Testing the priming, social script, and disinhibition predictions. *Journal of Personality and Social Psychology, 53,* 882–890.

*Krosnick, J. A., & Brannon, L. A. (1993a). The impact of the Gulf War on the ingredients of presidential evaluations: Multidimensional effects of political involvement. *American Political Science Review, 87,* 963–975.

Krosnick, J. A., & Brannon, L. A. (1993b). The media and the foundations of presidential support: George Bush and the Persian Gulf crisis. *Journal of Social Issues, 49,* 167–182.

*Krosnick, J. A., & Kinder, D. R. (1990). Altering the foundations of support for the president through priming. *American Political Science Review, 84,* 497–512.

Lagerspetz, K. M. J., & Bjorkqvist, K. (1994). Indirect aggression in boys and girls. In L. R. Huesmann (Ed.), *Aggressive Behavior: Current perspectives* (pp. 131–150). New York: Plenum Press.

*Langley, T., O'Neal, E. C., Craig, K. M., & Yost, E. A. (1992). Aggression-consistent, -inconsistent, and -irrelevant priming effects on selective exposure to media violence. *Aggressive Behavior, 18,* 349–356.

Lau, R. R. (1989). Construct accessibility and electoral choice. *Political Behavior, 11,* 5–32.

*Leyens, J., & Dunand, M. (1991). Priming aggressive thoughts: The effect of the anticipation of a violent movie upon the aggressive behavior of the spectators. *European Journal of Social Psychology, 21,* 507–516.

Lombardi, W. J., Higgins, E. T., & Bargh, J. A. (1987). The role of consciousness in priming effects on categorization. *Personality and Social Psychology Bulletin, 13,* 411–429.

*Malamuth, N. M., & Check, J. V. P. (1985). The effects of aggressive pornography on beliefs in rape myths: Individual differences. *Journal of Research in Personality, 19,* 299–320.

McCombs, M. E., & Shaw, D. L. (1972). The agenda-setting function of the mass media. *Public Opinion Quarterly, 36,* 176–187.

McCombs, M. E., & Shaw, D. L. (1993). The evolution of agenda-setting research: Twenty-five years in the marketplace of ideas. *Journal of Communication, 43*(2), 58–67.

*McGraw, K. M., & Ling, C. (2003). Media priming of president and group evaluations. *Political Communication, 20,* 23–40.

*McGraw, K. M., & Pinney, N. (1990). The effects of general and domain-specific expertise on political memory and judgment. *Social Cognition, 8,* 9–30.

McKoon, G., & Ratcliff, R. (1986). Inferences about predictable events. *Journal of Experimental Psychology: Learning, Memory, and Cognition, 12,* 82–91.

*Mendelberg, T. (1997). Executing Hortons: Racial crime in the 1988 presidential campaign. *Public Opinion Quarterly, 61,* 134–157.

*Mendelsohn, M. (1996). The media and interpersonal communications: The priming of issues, leaders, and party identification. *Journal of Politics, 58,* 112–125.

Meyers, D. E., & Schvaneveldt, R. W. (1971). Facilitation in recognizing pairs of words: Evidence of a dependence between retrieval operations. *Journal of Experimental Psychology, 90,* 227–234.

*Miller, J. M., & Krosnick, J. A. (2000). News media impact on the ingredients of presidential evaluations: Politically knowledgeable citizens are guided by a trusted source. *American Journal of Political Science, 44,* 301–315.

*Mutz, D. C. (1992). Mass media and the depoliticization of personal experience. *American Journal of Political Science, 36,* 483–508.

*Mutz, D. C. (1994). Contextualizing personal experience: The role of mass media. *The Journal of Politics, 56,* 689–714.

Neely, J. H. (1977). Semantic priming and retrieval from lexical memory: Roles of inhibitionless spreading activation and limited_capactiy attention. *Journal of Experiemntal Psychology: General, 106,* 225–254.

*Pan, Z., & Kosicki, G. M. (1997). Priming and media impact on the evaluations of president's performance. *Communication Research, 24,* 3–30.

Perry, D. K. (1996). *Theory and Research in Mass Communication.* Mahwah, NJ: Lawrence Erlbaum.

Potts, R., & Swisher, L. (1998). Effects of televised safety models on children's risk taking and hazard identification. *Journal of Pediatric Psychology, 23,* 157–163.

*Power, J. G., Murphy, S. T., & Coover, G. (1996). Priming prejudice: How stereotypes and counter-stereotypes influence attribution of responsibility and credibility among ingroups and outgroups. *Human Communication Research, 23,* 36–58.

Price, V., & Tewksbury, D. (1997). New values and public opinion: A theoretical account of media priming and framing. In G. A. Barnett & F. J. Boster (Eds.), *Progress in Communication Sciences: Advances in persuasion* (Vol. 13, 173–212). Greenwich, CT: Ablex Publishing.

Rogers, E. M. (1994). *A History of Communication Study.* New York: Free Press.

Rosenthal, R. (1991). *Meta-analytic Procedures for Social Research.* Newbury Park, CA: Sage.

Roskos-Ewoldsen, D. R. (1997). Attitude accessibility and persuasion: Review and a transactive model. In B. R. Burleson (ed.), *Communication Yearbook 20* (pp. 185–225). Thousand Oaks, CA: Sage.

Roskos-Ewoldsen, D. R., Apran-Ralstin, L. A., & St. Pierre, J. (2002). Attitude accessibility and persuasion. In J. P. Dillard & M. Pfau (Eds.), *Persuasion: Developments in theory and practice* (pp. 39–61). Thousand Oaks, CA: Sage.

Roskos-Ewoldsen, D. R., & Fazio, R. H. (1992). On the orienting value of attitudes: Attitude accessibility as a determinant of an object's attraction of visual attention. *Journal of Personality and Social Psychology, 63,* 198–211.

Roskos-Ewoldsen, D. R., Roskos-Ewoldsen, B, & Dillman Carpentier, F. (2002). Media priming: A synthesis. In J. B. Bryant & D. Zillmann (Eds.), *Media Effects in Theory and Research* (2nd ed., pp. 97–120). Mahwah, NJ: Lawrence Erlbaum.

Rule, B. G., Taylor, B. R., & Dobbs, A. R. (1987). Priming effects of heat on aggressive thoughts. *Social Cognition, 5,* 131–143.

*Scharrer, E. (2001). Men, muscles, and machismo: The relationship between television violence exposure and aggression and hostility in the presence of hypermasculinity. *Media Psychology, 3,* 159–188.

*Schleuder, J. D., White, A. V., & Cameron, G. T. (1993). Priming effects of television news bumbers and teasers on attention and memory. *Journal of Broadcasting and Electronic Media, 37,* 437–452.

Schramm, W. (1997). *The Beginnings of Communication Study in American.* S. H. Chaffee & E. M. Rogers (Eds.). Thousand Oaks, CA: Sage.

Shrum, L. J. (1999). The relationship of television viewing with attitude strength and extremity: Implications for the cultivation effect. *Media Psychology, 1,* 3–26.

Shrum, L. J., & O'Guinn, T. C. (1993). Processes and effects in the construction of social reality. *Communication Research, 20,* 436–471.

Srull, T. K., & Wyer, R. S. (1979). The role of category accessibility in the interpretation of information about persons: Some determinants and implications. *Journal of Personality and Social Psychology, 37,* 1660–1672.

Srull, T. K., & Wyer, R. S. (1980). Category accessibility and social perception: Some implications for the study of person memory and interpersonal judgment. *Journal of Personality and Social Psychology, 38,* 841–856.

Todorov, A., & Bargh, J. A. (2002). Automatic sources of aggression. *Aggression and Violent Behavior, 7,* 53–68.

*Valentino, N. A. (1999). Crime news and the priming of racial attitudes during evaluations of the president. *Public Opinion Quarterly, 63,* 293–320.

Wann, D. L., & Branscombe, N. R. (1990). Person perception when aggressive or nonaggressive sports are primed. *Aggressive Behavior, 16,* 27–32.

*Willnat, L., & Zhu, J. (1996). Newspaper coverage and public opinion in Hong Kong: A time-series analysis of media priming. *Political Communication, 13,* 231–246.

*Wyer, R. S., Bodenhausen, G. V., & Gorman, T. F. (1985). Cognitive mediators of reactions to rape. *Journal of Personality and Social Psychology, 48,* 324–338.

*Yi, Y. (1990a). Cognitive and affective priming effects of the context for print advertisements. *Journal of Advertising, 19,* 40–48.

*Yi, Y. (1990b). The effects of contextual priming in print advertisements. *Journal of Consumer Research, 17,* 215–222.

Zaller, J. R. (1998). Monica Lewinsky's contribution to political science. *PS: Political Science and Politics, 31,* 182–189.

Zillmann, D. (1999). Exemplification theory: Judging the whole by some of its parts. *Media Psychology, 1,* 69–94.

6

The Third-Person Effect: A Meta-Analysis of the Perceptual Hypothesis[*]

Bryant Paul
Indiana University

Michael B. Salwen
Michel Dupagne
University of Miami

Research on the social effects of mass communication has advanced markedly by examining individuals' perceptions of media messages and public opinion (Davison, 1983; Fields & Schuman, 1976; Glynn, Ostman, & McDonald, 1995; Mutz & Soss, 1997; Noelle-Neumann, 1974; O'Gorman & Garry, 1976; Sears & Freedman, 1967; Tyler & Cook, 1984; Vidmar & Rokeach, 1974). Among these approaches, Davison's (1983) the "third-person effect" has generated considerable research (for reviews, see Lasorsa, 1992; Perloff, 1993, 1996). The third-person effect's perceptual hypothesis, also known as the self-other discrepancy, perceptual bias, or the third-person perception (Davison, 1996; Perloff, 1993; Salwen, 1998), predicts that people will perceive a persuasive media message to have greater persuasive effects on others than on themselves.[1] Although the perceptual hypothesis has

---

*This shortened version reprinted with permission from Paul, B., Salwen, M. B., & Dupagne, M. (2000). The third-person effect: A meta-analysis of the perceptual hypothesis. *Mass Communication & Society, 3,* 57–85.

Department of Health and Human Services
Department of Health and Human Services

[1]The third-person effect also posits a behavioral hypothesis which predicts that perceiving others as more influenced than oneself will lead to increased support for restrictions on messages (Davison, 1983). The behavioral hypothesis has received mixed or qualified support (Gunther, 1995; Lee &

yielded robust empirical findings, research to adequately explain how people perceive themselves to be smarter and less resistant to media messages than others has yet to be done. Researchers have also failed to identify the contingent factors that might enhance or diminish the perceptions. The failure of predictive models to provide a clear explanation led one scholar to declare the third-person effect "a phenomenon without a clear process explanation" (Mason, 1995, p. 612).

In addition, despite the robustness of the effect, many individuals fail to exhibit the perception. In reviewing the literature, Lasorsa (1992) reported that about 50% of the members of a particular sample are susceptible to the third-person effect. This underscores the need to understand why the other 50% do not exhibit third-person perceptions, and in some instances display a reverse "first-person effect" to estimate greater effects on themselves (Gunther & Mundy, 1993; Innes & Zeitz, 1988). Perloff (1993) identified a number of conditions that mediate the third-person effect, such as message topic and demographics, adding that the effect may be "a function of the situation, and is more likely to show up in certain situations than in others" (p. 172). But, as research studies accumulate, the number of contingent conditions becomes imposing and daunting. This underscores the need to summarize the findings in a systematic manner.

In this chapter we will perform a meta-analysis to ferret out methodological and content variables that moderate the third-person effect.[2] It is based on a previous study (Paul, Salwen, & Dupagne, 2000). Where relevant, readers will be directed to that original article to acquire technical or in-depth information not included here. In this chapter, we will examine eight moderators: source, method, sampling, respondent, country, desirability, medium, and message. Meta-analysis, which has become increasingly popular in mass communication research (e.g., Allen, D'Alessio, & Brezgel, 1995; Glynn, Hayes, & Shanahan, 1997; Kim & Hunter, 1993; Morgan & Shanahan, 1997; Paik & Comstock, 1994; Ware &

Yang, 1996; McLeod, Eveland, & Nathanson, 1997; Rojas, 1994; Rojas, Shah, & Faber, 1996; Rucinski & Salmon, 1990; Salwen, 1998; Salwen, Dupagne, & Paul, 1998). Unfortunately, most behavioral results cannot be aggregated using meta-analytic procedures because these studies use multiple regression with different control variables (e.g., media use, self-knowledge, and demographics). Cumulation of regression weights for the purpose of a meta-analysis is only appropriate when the predictors are the same across studies (Hunter et al., 1982). Of the 62 third-person effect studies we located, 13 tested the behavioral hypothesis. Of those 13, only 5 reported a correlation coefficient between third-person perception and support for restrictions. Eight studies used multiple regression and quantified the relationship between third-person perception and restrictions using beta weights without reporting zero-order correlations between the predictor and the criterion variable.

[2]With most social-structural variables, such as gender, age, and education, a moderator analysis cannot be carried out unless studies report statistics for each category of these variables (e.g., effect sizes for male and female respondents in the case of gender) or focus on a single variable category that can be compared to another variable category (e.g., the effect size of a study using a sample of male respondents can be compared to the effect size of another study using a sample of female respondents).

Dupagne, 1994), enables researchers to draw generalizations concerning a hypothesis and make sense of diverse empirical findings. Before formulating the research questions and describing the methodology, we will review the theoretical foundations of the third-person effect.

THEORETICAL FOUNDATIONS

Researchers have drawn on a variety of psychological theories to justify the third-person effect. Few, however, explicitly linked these theories to the third-person effect. Although some researchers have used ego-involvement (e.g., Perloff, 1989; Vallone, Ross, & Lepper, 1985), the elaboration likelihood model (e.g., Stenbjerre & Leets, 1998; White, 1995, 1997) and social categorization theory (e.g., Stenbjerre, 1997), most have relied on attribution theory (e.g., Gunther, 1991; Hoffner et al., 1997; Rucinski & Salmon, 1990) and biased optimism (e.g., Brosius & Engel, 1996; Gunther & Mundy, 1993; Rucinski & Salmon, 1990) to explain the theoretical underpinnings of the third-person effect. In a reflective and candid essay, Davison (1996), a sociologist, writing 13 years after his seminal study and expressing surprise at the number of studies generated by his 1983 piece, confessed that he originally viewed the third-person effect as "an interesting phenomenon . . . but of minor theoretical significance" (p. 114).

Attribution Theory

In its broadest sense, attribution theory refers to the study of processes used by people to infer causes of behavior. Heider (1958) argued that people act like "naive psychologists" who seek to understand actions and events that are relevant to them and form beliefs based on observations. Attribution theory has four major assumptions: (a) people perceive behavior as being caused and intentional, (b) people possess dispositional properties (e.g., traits, abilities, and intentions), (c) people assess behavior as being caused by a combination of internal or dispositional (e.g., motivations, knowledge, attitudes, moods, needs, and opinions of others) and external or situational (e.g., task difficulty and luck) factors, and (d) people perceive that others have characteristics similar to theirs. Heider's principle of similarity appears to contradict the basic theoretical premise of the third-person effect, which posits that people perceive others to be different from, not similar to, themselves and more vulnerable to media influences.

However, Heider recognized that there are situations in which attributions to self and others can differ: "The person tends to attribute his own reactions to the object world, and those of another, when they differ from his own, to personal characteristics in o [the other]" (p. 157). Jones and Nisbett (1972) removed

Heider's phrase "when they differ from his own" and amplified his statement as a formal proposition about actor and observer differences. They postulated that "there is a pervasive tendency for actors to attribute their actions to situational requirements, whereas observers tend to attribute the same actions to stable personal dispositions" (p. 80; see also Zimbardo, 1972). For instance, a student (actor) who turns in an assignment late might explain to the professor that this tardiness was out of character and caused by an unusual computer problem (external or situational factor). On the other hand, the professor (observer) might believe that this tardiness was not due to the student's environment but instead to the student's laziness or ineptitude (internal or dispositional factor). These actor–observer differences in causal attributions are to be interpreted in the context of the so-called *fundamental attribution error,* defined as "the tendency for attributers to underestimate the impact of situational factors and to overestimate the role of dispositional factors in controlling behavior" (Ross, 1977, p. 183; see also Zebrowitz, 1990). It is this nonmotivational source of bias in attribution theory that has attracted the attention of third-person effect researchers (e.g., Gunther, 1991; Rucinski & Salmon, 1990; Standley, 1994).

Applied to a media message, attribution theory explains why a person may think he or she understands the underlying persuasive aspects of the message whereas others' dispositional flaws (e.g., gullibility, naiveté, or lack of intelligence) make them incapable of perceiving message persuasiveness. Because this explanation deals with circumstances and situations, attributions may vary based on message content. Gunther (1991) described the relevance of attribution theory to third-person perceptions: "Attribution theory is pertinent to the third-person effect simply because of the consistent bias in estimating the situational response. There may or may not be specific dispositional attributes assigned to the greater persuasibility of others, but the relevant point is that observers see others as less responsive to the situation" (p. 357). In a rare empirical test of attribution theory applied to the third-person effect, Standley (1994) found support for the proposition that people attribute their own actions to situational factors whereas they attribute others' actions to dispositional factors. Using a series of in-depth interviews, she reported that respondents were more likely to cite situational reasons than dispositional ones when asked to assess the effects of television on themselves. When asked to determine the effects of television on the audience, respondents were more likely to cite dispositional reasons than situational ones.

Biased Optimism

Another commonly used framework has been called biased optimism (Gunther, 1995; Gunther & Mundy, 1993), variations of which are also known as impersonal impact (Brosius & Engel, 1996; Glynn & Ostman, 1988; Tyler & Cook, 1984), unrealistic optimism (Glynn & Ostman, 1988; Weinstein, 1980; Weinstein &

Lachendro, 1982), and personal optimism or societal pessimism (Culbertson & Stempel, 1985; Weinstein, 1980). This explanation holds that people judge themselves less likely than others to experience negative consequences. Biased optimism explains why people believe they are better drivers than others (Svenson, 1981), receive better health care than others (Culbertson & Stempel, 1985), or are better off than others in a myriad of ways (Whitman, 1996). Biased optimism has two underlying assumptions: (a) that people can distinguish between societal–others and personal–self level effects and (b) that media messages influence people's perceptions of risk or harm (Tyler & Cook, 1984).

People's biased optimism has been explained by their attempts to reinforce self-esteem. People reinforce their self-esteem by estimating themselves smart enough to disbelieve media messages while others believe the messages. But the process is not that simple. Some media messages that advocate beneficial outcomes may be desirable to believe. As Gunther and Mundy (1993) stated, "The concept of harmful vs. beneficial outcome is a central one in theoretical research on the 'optimistic bias' phenomenon—the tendency for people to think they are less likely to have negative or undesirable experiences than others" (p. 60).

Biased optimism assumes the existence of a "self-serving" bias—that people evaluate themselves more favorably than they evaluate others and that they believe they are less likely than others to experience negative events (Weinstein & Klein, 1996). This bias is rooted in several social–psychological theories, such as social comparison theory and social evaluation theory (Brown, 1986). Central to biased optimism is the issue of "event desirability." Weinstein (1980) described event desirability as involving two hypotheses: "[1] People believe that negative events are less likely to happen to them than to others, and [2] they believe that positive events are more likely to happen to them than to others" (p. 807). Weinstein's first hypothesis describes the third-person effect whereas the second describes the first-person effect, the tendency to appraise oneself as more affected by desirable-to-believe media messages than others.

Third-person effect research overwhelmingly supports Weinstein's first hypothesis (see Perloff, 1993, 1996). Third-person effect research pertaining to Weinstein's second hypothesis suggesting a first-person effect is equivocal. Hoorens and Ruiter (1996) and Duck, Terry, and Hogg (1995) found individuals to be more strongly influenced by desirable messages than others, as Weinstein's second hypothesis posits. Other studies, however, indicate that desirable messages either diminish third-person perception or result in no perceptual difference (Brosius & Engel, 1996; Gunther & Mundy, 1993; Gunther & Thorson, 1992; Innes & Zeitz, 1988). These findings suggest that although a first-person effect may manifest itself with extremely desirable-to-believe messages, third-person perception is the norm. Furthermore, it seems reasonable to assume that absent any message desirability, the general undesirability associated with believing a media message will result in third-person perception.

RESEARCH QUESTIONS

In summary, there has been much recent research on the third-person effect. Almost all findings have supported the perceptual hypothesis. But what is the magnitude of the effect? This led to our first research question:

> *RQ1: What is the overall level of support for the third-person effect's perceptual hypothesis?*

In addition to determining overall level of support for third-person perceptions, it is necessary to map out the conditions that enhance or diminish third-person perceptions to make inferences about the underlying process. Therefore, a second research question was advanced:

> *RQ2: What study characteristics and content variables moderate the third-person effect's perceptual hypothesis?*

METHOD

Following the methodological procedures of Hunter, Schmidt, and Jackson (1982), Wolf (1986), and Rosenthal (1984), this section includes the five major steps of meta-analysis: (a) locating and searching the literature, (b) selecting a common metric, (c) computing an average effect size and testing for variance homogeneity across studies, (d) identifying moderators, and (e) computing a fail-safe *N*. Statistically, this meta-analysis involves two basic procedures: averaging zero-order correlation coefficients of studies weighted by their respective sample sizes and determining whether there is a significant difference in effect size across studies. If the test of homogeneity is statistically significant, then a moderator analysis is warranted to identify the source of this variation.

Literature Search

To locate published and unpublished third-person effect studies, three computer databases were searched: *Educational Resources Information Center* (*ERIC*), 1968 to 1997; *Dissertation Abstracts International,* 1861 to 1998; and *Periodical Abstracts,* 1982 to 1998. In addition, the following online databases were also used: *PapersFirst,* 1993 to 1998; *Article1st,* 1990 to 1998; and *Social Science Abstracts,* 1983 to 1998. Print copies of *Communication Abstracts* starting with volume 1 were also consulted. The reference sections of all studies located were scrutinized for relevant citations. Finally, several scholars with an interest and publication record in third-person effect research were contacted to locate studies they had or knew of that might have been overlooked. In some cases, they supplied unpublished papers, theses, dissertations, and citations. In all, 62 empirical studies were found using these resources.

Common Metric

All studies included in the meta-analysis were converted to a common statistical metric for comparison. This study used the Pearson's product-moment correlation coefficient *r*, the most widely used metric in meta-analysis (e.g., Glynn et al., 1997; Kim & Hunter, 1993; Morgan & Shanahan, 1997; Paik & Comstock, 1994; Ware & Dupagne, 1994). The data were coded so that a positive *r* indicated a third-person effect (i.e., greater perceived effects on others than on oneself), whereas a negative *r* indicated a first-person effect (i.e., greater perceived effects on oneself than on others).

Third-person effect studies typically report the difference between individuals' estimations of the mean level of influence of media messages on themselves and their perceptions of influence on others. The discrepancy between these perceptions (known as *third-person perception, perceptual discrepancy, perceptual bias,* and *self–others difference* in the literature) is then assessed using *t* or *F* statistics. Studies that provide *t*s or *F*s can usually be converted to *r*s using Wolf's (1986) *t*-to-*r* conversion formula. The formulas appear in the original journal article on which this chapter is based.

Two criteria were used to determine inclusion of studies in this meta-analysis: a study had to (a) include effect measures of the media on oneself and others and (b) report the self–others difference in a manner that permitted conversion to *r*s. Therefore, studies reporting only perceived self–others effects means without standard deviations (or other measures of dispersion that could be converted to standard deviations), as well as studies reporting only the percentages of self and others effects, could not be included in the meta-analysis.

Effect Size and Test of Homogeneity

After the study results were converted to a common metric, the effect size across studies was computed. This formula from Hunter et al. (1982) is described in the original journal article. According to Hunter et al. (1982), "If the population correlation is assumed to be constant over studies, then the best estimate of that correlation is not the simple mean across studies but a weighted average in which each correlation is weighted by the number of persons in that study" (pp. 40–41).

Before undertaking a moderator analysis, data were analyzed to determine whether the variance in effect size across studies is greater than would be expected by chance. Should this be the case, the effect size can be said to be heterogeneous, and a moderator analysis is warranted. A test of homogeneity was performed and, again, the formula is available in the original study.

Moderator Analysis

Eight moderators culled from the literature were examined: source, method, sampling, respondent, country, message desirability, medium, and message. Moderating variables were investigated to determine (a) whether there was a statistically significant difference (at the $p < .05$ level) between the average effect sizes (in terms of r) and (b) whether the mean variance of effect sizes was less than that of the overall mean effect size. Should both of these criteria be satisfied, the variable can be said to be a significant moderator (Hunter et al., 1982). Regarding the second condition, we applied a formula for correcting the across-studies variance for sampling error (see Paul et al., 2000).

Coding

The first author coded all the studies. Nine studies were randomly selected and recoded by a trained graduate student. Across the combined nine studies, which included 25 effect sizes, the overall intercoder reliability, computed as the simple percentage of agreement between the two coders (Holsti, 1969), was .94. Intercoder reliability figures for individual moderators are reported later.

Source

Studies were coded to determine whether significant differences in the reported level of third-person perception existed between published and unpublished studies. Glynn et al. (1997) used this moderator in an effort to examine the possible impact of the "file drawer problem" in a meta-analysis of spiral of silence studies. The file drawer problem, an enduring concern in meta-analysis, refers to the charge that journals are more likely to publish studies that report significant results than those that report nonsignificant results. If this were the case, it would suggest that published research leaves an overly optimistic impression of support for a body of research. Glynn et al. did not find source to be a significant moderator. Journal articles were coded as "published," whereas theses, dissertations, and conference papers or proceedings were coded as "unpublished" (intercoder reliability = 1.00).

Method

Third-person effect studies have used either surveys or experimental methods. In theory, findings should not be attributable to the method. If survey and experimental findings were in general agreement for a body of research, that would provide confidence in the findings. However, in an influential essay, Hovland (1963) reported the tendency of experiments to isolate variable relationships and to thereby increase the likelihood of finding significant outcomes. Paik and Comstock (1994) found that the average effect size for the relationship between exposure to television violence and antisocial behavior was larger for experiments than for surveys. To determine whether the third-person effect is moderated by research methods, studies were coded as either "survey" or "experiment" (intercoder reliability = .95). In studies that met inclusion criteria other methods were not used.

Sampling

For reasons of cost and tradition, survey and experimental researchers often use convenience samples of college students. Potter, Cooper, and Dupagne (1993) reported that 51% of quantitative mass communication articles selected from a sample of eight communication journals between 1965 and 1989 used nonprobabilistic sampling. But nonprobabilistic samples, such as convenience samples, may vary from other populations in unknown and unanticipated ways. In their meta-analysis investigating the impact of U.S. television programs on foreign audiences, Ware and Dupagne (1994) found that using a random sample produced a larger effect size than using a nonrandom sample, although the difference failed to attain statistical significance. To determine whether third-person perception is affected by sampling procedures, study samples were coded as "random" or "nonrandom" (intercoder reliability = .93).

Respondent

It is often, but not always, the case that nonprobabilistic samples consist of college students whereas probabilistic samples consist of noncollege students, hence the importance of considering type of respondent as a separate moderator. In our meta-analysis, one probabilistic study used college student respondents (Hoffner et al., 1997), and three nonprobabilistic studies used general population respondents (Faber, Shah, Hanyoun, & Rojas, 1997; Shah, Faber, Hanyoun, & Rojas, 1997; Youn, Faber, & Shah, 1998). Still the majority of nonprobabilistic studies relied on student samples ($n = 11$). Third-person effect research suggests a reason to expect differences in perceptions among college students. Research examining respondents' self-assessed knowledge indicates that respondents with high levels of self-assessed knowledge, such as college students, might exhibit greater third-person perception than others (Driscoll & Salwen, 1997; Lasorsa, 1989). In fact, it may be that student respondents' status as college students is the factor that allows them to assess themselves as being smarter than other people. Studies were coded as using either "college students" or"noncollege students" (intercoder reliability = .93).

Country

Several studies have investigated the third-person effect in nations other than the United States. For example, Gunther and Ang (1996) examined the third-person effect in Singapore to study the effect in an authoritarian society. If the third-person effect is solely a psychological effect attributable to human perception, then country and cultural variations should not moderate the effect. However, if sociological factors influence people's perceptions of media influence, then social/political factors associated with different countries may moderate the effect. For example, it may be that respondents in authoritarian Singapore perceive media effects differently because of severe government restrictions on the media. Because few third-person effect studies have been conducted outside the United States, studies were dichotomously coded as conducted in the "United States" or "other countries" (intercoder reliability = 1.00).

Desirability

Message desirability has received considerable attention. It is believed that messages perceived as undesirable to believe will enhance third-person perception because these are precisely the types of messages that vulnerable others will believe. On the other hand, the perceiver views himself or herself clever enough to see the foolishness in believing an undesirable-to-believe message (Bereck & Glynn, 1993; Cohen, Mutz, Price, & Gunther, 1988; Duck et al., 1995; Gunther & Mundy, 1993; Gunther & Thorson, 1992; Innes & Zeitz, 1988; Ognianova, Meeds, Thorson, & Coyle, 1996; Thorson & Coyle, 1994). Desirable-to-believe messages may result in reduced third-person perception, no perceptual difference, or even a reverse first-person effect to estimate greater effects on oneself (Gunther & Mundy, 1993; Gunther & Thorson, 1992; Innes & Zeitz, 1988). Studies were coded as "socially undesirable," "socially desirable," or "neither desirable nor undesirable."

Socially undesirable messages included messages or issues that the study authors *expressly stated* were socially undesirable to be believed. Socially undesirable messages also included issues selected because of their *obvious undesirability,* even if not directly stated. The undesirable messages included pornography, television violence, political scandals, and cultural taboos such as extramarital affairs and sexual deviancy. Socially desirable messages were those that the researchers *expressly stated* would be desirable to be believed. Socially desirable messages also included messages and issues selected because of their *obvious desirability.* The desirable issue was public service announcements. Finally, neither desirable nor undesirable messages were those that the researchers stated were neither desirable nor undesirable to believe or neither obviously desirable nor undesirable messages (intercoder reliability = .93). We recognize that it is of dubious validity to operationally define issues as desirable or undesirable based on researchers' assumptions, even if this definition appeared to achieve reasonable face validity. A more valid definition would have respondents evaluating message desirability.

Medium

Research indicates that mass media effects can vary according to the type of medium (Jeffres, 1997). Salwen (1998) reported that newspaper reading was associated with greater third-person perception of presidential election news than was local and network news viewing. He claimed that newspaper readers saw this medium as closely associated with news and public affairs. As a result, newspaper readers were more confident than non-newspaper readers in their superior news and public affairs knowledge. Medium categories included "media in general" (used when respondents were asked to estimate the perceived influence on self and others of no medium in particular or all media in general, such as "the media"), "television;" "radio;" "newspapers," and "other" (intercoder reliability = .94).

Message

Related to message desirability is message content. Third-person effect studies have examined messages concerning a variety of issues and contexts, including commercial product advertisements (Thorson & Coyle, 1994), television violence (Hoffner et al., 1997), pornography (Gunther, 1995), and political news (Hu & Wu, 1996; Salwen, 1998). In their meta-analysis of television violence effects on antisocial behavior, Paik and Comstock (1994) found differences in average correlation coefficients by program type, with cartoons and fantasies producing the largest effect sizes. Message type in this study included seven coding categories selected from third-person effect studies: "media messages in general" (referring to the influence of the media without reference to specific message content), "pornography," "television violence," "commercial ads," "politics" (when studies involved noncommercial political news, political debates, and political advertisements for political candidates and issues), "nonpolitical news" (when studies involved noncommercial news messages that did not relate to politics), and "other" (used when an issue did not fit into any of the other coding categories) (intercoder reliability = .97).

Fail-Safe N

As discussed earlier, the file drawer problem refers to a retrievability bias inherent in all research, but it can be especially acute when one computes aggregated statistical findings in meta-analysis (Rosenthal, 1984). As a result of this bias, generalizations made from published research are thought to be more affirmative than is warranted. Support for the file drawer problem appears to be based more on "common sense" than on empirical evidence. Nevertheless, because results of published studies only might provide an overly optimistic picture of the state of the research, the meta-analyst must use procedures to address the file drawer problem. In our original article, we reported Rosenthal's (1984) calculation of a fail-safe N to address this "availability bias."

FINDINGS

A total of 32 published and unpublished studies that met a priori standards for inclusion in the meta-analysis were examined. From these, 121 separate effect sizes were computed. When combined, a total of 45,729 respondents were included in the meta-analysis. The original study on which this chapter is based contains a table listing the 32 studies.

To address the issue of statistical nonindependence of effect sizes,[3] a t test was performed to determine whether a significant difference existed between the mean r when all effect scores were treated as statistically independent (including multiple scores from the same sample) and the mean r when the average of multiple effect sizes coming from the same samples was considered (see Paik & Comstock, 1994). No significant difference was found between the two groups, $t(153) = .78, ns$. As such, nonindependence was not considered a threat to validity, and the larger set of data made possible by considering each hypothesis test as independent could be used. The unit of analysis was the hypothesis test, not the study, and accordingly K refers to the number of hypothesis tests (individual effect sizes).

Overall Effect Size

Overall, the mean r coefficient for the third-person effect's perceptual hypothesis weighted by sample size was .50 ($r^2 = .25$). This correlation had a fail-safe N of 1,519 (Rosenthal, 1984). This means that 1,519 additional nonsignificant effect sizes would be needed for the mean effect size to fail to attain statistical significance. The corrected (for sampling error) variance for this average correlation coefficient was .034. The correlations were found to be heterogeneous across studies, $\chi^2(120, N = 45,729) = 2,845.36, p < .001$. This finding suggests the presence of at least one moderator.

Moderator Analysis

In Table 6.1, K refers to the number of effect sizes considered in a group for a particular moderator. Therefore, a K of 25 indicates that 25 separate effect sizes were included in a group. N refers to the total number of respondents included in each group. As mentioned earlier, for a moderator to be statistically significant, there

---

[3]Many third-person effect studies examine the perception of media influence on self and on others for a number of different media messages using the same sample of respondents. Each such effect score cannot be assumed to be independent. Hunter and Schmidt (1990) suggest two approaches to handle this problem. First, effect scores could be treated as independent, thereby contributing to a synthesis as separate values. Tracz (1984) conducted a statistical Monte Carlo simulation and found that the distribution of r was not affected by nonindependence when combining correlation coefficients in a meta-analysis (see also Allen et al., 1995). Second, these values could be averaged to contribute to an overall effect score. The first method is more commonly applied in meta-analyses (Hunter & Schmidt, 1990). However, to treat nonindependent data as independent, a meta-analyst must be assured that considering all effect scores separately will not produce results that would differ significantly from the averaging of scores. To avoid the risk of distortion attributable to nonindependence, Paik and Comstock (1994) compared the means of all combined hypothesis tests when each was treated as independent with the means of combined hypothesis tests when multiple effect scores from the same samples were averaged. The researchers found no significant difference between the two means and hence decided to treat all effect scores as though they were independent. We used the same diagnostic approach in this study.

TABLE 6.1
Summary of the Moderator Analyses

Moderator	Categories	Mean r	SD	Mean s_r^2 corrrected	N	K
Source	Published	.44	.24	.060	14,690	55
	Unpublished	.53	.13	.017	31,039	66
Method	Survey	.50	.18	.032	44,422	97
	Experiment	.56	.16	.027	1,307	24
Sampling	Random	.49	.18	.034	39,666	70
	Nonrandom	.56	.14	.021	6,063	51
Respondent	College students	.60	.14	.015	4,784	44
	Noncollege students	.49	.18	.033	40,945	77
Country	United States	.49	.15	.024	23,022	92
	Other countries	.51	.20	.041	22,707	29
Message desirability[a]	Undesirable	.47	.14	.020	10,888	30
	Desirable	.21	.29	.087	3,773	11
	Neither	.54	.14	.020	29,144	66
Medium	Media in general	.48	.17	.031	16,268	67
	Television	.50	.20	.040	22,707	40
	Radio	.56	.06	.004	2,155	3
	Newspapers	.55	.06	.004	2,515	7
	Other[b]	.56	.04	.002	2,084	4
Message	Media messages in general	.72	.05	.003	3,088	13
	Pornography	.37	.11	.013	3,022	6
	TV violence	.48	.08	.007	2,476	7
	Commercial ads	.42	.10	.010	1,267	8
	Politics	.58	.01	.001	21,654	49
	Nonpolitical news	.47	.17	.030	4,611	12
	Other[b]	.39	.07	.002	9,611	26

Note. Mean s_r^2 corrected represents the mean variance of the mean r corrected for sampling error. [a]Fourteen of the 121 hypothesis tests could not be categorized for message desirability. [b]Not included in the F test.

must be a significant difference in effect size between the moderator groups, and the mean variance of effect sizes must be less than that of the overall mean effect size.

Source

Analysis of studies as published and unpublished indicated that this variable was not a significant moderator of third-person perceptions (Table 6.1). Whereas there was a significant difference in effect size between published studies and unpublished studies, $t(119) = 2.42$, $p < .05$, the mean corrected variance (mean s_r^2 corrected $= .039$; thereafter mean s_r^2 cor) for the two groups was greater than that for the overall correlation coefficient of the perceptual hypothesis (.034).

Method

Analysis of the method indicated that this variable was not a significant moderator of third-person perception (Table 6.1). Although the mean corrected variance for the two groups was less than that for the overall r coefficient of the perceptual hypothesis (mean $s_r^2 = .030$), no significant difference was found between mean correlations for the two groups, $t(119) = 1.39$, ns.

Sampling

Sampling was found to be a significant moderator of third-person perception (Table 6.1). There was a significant difference in effect size between the random and nonrandom sample groups, $t(119) = 2.33$, $p < .05$, and the mean variance (mean $s_r^{2\ cor} = .028$) was less than that for the overall r of the perceptual hypothesis. On average, then, third-person perception was larger in nonrandom samples ($r = .54$, $SD = .14$) than in random samples ($r = .49$, $SD = .18$).

Respondent

Comparison of effect sizes between college student samples and noncollege student samples indicated that this variable was a significant moderator (Table 6.1). A significant difference test, $t(119) = 3.63$, $p < .001$, as well as a mean variance (mean $s_r^{2\ cor} = .024$) less than that for the overall r of the perceptual hypothesis, supported this finding. On average, college student samples ($r = .60$, $SD = .14$) yielded a greater third-person effect than noncollege student samples ($r = .49$, $SD = .18$).

Country

Country was not a significant moderator of third-person perception (Table 6.1). Significant variation was not found across studies, $t(119) = 1.45$, ns, and the mean variance found across studies (mean $s_r^{2\ cor} = .035$) was greater than the variance for the overall self–others correlation.

Desirability

Message desirability was not a significant moderator of third-person perception (Table 6.1). We found a significant difference between groups, $F(2, 104) = 12.69$, $p < .001$ (Levene statistic of homogeneity of variances $(2, 104) = 2.28$, ns). A Scheffé post hoc test revealed that the average effect size for "undesirable to be influenced" ($r = .47$, $SD = .14$) was significantly different from the average effect size for "desirable to be influenced" ($r = .21$, $SD = .29$) and that the average effect size for desirable to be influenced was significantly different from the average effect size for neither desirable nor undesirable to be influenced ($r = .54$, $SD = .14$). However, the mean variation for all three groups (mean $s_r^{2\ cor} = .042$) was greater than that for the overall mean correlation of the self–others discrepancy.

Medium

Medium was not a significant moderator of third-person perception (Table 6.1). Although the mean corrected variance for the category (mean $s_r^{2\ cor}$ = .016) was less than that for the overall mean correlation of the self–others discrepancy, no significant variation was found across categories, $F(3, 113)$ = .53, *ns*.

Message

Type of message was a significant moderator of third-person perception (Table 6.1). The mean combined variance across studies (mean $s_r^{2\ cor}$ = .018) was less than that for the overall perceptual hypothesis correlation coefficient. Additionally, there was a significant difference across groups, $F(5, 88)$ = 2.75, $p < .05$ (Levene $(5, 88)$ = .93, *ns*), although the Scheffé test failed to identify significant differences between pairs of effect sizes at the $p < .05$ level.

DISCUSSION

In this study we utilized meta-analytic procedures to investigate claims of "robust" support for the third-person effect's perceptual hypothesis. We also examined whether eight moderators addressed in the literature enhanced or diminished third-person perceptions. Data from 32 studies affirmed claims of at least moderate support for a third-person perception. The overall effect size between estimated media effects on self and on others was r = .50 (r^2 = .25), indicating a moderate relationship (Guilford, 1956). Compared with other meta-analyses in mass communication, this effect size is rather substantial. For instance, Paik and Comstock (1994) reported an r of .31 for the effect of television violence on antisocial behavior, Allen et al. (1995) reported an r of .13 for the effect of pornography on aggression, and Glynn et al. (1997), examining the spiral of silence, another perceptual theory, reported an r of .05 between perceptions of public opinion support and willingness to speak out.

The analyses yielded three significant moderators: type of sampling, type of respondent, and type of message. The findings that nonrandom samples and student samples yielded greater third-person perception than random samples and nonstudent samples are intriguing and perhaps disturbing. From a theoretical perspective, research suggests that respondents with high levels of self-assessed knowledge, such as college students who are often studied in nonrandom samples, might exhibit greater third-person perception because they evaluate themselves as being smarter than other people. An intriguing explanation grounded in self-assessed knowledge (Driscoll & Salwen, 1997; Lasorsa, 1989) holds that college students may perceive that their educational status makes them smarter and less vulnerable to harmful media messages than "others." It is also possible that the students' tendency to conform might make them especially more likely to express the desirable response that they are more resistant to media messages than others.

From a methodological perspective, a more disturbing explanation would be that greater third-person perception among college students is not a moderating variable at all. Instead it may be attributable to study designs relying on student samples. Some researchers have claimed that the use of nonprobabilistic samples, and of college students in particular, can skew findings and threaten external validity (Abelman, 1996; Courtright, 1996; Potter et al., 1993). Others have argued that there is a role for student samples in communication research and that randomization techniques can minimize or solve the nonprobabilistic sampling issue (Basil, 1996; Lang, 1996).

In this regard, it is important to note that method, coded as survey or experiment, was not a significant moderator. This is important because experiments are more likely than surveys to use student samples. Thus, it may not be the method but rather the use of student samples in experiments and surveys that causes generalization problems. Survey studies that use student samples are especially problematic because in surveys, unlike experiments, the primary goal is to ensure external validity. Experimental researchers who often use student samples would argue that, despite problems associated with external validity, their goal is to secure internal validity and determine whether variables are causally related (Lang, 1996; Sparks, 1995).

Although message content was found to be a significant moderator, the importance of this finding is mitigated by the fact that the post hoc test produced nonsignificant differences between pairs of correlation coefficients. Therefore, this moderator is at best ambiguous. The related variable of message desirability was not a significant moderator. This was somewhat surprising because researchers believe that third-person perception is a function of desirability to be influenced (Gunther, 1995; Gunther & Thorson, 1992; Thorson & Coyle, 1994). It is possible that the desirable messages in the research were not perceived as desirable or at least not perceived as desirable as the undesirable messages were perceived as undesirable. In fact, measurement of perceptions of messages as desirable or undesirable is problematic because message desirability is usually assumed without obtaining respondents' opinions. This underscores our earlier point for the need for researchers to directly obtain respondents' perceptions of issue or message desirability rather than ad hoc assuming desirability.

What does this study imply regarding the other nonsignificant moderators? Third-person perception was not moderated by country, operationalized as studies conducted in the United States and other nations. Although the number of foreign studies is small and perhaps differences by national settings may yet emerge as more studies in different countries are conducted, this finding suggests that third-person perception might be an enduring psychological characteristic that holds across national settings and social structures. As more studies are conducted in foreign countries, it will be necessary to move beyond a U.S./non-U.S.

dichotomy and distinguish among nations and aspects of national settings (e.g., democratic, authoritarian, First World, Third World, standard of living, amount of press freedom, availability of media, and level of development) that may explain national differences.

Medium was also a nonsignificant moderator. In one sense this is surprising because it might be argued that the assumed ubiquity and pervasiveness of television makes this medium more influential and persuasive than print media. On the other hand, from a perceptual perspective, because consumers of print media might see themselves as smarter than users of nonprint media, they might exhibit greater third-person perception (Salwen, 1998).

The fact that source, coded as published or unpublished, was not a significant moderator casts doubt on the common wisdom associated with the file drawer problem Perhaps too much is made of the file drawer problem. Certainly more research is needed to determine whether the file drawer problem is simply an untested truism in the academy. Perhaps journal editors are more open to well-designed studies than is often thought, even if results fail to attain significance. One would hope that this is the case. The publication of well-designed studies with nonsignificant findings can contribute to our knowledge. Likewise, perhaps unpublished studies remain unpublished simply because they—especially theses and dissertations—are more likely to be written by students, who do not have as much of an interest and a career stake in journal publication as faculty. Finally, in terms of coding this variable, a caveat is in order. Many unpublished studies become published studies, underscoring the variability of this moderator. During the course of data gathering we had to recode studies when unpublished conference papers were published in journals, and the recoding sometimes changed significance. We expect that several unpublished studies will be published by the time this manuscript is in print.

A limitation of this study is that we did not examine the behavioral hypothesis because of the dearth of behavioral studies and because behavioral studies often failed to report statistics suitable for meta-analysis. Although it is important to study the perceptual hypothesis because perceptions precede behaviors, the behavioral hypothesis makes the third-person effect relevant to social researchers and media practitioners. For example, the behavioral hypothesis offers an intriguing explanation of public support for media censorship—that is, that people support censorship to "protect" others from harmful media messages (Rojas et al., 1996; Salwen, 1998; Salwen & Driscoll, 1996). Another limitation associated with meta-analyses is that results are often based on small sample sizes of studies (not effect sizes). The relatively small number of studies means that the publication of even a few new studies can have an impact on the overall findings and alter outcomes. As noted, we became especially aware of this limitation during the course of this study when we coded the source variable.

So, what do our findings mean? They affirm that the third-person effect's perceptual hypothesis is a moderate to robust finding, not only in terms of the consistency of the findings but also in the overall effect size. They also affirm that moderators can affect third-person perceptions. The message moderator indicates that researchers need to be aware of how issue characteristics might affect third-person perceptions. The fact that sampling and types of respondents might moderate the effect warns of the need to be cautious when deviating from traditional random sampling with a general population. The fact that these methodological moderators were significant warns third-person effect researchers to be extra careful because other methodological matters such as question wording or sample size might affect outcomes.

Although desirability was not a significant moderator, we noted dissatisfaction with past conceptualizations and operationalizations of message desirability. Desirability is still an important variable worth studying, although more creative ways of studying this variable are needed. Finally, although theory was not part of our meta-analysis, we feel the need to comment its use in third-person effect research. Studies that drew on attribution theory, biased optimism, and other theories used them as theoretical rationales to gird third-person perception. Third-person effect research might profit if researchers went further and borrowed some of the operational measures and procedures in these theory-oriented bodies of research to more convincingly demonstrate the link between third-person perceptions and psychological theories.

We conclude with a comment of methodological nature regarding the use of meta-analysis. As Glynn et al. (1997) suggested, it would be helpful to meta-analysts if statistical data were reported in a manner that facilitated their combination. In many cases this would simply entail reporting a mean and standard deviation for the groups being compared. As such, presenting empirical research results in a manner that enables the effective combination and comparison of equivocal findings seems essential.

REFERENCES

Abelman, R. (1996). Can we generalize from Generation X? Not! *Journal of Broadcasting & Electronic Media, 40,* 441–446.

Allen, M., D'Alessio, D., & Brezgel, K. (1995). A meta-analysis summarizing the effects of pornography. II. Aggression after exposure. *Human Communication Research, 22,* 258–283.

Basil, M. D. (1996). The use of student samples in communication research. *Journal of Broadcasting & Electronic Media, 40,* 431–440.

Bereck, S. R., & Glynn, C. J. (1993, May). *Interpersonal interaction and the third-person effect in potential first time presidential election voters.* Paper presented at the annual meeting of the American Association for Public Opinion Research, St. Charles, IL.

Brosius, H., & Engel, D. (1996). The causes of third-person effects: Unrealistic optimism, impersonal impact, or generalized negative attitudes towards media influence? *International Journal of Public Opinion Research, 8,* 142–162.

Brown, J. D. (1986). Evaluations of self and others: Self-enhancement biases in social judgments. *Social Cognition, 4,* 353–376.

Cohen, J., Mutz, D., Price, V., & Gunther, A. (1988). Perceived impact of defamation. *Public Opinion Quarterly, 52,* 161–173.

Courtright, J. A. (1996). Rationally thinking about nonprobability. *Journal of Broadcasting & Electronic Media, 40,* 414–421.

Culbertson, H. M., & Stempel, G. H. (1985). Media malaise: Explaining personal optimism and societal pessimism about health care. *Journal of Communication, 35*(2), 180–190.

Davison, W. P. (1983). The third-person effect in communication. *Public Opinion Quarterly, 47,* 1–15.

Davison, W. P. (1996). The third-person effect revisited. *International Journal of Public Opinion Research, 8,* 113–119.

Driscoll, P. D., & Salwen, M. B. (1997). Self-perceived knowledge of the O. J. Simpson trial: Third-person perception and perceptions of guilt. *Journalism & Mass Communication Quarterly, 74,* 541–556.

Duck, J. M., Terry, D. J., & Hogg, M. A. (1995). The perceived influence of AIDS advertising: Third-person effects in the context of positive media content. *Basic and Applied Social Psychology, 17,* 305–325.

Faber, R. J., Shah, D., Hanyoun, S., & Rojas, H. (1997). *Advertising censorship: Factors accounting for a willingness to restrict commercial speech for legal products.* Manuscript submitted for publication.

Fields, J., & Schuman, H. (1976). Public beliefs about the beliefs of the public. *Public Opinion Quarterly, 40,* 427–448.

Glynn, C. J., Hayes, A. F., & Shanahan, J. (1997). Perceived support for one's opinions and willingness to speak out: A meta-analysis of survey studies on the "spiral of silence." *Public Opinion Quarterly, 61,* 452–463.

Glynn, C. J., & Ostman, R. E. (1988). Public opinion about public opinion. *Journalism Quarterly, 65,* 299–306.

Glynn, C., Ostman, R., & McDonald, D. (1995). Opinions, perception, and social reality. In T. Glasser & C. Salmon (Eds.), *Public opinion and the communication of consent* (pp. 249–277). New York: Guilford.

Guilford, J. P. (1956). *Fundamental statistics in psychology and education.* New York: McGraw-Hill.

Gunther, A. (1991). What we think others think: Cause and consequence in the third-person effect. *Communication Research, 18,* 355–372.

Gunther, A. (1995). Overrating the X-rating: The third person perception and support for censorship of pornography. *Journal of Communication, 45*(1), 27–38.

Gunther, A. C., & Ang, P. H. (1996). Public perception of television influence and opinions about censorship in Singapore. *International Journal of Public Opinion Research, 8,* 248–265.

Gunther, A. C., & Mundy, P. (1993). Biased optimism and the third-person effect. *Journalism Quarterly, 70,* 58–67.

Gunther, A. C., & Thorson, E. (1992). Perceived persuasive effects of product commercials and public service announcements: Third-person effects in new domains. *Communication Research, 19,* 574–596.

Heider, F. (1958). *The psychology of interpersonal relations.* New York: Wiley.

Hoffner, C., Plotkin, R. S., Buchanan, M., Schneider, S., Ricciotti, L. A., Kowalczyk, L. Silberg, K., & Pastorek, A. (1997, May). *The third-person effect in perceptions of the influence of television violence.* Paper presented at the annual meeting of the Association for Education in Journalism and Mass Communication, Montreal.

Holsti, O. R. (1969). *Content analysis for the social sciences and humanities.* Reading, MA: Addison-Wesley.

Hoorens, V., & Ruiter, S. (1996). The optimal impact phenomenon: Beyond the third-person effect. *European Journal of Social Psychology, 26,* 599–610.

Hovland, C. I. (1963). Reconciling conflicting results derived from experimental studies of attitude change. In E. P. Hollander & R. G. Hunt (Eds.), *Current perspectives in social psychology* (pp. 378–389). New York: Oxford University Press.

Hu, Y. W., & Wu, Y. C. (1996, August). *Testing a theoretical model on the third person effect: Perceived impacts of election polls.* Paper presented at the annual meeting of the Association for Education in Journalism and Mass Communication, Anaheim, CA.

Hunter, J. E., & Schmidt, F. L. (1990). *Methods of meta-analysis: Correcting error and bias in research findings.* London: Sage.

Hunter, J. E., Schmidt, F. L., & Jackson, G. B. (1982). *Meta-analysis: Cumulating research findings across studies.* New York: Sage.

Innes, J. M., & Zeitz, H. (1988). The public's view of the impact of the mass media: A test of the 'third person' effect. *European Journal of Social Psychology, 18,* 457–463.

Jeffres, L. W. (1997). *Mass media effects* (2nd ed.). Prospects Heights, IL: Waveland.

Jones, E. E., & Nisbett, R. E. (1972). The actor and the observer: Divergent perceptions of the causes of behavior. In E. E. Jones, D. E. Kanouse, H. H. Kelley, R. E. Nisbett, S. Valins, & B. Weiner (Eds.), *Attribution: Perceiving the causes of behavior* (pp. 79–94). Morristown, NJ: General Learning Press.

Kim, M. S., & Hunter, J. E. (1993). Attitude-behavior relations: A meta-analysis of attitudinal relevance and topic. *Journal of Communication, 43*(1), 101–142.

Lang, A. (1996). The logic of using inferential statistics with experimental data from nonprobability samples: Inspired by Cooper, Dupagne, Potter, and Sparks. *Journal of Broadcasting & Electronic Media, 40,* 422–430.

Lasorsa, D. L. (1989). Real and perceived effects of "Amerika." *Journalism Quarterly, 66,* 373–378, 529.

Lasorsa, D. L. (1992). How media affect policymakers: The third-person effect. In J. D. Kennamer (Ed.), *Public opinion, the press and public policy* (pp. 163–175). New York: Praeger.

Lee, C., & Yang, S. (1996, August). *Third-person perception and support for censorship of sexually explicit visual content: A Korean case.* Paper presented at the annual meeting of the Association for Education in Journalism and Mass Communication, Anaheim, CA.

Mason, L. (1995). Newspaper as repeater: An experiment on defamation and the third-person effect. *Journalism & Mass Communication Quarterly, 72,* 610–620.

McLeod, D. M., Eveland, W. P., Jr., & Nathanson, A. I. (1997). Support for censorship of violent and misogynic rap lyrics: An analysis of the third-person effect. *Communication Research, 24,* 153–174.

Morgan, M., & Shanahan, J. (1997). Two decades of cultivation research: An appraisal and meta-analysis. In B. R. Burleson (Ed.), *Communication yearbook 20* (pp. 1–45). Thousand Oaks, CA: Sage.

Mutz, D. C., & Soss, J. (1997). Reading public opinion: The influence of news coverage on perceptions of public sentiment. *Public Opinion Quarterly, 61,* 431–451.

Noelle-Neumann, E. (1974). The spiral of silence: A theory of public opinion. *Journal of Communication, 24*(2), 43–51.

Ognianova, E., Meeds, R., Thorson, E., & Coyle, J. (1996, August). *Political adwatches and the third-person effect.* Paper presented at the annual meeting of the Association for Education in Journalism and Mass Communication, Anaheim, CA.

O'Gorman, H., & Garry, S. (1976). Pluralistic ignorance—A replication and extension. *Public Opinion Quarterly, 40,* 449–458.

Paik, H., & Comstock, G. (1994). The effects of television violence on antisocial behavior: A meta-analysis. *Communication Research, 21,* 516–546.

Paul, B., Salwen, M. B., & Dupagne, M. (2000). The third-person effect: A meta-analysis of the perceptual hypothesis. *Mass Communication & Society, 3,* 57–85.

Perloff, R. M. (1989). Ego-involvement and the third person effect of televised news coverage. *Communication Research, 16,* 236–262.

Perloff, R. M. (1993). Third-person effect research 1983–1992: A review and synthesis. *International Journal of Public Opinion Research, 5,* 167–184.

Perloff, R. M. (1996). Perceptions and conceptions of political media impact: The third-person effect and beyond. In A. N. Crigler (Ed.), *The psychology of political communication* (pp. 177–191). Ann Arbor: The University of Michigan Press.

Potter, W. J., Cooper, R., & Dupagne, M. (1993). The three paradigms of mass media research in mainstream communication journals. *Communication Theory, 3,* 317–335.

Rojas, H. (1994). *Censorship and the third-person effect in mass communication.* Unpublished master's thesis, University of Minnesota, St. Paul.

Rojas, H., Shah, D. V., & Faber, R. J. (1996). For the good of others: Censorship and the third-person effect. *International Journal of Public Opinion Research, 8,* 162–185.

Rosenthal, R. (1984). *Meta-analytic procedures for social research.* Beverly Hills, CA: Sage.

Ross, L. (1977). The intuitive psychologist and his shortcomings: Distortions in the attribution process. In L. Berkowitz (Ed.), *Advances in experimental social psychology* (pp. 173–220). New York: Academic Press.

Rucinski, D., & Salmon, C. T. (1990). The 'other' as vulnerable voter: A study of the third-person effect in the 1988 U.S. presidential campaign. *International Journal of Public Opinion Research, 2,* 343–368.

Salwen, M. B. (1998). Perceptions of media influence and support for censorship: The third-person effect in the 1996 presidential election. *Communication Research, 25,* 259–285.

Salwen, M. B., & Driscoll, P. D. (1996, August). *Self-perceived knowledge and the third-person effect: Media influence during the O. J. Simpson trial.* Paper presented at the annual meeting of the Association for Education in Journalism and Mass Communication, Anaheim, CA.

Salwen, M. B., Dupagne, M., & Paul, B. (1998, August). *Perceptions of media power and moral influence: Issue legitimacy and the third-person effect.* Paper presented at the annual meeting of the Association for Education in Journalism and Mass Communication, Baltimore, MD.

Sears, D. O., & Freedman, J. L. (1967). Selective exposure to information: A critical review. *Public Opinion Quarterly, 31,* 194–213.

Shah, D. V., Faber, R. J., Hanyoun, S., & Rojas, H. (1997, August). *Censorship of political advertising: A third-person effect.* Paper presented at the annual meeting of the Association for Education in Journalism and Mass Communication, Chicago, IL.

Sparks, G. G. (1995). Comments concerning the claim that mass media research is "prescientific": A response to Potter, Cooper, and Dupagne. *Communication Theory, 5,* 273–280.

Standley, T. C. (1994). *Linking third-person effect and attribution theory.* Unpublished master's thesis, Southern Methodist University, Dallas.

Stenbjerre, M. N. (1997). *A social categorization model of the third-person effect in mass communication.* Unpublished master's thesis, Cornell University, Ithaca, NY.

Stenbjerre, M., & Leets, L. (1998, July). *Central and peripheral routes to the third-person effect: Media effects attribution to self and others as a function of message elaboration.* Paper presented at the annual meeting of the International Communication Association, Jerusalem.

Svenson, O. (1981). Are we all less risky and more skillful than our fellow drivers? *Acta Psychologica, 47,* 693–708.

Thorson, E., & Coyle, J. (1994). The third person effect in three genres of commercials: Product and greening ads, and public service announcements. In K. King (Ed.), *Proceedings of the American Academy of Advertising* (pp. 103–112). Athens: University of Georgia.

Tracz, S. M. (1984). The effect of the violation of the assumption of independence when combining correlation coefficients in a meta-analysis (Doctoral dissertation, Southern Illinois University, Carbondale, 1984). *Dissertation Abstracts International, 56,* 688.

Tyler, T. R., & Cook, F. L. (1984). The mass media and judgments of risk: Distinguishing impact on personal and societal level judgments. *Journal of Personality and Social Psychology, 47,* 693–708.

Vallone, R. P, Ross, L., & Lepper, M. R. (1985). The hostile media phenomenon: Biased perception and perceptions of media bias in coverage of the Beirut massacre. *Journal of Personality and Social Psychology, 49,* 577–585.

Vidmar, N., & Rokeach, M. (1974). Archie Bunker's bigotry: A study in selective perception and exposure. *Journal of Communication, 24*(1), 124–137.

Ware, W., & Dupagne, M. (1994). Effects of U.S. television programs on foreign audiences: A meta-analysis. *Journalism Quarterly, 71,* 947–959.

Weinstein, N. (1980). Unrealistic optimism about future life events. *Journal of Personality and Social Psychology, 39,* 806–820.

Weinstein, N. D., & Klein, W. M. (1996). Unrealistic optimism: Present and future. *Journal of Social and Clinical Psychology, 15,* 1–8.

Weinstein, N. D., & Lachendro, E. (1982). Egocentrism as a source of unrealistic optimism. *Personality and Social Psychology Bulletin, 8,* 195–200.

White, H. A. (1995, August). *Issue involvement and argument strength as mediating factors in the third-person effect.* Paper presented at the annual meeting of the Association for Education in Journalism and Mass Communication, Washington, DC.

White, H. A. (1997). Considering interacting factors in the third-person effect: Argument strength and social distance. *Journalism & Mass Communication Quarterly, 74,* 557–564.

Whitman, D. (1996, December 16). I'm OK, you're not. *U.S. News & World Report, 121,* 24–30.

Wolf, F. M. (1986). *Meta-analysis: Quantitative methods for research synthesis.* London: Sage.

Youn, S., Faber, R. J., & Shah, D. V. (1998). *Attitudes toward gambling advertising and the third-person effect.* Manuscript submitted for publication.

Zebrowitz, L. A. (1990). *Social perception.* Pacific Grove, CA: Brooks/Cole.

Zimbardo, P. (1972). The tactics and ethics of persuasion. In B. T. King & E. McGinnies (Eds.), *Attitudes, conflict and social change* (pp. 88–114). New York: Academic Press.

7

The Selective Exposure Hypothesis and Media Choice Processes

Dave D'Alessio
University of Connecticut–Stamford

Mike Allen
University of Wisconsin–Milwaukee

The theory of cognitive dissonance (Festinger, 1957) is often offered as the culmination of a line of thought that was an attempt to consider persuasive processes as being integrally based on an individual's expected preference for cognitive balance. The balance theories, including dissonance, held that rational persons should have a general preference for cognitive elements—beliefs, values, and/or attitudes—that are logically consistent.

This is of interest to students of media in that many of these cognitive elements, as well as individual communications designed to change them (e.g., advertisements), would be introduced via mediated messages. To present a particularly horrid example from recent headlines, if one believed that both Saddam Hussein and Osama bin Laden were enemies of the United States, then it would be cognitively consistent (and so "balanced") to conclude that the two were allied (i.e., "my enemy and my enemy are allies" is a logical construction). For most Americans, the first two beliefs would necessarily have been inculcated by mediated messages, as few Americans have had any first-hand contact with either madman.

The theory of cognitive dissonance is of particular interest here in that it not only provided a means of thinking about how people process mediated messages but it also went on to consider what the desire in a media user for cognitive balance might imply in terms of how people use media. One of its first predictions was that the desire for cognitive balance could induce people to expose themselves to certain types of media content in preference to others: Specifically, they would be expected to avoid exposure to dissonant messages and to prefer consonant messages, where *dissonant* basically means that messages or cognitive elements are inconsistent with one another and *consonant* means the reverse (consistency). Festinger's exact prediction was

> The avoidance of an increase in dissonance comes about as a result of the existence of dissonance . . . (when) support is sought for a new cognitive element to replace an existing one or when new cognitive elements are to be added. . . . A person would initiate discussion with someone he thought would agree with the new cognitive element but would avoid discussion with someone who might agree with the element he was trying to change. (p. 30)

This extremely powerful prediction was immediately seized on by researchers into mass media effects. It is probably an oversimplification to state baldly that effects researchers considered media audiences to be passive receivers and highly persuadable, but, for instance, Hyman and Sheatsley (1947/1971) felt obliged to explain in detail how and why mediated information campaigns did *not* achieve expected results: The underlying presupposition is that mediated information campaigns ought to work. Similarly, discovery of selective perception processes, in which viewers tend to interpret materials based on idiosyncratic frameworks, is also treated as though it is revelatory (historically speaking).

Research on the selective exposure hypothesis tends to consider it from two standpoints. *Selectivity* is a positive phenomenon—people deliberately selecting material congruent with their attitudes. In the absence of (or competing with) selectivity is *avoidance,* in which people turn away from material that disagrees with their preexisting attitudes.

Ultimately, selective exposure and other selectivity phenomena such as avoidance are among the cornerstones of Klapper's (1960) law of minimal effects, which holds that under many conditions the consumers of mediated messages are protected against persuasion by a variety of psychological, sociological, and cultural process that have the ultimate impact of creating mechanisms that support the reinforcement of preexisting attitudes in viewers as opposed to their change. The law of minimal effects, although problematic as a theory, forced recognition of the relative complexity of the social and psychological processes surrounding the consumption of mediated messages. Klapper, for instance, made explicit the idea of the media as competitive message environments: In a pluralistic programming environment, on subjects for whom there is general debate and legitimate differences of opinion, mediated messages summarizing and espousing any number of viewpoints may be accessible to a consumer. Which of these persuasive messages, if any of them, will sway the audience?

Klapper drew heavily on dissonance theory in discussing the psychological processes involved in message consumption and impact. In particular, he perceived the audience as being cognitively active rather than passive. Klapper saw a media consumer as one who would deliberately choose certain messages in preference to others, who would interpret (or misinterpret) ambiguous messages, and who would retain certain messages while forgetting others. He felt that dissonance theory supplied an explanation for how this would occur: To protect the integrity of their belief structures and so avoid or minimize cognitive dissonance, an audience would preferentially choose messages in accord with their preexisting attitudes (selective exposure), interpret messages as being supportive of their preexisting attitudes (selective perception), and retain supportive messages better than nonsupporting ones (selective retention).

The reliance on dissonance-related phenomena tied the law of minimal effects to the theory of cognitive dissonance. Critical reviews, however, suggested that Festinger's prediction was incorrect (and, by implication, that the law of minimal effects was incorrect as well). Freedman and Sears (1965) reviewed the literature on selective exposure and concluded that the results were inconclusive: Studies of the phenomenon were as likely to contradict dissonance theory as to support it. By 1967, Sears and Freedman (1967/1971) had located 23 tests of selective exposure: By their reckoning, in 7 of them participants had preferred consonant material as dissonance theory predicts, in 5 they chose dissonant materials (in direct opposition to Festinger's prediction), and in the remaining 11 their preferences were unclear or did not differ significantly. The conclusion was that "a considerable amount of experimental research has uncovered no general psychological preference for supportive information" (p. 232). This is a damning criticism if it is correct. The first step in revising our thinking on the subject of dissonance and its role in media consumption is to determine whether Sears and Freedman's conclusion is correct.

Since the mid-1960s one trend in the methodology of the social sciences has been an increase in the use of meta-analysis as a review technique (Glass, 1976; Rosenthal, 1978). Examination of the two reviews (Freedman & Sears, 1965; Sears & Freedman, 1967/1971) and the studies on which their conclusions are based from the standpoint of meta-analysis makes it clear that it is possible the original studies reviewed were heterogeneous in design and should, therefore, have been expected to yield the inconsistent results that Sears and Freedman found. Also, it is possible that studies of selective exposure would produce nonsignificant or even negative results simply due to sampling error (Hunter & Schmidt, 1990). ns of the various studies were as low as 18 for Freedman (1965a), suggesting a high potential for sampling error and also low statistical power.

Meta-analysis provides a means of accumulating the results of many studies into a comprehensive body of literature whose design permits the application of statistical tests to the results. Effect sizes from the set of studies are converted to a common metric, and the results are aggregated and subsequently tested for heterogeneity; that is, they are tested to assess whether the set of results vary simply due to sampling error or, conversely, whether they vary due to the action of moderating variables in creating subgroups in the studies under examination (Hunter & Schmidt, 1990).

The ability to test the overall set of results using a formal, statistical method makes meta-analysis an important tool for literature review, at least in a mature body of literature containing a large number of published studies (Cook & Leviton, 1980). The Sears and Freedman reviews were conducted as traditional literature reviews, begging the question of the value of meta-analysis: Will meta-analysis support the same conclusions as the original, traditional reviews?

STUDY 1: REPLICATING SEARS
AND FREEDMAN'S FINDINGS

The value of a dissonance prediction of selective exposure and the possibility that the findings of critical reviews may be flawed by sampling error and the inclusion of inappropriate or dissimilar tests suggest the value of a meta-analytic review of the ability of dissonance theory to predict selective exposure. To do this, we located as many of the works reviewed by Sears and Freedman (1967/1971) as proved to be recoverable and subjected this body of literature to meta-analytic testing.

The 23 tests of the selective exposure phenomenon cited by Sears and Freedman (1967/1971) had been made available publicly in 18 published papers, one published abstract (Freedman & Sears, 1963), and one U.S. Navy technical report (Sears & Freedman, 1963). The technical report has thus far been unrecoverable. The published abstract reported neither n nor the test statistic used, so no estimate of effect size could be made. Additionally, two of the reports, Mills and Ross (1964) and Rhine (1967), reported results in a manner that precluded a direct test of the selective exposure hypothesis.

For the remaining tests, the final association between attitude and either the selection of consonant material or the avoidance of dissonant material was restated as a Pearson product–moment correlation (r). r is generally the preferred statistic for meta-analytic purposes as it is not affected by sample size and because it is in common use and therefore readily interpretable (Hunter & Schmidt, 1990). The entire set of studies, with their ns and effect sizes, is reported as Table 7.1.

This set of studies yields a mean effect size of $r = .157$. With the aggregate total of 1953 participants, this r is significant at the $p < .001$ level. The positive sign of the result indicates that the body of findings as a whole supports the idea that people tend to expose themselves to media congruent with their preexisting attitudes or avoid material that contradicts them; that is, it supports the selective exposure hypothesis as predicted by dissonance theory. The statistical power of this test exceeds .99.

These tests do not form a homogeneous grouping, as the test of homogeneity yielded $\chi^2(16) = 125.23, p < .001$. This result indicates the operation of one or

TABLE 7.1

Tests of Selective Exposure Cited by Sears and Freedman

Study	n	Effect Size
Adams (1961)	66	.185
Brock (1965)	197	.635
Brodbeck (1956)	160	.187
Ehrlich et al. (1957)	125	.199
Feather (1962—smokers)	50	−.472
Feather (1962—non-smokers)	63	−.337
Feather (1963)	152	.412
Freedman & Sears (1963)	n and effect size unreported	
Freedman (1965a)	18	−.447
Jecker (1964)	59	.130
Mills (1965a) Study 1	70	.093
Mills (1965a) Study 2	73	.268
Mills (1965b)	80	.000
Mills, Aronson, & Robinson (1959)	356	.150
Mills & Ross (1964)	Effect size not estimable	
Rhine (1967)	Effect size not estimable	
Rosen (1961)	135	.243
Sears (1965)	92	−.271
Sears (1966)	80	.158
Sears & Freedman (1963)	U.S. Navy Technical Report (unrecoverable)	
Sears & Freedman (1965)	143	−.066

more moderating variables intervening between the preexisting attitudes of the participants and their choice of supportive material.

Searching the studies for one or more moderating variables proved problematic owing to the wide variety of different research designs, participant populations, media and topics, and the mixing of selectivity and avoidance processes included in the studies Sears and Freedman were reviewing. For instance, Ehrlich, Guttmann, Schoenbach, and Mills (1957) visited new car owners and asked them to select from a set of eight envelopes containing ads for various car models. Feather (1962) asked smokers to rank order 13 articles, one of which dealt with the smoking–lung cancer relationship, by interest in the contents. Freedman (1965b) asked college students to evaluate a confederate's academic qualifications and then offered them a choice between materials supporting or opposing their choice. Rosen (1961) asked introductory psychology students to choose between essay or multiple choice exams and then offered them a choice of six articles to read, three each supporting each type of exam. In view of this sort of study-to-study variety of conditions, we have so far been unable to coherently discern moderating variables.

On the whole, however, it must be stated that Sears and Freedman's overall conclusion is not exactly correct. The positive and significant overall effect size is evidence of a general preference for supportive information. It is not a large effect, and the heterogeneity of the results shows that it is an inconsistent effect, but on the whole people show a preference for material supportive of preexisting attitudes (or negative preference for material in opposition of preexisting attitudes), as Festinger predicted.

The perceived failure of dissonance theory to make consistent predictions about message selection by media users led to a three-way split of the research into selective exposure processes. The first set of literature focused more broadly on the consistent existence of demographic regularities in media use patterns, sometimes referred to as *selectivity*. In this view, selective exposure is considered to be in action whenever a distinct (and, one assumes, non-propinquity based) regularity in viewing audiences occurs, such as the preference of male viewers for football and female viewers for figure skating on television. Although such regularities have substantial commercial value, they are in and of themselves not theoretically interesting.

The second direction into which selective exposure leads is the question of the role of mood state in media choice (e.g., Boyanowsky, 1977; Wakshlag, Vial, & Tamborini, 1983; among many others). It is clear that mediated messages can evoke mood-state reactions in users, and from that recognition it is only a short step to the idea that users can choose media content teleologically, specifically, to achieve preferred mood states. It has been demonstrated numerous times that people choose media in part to achieve specific emotional responses, and this line of research is providing useful insights into the relationship of media and people. However, entire books (Bryant, Roskos-Ewoldsen, & Cantor, 2003) have been written on this topic, and it is impossible to adequately treat it here.

A final group of researchers has attempted to continue to explicate and refine the nature and predictions of dissonance theory (e.g., Frey, 1986). This will remain the primary focus of this chapter, and so it may be valuable to apply the methods of meta-analysis to this body of literature.

STUDY 2: DISSONANCE-BASED STUDIES

Although the wide variety of published literature containing estimates of selectivity or avoidance-type effects allows examination of a wide variety of processes, for the second study we chose to limit ourselves to the fundamental prediction of dissonance theory: that following a decision people will tend to select material supportive of that decision and reject material that contradicts the decision.

To gather studies for this review, a number of sources were considered. We first gathered a number of well-known works in the field and used their reference lists to generate leads to other articles. We added articles by looking in *Psychological Abstracts* under the heading of "selective exposure" and also by looking under the "media" heading and looking for the subheadings "attitude" and "selectivity." We also searched PsycINFO using the term "selective exposure." This led to the accumulation of a database of more than 120 publications.

From this database we selected all of the studies that met all four of the following criteria: (a) the study was conducted under controlled conditions; (b) participants underwent manipulation of a cognitive element such as attitude, belief, or opinion that involved making a choice; (c) participants were asked to make some form of selection of media; and (d) authors reported their statistical results in a form that permitted conversion to the common metric.

Field studies and studies involving mood manipulations were excluded. Also excluded were studies that did not require a choice as a means of creating dissonance, in other words, only studies that met the formal and strictest characteristics of direct tests of the theory of cognitive dissonance in its original form. For purposes of simplification we added an additional criterion: that experimental participants be asked to choose from between simultaneously presented materials. As we will see, recent methodological advances utilize a more realistic model of media selection behavior; however, as a recent formulation, this methodological advance has so far been deployed infrequently.

Typical experimental protocols meeting all of the preceding criteria included choosing between reading positive or negative performance evaluations of a job candidate after a decision on whether or not to interview him (Freedman, 1965b), choosing between consonant or dissonant information after being forced to write a counterattitudinal essay on the placement of nuclear power plants in populated areas (Cotton & Hieser, 1980), and choosing whether to read personality evaluations of a task partner after choosing between that partner and another (Jecker, 1964). Protocols such as these provided a set of studies conducted under conditions comparable to those used to test Festinger's specific claims.

It should be noted that a preliminary version of this analysis was reported on previously by D'Alessio and Allen (2002). Since that report, six more effect size measurements based on an additional 179 additional experimental participants have been recovered and added. It should further be noted that our conclusions have not been substantially affected. Finally, it should be noted that only 5 of the original 18 studies analyzed by Sears and Freedman (1967/1971) met all of the conditions discussed here. Of course, the report we were unable to recover for the first study remained unrecoverable.

This selection process yielded a set of 22 effect size estimates that directly tested Festinger's predictions (1957). Although several of the estimates were simultaneously published in the same report, Tracz (1984) demonstrated that this is not problematic for the purposes of meta-analytic estimation. As earlier, *r* is used as a common metric for effect size estimates. The 22 studies, their *n*s, and their converted effect sizes are presented in Table 7.2.

TABLE 7.2

Postdecisional Selections Between Simultaneously Presented Materials

Study	n	Effect Size
Adams (1961)	66	.185
Brock, Albert, & Becker (1970)	251	.218
Brodbeck (1956)	160	.187
Cotton & Hieser (1980)	60	.272
Feather (1963)	152	.412
Freedman (1965a)	116	.331
Freedman (1965b)	18	−.447
Frey (1981) Study 2	132	.293
Frey & Rosch (1984)	66	.120
Guerrero (1969)	38	.158
Innes (1978)	48	.292
Jecker (1964)	59	.130
Jonas et al. (2001) Study 1	18	.457
Jonas et al. (2001) Study 2	30	.671
Jonas, et al. (2001) Study 3	17	.546
Jonas, et al. (2001) Study 4	30	.436
Kleck & Wheaton (1967)	72	.272
LaVoie & Thompson (1972)	418	.172
McCroskey & Prichard (1967)	136	.183
Nemeth & Rogers (1996)	96	.204
Schulz-Hardt et al. (2000) Study 1	15	.653
Schulz-Hardt et al. (2000) Study 3	138	.206

The mean effect size, weighted for the n of each study, was calculated to be $r = .241$. The total n for the 22 studies was 2,101, so the results are significant at $p < .0001$. The positive sign of the result indicates support for Festinger's prediction of selecting consonant material or avoidance of dissonant material. Statistical power for this study exceeded .995.

The test of homogeneity yielded $\chi^2(21) = 31.0$, $p = ns$. Despite differences in magnitude from $r = -.447$ to $r = .412$, the nonsignificant χ^2 implies that the observed scores are within the limits expected of variation due to sampling error and that the studies can be said to form a single group with no moderators operating. Direct tests of postdecisional selective exposure support the predictions of the theory of cognitive dissonance, in contradiction to the conclusions of previous reviews. The reasons for this should be clear. First, the overall mean effect size of $r = .241$ clearly indicates that the effect is small in magnitude and so is easily obscured by the effects of sampling error in many of the studies.

Further, in their attempts to provide as complete a review as possible, Freedman and Sears included studies that either lacked experimental controls or (in several cases) did not require a decision as part of the experimental protocol. It should be noted that only five of the 18 studies reviewed by Sears and Freedman (1967/1971) met the four criteria we set to locate studies that comprised fair tests of Festinger's hypothesis. (Again, one proved unrecoverable.) To review the literature thoroughly, Sears and Freedman (1967/1971) attempted to aggregate field experiments, survey data results, and studies conducted under controlled conditions. They also included studies both with protocols that included decisions and protocols that did not. In the absence of meta-analytic rigor, it is easy for reviewers to inadvertently be comparing apples to oranges, in essence.

Most troubling was the inclusion by Sears and Freedman (1967/1971) of studies that did not include a choice between attractive alternatives as part of the experimental protocol. Although Festinger (1957) conceded that everyone always has some dissonance (the justification for such protocols), it is also clear that he expected dissonance to be largest and so provide the most motivation after a decision, which is why he consistently referred to *postdecisional* dissonance.

The statistical impact of this choice is easily examined. The effect size yield by our second study is significantly higher than that in the first ($z = .279, p < .01$) and the second is also significantly less heterogeneous than the first [$\chi^2(5) = 94.23, p < .001$]. This result implies that a number of the tests yielding what Sears and Freedman would call disconfirming or unclear tests were actually inappropriate tests. (In fact, the only disconfirming test to meet the criteria was Freedman, 1965b, which had an n of 18.) Including them both reduced the overall effect size and confounded their attempts to interpret the results of their review.

It should also be noted that 17 of the 22 tests in this meta-analysis were published after the original publication of the second Sears and Freedman (1967/1971) review. No study was found that they should have included but did not. Their reviews were comprehensive and appropriate under the conditions that prevailed in the mid-1960s, and the present study should not be interpreted as a criticism of theirs.

Although subject to ex post facto reanalysis, the Sears and Freedman reviews had the effect of expanding the ways that people looked at selective exposure in subsequent years, as discussed earlier. Herein we have decided to pursue only the examination of selective exposure using the framework of dissonance theory, and it must be noted that attempts to develop and modify dissonance theory to make it more powerfully predictive happened in part as a response to Sears and Freedman's critique.

These attempts have led to the development of two additional lines of research conducted by proponents of dissonance theory. One of the potential moderators of selective exposure is the utility of the information being offered. It may be that people are willing to look at material that disagrees with their attitudinal positions if that information is sufficiently useful to them (Frey, 1986). We are continuing to attempt to explicate the evaluation of utility, but so far have been unsuccessful in creating sensible valuations of usefulness and so will not examine this line of research further here.

The second, and newest, line of research includes attempts to modify the standard experimental approach to examining attitudinally based selective exposure by creating an experimental protocol that better models the choice processes of individuals. We will consider this line of research in our final study.

STUDY 3: SEQUENTIAL VERSUS SIMULTANEOUS CHOICE

The common experimental protocol for researching selective exposure involves having participants make some choice and then choose from a menu of media selections. For instance, Ehrlich et al. (1957) offered participants advertising materials for eight models of cars (including their own) or participants who had just made hire/not hire decisions on experimental confederates would be offered a choice of additional pro and con material (Jecker, 1964).

In the 1950s media milieu, this protocol may have been a viable model of choice. In the vast majority of TV markets there were only the three major networks whose programs would be readily displayed in *TV Guide* or the local newspaper; a town might have two newspapers, one each in allegiance to the major parties. Cable TV was largely unviable due to restrictive federal regulations on the rebroadcast of previously aired material, and movie theaters displayed their choices on single-page-menu-like marquees.

However, as Jonas, Schulz-Hardt, Frey, and Thelen (2001) pointed out, this model is probably no longer viable. Although theatrical film is still presented in the same way and the number of newspaper choices has actually declined, cable and satellite TV have come to permeate the marketplace, creating a processing overload that must be dealt with by users. Many cable operators provide linear, scrolling channel guides because there is far too much programming for the single-page menu to be viable, and cable remote control devices are frequently designed to permit users to scroll through either the entire network channel by channel or through a personalized "repertoire" or subset of channels (Heeter, 1988). In either instance, selections are made in a linear and binary "yes-no" manner rather than as a single selection from a single, potentially unmanageable, set.

As Jonas et al. also mention, the simultaneous mode of presentation developed probably in part for the convenience of experimental confederates. It is not a great leap to envision an unlucky graduate student standing on the doorstep of a new car buyer, fanning out a handful of envelopes containing ads in the manner of a magician and asking the participant to "Pick a card, any card!" But such a presentation places the messages into direct competition, requiring the participant to create ad hoc some form of simplification routine to narrow the set to one, possibly evoking any of several moderators. Making binary "yes-no" decisions is a much simpler process, does not require "naive" theorizing, and so probably evokes fewer cognitive processes.

To perform the third study, we examined our database, looking for research studies that met the same four main criteria as in Study 2 but that used experimental protocols calling for participants to be presented with stimuli sequentially rather than simultaneously. We found only one research report of four separate experiments. We also searched the literature review of that article but found no additional studies meeting all criteria. It should be noted that two of the possible reports were published in Germany (in German) and could not be examined.

Again, although published together, the results of four separate experiments designed differently to examine different elements of the simultaneous processing versus sequential processing question were included in the report of Jonas et al. The participants were different each time. Although this difference may violate the presumption of independence of tests, Tracz (1984) showed that meta-analysis is generally robust to such violations. We again restated the effect sizes as rs. The results are presented as Table 7.3.

The mean effect size is $r = .642, p > .001$. Because the four studies were designed using basically the same protocols and population sets, it is not surprising that they form a homogeneous set, $\chi^2(3) = 0.37, p = ns$.

Far more importantly, the mean effect size for this set of studies, despite the relatively low n of 95 for Study 3, is significantly as well as substantively higher than the mean effect size for Study 2, $z = 3.77, p < .001$. This finding is a clear indication that the role of selective exposure when participants choose among sequentially presented materials is greater than it is for simultaneously presented messages.

Jonas et al. attributed this finding to the decision focus hypothesis, which basically holds that each decision in a sequential series requires the participant to reflect back onto the original, dissonance-evoking choice. Cognitively, this effectively means that the participants re-persuade themselves constantly throughout the message choice process, as opposed to their behavior in the simultaneous choice situation, which requires only one decision and a single reflection back.

It is also possible that the development of ad hoc choice theories discussed earlier is contributory to the smaller manifestation of selective exposure in the simultaneous presentation protocol. This contribution would maximize the opportunity for moderating variables such as the utility of the information to come into

TABLE 7.3
Postdecisional Selections Between Sequentially Presented Materials

Study	n	Effect Size
Jonas et al. (2001) Study 1	18	.650
Jonas et al. (2001) Study 2	30	.663
Jonas et al. (2001) Study 3	17	.519
Jonas et al. (2001) Study 4	30	.686

play, because the participant will be faced with what amounts to an overload of information. Also, because the participant can reasonably expect that the experimental confederate conducting the test will expect the participant to have some reason for selecting a given message, the participant may form a "naive" theory of the value of the stimuli. In a sequential choice process, no participant knows whether the next choice will possess any given characteristic whatsoever, and so the participant is not in a position to develop a more sophisticated criterion set. This possibility has not been tested but can potentially explain the differences between the outcomes of Study 2 and Study 3.

We are not arguing that 100 of 100 people confronted by a handful of envelopes containing ads for cars will stop and form an ad hoc theory that allows simultaneous evaluation of each. Rather, it is distinctly likely that these 100 people will tend to follow one of three evaluative paths: One group will probably just grab an envelope at random, the second may engage in a selective exposure procedure, and only the third group—proportion unknown—will consider all the key elements of all the stimuli. But it need not be a large number of people doing so to moderate the impact of selective exposure. (Rosenthal, 1986, has pointed out the value of understanding what effect sizes translate into from the standpoint of raw numbers.)

GENERAL DISCUSSION

We have examined selective exposure from the standpoint of the theory of cognitive dissonance in its strictest sense: that of postdecisional dissonance. This term defines the realm of applicability of the specific conclusions we have been discussing. It needs to be explicitly stated that we have been discussing selective exposure that has occurred after a decision between attractive alternatives.

This area of research is interesting theoretically, as we will see, but of limited practical implication. By definition, a theory of postdecisional dissonance can predict neither behavior nor cognitive processing before a decision, including the decision-making process itself, and so it is of limited utility to people who have a vested interest in the valence of decisions. Our findings do imply that were we car salesmen, we would like to have available a number of brochures extolling the virtues of the cars we were selling to provide reinforcing information after the sale.

If we continue to consider our findings from the standpoint of practical utility, we would have to point out that selective exposure is of greatest utility in controlling future behavior. Selective exposure processes are, by their very nature, processes that support the reinforcement of existing behaviors, as an essential nature of mediated material people selectively expose themselves to is that it agrees with their preexisting positions. No one has ever had his or her mind changed by consuming messages that agree with existing beliefs and attitudes.

Rather, from a practical standpoint, the utility of selective exposure is that it implies a means of retaining an audience. In advertising terms, selective exposure to messages is valuable in the building of phenomena such as brand loyalty, in which people buy the same brand of product regardless of the blandishments of other similar products. It is also may be possible to find a practical application in the examination of sequential consumption processes: If one shopping decision can be shown to lead to a second shopping decision (e.g., the purchase of tortilla chips may be followed by the purchase of salsa or vice versa), it may be possible to tie products together cognitively to reinforce both behaviors simultaneously.

But it is clear that the existence of selective exposure processes is far more interesting from a theoretical rather than an applied level because it emphasizes the value of regarding audiences as active, decision-making entities rather than as static blobs. Ruben pointed out in 1984 that it was possible to divide TV show selection (and, by extension, other uses of other media) into two major categories, instrumental viewing and ritualized viewing. Instrumental viewing was conceptualized as goal-directed and implied a deliberate choice to maximize desired cognitive or emotional outcomes, whereas ritualized viewing was seen as essentially habitual: At a certain hour the TV goes on even if no one is paying much attention. Ruben found that instrumental viewing is associated with gratifications such as learning whereas ritualized viewers seek to pass time and desire companionship from having the medium on.

What is particularly interesting about this dichotomy is that it parallels the direction in which persuasion research is presently heading. Both the elaboration likelihood model (Petty & Cacioppo, 1984) and Chaiken's (1980) notion of systematic versus heuristic processing presuppose that incoming messages are typically processed in one of two ways: They can be processed thoughtfully, using rational reasoning and a number of possible cognitive responses, or they can be processed superficially, focusing on surface structure, context rather than content, the use of catchphrases, or whatever. It is almost certain that when Chaiken refers to systematic processing and Ruben to instrumental viewing, they are discussing decisions made via parallel processes and the same is true with heuristic processing and ritualized viewing.

The results of (particularly) our third study fairly strongly imply that selective exposure in the narrow sense that we have been discussing it is probably one of the decision criteria applied in each of the selection processes, but also that it plays a greater role in ritualized viewing selections. When one considers that it is likely that simultaneously presented materials force users into the formulation of a cognitive scheme designed to arrive at a solution, it seems reasonable to conclude that users are more likely to engage in instrumental processes with simultaneously presented media than they are with sequentially presented material. Although the interplay of potential criteria helps to moderate selective exposure effects, our statistically significant (and homogeneous) result for Study 2 indicates that selective exposure still plays a small role in instrumental decisions.

The results for Study 3, however, indicate much stronger selective exposure effects with sequentially presented materials. As discussed previously, this type of presentation of information almost forces the participant into a low cognitive-processing environment, because the sequential presentation does not allow the development of a competitive criterion set. Under these conditions, it seems very reasonable that the desire to select material to agree with oneself will come to the fore: Given that one is not trying to accomplish anything else with this material (i.e., one is engaged in ritualized rather than instrumental viewing), why would anyone deliberately select material that "fries their gizzards"?

To summarize, we have concluded that people routinely selectively expose themselves to messages in accord with their existing attitudinal structures and avoid incongruent messages (Study 1). In the specific realm of human behavior that dissonance theory was designed to explain, that is, behavior following decisions between attractive alternatives, people engage in selective exposure with a certain degree of consistency (Study 2). In specific situations designed to model ritualized viewing decisions (sequential presentation of stimuli), selective exposure is substantially more powerful than it is in decisions made between simultaneously presented stimuli (Study 3).

We suspect the reason for selective exposure being weaker with simultaneously presented material is that the simultaneous presentation forces users to consider a number of factors to appear to be making a rational choice, that is, to formulate an ad hoc theory. We suspect that the use of ad hoc theories is more prevalent in instrumental viewing (and media use generally) than it is in ritualized viewing.

Finally, on the whole, it is clear that psychological processes, including but also clearly not limited to cognitive dissonance, play a role in the consumption of media. It is critical as we study the role of media in society to remember that exposure is the first step in any media effects process model. If we want to know what media do to people, it behooves us to figure out what people do with media.

REFERENCES

Adams, J. S. (1961). Reduction of cognitive dissonance by seeking consonant information. *Journal of Abnormal and Social Psychology, 62,* 74–78.

Boyanowsky, E. O. (1977). Film preferences under conditions of threat. *Communication Research, 4,* 133–144.

Brock, T. C. (1965). Commitment to exposure as a determinant of information receptivity. *Journal of Personality and Social Psychology, 2,* 287–289.

Brock, T. C., Albert, S. M., and Becker, L. A. (1970). Familiarity, utility, and supportiveness as determinants of information receptivity. *Journal of Personality and Social Psychology, 14,* 292–301.

Brodbeck, M. (1956). The role of small groups in mediating the effects of propaganda. *Journal of Abnormal and Social Psychology, 52,* 166–170.

Bryant, J., Roskos-Ewoldsen, D., and Cantor, J. (2003). *Communication and Emotion.* Mahwah, NJ: Lawrence Erlbaum Associates.

Chaiken, S. (1980). Heuristic versus systematic information processing and the use of source versus message cues in persuasion. *Journal of Personality and Social Psychology, 39*, 752–766.

Cook, T., and Leviton, L. (1980). Reviewing the literature: a comparison of traditional methods with meta-analysis. *Journal of Personality, 48*, 449–472.

Cotton, J. L., and Hieser, R. A. (1980). Selective exposure to information and cognitive dissonance. *Journal of Research in Personality, 14*, 518–527.

D'Alessio, D., and Allen, M. (2002). Selective exposure and dissonance after decisions. *Psychological Reports, 91*, 527–532.

Ehrlich, D., Guttmann, I., Schonbach, P., and Mills, J. (1957). Post-decision exposure to relevant information. *Journal of Abnormal and Social Psychology, 54*, 98–102.

Feather, N. T. (1962). Cigarette smoking and lung cancer: a study of cognitive dissonance. *Australian Journal of Psychology, 14*, 55–64.

Feather, N. T. (1963). Cognitive dissonance, sensitivity, and evaluation. *Journal of Abnormal and Social Psychology, 66*, 157–163.

Festinger, L. (1957). *A theory of cognitive dissonance.* Stanford, CA: Stanford University Press.

Freedman, J. L. (1965a). Confidence, utility, and selective exposure. *Journal of Personality and Social Psychology, 2*, 778–780.

Freedman, J. L. (1965b). Preference for dissonant information. *Journal of Personality and Social Psychology, 2*, 287–289.

Freedman, J. L., and Sears, D. O. (1963). Voters' preferences among types of information. *American Psychologist, 18*, 375 (abstract).

Freedman, J. L., and Sears, D. O. (1965). Selective exposure. *Advances in Experimental Social Psychology, 2*, 57–97.

Frey, D. (1981). Postdecisional preference for decision-relevant information as a function of the competence of the source and the degree of familiarity with this information. *Journal of Experimental Social Psychology, 17*, 51–67.

Frey, D. (1986). Recent research on selective exposure to information. *Social Psychology, 19*, 41–80.

Frey, D., and Rosch, M. (1984). Information seeking after decisions: the role of novelty of information and decision reversibility. *Personality and Social Psychology Bulletin, 10*, 91–98.

Glass, G. V. (1976). Primary, secondary and meta-analysis of research. *Educational Researcher, 5*, 3–8.

Guerrero, J. L. (1969). Avoidance, relevance and exposure to discrepant information. *Journalism Monographs, 14*, 39–54.

Heeter, C. (1988). The Choice Process Model. In Heeter, C., and Greenberg, B. S. (eds.) *Cableviewing.* Norwood, NJ: Ablex.

Hunter, J. E., and Schmidt, F. L. (1990). *Methods of meta-analysis.* Newbury Park, CA: Sage.

Hyman, H. H., and Sheatsley, P. B. (1947/1971). Some reasons why information campaigns fail. In Schramm, W., and Roberts, D. F. (eds.) *The Process and Effects of Mass Communication* (Rev. Ed.). Urbana, IL: University of Illinois Press.

Innes, J. M. (1978). Selective exposure as a function of dogmatism and incentive. *The Journal of Social Psychology, 106*, 261–265.

Jecker, J. D. (1964). Selective exposure to new information. In L. Festinger (Ed.), *Conflict, decision and dissonance.* Stanford, CA: Stanford University Press. pp. 65–81.

Jonas, E., Schulz-Hardt, S., Frey, D., and Thelen, N. (2001). Confirmation bias in sequential information search after preliminary decisions: an expansion of dissonance theoretical research on selective exposure to information. *Journal of Personality and Social Psychology, 80*, 557–571.

Klapper, J. (1960). *The effects of mass communication.* New York: Free Press.

Kleck, R. E., and Wheaton, J. (1967). Dogmatism and responses to opinion-consistent and opinion-inconsistent information. *Journal of Personality and Social Psychology, 5*, 249–252.

LaVoie, A. L., and Thompson, S. K. (1972). Selective exposure in a field setting. *Psychological Reports, 31*, 433–434.

McCroskey, J. C., and Prichard, S. V. O. (1967). Selective-exposure and Lyndon B. Johnson's 1966 "State of the Union" address. *Journal of Broadcasting, 11,* 331–337.

Mills, J. (1965a). Avoidance of dissonant information. *Journal of Personality and Social Psychology, 2,* 10–19.

Mills, J. (1965b). Effect of certainty about a decision upon postdecision exposure to consonant and dissonant information. *Journal of Personality and Social Psychology, 2,* 749–752.

Mills, J., Aronson, E., and Robinson, H. (1959). Selectivity in exposure to information. *Journal of Abnormal and Social Psychology, 59,* 250–253.

Mills, J., and Ross, A. (1964). Effects of commitment and certainty on interest in supporting information. *Journal of Abnormal and Social Psychology, 68,* 552–555.

Nemeth, C., and Rogers, J. (1996). Dissent and the search for information. *British Journal of Social Psychology, 35,* 67–76.

Petty, R. E., and Cacioppo, J. T. (1984). The effects of involvement on responses to argument quantity and quality. *Journal of Personality and Social Psychology, 46*(1), 69–81.

Rhine, R. J. (1967). The 1964 presidential election and curves of information seeking and avoiding. *Journal of Personality and Social Psychology, 5,* 416–423.

Rosen, S. (1961). Post-decision affinity for incompatible information. *Journal of Abnormal and Social Psychology, 63,* 188–190.

Rosenthal, R. (1978). Combining results of independent studies. *Psychological Bulletin, 85,* 185–193.

Rosenthal, R. (1986). Media violence, antisocial behavior, and the social consequences of small effects. *Journal of Social Issues, 42,* 141–154.

Ruben, A. M. (1984). Ritualized and instrumental television viewing. *Journal of Communication, 34,* 67–77.

Sears, D. O. (1965). Biased indoctrination and selectivity of exposure to new information. *Sociometry, 28,* 363–376.

Sears, D. O. (1966). Opinion formation and information preferences in an adversary situation. *Journal of Experimental Social Psychology, 2,* 130–142.

Sears, D. O., and Freedman, J. L. (1963). Commitment, information utility and selective exposure. USN Technical Reports, number 12 (August).

Sears, D. O., and Freedman, J. L. (1965). The effects of expected familiarity with arguments upon opinion change and selective exposure. *Journal of Personality and Social Psychology, 2,* 420–426.

Sears, D. O., and Freedman, J. L. (1967/1971). Selective exposure to information: a critical review. In W. Schramm and D. F. Roberts (Eds.), *The process and effects of mass communication.* (Rev. ed.) Urbana, IL: University of Illinois Press. pp. 209–235.

Schulz-Hardt, S., Frey, D., Luthgens, C., and Moscovici, S. (2000). Biased information search in group decision making. *Journal of Personality and Social Psychology, 78,* 655–669.

Tracz, S. M. (1984). The effect of the violation of the assumption of independence when combining correlation coefficients in a meta-analysis (Doctoral dissertation, Southern Illinois University, Carbondale, 1984). *Dissertation Abstracts International, 56,* 688.

Wakshlag, J., Vial, V., and Tamborini, R. (1983). Selecting crime drama and apprehension about crime. *Human Communication Research, 10,* 227–242.

8

Meta-Analysis
of Television's Impact
on Special Populations

Robert Abelman
*Cleveland State
University*

David J. Atkin
*Cleveland State University
and University of
Connecticut*

Carolyn A. Lin
*University of
Connecticut*

Television viewing has evolved into the most time-consuming leisure activity of American youth and, as such, has been the topic of much scientific inquiry. As can be seen in the preceding chapters of this text and in numerous other texts (see Brown, 1976; Bryant & Anderson, 1983; Clifford, Gunter, & McAleer, 1995; Greenberg, 1980; Van Evra, 1998), literally thousands of studies have examined the content of television programs, the effect that different types of content has on child viewers, and the manner by which children process television information. The question of what types of children are most influenced by television is a recurrent theme in the scientific literature, particularly since Schramm, Lyle, and Parker's (1961) much cited conclusion that "for *some* children, under some conditions, some television is harmful" (p. 1, italics added). Until quite recently, however, virtually all of the research has focused on average or "normal" children rather than on the special populations for which television viewing and the impact of that viewing, under some conditions, is most significant.

Researchers have known for many years that children who have major difficulties in their relationships with their peers and/or parents and perform poorly in school tend to watch a great deal of television (e.g., Himmelweit, Oppenheim, & Vince, 1958; Liebert, Sprafkin, & Davidson, 1982). Children who behave aggressively have an increased preference for and reactivity to television violence (e.g., Dorr & Kovaric, 1980; Surgeon General's Scientific Advisory Committee on Television and Social Behavior, 1971), although this has not always held true for low-IQ children (Gadow & Sprafkin, 1987; Sprafkin, Gadow, & Grayson, 1987). Also, in studies of perceived reality, children less able to attend to and comprehend the persuasive intent of commercials are more vulnerable to their appeals (e.g., Ward, Wackman, & Wartella, 1977; Young, 1990). This line of work, in conjunction with perceptions of TV content generally, was not applied to special populations until recently (e.g, Sprafkin, Kelly, & Gadow, 1987; Donahue, 1978; Sprafkin & Gadow, 1988; Sprafkin, Liebert, & Poulos, 1975; Sprafkin & Rubinstein, 1982; Sprafkin, Watkins, & Gadow, 1990; Striefel, 1972; Striefel, 1974).

These characteristics—problems with interpersonal relationships, academic underachievement, aggressive behavior, and non-normative attention and comprehension skills—are common in children who have been labeled by their school districts as emotionally disturbed (ED)[1] (Morse, Cutler, & Fink, 1994; Quay, Morse, & Cutler, 1966), learning disabled (LD)[2] (Bryan, 1976; Cunningham & Barkley, 1978), or mentally retarded (MR)[3] (Eyman & Call, 1977; Rutter, Tizard, & Whitmore, 1970). It is, therefore, surprising that relatively little consideration has been given to exceptional individuals, that is, those "who require special education and related services if they are to realize their full human potential" (Hallahan & Kauffman, 1991, p. 6).

---

[1]According to Public Law 94-142, the Education for All Handicapped Children Act (U.S. Office of Education, 1977, p. 42478), the term *emotionally disturbed* means a condition exhibiting one or more of the following characteristics over a long period of time and to a marked degree, which adversely affect educational performance: (a) an inability to learn that cannot be explained by intellectual, sensory, or health factors; (b) an inability to build or maintain satisfactory interpersonal relationships with peers and teachers; (c) inappropriate types of behavior or feelings under normal circumstances; (d) a general pervasive mood of unhappiness or depression; or (e) a tendency to develop physical symptoms or fears associated with personal or school problems.

[2]According to Public Law 94-142 (U.S. Office of Education, 1977, p. 65083), *specific learning disability* means a disorder in one or more of the basic psychological processes involved in "understanding or in using language, spoken or written, which may manifest itself in an imperfect ability to listen, think, speak, read, write, spell, or do mathematical calculations. The term includes such conditions as perceptual handicaps, brain injury, minimal brain dysfunction, dyslexia, and developmental aphasia. The term does not include children who have learning problems which are primarily the result of visual, hearing, or motor handicaps, of mental retardation, of emotional disturbance, or of environmental, cultural, or economic disadvantage."

[3]According to Public Law 94-142 (U.S. Office of Education, 1977), *mentally retarded* means significantly subaverage general intellectual functioning concurrent with deficits in adaptive behavior and manifested during the developmental period, which adversely affects a child's educational performance. The degree of mental retardation can range in severity from mild to profound.

Failure to examine TV and children at the other end of the educational continuum, intellectually gifted children,[4] is an equal oversight although one might not ordinarily consider them vulnerable to the adverse effects of the medium in the same sense as disabled youngsters, and they are not. Yet the combination of natural curiosity (Franks & Dolan, 1982; Sternberg & Davidson, 1985) and the ease and swiftness with which they learn (Davis & Rimm, 1989; Griggs & Dunn, 1984) raises questions regarding their attraction to programming for which they are intellectually but not socially or emotionally prepared. Indeed, Salomon (1984) observed that the strongest debilitating effects of television are observed with high-ability children. They have the most negative views of the medium, expend the least mental effort in processing a presented program, and show the poorest inference-making performance (p. 62).

In addition, parents and special educators have long recognized that television holds unique promise as an educational tool for exceptional children (see Sprafkin, Gadow, & Abelman, 1992). For children who are frequently deficient in social skills, television offers direct demonstrations of appropriate social interactions that teachers can reinforce with classroom activities. For children who are often unresponsive to traditional learning techniques, television offers stimulating multisensory learning experiences. For children who need frequent repetition to learn new concepts or skills, television provides endless opportunities for repetition through the added technology of videocassette playback and TiVo (e.g., Lin & Atkin, 1989). Television has also proven to be a masterful medium for capturing the attention of children who cannot sit still and attend to anything else. Given the tremendous potential for television to supplement traditional teaching methods, one would expect that there would be scores of studies in the education literature demonstrating the effectiveness of television in enhancing learning in exceptional children. This is not the case.

The relative exclusion of exceptional populations may have been defensible in the early days of television research when attention was reasonably devoted to studying the normal majority, but television is the great common denominator in contemporary society, the one environmental experience that all children share. Whether television is considered a "vast wasteland" (Minow, cited in Sarnoff, 1961), a "plug-in drug" (Winn, 1977), a "double-edged sword" (Richert, 1981), a "home invader" (Wildmon, 1985), or a "magic window" (Dorr, 1986), an examination of its use by and impact on all children is justifiable. Furthermore, we are not referring to an insignificant segment of the viewing audience when we

---

[4]The definition in Public Law 97-35, the Education Consolidation and Improvement Act, which was passed by Congress in 1981, characterized *gifted children* as "children who give evidence of high performance capability in areas such as intellectual, creative, artistic, leadership capacity or specific academic fields and who require services or activities not ordinarily provided by the school in order to fully develop such capabilities" (Section 582).

consider exceptional children. Almost 3 million youngsters in the United States are currently classified as ED, LD, or MR by their local school districts (U.S. Department of Education, 1989), and an additional 1 million of the school-age population could be classified as intellectually gifted (Abelman, 1995b) or intellectually gifted with a learning disability (Barton & Starnes, 1989).

It is also surprising that, with rare exception, the mass media have traditionally ignored exceptional populations. In a landmark investigation, Greenberg (1980) analyzed the television landscape to identify major dimensions of television content. The singular criterion used to determine what dimensions to search out was "whether the content area was judged to have significant potential social implications. That is, was this content ... likely to have social effects on issues of some significance both to policy makers and to individual American families" (p. x). The portrayals of Hispanic-Americans, African-Americans, the elderly, and women were examined in dozens of studies conducted over the course of 5 years, whereas the portrayals of disabled and exceptionally abled populations were not. According to Harmonay (1977) in her book *Promise and Performance: Children with Special Needs*:

> The problems of children with special needs or handicaps have long been neglected by television. Perhaps this is due in part to our problem as a society in dealing with handicapped people in general. As society becomes more sophisticated and adept at doing this, we should be able to better use the mass media—and television in particular—toward this goal (pp. xiii–xiv).

This has not necessarily been the case. In *The Disabled, the Media, and the Information Age* Nelson (1994) reported that "writers and producers who mold so many attitudes of viewers began to show disability in a new light, featuring real human beings with feelings and goals and talents and personalities" (Morse, Cutler, & Fink, 1994; Nelson, 1994). Yet, not one chapter dealt with television entertainment and there was no discussion of television's portrayal of disabled children. In his examination of the 404 new prime-time television series that aired on the commercial networks from 1980 to 1995, R. Abelman (1995b) found that (a) approximately 26% of these programs portrayed children or teenagers as regularly appearing characters; (b) only eight programs (2%), most of which were comedies, featured a child who could be classified as intellectually gifted, (c) one program (0.2%) featured a child with a learning disability, (d) no programs featured exceptional children younger than age 15, and (e) gifted girls were uniformly depicted as socially isolated and physically unattractive compared with their nongifted counterparts.

It is particularly ironic that television and television researchers ignored exceptional children during a period when the development of educational, vocational, medical, and support services for them skyrocketed. The period from 1960 to 1980 was the most active in the creation of programs and the assurance of rights of individuals with disabilities. Deinstitutionalization, normalization, and the right to both special education and mainstreaming were all important goals of this era. The passing of the Education for All Handicapped Children Act of 1975 (Public Law 94-142), along with Section 504 of the Rehabilitation Act of 1973, guaranteed disabled individuals equal access to programs and services. PL 94-142 guaranteed free, appropriate, public education to every school-age person identified as disabled in the United States. In addition, general support for programs for gifted students rose dramatically after the 1957 Soviet launching of Sputnik (see Tannenbaum, 1979). Concern for American achievement in science motivated radical changes in public education, and human intellect became a valuable natural resource worthy of nurturance. More recently, the Americans with Disabilities Act of 1990 recognized exceptional populations and their telecommunications needs (see Brotman, 1990) and the Children's Television Act of 1990 (H.R. 1677) specifically reinforces the fact that an essential part of all broadcasters' obligations to the public is to "serve the specific educational and informational needs of children through programming" (104 Stat. 997), with no distinction between abled or disabled children.

CURRENT STUDY

Generally, the heterogeneity of populations and variables considered here augers against a single, tight theoretical framework (as one might see with, say, TV violence). For instance, research in this area highlights four different mental ability groupings: MR, LD, ED, and gifted. And, as the previous literature review suggests, researchers address a wide range of covariates (e.g., socioeconomic status and race) that tend to vary from study to study. For that reason, it is useful to consider a systems level framework that is applicable to children with special needs.

As Baran (1973) noted, broad-based, integrative frameworks can help contextualize the many characteristics and experiences that make lower-IQ children particularly susceptible to the influence of television (e.g., low self-esteem, a history of failure, little social contact, and high dependence). He maintains that research in this area could be informed by Bronfenbrenner's (1970) framework of ecological niches. Bronfenbrenner said that normal children, because of an increasing lack of parental attention at home, are turning more and more to peers and television for their socialization. Television presents them with frequent, available, attractive models of behavior. Institutionalized children also suffer from a lack of personal contacts, which leads to insecurity.

Employing Baran's and Bronfenbrenner's logic, we can assume that TV provides stable, generally "pleasant" companionship. According to Baran (1973, p. 38): "... from this relatively 'warm' relationship, the child will learn the social behaviors of the televised models who may represent one of the very few sources from which to acquire social skills." These sources may, in turn, provide a basis for the acquisition of either antisocial or prosocial behaviors, as mediated by parents or other coviewers. It is useful, then, to provide an overview of Bronfenbrenner's typology as it relates to the viewing context for exceptional children.

Bronfenbrenner's Theory of Ecologically Embedded Niches

Drawing from his earlier work, Bronfenbrenner (1979) articulated a hierarchy of embedded familial, social, and cultural contexts. Using past work with broadcast television as a guide (e.g., Atkin, 1994; Atkin, Greenberg, & Baldwin, 1991), we can examine family viewing from a developmental perspective based on Bronfenbrenner's (1979, p. 222) typology of settings, including (a) a *mesosystem,* involving interrelations among two or more settings in which the developing person actively participates (e.g., the child's relations among home media environments and school and peer groups); (b) an *exosystem,* involving one or more settings that do not involve the developing person as an active participant, but in which events occur that affect, or are affected by, what happens in the setting containing the developing person (e.g., television); (c) a *microsystem,* or pattern of activities, roles, and interpersonal relations experienced by the developing person in a given setting with particular physical and material characteristics (e.g., interpersonal interaction in the home); (d) a *macrosystem,* involving consistencies, in the form and content of lower-order systems (micro-, meso-, and exo-) that exist, or could exist, at the level of the subculture or the culture as a whole, along with any belief systems or ideology underlying such consistencies; and (e) an *ontogenic system,* which comprises the child's individual psychological competencies for development.

Although viewing has been analyzed in conjunction with each of these elements, Bronfenbrenner places television within the exosystem, because its programming enters the home from an external source:

> To the extent that this powerful medium exerts its influence not directly but through its effect on the parents and their interaction with their children, it represents ... a second-order effect, in this case operating not completely within a microsystem but rather across ecological orders as an exosystem phenomenon. (p. 242)

Given this focus on the exosystem, it is important to review how other ecologically nested settings influence viewing. Such an approach is necessitated by Bronfenbrenner's limited discussion of television, which he saw "freezing" family speech and action (Bronfenbrenner, 1979, p. 170). Many of those interactions that are "lost" to television may, in part, be recovered by parental supervision of viewing. Bronfenbrenner's (1979) review, however, included few studies beyond the 1950s, ignoring the role of the "ontogenic system" in relation to TV viewing. Although subsequent work (Atkin, 1994) has extended this framework to parental mediation of viewing across general populations—including different exosystem (media) settings—researchers have yet to consider the influence of new media use on exceptional children.

Where video programming represents an exosystem component, it influences interactive processes in the home, or microsystem. Studies of normal children, for instance, suggest that mediation is influenced by the number of parents and siblings within a given household (e.g., Atkin et al., 1991). Family uses and responses to TV may, in turn, be influenced by macrosystem (e.g., class) variables. For instance, Donohue and Donohue (1977) found that race influenced evaluations of perceived reality of TV among households with gifted and ED children.

This exosystem "guest" entering the home may motivate mediation behaviors, including (a) debriefing (or helping interpret) program content, (b) instilling general modes of responding so that the child can interpret similar events in the future, and (c) restraining the child from viewing potentially distressing material (see Atkin, 1994). Such mediation is more likely to occur in families with gifted children, in which perceptions of television's effects are also greater (Abelman, 1990).

The previously cited findings, taken together, can be integrated into an ecological perspective, in which the role of ontogenic factors on TV viewing, as mediated by macrosystem and microsystem variables, is considered. Past work (e.g., Abelman & Pettey, 1989) suggests that gifted children receive higher levels of mediation than general child audiences. Although the literature does not provide as thorough an accounting across differently abled groups, such ontogenic variables also present a more compelling raison d'être for parental concern, which may motivate parental intervention. Such mediation is often designed to enhance a child's learning from television. Two of the more frequently measured aspects of child learning from television, reviewed earlier, involve (a) the enhancement of a child's knowledge about TV, or perceived reality dimension, and (b) the acquisition of antisocial behaviors, such as the inducement of aggression. In discerning major themes from the literature, we pose the following research questions about the influence of television on exceptional children:

RQ1: For special ontogenic (IQ) populations, what are the interrelationships between the perceived reality of TV, advertisements, and knowledge about TV?

RQ2: What role does TV (exosystem) play in inducing violent responses from children across non-normal levels of IQ (ontogenic) classification?

METHODS

Data for the present study were collected from a search of the PsycINFO database, in conjunction with a review of secondary compendia on TV viewing and exceptional children (e.g., Sprafkin et al., 1992). Several studies were excluded because they represent unique instances in which (a) viewing of regular TV in a natural environment is not examined—e.g., educational TV studies—which (b) makes them distinctive from other viewing contexts in this book. Such studies (e.g., Fechter, 1971) could theoretically be grouped together in a "learning from TV" section. But even that type of comparison is difficult, as many of these studies address unique learning contexts (e.g., interactive learning) and hence cannot be compared. Consistent with other studies in this volume, we also excluded research focusing on adults, specialized training, nonmedia contexts, and/or designs in which the focus on criterion populations was incidental.

Although we had initially hoped to analyze another set of studies focusing on program preferences (e.g., Ahrens, 1977; Baran & Meyer, 1975; Sprafkin & Gadow, 1986; Striefel, 1974). Imitation of live and videotaped models. *Education and Training of the Mentally Retarded, 9,* 83–88, widely varying dependent measures (e.g., repertoires of favorite programs/characters) precluded meta-analytic comparisons. The same was true for perceptions of television among gifted children (e.g., R. Abelman, 1991, 1995; Donohue & Donohue, 1977; Hunter, 1992). Although it might be possible to pull baseline media use frequencies from a small portion of the latter studies, the varying measures of time spent with TV uncovered (e.g., R. Abelman, 1995; Ahrens, 1977) a methodological confound. Moreover, mixing the handful of media use estimates across our four non-normal populations may present a conceptual confound, owing to their widely differing cognitive capabilities.

We were, however, able to attain a critical mass of studies, comparable in methodological and conceptual scope, in two areas: (a) perceived reality of television and (b) inducement of aggression. Where applicable, we calculated the mean correlation, variance across studies, sampling error variance, variance of the population correlations, and standard deviation of the population correlation.

RESULTS

Research undertaken by the Stony Brook group (e.g., Sprafkin, Gadow, & Grayson, 1988), utilizing the Stony Brook Videotest (SBV), provided the focus for our first set of analyses. This group noted that the SBV was constructed to assess children's knowledge about the realism of people and situations shown on television.[5] The test is composed of two subtests: the first pertains to regular television programs (perceptions of realism of television) and the second to commercials (perceptions of realism of commercials). The perceived realism of television items are based on five concept categories identified as being relevant for media literacy (p. 148).

---

[5]Specifically, in the words of Sprafkin et al. (1986), the SBV assesses several viewing dimensions, beginning with PORT's treatment of (a) realism of aggressive content, (b) actors versus the roles played, (c) realism of nonaggressive content, (d) cartoons versus nonanimated programs, and (e) realism of human capabilities (e.g., superhuman portrayals). In addition, the PORT contains items from a "filler" category designed to test recall of factual content from the television sequence shown. Four or five questions were formulated for each of the six categories, yielding a total of 27 items. The POC items are based on various techniques used in television commercials: (a) promise of enhanced personal appeal, (b) exaggerated size, (c) exaggerated performance, (d) emphasis on irrelevant attributes of product, (e) jargon language, and (f) endorsements by famous or attractive people, and on the subjects' comprehension of disclaimers about (g) nutritional value, (h) toy assembly requirement, (i) accessories, and (j) aspects of product performance. The POC contains three questions from each of these 10 categories.

TABLE 8.1
Correlations between PORT, POC, and KATT

		Correlations		
Authors	*Sample Size*	*(PORT × POC)*	*(PORT × KATT)*	*(POC × KATT)*
Gadow et al. (1988)	333	.78	.77	.79
Sprafkin, Gadow, & Dussault (1986)	82	.70	—	—
Sprafkin et al. (1987)	41	.30	.67	.46
Sprafkin et al. (1987)	233	.77	.75	.77

Note. A certain number of students with IQs falling within normal ranges were included in the Stony Brook group's 1987 and 1988 studies, but they could not be statistically isolated based on reported findings. All correlations are significant at $p \leq .05$.

To examine the relationship between perceived realism of TV and perceptions of various production techniques across our populations (RQ1), a meta-analysis of five studies encompassing five samples of low-IQ (ED and/or LD) subjects was conducted. A list of the authors of those studies, the sample size, and correlations between variables common to them is shown in Table 8.1. To the extent possible, we identified variables with names utilized by study authors, as they appeared in the original tables. The first analysis examines interrelationships between perceived realism of television (PORT) and perceived realism of commercials (POC) and knowledge of TV techniques (KATT). This is followed by the correlation between perceived realism of TV commercials (POC) and knowledge of TV techniques (Table 8.1).

Focusing on the relationship between perceived realism of TV and perceived realism of commercials, the Stony Brook studies yielded a mean correlation of .74. There was also a variance across studies of .0128, sampling error variance of .0012, and variance of the population correlation of .0016. The standard deviation of the population correlation was .034. The 95% confidence interval ranges from $.67 \leq .74 \leq .81$ ($z = 21.76 > 1.96$). As Table 8.2 shows, this significant z value suggests that the relationship is significant beyond the range of expected sampling error.

Next, we looked at the relationship between perceived realism of TV and knowledge of TV techniques, which generated a mean correlation of .76. Variance across studies was .00064, with a sampling error variance of .00089, and variance of the population correlation of .000251. The standard deviation of population correlation was 0.0. The z value is 10.13, indicating a statistically significant correlation between these variables.

Finally, with regard to the relationship between perceived realism of TV commercials and knowledge of TV techniques, those studies yielded a mean correlation

TABLE 8.2
Effect Sizes for Studies on PORT, POC, and KATT

Relationship	Mean Correlation	Variation across Studies	Sampling Error	Variation of Population r
PORT × POC	.74	.0128	.0012	.0016
PORT × KATT	.76	.00064	.00089	.00025
POC × KATT	.76	.0066	.00089	.00057

of .76. There was also a variance across studies of .0066, sampling error variance of .00089, and variance of the population correlations of .00057. The standard deviation of the population correlation was .075. The 95% confidence interval ranges from .70 ≤ .76 ≤ .82 ($z = 21.76 > 1.96$), a reading suggesting that the magnitude of this relationship is significant, beyond the range of expected sampling error. On balance, these studies find very large positive correlations between the various perceived reality measures, even after correcting for sampling error.

Studies on Aggression

Once again, research by the Stony Brook group serves as the focus for our analysis. Their aggression studies were conducted in a school setting in which ED children were exposed to both aggressive and control cartoons. As Gadow et al. (1987) noted: "Our interest in the clinical significance of the purported induction phenomenon led us to select settings and procedures to resemble as great a degree as possible the real world (p. 258)."

Unfortunately, this decision almost always leads to a compromise with the desire to achieve methodological elegance. Hence these studies are typically based on experimental samples, numbering in the single digits, in which students were exposed to control versus baseline stimuli (as opposed to being divided into control and treatment groups). Because the studies do not involve correlations, per the perceived reality measures discussed previously, we focus our analysis on effects sizes from the experiments summarized in Table 8.3.

Per RQ2, these studies generated a mean effect size of .06, as exposure to aggressive fare was related to reduced physical aggression ($r = -.03$]). The variance of effect sizes across studies was .004, whereas sampling error variance across studies was .1396. The variance of the effect size for the population was $-.1356$, whereas the standard deviation of the effect size for the population was 0. Variations between the effect sizes of these different studies is due to sampling error. The mean effect size is a negative one, consistent with effect sizes across studies.

TABLE 8.3
Effects Sizes for Studies on Aggression

Authors	Sample Size	Effect Size
Gadow, Sprafkin, & Ficarrotto (1987)	14	−.20*
Sprafkin et al. (1988)	26	−.02*
Sprafkin et al. (1987)	46	−.06*

Note. *These are all significant effect sizes, in a negative direction.

DISCUSSION

The inability to draw a wide number of comparisons within and across our research on MR, LD, ED, and gifted students reflects, to an extent, the relative immaturity of study on media effects in these contexts. That our literature search on these populations turned up several more studies on otitis media (ear disorder) than on media use stands as a testament to the relative youth of this line of inquiry. Only a small fraction of these studies were conducted by communication scholars, and the proportion appearing in communication journals is smaller still (i.e., R. Abelman, 1995). The preponderance of studies coming from psychology no doubt contributes to the near-monopoly of experimental (as opposed to survey) methods.

As a rule, studies offered by communication scholars (e.g., R. Abelman, 1991, 1995; Baran & Meyer, 1975; Donohue & Donohue, 1977) were breaking new ground; that is, each offered a unique focus on topics varying from, say, critical viewing to perceived reality to preferences for violent fare. Although this tendency to offer new perspectives can be expected from a discipline that was not officially classified by the Department of Education until the late 1960s, the focus on unique dependent variables lamentably complicates the process of meta-analysis.

By contrast, in the studies offered by psychologists—notably the Stony Brook group (e.g., Gadow, Sprakfin, Kelly & Ficarrotto, 1988)—a standardized set of measures was developed and repeated (e.g., the SBV). That adherence to strictly replicable design reflects the relative maturity of the psychology discipline, in which the unique contribution of each study was more likely to involve extensions of past findings to new groups. Although these standardized measures are useful in providing grist for our meta-analyses, the fact that they were based on rather small samples perhaps represents the relative premium that psychologists place on internal (as compared with external) validity.

The consistently strong relations between the Stony Brook group's measures of perceived realism of TV and commercials and knowledge of TV techniques attests to the stability and consistency of their measures. Stability was evident from the fact that these measures yielded highly similar readings across four different samples, with each falling within the range of expected sampling error. The fact that those authors were able to tap the concept of perceived reality with three measures—in addition to others unique to particular studies—establishes the reliability of those core measures.

Although the Stony Brook group's investigations of induced aggression employed a narrower set of measures, we see similarly robust findings across studies. The finding that exposure to cartoons results in slightly lower levels of aggression would seem to favor the catharsis hypothesis, which also seemed to hold true only for other special populations (e.g., children predisposed toward aggression; see Feshbach & Singer, 1971). Although this "catharsis versus stimulation" debate has received considerable attention in the TV violence literature, this finding contradicts research on normal populations, the bulk of which fails to support a catharsis dynamic (see chaps. 10 and 20, in this volume).

It should be noted that individual studies did show countervailing evidence of an inducement effect with nonphysical aggression, although it was not measured in as many studies. Thus, questions concerning the larger inducement dynamic with special populations cannot be easily answered here. Research in this area remains in its nascent phase, and more work needs to be done across a wider range of respondents before we can draw firm conclusions. However, owing to the particular ontogenic concerns accompanying these children's ability to distinguish between reality and fantasy (reviewed earlier), the nature of this influence should be of particular concern to scholars of the mass media.

By contrast, studies done by communication scholars were more likely to employ sample sizes numbering in the hundreds (see R. Abelman, 1991, 1995; Donohue & Donohue, 1977). This may reflect, to an extent, the communication discipline's relatively greater concern with external validity, particularly in issues related to statistical power. External validity concerns notwithstanding, survey approaches are virtually absent from this literature, as only one study identified in our literature search utilized such an approach. This may reflect the relative difficulty of accessing institutionalized or other low-IQ respondents by conventional phone and mail survey methods. The lone survey was conducted by an Australian physician (Ahrens, 1971) and ultimately could not be included in the meta-analysis owing to its unique scope—program preferences of mentally retarded children.

Thus, the scarcity of work in this area is further compounded by the relative youth of communication as a discipline. This paucity of literature did not enable us to test all components of Bronfenbrenner's framework. Nevertheless, the findings concerning interrelationships between perceived reality measures and induced aggression are instructive at the level of ontogenic (IQ) classification levels. Hopefully Bronfenbrenner's typology of embedded ecological niches can serve as a template for the further systematic investigation of media uses across these special populations. Researchers might fruitfully move to consider, for instance, the mediating influences of family size (microsystem) or race and class dimensions (macrosystem) on televiewing across the ontogenic classifications reviewed here. Even within the level of exosystem (media environment) variables, it will be important to consider characteristic uses of new media—such as VCRs, cable and computers—across special populations (see Figure 8.1).

As Donohue and Donohue (1977) note, access issues will continue to present challenges for researchers, particularly in large institutions that might otherwise present useful survey venues. Public policy initiatives to safeguard the privacy and rights of the institutionalized MR population over the past three decades have probably complicated that process. However, given the significance of these issues, it will be important for scholars from a range of disciplines to continue

a) **Background variables**

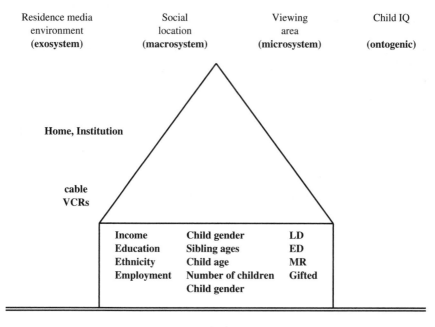

| Residence media environment (exosystem) | Social location (macrosystem) | Viewing area (microsystem) | Child IQ (ontogenic) |

Home, Institution

cable VCRs

Income	Child gender	LD
Education	Sibling ages	ED
Ethnicity	Child age	MR
Employment	Number of children	Gifted
	Child gender	

HOME

b) **Mediating variables:**
   Parental or caregiver mediation

c) **Viewing outcomes:**
   Perceived reality and critical viewing skills
   Antisocial or prosocial behaviors
Note. Adapted from Atkin (1994) and Bronfenbrenner (1972).

FIG. 8.1. Ecology of televiewing for special populations.

gaining access to these special populations. As Gadow et al. (1988) suggest, this is particularly true in the realm of cultivating critical viewing skills for children who may be at greater risk for the negative influence of the medium: "... children who are most likely to perceive television content as realistic are less able intellectually, come from poorer socioeconomic backgrounds, and have less social interaction with others. One group of students in our public schools who exhibit greater degrees of these characteristics then their unlabeled peers are learning-disabled (LD) children" (p. 270).

To be sure, the same might be said of ED and MR children who, along with LD children, may also prove to be more susceptible to antisocial media influences, as our earlier study outlines. Yet, it is striking that only a few dozen studies have addressed these very important populations—scarcely 1% of the more than 4,000 interdisciplinary studies conducted to determine the effects of TV on children since 1961 (see Sprafkin et al., 1992).

It will be important in later work to reduce the number of methodological and conceptual confounds to further advance the cause of replication in this area. One possible strategy could involve the aggregation of children into "exceptionally abled" versus "exceptionally disabled" groupings, bearing in mind that the latter would remain relatively small. Any further combinations—say, a "non-normal" IQ grouping—might present a conceptual confound for the aggregation of data, given the opposing polarities along that dimension. Although it is certainly legitimate to study gifted children along with LD and other special groupings, researchers should take care to report separate effects sizes for each group so that the influence of IQ can be isolated.

Only through the confluence of various study approaches can we hope to complete our understanding of television's influence on special populations. The limited collaborations appearing between communication scholars and psychology (e.g., Sprafkin et al., 1992) represent a preliminary step in this direction. It will be important, in later work, to refine these measures and repeat them for various populations across more geographically varied samples.

REFERENCES

Abelman, R. (1995a). *Reclaiming the wasteland: TV & gifted children.* Cresskill, NJ: Hampton Press.

Abelman, R. (1995b). Gifted, LD and gifted/LD children's understanding of temporal sequencing on television. *Journal of Broadcasting & Electronic Media, 39,* 297–312.

Abelman, R. (1990). Determinants of parental mediation of children's television viewing. In J. Bryant (ed.), *Television and the American Family* (pp. 311–326). Hillsdale, NJ: Lawrence Erlbaum Associates.

Abelman, R. (1991). TV literacy III—The gifted and learning disabled: Amplifying prosocial learning through curricular intervention. *Journal of Research and Development and Development in Education, 24*(4), 51–60.

Abelman, R., & Pettey, G. R. (1989). Child attributes as determinants of parental television-viewing mediation: The role of child giftedness. *Journal of Family Issues, 10*(2), 251–266.

Ahrens, M. G. (1977). Television viewing habits of mentally retarded children. *Australian Journal of Mental Retardation, 4,* 1–3.

Atkin, D. (1994). An integrative perspective on parental mediation of children's TV viewing habits across traditional and new program environments. *World Communication, 23,* 22–34.

Atkin, D., Greenberg, B., & Baldwin, T. (1991). The home ecology of children's television viewing: Parental mediation and the new video environment. *Journal of Communication, 41,* 40–53.

Baran, S. J. (1973). TV and social learning in the institutionalized MR. *Mental Retardation, 11*(3), 36–38.

Baran, S. J., & Meyer, T. P. (1975). Retarded children's perceptions of favorite television characters as behavioral models. *Mental Retardation, 13*(4), 28–31.

Barton, J. N., & Starnes, W. T. (1989). Identifying distinguishing characteristics of gifted and talented/learning disabled students. *Roeper Review, 12,* 23–28.

Bronfenbrenner, U. (1970). *Two worlds of childhood.* New York: Russell Sage Foundation.

Bronfenbrenner, U. (1979). *The ecology of human development.* New York: Russell Sage Foundation.

Brotman, S. N. (1990). *Extending telecommunications service to Americans with Disabilities Act of 1990.* Washington, DC: Northwestern University.

Brown, R. (Ed.). (1976). *Children and television.* Beverly Hills, CA: Sage.

Bryan, T. (1976). Peer popularity of learning disabled children: A replication. *Journal of Learning Disabilities, 9,* 307–311.

Bryant, J., & Anderson, D. R. (Eds.). (1983). *Children's understanding of television: Research on attention and comprehension.* New York: Academic Press.

Clifford, B. R., Gunter, B., & McAleer, J. (1995). *Television and children.* Hillsdale, NJ: Lawrence Erlbaum Associates.

Cunningham, C. E., & Barkley, R. A. (1978). The role of academic failure in hyperactive behavior. *Journal of Learning Disabilities, 11,* 274–280.

Davis, G. A., & Rimm, S. B. (1989). *Education of the gifted and talented.* Englewood, NJ: Prentice-Hall.

Donohue, T. R. (1978). Television's impact on emotionally disturbed children's value systems. *Child Study Journal, 8,* 187–201.

Donohue, W. A., & Donohue, T. R. (1977). Black, white, and white gifted and emotionally disturbed children's perceptions of the reality in television programming. *Human Relations, 30,* 609–621.

Dorr, A. (1986). *Television and children: A special medium for a special audience.* Beverly Hills, CA: Sage.

Dorr, A., & Kovaric, P. (1980). Some of the people some of the time—But which people? Televised violence and its effects. In E. L. Palmer & A. Dorr (Eds.), *Children and the faces of television: Teaching, violence, selling* (pp. 183–199). New York: Academic Press.

Eyman, R. K., & Call, T. (1977). Maladaptive behavior and community placement of mentally retarded persons. *American Journal of Mental Deficiency, 82,* 137–144.

Fechter, J. V. (1971). Modeling and environmental generalization by mentally retarded subjects of televised aggressive or friendly behavior. *American Journal of Mental Deficiency, 76*(2), 266–267.

Feshbach, S., & Singer, R. (1971). *Television and aggression.* San Francisco: Jossey Bass Publishers.

Franks, B., & Dolan, L. (1982). Affective characteristics of gifted children: Educational implications. *Gifted Child Quarterly, 26,* 172–178.

Gadow, K. D., & Sprafkin, J. (1987). Effects of viewing high versus low aggression cartoons on emotionally disturbed children. *Journal of Pediatric Psychology, 12,* 413–427.

Gadow, K. D., Sprafkin, J., & Ficarrotto, T. (1987). Effects of viewing aggression-laden cartoons on preschool-aged emotionally disturbed children. *Child Psychiatry and Human Development, 17,* 257–274.

Gadow, K. D., Sprafkin, J., Kelly, E., & Ficarrotto, T. (1988). Reality perceptions of television: A comparison of school-labeled learning disabled and nonhandicapped children. *Journal of Clinical Child Psychology, 17,* 25–33.

Greenberg, B. S. (Ed.). (1980). *Life on television: Content analyses of U.S. TV drama.* Norwood, NJ: Ablex Press.

Griggs, S., & Dunn, R. (1984). Selected case studies of the learning style preferences of gifted students. *Gifted Child Quarterly, 28,* 115–119.

Hallahan, D. P., & Kauffman, J. M. (1991). *Exceptional children: Introduction to special education.* Englewood Cliffs, NJ: Prentice-Hall.

Harmonay, M. (Ed). (1977). *Promise and performance: Children with special needs.* Cambridge, MA: Ballinger.

Himmelweit, H., Oppenheim, A. N., & Vince, P. (1958). *Television and the child: An empirical study of the effects of television on the young.* London: Oxford University Press.

Hunter, P. (1992). Teaching gifted television viewing: An approach for gifted learners. *Roper Review, 15*(2), 84–89.

Liebert, R. M., Sprafkin, J. N., & Davidson, E. M. (1982). *The early window: Effects of television on children and youth.* New York: Pergamon Press.

Lin, C. A. & Atkin, D. (1989). Parental mediation adolescent uses of VCRs. *Journal of Broadcasting & Electronic Media, 33,* 3–67.

Morse, W. C., Cutler, R. L., & Fink, A. H. (1994). *Public school classes for the emotionally handicapped: A research analysis.* Washington, DC: Council for Exceptional Children.

Nelson, J. A. (1994). *The disabled, the media, and the information age.* Westport, CT: Greenwood Press.

Quay, H. C., Morse, W. C., & Cutler, R. L. (1966). Personality patterns of pupils in special classes for the emotionally disturbed. *Exceptional Children, 32,* 297–301.

Richert, S. (1981). Television for the gifted: A double-edged sword. *Roeper Review, 3*(4), 17–20.

Rutter, M., Tizard, J., & Whitmore, K. (Eds.) (1970). *Education, health, and behavior.* London: Longman.

Salomon, G. (1984). Investing effort in television viewing. In J. P. Murray & G. Salomon (Eds.), *The future of children's television* (pp. 59–64). Boys Town, NE: The Boys Town Center.

Sarnoff, R. W. (1961, July 1). What do you want from television. *The Saturday Evening Post,* pp. 13–15, 44–46.

Schramm, W., Lyle, J., & Parker, E. B. (1961). *Television in the lives of our children.* Stanford, CA: Stanford University Press.

Sprafkin, J., & Gadow, K. D. (1986). Television viewing habits of emotionally disturbed, learning disabled, and mentally retarded children. *Journal of Applied Developmental Psychology, 7,* 45–59.

Sprafkin, J., & Gadow, K. D. (1988). The immediate impact of aggressive cartoons on emotionally disturbed and learning disabled and learning disabled children. *Journal of Genetic Psychology, 149,* 35–44.

Sprafkin, J., Gadow, K. D., & Abelman, R. (1992). *Television and the exceptional child: A forgotten audience.* Hillsdale, NJ: Lawrence Erlbaum Associates.

Sprafkin, J., Gadow, K. D., & Dussault, M. (1986). Reality perceptions of television: A preliminary comparison of emotionally disturbed and nonhandicapped children. *American Journal of Orthopsychiatry, 56,* 147–152.

Sprafkin, J., Gadow, K. D., & Grayson, P. (1987). Effects of viewing aggressive cartoons on the behavior of learning disabled children. *Journal of Child Psychology and Psychiatry, 28,* 387–398.

Sprafkin, J., Gadow, K. D., & Grayson, P. (1988). The effects of cartoons on emotionally disturbed children's social behavior in school settings. *Journal of Child Psychology and Psychiatry, 29,* 91–99.

Sprafkin, J., Gadow, K. D., & Kant, J. (1987). Teaching emotionally disturbed children to discriminate reality from fantasy on television. *Journal of Special Education, 21*(9), 99–107.

Sprafkin, J., Kelly, E., & Gadow, K. D. (1987). Reality perceptions of television: A comparison of emotionally disturbed, learning disabled, and nonhandicapped children. *Journal of Developmental and Behavioral Pediatrics, 8*(3), 149–153.

Sprafkin, J. N., Liebert, R. M., & Poulos, R. W. (1975). Effects of a prosocial televised example on children's helping. *Journal of Experimental Child Psychology, 20,* 119–126.

Sprafkin, J., & Rubinstein, E. A. (1982). Using television to improve the social behavior of institutionalized children. *Prevention in Human Services, 2,* 107–114.

Sprafkin, J., Watkins, L. T., & Gadow, K. D. (1990). Efficacy of a television literacy curriculum for emotionally disturbed and learning disabled children. *Journal of Applied Developmental Psychology, 11,* 225–244.

Sternberg, R., & Davidson, J. E. (1985). Cognitive development in the gifted and talented. In F. D. Horowitz & M. O'Brien (Eds.), *The gifted and talented: Developmental perspectives* (pp. 37–74). Hyattsville, MD: American Psychological Association.

Striefel, S. (1972). Television as a language training medium with retarded children. *Mental Retardation, 10*(2), 27–29.

Striefel, S. (1974). Isolating variables which affect TV preferences of retarded children. *Psychological Reports, 35,* 115–122.

Surgeon General's Scientific Advisory Committee on Television and Social Behavior (1971). *Television and growing up: The impact of televised violence.* Washington, DC: National Institute of Health.

Tannenbaum, P. H. (1979). Post-Sputnik post-Watergate concern about the gifted. In A. H. Passow (Ed.), *The gifted and the talented: Their education and development* (pp. 5–27). Chicago: University of Chicago Press.

U.S. Department of Education (1989). *Twelfth annual report to Congress on the implementation of the education of the Handicapped Act.* Washington, DC: U.S. Government Printing Office.

U.S. Office of Education (1977). *Federal Register, 42,* 42478.

Van Evra, J. (1998). *Television and child development.* Mahwah, NJ: Lawrence Erlbaum Associates.

Ward, S., Wackman, D. B., & Wartella, E. (1977). *How children learn to buy.* Beverly Hills, CA: Sage.

Wildmon, D. E. (1985). *The home invaders.* Wheaton, IL: Victor Books.

Winn, M. (1977). *The plug-in drug.* New York: Bantam Books.

Young, B. M. (1990). *Television advertising and children.* London: Oxford University Press.

9

"And Miles to Go ...": Reflecting on the Past and Future of Mass Media Effects Research

Robin I. Nabi
University of California, Santa Barbara

The study of media effects is as diverse as it is compelling. Yet, it is this diversity—in outcomes assessed, stimuli considered, and methods employed—that makes conclusions about the psychological and social effects of the media so difficult to pin down. This is not to suggest that the accumulation of research does not offer meaningful insights into the effects of certain forms of media. Indeed, the meta-analyses in this volume show quite clearly that the media can affect important outcomes such as aggressive and antisocial behavior, gender stereotyping, and altruistic behavior. Most striking about this set of analyses, however, is not what we know, but rather how much we do not yet know about media effects, specifically, the conditions under which certain effects are likely to occur, in whom, and the psychological processes underlying them. The answers to these questions are critical to the design of appropriate interventions to mitigate the negative social influences of the media and to better inform the policy debates that have served as the impetus for much of the research undertaken thus far. This chapter highlights and explores some themes common to the analyses presented in the following chapters to help assess not only where we have been with media effects study but also what the future might hold for media effects research.

SMALL BUT MEANINGFUL EFFECTS

Several commonalities are readily spotted across the domains of effects inquiry. First, there are consistent effects of media exposure on a range of both antisocial and prosocial attitudes and behaviors. These effects are generally categorized as small to moderate in size (e.g., $r = .15–.30$), and larger in laboratory versus nonexperimental research. The small overall effect sizes, however, should not be confused with unimportant effects. As Christensen and Wood (chap. 10, this volume) argue in their review of media violence–aggression research, these effects may be comparable in size to those based on individual differences, such as gender, empathy, or social class, and can translate into meaningful real world consequences, especially when repeated exposure over long periods of time is considered. These points hold true not only for antisocial attitudes and behaviors, such as aggression, but also for prosocial effects, as Mares and Woodard (chap. 17, this volume) explain in their review of the positive effects of children's programming.

THE IMPORTANCE OF
MODERATING VARIABLES

For many outcomes there are multiple forces working at times in conjunction with and at times in opposition to media influence, thus complicating our understanding of the link between media exposure and outcomes. A second theme arising from this research, then, is the critical need to investigate variables that might moderate media effects. In some cases, moderators have been identified, but not enough research exists to be sure of their impact. Hoffner and Levine (chap. 14, this volume) note this concern with regard to specific program characteristics, respondent demographics, and type of research design in the study of the enjoyment of mediated horror. In other cases, as with parasocial relationships, moderators appear to be operational but not yet identified. Still, across the domains of inquiry, certain categories of moderators, such as content features and individual differences, have proven important to understanding the conditions under which effects are more or less likely to occur.

Focusing on message content, the literature has successfully identified presentational features and media character issues that serve to moderate related outcome. The effects of violent media, for example, may be mitigated or enhanced if presented as punishable or with humor (Christensen & Wood), as human or fantasy violence (Sherry, chap. 15, this volume), or as more or less graphic (Hoffner & Levine). Further, character features, such as similarity or attractiveness, may affect the degree of gender stereotyping (Opplinger, chap. 13, this volume) or development of parasocial relationships (Schiappa, Allen, & Gregg, chap. 18, this volume). Yet across contexts, gaps in our understanding are evident. For example, not enough research exists to adequately assess the effects of different types of music on antisocial outcomes (Allen, Herrett-Skjellum, Jorgenson, Kramer, Ryan, & Timmerman, chap. 16, this volume) or how character development might impact parasocial relationships (Schiappa et al.). More broadly, message characteristics, such as perceived reality in portrayals, have been identified as relevant to multiple forms of media, but limited research precludes our ability to draw further conclusions at this point.

Similar to the work on program features, the research on individual differences offers some clear conclusions amidst many unknowns. Age may be the most consistently studied individual difference variable, with results suggesting that preadolescent children seem particularly susceptible to media influence in terms of aggression, gender socialization, and prosocial behavior. Adolescents seem to enjoy horror more than other age groups, and effects of video games and popular music seem to get stronger with age. Yet, for all the work focused on age, too few studies consider effects across the lifespan to make definitive claims about media effects in older populations. Moreover, age itself is probably a proxy for the cognitive and/or emotional developmental factors that underlie the demonstrated effects. Although age may be useful for targeting messages or interventions, scholars may be particularly interested in pursuing the developmental issues that are the hallmarks of the age-related findings.

In contrast with age, personality traits, such as empathy, sensation seeking, aggressiveness, and shyness, are generally stable tendencies that are first evidenced in early childhood. Alone or in combination, traits might serve as factors that make one vulnerable or resistant to media influence. For example, empathy may reduce enjoyment of horror whereas sensation seeking may enhance it (Hoffner & Levine). Despite the intuitive appeal of such variables and their recognized importance as moderators in some contexts, violent programming in particular, they appear to be overlooked in other domains, such as video games, popular music, and prosocial programming. The consideration of a range of traits is important not only for their role as moderators of media effects but also for their impact on exposure to certain media forms, an issue addressed in the next section.

THE ACTIVE AUDIENCE

Concerns about media effects stem somewhat from the knee-jerk reaction that audience members, children and adolescents in particular, might be helpless to resist the influence that negative portrayals might have on their cognitive and emotional orientations to the world. In contrast to this view of audiences as passive and vulnerable is the conception of audiences as active, selectively exposing themselves to media content and interpreting that content in ways suited to their unique needs. Although the meta-analyses do not directly test issues related to audience activity, assumptions about activity level inform the authors' interpretations of the likely effects and the processes through which they might occur.

Activity can be conceptualized in multiple ways, including activity in message selection, processing, and interpretation. As to selection, some media content, such as pornography, requires greater initiative for exposure to even occur, and still other media forms, such as popular music or horror, might be actively selected based on expectations of how well such messages might satisfy existing needs or desires. For example, perhaps aggressive adolescents choose to expose themselves to violent media, or disenfranchised youth choose to listen to rebellious music because it resonates with their world view. As to processing, some media forms may require greater cognitive effort during exposure. For example, Sherry noted that compared with television programming, video games require intense levels of concentration throughout the duration of exposure. Finally, in considering interpretation, an active audience perspective makes clear that the message sent is not always the message received. For example, Mundorf, Allen, D'Alessio, and Emmers-Sommer (chap. 12, this volume) note that the audience may determine what constitutes pornography not based on content but based on how that content is interpreted and the functional purpose it serves.

In all, the notion of the active audience suggests that individuals experience heightened exposure to certain forms of personally desirable media. Thus, consideration of audience motivations and perceptions is particularly important to factor into the modeling of media effects processes. Untangling whether resulting effects are caused by media exposure or whether those same individual differences that lead to media selection are also associated with certain preexisting attitudes and behaviors is an issue that the authors of each of the upcoming chapters recognize as important but are unable to adequately address, given the state of the literature thus far. Nonetheless, it is clear that we must respect the complexity of the relationships among individual differences, selective exposure and perception, and paths of media influence if we are to appreciate the media's role not only in shaping audience attitudes and behavior, but also, equally importantly, in reinforcing the beliefs and behaviors already present in media consumers.

THE CALL FOR THEORETICAL ADVANCEMENT

Perhaps above all else, the upcoming chapters make clear the need for theoretical advancement in the study of media effects. As the reader will surely notice, two theoretical perspectives—social learning/cognitive theory (SLT) (Bandura, 1977, 1986) and excitation transfer theory (ETT) (Zillmann, 1971)—frequently serve as frameworks for the assessment of media messages, including the effects of video games (Sherry), pornography (Mundorf et al.), popular music (Allen et al.), and gender stereotyping (Opplinger). Yet, these explanations are not necessarily supported by the meta-analyses results. For example, Sherry provides a nice comparison of theoretical predictions, concluding that no existing theory, including SLT, ETT, or priming, can sufficiently account for the pattern of findings of the impact of video games on aggressive behavior. Similarly, Mundorf et al. conclude that there is only mixed support for SLT and ETT in the pornography literature, and Hoffner and Levine point out that although ETT is used to explain enjoyment of horror, the theory cannot fully account for the evidence, particularly the lack of association between arousal and horror enjoyment.

The authors further lament the paucity of research designed to test theoretical predictions. Opplinger indicates that there is not enough research to assess uses and gratifications as an explanation for the effects of gender stereotypes. Mares and Woodard note that the process explaining prosocial effects is assumed to be the same as that for antisocial effects, although there is not enough evidence to support this conclusion, and Mundorf et al. assert the need for research to explore the psychological and cognitive mechanisms that people might use as filters (or frames) when processing pornographic materials.

It is clear that media effects research is in need of theoretical with advancement, and there are multiple ways in which this need might be met. First, as media researchers frequently turn to social psychology for theoretical guidance, we could consider previously overlooked psychological theories and their implications in the media context. For example, Christensen and Wood apply McGuire's (1972) information processing paradigm to understand how individual characteristics might differentially affect reception and yielding to a media message. This, in turn, might help to identify groups particularly vulnerable to certain types of effects. Second, existing theories can be reconfigured to explain documented patterns of media effects, as Sherry attempts with his proposed primed arousal model, which integrates the theoretical concepts of priming and arousal, each of which partially accounts for video game effects. A third approach focuses on model building based on documented findings, as suggested by Schiappa et al. in the context of parasocial relationship development. A combination of these approaches across media contexts will surely help to jump-start both our thinking and research in these important areas of inquiry.

INTERVENTION DESIGN AND POLICY DEBATE

Ultimately, understanding the effects of media messages, as well as the process through which they occur, is critical to contributing effectively to the public debate on interventions to mitigate their negative effects (and to promote their positive outcomes). Policy initiatives of warning labels, program ratings, and programming or distribution restrictions are based on the assumption that the most effective way to minimize negative effects is to limit exposure. However, the results of the meta-analyses in this volume offer a different perspective. In several of the upcoming chapters, the effectiveness of providing alternative frames through which to view messages with the potential for antisocial effects is supported. Indeed Mundorf et al. note that educational materials may not only eliminate the harmful effects of exposure to pornographic materials but may actually promote prosocial outcomes. If indeed some negative media effects may be mitigated by offering alternative interpretative frames, media literacy efforts may be better informed. For example, as several authors suggest, encouraging active awareness of unrealistic portrayals in media messages may serve to defend against the media's more pernicious effects. Further, altering media content to include modeling of desirable behaviors can help to change troubling effects, such as gender stereotypes (Opplinger) as well as to promote altruistic behavior (Mares and Woodard).

In addition to suggesting how media messages might be presented or interpreted to maximize positive outcome, this research also provides insight into who to target for literacy interventions and when to intervene. For example, if preadolescents are especially vulnerable to the effects of media violence, interventions at this age are critical. Parents and educators, rather than policymakers, may be particularly influential at this point. Further, if effects are short term, as suggested by the video game and aggression literature, any proposed interventions should be sensitive to potential attitudinal or behavioral by-products in the immediate social environment as well as more distal contexts. Despite the wealth of evidence related to media effects, the limitations of the research pose similar limitations on the ability to inform effective intervention. By better understanding the processes of media influence, educational and policy-level interventions sensitive to issues of both free speech and protection of the public good might be forthcoming.

ADDITIONAL CONSIDERATIONS FOR FUTURE RESEARCH

The above themes highlight a number of directions for future research, although there are three additional points that warrant attention, if for no other reason than that they appear to have been understudied in the general scheme of media effects research: affective response, social context of media consumption, and longevity of effects. Variables relating to affective response appear to varying degrees of explicitness in each of the chapters in this section: as a potential explanatory mechanism (i.e., negative mood and arousal) in research on violence/horror, video games, pornography, and popular music; as predictors of effects in the form of affect-related traits (e.g., empathy and shyness) in research on horror and parasocial relationships; and as dependent measures in the form of enjoyment and altruism. Despite the apparent prominence of emotion-related constructs in media research, there is surprisingly little theorizing to systematically address the role of emotions per se (e.g., fear, anger, or sadness) at different stages of the media consumption process. As discrete emotions are garnering increased attention in various domains of social psychology, including those related to stereotyping, message processing, and persuasion, it seems reasonable to pay closer attention to their role in the processes of media effects.

Second, the social context of media consumption is rarely mentioned in the upcoming chapters. This omission is, of course, no fault of the authors, but rather a reflection of the general neglect of this variable in media effects research. This neglect may be due, in part, to the wealth of laboratory research designed to control such factors rather than investigate them and to survey research not being well suited to assess such influences. Yet, much engagement with the media, including television viewing, video game play, and popular music consumption, takes place in the presence of others. Apart from media literacy efforts, too little attention has been paid to the impact of the social environment on media consumption, interpretation, and effects, and thus this impact remains an important consideration for future research.

Finally, across media contexts, the authors are hesitant to project effects, positive or negative, as being long lived. This is not because long-lived results are not possible or even likely, but rather because research efforts, particularly experimental studies, have not been geared to systematically examine the longevity of effects. There are, however, theoretical reasons to believe that effects might be long lasting. For example, SLT suggests that media exposure can make enduring changes to schemas that might, in turn, guide behaviors, such as gender stereotypical judgments and prosocial action, in the longer run. Also, the cumulative effect of repeated exposure to similar messages over time (cultivation theory, Gerbner, 1969) might make certain beliefs chronically accessible and thus able to guide behavior, even away from the presence of a mediated stimulus. Theoretically, exploring the longevity of effects in multiple contexts will help with the modeling of media effects processes. Practically speaking, for the design of effective intervention, it is important to understand when effects are likely to occur and how long they might last.

In conclusion, as the upcoming chapters make clear, the process of articulating the route through which media effects occur is far more complicated than one might first imagine. Cultural, contextual, and individual differences likely interact to shape message exposure and perceptions which, in turn, blend to influence the effects those messages might have in the short and long term. As a method, meta-analysis is tremendously helpful in encouraging the scholarly community to stop and take stock of what we know, what we would like to know, and how we might know it. The authors in this volume offer a great service in this regard, not only to researchers but also to the broader community of parents, educators, and policymakers concerned about the psychological and social consequences of mass media exposure.

REFERENCES

Bandura, A. (1977). *Social learning theory.* Englewood Cliffs, NJ: Prentice-Hall.

Bandura, A. (1986). *Social foundations of thought and action: A social cognitive theory.* Englewood Cliffs, NJ: Prentice-Hall.

Gerbner, G. (1969). Toward "cultural indicators": The analysis of mass mediated message systems. *AV Communication Review, 17*(2), 137–148.

McGuire, W. J. (1972). Attitude change: The information processing paradigm. In C. G. McClintock (Ed.), *Experimental social psychology* (pp. 108–141). New York: Holt, Rinehart, & Winston.

Zillmann, D. (1971). Excitation transfer in communication-mediated aggressive behavior. *Journal of Experimental Social Psychology, 7,* 419–435.

10

Effects of Media Violence on Viewers' Aggression in Unconstrained Social Interaction*

P. Niels Christensen
Radford University

Wendy Wood
Duke University

This chapter is an update of Wood, Wong, and Chachere's (1991) meta-analytic synthesis of research on media violence and aggressive behavior in unconstrained social contexts. Our primary goal in writing this chapter is to determine whether research published since Wood et al. completed their literature review in 1987 reaffirms the causal effect they documented of exposure to media violence on naturally-occurring aggression. At the time of the original article, the relationship between media violence and aggression was still closely debated in both social policy and academic circles. In an especially pessimistic review, McGuire (1986) claimed that media effects in general "range from statistically trivial to practically insubstantial" (p. 213). Freedman (1988) similarly concluded that the available empirical "evidence does not support the idea that viewing television violence causes aggression" (p. 158).

Since the early research, the overwhelming majority of reviews of this literature have recognized a significant effect of media violence on aggression. Although news coverage increasingly describes the evidence as modest or equiv-

*This chapter is based in large part on Wood, Wong, and Chachere's (1991) meta-analysis of media violence and aggression. We thank Frank Y. Wong and J. Gregory Chachere for their contribution to the earlier meta-analysis.

145

ocal (Bushman & Anderson, 2001), the effect of media violence now seems to be an accepted phenomenon among scientists (e.g., Felson, 1996; Geen, 1998; Heath, Bresolin, & Rinaldi, 1989; Paik & Comstock, 1994; Roberts & Maccoby, 1985). The Wood et al. (1991) meta-analysis was a cornerstone in this conclusion because the authors addressed the fundamental question of causality and furthermore examined media impact on everyday social interaction. Specifically, they designed the review to address whether there is a *causal* relationship between viewing violent programming and subsequent *unconstrained* aggressive behavior.

The importance of demonstrating causal direction is underscored by research suggesting that the relation between media violence and aggression is bidirectional (e.g., Gunter, 1985; Slater, Henry, Swaim, & Anderson, 2003). It seems that individual dispositions such as level of aggressiveness can produce a liking or disliking for media violence that then leads to a general tendency to be a consumer of violent media. Thus, evidence of causality is critical for any argument that media violence enhances aggression. This evidence emerges most clearly from experiments in which participants are randomly assigned to view media violence or not. The importance of examining unconstrained aggressive behavior is less obvious. To understand the implications of this aspect of our review, it is helpful to consider previous reviews of the literature examining media–violence effects.

PREVIOUS INTERPRETATIONS OF MEDIA EFFECTS

Authors of previous reviews typically have evaluated the findings from laboratory and field investigations separately. Laboratory experiments are reputed to demonstrate the strongest evidence for media effects and are thought to provide information about the upper bounds of media impact (Cook, Kendzierski, & Thomas, 1983; Freedman, 1984; Friedrich-Cofer & Huston, 1986; McGuire, 1986; Paik & Comstock, 1994). The settings and manipulations in laboratory research have a number of features that might maximize the likelihood of aggression, including angering or arousing participants before media exposure and legitimizing aggressive responses as punishment for others' poor task performance.[1]

The magnitude of laboratory effects has been estimated in three previous reviews using meta-analytic techniques (Andison, 1977; Hearold, 1986, based on her 1979 dissertation; Paik & Comstock, 1994). Meta-analysis is a statistical procedure that yields an exact effect estimate. In a meta-analysis, the outcomes of

---

[1]This is not, of course, a completely accurate characterization of the intent of laboratory research. Often laboratory experiments are designed to assess moderators of media effects. Certain experimental conditions are constructed so that they show an effect and others so that they reveal no effect. Generalizing across the conditions in such a study to achieve some overall assessment would not necessarily overestimate the size of the effect.

individual studies are calculated in a standardized metric, and these outcomes then are aggregated to yield an estimate of effect across a body of literature.

Andison (1977) calculated, for each experiment in his sample, the correlation between viewing versus not viewing violent media and participants' subsequent levels of aggression. The 31 laboratory experiments in the review yielded a modal finding of enhanced aggression with exposure to media violence (i.e., 52% of the studies obtained rs between .31 and .70). Hearold (1986) evaluated antisocial behavior in general and included, in addition to aggression, rule breaking, materialism, and perceiving oneself as powerless in society. Although this broad sampling of outcomes renders the review only tangentially relevant to the present investigation, we consider it here because it is often interpreted as a study of viewers' aggressive behavior. Hearold calculated effect size in terms of d, which represents, for each study, the mean antisocial behavior of the group exposed to media violence minus the mean for the control group not exposed to violent media, divided by the common standard deviation. Effect sizes were then aggregated across studies. The 131 laboratory experiments included in the review again yielded evidence of higher antisocial behavior in the conditions with exposure to violent media compared with the no-exposure control conditions ($d = 0.73$ and $d = 0.34$ for designs using prosocial media presentations as a control and for designs with other types of controls, respectively). Paik and Comstock (1994) updated Hearold's (1986) review and used a slightly more narrow definition of antisocial behavior. Their 217 reports yielded a comparable overall result for the effect of media violence ($d = 0.65$).

Laboratory investigations not only have been criticized for overestimations of media impact but they also have been faulted for possessing poor external and construct validity (e.g., Freedman, 1984; McGuire, 1986). External validity in this case refers to generalizability to natural (i.e., nonlaboratory) contexts and to the noncollege population (Cook & Campbell, 1979). If studies have poor external validity, then media violence effects documented in the laboratory with college students may have few implications for other settings and populations. Construct validity refers to the fit between operations and conceptual definitions or the validity with which one can make generalizations about higher-order constructs from research operations (Cook & Campbell, 1979). Media violence studies have poor construct validity to the extent that they use artificial and contrived media presentations and to the extent that participants are evaluated engaging in atypical or unusual means of aggression.

In contrast to laboratory experiments, the findings from field experiments are often reputed to provide more valid estimates of real-world impact. The assumption is that natural measures of aggression, as opposed to laboratory analogues, will ensure high construct validity of field results. Furthermore, the variety of participants available in field settings and the varying situational factors in natural contexts plausibly ensures the external validity of these findings.

Narrative reviews by Freedman (1984, 1986) and Friedrich-Cofer and Huston (1986) identified only five published sets of true field experiments. Freedman emphasized the methodological flaws in this work, the findings from one set of experiments that demonstrated a catharsis effect of exposure to violent media (i.e., Feshbach & Singer, 1971), and the findings from the remainder of the research that were moderated by a large number of additional variables (i.e., significant effects of media violence were obtained only for some participant samples, some methods of assessment, and some situations). In contrast, Friedrich-Cofer and Huston (1986) argued that field experiments most plausibly underestimate effects of exposure to media violence because, for example, treatments tend to be relatively weak and of short duration, and many extraneous variables exist in natural contexts that might obscure effects. Furthermore, they argued that the best designed studies, which presumably provide the most accurate estimates, reveal the strongest evidence for impact.

The meta-analytic reviews by Andison (1977), Hearold (1986), and Paik and Comstock (1994) also estimated the outcomes obtained through field research. Although the heterogeneity of designs and dependent measures of the studies included in the reviews limits the utility of these reviews for estimating outcomes in field settings, the results are interesting to note. Andison (1977) obtained a modal result of a small, positive correlation between exposure and subsequent aggression (i.e., 41% of the studies obtained rs between .10 and .30). Hearold (1986) also obtained somewhat greater antisocial behavior with the conditions exposed to violent media than with no-exposure control conditions, reporting mean effects of $d = 0.30$ and $d = 0.07$ for research designs with prosocial media controls and with other types of controls, respectively. Finally, Paik & Comstock (1994) reported a mean d of 0.62 when reviewing both correlational and experimental results in field settings.

THE DOMAIN OF THE PRESENT REVIEW

Past literature reviews yielded only a limited view of media impact in natural settings in part because so few field studies were identified and in part because of the way field experiments were defined. Field research can take many forms, and the definition of "field" can emphasize the research setting, the experimental treatment, or the outcome measure. Each classification results in a selection of studies with certain properties of external and construct validity.[2]

In previous reviews, researchers generally relied on the setting in which the aggressive behavior was observed to define field investigations. This justified inclusion of study outcomes that were not optimal measures of the aggression con-

---

[2]Many factors must be considered in evaluating a study's external and construct validity, most importantly the research question addressed (cf. Berkowitz & Donnerstein, 1982; Mook, 1983; see also Greenberg & Folger's, 1988, excellent summary of controversies concerning the validity of field vs. laboratory research).

struct, such as vandalism and other antisocial behavior (e.g., stealing money from charity boxes; Milgram & Shotland, 1973). As Geen (1998) noted, most social psychologists accept the definition that "aggression is any form of behavior directed toward the goal of harming or injuring another living being who is motivated to avoid such treatment" (Baron, 1977, p. 7). Thus, although previous reviewers may have succeeded in evaluating media effects in naturalistic contexts, they did not necessarily capture the essence of the concept of aggression.

In the present review, we relied on the validity of the dependent measure as the sample selection criterion. Because we sought to estimate the impact of media violence on aggressive behavior in naturally occurring social interaction, studies in our review assessed aggressive responses that were part of the research participants' existing action repertoire and were not evoked by experimental stimuli. Specifically, aggression was assessed as it occurred in the free-play behavior of children or in unconstrained social interaction among adults.

Our focus on the validity of the dependent measure yields a sample of studies particularly suited to reveal the impact of media violence. The assessed behaviors possess high construct validity. Spontaneously exhibited interpersonal aggression is unlikely to represent obedience, helpfulness, or impression management (Melburg & Tedeschi, 1989; Gottfredson & Hirschi, 1993). Furthermore, the aggression measure in the studies in our review was not limited to intensity of response, which is the typical laboratory index (Krebs & Miller, 1985). Instead, the reviewed studies captured a range of reactions that reflect whether, to what extent, and how often to behave aggressively.

Relying on the measure of aggression to define the limits of the review does not compromise the external validity of our conclusions about aggression in everyday settings. External validity is ensured in part because, regardless of whether the aggressive behavior was assessed in a laboratory playroom, a lunchroom at school, or in participants' residences, another person was always present in the research setting as a target for aggressive responses. Many real-world inhibitions and inducements to aggression are intrinsic to social interaction. These are not specified by the experimenter and reflect the naturally occurring contingencies that arise in everyday settings.

The definition of our sample thus led us to consider the results from laboratory as well as field settings. In a typical laboratory study, a movie was presented, and participants were told to wait in the viewing room until the experimenter was ready for them. The participants most likely believed that the study terminated at this point, and indeed in a few cases this instruction was explicitly mentioned in the report. Toys were provided for the children to play with, and behavior coding was conducted in an unobtrusive manner. Because participants were not interacting with others for research purposes, behavior in the laboratory should be comparable on important dimensions to that in natural settings.

Laboratory settings, however, differ from other contexts in a variety of ways. The laboratory provides particularly good control over extraneous variables (e.g., duration of the interaction opportunity and the presence of a teacher or other authority figure). Control over such variables is likely to be less in the present set of studies than in standard experimental investigations of aggression, in part because of the naturally occurring responses of participants' interaction partners. However, it is still possible that the studies with experimental settings in our review will exert greater control over random error than studies in other settings and thus yield slightly larger media effects.

A potential confound to interpreting participants' responses in the laboratory is that these behaviors might reflect experimental demand. Experimenters who show violent films might appear to the research participants to condone violence (e.g., Felson, 1996; Freedman, 1988). Participants' aggressive behavior thus supposedly reflects their beliefs about what is expected of them, or what is permissible, rather than any direct film effects. We believe, however, that this kind of "demand" effect is an intrinsic feature of violent media presented in all contexts. Generally, viewers are likely to believe that violent presentations are condoned by media sponsors, whether the sponsor is an experimenter, one's family, the television networks or movie studios, or society in general. Wood et al. (1991) labeled this aspect of experimental demand a *sponsor effect,* and concluded that it occurs regardless of who provides the media presentation. Sponsor effects are not artifacts of laboratory procedures; they also occur in field settings.

We recognize that participants' beliefs about the experimenter's hypothesis in a research study add a dimension of complexity to sponsor effects in the laboratory that does not occur in natural settings. In the laboratory, sophisticated participants may differentiate between what experimenters personally endorse and what they present for research purposes. These beliefs about why violent media are being presented in experimental research might then affect participants' aggressive responding. However, we wonder whether children easily can generate such complex meta-perspectives. Given that the laboratory research in our review relied largely on children as participants, these complex forms of sponsor effects may not have been prominent in the reviewed research.

THE PRESENT RESEARCH

Our review is limited to experiments that assessed unconstrained interpersonal aggression. In the prototypic study, children or adolescents were exposed to either aggressive or nonaggressive films in their school or in their institution of residence. Then participants either were told to play with others for a while in the viewing room or were allowed to return to their classroom or lunchroom and interact with nonparticipants. Participants' behavior was unobtrusively observed in these contexts by trained coders, and the amount of aggressive activity was noted.

We used the technique of meta-analysis to evaluate study outcomes (Wood & Christensen, 2004). Meta-analysis is particularly appropriate for the present investigation because estimates of effect size do not depend on the significance level attached to the result in the original research. When a given research paradigm tends to use few participants, as is likely to be the case with studies that code ongoing behaviors in social interaction, nonsignificant findings may be obtained because of inadequate power to detect effects. Narrative reviews that rely on statistical significance thus may underestimate or fail to detect existing relations (cf. Cooper & Rosenthal, 1980).

Meta-analysis is also useful to identify moderators of an effect. Moderator analyses in meta-analytic syntheses take advantage of the wider range of participant types, settings, and operations across a body of literature than is available in any single investigation. We examined several features of the original experiments that have been identified in prior work as potential moderators of exposure effects.

Because the studies in our review range in context from field to laboratory experiments, we were able to evaluate the effects of setting. It is correct to describe this attribute of research as a range and not a dichotomy because no clear criteria separated field and laboratory settings (see Aronson, Wilson, & Brewer, 1998). Because we included only true experiments in our review, our field and laboratory studies did not differ on the variety of dimensions that Aronson et al. (1998) noted as likely to differentiate these settings (e.g., less possibility of random assignment in the field and less possibility of precise manipulation of the independent variable in the field). The critical factor that differentiated laboratory from field settings in our sample was whether participants appeared to believe they were in an experiment. Thus if the research was conducted in an "experimental room" or we could not evaluate participants' awareness of the experimental procedure, we classified the setting for media exposure and for assessment of aggressive behavior as involving a laboratory. However, if participants were children who were taken with classmates from their normal schoolroom to a viewing room in the school building to see a movie, they most plausibly experienced the research as part of their school day. Thus, we considered that such studies were conducted in a field setting. Other field settings used in the reviewed research included playgrounds at school, athletic fields, and participants' residences.

METHODOLOGY OF THE
META-ANALYTIC REVIEW

The sample of 24 research reports was identified by searching citations in earlier reviews and computerized searches of *PsycINFO* (1967–2004), Educational Resources Information Center documents (1966–2004), and *Dissertation Abstracts International* (1950–2004).[3] The key words used in the searches included *media, television, violence, aggression,* and *antisocial behavior.* The

---

[3]An unpublished experiment by Wells (1973) cited in earlier reviews (e.g., Freedman, 1986) was not included in our analyses because we could not obtain a copy of the research report.

present sample thus updates the Wood et al. (1991) earlier review with the addition of one study that met the selection criteria (i.e., Ling & Thomas, 1986).

The criteria for including studies in the sample were as follows: (a) participants were randomly assigned to experimental (i.e., exposure to violent media) and control conditions, (b) the dependent measure was aggressive acts directed toward another person who was physically present and in some cases also included aggression toward inanimate objects, and (c) aggression was assessed through raters' direct observation of participants' behavior. We did not include research that used highly structured interaction contexts, such as competition for space among children (e.g., Hapkiewicz & Roden, 1971; Hapkiewicz & Stone, 1974) or research that assessed aggression on a single behavioral dimension, such as harassing telephone calls (e.g., Milgram & Shotland, 1973). Narrow definitions or samples of behavior may underestimate media effects (when aggression is expressed in alternate forms that are not evaluated) or may exaggerate effects (when aggression is limited only to the dimension assessed and does not occur in other forms). Several studies also were excluded because they relied on raters' subjective recall of participants' aggressive behavior or because they included in the outcome score behaviors not representative of the aggression construct, such as restlessness, sullen facial expression, and sleep disturbance (Cameron & Janky, 1971; Feshbach & Singer, 1971; Loye, Gorney, & Steele, 1977).[4]

We initially considered the effects of all of the study attributes that were evaluated in the earlier review (Wood et al., 1991). However, because only two of the coded variables yielded any effects in the earlier analyses, we report the findings just for these two: (a) setting for media exposure and for observation of aggression (laboratory–experimentally constructed room vs. field–classroom or other schoolroom, playground, or residence) and (b) age of participants (younger than 6 years old vs. between 6 and 10 years old vs. 10 years and older).[5] It is also

---

[4]We did calculate the outcomes from the three studies that used subjective ratings of viewers' aggressive behavior. These studies demonstrated no consistent pattern of effects; Cameron and Janky (1971) and Loye et al. (1977) reported somewhat greater aggressiveness in the media violence than control conditions ($d = 0.26$ and $d = 0.20$, respectively), and Feshbach and Singer (1971) reported greater aggressiveness in the control condition than in the media-violence condition ($d = -0.25$).

[5]None of the other study attributes that we evaluated as moderators of media violence effects proved to be significant predictors (i.e., publication status of the report or sex composition of sample). It was not possible to evaluate the effects of type of control condition because 11 outcomes represented a comparison with a neutral film control, 1 represented a comparison with no film plus neutral film conditions combined, and 1 used a prosocial control film. It was not possible to evaluate the effects of interaction partner because in the majority of studies, participants were observed interacting with schoolmates or housemates ($n = 11$) or the nature of interaction partners could not be classified ($n = 2$). Furthermore, in only one study were participants angered or frustrated before their aggressive behavior was observed, and in only one study was there a delay between exposure to violent media and assessment of aggression. It is also worth noting that we failed to replicate the effects of type of research participants obtained in the original Wood et al. (1991) meta-analysis. Although they reported a stronger effect for normal populations versus emotionally disturbed or delinquent populations, this factor was not a significant predictor in the present analyses.

worth noting that we were not able to evaluate some potentially important moderators of media effects, such as the specific content of the program. Although little systematic information was provided in the research reports about program content (e.g., whether the aggressive models were successful), we recognize that program attributes are likely to be important moderators of media violence effects. For example, viewer aggression is especially likely following portrayals of successful violence (Betsch & Dickenberger, 1993) and when the violence is justified (Hogben, 1994). Similarly, attitudes toward violence become less favorable after viewing public service announcements that suggest death as consequence of handgun violence versus announcements that depict no consequence (National Television Violence Study, 1998).

We made a number of a priori decisions about selection and presentation of findings from the various reports. Several of our studies included findings from multiple experiments. in total, the 24 studies yielded 29 experiments on separate participant samples. When adequate data were available, an effect size (g) was calculated. This statistic represents the magnitude of an effect and is calculated from the difference between the means of the experimental and control groups divided by the standard deviation assumed to be common to the two conditions (Hedges & Olkin, 1985). Effect size calculations were performed with D-STAT (Johnson, 1993). Effect size was calculated from means and standard deviations in nine studies and from a t or F statistic in four studies. Effect sizes were corrected for the bias associated with small sample sizes and reported as ds (Hedges & Olkin, 1985).[6]

Some studies reported both immediate and delayed outcome measures. In all cases but one (Parke, Berkowitz, Leyens, West, & Sebastian, 1977), we were able to base our analyses on just the immediate outcomes. Furthermore, because we are primarily interested in interpersonal aggression, whenever possible we selected this measure from each study. When data from more than one type of control condition were provided for a given study, we selected as the control a neutral, nonaggressive presentation condition rather than a prosocial media or no media presentation control. Finally, for some reports it was possible to calculate effect sizes to represent both gain scores (i.e., change from an initial level of aggression in the experimental vs. control conditions) and final status scores (i.e., the final level of aggression in each condition). In these cases, final status scores were selected to represent study outcomes in the overall analysis. Supplementary analyses that evaluated change scores yielded results comparable to those we report.

The data obtained from each study are presented in Table 10.1.

---

[6]This present meta-analysis is largely based on the results of experimental studies, which is best represented by the effect size d. Effect sizes are also reported as rs (transformed from the ds; Rosenthal, 1994) to be consistent with the other chapters in this book.

TABLE 10.1

Studies Included in the Meta-Analysis

Study	Participant Population	Setting[a]	Total N	Control Conditions	Direction of Effect	Effect Size[b] r	Effect Size[b] d	95% CI (d) Lower	95% CI (d) Upper
Biblow (1973)	Fifth graders	1/1	30	Neutral film	E > C	.16	0.32	−0.19	0.83
			40	No film	C > E	−.23	−0.47	−1.09	0.16
Cooper & Axsom (1981)	Kindergartners to fifth graders	2/3	119	Neutral film					
Drabman & Thomas (1977)	Preschool boys	2/1	20	Prosocial film	C > E				
Ellis & Sekyra (1972)	First graders	2/2	51	Neutral film & no film (combined)	E > C	.36	0.78	0.18	1.39
Fechter (1971)	Mentally retarded 8- to 38-year-olds	2/4	40	Prosocial film	E > C				
Friedrich & Stein (1973)	Nursery school	2/2	65	Neutral film	E > C				
			65	Prosocial film	E > C				
Gadow & Sprafkin (1987)	Emotionally disturbed 8- to 12-year olds	2/2	11	Neutral film	E > C				
	Emotionally disturbed 5- to 8-year-olds	2/2	9	Neutral film	E > C	.43	0.94	−0.03	1.91
	Emotionally disturbed 3- to 5-year-olds	2/2	9	Neutral film					
Gadow, Sprafkin, & Ficarrotto (1987)	Emotionally disturbed 2- to 5-year olds	2/2	14	Neutral film	C > E	−.17	−0.34	−1.09	0.40

154

Study	Sample			Comparison	Direction				
Guralnick (1980)	Male juvenile offenders								
Hall & Cairns (1984)	First- and second-grade boys	2/2 1/1	39 30[c]	Neutral film No film	E > C	.39	0.84	.05	1.63
Huston-Stein, Fox, Greer, Watkins, & Whitaker (1981)	Preschoolers	1/1	33	No film	E > C				
Josephson (1987)	Second- and third-grade boys	2/3	50 66[c]	Neutral film Neutral film	C > E E > C	.17	0.35	−0.17	0.86
Leyens, Camino, Parke, & Berkowitz (1975)	Adolescent boys in a residential school	3/4	85	Neutral film	E > C				
Ling & Thomas (1986)	Maori and European 8-year-olds	1/3	52	Prosocial film	E > C	.49	1.12	0.54	1.71
McCabe & Moriarity (1977)	Study 1: 6- to 17-year-olds	1/3		Neutral film Prosocial film	E > C C > E				
	Study 2: 7- to 20-year-olds	1/3		Neutral film Prosocial film	E > C C > E				
	Study 3: 6- to 12-year-old boys	1/3		Neutral film Prosocial film	C > E C > E				
Parke, Berkowitz, Leyens, West, & Sebastian (1977)	First American study: male juvenile offenders	3/4	37	Neutral film	E > C	.31	0.65	−0.01	1.32
	Second American study: male juvenile offenders	3/4	74	Neutral film					
Potts, Huston, & Wright (1986)	Preschool boys	1/1	32[c]	Neutral film	E > C	.27	0.56	−0.15	1.26

(Continued)

155

TABLE 10.1 (Continued)
Studies Included in the Meta-Analysis

Study	Participant Population	Setting[a]	Total N	Control Conditions	Direction of Effect	Effect Size[b]		95% CI (d)	
						r	d	Lower	Upper
Ross (1972)	Kindergartners	2/2	64	Neutral film	E > C	0.14	0.29	−0.20	0.79
			64	No film	E > C	0.44	0.97	0.45	1.49
Sawin (1974)	Nursery schoolers	2/2	8[c]	Neutral film	C > E				
Siegel (1956)	Nursery schoolers	1/1	24	Neutral film	E > C				
Simonson (1992)	10- to 13-year-old boys	2/2	96	Neutral film	C > E	−.09	−0.19	−0.59	0.21
Sprafkin, Gadow, & Grayson (1987)	Learning-disabled 6- to 10-year-olds	2/2	46	Neutral film					
Sprafkin, Gadow, & Grayson (1988)	Emotionally disturbed 6- to 9-year-olds	2/2	26	Neutral film	C > E	−.03	−0.07	−0.62	0.47
Steuer, Applefield, & Smith (1971)	Preschoolers	1/1	10	Neutral film	E > C	.46	1.04	−0.28	2.36

Note. Effects sizes are scored so that positive numbers reflect greater aggressiveness of participants exposed to violent media, and negative numbers reflect greater aggressiveness of participants in control conditions. E, experimental condition; C, control condition.

[a]Setting is coded such that the first numeral reflects exposure setting (1 = experimentally constructed viewing room, 2 = classroom or viewing room in school, 3 = residence), and the second numeral reflects setting for behavioral observation of viewers' aggression (1 = experimentally constructed viewing room, 2 = classroom, viewing room in school, or school lunchroom, 3 = playground or athletic field, 4 = residence). [b]Effect sizes are corrected to remove bias associated with small sample size. Correlations (r) are converted from d. [c]Sample size reflects the number of interacting groups of participants rather than the number of individual participants.

INTERPRETATION AND REPORT
OF FINDINGS OF THE REVIEW

A summary of the study attributes is presented in Table 10.2. Exact effect sizes could be calculated for 13 independent studies.

Our first concern was whether the distribution of effect sizes approximated a normal curve. As can be seen in Table 10.3, the distribution was not skewed in either direction; skewness can be an indicator of selective representation of study outcomes (Light, Singer, & Willett, 1994). Selectivity could result from publication biases in a particular literature set, such as editorial decisions favoring publication of significant results in a given direction or from authors presenting inadequate information to calculate effect sizes when these effects are inconsistent with accepted theory. Thus, the shape of the distribution of effect sizes does not suggest that such factors distorted the findings of our review.

We then aggregated across the effect sizes to answer our central question: Does exposure to media violence increase viewers' aggression? Our approach to meta-analysis was to use approximate data pooling and to rely on the participant as the unit of analysis (Hedges & Olkin, 1985). We report two versions of effect size calculations. In one analysis, study outcomes were weighted by the inverse of the

TABLE 10.2
Summary of Study Attributes

Variable	Reports with Known Effect Sizes (n = 13)	All Reports (n = 29)
Mean publication year	1982	1979
Sex of participants		
Male only	5	10
Mixed sex	8	19
Angered/frustrated participants[a]		
Yes	1	1
No	11	26
Observer present[b]		
Yes	10	23
No or do not know	3	5
Media presentation		
Commercial	10	21
Experimentally constructed or do not know	3	8

Note. [a]For the sample with known effect sizes, in one report this variable was manipulated across experimental conditions. For the total sample, this variable was manipulated across conditions in two reports. [b]For the total sample, in one report this variable was manipulated across experimental conditions.

TABLE 10.3

Distribution of EffectSizes (*r*) on a Stem-and-Leaf Plot

Stem	Leaf
+0.4	2, 6, 8
+0.3	0, 6, 8
+0.2	7
+0.1	4, 6, 7
+0.0	
−0.0	3, 9
−0.1	7

Note. Each effect size estimate is composed of one stem and one leaf. The numbers in the left column represent the stems or first numerals in the estimates, and the numbers in the right column represent the leaves or second numerals in the estimates. Multiple entries in a row indicate that more than one estimate is composed of a given stem. Positive numbers reflect greater aggressiveness of participants exposed to violent media, and negative numbers reflect greater aggressiveness of control participants.

variance associated with each outcome before findings were aggregated. Variance is a function of sample size, and thus the studies with the greatest precision of measurement were weighted most heavily. The second analysis did not use weighting procedures. In the weighted analyses, the mean effect size revealed a significant increase in aggression after exposure to violent media ($d = 0.35$, 95% confidence interval [CI] = 0.18/0.52, $r = .17$). A comparable finding was obtained with the unweighted mean ($d = 0.48$, $r = .23$). The homogeneity statistic, Q, indicates whether the weighted effect sizes are sufficiently different from each other to reject the null hypothesis that they are drawn from a common population. This estimate has an approximate chi-square distribution with $k - 1$ degrees of freedom, in which k is the number of effect sizes. The significant effect suggested rejection of homogeneity, $Q = 26.54$, $p < .01$.

Thus, our review of 13 experiments examining children's and adolescents' spontaneous aggression during unconstrained social interaction reaffirms Wood et al.'s (1991) earlier conclusion: The experimental literature reveals that exposure to media violence enhances viewers' unconstrained aggression. It also appears that the size of the effect varies across the specific studies in the review.

Size of the Effect

How important are the media effects identified in this review? Importance is sometimes equated with size, and size comparisons are necessarily relative. Thus, to answer this question we need to know the typical effect size associated with social–psychological variables. According to Cohen's (1992) intuitive rule of thumb, effect sizes (in the metric of d) of 0.20 or less are small ($rs < .10$) and 0.80 or greater are large ($rs > .50$). Cohen identified small effects as representative of personality, social, and clinical psychology research, whereas large effect sizes are more common in physiological and experimental psychology. Supporting Cohen's assessment, a meta-analysis of 322 meta-analyses on social psychological phenomena revealed a mean effect size of $r = .21$ (Richard, Bond, & Stokes-Zoota, 2003). According to these guidelines, the mean effect of exposure to violent media on unconstrained aggression is slightly larger that the average effect in social psychology and would fall within the small to moderate range. For comparison, consider that the media violence effect is stronger than many effects deemed important by society, including the effects of condom use on HIV transmission, lead exposure on children's intelligence, and calcium intake on bone mass (Bushman & Anderson, 2001).

The labels *small* and *moderate* might suggest a phenomenon that is of limited importance. However, meaningfulness of an effect depends on a variety of considerations. As Prentice and Miller (1992) noted, small magnitude effects may be highly noteworthy when they occur in settings that would plausibly inhibit the effect. We believe that the small to moderately sized effects that emerged in our analysis are impressive, given that the reviewed research assessed participants' spontaneous aggressive behavior in relatively uncontrolled settings that involved interaction with peers. To investigate directly the effect of setting, we conducted moderator analyses to evaluate whether media violence effects were larger in laboratory contexts than in field contexts. The moderator analyses were conducted with weighted effect sizes and involved calculating a comparison between classes (Q_B) analogous to testing for main effects in analysis of variance models. The estimated Q_B has an approximate chi-square distribution with $p - 1$ degrees of freedom, in which p represents the number of classes (Hedges & Olkin, 1985).

Replicating Wood et al.'s (1991) earlier findings, we found that the outcomes for laboratory settings ($d = 0.69$, 95% CI 0.39/1.00, $r = .33$, $n = 5$) were larger than those for field settings ($d = 0.20$, 95% CI $= 0.00/0.40$, $r = .10$, $n = 8$), $Q_B = 7.13$, $p < .01$. For estimates in field settings, the hypothesis of homogeneity was rejected at a marginal level of significance, $Q_W = 14.78$, $p < .10$. The larger findings in laboratory contexts plausibly arise from the greater control over extraneous variables and less random variation in relevant variables afforded by the laboratory. This variation according to setting highlights the importance of considering the overall variability in a given context when one interprets effect size magnitude.

The importance of the effect obtained in the present review also can be understood in terms of the binomial effect-size display (Rosenthal and Rubin, 1982; Rosenthal, 1986), which illustrates empirically the social consequences of a finding. This procedure was developed with reference to biomedical research and in general demonstrates the effect of a treatment, or independent variable (i.e., exposure to media violence), on success rate, or dependent variable (i.e., increases in the percentage of the experimental group exhibiting greater than the mean-level aggressive response). Using the binomial effect size display, we can calculate the increase in the percentage of high- and low-aggression viewers as a function of the type of media exposure. Based on the weighted analyses, we would expect approximately 59% of participants to display greater than average aggressiveness in the media violence condition, compared with only 41% of participants in control conditions. This suggests that almost a fifth more people would show greater than average aggressive behavior after exposure to violent media. Use of the unweighted analyses yields even stronger effects; 24% more participants would be expected to show more aggression than the mean.

The importance of the findings can also be interpreted in the context of aggregation of effects (Eagly & Wood, 1994). Exposure to media violence may have a small to moderate impact on any single behavior, but the impact may be substantial when cumulated across multiple exposures and multiple social interactions. The research in our review typically exposed participants to only one or a few episodes of media violence. The cumulative impact across a lifetime of media exposure might plausibly be greater. Furthermore, if the form of media impact followed a nonlinear pattern, then media effects would only be apparent in cumulated data and would be captured inadequately by the one-shot exposure studies typical in our review (e.g., if an exposure threshold exists with media effects discernible only above some minimum level; McGuire, 1986). It is possible that the full impact of media violence is apparent when viewers interact with others. Aggregation across aggressive acts may also be required to document substantial media impact. Particularly if we assume that one person's aggression begets corresponding hostility in others (Kiesler, 1983; Leary, 1957; Orford; 1986), small increases in an individual's aggression may have significant impact across sequences of interaction with other people.

To interpret effect size, we might also ask whether exposure to media violence is an important determinant of aggression in comparison with other known predictors. It is not possible to present a comprehensive literature review here, but we present some representative findings from the host of predictors of aggression. As an example of individual differences, the median sex difference in aggressive behavior is $r = .19$ (Bettencourt & Miller, 1996). A similar size effect is found in developmental research: Parents who use corporal punishment have children who are more likely to be nominated by peers as being aggressive ($d = .36$, Gershoff, 2002). As evidence of a situational factor, Bushman and Cooper's (1990) meta-analytic synthesis found that alcohol enhanced laboratory-based aggression (mean rs ranged from 0.12 to 0.29, depending on the type of control condition). Finally, well-conducted studies examining the effect of video game violence on aggression yield mean rs that range from .19 to .27 (Anderson et al., 2004). Thus the media effects documented in the present review are of a magnitude comparable to these other predictors of aggression.

Yet media violence effects do not appear especially significant if we consider the macrosocial variables that have been used to account for aggregate, population-level indicators of aggression. It is easy to find substantial predictors of aggression in this literature. For example, Baron and Straus (1987) found that the reported incidence of rape across the United States was highly associated ($r = 0.68$) with an index representing level of social disorganization (including divorce and geographic mobility). Violent crime also seems to have a substantial relation with the climate of a city, even after controlling for population, socio-economic status, and "Southernness" (Anderson, Anderson, Dorr, DeNeve, & Flanagan, 2000). Furthermore, 60% to 70% of the variability in homicide rates across communities appears to be accounted for by three variables: percentage of the population who are poor, population size, and percentage who are Black (Williams, 1984). Although these findings might be only tangentially relevant to the present investigation because they deal with extreme, relatively low-frequency forms of violent behavior and with aggregate, population-level data, they do demonstrate the effectiveness of certain types of predictors of aggression.

At the least, these various findings reveal that aggression is multiply determined; a variety of individual and social variables predict aggressive activity. We doubt that future investigations will find that exposure to violent media features prominently among the most important determinants of aggression in our society. Yet the impact of media violence on individual behavior is not trivial in comparison with the size of effects typically obtained with social–psychological predictors.

Adequacy of the Experimental Manipulations

In experimental research, understanding the form and strength of the experimental manipulations must be considered when interpreting effect size. In one important aspect, the form of media exposure in the studies in our review is highly similar to real-world conditions. That is, the majority of studies used commercially available media presentations (see Table 10.2). In only 8 of the 29 experiments did the researchers either construct their own films or fail to report the type of film. However, unlike real-world exposure settings, participants in the studies were most often shown the media presentations without interruptions and with minimal social contact (although other participants were typically present). Furthermore, media presentations were typically edited to remove interruptions. The overall impact of these characteristics of the experimental manipulations is unclear, but these attributes are worth noting in interpreting the obtained results.

The strength of the media violence manipulation in the original studies was determined in a general way by real-world conventions, given that the majority of media excerpts were drawn from commercial presentations. The original researchers uniformly selected violent films representative of mainstream programming: Cartoons, feature films, and popular television serials were used as violent media rather than the more extreme examples currently available in many video stores and showing in some theaters (e.g., horror films and slasher films). It is unclear what effects would be associated with these more extreme examples of media violence.

Although study authors presumably were careful in selecting violent and control films, few authors used manipulation checks to substantiate the intended differences between film presentations. Thus, we were unable to evaluate the adequacy with which high-violence versus low-violence films were operationalized or the extent to which these manipulations varied on dimensions other than amount of violence. A meta-analysis by Paik and Comstock (1994), which used a different and larger sample of studies, was able to analyze characteristics of the films used in the primary reports. Although there was some variation in the size of the effect (e.g., studies that included manipulation checks yielded slightly larger effects than those without checks), all types of films had significant, positive effects on viewer aggression. So, despite the importance of having an internally valid experiment, there is no evidence to suggest that the media violence and aggression relationship hinges on such study qualities.

Age of Viewers

Because our data set included an additional experiment that Wood et al. (1991) failed to locate, we had sufficient data to examine systematically whether age of the viewer affected the impact of media violence. One hypothesis about the effects of age is that younger children have less capacity to comprehend and attend to violent media and thus might be less influenced than older viewers (Hughes, 1989). On the other hand, older children's greater experience and more crystallized attitudes might make them more resistant to media impact than younger viewers. These two seemingly competing perspectives can be reconciled in the Yale–McGuire model of individual differences in susceptibility to persuasive messages (Hovland, Janis, & Kelly, 1953; McGuire, 1985; Rhodes & Wood, 1992). In this model, people are influenced by media and other persuasive messages when they *receive* the media information and when they *yield* to it. The varying effects of mental age on influence can be understood in terms of information-processing ability, specifically on reception and yielding.

Because adolescents and adults are more likely than young children to understand media arguments (i.e., receive them), the relation between age and *reception* should be positive. However, older people also are more likely to be knowledgeable and to hold established behavioral patterns. Therefore, they should be less likely to adopt the recommendations offered by the media. Thus, the relation between age and *yielding* should be negative. The opposing effects of age on reception and yielding lead to the prediction of an inverted U-shaped relationship between the age and media effects. Although very young participants may be influenced (high yielding), they should not fully comprehend the message of the violent media that people act aggressively (low reception, see Collins, Berndt, &

Hess, 1974). Therefore, very young participants are unlikely to respond to media exposure by acting aggressively themselves. Adolescents, however, should understand the violent behaviors they watch (high reception) but also should have more established patterns of social behavior (low yielding) and therefore are unlikely to yield to the media images. If the Yale–McGuire model is correct, children in between these two age groups would be the most susceptible to viewing violent media: These children should understand the violent behaviors being presented (moderate reception) and accept others' behavior as a standard for their own (moderate yielding), and thus they should demonstrate the strongest reactions to the presentations.

To test the moderating effects of age, we classified the studies in our review into three groups, representing the age of participants as very young (preschool and kindergarten), mid-childhood to preadolescent (6 to 10 years of age), and adolescent. As the Yale–McGuire model anticipates, a small effect of media violence emerged for studies examining media effects on very young children ($d = 0.27$, 95% CI $= -0.07/0.61$, $r = .13$, $n = 4$) and a small effect emerged for studies examining media effects on adolescents ($d = 0.12$, 95% CI $= -0.16/0.41$, $r = .06$, $n = 3$). However, a significantly larger effect was obtained in the six studies of preadolescent children ($d = 0.66$, 95% CI $= 0.43/0.89$, $r = .31$, $n = 6$). The difference across age groups was significant, $Q_B = 8.85$, $p < .05$, and the assumption of homogeneity was rejected for estimates within the middle age group, but not the others, $Q_W = 13.92$, $p < .05$.

This inverted U-shaped relationship between age and media effects contributes to the growing evidence that recipients' dispositions often have a nonlinear relation to the influence of media and other persuasive information. In an earlier meta-analytic synthesis, Rhodes and Wood (1992) discovered an inverted U-shaped relation between recipients' self-esteem and their influenceability when presented with persuasive appeals. Like the very young children in the present review, low self-esteem participants in Rhodes and Wood's (1992) review were relatively unaffected by influence appeals, presumably because their low self-esteem rendered them too defensive to receive much information discrepant from their own beliefs. Similarly, like the adolescents in the present review, high self-esteem participants were little influenced, presumably because they had considerable confidence in their own initial position and did not yield to the position presented in the message. Much like the mid-childhood aged participants in the present research, the greatest influence in the Rhodes and Wood review emerged among those of mid-level self-esteem.

In the present review, we were only able to document the outcome of media impact, and additional research is necessary to substantiate the mediating processes specified in the Yale–McGuire model. Measures that directly assess viewers' reception of violent media should reveal that increasing age is associated with increasing reception of the media message that violent behavior is performed in certain ways, is normative, or is an acceptable response to frustration and to desire.

In addition, direct measures of yielding should reveal that increasing age is associated with decreasing yielding to the message concerning violent behavior.

CONCLUSION

Our analysis revealed that media violence enhances children's and adolescents' aggression in interactions with strangers, classmates, and friends. The findings cannot be dismissed as representing artificial experimental constructions because the studies included in our review evaluated media exposure on aggression as it naturally emerged in unconstrained social interaction. Despite such strong evidence, television programming continues to feature violent behaviors in shows that are targeted toward both children and adults (National Television Violence Study, 1998).

The review was not designed to test theoretical accounts of the effects of media violence but rather to evaluate the magnitude of the effect in naturally occurring interactions. However, the results are worth considering in terms of their theoretical implications. Our findings are best interpreted as short-term media impact; in all but one study observation of viewers' behavior commenced almost immediately after the film presentation. The behavioral observation period may have extended over several hours or days, but the reported results cannot be disentangled from effects during the initial postexposure period. For this reason, temporary state changes, such as increases in thoughts, affect, and arousal (Anderson & Bushman, 2002), may be implicated in the effects in addition to longer-term processes such as modeling (Bandura, 1994) and the learning of aggressive behavioral scripts (Huesmann, 1986).

The findings from the highly structured experiments in our review speak to one of the important issues raised in the debate over media violence. That is, they illustrate the *causal* relation between media exposure and naturally occurring aggression. From an applied perspective, a number of important issues remain concerning media effects, including viewer selection of violent versus nonviolent programs and the cumulative impact of exposure over time. Our demonstration of a causal relation between media violence and aggression is an important foundation for understanding these complex relations that occur with viewers' real-world use of violent media.

REFERENCES

References marked with an asterisk indicate studies included in the meta-analysis.

Anderson, C. A., Anderson, K. B., Dorr, N., DeNeve, K. M., & Flanagan, M. (2000). Temperature and aggression. In M. Zanna (Ed.), *Advances in experimental social psychology* (Vol. 32, pp. 63–133). New York: Academic Press.

Anderson, C. A., & Bushman, B. J. (2002). Human aggression. *Annual Review of Psychology, 53,* 27–51.

Anderson, C. A., Carnagey, N. L., Flanagan, M., Benjamin, A. J., Jr., Eubanks, J., & Valentine, J. C. (2004). Violent video games: Specific effects of violent content on aggressive thoughts and behavior. In L. Berkowitz (Ed.), *Advances in Experimental Social Psychology* (Vol. 36, pp. 199–249). New York: Academic Press.

Andison, F. S. (1977). TV violence and viewer aggression: A cumulation of study results. *Public Opinion Quarterly, 41,* 314–331.

Aronson, E., Wilson, T. D., Brewer, M. B. (1998) Experimention in social psychology. In D T. Gilbert, S. T. Fiske (Eds.), *Handbook of social psychology* (4th ed., pp. 99–142). New York, NY, US: McGraw-Hill.

Bandura, A. (1994). Social cognitive theory of mass communication. In J. Bryant & D. Zillmann (Eds.), *Media effects: Advances in theory and research* (pp. 61–90). Hillsdale, NJ: Lawrence Erlbaum Associates.

Baron, L., & Straus, M. A. (1987). Four theories of rape: A macrosocial analysis. *Social Problems, 34,* 467–489.

Baron, R. A. (1977). *Human aggression.* New York: Plenum Press.

Berkowitz, L., & Donnerstein, E. (1982). External validity is more than skin deep: Some answers to criticisms of laboratory experiments. *American Psychologist, 37,* 245–257.

Betsch, T., & Dickenberger, D. (1993). Why do aggressive movies make people aggressive? An attempt to explain short-term effects of the depiction of violence on the observer. *Aggressive Behavior, 19,* 137–149.

Bettencourt, B. A., & Miller, N. (1996). Gender differences in aggression as a function of provocation: A meta-analysis. *Psychological Bulletin, 119,* 422–427.

*Biblow, E. (1973). Imaginative play and the control of aggressive behavior. In J. L. Singer (Ed.), *The child's world of make believe* (pp. 104–128). San Diego, CA: Academic Press.

Bushman, B. J., & Anderson, C. A. (2001). Media violence and the American public: Scientific facts versus media misinformation. *American Psychologist, 56,* 477–489.

Bushman, B. J., & Cooper, H. M. (1990). Effects of alcohol on human aggression: An integrative research review. *Psychological Bulletin, 107,* 341–354.

Cameron, P., & Janky, C. (1971, September). *Effects of TV violence on children: A naturalistic experiment.* Paper presented at the 79th Annual Convention of the American Psychological Association, Washington, DC.

Cohen, J. (1992). A power primer. *Psychological Bulletin, 112,* 155–159.

Collins, W. A., Berndt, T. J., & Hess, V. L. (1974). Observational learning of motives and consequences of television aggression: A developmental study. *Child Development, 45,* 799–802.

Cook, T. D., & Campbell, D. T. (1979). *Quasi-experimentation: Design and analysis issues for field settings.* Boston: Houghton Mifflin.

Cook, T. D., Kendzierski, D. A., & Thomas, S. V. (1983). The implicit assumptions of television research: An analysis of the 1982 NIMH report on Television and Behavior. *Public Opinion Quarterly, 47,* 161–201.

Cooper, H. M., & Rosenthal, R. (1980). Statistical-versus traditional procedures for summarizing research findings. *Psychological Bulletin, 87,* 442–449.

*Cooper, J., & Axsom, D. (1981, August). The impact of televised aggression on children: A developmental field study. Paper presented at the 89th Annual Convention of the American Psychological Association, Los Angeles, CA.

*Drabman, R. S., & Thomas, M. H. (1977). Children's imitation of aggressive and prosocial behavior when viewing alone and in pairs. *Journal of Communication, 27,* 199–205.

Eagly, A. H., & Wood, W. (1994). Using research syntheses to plan future research. In H. M. Cooper & L. V. Hedges (Eds.), *The handbook of research synthesis* (pp. 485–502). New York: Russell Sage Foundation.

*Ellis, G. T., & Sekyra, F., III. (1972). The effects of aggressive cartoons on the behavior of first grade children. *The Journal of Psychology, 81,* 37–43.

Felson, R. B. (1996). Mass media effects on violent behavior. *Annual Review of Sociology, 22,* 103–128.

Feshbach, S., & Singer, R. D. (1971). *Television and aggression.* San Francisco: Jossey-Bass.

*Fechter, J. V., Jr. (1971). Modeling and environmental generalization by mentally retarded participants of televised aggressive or friendly behavior. *American Journal of Mental Deficiency, 76,* 266–267.

Freedman, J. L. (1984). Effects of television violence on aggressiveness. *Psychological Bulletin, 96,* 227–246.

Freedman, J. L. (1986). Television violence and aggression: A rejoinder. *Psychological Bulletin, 100,* 372–378.

Freedman, J. L. (1988). Television violence and aggression: What the evidence shows. In S. Oskamp (Ed.), *Applied social psychology annual: Television as a social issue* (Vol. 8, pp. 144–162). Newbury Park, CA: Sage.

*Friedrich, L. K., & Stein, A. H. (1973). Aggressive and prosocial television programs and the natural behavior of preschool children. *Monographs of the Society for Research in Child Development, 38* (Whole No. 151).

Friedrich-Cofer, L., & Huston, A. C. (1986). Television violence and aggression: The debate continues. *Psychological Bulletin, 100,* 364–371.

*Gadow, K. D., & Sprafkin, I. (1987). Effects of viewing high versus low aggression cartoons on emotionally disturbed children. *Journal of Pediatric Psychology, 12,* 413–427.

*Gadow, K. D., Sprafkin, J., & Ficarrotto, T. J. (1987). Effects of viewing aggression-laden cartoons on preschool-aged emotionally disturbed children. *Child Psychiatry and Human Development, 17,* 257–273.

Geen, R. G. (1998). Aggression and antisocial behavior. In D. T. Gilbert, S. T. Fiske, & G. Lindzey (Eds.), *The handbook of social psychology* (4th ed., Vol. 2, pp. 317–356). Boston: McGraw Hill.

Gershoff, E. T. (2002). Corporal punishment by parents and associated child behaviors and experiences: A meta-analytic and theoretical review. *Psychological Bulletin, 128,* 539–579.

Gottfredson, M. R., & Hirschi, T. A. (1993). Control theory interpretation of psychological research on aggression. In R. B. Felson & J. T. Tedeschi (Eds.), *Aggression and violence: Social interactionist perspectives* (pp. 47–68). Washington, DC: APA.

Greenberg, J., & Folger, R. (1988). Controversial issues in social research methods. New York: Springer-Verlag.

Gunter, B. (1985). Determinants of television viewing preferences. In D. Zillmann & J. Bryant (Eds.), *Selective exposure to communication* (pp. 93–112). Hillsdale, NJ: Lawrence Erlbaum Associates.

*Guralnick, E. A.(1980). *The effects of televised violence and frustration on the aggressiveness of delinquents.* Unpublished doctoral dissertation, Boston University.

*Hall, W. M., & Cairns, R. B. (1984). Aggressive behavior in children: An outcome of modeling or social reciprocity? *Developmental Psychology, 20,* 739–745.

Hapkiewicz, W. G., & Roden, A. H. (1971). The effect of aggressive cartoons on children's interpersonal play. *Child Development, 42,* 1583–1585.

Hapkiewicz, W. G., & Stone, R. D. (1974). The effects of realistic versus imaginary aggressive models on children's interpersonal play. *Child Study Journal, 4,* 47–58.

Hearold, S. (1986). A synthesis of 1043 effects of television on social behavior. In G. Comstock (Ed.), *Public communication and behavior* (Vol. 1, pp. 65–133). San Diego, CA: Academic Press.

Heath, L., Bresolin, L. B., & Rinaldi, R. C. (1989). Effects of media violence on children. *Archives of General Psychiatry, 46,* 376–379.

Hedges, L. V., & Olkin, I. (1985). *Statistical methods for meta-analysis.* San Diego, CA: Academic Press.

Hogben, M. (1994). Factors moderating the effect of televised aggression on viewer behavior. *Communication Research, 25,* 220–247.

Hovland, C. I, Janis, I. L., & Kelly, H. H. (1953). *Communication and persuasion: Psychological studies of opinion change.* New Haven: Yale Univ. Press.

Huesmann, L. R. (1986). Psychological processes promoting the relation between exposure to media violence and aggressive behavior by the viewer. *Journal of Social Issues, 42,* 125–139.

Hughes, C. E. (1989). Young children and information on television: A review of methods and results. In B. Dervin & M. J. Voight (Eds.), *Progress in Communication Sciences* (9th ed., pp. 79–103). Norwood, NJ: Ablex.

*Huston-Stein, A., Fox, S., Greer, D., Watkins, B. A., & Whitaker, J. (1981). The effects of TV action and violence on children's social behavior. *Journal of Genetic Psychology, 138,* 193–191.

Johnson, B. T. (1993). *D-STAT 1.10: Software for the meta-analytic review of research literatures.* Hillsdale, NJ: Lawrence Erlbaum Associates.

*Josephson, W. L. (1987). Television violence and children's aggression: Testing the priming, social script, and disinhibition predictions. *Journal of Personality and Social Psychology, 53,* 882–890.

Kiesler, D. J. (1983). The 1982 interpersonal circle: A taxonomy for complementarity in human transactions. *Psychological Review, 90,* 185–214.

Krebs, D. L., & Miller D. T. (1985). Altruism and aggression. In G. Lindzey & E. Aronson (Eds.), *Handbook of social psychology* (3rd ed., Vol. II, pp. 1–72). New York: Random House.

Leary, T. (1957). *Interpersonal diagnosis of personality.* New York: Roland.

Lesser, H. (1977). *Television and the preschool child.* San Diego, CA: Academic Press.

*Leyens, J. P., Camino, L., Parke, R. D., & Berkowitz, L. (1975). Effects of movie violence on aggression in a field setting as a function of group dominance and cohesion. *Journal of Personality and Social Psychology, 32,* 346–360.

Light, R. J., Singer, J. D., & Willett, J. B. (1994). The visual presentation and interpretation of meta-analysis. In Cooper, H. & Hedges, L. V. (Eds.), *The handbook of research synthesis.* New York: Russell Sage Foundation.

*Ling, P. A., & Thomas, D. R. (1986). Imitation of television aggression among Maori and European boys and girls. *New Zealand Journal of Psychology, 15,* 47–53.

Loye, D., Gorney, R., & Steele, G. (1977). An experimental field study. *Journal of Communication, 27,* 206–216.

*McCabe, A. E., & Moriarity, R. J. (1977, March). A laboratory/field study of television violence and aggression in children's sports. Paper presented at the biennial meeting of the Society for Research in Child Development, New Orleans, LA.

McGuire, W. J. (1985). Attitudes and attitude change. In G. Lindzey & E. Aronson (Eds.), *Handbook of social psychology* (3rd ed., Vol. 2, pp. 233–346). New York: Random House.

McGuire, W. J. (1986). The myth of massive media impact: Savagings and salvagings. In G. Comstock (Ed.), *Public communication and behavior* (Vol. 1, pp. 173–257). San Diego, CA: Academic Press.

Melburg, V., & Tedeschi, J. T. (1989). Displaced aggression: Frustration or impression management? *European Journal of Social Psychology, 19,* 139–145.

Milgram, S., & Shotland, R. L. (1973). *Television and antisocial behavior: Field experiments.* San Diego, CA: Academic Press.

Mook, D. G. (1983). In defense of external invalidity. *American Psychologists, 38,* 379–387.

National Television Violence Study (1998). Thousand Oaks: Sage.

Orford, J. (1986). The rules of interpersonal complementarity: Does hostility beget hostility and dominance, submission? *Psychological Review, 93,* 365–377.

Paik, H., & Comstock, G. (1994). The effects of television violence on antisocial behavior: A meta-analysis. *Communication Research, 21,* 516–546.

*Parke, R. D., Berkowitz, L., Leyens, J. P., West, S. G. & Sebastian, R. J. (1977). Some effects of violent and nonviolent movies on the behavior of juvenile delinquents. In L. Berkowitz (Ed.), *Advances in experimental social psychology* (Vol. 10, pp. 135–172). San Diego, CA: Academic Press.

*Potts, C. R., Huston, A. C., & Wright, J. C. (1986). Effects of television form and content on boy's attention and social behavior. *Journal of Experimental Child Psychology, 41,* 1–17.

Prentice, D. A., & Miller, D. T. (1992). When small effects are impressive. *Psychological Bulletin, 112,* 160–164.

Rhodes, N. D., & Wood, W. (1992). Self-esteem and intelligence affect influenceability: The mediating role of message reception. *Psychological Bulletin, 111,* 156–171.

Richard, F. D., Bond, C. F., & Stokes-Zoota, J. J. (2003). One hundred years of social psychology quantitatively described. *Review of General Psychology, 7,* 331–363.

Roberts, D. F., & Maccoby, N. (1985). Effects of mass communication. In G. Lindzey & E. Aronson (Eds.), *Handbook of social psychology* (3rd ed., Vol. 2, pp. 539–598). New York: Random House.

Rosenthal, R. (1986). Media violence, antisocial-behavior, and the social consequences of small effects. *Journal of Social Issues, 42,* 141–154.

Rosenthal, R. (1994). Parametric measures of effect size. In H. Cooper & L. V. Hedges (Eds.), *Handbook of research synthesis* (pp. 231–244). New York: Russell Sage Foundation.

Rosenthal, R., & Rubin, D. B. (1982). A simple, general purpose display of magnitude of experimental effect. *Journal of Educational Psychology, 74,* 166–169.

*Ross, L. B. (1972). *The effect of aggressive cartoons on the group play of children.* Unpublished doctoral dissertation, Miami University, Oxford, OH.

*Sawin, D. B. (1974). *Aggressive behavior among children in small play group settings with violent television.* Unpublished doctoral dissertation, University of Minnesota, Minneapolis.

*Siegel, A. E. (1956). Film-mediated fantasy aggression and strength of aggressive drive. *Child Development, 27,* 365–378.

*Simonson, H. M. (1992). Interaction effects of television and socioeconomic status on teenage aggression. *International Journal of Adolescence and Youth, 3,* 333–343.

Slater, M. D., Henry, K. L., Swaim, R. C., & Anderson, L. I. (2003). Violent media content and aggressiveness in adolescents. *Communication Research, 30,* 713–736.

*Sprafkin, J., Gadow, K. D., & Grayson, P. (1987). Effects of viewing aggressive cartoons on the behavior of learning disabled children. *Journal of Child Psychiatry, 28,* 387–398.

*Sprafkin, J., Gadow, K. D., & Grayson, P. (1988). Effects of cartoons on emotionally disturbed children's social behavior in school settings. *Journal of Child Psychology, 29,* 91–99.

*Steuer, F. B., Applefield, J. M., & Smith, R. (1971). Televised aggression and the interpersonal aggression of preschool children. *Journal of Experimental Child Psychology, 11,* 442–447.

Wells, W. D. (1973). Television and aggression: Replication of an experimental field study . Unpublished manuscript, University of Chicago.

Williams, K. R. (1984). Economic sources of homicide: Reestimating the effects of poverty and inequality. *American Sociological Review, 49,* 283–289.

Wood, W., & Christensen, P. N. (2004). Quantitative research synthesis across studies, paradigms, and time. In C. Sansone, C. C. Morf, & A. T. Panter (Eds.), *Handbook of methods in social psychology* (pp. 335–356). Thousand Oaks, CA: Sage

Wood, W., Wong, F. Y., & Chachere, J. G. (1991). Effects of media violence on viewers' aggression in unconstrained social interaction. *Psychological Bulletin, 109,* 371–383.

11

The Effects of
Advertising on Children
and Adolescents:
A Meta-Analysis

Roger Desmond
University of Hartford

Rod Carveth
Marywood University

The power of advertising to elicit consumer behavior in children and adolescents is the second most investigated problem in the literature on communication and behavior. Second only to the links between TV viewing and aggression in terms of the volume of published research, advertising effects occupy research professionals in communication, medicine, psychology, marketing, economics, nursing, and a number of other disciplines. However, there is no consensus among researchers regarding the role of advertising in children's consumer behavior.

Despite this lack of consensus among scholars, strong claims for powerful advertising effects are common. For example, one analysis suggested the potent effects of advertising in this manner: "Collectively, these studies provide compelling evidence that cigarette advertisements are seen by adolescents and that they respond to the advertiser's intent. Some health experts therefore, now believe that cigarette advertising is causally linked to smoking behavior" (Fischer, Schwartz, Richards, Goldstein, & Rojas, 1991, p. 3146). Another, more direct statement of causality (based on correlational data, however) asserted: "Tobacco marketing campaigns between 1988 and 1997 are responsible for 6 million adolescents experimenting with cigarettes. Of those, 2.6 million kids took their first puffs as a result of the Joe Camel campaign; another 1.4 million tried smoking because of the Marlboro campaign" (Thorp, 1998).

In the popular press, a major role for advertising in various domains of child and adolescent socialization is commonly claimed. Such claims for robust advertising effects extend from the recent concerns about smoking, drinking, and drug use to a pronounced acceptance of advertising as a force that elicits greater consumer demand for all products, including toys, snack foods, and athletic equipment (Amaral, 1998).

Even though the debate about advertising effects on children and adolescents continues in the academic community, the press, politicians, and many of the therapeutic community are more vocal in their certainty of the power of advertising than are those who conduct research.

REVIEW OF THE LITERATURE

A variety of research reviews have appeared in the literature at several moments in history. Early reviews typically concluded that advertising generates moderate to strong effects on young TV viewers (Sheikh, Prasad, & Rao, 1974; Feschbach, Dillman & Jordan, 1979; Rossiter, 1977). The two aspects of child susceptibility most frequently addressed are (a) the outcomes of advertising on children's attitudes and behavior and (b) comprehension of commercials (i.e., do children understand the persuasive intent of commercials and can they distinguish them from programs?). These early reviews generally concluded that children younger than ages 7 or 8 experience difficulty identifying commercials and are therefore more susceptible to advertising appeals than are adults. Another recurring finding in the early reviews is that advertising elicits product requests by young children. A number of studies included in the reviews suggested a high degree of parental yielding to product requests, especially if parents were not product users (e.g., breakfast cereals).

As research on advertising and children became more frequent and more sophisticated in the 1980s and 1990s, literature reviews became more qualified and narrower in scope than they had been previously. In a review of advertising effects literature from the 1980s, Van Evra (1998, p. 97) stated: "Even when they are able to discern differences between programs and ads, however, young children still show very limited knowledge of the commercials and their purpose." She also found that 8- to 14-year-olds are more susceptible to celebrity endorsements than are their older counterparts, especially when celebrities are used in live action commercials. As is the case with the majority of literature reviews in this area, the paraphrased general conclusion is that advertising has powerful effects on the consumer behavior of young children and adolescents. These effects are powerful because (a) commercials directed to children use powerful multimedia techniques to attract attention, (b) children have less ability to discriminate between commercials and programs than do adults, and (c) children have not developed adult cynicism about advertising, nor do they possess the critical viewing skills that adults gain by experience.

Unnikrishnan and Bajpai (1996) presented a review of advertising and children studies from several nations and used the review to design an 8-month study of how television would affect a large sample of Indian children and adolescents aged 3 to 15. Their conclusion from reviewing relevant literature and from a qualitative and quantitative study of 730 research participants was summarized as, "Our experience with these children strongly indicates that their innocence and lack of defenses against the influence of advertising make them particularly easy prey" (p. 164). Throughout the study, many similar pronouncements of strong effects are found, but evidence for them came from personal interviews of an introspective nature.

Although both selective and comprehensive reviews of research literature may contribute to a greater understanding of advertising effects, both of these traditional approaches pose limitations for policy analysts. In the scientific debates about the dangers of second-hand cigarette smoke, policy was made on the basis of 33 studies, only 17 of which showed a positive and significant relationship between second-hand tobacco smoke and lung diseases. Two studies found negative relationships and in the remaining investigations, the $p > .05$ significance level was abandoned in favor of a $p > .10$ level. Nevertheless, partisan research analysts pronounced a clear causal relationship, and the conclusion became canon. In fact, in July 1998, federal judge William Osteen threw out the findings of the Environmental Protection Agency (EPA) study, citing: "EPA's study selection is disturbing. First, there is evidence in the record supporting the accusation that EPA 'cherry picked' its data. Second, EPA's excluding nearly half of the available studies directly conflicts with EPA's purported purpose for analyzing the epidemiological studies and conflicts with EPA's Risk Assessment Guidelines." (Federal Ruling, 1998; U.S. Environmental Protection Agency, 1992).

THE META-ANALYSIS

The most effective research technique for assessing the size of an effect in an area in which considerable social scientific research has been conducted is meta-analysis, the measurement of effect sizes across a large body of investigations. The procedure also permits the investigator to determine whether those effect sizes are homogeneous or variable across studies. Meta-analysis reduces potential bias from time periods that may indicate shifts in effects in the population, that is, if television industry policies over time render children more or less susceptible to advertising effects, the investigation of time period as a moderator variable should reveal the bias.

A search of the advertising effects literature yielded one published meta-analysis of an important aspect of advertising effects, children's understanding of the *informative* and *persuasive intent* of television advertising (Martin, 1997). The author analyzed 23 published articles that met data-reporting criteria for inclusion and found an effect size of $r = .37$ between advertising exposure and understanding advertising intent, which has long been used as a proxy for other advertising effects in the research tradition. Because homogeneity across studies was not found, a search for possible moderator variables was conducted. A significant moderator effect was found for *year of publication,* in that studies published before 1984 had a much larger effect size than those published after that year (from an average of .40 to .17), indicating an increase in children's understanding of intent in more recent investigations. The author suggested that regulatory shifts in industry policy were responsible for the shift, including the elimination of host selling, elimination of program-length commercials, and after a brief period of deregulation from 1984 to 1990, the introduction of the Children's Television Act of 1990, which reinforced the ban on program-length commercials and reduced total nonprogram time in the hours most frequently watched by children.

In the present study, we sought to investigate the effect sizes of studies published after 1984 that were designed to investigate the more direct dimensions of advertising: comprehension of advertising by children and adolescents, attitude toward advertised products, and changes in consumer behavior elicited by advertising. Even though vast numbers of advertising studies were published in the 1970s and early 1980s, we chose to examine more recent studies because of (a) the regulatory shifts described by Martin's (1997) analysis; (b) the increased methodological sophistication of more recent research, using multivariate designs and dependent measures other than perception of intent; and (c) the enormous organized media education efforts by a number of public and private agencies in recent years designed to increase children's critical evaluation of advertising.

Research Questions

In this meta-analysis we addressed the following questions:

Do studies assessing the persuasive effects of advertising among children and adolescents demonstrate a large effect size?

Do the studies share a common effect size; that is, are they homogeneous? If not, what study characteristics (moderators) account for the variance in effect size across studies?

Methodology

Literature Search

The literature search was conducted using a variety of electronic databases deemed relevant for the investigation (*Communication Abstracts,* ERIC, PsycLIT, SocInfo, Nexis, and EBSCOhost). Studies included had to contain some measure of advertising exposure (either experimentally controlled or by self-report) and some measure of effect (attitudes toward the brand, product selection, etc.). Tables 11.1, 11.2, and 11.3 contain a list of studies included in this analysis.

Studies were excluded if they focused on issues about the content of the ads or policy implications of advertising and children or did not include a specific and/or consistent measure of advertising exposure. For example, DiFranza et al.'s 1991 study of the recognition of Joe Camel was excluded, because there was no comparative measure of advertising exposure. Additionally, Robertson et al.'s 1989 study of advertising effects across cultures was excluded, because the measure of advertising exposure was not consistent (television exposure within each culture was used as a measure of advertising exposure; the number of ads and even type of ads vary across the four cultures studied).

Statistical Analysis

The statistical analysis involves three basic sets: (a) conversion to a common metric, (b) averaging the estimates, and (c) examining the degree of variability in the data set. In this meta-analysis we used the metric of the correlation coefficient because of the ease of statistical manipulation and interpretation of information. The individual effects were averaged using a procedure that weighted the study by size of the sample. The procedures used in this analysis are those outlined by Hunter and Schmidt (2004). Studies were grouped into three cate-

TABLE 11.1
Studies

Authors	Sample Size	Correlation
Austin & Freeman (1997)	137	.156
Austin & Mieli (1994)	154	.070
Boush, Friestad, & Rose (1994)	426	.304
Brand & Greenberg (1994)	827	.089
Gorn & Florsheim (1985)	70	.200
Gorn & Goldberg (1987)	228	.111
Lee & Browne (1995)	161	.393
Martin (1997) (Study 1)	40	.233
Martin (1997) (Study 2)	40	.427
Martin & Gentry (1997)	268	.152
Martin & Kennedy (1993)	144	.111
Meier (1991)	1085	.179
Pechmann & Ratneshwar (1994)	304	.134
Phelps & Hoy (1996)	111	.122
Silverman, Jaccard, & Burke (1988)	56	.197
Wyllie & Zhang (1998)	500	.130

TABLE 11.2
Comprehension Studies

Authors	Sample Size	Correlation
Austin & Johnson (1997)	225	.156
Collins (1990)	266	.101
Fischer et al. (1991)	229	.105
Goldberg (1990)	483	.202
Grube & Wallack (1994)	468	.233
Macklin (1987) (Study 1)	40	.109
Macklin (1987) (Study 2)	40	.042
Prasad & Smith (1994)	95	.055
Slater, Rouner, Beauvais, Van Leuven, & Rodriguez (1996)	408	.174
Wilson & Weiss (1992)	94	.134

TABLE 11.3
Product Selection (Behavior) Studies

Authors	Sample Size	Correlation
Butter, Weikel, Otto, Wright, & Deinzer (1991) (Study 1)	115	.088
Butter et al. (1991) (Study 2)	234	.128
Connelly & Caswell (1994)	500	.363
Dawson, Jeffrey, & Walsh (1988)	80	.327
Goldberg (1990)	483	.169
Gorn & Goldberg (1987)	228	.112
Slater et al. (1996)	157	.174
While et al. (1996)	833	.020

gories: (a) advertising effects on comprehension, (b) advertising effects on attitudes, and (c) advertising effects on product consumption.

Results

Advertising Effects on Attitudes

The results indicate that exposure to advertising affects attitudes toward brands and ads (average $r = .153$, $k = 16$, $N = 4,551$). An analysis of the variability demonstrates that the observed average effects is based on a sample of correlations that is heterogeneous [$\chi^2(15, N = 4,551) = 32.92, p < .05$]. This result indicates the probable existence of a moderator variable.

Further examination indicated that two studies (Austin & Freeman, 1997; Lee & Browne, 1995) utilized exclusively African-American samples. Deleting these two studies from our sample resulted in an average $r = .140$ ($k = 14$, $N = 4,253$). Confidence intervals for attitudes are $.039 < r < .249$. A test of significant differences between the African-American samples versus the others revealed a significant difference, $Z = 3.74$, $p < .001$. The revised analysis of variability shows that the observed average effects is based on a sample of correlations that is homogeneous [$\chi^2(13, N = 4,253) = 19.49$, $p > .05$]. Thus, race is a possible moderator variable in the relationship of advertising exposure to brand/advertising-related attitudes.

Advertising Effects on Comprehension

The results indicate that exposure to advertising improves comprehension of brands advertised (average $r = .175$, $k = 10$, $N = 2,431$). Confidence intervals for comprehension are $.051 < r < .229$. An analysis of the variability demonstrates that the observed average effects is based on a sample of correlations that is homogeneous ($\chi^2[(9), N = 2431] = 7.42$, ns). Consequently, no moderator variable appears to be present.

Advertising Effects on Product Selection (Behavior)

The results here indicate that exposure to advertising leads to greater selection of the product advertised (average $r = .154$, $k = 8$, $N = 2,630$). An analysis of the variability demonstrates that the observed average effects is based on a sample of correlations that is heterogeneous ($\chi^2[(7), N = 2,630] = 41.35$, $p < .0001$). This result indicates the presence of a probable moderator variable.

Further examination indicated that two studies (Connelly & Caswell, 1994; While, Kelly, & Huang, 1996) utilized exclusively international samples. Deleting these two studies from our sample resulted in an average $r = .155$ ($k = 6$, $N = 1,297$). The revised analysis of variability shows that the observed average effects is based on a sample of correlations that is homogeneous ($\chi^2[(5), N = 1,297] = 3.81$, ns). Confidence intervals for behavior are $.025 < r < .285$. Thus, country of origin of the sample is a possible moderator variable in the relationship of advertising exposure to product selection behavior.

Summary of Results

Overall, the results here indicate that advertising exposure results in more positive associations with the brands advertised, increases brand comprehension, and leads young consumers to select the products advertised. However, these effects are small, representing 1.96%, 3.06%, and 2.40% of the variance explained, respectively. Hence, the concern of critics of an all-powerful effect of advertising on children and adolescents appears to be unwarranted.

In addition, the discovery of two moderator variables in our analyses (race and country of origin of the sample) suggests that researchers in the area of advertising and children consider the influence of these two variables. For example, research has consistently indicated that African-American children and adolescents watch more television than children from other demographic groups and thus have more consistent exposure to advertising. In addition, income and race have been shown to have a consistent relationship to one another, so not only are African-American children more likely to be exposed to television advertising but they are also less likely to have other sources of diversion (e.g., magazines or computers) in their homes to lessen the influence of such advertising.

In terms of international samples, researchers may need to beware of how the results in other countries compare with those in the United States. The number and types of ads allowed, as well as the prevalence of certain advertising formats over others, may mean that comparing the effects of advertising with U.S. samples to the effects of advertising with international samples may be comparing apples to oranges.

Discussion

The relatively low correlation coefficient indicates that advertising has a statistically significant, but practically insignificant, effect on children's brand comprehension, attitudes, and purchase behavior. This finding flies in the face of research on exposure to media, which indicates that the average 18-year-old has already watched 22,000 hours of television (significantly more than the 12,000 hours spent in school), including 350,000 commercials. Our findings suggest that advertising is less powerful than its critics fear. One reason that advertising lacks the perceived power of its critics is that consumers understand its purpose: persuasion. They know that sellers compose advertising messages to sell products, and they understand that those messages will inevitably emphasize the positive aspects of the product. As a result, they do not trust advertising. Even second graders understand that the goal of advertising is to sell a product, and by ages 11 or 12, children are as skeptical of advertising as are adults. Whether directed to children or adults, advertising is not subtly manipulating defenseless consumers. Rather, it is battling to overcome entrenched skepticism. Consumers, of course, also have sources of information other than advertising, such as news media and opinion leaders (including young peers).

In the past decade, media education inspired by a loose knit but effective media literacy movement across the United States has demonstrated that when children are educated about advertising, they become more critical consumers of its content (Kubey, 1998). School districts, religious organizations, and even the HBO network, with its "Buy Me That" series, have had a demonstrable impact on consumer socialization, and the results of this study offer more support for the efficacy of consumer education.

The moderator variable of race was a surprising but not unprecedented result. Several studies have found that black children are less critical of television advertising than are white children and that they are less able to perceive the persuasive intent of TV commercials (Donohue, 1975; Condry, 1989). The analysis of the race moderator in this investigation simply shows that black children are more variable as a group in their comprehension of advertising than are their white counterparts.

The moderator variable of international citizenship was another unexpected result. The best strategy for future research and for policy recommendations is to avoid cross-national samples in advertising research in light of possible differences in scheduling, commercial placement, and other differences that mitigate comparison.

Finally, today's children and adolescents are exposed to more advertising from more sources than they were in the 1970s and 1980s. Children now are born into a universe that includes cable and satellite TV, the Internet, and other new media. Thus, the impact of any specific ad (as was typical of protocols used in earlier studies) may be reduced.

Attacks on advertising will probably remain a part of the political landscape. The target is highly visible, and 70% of consumers are skeptical about it to begin with. Blaming advertising for what ails us is therefore likely to remain a recurring theme. Regulating advertising may do little to correct the problem, but it can demonstrate concern for the issue.

REFERENCES

References marked with an asterisk indicate studies included in the meta-analysis.

Amaral, J. (1998, May 21). Keep Channel One out of schools. *Providence (R.I.) Journal-Bulletin,* 7b.

Austin, E., & Freeman, C. (1997). Effects of media, parents and peers on African American adolescents' efficacy toward the media and the future. *Howard Journal of Communications, 8,* 275–290.

*Austin, E., & Johnson, K. (1997). Effects of general and alcohol-specific media literacy training on children's decision making about alcohol. *Journal of Health Communication, 2,* 17–43.

*Austin, E. W., & Meili, H. (1994). Effects of interpretations of televised alcohol portrayals on children's alcohol beliefs. *Journal of Broadcasting and Electronic Media, 34,* 417–435.

*Boush, D., Friestad, M., & Rose, G. (1994). Adolescent skepticism toward TV advertising and knowledge of advertiser tactics. *Journal of Consumer Research, 21,* 165–174.

*Brand, J., & Greenberg, B. (1994). Commercials in the classroom: The impact of Channel One advertising. *Journal of Advertising Research, 34*(1), 18–28.

*Butter, E., Weikel, K., Otto, V., Wright, K., & Deinzer, G. (1991). TV advertising of OTC medicines and its effects on child viewers. *Psychology and Marketing, 8*(2), 117–129.

*Collins, C. (1990). Television and primary schoolchildren in Northern Ireland: The impact of advertising. *Journal of Educational Television, 16,* 23–40.

Condry, J. (1989). *The psychology of television.* Hillsdale, NJ: Lawrence Erlbaum Associates.

*Connolly, G., & Caswell, S. (1994). Alcohol in the mass media and drinking by adolescents. *Addiction, 89,* 1255–1264.

*Dawson, B., Jeffrey, D. B., & Walsh, J. (1988). Television food commercials' effect on children's resistance to temptation. *Journal of Applied Social Psychology, 18,* 1353–1360.

Difranza, J., Richards, J., Paulman, P., Wolf-Gillespie, N., Fletcher, C., Jaffe, R., & Murray, D. (1991). RJR Nabisco's cartoon camel promotes Camel cigarettes to children. *Journal of the American Medical Association, 266,* 3149–3153.

Donohue, T. (1975). Effect of commercials on black children. *Journal of Advertising Research, 15*(6), 41–47.

Federal ruling overturning EPA report on environmental tobacco smoke should cause re-evaluation of smoking bans and restrictions (1998, July 13). Retrieved March 7, 2004, from http://www. speakup.org/re072098.html.

Feschbach, N., Dillman, A. & Jordan, T. (1979) Children and television advertising: Some research and some perspectives. *Journal of Clinical Child Psychology, 8,* 26-31.

*Fischer, M., Schwartz, P., Richards, J., Goldstein, A., & Rojas, T. (1991). Brand logo recognition by children aged 3 to 6 years. Mickey Mouse and Old Joe the Camel. *Journal of the American Medical Association, 266,* 3145–3148.

*Goldberg, M. (1990). A quasi-experiment assessing the effectiveness of TV advertising directed to children. *Journal of Marketing Research, 22,* 445–454.

*Gorn, G., & Florsheim, R. (1985). The effects of commercials for adult products on children. *Journal of Consumer Research, 11,* 962–967.

Greenberg, B., & Brand, J. (1994). Commercials in the classroom: The impact of Channel One advertising. *Journal of Advertising Research, 34,* 18–27

*Grube, J., & Wallack, L. D. (1994). Television beer advertising and drinking knowledge, beliefs and intentions among schoolchildren. *American Journal of Public Health, 84,* 254–260.

Hunter, J. & Schmidt, F. (2004). (2nd. Ed.) Methods of meta-analysis: Correcting error and bias in research findings. Los Angeles: Sage.

Kubey, R. (1998). Obstacles to the development of media education in the united states. *Journal of Communication, 48,* 58-70.

*Lee, E., & Browne, L. (1995). Effects of television advertising on African American teenagers. *Journal of Black Studies, 25,* 523–536.

*Macklin, M. C. (1987). Preschoolers' understanding of the informational function of television advertising. *Journal of Consumer Research, 14,* 229–239.

*Martin, M. (1997). Children's understanding of the intent of advertising: A meta-analysis. *Journal of Public Policy and Marketing, 16,* 205–216.

*Martin, M., & Gentry, J. (1997). Stuck in the model trap: The effects of beautiful models in ads on female pre-adolescents and adolescents. *Journal of Marketing, 26,* 19–33.

*Martin, M., & Kennedy, P. (1993). Advertising and social comparison: Consequences for female preadolescents and adolescents. *Psychology and Marketing, 10,* 513–530.

Meier, K. (1991). Tobacco truths: The impact of role models on children's attitudes toward smoking. *Health Education Quarterly, 18,* 173–183.

*Pechmann, C., & Ratneshwar, S. (1994). The effects of antismoking and cigarette advertising on young adolescents' perceptions of peers who smoke. *Journal of Consumer Research, 21,* 236–251.

*Phelps, J., & Hoy, M. (1996). The Aad-Ab-PI relationship in children: The impact of brand familiarity and measurement timing. *Psychology and Marketing, 13,* 77–105.

*Prasad, V., & Smith, L. (1994). Television commercials in violent programming: An experimental evaluation of their effects on children. *Journal of the Academy of Marketing Sciences, 22,* 340–351.

Robertson, T., Ward, S., Gatignon, H., & Klees, S. (1989). Advertising and children: A cross-cultural study. *Communication Research, 16,* 459–481.

Rossiter, T. S. (1977). Children's responsiveness to commercials. *Journal of Communication, 27,* 101–116.

Sheikh, A. A., Prasad, V. K., & Rao, T. R. (1974). Children's TV commercial: A review of research. *Journal of Communication, 24,* 126–136.

*Silverman, W., Jaccard, J., & Burke, A. (1988). Children's attitudes toward products and recall of product information over time. *Journal of Experimental Children Psychology, 45,* 365–381.

*Slater, M., Rouner, D., Beauvais, F., Van Leuven, J., & Rodriguez, M. (1996, July). Male adolescents reactions to TV beer advertisements: The effects of sports content and program context. *Journal of Studies on Alcohol,* 425–433.

Thorp, J. (1998, August 3). Research shows cigarette campaigns will be responsible for 600,000 smoking related deaths. *PR Newswire.* Retrieved Sept. 19, 2000, from: http://media.prnewswire.com/en/jsp/

U.S. Environmental Protection Agency (1992, December). *Respiratory health effects of passive smoking: Lung cancer and other disorders* (Publication EPA/600/6–90/006F). Washington, DC: U.S. Government Printing Office.

Unnikrishnan, N., & Bajpai, S. (1996). *The impact of television advertising on children.* Thousand Oaks, CA: Sage.

Van Evra, J. (1995). Advertising's impact on children as a function of viewing purpose. *Psychology and Marketing, 12,* 423–432.

Van Evra, J. (1998) Television and child development (2nd. Ed.). Mahwah, N.J.: Lawrence Erlbaum Associates.

*While, D., Kelly, S., & Huang, W. (1996). Cigarette advertising and onset of smoking in children. *British Medical Journal, 7504,* 398–401.

*Wilson, B., & Weiss, A. (1992). Developmental differences in children's reactions to a toy advertisement linked to a toy-based cartoon. *Journal of Broadcasting and Electronic Media, 36,* 371–394.

*Wyllie, A., & Zhang, G. (1998). Responses to television advertising associated with drinking behavior of 10–17 yr. olds. *Addiction, 93,* 361–372.

12

Effects of Sexually Explicit Media

Norbert Mundorf
University of Rhode Island

Mike Allen
University of Wisconsin–Milwaukee

Dave D'Alessio
University of Connecticut

Tara M. Emmers-Sommer
University of Arizona

The potential antisocial impact of sexually explicit material has concerned modern mass media scholars. The governments of the United States, Canada, Great Britain, Australia, and South Africa have all commissioned official investigations, taking the available literature into consideration. The prevailing concern is that exposure to pornography may constitute a factor in the commission of sexual crimes (rape, incest, pedophilia, etc.). While the pornography industry invokes freedom of the press, such entertainment material may constitute a source of danger to the public. If sexually explicit material generates negative social consequences identified through social scientific investigations, then legislative or judicial bodies may consider whether some type of restriction or limitation is warranted.

Pornography is defined as "media material used or intended to increase sexual arousal." This definition, in some form, is one used in previous meta-analytic summarizations (Allen, D'Alessio, & Brezgel, 1995a; Allen, D'Alessio, & Emmers-Sommers, 1997; Allen, D'Alessio, Emmers, & Gebhardt, 1996; Allen, Emmers, Gebhardt, & Giery, 1995; Hall, Shondrick, & Hirschman, 1993; Lalumiere & Quinsey, 1994; Paik & Comstock, 1994). The definition employs a functional approach to material by considering how a consumer chooses material. The argument is that such material is created, selected, and consumed to fulfill some purpose. A functional definition is contrasted with some type of structural definition that would define pornographic materials as the display of particular content (sexual acts) or body parts (e.g., breasts, penis, etc.). A functional definition means that material can serve as pornographic for some audiences and not others because of differing sexual practices. A functional definition also allows one to ask the question of how content is used by the audience rather than to seek to understand some aspect of effect that is inherent in the display of some material. The problem with a functional definition is the deficiency such an approach has for policymaking. The inability to specify the particular content that generates a specific outcome does not generate a corresponding basis for any type of limitation that a legislative or judicial body would find acceptable. For scientific purposes, such a definition not only is acceptable, but such an approach is also preferable because it allows one to seek an understanding between conceptual entities (variables) rather than the concrete and unchanging quantities (constants) that a structural definition requires.

The implications for theoretical understanding and practical outcome consider such choices for content and the function that such material serves for the consumer. The next section outlines the three dominant theoretical perspectives used to assess the impact of sexual materials (social learning, excitation transfer, and social cognition). Each perspective indicates that sexual materials offer the consumer a vicarious experience that serves as the basis for social behavior. The critical feature is an understanding of how a mediated event, represented as fantasy, could serve as the basis for a type of behavior for an individual. The theories offer explanations and understanding of the relationship between media representations and corresponding real life activities.

THEORETICAL CONSIDERATIONS

Social Learning

Social learning theory argues that the media serve as a basis of vicarious experience that the person uses to form his or her own judgments. Bandura (1973, 1977) argued that the key is a determination of the experience as negative (punishing) or positive (rewarding). The learning is based on the function that the representation provides for the individuals viewing the material. Media events provide an unambiguous representation of the lesson with simple and direct connections between events. The characters in the media portray how actions can generate personal or social rewards and serve as role models to imitate.

For sexually inexperienced college students, pornography serves as a source of information (Bryant & Brown, 1989; Duncan, 1990; Duncan & Donnelly, 1991; Duncan & Nicholson, 1991). Mediated sexual representations may serve as the first experience that a person has with sexual behavior. The sexual representation not only serves as a source of information about the physical aspects of sexual behavior but also may provide information on the social parts of sexual behavior. When the material depicts coercive sexual activity and suggests that persons have motivations and reactions to behavior, the consumer may learn about the process of sexual behavior and how persons interact and the appropriateness of various sexual interactions.

The process of identification serves as a link between the consumer of the mass media and the depictions of the character. Identification provides an empathic link for the rewards and punishments received by the character and the viewer. The consumer shares the pain, joy, and outcome of the person in the material. In sexually explicit material, the actions (and subsequent rewards) are shared by the consumer. If a consumer finds that the model of sexual behavior constitutes a rewarding experience, the consumer may wish to imitate that behavior. The link between the experience of a vicarious fantasy and the desire to live that fantasy may be important for sexual behavior. The consumer learns how the main character (typically a male) finds sexual rewards by participation in various sexual encounters. If these encounters are sexually coercive or women are treated as simply objects of sexual gratification, than the consumer is "learning" how successful characters receive rewards in sexual encounters. The identification with such a character may generate the desire by the consumer to imitate the character and receive the same rewards depicted by the content of the mass media.

Some social learning theorists argue that it is not the sexual content of the material but rather the violence associated with the sexual material that is the source of the harm (Donnerstein, 1984). Allen et al. (1995) argued that the theory provides for a cue hypothesis, that the violence in the material serves as a social cue that links sexual behavior with coercion. If the link between sexual material and violent content is the source of the antisocial outcome, then the harms would be demonstrated on the basis of content of the material. For example, investigations utilizing violent material should demonstrate a positive association between exposure and antisocial outcomes. However, nonviolent sexual materials should demonstrate no negative consequences as a result of exposure. This version of the social learning theory argues that the negative consequences of sexually explicit material are based on particular associations between content within the material rather than for some generalized effect for sexual materials. The learning in this version simply is the paired association (not between a bell and the serving of meat) between the sexual content and violent or coercive behavior.

Social learning theory is an argument for the vicarious nature of experience serving as a guide for behavior. Even if the association is based on the connection of various content, the experience still provides a vicarious event from which the consumer learns and applies to his or her own life. Social learning theory provides a content-based explanation; that focus requires an examination between the content of the media and how such content is translated ultimately into the actions of the consumer.

Excitation Transfer

Zillmann, Hoyt, and Day (1974) argued that "the observed effects of aggressive communication are not so much the consequences of exposure to aggressive stimuli per se as they are the result of excitatory potential associated with these communications" (p. 286). The theory suggests that media material viewed while a person is in a state of provocation, for example, can translate into action when the person is given an opportunity to act and the state of excitement is transferred. The key to the transfer and the subsequent action is that pornographic material translates into aggression because the material creates arousal not because the material involves sexual content (Zillmann, Bryant, Comisky, & Medoff, 1981).

The typical design of the investigations involving excitation transfer and sexual material involves the following: (a) make the participant angry, (b) show the person a sexually explicit film to create increased physiological arousal, and (c) then, finally, create an opportunity for the participant to behave aggressively against the target of the anger. A comparison is made to a group that is not angered (condition a). The distinction is that the second group should not demonstrate the same level of aggression because that group of participants was not angered before exposure to the sexual material. The transfer occurs because the anger is what cognitively frames the arousal felt when the sexually explicit material is viewed. The subsequent situation provides the ability to act out the provocation in the context of the physiological cue provided by the sexually explicit material. By contrast, the level of aggression is lower without the prior anger because the cognitive frame for the arousal (the anger) is not present when the sexually explicit material is viewed.

Sexually explicit materials are designed for sexual arousal and are successful in generating high levels of physiological arousal (Allen & D'Alessio, 1993). But excitation transfer theory is not simply a theory that linearly relates the level of arousal to the outcome. Instead, the arousal only increases aggression if the material is viewed by a person in a psychological state that provides a mediating condition termed as pleasant or irritating and becomes the basis for later application to behavior. The meta-analysis of Allen et al. (1996) that examined the theoretical aspects in detail showed ambiguous support for the theory. The results reported in this update of that analysis do not provide all of the detailed subanalyses, and the reader is referred to the earlier report for more details relating to the analysis of this theory.

COGNITIVE CONSIDERATIONS

Even though the facilitation of aggression resulting from exposure to SEM is troubling, most males will not engage in sexual violence. However, the impact on views and attitudes towards human relations is also relevant, because it has the potential to impact male-female relations on a broader base. SEM exposure has been related to attitudes towards rape, having children, happiness with one's sex life, the desire to have children as well as frequency estimates of others' sexual behaviors (Zillmann & Bryant, 1988). Such distortions may be partially explained through arousal and modelling considerations, but other cognitive processes come into play, as well. Most pornography is nonviolent, featuring consenting, if overly eager, adults. What aspect of this type of content leads to undesirable attitudes?

Weaver (1987) explains the findings resulting from nonviolent as well as violent SEM from a social cognition perspective: This theoretical approach posits that people create social categories or schemata to simplify perception of complex relationships and to facilitate processing of new information. New information is then put into existing categories based on perceived similarities. When a category is repeatedly activated, category differences are "exaggerated and distorted" (p. 31). These categories form the basis for social judgments and influence behaviors. Such social judgments are typically not subject to extensive search and reflexion. Instead, they often follow a 'rule of thumb,' based on recently activated categories (Sherman & Corty, 1984). One of these categories is female sexual promiscuity, the tendency to categorize women in 'good girls/bad girls,' permissive/restrictive, etc. Exposure to SEM not only activates this category, but it also appears to exaggerate perceptions of female permissiveness.

Leonard and Taylor (1983) found that men had significantly more aggressive responses towards a confederate who exhibited *permissive cues* displaying eager sexual openness compared to men in other conditions. They explain this effect based on the more callous reactions of subjects whose aggressive responses towards a permissive confederate were disinhibited. Weaver compared the impact of different portrayals on recommended incarceration in a mock rape trial. He found by far the strongest reduction after exposure to sexual material featuring insatiable, indiscriminate women (37%), more so than 'rape and terror,' (28%) and far more than 'lover's sex' (11%). The first condition is typical for most SEM. It should be noted, that the effect was strongest for nonviolent pornography. Apparently, the portrayal of women as nymphomaniacs rather typical for this genre leads viewers to a generalized view of women as sexually nondiscriminating, which makes rape a more excuseable offense. Terrorization of women as found in slasher films such as "Toolbox Murders" also had a strong impact. The type of portrayal in nonviolent erotica contributed a sizeable difference: the type of portrayal found in the 'nymphomaniac' condition is more likely to trigger perceptions associated with promiscuity and related social judgments. Socially cognitive reasoning can also explain the impact of SEM on attitudes towards relationships, marriage, and the desire to have children (Zillmann & Bryant, 1988). Cognitions activated by the free-spirited, varied sexual encounters in SEM will produce a sharp contrast versus the restrictions, commitment and responsibilities associated with family and relationships and make the latter appear as particularly limiting. In fact, they can even lead to trivialization of rape as a criminal offense not only for males, but even for females exposed to nonviolent pornography (Zillmann & Bryant, 1982).

In their meta-analysis, Oddone-Paolucci, Genuis, and Violato (2000) found robust effects of pornography exposure in four different outcome areas (which relate to all three theoretical approaches discussed here), specifically *sexual deviancy, sexual perpetration, attitudes towards intimate relationships, and belief in the rape myth.* It is expected that the current chapter will further add to the understanding of such effects.

METHODS

Literature Search

This project represents nearly a decade of literature collection in which more than 2,200 manuscripts have been amassed for examination. These manuscripts were assembled through examination of various computer and manual indexes of material (ComIndex, ERIC, Index to Legal Periodicals, Medline, PsycINFO, PsycLIT, and *Sociological Abstracts*). A copy of the complete bibliography is available from the second author. The results of this section reflect an updated analysis since the publication of the original articles (Allen et al., 1995; Allen et al., 1996; Allen, Emmers, et al., 1995). Meta-analysis is an ongoing process and estimates gain in accuracy as more material becomes available for inclusion.

Statistical Analysis

The analysis was conducted using the Hunter–Schmidt form of meta-analysis (Hunter & Schmidt, 1990). The analysis provides for the generation of an average effect, weighted by sample size. The other part of the statistical analysis is the examination of whether a moderator variable is present. The test for moderator variables determines whether the differences between individual observations of the associations are the result of sampling error or potentially some moderator variable.[1] If the results are homogeneous, the comparison of the actual variability in the data sets to the expected variability (based on the observed mean effect) will be nonsignificant, as measured by chi-square test. A significant chi-square test indicates that the observed variability in effects is greater than sampling error would expect. Under those conditions a moderator variable may be present and interpretation of the average effect should be cautious.

RESULTS

Attitudinal Effects

This dependent measure in the investigations is an examination of what impact the exposure to pornography has on the attitudes of individuals. The attitudes indicate an acceptance of violence in interpersonal relationships, acceptance of the rape myth, or the belief that sexual relationships are adversarial. A person endorsing such attitudes would believe that violence is an acceptable and expected part of

---

[1]A number of potential moderators exist. This updated analysis for space reasons does not present those analyses. The analysis of moderator variables is currently being undertaken and should be reported in the future. The available analyses referred to in the text provide a more detailed summary of the statistical information as well as additional tests.

sexual relationships and that men should dominate relationships and women should be objectified as sexual objects. Such attitudes are considered antisocial and are usually considered one form of subordination of women. The concern is whether the exposure to sexually explicit materials contributes to the development or serves as a reinforcement to such attitudes. A complete listing of items associated with these scales is found in Burt and Albin (1981).

The studies were divided into those employing experimental and nonexperimental designs. Experimental designs are those investigations that use a design in which the participants are exposed to some material selected by the investigator. The typical experimental design has a number of exposure conditions with participants consuming material of one particular content type. The experimental comparison is the difference between various exposure conditions that are usually randomly assigned. A nonexperimental design is an investigation in which the exposure to sexually explicit materials is self-selected and reported. A survey that asks the type and frequency of material consumed is then correlated with the outcome variables. The nonexperimental investigations demonstrate a small positive effect between reported exposure to sexually explicit materials and acceptance of rape myths (average $r = .056$, $N = 2,020$). The experimental studies report a larger positive effect (average $r = .146$, $N = 2,248$). Both of these summaries indicate a positive association such that increased exposure to sexual materials increases the probability that a person accepts rape myths and interpersonal violence in relationships or views sexual relationships as adversarial (Table 12.1).

These attitudinal effects in experimental settings indicate some potentially useful comparisons when one examines the content of pornography. In experimental studies in which a control condition was compared with nonviolent pornography (average $r = .125$, $k = 7$, $N = 1,048$) or with violent pornography (average $r = .112$, $k = 5$, $N = 719$), the average effects indicated positive correlations. Both of these comparisons demonstrated homogeneous results, indicating the lack of potential moderating conditions. The results indicate little distinction between violent and nonviolent material; that is, violent material did not increase the size of the effect.

Behavioral Effects

Studies examining behavioral effects all employed experimental designs. The investigators had participants consume some form of sexually explicit material and then permitted some situation in which the participant could act aggressively toward another person. The definition of behavioral aggression used includes attempts to harm a person physically, psychologically, or materially. The key to the decision is not whether such harms did in fact occur (usually the harm did not occur) but rather whether the participant believed that the action would generate the particular harm. Some forms of aggression were intended to harm the other person (usually a confederate) by performing some behavior unrelated to the media exposure but occurring soon after exposure to the sexually explicit mater-

TABLE 12.1
Attitudinal Effects

Author	Date	r^2	N	Design
Burt	1980	.094	598	Nonexperiment
Check Study I	1985	.098	431	Experiment
Check Study II		.111	434	Nonexperiment
Demare, Briere, & Lips	1988	.041	198	Nonexperiment
Donnerstein & Berkowitz	1981	.282	60	Experiment
Garcia	1986	−.010	115	Nonexperiment
Herrett	1993	.180	417	Experiment
Krafka	1985	.017	136	Experiment
Linz	1985	.112	99	Experiment
Malamuth	1986	.284	95	Experiment
Malamuth & Ceniti	1986	.000	42	Experiment
Malamuth & Check	1984	.260	74	Experiment
Malamuth & Check	1981a, 1981b	.072	265	Experiment
Malamuth & Check Study I	1985	.207	111	Experiment
Study II	1985	.322	122	Nonexperiment
Malamuth, Haber, & Feshbach	1980	.041	91	Experiment
Mayerson & Taylor	1987	.405	96	Experiment
Mosher	1971	−.080	377	Experiment
Padgett, Brislin-Slutz, & Neal	1989	.092	118	Nonexperiment
		−.308	59	Nonexperiment
		.071	66	Experiment
Smeaton & Bryne	1987	.000	70	Experiment
Stock	1983	.320	75	Experiment
Zillmann, Bryant, Comisky, & Medoff	1981	.175	120	Experiment

[a]A positive correlation indicates that exposure to sexually explicit materials increases the effect.

ial. In many of the investigations (often those examining excitation transfer theory) the participants were provided with provocation against the target.

One issue is whether the size of the effect is related to the level of sexual arousal generated by the material. Those studies reporting a manipulation check, providing an estimate of the level of sexual arousal, were correlated with the size of the aggressive effect reported by the investigation. The correlation between the level of sexual arousal and amount of behavioral aggression was negative ($r = -.13$, $N = 1,438$). The low (and negative) correlation indicates that simply explaining the level of aggression in terms of physiological arousal is not supported. The explanation that the more arousing the material the greater the impact on the consumer is not supported. The connection between exposure to sexual depictions and aggressive behavior is not simply a linear function of the level of sexual arousal.

Analyses were performed to compare the impact of various sexually explicit materials on the basis of the type of content: (a) violent, (b) nonviolent explicit sexual material, and (c) nude pictorials (Table 12.2). Violent sexual material refers to material in which the actions depicted involved either coercion of one of the participants through the use of emotional, psychological, or physical efforts to gain sexual compliance. These efforts are viewed as coercive even if the persons willingly engage in this behavior; for example, sadistic or masochistic sexual behavior would be viewed as violent. Nonviolent material involves consensual

TABLE 12.2
Behavioral Effects

		Nude Pictorials		Stimulus Type Nonviolent		Violent	
Author	Date	r	N	r	N	r	N
Baron	1974a	−.445	36				
Baron	1974b	−.098	40				
Baron	1979	−.338	33	.408	22		
Baron & Bell	1973	−.110	80				
Baron & Bell	1977	−.137	51	−.137	34		
Cantor, Zillman, & Einsiedel	1978			.301	40		
Donnerstein	1980			.143	80	.341	80
Donnerstein & Barrett; Donnerstein & Hallam	1978			.097	72		
Donnerstein & Berkowitz Study I	1981			.000	40	.313	60
Study II				.000	40	.313	60
Donnerstein,Donnerstein, & Evans	1975	.109	54	.316	40		
Leonard & Taylor	1983			.154	40		
Malamuth & Ceniti	1984			.000	28	.000	28
Meyer	1972			.392	24		
Mosher; Mosher & Katz	1971			.266	80		
Mueller & Donnerstein Study I	1981			.000	28		
Study II				.401	40		
Ramirez, Bryant, & Zillman	1982	−.116	48	.116	48		
Rosene	1971			.130	60	.226	60
Sapolsky & Zillman Study I	1981			.000	120		
Study II				.136	60		
Tannenbaum	1971			.407	45		
Tascher	1983					−.176	45
White	1979			.102	95		
Zillmann	1971			.511	63		
Zillmann, Bryant, & Carveth	1981	−.213	20	.284	20		
Zillmann, Hoyt, & Day	1974			.353	30		
Zillmann & Sapolsky	1977	−.091	44	−.091	44		

sexual interactions in which no attempt to injure the other person exists and both parties are portrayed as consenting parties. Nonviolent sexual material not only involves vaginal intercourse but can also include oral sexual behavior, autoerotica, and petting. Nude pictures are pictures of one person that display bare breasts, a penis, an anus, or vaginal areas but do not include explicit sexual touching or the use of sexual stimulators.

The viewing of violent sexual materials demonstrates a homogeneous $\chi^2 = 11.55_{(6, 353)}$ positive correlation (average $r = .216$, $k = 7$, $n = 353$). This effect indicates that the viewing of violent sexual materials increased the probability of subsequent aggressive acts. The homogeneity indicates that the differences in observed effects (the "inconsistency" in outcomes) is simply the result of normal sampling error.

Nonviolent sexual materials also produce an increase in aggressive behavior after a person viewed the material (average $r = .171$, $k = 24$, $n = 1,229$) based on a homogeneous set of estimates, $\chi^2 = 33.71_{(23, 1,229)}$. This finding indicates that exposure to nonviolent sexual materials increased the subsequent behavioral aggression. Thus, this finding contradicts some approaches or representations of social learning theory because the aggression occurs in the absence of cues in the material that link sexual gratification to violent behavior. This absence indicates findings that run contrary to an argument that the violence in sexual materials causes increases in aggression and not the sexually explicit content.

Nude pictorials produce diminished physical aggression compared with behavior of a control group (average $r = -.137$, $k = 9$, $n = 403$). This set of correlations came from a homogeneous set of estimates, $\chi^2 = 0.00_{(8, 403)}$. This finding indicates that nudity in the form of pictures typical of magazines such as *Playboy* and *Penthouse* (the source of stimuli in several investigations) diminished aggressive behavior and is contrary to the prevailing theoretical views of the impact of sexual material. For these stimuli, the exposure to this form of sexual materials actually diminished the level of subsequent aggressive behavior.

Educational Possibilities

One issue is whether it is possible to educate through the use of educational materials as a form of pre- or debriefing to reduce the available harm. A consideration is the ethical implications of continued investigation when current meta-analyses indicate the potential for harm. The continued empirical investigation, particularly in experimental studies on university campuses, would appear unethical if the outcomes of the meta-analyses are accurate. Experimental investigations would involve exposing individuals to materials with harms as suggested in the previous analyses (development of antisocial attitudes toward women and subsequent behavioral aggression). To justify continued research, effort must be expended to demonstrate that some postexposure procedure can alleviate any potential negative consequences.

TABLE 12.3
Effects of Educational Materials

Study	Date	r^2	N	Type of Briefing
Check & Malamuth	1984	.120	158	Debriefing
Donnerstein & Berkowitz	1981	.230	62	Debriefing
Intons-Peterson et al.	1989	.560	90	Prebriefing
Krafka	1985	.030	136	Debriefing
Linz Study I	1985	.240	136	Debriefing
Study II		.200	34	Debriefing
Linz, Connerstein, Bross, & Chapin	1986	.320	30	Prebriefing
Linz, Fuson, & Donnerstein	1990	.290	44	Prebriefing
Malamuth & Check	1984	.150	150	Debriefing
Rapaport	1984	.680	162	Debriefing

[a]A positive correlation indicates that exposure to an educational effort diminished the effect.

The current findings indicate that educational materials eradicate any harmful effect of exposure to sexual materials (average $r = .29$, $k = 10$, $n = 1,002$). The conclusions indicate that any harmful effects vanished, and the attitudes of the individuals were less -antisocial than they were before the investigation. Not only did the investigations demonstrate the elimination of harmful effects, but also the net impact of the experiment was a small change in attitudes in a positive direction. The results indicate that both pre- and debriefing techniques were effective in either alleviating existing harm (debriefing) or inoculating persons against harm (prebriefing) (Table 12.3).

DISCUSSION

Theoretical Issues

The findings indicate mixed support for social learning and excitation transfer theory. The support for basic positive correlations between exposure and various negative outcomes indicates some support for the theories. The attitudinal and most of the behavioral outcomes indicate support for a conclusion that exposure to sexually explicit material is related to antisocial behavior. Any theoretical position must have an explanation and prediction consistent with the available data. The problem is that the current theories, although predicting some of the outcomes, do not confirm or predict all the outcomes generated by the data.

Social learning theory predicts a positive correlation between exposure and the development of antisocial attitudes as well as aggressive behavior. However, the expectations for the theory would be a positive correlation for all materials and not the negative impact that exists in the behavioral aggression data for nudity. This anomalous finding represents a significant and unexplained departure from the general pattern expected by most theoretical formulations. Creating an alternative for this material would require some explanation that posits that the "learning" from this material comes from some other association or cue within the content of the material. The unanswered question, consistent with Bandura's (1977) concerns, deals with understanding the nature of rewards/punishments and identification. The fundamental problem is that the current data deal with an association between exposure and outcome without examination of the psychological or cognitive interpretive mechanisms that people use as a lens to filter or understand the media experience. Most media events do not explicitly provide the moral or ethical lesson that a consumer should learn; the learning is an inference from the action or content of the material. The probable existence of multiple interpretations of the same material prevents a simple correspondence of understanding of how media content generates a particular outcome.

Excitation transfer has not fully been tested by most investigations. The assumption of an emotional lens or framework for the material that is recreated or transferred is not fully demonstrated in the current data. The results indicate some possibility that the relationship described in the theory may in fact be supported, but the nature of the association is complicated and the process not fully articulated. At this point the theory remains a possibility, but little formal assessment or evaluation is possible. One practical problem is fully understanding the combination of emotional and cognitive frames that any consumer brings to a media exposure. Excitation transfer requires an understanding of this frame to predict the potential outcome. Full evaluation of this theory still awaits appropriate data collection and articulation.

Practical and Policy Implications

One interpretation of the findings would provide for a causal role of sexual materials in antisocial actions within society. The observed positive correlations between exposure to the material in experimental settings and subsequent anti-female attitudes and increased aggressive behavior are a source of concern. However, the same procedure demonstrates that educational pre- or debriefings mitigate the harm due to the exposure (at least as far as attitudinal outcomes have been measured). The findings indicate that simply banning the material may not be required, and, possibly ineffective, educational efforts instead provide a better alternative for the majority of media consumers.

However, the findings represent a condition necessary to demonstrate causality; they are not a sufficient condition to make the argument for causality. If a causal connection exists between sexually explicit materials and various social outcomes then the observed correlations would be necessary to sustain that argument. But a correlation between exposure and outcome of the kind reported in this chapter, although consistent with an explanation of causality, does not rule out alternative explanations that posit noncausal roles for media exposure.

Another problem with the practical issues of reducing the quantity of material is that for aggressive behavior, nudity actually decreased the subsequent aggressive behavior. This result indicates that the nudity found in magazines such as *Playboy* does not increase antisocial outcomes and may, in fact, reduce such outcomes. This difference represents an anomaly that requires further development and indicates the problems associated with the establishment of potential policies consistent with the findings described in this chapter. The argument for reducing aggressive behavior indicates that increased exposure to nude pictures should increase to serve the public good. The basis for this claim would appear unwarranted because no sound theoretical explanation exists for the observed effects. Similarly, any other action taken on the basis of the current data would be based on a lack of sound understanding of the issues that may be a basis for the observed relationships.

The problem is that the persons most likely to be affected by sexual materials and having them serve as an inducement for sexual crimes are probably a sample of individuals least likely to benefit from educational efforts. Most educational materials are designed to remind the consumer that the material represents a fantasy or fictional representation about sexual behavior. For the majority of the male audience, this reminder just reinforces the view that the depictions lack a characterization of reality. For persons already predisposed to commit antisocial sexual acts, exposure to educational materials may not work because the premise (that the sexual materials are fiction) becomes inconsistent with the view of this particular consumer. This consumer has already developed a view of sexual relationships that the material reinforces rather than develops. The material may reinforce an existing attitude about the nature of sexual relations but does not serve as the basis for the development of a new attitude where no attitude previously existed.

FUTURE CONSIDERATIONS

The primary consideration for future research in this area is the development of explanations for the web of contradictory findings generated thus far. Although some general findings or trends are apparent in the data, a number of anomalies that require attention exist. For example, why research reports examining behavioral aggression using nude pictorial stimulus actually show a negative relationship deserves exploration. The fact that in the original report, Allen et al. (1995) found no relationship between sexual arousal and behavioral aggression is important. The findings suggest that viewers are more active in processing this information and that the models assuming a passive audience that is captive and simply reacting to the material represent a dramatic oversimplification of the probable relationship that exists. The ability of educational materials to reframe mediated experience and eliminate or reduce the possible pernicious outcomes indicates that persons are not simply objects acted on by the media consumed.

The next step in meta-analytic summaries is an examination of particular populations and the response those persons have to pornography. A current unpublished meta-analysis (Allen et al., 1997) indicated thatgeneral exposure rates of convicted sexual offenders to sexually explicit materials do not differ from those of nonoffenders. One difference is that convicted sexual offenders use the material more often before engaging in sexual behavior than nonoffenders. The other finding was that the physiological arousal to the material was greatest when the particular sexual crime of which the individual was convicted was considered. The key was to note that it was not simply the level of exposure to sexual materials that indicated an association with criminal behavior but rather the function that the material served and the preference or reaction to particular kinds of sexual material. This finding creates the need for an analysis of the audience based on individual difference models or situation models that examine the nature of predisposition or framing as a method of understanding the relationship between media content and the impact that this material creates on viewers.

This finding suggests that rather than simply viewing "exposure" as the critical feature, the concern ought to be how someone exposed to such material "reacts." This viewpoint argues for a stimulus arrangement approach that has a person choosing to utilize media material for particular ends. This assumption indicates that attention needs to be focused on the context of consumption of materials by consumers as a reaction that creates a kind of psychological interaction. The relationship is ongoing because a consumer can self-select materials and create an individualized media environment. Not only is media consumption voluntary but also for most sexually explicit materials the consumption requires the expenditure of resources. The consumer is paying for the media experience. This relationship evolves and is subject to change and the availability of alternatives. Research must consider selective exposure, how consumers select among available alternatives.

Examining the interaction between the media content and the consumer indicates a possible method to interpret the findings of educational studies that consider how to eliminate potential negative social consequences from exposure to the material. Educational efforts assume that the problem of media is the misapplication of content to real life. A vicarious fantasy experience creates an emotional reaction. The educational material recontextualizes this experience, perhaps reminding the consumer that such material is in fact a fantasy and not a reflection of real life.

The controversy over the impact of sexually explicit materials will continue. No single meta-analysis or even group of meta-analyses can resolve this issue. The ultimate resolution requires the development and empirical testing of a number of complementary models. The current results indicate cause for concern and continued testing, but the current state of knowledge requires additional investigation.

REFERENCES

Allen, M., & D'Alessio, D. (1993). Comparing the physiological responses of males and females to pornography: A preliminary report. *Women & Language, 15,* 60.

Allen, M., D'Alessio, D., & Brezgel, K. (1995). A meta-analysis summarizing the effects of pornography. II: Aggression after exposure. *Human Communication Research, 22,* 258–283.

Allen, M., D'Alessio, D., Emmers, T., & Gebhardt, L. (1996). The role of educational briefings in mitigating effects of experimental exposure to violent sexually explicit material: A meta-analysis. *Journal of Sex Research, 33,* 135–141.

Allen, M., D'Alessio, D., & Emmers-Sommer, T. (1997, November). *Reactions of criminal sex offenders to pornography: A meta-analytic summary.* Paper presented at the National Communication Association Convention, Chicago, IL.

Allen, M., Emmers, T., Gebhardt, L., & Giery, M. (1995, Winter). Pornography and rape myth acceptance. *Journal of Communication, 45*(1), 5–26.

Bandura, A. (1973). *Aggression: A social learning analysis.* Englewood Cliffs, NJ: Prentice Hall.

Bandura, A. (1977). *Social learning theory.* Englewood Cliffs, NJ: Prentice Hall.

Baron, R. (1974a). The aggression-inhibiting influence of heightened sexual arousal. *Journal of Personality and Social Psychology, 30,* 318–322.

Baron, R. (1974b). Sexual arousal and physical aggression: The inhibiting influence of "cheesecake" and nudes. *Bulletin of Psychonomic Society, 3,* 337–339.

Baron, R. (1979). Heightened sexual arousal and physical aggression: An extension to females. *Journal of Research in Personality, 13,* 91–102.

Baron, R., & Bell, P. (1973). Effects of heightened sexual arousal on physical aggression. In *Proceedings of the 81st Annual Convention of the American Psychological Association,* pp. 171–172.

Baron, R., & Bell, R. (1977). Sexual arousal an aggression by males: Effects of type of erotic stimuli and prior provocation. *Journal of Personality and Social Psychology, 35,* 79–87.

Bryant, J., & Brown, D. (1989). Uses of pornography. In D. Zillmann & J. Bryant (Eds.), *Pornography: Research advances & policy considerations* (pp. 25–56). Hillsdale, NJ: Lawrence Erlbaum Associates.

Burt, M. (1980). Cultural myths and supports for rape. *Journal of Personality and Social Psychology, 38,* 217–230.

Burt, M., & Albin, R. (1981). Rape myths, rape definitions, and probability of conviction. *Journal of Applied Social Psychology, 11,* 212–230.

Cantor, J., Zillmann, D., & Einsiedel, E. (1978). Female responses to provocation after exposure to aggressive and erotic films. *Communication Research, 5,* 395–412.

Check, J. (1985). *The effects of violent and nonviolent pornography.* Ottawa, Ontario, Canada: Department of Justice (Department of Supply and Services Contract No. 05SV 19200–3-0899).

Check, J., & Malamuth, N. (1984). Can there be positive effects of participation in pornography experiments? *Journal of Sex Research, 20,* 14–31.

Demare, D., Briere, J., & Lips, H. (1988). Violent pornography and self-reported likelihood of sexual aggression. *Journal of Research in Personality, 22,* 140–153.

Donnerstein, E. (1980). Aggressive erotica and violence against women. *Journal of Personality and Social Psychology, 39,* 269–277.

Donnerstein, E. (1984). Pornography: ts effect on violence against women. In N. Malamuth & E. Donnerstein (Eds.), *Pornography and sexual aggression* (pp. 53–82). Orlando, FL: Academic Press.

Donnerstein, E., & Barrett, G. (1978). The effects of erotic stimuli on male aggression towards females. *Journal of Personality and Social Psychology, 36,* 180–188.

Donnerstein, E., & Berkowitz, L. (1981). Victim reactions in aggressive erotic film as a factor in violence against women. *Journal of Personality and Social Psychology, 41,* 710–724.

Donnerstein, E., Donnerstein, M., & Evans, R. (1975). Erotic stimuli and aggression: Facilitation or inhibition. *Journal of Personality and Social Psychology, 32,* 237–244.

Donnerstein, E., & Hallam, J. (1978). The facilitating effects of erotica on aggression toward females. *Journal of Personality and Social Psychology, 36,* 1270–1277.

Duncan, D. (1990). Pornography as a source of sex information for university students. *Psychological Reports, 66,* 442.

Duncan, D., & Donnelly, J. (1991). Pornography as a source of sex information for students at a private Northeastern university. *Psychological Reports, 68,* 782.

Duncan, D., & Nicholson, T. (1991). Pornography as a source of information for students at a Southeastern university. *Psychological Reports, 68,* 802.

Garcia, L. (1986). Exposure to pornography and attitudes about women and rape: A correlation study. *Journal of Sex Research, 22,* 378–385.

Hall, G., Shondrick, D., & Hirschman, R. (1993). The role of sexual arousal in sexually aggressive behavior: A meta-analysis. *Journal of Consulting and Clinical Psychology, 61,* 1091–1095.

Herrett, J. (1993). *The effects of exposure to female oriented pornography on viewer's attitudes toward women: A social learning theory analysis.* Unpublished master's thesis, University of Wisconsin–Milwaukee, Milwaukee.

Hunter, J. E., and Schmidt, F. L. (1990). *Methods of meta-analysis.* Newbury Park, CA: Sage.

Intons-Peterson, M., & Roskos-Ewoldsen, B. (1989). Mitigating the effects of violent pornography. In S. Gubar & J. Hoff (Eds.), *The dilemma of violent pornography: For adult users only* (pp. 218–239). Bloomington, IN: Indiana University Press.

Krafka, C. (1985). *Sexually explicit, sexually violent, and violent media: Effects of multiple naturalistic exposures and debriefing on female viewers.* Unpublished doctoral dissertation, University of Wisconsin–Madison, Madison.

Lalumiere, M., & Quinsey, V. (1994). The discrimination of rapists from non-sex offenders using phallometric measures: A meta-analysis. *Criminal Justice and Behavior, 21,* 150–175.

Leonard, K., & Taylor, S. (1983). Exposure to pornography, permissive, and nonpermissive cures, and male aggression toward females. *Motivation and Emotion, 7,* 291–299.

Linz, D. (1985). *Sexual violence in the media: Effects on male viewers and implications for society.* Unpublished doctoral dissertation, University of Wisconsin–Madison, Madison.

Linz, D., Donnerstein, E., Bross, M., & Chapin, M. (1986). Mitigating the influence of violence of television and sexual violence in the media. In R. Blanchard (Ed.), *Advances in the study of aggression* (Vol. 2, pp. 165–194). New York: Academic Press.

Linz, D., Fuson, I., & Donnerstein, E. (1990). Mitigating the negative effects of sexually violent mass communications through preexposure briefings. *Communication Research, 17,* 641–674.

Malamuth, N. (1986). Predictors of naturalistic sexual aggression. *Journal of Personality and Social Psychology, 50,* 953–962.

Malamuth, N., & Ceniti, J. (1984). Repeated exposure to violent and nonviolent pornography: Likelihood of raping ratings and laboratory aggression against women. *Aggressive Behavior, 12,* 129–137.

Malamuth, N., & Check, J. (1981a). Penile tumescence and perceptual responses to rape as a function of victim's perceived reactions. *Journal of Applied Social Psychology, 10,* 528–547.

Malamuth, N., & Check, J. (1981b). The effects of mass media exposure on acceptance of violence against women:A field experiment. *Journal of Abnormal Psychology, 92,* 55–67.

Malamuth, N., & Check, J. (1984). Debriefing effectiveness following exposure to pornographic rape depictions. *Journal of Sex Research, 20,* 1–13.

Malamuth, N., & Check, J. (1985). The effects of aggressive pornography on beliefs in rape myths: Individual differences. *Journal of Research in Personality, 19,* 299–320.

Malamuth, N., Haber, S., & Feshbach, S. (1980). Testing hypotheses regarding rape: Exposure to sexual violence, sex difference, and the "normality" of rapists. *Journal of Reseach in Personality, 14,* 121–137.

Mayerson, S., & Taylor, D. (1987). The effects of rape myth pornography to women's attitudes and the mediating role of sex role stereotyping. *Sex Roles, 17,* 321–338.

Meyer, T. (1972). The effects of sexually arousing and violent films on aggressive behavior. *Journal of Sex Research, 8,* 324–331.

Mosher, D. (1971). Sex callousness toward women. In *Erotica and social behavior: Technical report of the commission on obscenity and pornography* (Vol. 8, pp. 313–324). Washington, DC: Government Printing Office.

Mosher, D., & Katz, H. (1971). Pornographic films, male verbal aggression against women, and guilt. In Presidential Commission on Obscenity and Pornography (Ed.), *Technical report of the Presidential Commission on Obscenity and Pornography: Vol. 8. Erotica and social behavior* (pp. 357–379). Washington, DC: Government Printing Office.

Mueller, C., & Donnerstein, E. (1981). Film-facilitated arousal and prosocial behavior. *Journal of Experimental Social Psychology, 17,* 31–41.

Oddone-Paolucci, E., Genuis, M., & Violato, C. (2000). A meta-analysis of the published research on the effects of pornography. In C. Violato, E. Oddone-Paolucci, M. Genuis (Eds.), *The changing family and child development* (pp. 48–59). Aldershot, England: Ashgate Publishing.

Padgett, V., Brislin-Slutz, J., & Neal, J. (1989). Pornography, erotica, and attitudes toward women: The effects of repeated exposure. *Journal of Sex Research, 26,* 479–491.

Paik, H., & Comstock, G. (1994). The effects of television violence on antisocial behavior: A meta-analysis. *Communication Research, 21,* 516–546.

Ramirez, J., Bryant, J., & Zillmann, D. (1982). Effects of erotica on retaliatory behavior as a function of level of prior provocation. *Journal of Personality and Social Psychology, 43,* 971–978.

Rapaport, R. (1984). *Sexually aggressive males: Characterological features and sexual responsiveness to rape depictions.* Unpublished doctoral dissertation, Auburn University, Auburn, AL.

Rosene, J. (1971). *The effect of violent and sexually arousing film content: An experimental study.* Unpublished doctoral dissertation, Ohio University, Athens.

Sapolsky, B., & Zillmann, D. (1981). The effect of soft-core and hard-core erotica on provoked and unprovoked hostile behavior. *Journal of Sex Research, 17,* 319–343.

Sherman, S. J., & Corty, E. (1984). Cognitive heuristics. In R. S. Wyer & T. K. Srull (Eds.). *Handbook of Social Cognition* (Vol 1, pp. 189–286). Hillsdale, NJ: Erlbaum.

Smeaton, G., & Byrne, D. (1987). The effects of R-rated violence and erotica, individual differences, and victim characteristics on acquaintance rape proclivity. *Journal of Research in Personality, 21,* 171–184.

Stock, W. (1983). *The effects of violent pornography on the sexual responsiveness and attitudes of women.* Unpublished doctoral dissertation, State University of New York at Stony Brook, Stony Brook.

Tannenbaum, P. (1971). Emotional arousal as a mediator of erotic communication effects. In Presidential Commission on Obscenity and Pornography (Ed.), *Technical report of the Presidential Commission on Obscenity and Pornography: Vol. 8. Erotica and social behavior* (pp. 326–356). Washington, DC: U.S. Government Printing Office.

Tascher, D. (1983). *The effects of sex role stereotypes and sexually-aggressive film content on aggression against women.* Unpublished doctoral dissertation, Hofstra University, Hempstead, NY.

Weaver, J. B. (1987). *Effects of portrayals of female sexuality and violence against women on perceptions of women.* Unpublished doctoral dissertation. Indiana University, Bloomington, IN.

White, L. (1979). Erotica and aggression: The influence of sexual arousal, positive affect, and negative affect on aggressive behavior. *Journal of Personality and Social Psychology, 37,* 591–601.

Zillmann, D. (1971). Excitation transfer in communication-mediated aggressive behavior. *Journal of Experimental Social Psychology, 7,* 419–434.

Zillmann, D., & Bryant, J. (1982). Pornography, sexual callousness, and the trivialization of rape. *Journal of Communication, 32*(4), 10–21.

Zillmann, D., & Bryant, J. (1988). Effects of prolonged consumption of pornography on family values. *Journal of Family Issues, 9,* 518–544.

Zillmann, D., Bryant, J., & Carveth, R. (1981). The effect of erotica featuring sadomasochism and bestiality on motivated intermale aggression. *Personality and Social Psychology Bulletin, 7,* 153–159.

Zillmann, D., Bryant, J., Comisky, P., & Medoff, N. (1981). Sexual material, anger, and aggression. *European Journal of Social Psychology, 11,* 233–252.

Zillmann, D., Hoyt, J., & Day, K. (1974). Strength and duration of the effect of aggressive, violent, and erotic communications of subsequent aggressive behavior. *Communication Research, 1,* 286–306.

Zillmann, D., & Sapolsky, B. (1977). What mediates the effect of mild erotica on annoyance and hostile behavior in males. *Journal of Personality and Social Psychology, 35,* 587–596.

13

Effects of Gender Stereotyping on Socialization

Patrice A. Oppliger
La Salle University

Early media researchers were mostly concerned with the relationship between pro-gramming and aggressive behavior of consumers. The Civil Rights and Women's movements of the 1960s prompted exploration of the media content and its pos-sible contribution to the oppression of women and minorities. The movements encouraged a questioning of stereotypical media portrayals (Zuckerman, Singer, & Singer, 1980). Durkin (1985a) defined *stereotyping* as attributing qualities of a group to individuals within that group, without regard to the uniqueness of the individual. These qualities tend to be extreme and are assigned a value, mostly negative. The term *sexism* is the prejudice associated with sex-role stereotypes, negative feelings about either sex. The media are under scrutiny for presenting stereotyped portrayals of characters, which can influence inequality and perpetu-ate myths of women's incompetence.

The U.S. Commission on Civil Rights (1977) report *Window Dressing on the Set: Women and Minorities in Television* found that from the 1950s to the 1970s females were underrepresented as characters in television shows. When women did appear, they were frequently seen in token or stereotyped roles. The National Commission on Working Women found that female representation in the media had gotten a little better by the mid-1980s. Female characters were more numer-ous, more diverse in age and occupation, and more independent financially and socially than in previous television seasons (Reep & Dambrot, 1988). Content analysis studies, however, have consistently indicated that the media present a distorted view of reality especially in regard to gender roles: Men outnumber women three to one; women are likely to be younger than men and cast in traditional and stereotypical roles; women are less aggressive and more likely to be victimized than men; women are limited in their employment possibilities; and women are more likely to be married than men (Signorielli, 1990).

Past research has focused on the gender stereotyping effects of different types of media such as advertising, children's programming, daytime and prime-time television, television news, magazine advertising, magazine fiction, newspapers, child-oriented print media, textbooks, comic books, literature, and film (see Busby, 1975). A majority of research, however, has focused on television as the prime source of effects. Research suggests that, except for sleeping, Americans spend more time viewing television than engaging in any other single waking activity (Jennings-Walstedt, Geis, & Brown, 1980). Signorielli (1990) argued that of all the media, television may be the one most suited for socialization, especially for children. "[Televisions] are found in practically every home; requires minimal skills for understanding; visual nature is appealing to youngsters" (Signorielli, 1990, p. 50). Morgan (1982) noted the stability of the medium's basic messages over time and across genres. This stability and consistency, therefore, create reinforcement of the ideas being presented. Television is credited with being the great socializer in American society, teaching children how to behave and immigrants how to assimilate (Davis, 1990). Television has the same capacity to teach violence, fearfulness, and cynicism, as it does sex role stereotyping.

THEORETICAL PERSPECTIVES

Early stimulus-response theories such as the hypodermic needle theory have been replaced with a model of limited effects (Tuchman, 1979). The limited effects model is linear in that it predicts that the more media exposure the more influence on consumers. Unlike the hypodermic needle theory, the model recognizes that the effects are mediated by social variables such as family and peer influence. Theorists debate about other moderating factors such as the required length and intensity of exposure that are necessary for an effect to occur. Two views have emerged; the *drench* or high-impact television effect and the *drip, drip* or frequent-viewing effect (Reep & Dambrot, 1989). Advocates of the drip, drip effect—cultivation theorists—argue that the more time people spend watching television, the more likely they are to perceive the real world in ways that reflect the patterns found in television portrayals (Morgan, 1982). Researchers have also argued that some particular characters or programs may have an intense and significant impact on viewers and are far more influential than accumulated images. Two heavy viewers who watch totally different types of programs may hold two disparate sets of beliefs about television (Gunter, 1995). Reep and Dambrot (1989) found some evidence of the drench effect, that some specific characters had a stronger influence on audience responses than others regardless of the amount of viewing. They ultimately concluded that the single versus repeated exposure effects may not be mutually exclusive but rather are interrelated in explaining television effects.

Another important theoretical perspective, the uses and gratifications model, rejects the stimulus-response effects model. Instead of focusing on how the media act upon their passive audiences, the model acknowledges active viewers—viewers who select specific types of programs to fulfill the need for information, entertainment, relief from boredom, etc. Individuals make conscious decisions about what to consume, how to consume, how to interpret, and what to remember based on a desire for similarity to their attitudes, beliefs, and values. Viewers seek reinforcement for their sense of personal identity, including gender identity, from media models. Not surprisingly, Orlofsky, Cohen, and Ramsden (1985) found that individuals with more traditional sex role attitudes are more likely to have sex-typed interests and behaviors. According to the uses and gratification perspective, viewers consume media that closely adheres to their sense of sex-role identification. Therefore, an individual's gender perceptions affect media choices, unlike the effects model, which argues that the media affect gender perceptions.

Particular interest in media effects research has always been paid to children. Because young children make little distinction between the real and unreal in the media, social scientists argue that messages will have more influence on behavior, comprehension, and attitudes (Nikken & Peeters, 1988). Theories of sex-role development that rely heavily on observational learning without direct interaction between the learner and a teacher have gained acceptance in the academic community. Two competing theories of sex-role development and its relationship to observational learning are advanced by Mischel's (1966) social learning approach and Kohlberg's (1966) cognitive-development approach.

The social learning theory, advanced by Bandura (1965), asserts that individuals model behavior, taking into account the role of vicarious reinforcement. Attitudes and behaviors are either rejected or accepted, depending on the consequences, rewards, and punishments that follow. According to Mischel's (1966) approach, the acquisition and performance of sex-typed activities are influenced by a child's exposure to modeling. In a society, the appropriateness of male and female behaviors, attitudes, emotions, and personality traits is transmitted to the young through observation of modeling behavior (Peirce, 1989). Mischel (1976) argued that children value same-sex behavior because they traditionally see models rewarded for such behavior.

Kohlberg's (1966) perspective expanded on the work of cognitive developmental psychologists. He argued that children are motivated to develop an organized worldview that is consistent with a perception of self-worth. Children, therefore, will not selectively attend to and imitate same-sex models until they have developed an understanding of gender constancy. Research has shown that sex-role stereotypes develop as early as nursery school and influence belief systems, self-concept, self-esteem, and activities (Drabman et al., 1981). Repetti (1984) found children as young as 2 years old showing understanding of traditional sex roles in toys, chores, and occupations. A child's notion of gender develops in these stages until he or she recognizes that gender is an invariant part of an individual (Ruble, Balaban, & Cooper, 1981). According to Kohlberg's reasoning, children become interested in same-sex models and perceive sex-appropriate behaviors as reinforcing because of their newly acquired sense of the inevitability of their gender, rather than the reverse as explained by social learning theory (Perloff, Brown, & Miller, 1982). Cognitive development perspective overlaps with uses and gratifications theory. The child is not seen as passive and acted upon by the media but actively seeks out sex-role reinforcement and information (Ruble et al., 1981). For examples, boys will seek out programs such as action shows because these shows consistently reward traditional male-typed behavior.

The debate over the relationship between an individual's attitude and behavior has become particularly sharp in the area of sex-role research (Morgan, 1987). Although many researchers have argued whether attitudes guide behaviors or behaviors cue attitudes, the bigger question revolves around whether attitudes and behaviors are related at all. In their meta-analysis on the relationship between attitudes and behaviors, Kim and Hunter (1993) found a strong correlation between the two ($r = .80$). Behavioral and attitudinal measures in the present analysis were analyzed separately and are reported in the results section.

META-ANALYSIS

The primary question investigated in this meta-analysis is, Does a relationship exist between media use and gender stereotyping, and, if so, how strong is the relationship? In addition to an analysis of the main effect of media exposure on gender stereotyping attitudes and behaviors, several moderating variables such as participants' age, sex, and culture were investigated.

Results of individual studies differ to some degree depending on the sample, procedures, and measurement tool employed. Meta-analysis is a method of statistically combining the results of independent studies and using inferential statistics to aid in the evaluation of a body of research literature (Whitley, 1983). The combination of the results provides overall effect-size estimates for a set of studies and gives a richer, more in-depth view of what, if any, relationship exists between the media and their audience. The power of statistical analysis is not available to the traditional literature review, which uses qualitative techniques. Narrative reviews of studies offer valuable analysis; however, interpretations of results can be inaccurate because of the biases of the reviewer. Reviewers may inflate the importance of studies with small samples or give equal weight to statistical and anecdotal evidence. Researchers should take into consideration effect sizes, stringency of method, and sample sizes in order to draw more accurate conclusions.

Herrett-Skjellum and Allen (1995) conducted an earlier meta-analysis on television programming and sex stereotyping. In their analysis of nonexperimental studies, they found a positive correlation between self-reported amount of television viewing and acceptance of sexual stereotypes ($r = .101$). Further investigation revealed a significant difference between dependent measures of occupation attitudes, sex-role attitudes, and behavior; all findings were significant and positive. Results of experimental analyses were also positive ($r = .207$) but with no moderating variable affecting the outcome. Age and sex of participants had no significant effect on the outcome of the experimental and nonexperimental studies. Hearold's (1986) analysis of 230 studies, showed that among the types of antisocial behavior, stereotyping had a very high effect size (.90).

METHOD

Procedure

Online services such as PsychLIT, Communication Abstracts, and InfoTrac Expanded Academic Index were accessed in the initial search for relevant studies. After starting with the key words *gender, stereotyping, television,* and *media,* replacing *gender* with *sex* and *sex-roles* produced much better results. The reference sections of the relevant studies were used to trace backward to other studies until all citations had been investigated. A search of Social Science Citation Index identified new research that referenced key studies previously found. Studies cited in reviews by Singorielli (1990), Durkin (1985b, 1985c), and Herrett-Skjellum and Allen (1995) were added to the preliminary list. After exhausting these avenues, the most recent publications of journals in the communication and psychology fields were reviewed for additional studies.

Selection of Studies

To achieve constancy across media studies in other areas, studies for this analysis were chosen according to the guidelines established by the editors of this book. Selection began by including only articles in refereed journals that had undergone peer review. Studies that were content analyses, used qualitative measures, or were simply descriptions of previous research were eliminated. Also included were studies that reported secondary analysis of primary data (see Morgan, 1987, and Signorielli, 1989). The total process produced 52 studies that met the initial criteria. Although this analysis was not limited to a specific medium, television was the prevalent focus. There are several possible reasons for this trend: the importance of the medium in our culture; its delivery channels to consumers, both audio and visual; and researchers' ability to manipulate stimulus materials in experimental studies.

After the initial screening, additional studies were excluded from analysis. Studies that did not supply sufficient information such as means and standard deviations for each variable to allow for the computation of correlations or reported multivariate analyses of covariance and multiple regression analysis without zero-order correlation tables were dropped (see Davidson, Yasuna, & Tower, 1979; Fisher, 1989; Luecke-Aleksa, Anderson, Collins, & Schmitt, 1995; Meyer, 1980; Zuckerman et al., 1980). Because many of the studies were conducted two or more decades ago, much of the data analysis and statistical information is no longer available from the orginal researchers.

The present analysis did not include studies whose dependent measure was respondents' description or stereotype ratings of television characters. These studies were considered too similar to content analyses. Although providing important information about viewers' perceptions of individual characters, results do not significantly contribute to the understanding of media effect on sex-role attitudes of viewers. Studies in this category include Atwood, Zahn, and Webber (1986); Dambrot, Reep, and Bell (1988); Goff, Goff, and Lehrer (1980); Kolbe and Langefeld (1993); Lull, Hanson, and Marx (1977); Mayes and Valentine (1979); Melville and Cornish (1993); Popovich and Butler (1983); Reep and Dambrot (1988, 1989); and Reeves and Greenberg (1977).

Studies were also excluded if there was no measure of media exposure. Katz and Walsh (1991), for example, only reported media preference, not amount of viewing. Rosenwasser, Lingenfelter, and Harrington (1989) measured knowledge of three popular television programs, but again did not measure amount of viewing. In this case, children could have learned about the programs from friends without having seen an episode. Also excluded were experimental studies with no comparison group. Experiments by Drabman et al. (1981) and Eisenstock (1984) exposed all participants to a single video condition. Without a comparison or control group, confounding variables and alternative explanations for the effect cannot be eliminated. Although identified as an experiment, Peevers' study (1979) incorporated six to eight trained coders to code dramatic television programs. This study was considered to be more of a content analysis than an effects study and was eliminated from analysis.

Results collected from Newton and Buck's (1985) study from Chicago and Northampton, Great Britian, were included in the analysis, whereas samples from non-English-speaking cities (Seoul, Tokyo, and Manila) were excluded. Although it was found that the content of television was heavily sex-role stereotyped in all five cultures studied, results showed notable cross-cultural differences, most consistently between Chicago and the Asian cities. Findings illustrated that exposure to television does not operate in the same way across cultures. Too few studies with non-English-speaking, international samples fit the current criteria to test these effects further.

The final process yielded 31 studies.

Coding of Variables

A majority of the studies, 18 out of 31 or 58%, employed survey methods. The remaining 11 studies were experimental. As a follow-up analysis, experimental results were categorized into two types of dependent measurements: attitudinal (three studies) and behavioral measures (seven studies). Results of three studies that reported both measures were averaged and included in the general analysis.

Independent Variables

Participant's media exposure was a consistent independent measure in the studies analyzed. Survey studies measured amount of viewing or general media consumption through self-reports. Experimental studies controlled participant exposure to stimulus, creating conditions of sex-typed, counter–sex-typed, or neutral programs. In the experimental research, manipulation of stimulus material included male models playing with traditionally female toys (e.g., dolls) or female models playing with traditionally male toys (e.g., a firetruck) and stories about boys and girls growing up to be in either traditional (e.g., male pilots and female stewardesses) or nontraditional careers (e.g., male nurses and female doctors).

Dependent Variables

The studies reported a variety of instruments that measure sex-role attitudes and behaviors. Attitudes about women and sexist views were measured from questions about home, family, marital status, romance, employment, and chores as well as more abstract psychological sex-stereotypical characteristics such as aggressiveness, confidence, gentleness, and emotionality. More standardized measures such as the Bem Sex-Role Inventory (Bem, 1974) and the Attitude Toward Women Scale (Benson & Vincent, 1980) were also employed.

In other studies, participants were asked to estimate the percentage of females in counter-stereotypical jobs: doctors, lawyers, teachers, police officers, and laborers. Responses were then compared with prime-time television portrayal and U.S. Census statistics about real life representation. Questions also included the appropriateness of occupations for men and women and appropriateness of playing with a sex-typed toys. Children were asked how much they would consider "feminine" (model, secretary, dental hygienist) and "masculine" (lawyer, police officer, dentist) occupations for themselves. Paper and pencil measurements are often difficult for some respondents. Researchers adapted data collection for children who were too young to effectively complete the self-report measurements. For example, children were asked questions orally such as "which is the smartest doll?" and "which one would rake leaves or set the table?" and then were asked to give their answers by pointing to male or female dolls.

Behavioral-dependent variables included amount of time playing with gender-inappropriate toys, reported performance of gender-specific chores, and recall of sex-typed program materials. Experiments assessed children's imitation of a model by showing either models playing with a sex-inappropriate toy or models performing sex-inappropriate acts such as a male hugging and kissing a toy and a female performing a daring feat with a toy. After viewing stimulus material, the time child participants spent playing with similar toys was then recorded. Other measures included recall of sex-typed material, which was tested with multiple choice questions about the program viewed, and self-reports of performing sex-typed chores. Adult females' independence of judgment and self-confidence was also assessed in one study (see Jennings-Walstedt et al., 1980).

Moderating Variables

Studies were also coded for moderating variables. Moderating variables reflect additional theoretical or methodological features that may change the nature of the effect. Separate analyses were conducted to test for possible moderating variables: participant age (adults/children), participant sex (male/female), measurement (attitudes/behaviors), and culture (international/domestic populations). Studies were split into either adult (older than 18 years of age) or child (preschoolers to 18-year-old high school students) participants; no one study included samples from both populations. Although Herrett-Skjellum and Allen (1995) found no trend of increase or decrease based on age of participants, age was considered in this analysis. Reep and Dambrot (1989) argue that children perceive different aspects of television content than adults do; therefore, results cannot be extended to an adult population.

International respondents, including samples from Great Britain (Gunter & Wober, 1982; Newton & Buck, 1985) and Israel (Zemach & Cohen, 1986) were compared with results from samples selected from a domestic population. Studies were limited to those from places where English is spoken and whose television fare is similar, with some programming being identical, to that in the United States. Individual studies included investigations of moderating factors such as participant's IQ, education level, or occupation of parents and socioeconomic status. These variables were not considered here because no consistent effects were reported in the individual analyses.

Statistical Procedures

The first step of the statistical analysis was to record sample sizes and the zero-order correlations between the independent and dependent variables of each individual study. Significance test statistics were converted to correlations using conversion formulas (see Weiss & Hassett, 1993). In studies that indicated separate results for similar measures (e.g., Tan, 1979), correlations were averaged and reported as a single study (see Kim & Hunter, 1993).

The next step in the analysis was to calculate the mean correlation of the study correlations, the variance across studies, the sampling error variance, the estimate of the variance of population correlations, the corrected population standard deviation, and a 95% confidence interval (Hunter & Schmidt, 1990). Follow-up analyses were conducted to test for effects of moderating variables such as age, culture, and participant sex.

RESULTS

In the 31 studies in this analysis, the total number of respondents was 12,597. An overwhelming majority of respondents were in nonexperimental studies ($n = 11,417$). Adult respondents ($n = 10,485$) outnumbered children younger than age 18 ($n = 2,112$). International participants made up 14% of the sample ($n = 1,805$). For studies reporting participants' sex, participants were split fairly evenly between males ($n = 2,555$) and females ($n = 2,859$).

Effect sizes were computed for nonexperimental studies (Table 13.1) and experimental studies (Table 13.2).[1] The nonexperimental average correlation ($r = .117$) was significant and positive. The average correlation for experimental studies was stronger ($r = .235$) but not significantly different from nonexperimental studies. Two possible explanations for the difference are, first, that the stimulus materials selected in experiments were distinct representations of sex roles, which made a more substantial impression. Second, experimentation controlled for extraneous variables that may have confounded results of the survey results.

Analyses comparing results for moderator variables (Table 13.3) demonstrated some interesting findings. No significant difference was found between behavioral measures ($r = .305$) and attitudinal measures ($r = .156$), although behaviors tended to be more strongly correlated with media exposure than attitudes. Correlations from the U.S. samples ($r = .099$) did not significantly differ from those for the international samples ($r = .211$). These correlations were computed for nonexperimental studies only because all experimental studies were done with domestic samples.

---

[1]Special consideration was given to studies with outliers: Frueh and McGhee (1975), McGhee and Freuh (1980), and List et al. (1983). The average correlation calculated including the Freuh and McGhee studies ($r = .115$) was similar to the correlation without ($r = .106$). Average correlations with ($r = .235$) and without ($r = .191$) the List et al. results were also not significantly different. Signorelli's study (1989), which represented a disportionally large sample ($n = 7,049$ or 36% of the total), presented a greater difference with ($r = .115$) than without ($r = .206$), although not a statistically significant difference.

TABLE 13.1
Effect Size Estimates for Nonexperimental Studies

Study	r	N	Age[a]	Male	Female
Beuf (1974)	.330	63	C		
Frueh & McGhee (1975)	.867	80	C		
Gunter & Wober (1982)	.100	503	A		
McCauley et al. (1988)	.003	173	A	−.01	.02
McGhee & Frueh (1980)	.818	64	C		
Miller & Reeves (1976)	.125	200	C		
Morgan (1987)[b]	.139	287	C	.17	.11
Morgan (1982)[b]	.223	349	C	.27	.19
Morgan & Rothchild (1983)	.190	287	C	.20	.15
Newton & Buck (1985) Chicago	.155	100	A	.10	.29
Newton & Buck (1985) Northampton	.185	100	A	.24	.27
Perloff (1977)	.082	95	C		
Repetti (1984)	.041	40	C		
Ross, Anderson, & Wisocki (1982)	.363	97	A		
Signorielli (1989) Study I	.070	3743	A		
Signorielli (1989) Study II	.046	3306	A		
Signorielli & Lears (1992)	.100	530	C	.10	.08
Volgy & Schwarz (1980)	.410	133	A		
Wroblewski & Huston (1987)	.444	65	C		
Zemach & Cohen (1986)	.260	1202	A		

[a]C, children; A, adult.
[b]Reported findings at two separate times. For the overall analysis of findings, the first measures were used to be consistent with other cross-sectional studies.

Although a significant difference was not found between adult samples ($r = .096$) and children ($r = .210$), results suggest that children tended to be more susceptable to media effects. Age comparisons were conducted for nonexperimental studies only; all experiments were done with children except for a sample of 52 adults in the study by Jennings-Walstedt et al. (1980). For studies reporting gender, there was little difference between overall male ($r = .157$) and female samples ($r = .170$). This finding is not unusual since few individual studies reported interaction effects with participant sex. Gender differences were only computed for nonexperimental studies because too few studies in experimental conditions reported results separately.

DISCUSSION

There is little doubt that the media have some effect on consumers. Results of the meta-analysis show a consistent, positive correlation; as exposure to gender

TABLE 13.2

Effect Size Estimates for Experimental Studies

Study	r	N	Age[a]	Measure[b]	Male	Female
Cobb, Stevens-Long, & Goldstein (1982)	.542	24	C	B	.795	.289
Flex, Fidler, & Roger (1976)	.400	31	C	A		
Grusec & Brinker (1972)	.082	144	C	B		
Jennings-Walstedt et al. (1980)[c]	.400	52	A	B	.400	
List, Collins & Westby (1983)	.820	83	C	B		
McArthur & Eisen (1976)	.305	40	C	B	.330	.380
O'Bryant & Corder-Bolz (1978)	.323	67	C	A		
Pingree (1978)	.173	227	C	A		
Ruble et al. (1981)	.100	100	C	B		
Silverman-Watkins, Levi, & Klein (1986)	.100	96	C	A/B		
Tan (1979)[c,d]	.082	56	C	A/B	.082	
Tan, Raudy, Huff, & Miles (1980)	.207	120	C	A/B		
Wolf (1975)	.210	140	C	B		

[a]C, children; A, adult.
[b]B, behavioral measure; SS, sexism scale.
[c]All female respondents in the study.
[d]In the Tan study, unequal cell sizes were corrected in the one-way analysis of variance.

TABLE 13.3

Correlations and 95% Confidence Intervals for Moderating Variables

Variable	r	Confidence Interval
Experimental	.235	.040 to .431
Nonexperimental	.117	.036 to .198
Behavior[a]	.305	.111 to .500
Attitude	.156	−.036 to .348
Adult[b]	.096	.036 to .157
Children	.209	.072 to .347
Male[b]	.143	−.025 to .311
Female	.133	−.037 to .304
Domestic[b]	.099	.017 to .181
International	.211	.135 to .288

[a]Computed for experimental studies only.
[b]Computed for nonexperimental studies only.

stereotyping increases, sex-typed behavior and sex-role stereotyped attitudes increase. Because correlations for the experimental studies were stronger than the nonexperimental studies, results would appear to support the drench hypothesis: that intensity of media exposure is more influential than length. However, these experiments were done almost exclusively with children. When the experimental scores are compared with children's nonexperimental scores, there is little difference. Survey methods used in the nonexperimental studies did not consistently measure the type of programs or intensity of viewing in addition to amount of viewing, a common criticism of cultivation research. Support for the drip, drip hypothesis, therefore, remains tentative because it is unclear whether or not the amount of exposure is modified by intensity of exposure.

The reseach methods of the studies analyzed make it difficult to test the uses and gratifications model. First, most survey studies did not allow for order testing. There is no way to determine whether viewing affected perceptions or whether an individual's gender perceptions affected media choices. Second, experimental studies did not allow individuals to select programs. Experimental researchers often sacrifice ecological validity in favor of internal validity and control of extraneous variables. Results of one-shot experiments appear to weaken support for the uses and gratification model because individuals' gender peceptions and motivation differences were controlled for by random assignment to condition.

The current analysis demonstrates that children's scores correlate strongly with media consumption as predicted. Observational learning appears to be more important for children than adults—because as individuals age, they are exposed to a wider variety of experiences that may lessen the impact of the media. The results of the meta-analysis favor the social learning perspective over the cognitive approach in that it offers a more plausible explanation. According to the cognitive theory, sex-typed attitudes and behaviors should have already been established; therefore, the experiment's one-shot exposure should have had no effect. Because children begin watching television at a very young age, early development of gender identity and what it means to be "male" or "female" seems highly unlikely without the influence of modeling.

Results of this study indicate no statistically signficant differences in the moderating variables chosen for analysis. For example, correlations were very similar for male and female participants. Although overall scores often differed between male and female respondents in individual studies, gender was not a factor in the effect size or direction of correlations. International respondents tended to be more strongly affected than respondents from the United States, but not significantly. Too few studies were included to make a valid comparison. Age revealed the greatest disparity, however, not significantly. A serious problem for both correlational and experimental effects studies, according to Durkin (1985c), is how to separate the effects of the consumers' interaction with other aspects of the environment from the reported effects of the media. The sheer variety and number of moderating variables (e.g., biology, parents, siblings, peers, teachers, and institutional structures), not to mention the complex interactions between them, makes it difficult to measure their relationship.

No significant differences were found between behavioral and attitudinal measures. Behavioral measures tended to be more strongly correlated with media consumption than attitudinal measures. Behaviors such as playing with a sex-inappropriate toy for a specific length of time can be measured more accurately than an attitude can be measured by assigning it a number on a Likert scale. Behaviors may be the better measure if the goal of the research is to investigate media's effect on overt sex discrimination in the real world.

The results of the meta-analysis indicate that modeling can have a significant effect on consumer's gender perceptions, especially for children. Modeling should also be effective in changing stereotypes. Activists in the Women's Rights Movement demand a more democratic representation of women in the media, not simply an increase in the body count. Content analyses repeatedly show that male and female representations in the media differ significantly in categories such as age, martial status, and employment. The goal is not only to create characters who are counterstereotypical of traditional women, but also to portray females as positive and women's roles as valued. Gunter (1995) proposed not only hiring more women writers and producers and developing alternative media environments in which programs are run by women for women but also training professionals and educating viewers.

Pessimists contend that if men continue to hold the majority of power positions, major changes in women's media portrayals is unlikely. According to the cultural ratification model, those who control the media are interested in perpetuating images and worldviews compatible with their own goals (Durkin, 1985d). Recently more than 68% of network television shows have no women as executive producers or producers, 72% have no female writers, and only 11% have female directors (Stanley, 1996). As cable and satellite systems offer more channels, more opportunities should be available for new roles for women.

REFERENCES

Atwood, R. A., Zahn, S. B., & Webber, G. (1986). Perceptions of the traits of women on television. *Journal of Broadcasting & Electronic Media, 30*, 95–101.

Bandura, A. (1965). Influence of models' reinforcement contingencies on the acquistion of imitative responses. *Journal of Personality and Social Psychology, 1*, 589–595.

Bem, S. L. (1974). The measurement of psychological androgyny. *Journal of Consulting and Clinical Psychology, 42*, 155–162.

Benson, P., & Vincent, S. (1980). Development and validation of the Sexist Attitudes Towards Women scales (SATWS). *Psychology of Women Quarterly, 5*, 276–291.

Beuf, A. (1974). Doctor, lawyer, household drudge. *Journal of Communication, 24*(2), 142–145.

Busby, L. J. (1975). Sex-role research on the mass media. *Journal of Communication, 25*(3), 107–131.

Cobb, N. J., Stevens-Long, J., & Goldstein, S. (1982). The influence of television models on toy preferences in children. *Sex Roles, 8*, 1075–1080.

Dambrot, F. H., Reep, D. C., & Bell, D. (1988). Television sex roles in the 1980s: Do viewers' sex and sex role orientation change the picture? *Sex Roles, 19*, 387–401.

Davidson, E. S., Yasuna, A., & Tower, A. (1979). The effects of television cartoons on sex-role stereotyping in young girls. *Child Development, 50*, 597–600.

Davis, D. M. (1990). Portrayals of women in prime-time network television: Some demographic characteristics. *Sex Roles, 23*, 332.

Drabman, R. S., Robertson, S. J., Patterson, J. N., Jarvie, G. J., Hammer, D., & Cordua, G. (1981). Children's perception of media-portrayed sex roles. *Sex Roles, 7*, 379–389.

Durkin, K. (1985a). Television and sex-role acquisition. 1: Content. *British Journal of Social Psychology, 24*, 101–113.

Durkin, K. (1985b). Television and sex-role acquisition. 2: Effects. *British Journal of Social Psychology, 24*, 191–210.

Durkin, K. (1985c). Television and sex-role acquisition. 3: Counter-stereotyping. *British Journal of Social Psychology, 24*, 211–222.

Durkin, K. (1985d). *Television, sex roles and children: A developmental social psychological account.* Philadelphia: Open University Press.

Eisenstock, B. (1984). Sex-role differences in children's identification with counterstereotypical television portrayals. *Sex Roles, 10*, 417–430.

Fisher, G. (1989). Mass media effects on sex role attitudes of incarcerated men. *Sex Roles, 20*, 191–203.

Flex, V. C., Fidler, D. S., & Roger, R. W. (1976). Sex role stereotypes: Developmental aspects and early intervention. *Child Development, 47*, 998–1007.

Frueh, T., & McGhee, P. E. (1975). Traditional sex role development and amount of time spent watching television. *Developmental Psychology, 11*, 109.

Goff, D. H., Goff, L. D., & Lehrer, S. K. (1980). Sex-role portrayals of selected female television characters. *Journal of Broadcasting, 24*, 467–478.

Grusec, J. E., & Brinker, D. B. (1972). Reinforcement for imitation as a social learning determinant with implications for sex-role development. *Journal of Personality and Social Psychology, 21*, 149–158.

Gunter, B. (1995). *Television and gender representation.* London: John Libby.

Gunter, B., & Wober, M. (1982). Television viewing and perceptions of women's roles on television and in real life. *Current Psychological Research, 2*, 277–288.

Hearold, S. (1986). A synthesis of 1043 effects of television on social behavior. In G. Comstock (Ed.), *Public Communication and Behavior* (Vol. I, pp. 65–133). Orlando, FL: Academic Press.

Herrett-Skjellum, J., & Allen M. (1995). Television programming and sex stereotyping: A meta-analysis. In B. R. Burleson (Ed.), *Communication Yearbook 19* (pp. 157–185). Troy, NY: Sage.

Hunter, J. E., & Schmidt, F. L. (1990). *Methods of meta-analysis: Correcting for error and bias in research findings.* Newbury Park, CA: Sage.

Jennings-Walstedt, J., Geis, F. L., & Brown, V. (1980). Influence of television commercials on women's self-confidence and independent judgment. *Journal of Personality and Social Psychology, 38*, 203–210.

Katz, P., & Walsh, P. (1991). Modification of children's gender-stereotyped behavior. *Child Development, 62*, 338–351.

Kim, M., & Hunter, J. (1993). Relationships among attitudes, behavioral intentions, and behavior. *Communication Research, 20*, 331–364.

Kohlberg, L. (1966). A cognitive-development analysis of children's sex-role concepts and attitudes. In E. E. Maccoby (Ed.), *The development of sex differences* (pp. 82–173). Stanford, CA: Stanford University Press.

Kolbe, R. H., & Langefeld, C. D. (1993). Appraising gender role portrayals in tv commercials. *Sex Roles, 28*, 393–417.

List, J. A., Collins, W. A., & Westby, S. (1983). Comprehension and inferences from traditional and nontraditional sex-role portrayals on television. *Child Development, 54*, 1579–1587.

Luecke-Aleksa, D., Anderson, D. R., Collins, P. A., & Schmitt, K. L. (1995). Gender constancy and television viewing. *Developmental Psychology, 31,* 773–780.

Lull, J. T., Hanson, C. A., & Marx, M. J. (1977). Recognition of female stereotypes in TV commercials. *Journalism Quarterly, 54,* 153–157.

Mayes, S. L., & Valentine, K. B. (1979). Sex role stereotyping in Saturday morning cartoon shows. *Journal of Broadcasting, 23,* 41–50.

McArthur, L. Z., & Eisen, S. V. (1976). Television and sex-role stereotyping. *Journal of Applied Social Psychology, 6,* 329–351.

McCauley, C., Thangavelu, K., & Rozin, P. (1988). Sex stereotyping of occupations in relation to television viewing and the learning of sex-role stereotypes. *Sex Roles, 6,* 179–188.

McGhee, P. E., & Frueh, T. (1980). Television viewing and the learning of sex-role stereotypes. *Sex Roles, 6,* 179–188.

Melville, D. J., & Cornish, I. M. (1993). Conservatism and gender in the perception of sex-roles in television advertisements. *Perceptual and Motor Skills, 77,* 642.

Meyer, B. (1980). The development of girls' sex-role attitudes. *Child Development, 51,* 508–514.

Miller, M. M., & Reeves, B. (1976). Dramatic TV content and children's sex-role stereotypes. *Journal of Broadcasting, 20,* 35–50.

Mischel, W. (1966). A social learning view of sex differences in behavior. In E. E. Maccoby (Ed.), *The development of sex differences* (pp. 56–81). Stanford, CA: Stanford University Press.

Mischel, W. (1976). *Introduction to personality* (2nd ed.). New York: Holt, Rinehart & Winston.

Morgan, M. (1987). Television, sex-role attitudes, and sex-role behavior. *Journal of Early Adolescence, 7,* 269–282.

Morgan, M. (1982). Television and adolscents' sex role stereotypes: A longitudinal study. *Journal of Personality and Social Psychology, 43,* 947–955.

Morgan, M., & Rothchild, N. (1983). Impact of the new television technology: Cable TV, peers, and sex-role cultivation in the electronic environment. *Youth & Society, 15,* 33–50.

Newton, B. J., & Buck, E. B. (1985). Television as significant other: Its relationship to self-descriptors in five countries. *Journal of Cross-Cultural Psychology, 16,* 289–312.

Nikken, P., & Peeters, A. L. (1988). Children's perception of television reality. *Journal of Broadcasting & Electronic Media, 32,* 441–452.

O'Bryant, S. L., & Corder-Bolz, C. R. (1978). The effects of television on children's stereotyping of women's work roles. *Journal of Vocational Behavior, 12,* 233–244.

Orlofsky, J. L., Cohen, R. S., & Ramsden, M. W. (1985). Relationship between sex-role attitudes and personality traits and the revised sex-role behavior scale. *Sex Roles, 12,* 377–391.

Peevers, B. H. (1979). Androgyny on the TV screen? An analysis of sex-role portrayal. *Sex Roles, 5,* 797–809.

Peirce, K. (1989). Sex-role stereotyping of children on television: A content analysis of the roles and attributes of child characters. *Sociological Spectrum, 9,* 321–328.

Perloff, R. (1977). Some antecedents of children's sex-role stereotypes. *Psychological Reports, 40,* 463–466.

Perloff, R. M., Brown, J. D., & Miller, M. M. (1982). Mass media and sex-typing: Research perspectives and policy implications. *International Journal of Women's Studies, 5,* 35–44.

Pingree, S. (1978). The effects of nonsexist television commercials and perceptions of reality on children's attitudes about women. *Psychology of Women Quarterly, 2,* 262–277.

Popovich, P. M., & Butler, P. M. (1983). Recognition of sex-role stereotypes in prime time television. *Psychology and Human Development, 1,* 33–40.

Reep, D. C., & Dambrot, F. H. (1988). In the eye of the beholder: Viewer perceptions of TV's male/female working partners. *Communication Research, 15,* 51–69.

Reep, D. C., & Dambrot, F. H. (1989). Effects of frequent television viewing on stereotypes: 'Drip, drip' or 'drench'? *Journalism Quarterly, 66,* 542–550.

Reeves, B., & Greenberg, B. S. (1977). Children's perceptions of television characters. *Human Communication Research, 3,* 113–127.

Repetti, R. L. (1984). Determinants of children's sex stereotyping: Parental sex-role traits and television viewing. *Personality and Social Psychology, 10,* 457–468.

Rosenwasser, S. M., Lingenfelter, M., & Harrington, A. F. (1989). Nontraditional gender role portrayals on television and children's gender role perceptions. *Journal of Applied Developmental Psychology, 10,* 97–105.

Ross, L., Anderson, D. R., & Wisocki, P. A. (1982). Television viewing and adult sex-role attitudes. *Sex Roles, 8,* 589–592.

Ruble, D. N., Balaban, T., & Cooper, J. (1981). Gender constancy and the effects of sex-typed television toy commercials. *Child Development, 52,* 667–673.

Signorielli, N. (1989). Television and conceptions about sex roles: Maintaining conventionality and the status quo. *Sex Roles, 21,* 341–360.

Signorielli, N. (1990). Children, television, and gender roles. *Journal of Adolescent Health Care, 11,* 50–58.

Signorielli, N., & Lears, M. (1992). Children, television, and conceptions about chores: Attitudes and behaviors. *Sex Roles, 27,* 157–170.

Silverman-Watkins, L., Levi, S., & Klein, M. (1986). Sex-stereotyping as a factor in children's comprehension of television news. *Journalism Quarterly, 63,* 3–11.

Stanley, T. L. (1996). Only one of 4 behind camera is female. *Mediaweek, 6,* 28.

Tan, A. (1979). TV beauty ads and role expections of adolescent female viewers. *Journalism Quarterly, 56,* 283–288.

Tan, A., Raudy, J., Huff, C., & Miles, J. (1980). Children's reaction to male and female newscasters: Effectiveness and believability. *Quarterly Journal of Speech, 66,* 201–205.

Tuchman, G. (1979). Women's depiction by the mass media. *Signs, 4,* 529–542.

U.S. Commission on Civil Rights (1977). *Window dressing on the set: Women and minorities in television.* Washington, D.C.: Author.

Volgy, T. J., & Schwarz, J. E. (1980). TV entertainment programming and sociopolitical attitudes. *Journalism Quarterly, 57,* 150–155.

Weiss, N. A., & Hassett, M. J. (1993). *Introductory statistics* (3rd ed.). Reading, MA: Addison-Wesley.

Whitley, B. (1983). Sex role orientation and self-esteem: A critical meta-analytic review. *Journal of Personality and Social Psychology, 44,* 765–778.

Wolf, T. M. (1975). Response consequences to televised modeled sex-inappropriate play behavior. *The Journal of Genetic Psychology, 127,* 35–44.

Wroblewski, R., & Huston, A.C. (1987). Televised occupational stereotypes and their effects on early adolescents: Are they changing? *Journal of Early Adolescence, 7,* 283–297.

Zemach, T., & Cohen, A. A. (1986). Perception of gender equality on television and in social reality. *Journal of Broadcasting and Electronic Media, 30,* 427–444.

Zuckerman, D. M., Singer, D. G., & Singer, J. L. (1980). Children's television viewing, racial and sex-role attitudes. *Journal of Applied Social Psychology, 10,* 281–294.

14

Enjoyment of Mediated Fright and Violence: A Meta-Analysis

Cynthia A. Hoffner
Georgia State University

Kenneth J. Levine
University of Tennessee

Fright and violence have been featured in film and television since the early days of these media. For example, *The Cabinet of Dr. Caligari* (1919) is viewed as a classic of cinematic horror, and the television series *Alfred Hitchcock Presents* (1955–1962) focused on "stories of terror, horror, suspense" (Brooks & Marsh, 1988, p. 24). Researchers have long been interested in why people apparently enjoy entertainment that features the actual or threatened victimization of others. This meta-analysis examined some of the reasons people enjoy this type of media content. Specifically, any media offerings described as frightening, horrifying, or violent were considered. Violent media generally depict characters being attacked or physically injured by others. Scary media and horror often feature violence as well, but are designed to frighten or terrify audiences. Horror also typically involves supernatural or unnatural elements (Sapolsky & Molitor, 1996; Sparks & Sparks, 2000; Tamborini & Weaver, 1996). Although these types of content can be conceptually differentiated, they share key elements, most notably the depiction of actual or threatened physical harm to media characters, typically at the hand of external forces (e.g., other characters, natural disasters, or supernatural events). Throughout this paper these different types of content are treated similarly, except when their unique characteristics become relevant to the discussion (cf. Sparks & Sparks, 2000).

Several traditional reviews have addressed the enjoyment of fright and violence. Although some reviews consider a range of explanations for enjoyment (e.g., Cantor, 1998; Sparks & Sparks, 2000; Tamborini, 1991; Wober, 1988), many have focused on specific issues. For example, based on his excitation-transfer paradigm, Zillmann (1996) developed a theory of suspense enjoyment, where "suspense" is defined as audience members' "acute, fearful apprehension about deplorable events that threaten liked protagonists" (p. 208). In a recent book on horror films, several chapters are devoted to factors that affect the enjoyment of horror, notably sensation seeking and arousal needs (Lawrence & Palmgreen, 1996; Zuckerman, 1996), empathic responses to characters (Tamborini, 1996), and gender-role socialization (Zillmann & Weaver, 1996). Both Gunter (1994) and Fenigstein and Heyduk (1985) considered whether aggressive tendencies make violence more appealing.

As indicated by the topics of these reviews, recent research and theorizing in mass communication emphasize the need to consider individual differences in understanding responses to fright and violence. Another research approach investigates the role of content factors in enjoyment, such as the presence of destruction or sexual imagery, the characteristics of victims, or the resolution of the storyline. However, a search of the literature revealed very little commonality across studies in terms of the content factors examined or how they were operationalized, making a meta-analysis of these factors untenable. Thus, this meta-analysis focused on the role of individual differences in the enjoyment of fright and violence. Specifically, the studies selected for the meta-analysis (1) examined frightening or violent media content; (2) used self-report measures of enjoyment or preference for such content (the dependent variable); and (3) examined independent variables that had been given theoretical consideration in the literature and that were examined often enough in research to permit their inclusion in a meta-analysis. The independent variables included were negative affect and arousal during viewing, empathy, sensation seeking, aggressiveness, and the respondents' gender and age.

A review of the theoretical issues and research trends in each topic area is presented next. Many explanations for the enjoyment of fright and violence are derived from other fields of study (e.g., psychology) and are based on relatively little data pertaining to the mass media context. Although the research base is not extensive, it was deemed sufficient to justify a meta-analysis (for example, see Dillard & Spitzberg, 1984; Segrin, 1990). Hale and Dillard (1991, p. 465) contended that when the number of available studies is not large, "meta-analysis is most useful *not* as a mechanism for determining the final word in an area of research, but rather as a means of taking stock and providing directions for future research." Thus, the goals of this project are to synthesize the existing data and provide guidelines for future research.

EMOTIONAL RESPONSES DURING
VIEWING: NEGATIVE AFFECT
AND AROUSAL

A common element in horror films and other genres that feature threatening situations or events is suspense, which arouses fear in audience members about potentially disturbing outcomes (e.g., Mikos, 1996). One explanation of people's enjoyment of such presentations relies on the conversion of negative affect to euphoria that follows a satisfying resolution to a threat. According to Zillmann (1996), suspenseful drama, in which liked characters experience or are threatened with victimization, arouses dysphoric emotional reactions or "empathic distress." Based on his excitation-transfer theory, he argued that enjoyment of suspenseful drama is a function of both the level of negative emotional response produced during the program (characterized by subjective fear or distress and physiological arousal) and the viewer's affective reaction to the resolution. He contended that individuals cannot or do not perceive differences in the physiological arousal produced by different sources. Consequently, arousal from suspenseful scenes should carry over and intensify the viewer's positive response to a satisfying resolution, thus producing a rewarding, enjoyable emotional experience. Conversely, if the resolution is unhappy and produces sadness or disappointment, the residual arousal produced by suspense should intensify viewers' dysphoria.

Few published studies have investigated the extent to which negative affective responses that occur during viewing enhance the enjoyment of media presentations. Zillmann, Hay, and Bryant (1975) showed children an animated adventure program that varied in level of suspense. They found that physiological arousal, facial expressions of both fearfulness and positive affect, and liking for the program increased as the degree of suspense increased, especially when the threat was successfully overcome. However, the study did not directly examine the relationship between fear or arousal and liking for the program. More recent studies reported evidence that more negative affect is associated with greater enjoyment (Hoffner & Cantor, 1991a; Sparks, 1991; Zillmann, Weaver, Mundorf, & Aust, 1986), but this pattern occurred regardless of whether the threat was successfully resolved within the program.

Zillmann's model of suspense cannot easily account for enjoyment of scary programs that do not end happily. Many current horror films show sympathetic characters undergoing severe trauma and dying in brutal, terrifying ways. Zillmann (1996, p. 226) contended that "removal of the threat that produced empathic distress may be regarded [as] a minimal stimulus condition for the cognitive switch from dysphoria to euphoria." Thus, residual arousal can enhance enjoyment as long as viewers positively appraise their responses to the ending, even the simple termination of a threat (Tamborini, 1991). Other research suggests that people like frightening films because they feature destruction, or provide thrills, excitement, and unpredictability (Sparks, 1986; Tamborini & Stiff, 1987; Tamborini, Stiff, & Zillmann, 1987). It is also possible that some program elements that produce negative emotions elicit interest or enjoyment as well. This meta-analysis examined whether negative affect and arousal that occur during viewing are positively related to the enjoyment of programs featuring violence and fright.

PERSONALITY CHARACTERISTICS

Empathy. Many researchers have argued that empathy with characters' experiences is an important mediator of viewers' emotional responses to television and films (e.g., Oliver, 1993b; Tamborini, 1996). Empathy has been described broadly as an individual's reaction to the observed experiences of another person (Davis, 1994), but there has been much debate about the boundaries of this concept. However, there is a growing consensus that dispositional empathy is best conceptualized as a multidimensional construct that includes both cognitive and affective components (e.g., Davis, 1994; Stiff, Dillard, Somera, Kim, & Sleight, 1988). Perspective-taking, or sharing the viewpoint of another person, is the most often examined cognitive component of empathy. Affective components of empathy include sympathy or concern for another's welfare, and sharing of witnessed negative affect, although the definitions of specific components differ (e.g., Davis, 1994; Eisenberg & Fabes, 1990; Stiff et al., 1988).

Tamborini (1996) proposed a model of how individual differences in empathy are related to people's emotional responses to horror, although his model is relevant to any media presentation in which characters are threatened or victimized. He contends that cognitive components of empathy precede affective components, which have a direct effect on viewers' emotional reactions. The more that viewers tend to emotionally respond to or share the responses of others, the more negative affect they should experience while viewing horrifying presentations. Tamborini speculated that viewers who are highly empathic should dislike horror films as a result of their strong negative reactions to the pain and suffering of others.

Tamborini's (1996) proposed relationship between empathy and enjoyment initially appears inconsistent with Zillmann's (1996) model, which contends that "empathic distress" should facilitate liking of horror, at least after a satisfying resolution. In fact, Tamborini, Stiff, and Heidel (1990) argued that empathic distress should not readily intensify the enjoyment of horror, although enjoyment may be enhanced by arousal produced by other sources in a film. Two points can help to clarify this issue. First, as noted above, many recent horror movies conclude with scenes of further terror and victimization. As long as viewers do not consider such conclusions "satisfying," both models would predict that greater empathic response should be associated with less enjoyment. Second, perhaps what Zillmann referred to as "empathic distress" contributes to enjoyment of successfully resolved horror for people who do not identify deeply with the suffering of victims. However, viewers who appraise their reaction to violence as intensely dysphoric may have difficulty shifting to a positive state after a successful resolution. This type of response seems likely for individuals who experience high levels of empathy, especially what Davis (1994) has referred to as personal distress. Zillmann et al. (1986) advanced a similar rationale to account for the fact that distress did not enhance enjoyment of horror among women in their study, despite a satisfying resolution. This meta-analysis examined whether empathy is negatively related to the enjoyment of violence and fright.

Sensation seeking. Sensation seeking is another personal characteristic that is regarded as contributing to viewers' enjoyment of violence and fright. Zuckerman (1994, p. 27) defined sensation seeking as a trait characterized by "the seeking of varied, novel, complex, and intense sensations and experiences, and the willingness to take physical, social, legal, and financial risks for the sake of such experience."

In Zuckerman's original conceptualization, sensation seeking was viewed as related to an individual's optimal level of arousal, with high sensation seekers feeling better at higher levels of stimulation and arousal. From this perspective, high sensation seekers enjoy stimuli that elicit negative emotions, such as fear, because the intensity of these emotions helps them reach their optimal level of arousal. However, more recent evidence suggests that arousal in brain structures associated with positive affect provides rewards to high sensation seekers (Zuckerman, 1994, 1996). Zuckerman reconciled their taste for stimuli that induce fear and shock by suggesting that high sensation seekers may interpret the experience of these emotions positively, whereas low sensation seekers regard them as unpleasant (Zuckerman, 1996). Moreover, high sensation seekers also may be less likely to imagine themselves as personally vulnerable to threats depicted in horror and violent media (Franken, Gibson, & Rowland, 1992). This may enable them to better enjoy such presentations as a form of entertainment.

Zuckerman and Litle (1986) found that sensation seeking was positively related to frequency of attendance at horror films, but enjoyment of such content was not assessed. Two studies reported in book chapters (Edwards, 1991; Lawrence & Palmgreen, 1996) found strong evidence that sensation seeking and need for arousal are associated with a preference for horror. Although the importance of sensation seeking in comparison with other predictors of enjoyment has been questioned, there may be methodological reasons for why sensation seeking has not been a stronger predictor in some studies (see Lawrence & Palmgreen, 1996; Zuckerman, 1996). This meta-analysis examined the evidence for a positive correlation between sensation seeking and enjoyment of fright and violence.

Aggressiveness. It is often suggested that aggressive individuals are attracted to entertainment that features violence and brutality. The long line of research on televised violence has been concerned primarily with how viewers are affected by exposure to violent portrayals. But early on, researchers also recognized that a correlation between viewing violence and aggressiveness might reflect not only the effects of violence, but selective exposure, with more aggressive individuals choosing more violent media. Numerous surveys in the 1970s found that more aggressive children watched more violent television, although the causal direction of the relationship was difficult to establish in correlational research (see Fenigstein & Heyduk, 1985; Gunter, 1983; Wober, 1988). However, longitudinal studies using panel designs have provided evidence for selective exposure to violence by more aggressive children (e.g., Atkin, Greenberg, Korzenny, & McDermott, 1979; Huesmann, Lagerspetz, & Eron, 1984).

Fenigstein and Heyduk (1985) contended that individuals who are preoccupied with aggressive thoughts and fantasies are more interested in viewing violence performed by others. The processes that may lead aggressive individuals to enjoy such content have received little research attention. According to Atkin (1985, p. 76), "some persons with aggressive attitudes and behavior patterns ... may exalt in viewing content glorifying the acts that they commit, or they may feel satisfaction when characters express the sentiments that they value." In addition, aggressive individuals may like violent content because it enables them to justify their own behavior and feel less guilt about their actions (Atkin, 1985). This meta-analysis examined the evidence that aggressiveness is associated with greater enjoyment of fright and violence.

DEMOGRAPHIC CHARACTERISTICS

Gender differences. Numerous studies have noted that, compared with females, males tend to view more violent television, attend horror films more frequently, and report that they enjoy such presentations more. This pattern may derive from gender-role socialization of behavior and affect expression (Cantor, 1998; Oliver, 2000; Zillmann & Weaver, 1996). According to Fenigstein and Heyduk (1985), men are more likely than women to behave aggressively and to have aggressive fantasies, due in part to the process of socialization. Cantor (1998) argued that boys might be attracted to violence because they learn that such behavior is typically masculine and distinguishes them from girls.

Zillmann and Weaver (1996) developed a gender socialization theory to explain gender differences in the appeal of horror films. Research suggests that boys are socialized to avoid the outward expression of fear and distress, and may experience social disapproval for doing so, whereas girls are permitted or even encouraged to express these emotions (e.g., Saarni, 1989; Zaslow & Hayes, 1986). Zillmann and Weaver (1996) contended that in today's society, there are few circumstances where youth can develop and demonstrate mastery of gender-appropriate emotional behaviors. They suggested that horror films provide such a context for adolescents, in which boys can "prove to their peers, and ultimately to themselves, that they are unperturbed, calm, and collected in the face of terror," and girls can "demonstrate their sensitivity by being appropriately disturbed, dismayed, and disgusted" (p. 83). In part, then, gender differences in the enjoyment of horror may reflect the internalization of social expectations for males and females. This view suggests that gender differences in the enjoyment of fright and violence may increase from childhood through adolescence.

An interesting pattern of findings related to gender differences was first reported by Zillmann et al. (1986). Consistent with Zillmann's model of suspense enjoyment, the study found a positive association between distress and enjoyment of horror among males. However, no such relationship was observed among females. As noted earlier, the authors speculated that women who were intensely distressed by the horror film may have had difficulty reappraising their arousal as positive, despite an apparently successful outcome. This meta-analysis examined the evidence that males enjoy fright and violence more than females. In addition, this study assessed whether negative affect and arousal enhance enjoyment to a greater extent for males than for females.

Age differences. Researchers have considered whether enjoyment of violence and frightening media changes developmentally (Cantor, 1998). The literature on emotional development, especially in the area of emotion regulation, suggests that the ability to enjoy fear-arousing experiences develops with age. Campos and Barrett (1984, p. 251) argued that the development of coping skills "can help children transform negative emotions into pleasurable feelings of efficacy." It may be that adolescents can enjoy the experience of viewing fright and violence because they have better resources for coping with negative affect and can therefore feel satisfied with their ability to withstand vicarious terrors. In addition, there is some evidence that the cognitive switch from fear to happiness may not occur as readily among children as it does among older individuals (Barden, Garber, Leiman, Ford, & Masters, 1985; Hoffner & Cantor, 1990).

Twitchell (1989) argued that interest in violent media peaks during adolescence, when teens, especially males, are struggling to deal with aggressive impulses (Cantor, 1998). If this is true, then a curvilinear relationship should exist between age and liking for violence and fright, with an increase during childhood, a peak in adolescence, and a decline thereafter. However, Cantor (1998) contended that interest in violence at different ages varies by program genre, with certain types of child-oriented violence (e.g., action cartoons) appealing especially to younger children. She argued that children (particularly boys) in preschool and early elementary school enjoy such fare because they too are experiencing changes in their impulses and physical capabilities. This meta-analysis sought to determine whether there is a curvilinear relationship between age and enjoyment of violence and fright (as described above) and whether this pattern differs for child-oriented programs.

METHOD

The literature was collected in a search of four computer databases that index research in communication and psychology (ComAbstracts, PsycINFO, Social Science Index, and Sociological Abstracts). In an effort to identify all relevant articles, the search process used multiple search terms related to three basic concepts: media type (film, mass media, motion picture, television, TV), frightening or violent content (fright, frightening, horror, scary, violence, violent), and enjoyment or positive affective response (affect, appeal, enjoy, enjoyment, entertainment, like, liking). All abstracts were reviewed, and any articles that appeared relevant were obtained and examined. Additional articles were identified by examination of the references of all selected articles, as well as of the references in relevant books, book chapters, and review articles. The meta-analysis included only studies that were published in scholarly journals in 2002 or earlier.

Selection of Studies

To be included in the meta-analysis, a study had to meet several requirements. First, the study must examine frightening or violent entertainment and be written in English. Reality-based messages such as news and sports were excluded.[1] The content examined in each study was classified as (1) scary media, (2) horror, or (3) violent media. The classifications were made on the basis of the labels used and/or the descriptions of the media content in the studies.

Second, a self-report measure of enjoyment or preference for fright or violence must be used as a dependent variable. Three primary types of dependent

---

[1]It is common for scholars to treat news media and sports as distinct from non-reality-based entertainment (e.g., Guttmann, 1998; McCombs & Reynolds, 2002). Fictional media offerings, for example, are staged for the purpose of entertainment, and framing a presentation as fiction changes the ways in which audience members respond (McCauley, 1998). Certainly news and sports may be violent and/or frightening, and are often entertaining, but these genres each have a unique structure and purpose. News is primarily intended to inform rather than entertain, although the line between these two functions has been blurred in recent years. Sporting events often involve aggression, but without the intent to inflict injury or death (except in rare cases, e.g., boxing), as is typical in narrative depictions of violence. Thus, this meta-analysis focused on non-reality-based media presentations in which characters are threatened or involved in violence.

measures were evident in the research: (1) enjoyment of or liking for a genre of programming (e.g., horror films, violent content); (2) enjoyment of or liking for a specific program, usually viewed in a laboratory setting; (3) an expressed preference for viewing programs or films (e.g., based on film synopses). Measures of exposure (e.g., amount of violent television viewing) were not examined.[2]

Third, the study must include at least one of the independent variables of interest. These variables were selected because of theoretical interest, and because they were examined most often in the published literature (in at least four studies with useable data for this meta-analysis). The independent variables were: negative affect and arousal during viewing, empathy, sensation seeking, aggressiveness, and gender and age of respondent.[3]

Fourth, sufficient information to compute an effect size must be provided in the study or must be available from the author(s).[4]

The literature search found 47 journal articles that included both independent and dependent variables of interest. Of these, 11 articles were excluded because effect sizes could not be computed from the available data, or effects associated with the specific variables of interest were not reported and could not be obtained from the author(s) (Berry, Gray, & Donnerstein, 1999; Blanchard, Graczyk, & Blanchard, 1986; Botha & van Vuuren, 1993; Diener & Woody, 1981; Hansen & Hansen, 1990; King, 2000; Mundorf, Weaver, & Zillmann, 1989; Weiss, Imrich, & Wilson, 1993; Wober, 1997; Zillmann et al., 1975; Zillmann & Mundorf, 1987). Another study (Wilson, Hoffner & Cantor, 1987, Study 1) was excluded because of problems with the data from young children. Finally, one article (Lynn, Hampson, & Agahi, 1989) was excluded because of its unusually large sample size of

---

[2]Enjoyment of content that was not clearly identified as frightening or violent (e.g. action-adventure programs) was excluded. Studies that measured violence in favorite television programs (usually weighted by frequency of viewing) were also excluded, because this variable reflects both exposure and liking. Moreover, studies using this measure typically examined the link with aggressiveness, which presents the problem of directionality, since violent favorite programs may exert a strong influence on aggressiveness (Gunter, 1983).

[3]This meta-analysis examined all of the individual difference characteristics for which sufficient data were available. Several other personal characteristics were identified in the literature search (e.g., psychoticism, previewing anxiety or apprehension, gender-role identity), but either fewer than four studies were located that examined the characteristic, or the information needed to calculate an effect size could not be obtained for at least four studies.

[4]Several articles reported nonsignificant effects, but provided no statistical information. In other cases, significant results were reported but additional information was needed to estimate a correlation between the variables of interest. Additional statistical analyses or information were supplied for several studies (Cantor & Reilly, 1982; Harris, Hoekstra, Scott, Sanborn, Karafa, & Brandenburg, 2000; Hirschman, 1987; Hoekstra, Harris, & Helmick, 1999; Hoffner, 1995; Hoffner & Cantor, 1991a; Jablonski & Zillmann, 1995; Johnston, 1995; Oliver, 1993a; Raney, 2002; Valkenburg & Janssen, 1999). If the author could not be located, did not respond to the request, or did not have the information available, effects specifically reported as nonsignificant were treated as $r = .00$. This occurred in five instances. Other effects were excluded from the analysis.

2093.[5] Hunter, Schmidt, and Jackson (1982) indicate that this is one way to avoid skewing the meta-analysis results toward the findings of one large-sample study. Thus, this meta-analysis is based on data from 35 journal articles (reporting 38 different studies).

Analysis

To compute a meta-analysis, the results of all studies need to be converted into a common effect size metric. The correlation coefficient was chosen for this study because it is widely used and easily interpreted. When data were reported in some other format (e.g., t-test), techniques described in Hunter and Schmidt (1990) were used to convert the effects into their correlational equivalent. Because many studies used either single item measures or did not report reliabilities, correlations were not corrected for measurement error in the meta-analysis.

When a study included multiple measures of the same variable using the same mode of operationalization (e.g., rated enjoyment of two specific films), correlations involving those measures were combined (cf. Allen, Emmers, Gebhardt, & Giery, 1995; Segrin, 1990), using the r to z transformation (Corey & Dunlap, 1998).[6] However, three studies measured two different types of dependent variables (in all cases, enjoyment of a genre and enjoyment of a specific film). Each of these studies contributed separate correlations for the two types of dependent variables. When correlations were reported or could be computed only for separate subgroups (e.g., males and females), the correlation for the total sample was computed by combining the correlations for the subgroups (Hunter & Schmidt, 1990), using the r-to-z transformation.

---

[5]In a study of children aged 3 to 11, Wilson et al. (1987), Study 1, reported no age difference in liking for scary programs (answered yes or no). However, there was a strong tendency toward "yea-saying" among preschoolers on many questions, which, the authors argued, compromised the accuracy of the data. Thus, this study was excluded. Study 2 avoided this problem by having children rate their liking for scary programs. Lynn et al. (1989) surveyed adolescents and used a self-report scale of enjoyment of TV violence. The study reported correlations that were similar to those in the meta-analysis for aggressiveness ($r = .35$) and age ($r = .01$) but stronger for gender ($r = -.46$). However, the large sample size of 2093 greatly affected the homogeneity of variance. Thus it was deemed best to eliminate this study from further consideration.

[6]In all but two cases, the correlations that were combined involved multiple measures of the same type of dependent variable (e.g., enjoyment of two specific horror films, or enjoyment of several violent TV genres). The other cases involved multiple measures of the same independent variable: (a) two types of physiological arousal (Hoffner & Cantor, 1991a) and (b) four dimensions of the sensation seeking scale (Tamborini et al., 1987), which were combined so that the results would be comparable to those of the other studies that used a measure of total sensation seeking. In one study, aggressiveness was manipulated in two ways, but the effect of one manipulation was available for only a subset of the sample (Fenigstein, 1979, Study 2). The correlation for the total sample is included in the meta-analysis.

The meta-analysis was conducted with procedures described by Hunter and Schmidt (1990). For each independent variable, the correlations were weighted by sample size, and a mean correlation and confidence interval were calculated. To determine the likelihood that moderator variables were present, the chi-square test for homogeneity of variance, and the percentage of variance attributable to sampling error were computed. A significant chi-square indicates real variation among sample correlations, which suggests the presence of a moderator variable, whereas a nonsignificant chi-square indicates that differences among correlations are probably due to sampling error. An alternative approach recommended by Hunter and Schmidt (1990) is the 75% rule, which says that if at least 75% of the variance among correlations is due to sampling error, it is likely that the remaining 25% is due to uncorrected artifacts, and thus no moderator is present.

RESULTS

Table 14.1 lists the correlations and other descriptive information for each of the studies, and Table 14.2 presents the results of the initial meta-analysis for each independent variable. The initial meta-analyses were followed by a search for moderators, if warranted by theoretical concerns or significant variation in correlations across samples. Table 14.3 reports these results. Conclusions about significance are based on confidence intervals.

Negative Affect and Arousal During Viewing[7]

Negative affect during viewing was defined as the subjective experience of a negative emotional state, such as fear, anxiety, or distress, and was measured by self-reports in all studies. Consistent with Zillmann's (1996) model of suspense enjoyment, there was a significant positive correlation between enjoyment and negative affect during viewing. As Table 14.2 shows, correlations across the studies were homogeneous. The type of conclusion presented in the programs ranged from the defeat of the antagonist to an ongoing pursuit, but there was no indication that this factor played a role.

---

[7]Koukounas and McCabe (2001) also measured negative affect (anxiety, disgust, anger) and subjective arousal in response to violent film content. However, because they used a randomly ordered series of two-minute clips of violent and neutral scenes rather than a developed narrative sequence, the data are not relevant to Zillmann's (1996) model of suspense enjoyment. Thus, this study was excluded from analyses involving negative affect and arousal.

TABLE 14.1

List of Effects for Each Independent Variable's Association With Enjoyment

	Date	r	N	Dependent Variable Type[1]	Content[2]	Age Level[3]
Negative Affect						
During Viewing						
Hoffner & Cantor	1991a	.32	186	Enjoy Program	Scary	7–11 years
Sparks	1991					
Study 1		.24	110	Enjoy Program	Scary	Undergrads
Study 2		.42	44	Enjoy Program	Scary	Undergrads
Zillmann, Weaver, Mundorf, & Aust	1986	.32	72	Enjoy Program	Horror	Undergrads
Arousal During						
Viewing						
Hoffner & Cantor	1991a	.07	173	Enjoy Program	Scary	7–11 years
Sparks, Study 2	1991	.42	44	Enjoy Program	Scary	Undergrads
Sparks & Spirek	1988	.00+	59	Enjoy Program	Scary	Undergrads
Tamborini, Stiff, & Heidel	1990	−.26	95	Enjoy Program	Horror	18–22 years
Empathy						
Empathic Concern						
Harris et al.	2000	−.05	233	Enjoy Genre	Scary	Undergrads (M age: 19.2)
Hoekstra, Harris, & Helmick						
Study 2	1999	−.12	136	Enjoy Genre	Scary	Undergrads (M age: 20.1)
Hoffner	1995	−.08	228	Enjoy Genre	Scary	Grades 9–10 (M age: 15.0)
Johnston	1995	−.40	220	Enjoy Genre	Horror	13–16 years
Raney	2002	−.05	139	Enjoy Program	Violent	Undergrads
Tamborini, Stiff, & Heidel	1990	−.17	95	Enjoy Program	Horror	18–22 years
Personal Distress						
Harris et al.	2000	−.09	233	Enjoy Genre	Scary	Undergrads (M age: 19.2)
Hoekstra et al.,						
Study 2	1999	−.07	136	Enjoy Genre	Scary	Undergrads (M age: 20.1)
Hoffner	1995	−.25	228	Enjoy Genre	Scary	Grades 9–10 (M age: 15.0)
Tamborini et al.	1990	−.22	95	Enjoy Program	Horror	18–22 years
Sensation Seeking						
Aluja-Fabregat & Torrubia-Beltri	1998	.25	470	Enjoy Genre	Violent	Grade 8 (M age: 13.6)
Harris et al.	2000	.07	233	Enjoy Genre	Scary	Undergrads (M age: 19.2)
Hirschman	1987	.24	364	Enjoy Genre	Horror	20% Undergrads 80% Non-students

(Continued)

TABLE 14.1 (*Continued*)
List of Effects for Each Independent Variable's Association With Enjoyment

	Date	r	N	Dependent Variable		
				Type[1]	Content[2]	Age Level[3]
Sensation Seeking (continued)						
Neuendorf & Sparks	1988	.16	121	Enjoy Program	Horror	Undergrads
Tamborini & Stiff	1987	.19	155	Enjoy Genre	Horror	15–45 years
Tamborini, Stiff,						
& Zillmann	1987	.16	94	Preference	Horror	Undergrads
Aggressiveness						
Bjorkvist & Lagerspetz	1985	.50	87	Enjoy Program	Violent	5–9 years
Cantor & Nathanson	1997	.22	285	Enjoy Genre	Violent	Parents of
						5–10-year-olds
Diener & DeFour,						
Study 2	1978	−.05	54	Enjoy Program	Violent	Undergrads
Fenigstein	1979					
Study 1		.33	45	Preference	Violent	Undergrads
Study 2		.50	64	Preference	Violent	Undergrads
Haridakis	2002	.15	296	Enjoy Genre	Violent	Undergrads
						(M age: 20.5)
Langley, O'Neal,						
Craig, & Yost	1992	.55	20	Preference	Violent	Undergrads
Walker & Morley	1991	.42	332	Enjoy Genre	Violent	High school
						students
						(M age: 16.5)
Gender of Respondent						
Aluja-Fabregat &						
Torrubia-Beltri	1998	−.38	470	Enjoy Genre	Violent	Grade 8
						(M age = 13.6)
Apanovitch. Hobfoll,						
& Salovey	2002	−.21	188	Enjoy Program	Violent	Undergrads
						(M age: 19.4)
Bahk	2000	−.49	185	Preference	Violent	Undergrads
						(M age: 21.1)
Bjorkvist & Lagerspetz	1985	.00+	87	Enjoy Program	Violent	5–9 years
Cantor & Nathanson	1997	−.21	285	Enjoy Genre	Violent	Parents of
						5–10-year-olds
Cantor & Reilly	1982	−.23	232	Enjoy Genre	Scary	Grades 6 & 10
Cantor, Ziemke						
& Sparks	1984	−.26	43	Enjoy Genre	Scary	Undergrads
		.00+	43	Enjoy Program	Scary	
Fenigstein, Study 1	1979	−.56	87	Preference	Violent	Undergrads
Haridakis	2002	−.01	296	Enjoy Genre	Violent	Undergrads
						(M age: 20.5)
Harris et al.	2000	−.19	233	Enjoy Genre	Scary	Undergrads
						(M age: 19.2)
Hoekstra et al.	1999					
Study 1		−.24	202	Enjoy Genre	Horror	Undergrads
						(M age: 19.0)
Study 2		−.09	136	Enjoy Genre	Scary	Undergrads
						(M age: 20.1)

(*Continued*)

TABLE 14.1 (*Continued*)
List of Effects for Each Independent Variable's Association With Enjoyment

				Dependent Variable		
	Date	r	N	Type[1]	Content[2]	Age Level[3]
Gender of Respondent (continued)						
Hoffner	1995	−.13	228	Enjoy Genre	Scary	Grades 9–10 (M age: 15)
Hoffner & Cantor	1991a	−.08	186	Enjoy Genre	Scary	5–11 years
		.02	186	Enjoy Program	Scary	
Jablonski & Zillmann	1995	.00+	87	Enjoy Program	Violent	Undergrads
Johnston	1995	−.32	220	Enjoy Genre	Horror	13–16 years
Koukounas & McCabe	2001	−.73	40	Enjoy Program	Violent	University sample (M age: 26.4)
Neuendorf & Sparks	1988	−.20	121	Enjoy Program	Horror	Undergrads
Oliver	1993a	.04	96	Enjoy Program	Horror	Grades 9–12 (Median age: 16)
Oliver	1994	−.21	189	Enjoy Genre	Horror	17–27 years
		−.23	189	Enjoy Program	Horror	
Sparks	1986	−.13	220	Enjoy Genre	Scary	Undergrads
Sparks	1991					
Study 1		−.28	110	Enjoy Program	Horror	Undergrads
Study 2		−.07	44	Enjoy Program	Horror	Undergrads
Tamborini & Stiff	1987	−.12	155	Enjoy Genre	Horror	15–45 years
Valkenburg & Janssen	1999	−.48	200	Enjoy Genre	Violent	6–11 years
Wakshlag, Vial & Tamborini	1983	−.33	84	Preference	Violent	Undergrads
Zillmann et al.	1986	−.40	72	Enjoy Program	Horror	Undergrads
Age of Respondent						
Bjorkvist & Lagerspetz	1985	.43	87	Enjoy Program	Violent	5–9 years
Cantor & Nathanson	1997	−.22	285	Enjoy Genre	Violent	Parents of 5–10-year-olds
Cantor & Reilly	1982	.00+	232	Enjoy Genre	Scary	Grades 6 & 10
Hoffner & Cantor	1991a	.27	186	Enjoy Genre	Scary	7–11 years
		−.31	186	Enjoy Program	Scary	
Koukounas & McCabe	2001	.28	40	Enjoy Program	Violent	University sample (M age: 26.4)
Palmer, Hockett & Dean	1983	.23	89	Enjoy Genre	Scary	Grades 2 & 6
Tamborini & Stiff	1987	−.20	155	Enjoy Genre	Horror	15–45 years
Valkenburg & Janssen	1999	−.01	200	Enjoy Genre	Violent	6–11 years
Wilson, Hoffner, & Cantor, Study 2	1987	.05	115	Enjoy Genre	Scary	4–11 years

[1]Three primary types of dependent variables were used in the sample of studies: (1) Enjoy Genre: Enjoyment of or liking for a particular genre or type of programming; (2) Enjoy Program: enjoyment of or liking for a specific program or film; (3) Preference: Expressed preference for programs or films, based on brief descriptions.

[2]The studies examined three basic types of content: (1) scary media, (2) horror, and (3) violent media.

[3]The age range of respondents is listed if this information was provided in the article. If no age information is listed, then none was reported.

+This was a nonsignificant finding; the actual effect size was not reported and was not available from the author(s).

TABLE 14.2

Initial Meta-analysis Results for Independent Variables' Association
with the Enjoyment of Fright and Violence

Independent Variable	K	r	95% Confidence Interval	N	χ^2	% of Variance Attributable to Sampling Error
Responses During Viewing						
Negative Affect	4	.31	.22 to .40	412	1.33	100%
Arousal	4	.02	−.18 to .21	371	14.78***	27%
Empathy						
Empathic Concern	6	−.15	−.26 to −.04	1051	19.51***	31%
Personal Distress	4	−.16	−.24 to −.08	692	4.62	87%
Sensation Seeking	6	.20	.15 to .25	1437	5.53	92%
Aggressiveness	8	.29	.19 to .40	1183	32.20***	25%
Gender of Respondent	30	−.22	−.27 to −.16	4914	130.05***	23%
Age of Respondent	10	−.02	−.15 to .12	1575	74.73***	13%

Note: Gender of respondent was coded as male (0), female (1).
***$p < .001$

When males and females were considered separately, the correlation with negative affect was significantly stronger for males than for females. However, negative affect was associated with greater enjoyment for both groups. Again, the subsamples themselves were homogeneous.

Arousal during viewing was measured by various physiological measures, including skin conductance, skin temperature, and heart rate, with all data coded so that higher scores reflect more arousal. There was no support for Zillmann's model in the analysis of arousal, either overall or for males and females examined separately. The heterogeneity in correlations could not be accounted for by any moderator. However, because there were so few studies and they used different measures of arousal, such an outcome is not surprising.

Empathy

The six studies that examined empathy used a variety of different self-report scales, but all measured one or more affective components of empathy. All of the studies measured sympathy or concern for others' welfare (i.e., empathic concern, emotional empathy, humanistic orientation), and four of the studies measured the

TABLE 14.3
Meta-analysis Results Associated with Moderator Variables

Independent Variable Subgroup	K	r	95% Confidence Interval	N	χ^2	% of Variance Attributable to Sampling Error
Negative Affect During Viewing						
Males	4	.44	.32 to .56	185	1.89	100%
Females	4	.20	.07 to .32	227	1.47	100%
Arousal During Viewing						
Males	2	.18	−.08 to .44	131	3.66	55%
Females	2	.10	−.07 to .27	99	1.45	100%
Aggressiveness						
Enjoy Genre	3	.27	.14 to .40	913	14.43***	21%
Preference	3	.45	.31 to .59	129	1.54	100%
Enjoy Program	2	.29	−.08 to .64	141	11.84***	17%
Gender of Respondent						
Enjoy Genre						
Horror/Scary Media	11	−.18	−.22 to −.14	2044	11.40	96%
Violence	4	−.27	−.43 to −.10	781	41.21***	10%
Preference	3	−.47	−.56 to −.37	356	4.32	69%
Enjoy Program						
Blood & gore:						
Extreme	4	−.24	−.32 to −.16	570	2.48	100%
Moderate/minimal	7	−.04	−.12 to .04	653	7.94	88%
Age of Respondent						
Enjoy Genre						
Horror/scary media						
Children	3	.20	.09 to .30	390	3.83	78%
Adolescents	1	.00	−.13 to .13	232	—	—
Adults	1	−.20	−.35 to −.05	155	—	—
Enjoy Children's Media	4	−.11	−.33 to .11	758	39.03***	10%

Note: Gender of respondent was coded as male (0), female (1).
***p < .001

tendency to share witnessed emotional states (i.e., personal distress, emotional contagion). For the purpose of the meta-analysis, these two components are referred to as empathic concern and personal distress.[8]

---

[8]Other aspects of empathy (e.g., perspective taking, fantasy empathy) were reported in two or fewer studies and thus were not included in the meta-analysis.

Both empathic concern and personal distress were negatively correlated with enjoyment of fright and violence. The correlations with personal distress were homogeneous across studies, but those with empathic concern were not.

An examination of the studies suggested that the nature of the media content might account for the lack of homogeneity in the correlations with empathic concern. The two studies that reported the strongest negative correlations both examined enjoyment of horror films, specifically enjoyment of graphic violence such as torture (Johnston, 1995) or enjoyment of violent horror clips that concluded with brutal murders and *no satisfactory resolution* (Tamborini et al., 1990). In other words, these studies specifically focused on enjoyment of victimization. When these two studies were eliminated, the average correlation in the remaining four studies did not differ significantly from zero ($r = -.07, N = 736$), and the correlations were homogeneous ($\chi^2 (3) = 0.51$, ns, 100% of the variance attributable to sampling error). These studies measured enjoyment of scary films as a genre, with no specification of the content, with the exception that one study (Raney, 2002) examined responses to a violent drama with a likable victim but a *satisfactory resolution:* retribution against the villain.

Sensation Seeking[9]

There was a significant positive correlation between sensation seeking and enjoyment of fright and violence. The distribution of correlations across the studies was homogeneous.

Aggressiveness

The analysis of aggressiveness showed a moderate positive correlation with enjoyment of violence (the type of content referred to in all of these studies), but the correlations were not homogeneous.

The type of dependent variable was considered a possible moderator variable, because perceptions of program genres may differ greatly from responses to specific media offerings, which vary widely. When the studies were subdivided on this basis, correlations for the studies that examined enjoyment of the genre (in this case, violent media) were not homogeneous. However, all three surveys (individually) reported significant positive correlations between aggressiveness and enjoyment of violence, and the difference in magnitude may be due to a variety of methodological factors, such as the fact that the three studies examined three different age groups. The two studies examining responses to specific programs

---

[9]Johnston (1995) also measured sensation seeking, but only two short subscales were reliable (proclivity for substance abuse and adventure seeking). Since these subscales are not comparable to the entire sensation seeking scale used in other studies, the study was excluded from this analysis.

also were not homogeneous, undoubtedly because of methodological differences (i.e., children's responses to violent cartoons vs. adults' responses to a violent TV drama).

The possible role of gender in the differences among studies cannot be fully examined because only two studies (Deiner & DeFour, 1978; Fenigstein, 1979, study 1) reported data that could be used to calculate the association between aggressiveness and enjoyment of violence separately for males and females. When the data for these two studies were combined, the average correlation was positive for males ($r = .46, N = 48$) and was significantly greater than the average correlation for females ($r = -.20, N = 51$), which did not differ significantly from zero. The correlations were homogeneous for both males ($\chi^2 (1) = 2.68$, ns) and females ($\chi^2 (1) = 1.81$, ns), with 100% of variance in both groups attributable to sampling error. However, the sample sizes are so small that the findings should be treated with great caution.

Gender of Respondent

The analysis showed that males enjoy fright and violence more than females, but the correlations were not homogeneous across studies. The type of dependent variable was again considered a possible moderator variable, especially because it seemed likely that gender differences might vary, depending on the content features of specific programs.

The enjoyment of the genre of fright or violence yielded a significant negative correlation ($r = -.22, N = 2825$), with more enjoyment among male viewers, but the studies were not homogeneous ($\chi^2 (14) = 57.21, p < .001$). The studies were further divided based on whether they examined enjoyment of scary media and horror or enjoyment of violence. Table 3 shows that the correlations for enjoyment of scary media/horror were homogeneous, with more enjoyment among males than females. The correlations for enjoyment of violence as a genre were not homogeneous, perhaps because three studies involved children (and reported significant negative correlations), and the other involved adults (and reported a near-zero correlation).

The three studies that measured preference for or choice of a program in a laboratory setting found a much stronger gender difference than that observed for liking of horror or violence as a genre. The distribution of correlations across the studies was homogeneous, based on the chi-square.

The analysis of liking for specific programs produced a significant negative correlation ($r = -.15, N = 1223$), but the studies were not homogeneous ($\chi^2(11) = 37.36, p < .001$). This variation could be due to various content features of the specific programs employed. One such content feature is the visual depiction of blood and gore. Programs were classified as depicting extreme, moderate, or minimal blood and gore, based on descriptions in the studies or evaluations of the authors.[10] When studies using programs classified as extreme were compared with the others, meta-analyses yielded two homogeneous subsets of studies with significantly different average correlations. For the studies that used very graphic stimuli, males reported significantly more enjoyment than females, whereas the gender difference was not significant for programs with less graphic depictions.

To examine the possibility that the gender difference in enjoyment of the genre (fright or violence) changes with age, an additional analysis was conducted to compare age groups on this dependent variable. The resulting average correlations (which all differed significantly from zero, based on confidence intervals) were as follows: children, $r = -.25$ ($N = 671$; $K = 3$); adolescents, $r = -.29$ ($N = 1150$; $K = 4$); adults, $r = -.14$ ($N = 1474$; $K = 8$).[11] The correlations for adolescents and adults were homogeneous, but those for children were not. The correlation for adults was significantly smaller than the correlations for children and adolescents (which did not differ from each other), reflecting a smaller gender difference among adults than among younger individuals.

Age of Respondent

The average correlation between enjoyment and age did not differ significantly from zero, but the sample was heterogeneous, which is not surprising, since the age level of the participants varied widely.

As noted earlier, a curvilinear relationship between age and enjoyment of fright and violence has been proposed, with enjoyment increasing during childhood, peaking during adolescence, and declining thereafter. Cantor (1998), however, argues that this pattern varies by genre, with the preference for violent children's media declining during childhood. To investigate these possibilities, the effects were first subdivided into those that examined enjoyment of violent children's media (e.g., cartoons, a Disney sequence) and those that did not. This latter group—reflecting enjoyment of scary media or horror as a genre—was further separated based on the age level of participants (children, adolescents, or adults).[12]

Despite the very small number of studies, the data in Table 3 are somewhat consistent with both of the proposals outlined above. For the studies that examined enjoyment of horror or scary media as a genre, the pattern across age levels is con-

---

[10]One study was excluded because the violent program content was not described in sufficient detail to assess the degree of blood and gore (Koukounas & McCabe, 2001).

[11]Tamborini and Stiff (1987) included mostly adults (M age: 21), but some were as young as 15. When this study was eliminated from the analysis of adults, the results were essentially unchanged.

[12]The "enjoy program" effect from Hoffner and Cantor (1991a) was included with violent children's media because it involved responses to a sequence from a Disney film that could be considered violent (a boy being attacked by a snake). The Koukounas and McCabe (2001) study was excluded from further analysis of age differences for two reasons: (1) it was the only study not focusing on children's media that examined responses to specific programs, and (2) the age range for the sample was not reported, making it difficult to interpret the correlation with age.

sistent with the curvilinear hypothesis. For the three child samples (preschool through grade 6) the correlation is positive, for the adolescent sample (grades 6 to 10) the correlation is approximately zero, and for the community sample of adults the correlation is negative.[13] For the four studies dealing with children's media, age was not consistently related to enjoyment. However, the studies operationalized enjoyment in a variety of ways. Two studies measured children's overall enjoyment of violent children's TV genres (e.g., cartoons) or a Disney film sequence, and both reported significant negative correlations with age (Cantor & Nathanson, 1997; Hoffner & Cantor, 1991a). The other two studies specifically assessed enjoyment of the violence in children's TV programs and found either no age difference (Valkenburg & Janssen, 1999) or an increase in enjoyment with age (Bjorkvist & Lagerspetz, 1985).

DISCUSSION

This meta-analysis synthesizes research from published journal articles that has investigated viewers' enjoyment of fright and violence. Given the long-term interest in many of the explanations examined, it is surprising that so few relevant studies have been published. Yet in discussing the uses of meta-analysis, Hale and Dillard (1991) contend that knowledge claims are stronger if they are based on observations combined across even a few studies rather than on only one study involving a single sample. Given the limited research, this meta-analytic review should be regarded primarily as a way of summarizing the current state of knowledge and developing directions for future research.

The meta-analysis revealed that negative affect during viewing was associated with greater enjoyment of fright and violence. Although this pattern is consistent with an explanation based on Zillman's (1996) model of suspense enjoyment and excitation transfer theory, more research is needed to clarify certain issues. First, the lack of a similar pattern for physiological arousal presents a problem, although the limitations of physiological measurement must be recognized (Hoffner & Cantor, 1991a). Second, the research does not demonstrate that negative affect enhances enjoyment of a program to a greater extent when the threat is successfully resolved, as predicted by Zillmann's model. In fact, Hoffner and Cantor (1991) manipulated the resolution and found that the contribution of negative affect to program enjoyment was similar for the resolved and unresolved versions. Of course, very few published studies report data relevant to this issue. Zillmann (1996) notes that episode resolutions within a program may contribute to positive affect, and simple termination of the threat may be regarded as satisfy-

---

[13]The correlation for adolescents was reported as nonsignificant, but the actual statistic was unavailable. However, it should be noted that the large-sample study by Lynn et al. (1989) reported a similar correlation with age ($r = .01$) among adolescents aged 11 to 16.

ing by some viewers. However, there does not appear to be any evidence on these points. Laboratory research needs to examine more thoroughly how narrative structure interacts with affective responses and arousal during viewing.

The meta-analysis found some evidence that empathy is associated with less enjoyment of fright and violence. Some insight into the underlying processes may be gained by considering empathy in relation to Zillmann's (1996) model of suspense enjoyment. The self-focused nature of personal distress suggests that this component of empathy should be associated with less enjoyment of horror, regardless of the outcome of the program. In other words, those who tend to share the negative emotions of others should strongly dislike any depiction of violence or character endangerment. In contrast, empathic concern reflects an other-oriented focus of concern and caring for others (Davis, 1994). In accordance with Zillmann's model, this type of response may not reduce (and may even enhance) enjoyment of fright and violence, but only if threatened characters successfully escape or triumph. With no satisfactory resolution, concern for suffering characters should result in much less enjoyment. The meta-analysis results are basically consistent with these interpretations. However, there is no direct evidence regarding Tamborini's (1991) contention that empathy interferes with enjoyment primarily by producing an aversive emotional response to pain and suffering. Clearly there is a need for more studies that examine how empathy influences the way viewers respond to particular depictions of violence and victimization (cf. Raney, 2002). For example, individuals could view a film sequence that has been manipulated so that the emotional responses of the victim—such as facial and vocal expressions of pain—are either included or edited out, and a resolution in which the victim escapes from the attacker is either included or excluded. This type of research could begin to identify the process by which empathy (and associated negative affect) influences enjoyment of fright and violence, and how this process varies according to the narrative structure of the program.

Evidence also emerged that sensation seeking is associated with more enjoyment of fright and violence, which is consistent with other research reported in book chapters (Edwards, 1991; Lawrence & Palmgreen, 1996). The sensation-seeking scale includes four dimensions (thrill and adventure seeking; experience seeking; disinhibition; boredom susceptibility), but only three studies in this meta-analysis examined separate dimensions of the scale (Aluja-Fabregat & Torrubia-Beltri, 1998; Harris et al., 2000; Tamborini et al., 1987). Two of these studies, and other evidence, suggest that disinhibition (i.e., preference for a hedonistic lifestyle) is more strongly associated with interest in and exposure to fright and violence than the other dimensions (Zuckerman, 1996). This pattern awaits confirmation in further research that examines the separate dimensions of sensation seeking.

The reasons that high sensation seekers enjoy fright and violence also require further analysis. For example, do high sensation seekers actually enjoy the experience of fear? If these individuals tend to see themselves as personally invulnerable to threats (Franken et al., 1992), then they also may be less likely to experience lingering fright reactions to horror, such as fears about personal safety (Sparks, Spirek, & Hodgson, 1993). This may enable them to enjoy temporary states of fear without expecting long-term negative consequences. There is also limited evidence regarding the specific types of content that sensation seekers enjoy. If high sensation seekers interpret even aversive arousal positively (Zuckerman, 1996), these individuals should enjoy of any type of content that contributes to fear or arousal—such as suspense, destruction, action, violence, or death—to a greater extent than low sensation seekers. The role of these components could be examined in surveys in which respondents rate the appeal of different kinds of content, or rate their expected enjoyment of film synopses featuring different content elements. However, it should be noted that almost all of the studies in this meta-analysis examined sensation seeking with the use of survey methodology. Thus, there is little evidence regarding how sensation seeking affects enjoyment of specific frightening or violent presentations. Experimental research would be ideal for assessing responses to particular content elements and would clearly be the best way to examine the impact of production elements such as sound and visual effects (e.g., screams, rapid editing, music) that may contribute to the appeal of fright and violence among high sensation seekers. Finally, research should examine the combined role of empathy and sensation seeking in enjoyment. It seems likely that individuals low in empathy and high in sensation seeking would enjoy fright and violence the most, and that those high in empathy and low in sensation seeking would enjoy such content the least (Tamborini, 1991).

The meta-analysis produced some evidence that violence is enjoyed more by aggressively inclined individuals. This association was quite strong for studies that examined preference for violent media in a laboratory setting, and that manipulated aggressive thoughts and fantasies. Surveys also showed that enduring aggressive tendencies were associated with greater liking for violent media as a genre. However, there is little research regarding the reasons for this, such as whether more aggressive individuals enjoy seeing behavior like their own depicted as normative and appropriate (Fenigstein & Heyduk, 1985). Researchers need to examine aggressive and nonaggressive viewers' perceptions of violent content, and their affective reactions in response to different types of violent depictions. Studies examining responses to specific programs in a laboratory setting may be able to obtain a more precise understanding of the elements of violent portrayals that aggressive individuals find appealing. The meta-analysis also revealed a positive association between aggression and enjoyment for males, but not for females. However, the two studies for which data were available for both genders were conducted in the 1970s. It may be that changes in gender roles within society and/or an increase in powerful, aggressive female characters on TV and in films (e.g., *Buffy, the Vampire Slayer;* the *Alien* film series) have reduced or eliminated any gender difference in the association between aggression and enjoyment of violence. If such a difference does still exist, then the reasons for it (e.g., socialization processes, gender of the aggressors and victims in films) need to be explored.

The meta-analysis confirmed that enjoyment of fright and violence is higher for males than for females, particularly for preference for violence in a laboratory setting. In addition, there was clear evidence that males enjoy horror and scary media as a genre more than females do. Zillmann and Weaver (1996) propose that this pattern reflects the influence of gender role socialization. Although there is little direct evidence of this process, Zillmann et al. (1986) found that viewers enjoyed a horror film more when an opposite-gender coviewer expressed gender-appropriate reactions to the film. If the gender difference in enjoyment is due at least partially to socialization, then the difference should increase with age, at least through adolescence. The meta-analysis did not reveal any evidence to support this view. In fact, the meta-analysis showed that the gender difference in enjoyment of the genre of frightening and violent media was smaller among adults than among younger individuals. However, the age groupings were very broad, and the number of studies involving children and adolescents was relatively small. Research should examine how the gender difference in the enjoyment of fright and violence changes across the life span and should further investigate the role of socialization processes. This type of data could come from survey research that explores individuals' viewing motivations (cf. Johnston, 1995) and assumptions about gender-appropriate viewing behaviors at different ages, as well as from observational studies of children, adolescents, and adults watching scary or violent programs in same-gender and mixed-gender groups.

Program content was identified as a significant moderator of gender differences in liking for particular programs. Specifically, the gender difference was greater if the blood and gore in the program were judged to be extreme rather than mild or moderate. In a related finding, negative affect was more strongly related to enjoyment for males than for females. What can account for these results? One possibility is the fact that empathy is typically higher for females than for males (Eisenberg, Fabes, Schaller, & Miller, 1989). Perhaps females tend to dislike extreme violence because they are more likely than males to empathize with the victims. As suggested earlier, females may have more difficulty interpreting responses to horror as positive in the aftermath of empathic distress (Sparks, 1991; Zillmann et al., 1986). Research that probes the cognitive and emotional responses of males and females to different types of violent and frightening portrayals and measures relevant personal characteristics on which males and females typically differ (e.g., empathy, sensation seeking, aggressiveness) may provide some insight into the reasons for the gender difference.

Regarding age differences, there was limited support (based on very few studies) for the curvilinear hypothesis that enjoyment of violence and fright increases during childhood, peaks during adolescence, and declines thereafter. It should be noted that the observed pattern of correlations does not actually demonstrate that enjoyment was higher among adolescents than among individuals who were younger or older. More direct evidence for a curvilinear pattern would come from research involving people across the life span. For example, in their book chapter,

Lawrence and Palmgreen (1996) obtained a strong negative correlation between age and liking for horror films in a sample ranging in age from 18 to 82. If a similar study were to extend the age range to include children, a curvilinear pattern might emerge. Longitudinal data showing a change within individuals as they mature would provide even stronger support. Future research also needs to consider explanations for age differences. One possibility is that a preference for fright and violence parallels the age-related change (possibly biologically based) in sensation seeking, which has been shown to follow a similar curvilinear pattern (Zuckerman, 1994).

Based on this meta-analysis and the preceding discussion, some general guidelines for future research can be suggested. The meta-analysis revealed differences between enjoyment of fright or violence as a genre and enjoyment of specific programs. The reasons for these differences need to be explored. For example, reports of genre enjoyment undoubtedly reflect the elements that are typically featured in that genre and the social context in which it is usually viewed. In contrast, enjoyment of specific films depends on a wide variety of unique program characteristics; in addition, the experimental context in which such research is usually conducted overlooks the influence of social factors. Nonetheless, more experimental research is needed to examine the specific elements within programs that contribute to enjoyment of fright and violence, such as character portrayals (e.g., hero, villain), the type of threat or violence, the narrative structure, the type of resolution, and aesthetic elements such as music. Clearly these factors have been examined (e.g., Hoffner & Cantor, 1991a; Raney, 2002; Zillmann et al., 1975), but much more research is needed. For example, the meta-analysis revealed a gender difference in the enjoyment of fright and violence primarily for more graphic depictions, but there was not enough evidence to examine the role of content features in most analyses. Further research should examine not only how various content features contribute to the enjoyment of fright and violence, but also how they interact with personal characteristics like empathy, sensation seeking, or gender to influence enjoyment.

Related to the need for greater attention to content elements, more research needs to consider predictions derived from disposition theory (e.g., Raney, 2004; Zillmann, 1996), which focuses on the audience's judgments of and responses to characters in media entertainment. Although disposition theory has been used to explain audiences' enjoyment of many forms of entertainment, such as humor, sports, and drama, relatively few empirical investigations have applied this perspective to the enjoyment of fright and violence (e.g., Hoffner & Cantor, 1991; King, 2000; Oliver, 1993a; Raney, 2002; Raney & Bryant, 2002). Disposition theory can help researchers identify the elements of narrative structure and character portrayals that are likely to facilitate or minimize the enjoyment of a frightening or violent presentation, although the influence of other factors (e.g., action, aesthetics) should be recognized as well (McCauley, 1998). The role of empathy (as a personal characteristic) in mediating responses to fright and violence could be productively examined within this theoretical framework (cf. Raney, 2002). Surprisingly, virtually no research on enjoyment of fright or violence seems to have examined dramas featuring known characters, such as those on familiar television series. Given that parasocial relations can mediate viewers' responses to characters' experiences (Hoffner & Cantor, 1991b) and that audiences' affective responses to characters and evaluation of their behaviors play a key role in enjoyment of narratives, these are important factors to consider.

One issue that emerged in the literature within several different theoretical contexts is the importance of considering how viewers interpret or appraise their reactions to violence and fright. For example, Zuckerman (1996) argues that high sensation seekers may interpret fear-arousing experiences positively, whereas low sensation seekers regard them as aversive. A psychological concept relevant to this position is the "meta-experience" of an emotion (Mayer & Gaschke, 1988; Oliver, 1993b). Mayer and Gaschke (1988) contend that an emotion can be experienced not only directly, but also at a reflective level, which involves feelings and impressions about the emotion (i.e., the meta-experience). Within the domain of mass communication, Oliver (1993b, p. 319) argues that, "viewers may enjoy sad films not necessarily because the films ultimately succeed in evoking positive affect but, rather, because the experience of sadness itself is perceived as gratifying." By explicitly considering the meta-experience of fear and distress, researchers may gain a better understanding of individual differences in response to entertainment featuring terror and brutality.

Limitations to this meta-analysis should be acknowledged. As already noted, relatively few published studies have investigated the variables of interest. Thus, the conclusions reported here should be regarded with caution. In addition, the limited research prevents sophisticated tests of moderator variables, such as type of research design, demographics of respondents, or specific program characteristics. For example, although individual studies have examined the role of content features such as sexual portrayals in the enjoyment of horror (e.g., Oliver, 1993a), the uniqueness of individual programs suggests the need for multiple messages (Jackson & Jacobs, 1983). Given the impracticality of including several examples of complex media messages within individual studies (Hewes, 1983), one of the values of meta-analysis is the opportunity to uncover the effects of message features that vary across a sample of studies. The available data were rarely adequate for this type of analysis.

This meta-analysis summarizes the research on the relationship between enjoyment of fright and violence and several affective, personality, and demographic variables. Evidence for basic linkages among these variables is accumulating, but less is known about underlying processes, and more research support is needed for the various theoretical accounts. As suggested above, there is also a need to more thoroughly examine interactions between personality factors and program features, such as graphic violence and narrative structure. It is hoped that this meta-analytic review will stimulate theoretically based research that addresses these issues and which moves toward integrating separate lines of inquiry in a unified approach to understanding entertainment.

REFERENCES

References marked with an asterisk indicate studies included in the meta-analysis.

Allen, M., Emmers, T., Gebhardt, L., & Giery, M. A. (1995). Exposure to pornography and acceptance of rape myths. *Journal of Communication, 45*(1), 5–26.

*Aluja-Fabregat, A., & Torrubia-Beltri, R. (1998). Viewing of mass media violence, perception of violence, personality and academic achievement. *Personality and Individual Differences, 25,* 973–989.

*Apanovitch, A. M., Hobfoll, S. E., & Salovey, P. (2002). The effects of social influence on perceptual and affective reactions to scenes of sexual violence. *Journal of Applied Social Psychology, 32,* 443–464.

Atkin, C. (1985). Informational utility and selective exposure to entertainment media. In D. Zillmann & J. Bryant (Eds.), *Selective exposure to communication* (pp. 63–91). Hillsdale, NJ: Erlbaum.

Atkin, C., Greenberg, B., Korzenny, F., & McDermott, S. (1979). Selective exposure to televised violence. *Journal of Broadcasting, 23,* 5–13.

*Bahk, C. M. (2000). College students' responses to content-specific advisories regarding television and movies. *Psychological Reports, 87,* 111–114.

Barden, R. C., Garber, J., Leiman, B., Ford, M. E., & Masters, J. C. (1985). Factors governing the effective remediation of negative affect and its cognitive and behavioral consequences. *Journal of Personality and Social Psychology, 49,* 1040–1053.

Berry, M., Gray, T., & Donnerstein, E. (1999). Cutting film violence: Effects on perceptions, enjoyment, and arousal. *The Journal of Social Psychology, 139,* 567–582.

*Bjorkqvist, K., & Lagerspetz, K. (1985). Children's experience of three types of cartoon at two age levels. *International Journal of Psychology, 20,* 77–93.

Blanchard, D. C., Graczyk, B., & Blanchard, R .J. (1986). Differential reactions of men and women to realism, physical damage, and emotionality in films. *Aggressive Behavior, 12,* 45–55.

Botha, M. P., & van Vuuren, D. P. (1993). Reactions of black and white children to TV violence in South Africa: 1987-1991. *South African Journal of Psychology, 23,* 71–80.

Brooks, T., & Marsh, E. (1988). *The complete directory to prime time network TV shows 1946-present.* New York: Ballantine Books.

Campos, J .J., & Barrett, K. C. (1984). Toward a new understanding of emotions and their development. In C. E. Izard, J. Kagan, & R. B. Zajonc (Eds.), *Emotions, cognition, and behavior* (pp. 229–263). New York: Cambridge University Press.

Cantor, J. (1998). Children's attraction to violent television programming. In J. H. Goldstein (Ed.), *Why we watch: The attractions of violent entertainment* (pp. 88–115). New York: Oxford University Press.

*Cantor, J., & Nathanson, A. I. (1997). Predictors of children's interest in violent television programs. *Journal of Broadcasting & Electronic Media, 41,* 155–167.

*Cantor, J., & Reilly, S. (1982). Adolescents' fright reactions to television and films. *Journal of Communication, 32*(1), 87–99.

*Cantor, J., Ziemke, D., & Sparks, G. G. (1984). Effect of forewarning on emotional responses to a horror film. *Journal of Broadcasting, 28,* 21–31.

Corey, D. M., & Dunlap, W. P. (1998). Averaging correlations: Expected values and bias in combined Pearson rs and Fisher's z transformations. *Journal of General Psychology, 125,* 245–261.

Davis, M. H. (1994). *Empathy: A social psychological approach.* Madison, WI: Brown & Benchmark.

*Diener, E., & DeFour, D. (1978). Does television violence enhance program popularity? *Journal of Personality and Social Psychology, 36,* 333–341.

Diener, E., & Woody, L.W. (1981). Television violence, conflict, realism, and action: A study in viewer liking. *Communication Research, 8,* 281–306.

Dillard, J. P., & Spitzberg, B. H. (1984). Global impressions of social skills: Behavioral predictors. In R. N. Bostrom (Ed.),*Communication yearbook* (Vol. 9, pp. 446–463). Beverly Hills, CA: Sage.

Edwards, E. (1991). The ecstasy of horrible expectations: Morbid curiosity, sensation seeking, and interest in horror movies. In B. Austin (Ed.), *Current research in film: Audience, economics, and law* (Vol. 5, pp. 19–38). Norwood, NJ: Ablex.

Eisenberg, N., & Fabes, R. A. (1990). Empathy: Conceptualization, measurement, and relation to prosocial behavior. *Motivation and Emotion, 14,* 131–149.

Eisenberg, N., Fabes, R. A., Schaller, M., & Miller, P. A. (1989). Sympathy and personal distress: Development, gender differences, and interrelations of indexes. In N. Eisenberg (Ed.), *Empathy and related emotional responses* (pp. 107–126). San Francisco: Jossey-Bass.

*Fenigstein, A. (1979). Does aggression cause a preference for viewing media violence? *Journal of Personality and Social Psychology, 37,* 2307–2317.

Fenigstein, A., & Heyduk, R. G. (1985). Thought and action as determinants of media exposure. In D. Zillmann & J. Bryant (Eds.), *Selective exposure to communication* (pp.113–139). Hillsdale, NJ: Erlbaum.

Franken, R. E., Gibson, K. J., & Rowland, G. L. (1992). Sensation seeking and the tendency to view the world as threatening. *Personality and Individual Differences, 13,* 31–38.

Gunter, B. (1983). Do aggressive people prefer violent television? *Bulletin of the British Psychological Society, 36,* 166–168.

Gunter, B. (1994). The question of media violence. In J. Bryant & D. Zillmann (Eds.), *Media effects: Advances in theory and research* (pp. 163–211). Hillsdale, NJ: Erlbaum.

Guttmann, A. (1998). The appeal of violent sports. In J. H. Goldstein (Ed.), *Why we watch: The attractions of violent entertainment* (pp. 1–26). New York: Oxford University Press.

Hale, J. L., & Dillard, J. P. (1991). The uses of meta-analysis: Making knowledge claims and setting research agendas. *Communication Monographs, 58,* 463–471.

Hansen, C. H., & Hansen, D. R. (1990). The influence of sex and violence on the appeal of rock music videos. *Communication Research, 17,* 212–234.

*Haridakis, P. M. (2002). Viewer characteristics, exposure to television violence, and aggression. *Media Psychology, 4,* 323–352.

*Harris, R. J., Hoekstra, S. J., Scott, C. L., Sanborn, F. W., Karafa, J. A., & Brandenburg, J. D. (2000). Young men's and women's different autobiographical memories of the experience of seeing frightening movies on a date. *Media Psychology, 2,* 245–268.

Hewes, D. (1983). Confessions of a methodological puritan: A response to Jackson and Jacobs. *Human Communication Research, 9,* 187–191.

*Hirschman, E. C. (1987). Consumer preferences in literature, motion pictures, and television programs. *Empirical Studies of the Arts, 5,* 31–46.

*Hoekstra, S. J., Harris, R. J., & Helmick, A. L. (1999). Autobiographical memories about the experience of seeing frightening movies in childhood. *Media Psychology, 1,* 117–140.

*Hoffner, C. (1995). Adolescents' coping with frightening mass media. *Communication Research, 22,* 325–346.

Hoffner, C., & Cantor, J. (1990). Forewarning of a threat and prior knowledge of outcome: Effects on children's emotional responses to a film sequence. *Human Communication Research, 16,* 323–354.

*Hoffner, C., & Cantor, J. (1991a). Factors affecting children's enjoyment of a frightening film sequence. *Communication Monographs, 58,* 41–62.

Hoffner, C., & Cantor, J. (1991b). Perceiving and responding to mass media characters. In J. Bryant & D. Zillmann (Eds.), *Responding to the screen: Reception and reaction processes* (pp. 63–101). Hillsdale, NJ: Erlbaum.

Huesmann, L. R., Lagerspetz, K., & Eron, L. D. (1984). Intervening variables in the TV-aggression relation: Evidence from two countries. *Developmental Psychology, 20,* 746–775.

Hunter, J. E., & Schmidt, F. L. (1990). *Methods of meta-analysis: Correcting error and bias in research findings.* Newbury Park, CA: Sage.

Hunter, J. E., Schmidt, F. L., & Jackson, G. B. (1982). *Meta-analysis: Cumulating findings across studies.* Beverly Hills, CA: Sage.

*Jablonski, C. K., & Zillmann, D. (1995). Humor's role in the trivialization of violence. *Medienpsychologie, 7,* 122–133.

Jackson, S., & Jacobs, S. (1983). Generalizing about messages: Suggestions for design and analysis of experiments. *Human Communication Research, 9,* 169–181.

*Johnston, D. D. (1995). Adolescents' motivations for viewing graphic horror. *Human Communication Research, 21,* 522–552.

King, C. M. (2000). Effects of humorous heroes and villains in violent action films. *Journal of Communication, 50*(1), 5–24.

*Koukounas, E., & McCabe, M. P. (2001). Emotional responses to filmed violence and the eye blink startle responses. *Journal of Interpersonal Violence, 16,* 476–488.

*Langley, T., O'Neal, E. C., Craig, K. M., & Yost, E. A. (1992). Aggression-consistent, -inconsistent, and -irrelevant priming effects on selective exposure to media violence. *Aggressive Behavior, 18,* 349–356.

Lawrence, P. A., & Palmgreen, P. C. (1996). A uses and gratifications analysis of horror film preference. In J. B. Weaver & R. Tamborini (Eds.), *Horror films: Current research on audience preferences and reactions* (pp. 161–178). Mahwah, NJ: Erlbaum.

Lynn, R., Hampson, S., & Agahi, E. (1989). Television violence and aggression: A genotype-environment, correlation and interaction theory. *Social Behavior and Personality, 17,* 143–164.

Mayer, J. D., & Gaschke, Y. N. (1988). The experience and meta-experience of mood. *Journal of Personality and Social Psychology, 55,* 102–111.

McCauley, C. (1998). When screen violence is not attractive. In J. H. Goldstein (Ed.), *Why we watch: The attractions of violent entertainment* (pp. 144–162). New York: Oxford University Press.

McCombs, M., & Reynolds, A. (2002). News influence on our pictures of the world. In J. Bryant & D. Zillmann (Eds.), *Media effects: Advances in theory and research* (2nd ed., pp. 1–18). Mahwah, NJ: Erlbaum.

Mikos, L. (1996). The experience of suspense: Between fear and pleasure. In P. Vorderer, H. J. Wulff, & M. Friedrichsen (Eds.), *Suspense: Conceptualizations, theoretical analyses, and empirical explorations* (pp. 37-49). Mahwah, NJ: Erlbaum.

Mundorf, N., Weaver, J., & Zillmann, D. (1989). Effects of gender roles and self-perceptions on affective reactions to horror films. *Sex Roles, 20,* 655–673.

*Neuendorf, K. A., & Sparks, G. G. (1988). Predicting emotional responses to horror films from cue-specific affect. *Communication Quarterly, 36,* 16–27.

*Oliver, M. B. (1993a). Adolescents' enjoyment of graphic horror: Effects of viewers' attitudes and portrayals of victim. *Communication Research, 20,* 30–50.

Oliver, M. B. (1993b). Exploring the paradox of the enjoyment of sad films. *Human Communication Research, 19,* 315–342.

*Oliver, M. B. (1994). Contributions of sexual portrayals to viewers' responses to graphic horror. *Journal of Broadcasting & Electronic Media, 38,* 1–17.

Oliver, M. B. (2000). The respondent gender gap. In D. Zillmann & P. Vorderer (Eds.), *Media entertainment: The psychology of its appeal* (pp. 215–234). Mahwah, NJ: Erlbaum.

*Palmer, E. L., Hockett, A. B., & Dean, W. W. (1983). The television family and children's fright reactions. *Journal of Family Issues, 4,* 279–292.

*Raney, A. A. (2002). Moral judgment as a predictor of enjoyment of crime drama. *Media Psychology, 4,* 305–322.

Raney, A. (2004). Expanding disposition theory: Reconsidering character liking, moral evaluations, and enjoyment. *Communication Theory, 14,* 348–369.

Raney, A. A., & Bryant, J. (2002). Moral judgment and crime drama: A integrated theory of enjoyment. *Journal of Communication, 52*(2), 402–415.

Saarni, C. (1989). Children's understanding of strategic control of emotional expression in social transactions. In C. Saarni & P. L. Harris (Eds.), *Children's understanding of emotion* (pp. 181–208). New York: Cambridge University Press.

Sapolsky, B. S., & Molitor, F. (1996). Content trends in contemporary horror films. In J. B. Weaver & R. Tamborini (Eds.), *Horror films: Current research on audience preferences and reactions* (pp. 33–48). Mahwah, NJ: Erlbaum.

Segrin, C. (1990). A meta-analytic review of social skill deficits in depression. *Communication Monographs, 57,* 292–308.

*Sparks, G. G. (1986). Developing a scale to assess cognitive responses to frightening films. *Journal of Broadcasting & Electronic Media, 30,* 65–73.

*Sparks, G. G. (1991). The relationship between distress and delight in males' and females' reactions to frightening films. *Human Communication Research, 17,* 625–637.

Sparks, G. G., & Sparks, C. W. (2000). Violence, mayhem, and horror. In D. Zillmann & P. Vorderer (Eds.), *Media entertainment: The psychology of its appeal* (pp. 73–91). Mahwah, NJ: Erlbaum.

*Sparks, G. G., & Spirek, M. M. (1988). Individual differences in coping with stressful mass media: An activation-arousal view. *Human Communication Research, 15,* 195–216.

Sparks, G. G., Spirek, M. M., & Hodgson, K. (1993). Individual differences in arousability: Implications for understanding immediate and lingering emotional reactions to frightening mass media. *Communication Quarterly, 41,* 465–476.

Stiff, J. B., Dillard, J. P., Somera, L., Kim, H., & Sleight, C. (1988). Empathy, communication, and prosocial behavior. *Communication Monographs, 55,* 198–213.

Tamborini, R. (1991). Responding to horror: Determinants of exposure and appeal. In J. Bryant & D. Zillmann (Eds.), *Responding to the screen: Reception and reaction processes* (pp. 305–328). Hillsdale, NJ: Erlbaum.

Tamborini, R. (1996). A model of empathy and emotional reactions to horror. In J. B. Weaver & R. Tamborini (Eds.), *Horror films: Current research on audience preferences and reactions* (pp. 103–123). Mahwah, NJ: Erlbaum.

*Tamborini, R., & Stiff, J. (1987). Predictors of horror film attendance and appeal: An analysis of the audience for frightening films. *Communication Research, 14,* 415–436.

*Tamborini, R., Stiff, J., & Heidel, C. (1990). Reacting to graphic horror: A model of empathy and emotional behavior. *Communication Research, 17,* 616–640.

*Tamborini, R., Stiff, J., & Zillmann, D. (1987). Preference for graphic horror featuring male versus female victimization: Personality and past film viewing experiences. *Human Communication Research, 13,* 529–552.

Tamborini, R., & Weaver, J. (1996). Frightening entertainment: A historical perspective of fictional horror. In J. B. Weaver & R. Tamborini (Eds.), *Horror films: Current research on audience preferences and reactions* (pp. 1–13). Mahwah, NJ: Erlbaum.

Twitchell, J. B. (1989). *Preposterous violence.* New York: Oxford University Press.

*Valkenburg, P. M., & Janssen, S. C. (1999). What do children value in entertainment programs? A cross-cultural investigation. *Journal of Communication, 49*(2), 3–21.

*Wakshlag, J., Vial, V., & Tamborini, R. (1983). Selecting crime drama and apprehension about crime. *Human Communication Research, 10,* 227–242.

*Walker, K. B., & Morley, D. D. (1991). Attitudes and parental factors as intervening variables in the television violence-aggression relation. *Communication Research Reports, 8,* 41–47.

Weiss, A. J., Imrich, D. J., & Wilson, B. J. (1993). Prior exposure to creatures from a horror film: Live versus photographic representation. *Human Communication Research, 20,* 41–66.

*Wilson, B. J., Hoffner, C., & Cantor, J. (1987). Children's perceptions of the effectiveness of techniques to reduce fear from mass media. *Journal of Applied Developmental Psychology, 8,* 39–52.

Wober, M. (1988). The extent to which viewers watch violence-containing programs. *Current Psychology: Research & Reviews, 7,* 43–57.

Wober, J. M. (1997). Violence or other routes to appreciation: TV program makers' options. *Journal of Broadcasting & Electronic Media, 41,* 190–202.

Zaslow, M. J., & Hayes, C. D. (1986). Sex differences in children's responses to psychosocial stress: Toward a cross-context analysis. In M. E. Lamb, A. L. Brown, & B. Rogoff (Eds.), *Advances in developmental psychology* (vol. 4, pp. 285–337). Hillsdale, NJ: Erlbaum.

Zillmann, D. (1996). The psychology of suspense in dramatic exposition. In P. Vorderer, H. J. Wulff, & M. Friedrichsen (Eds.), *Suspense: Conceptualizations, theoretical analyses, and empirical explorations* (pp. 199–231). Mahwah, NJ: Erlbaum.

Zillmann, D., Hay, T. A., & Bryant, J. (1975). The effect of suspense and its resolution on the appreciation of dramatic presentations. *Journal of Research in Personality, 9,* 307–323.

Zillmann, D., & Mundorf, N. (1987). Image effects in the appreciation of video rock. *Communication Research, 14,* 316–334.

Zillmann, D., & Weaver, J. B. (1996). Gender-socialization theory of reactions to horror. In J. B. Weaver & R. Tamborini (Eds.), *Horror films: Current research on audience preferences and reactions* (pp. 81–101). Mahwah, NJ: Erlbaum.

*Zillmann, D., Weaver, J. B., Mundorf, N., & Aust, C. F. (1986). Effects of opposite-gender companion's affect to horror on distress, delight, and attraction. *Journal of Personality and Social Psychology, 51,* 586–594.

Zuckerman, M. (1994). *Behavioral expressions and biosocial bases of sensation seeking.* Cambridge, UK: Cambridge University Press.

Zuckerman, M. (1996). Sensation seeking and the taste for vicarious horror. In J. B. Weaver & R. Tamborini (Eds.), *Horror films: Current research on audience preferences and reactions* (pp. 147–160). Mahwah, NJ: Erlbaum.

Zuckerman, M., & Litle, P. (1986). Personality and curiosity about morbid and sexual events. *Personality and Individual Differences, 7,* 49–56.

15

Violent Video Games and Aggression: Why Can't We Find Effects?

John L. Sherry
Michigan State University

A number of years ago, I embarked on a review of the video game literature. What I found was a body of literature that was large, diffuse, and contradictory. There was work on the effects of violent video games, the causes of video game addiction, the use of video games in clinical settings (e.g., to treat autism), the effects of games on health and on cognitive development, and research on usage by groups such as girls and the elderly. The research stream was wide, but shallow with few studies in any one area. With growing media attention on ever more sophisticated violent games such as *Doom* and *Mortal Kombat,* I decided to focus my attention on the effect of violent video games on aggression. Certainly the gory and interactive nature of these games would stimulate greater aggression in users than the relatively passive experience of television and film viewing. I expected to find fairly clear, compelling, and powerful effects.

Instead, the literature is inconsistent. The researchers, primarily from psychology, had also expected to find powerful effects but were unable to demonstrate these effects in their research. In fact, whereas some studies found support for the proposition that violent video games lead to aggression (Anderson & Ford, 1986; Ballard & Wiest, 1995; Irwin & Gross, 1995; Schutte, Malouff, Post-Gordon, & Rodasta, 1988; Silvern & Williamson, 1987), a number of other studies showed no such relationship (Cooper & Mackie, 1986; Graybill, Kirsch, & Esselman,

245

1985; Graybill, Strawniak, Hunter, & O'Leary, 1987; Scott, 1995; Winkel, Novak, & Hopson, 1987). Still, researchers are committed to the notion of powerful effects (e.g., Funk, 1993; Gentile & Anderson, 2003). Complicating matters further, the literature on video game effects was littered with mixed findings from studies that used a wide range of games, treatment exposure times, and subject pools, obscuring clear conclusions.

Adding additional complication to the review, researchers theorized a variety of mechanisms to account for the effect of violent games on aggression. Naturally, different mechanisms dictate different variables that need to be accounted for in the studies. The theories were drawn directly from research on the effects of violent television including social learning, neo-associative networks (priming), excitation transfer, and catharsis. The decision to use these theories revealed a flawed assumption on the part of the researchers: that the video game-playing situation is simply an amplification of television viewing. Dominick (1984) pointed out that although video games share some characteristics with television, the medium is different in several ways that impact on theoretical mechanisms. For example, television is an essentially passive experience, whereas video games are highly active, requiring intense concentration and physical activity. Television viewers can break concentration and still follow the story, but video game players cannot break concentration except during programmed rest periods. Further, video game violence tends to be highly abstract versus the realistic violence portrayed on television. Studies of television and film effects have shown that greater aggression results from the viewing of more realistic or realistically perceived violence (Atkin, 1983; Berkowitz & Alioto, 1973). The amount of exposure to violence in a given amount of time varies by individual player, depending on skill level. Highly skilled players may engage in more violence more rapidly than players just learning the game.

In addition to structural features of the games, there were a number of social contextual factors influencing the game-playing experience that had not been accounted for by researchers. Sherry and Lucas (2003) used a uses and gratifications approach to point out that players' orientation to video games is much different from viewers' orientation to television. Traditionally, researchers have found that the main reasons for using television and film were to learn about society and about how you should behave, for diversion and arousal, and as a way of keeping up with friends (Blumer, 1933; Greenberg, 1974; Rubin, 1994). Sherry and Lucas found that the primary reasons for using video games were for the challenge of beating the game or friends, for the fantasy enjoyment of doing something you cannot do in real life (e.g., flying), as a reason to get together, and for diversion and arousal. There are clear overlaps, but the main reasons for using the two media are different.

Because of the inconsistent theories, findings, and number of subjects across studies, it would have been difficult to get an accurate sense of the state of the research using a qualitative approach based on reports of statistical significance.

Such an approach would also have made it difficult to locate important trends among the plethora of variables. Therefore, I decided to conduct a meta-analysis to test overall effect size and look for trends within the research reports (see Sherry, 2001). Meta-analysis provides an effective tool for discerning trends in the current research from which productive, theory-building research can emerge. I felt that meta-analysis was necessary at this stage of video game research to locate important causal variables and focus inquiry in a more systematic, productive manner.

In this chapter I continue the work started in the meta-analysis by addressing theoretical implications of the meta-analytic findings. The main question addressed here is whether television theories apply to the video game situation. I evaluate the four television theories in light of the meta-analysis results and results of other research that was informed by the meta-analysis findings. First, the set of meta-analysis results will be presented (Sherry, 2001). Next, each television theory will be evaluated in turn to determine whether the theory's mechanisms are consistent with the meta-analytic findings. I will then offer an overall assessment and directions for future research.

META-ANALYTIC FINDINGS

The overall estimate of the correlation between video game play and aggression in the 25 studies included in this meta-analysis ($r = .15$, $n = 2,722$) is associated with a Type I error probability of $\alpha < .0001$ and a Type II error probability of $\beta < .05$ (for details on calculations see Sherry, 2001). Cohen (1988) provided a guideline for understanding magnitude of effect size in terms of small ($d = .20$), medium ($d = .50$) and large ($d = .80$) effect. Converting the overall effect size of video game play on aggression into Cohen's d metric reveals a small effect size of $d = .30$. For comparison, Paik and Comstock (1994) arrived at an effect size estimate for the effect of television violence on aggression nearing the large effect range ($d = .65$). Overall, this analysis suggests that there is a correlation between playing violent video games and aggression, but that relationship is smaller than that found for viewing violent television content.

A search for moderator variables in the experimental studies revealed two important variables: type of game violence and time spent playing the games. More recent games that contain human or fantasy characters engaging in destructive violence registered greater effect sizes ($r = .15$) than games in which the portrayed violence was socially sanctioned ($r = .08$) as is found in sports genre games. This pattern of effect sizes suggests that players are reacting to some aspect of the message that differs by game type. This same pattern of differing effects by content has also been found in studies of violent television (Paik & Comstock, 1994). What is it about destructive violence that resulted in greater aggression? To better understand this relationship, future researchers will need to conduct a more focused analysis of game elements. Perhaps the destructive violence games contained a greater amount of action, thus raising nonspecific arousal. However, it would be difficult to contend that sports genre games are less action packed than fighter and shooter genre games. A closer analysis of the games included in the meta-analysis shows that sports games are represented by *Boxing* (c. 1985) whereas the human violence category is represented by recent violent games such as *Mortal Kombat* and *Wolfenstien 3D*. The chief difference would be richer three-dimensional graphics that are more likely to contain weapons and to depict blood and gore. Researchers have found that the presence of weapons increases effects in television studies (Carlson, Marcus-Newhall, & Miller, 1990) and that extensive violence lowers sensitivity to violence in television studies (Mullin & Linz, 1995).

Interestingly, effect size is negatively related to playing time, when one controls for age of players and year of study ($\beta = -.19$). If one examines the partial plot of playing time on effect size while controlling for age of subjects and year of study (Fig. 15.1), it appears that much of this relationship is anchored by two studies, with the remainder of the studies grouped in the center and supporting the general trend. The two studies anchoring the negative slope are interesting because they were performed using the same game (*Mortal Kombat*), the same type of subject pool (university undergraduates), and the same outcome measure but with widely differing playing times of 10 and 75 minutes (Ballard & Wiest, 1995, and Hoffman, 1995, respectively). Ballard and Wiest found an effect size of $r = .90$ using the Buss–Durkee measure of aggression, whereas Hoffman found an effect size of only $r = .05$ using the same scale. The results suggest that playing even the most violent of games for extended times may not increase aggression. This dramatic effect is important for both methodological and social reasons. Methodologically, the results suggest that most of the

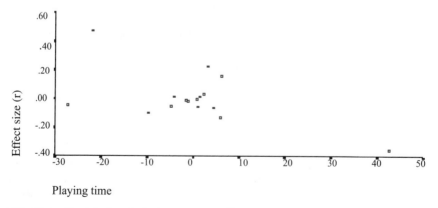

Playing time

FIG. 15.1   Partial plot of playing time on effect size, controlling for age of subjects and year of study.

studies may be measuring an initial arousal effect that may fall off dramatically after extended play. Therefore, a number of different playing time inductions need to be compared using the same game to trace out the trajectory of the effect. The results also have socially significant implications. Children and adolescents playing games in long stretches may transfer less aggression from the game playing situation to the external world than those playing for brief periods. Parents' intuitive reaction to limit playing time may actually be counterproductive, pulling the child from the game at a time when the largest aggressive effects are likely.

An important methodological trend was found among the studies. The average effect size differed according to whether a behavioral ($r = .09$) or pen and paper ($r = .19$) outcome measure of aggression was used. This finding does not change despite the possible confound that behavioral measures were used with younger children and attitude measures were used with university age subjects (analysis of covariance with age as covariate, $F(1, 11) = .21$ *ns*). Additionally, there was a difference according to whether the data were collected in an experiment ($r = .11$) or survey ($r = .16$). These two findings are somewhat confounded because surveys did not use behavioral measures only pen and paper measures. Nonetheless, these findings suggest that actual aggressive behavior is much more difficult to stimulate in experimental situations than simple feelings of aggression. The theoretical implications of this finding are interesting. Supporters of a neo-associative network approach would contend that this finding supports a priming of hostile/aggressive thoughts because measures such as adjective checklists are showing greater effects than behavioral measures such as free play. The presence of primed aggressive thoughts is confirmed by the adjective checklist; behavioral measures simply show the translation of the primed aggressive thoughts to the play environment. Social learning theorists could contend that the presence of aggressive thoughts simply represents the rehearsal of aggression before the imitative play that is evident when behavioral measures are used. In other words, both theories can account for the observed behavior and, as such, the studies do little to advance the understanding of the mechanism underlying the effect. A reading of the methodologies used in these studies confirms this assumption. There is little in the studies to explain or predict which mechanism is operating.

The mean effect size found in experiments that used nonviolent games in the control condition versus experiments that did not use a game in the control condition were slightly different ($r = .13$ and $r = .19$, respectively). This finding suggests a narrowing of aggression between the violent game condition and the nonviolent game condition as opposed to the nongame condition, which may be due to some level of arousal in the nonviolent game that is not present when subjects do not play a game.

Conspicuously absent from the literature are other designs used in the study of television violence such as longitudinal designs and field experiments. These types of research designs are more complex and expensive to undertake, so their absence may merely reflect the fact that video game research began fairly recently. However, these designs often provide the greatest ecological validity and allow researchers to make stronger predictions of social significance. These types of designs are crucial to understanding some of the relationships whose explanation is missing in the existing studies. For example, there is a small indication that the effect size increases as the subjects get older ($\beta = .25$), controlling for playing time and game type (year of study). This finding seems counterintuitive: We would expect younger children to be more vulnerable to the effects of video games. A longitudinal design would be helpful in assessing the effects of the games throughout the life span. A cohort study would also be helpful in settling the priming effects versus social learning debate, as social learning predicts relatively enduring effects whereas priming effects predicts short term effects. How long do the effects last? Are they translated into the real world? Field experiments would be helpful in assessing the social significance of the video game effects.

The main findings of the meta-analysis can be summarized as:

- There is a small, but significant, overall effect of video game play on aggression, but the effect is smaller than the effect of violent television on aggression.
- Within the range of games studied, the type of violence contained in the games is a moderately strong predictor of aggression, with human violence being associated with greater effects than fantasy or sports violence. The effect of video games with human violence themes approaches effects found in violent television studies.
- There is a trend suggesting that longer playing times result in less aggression.
- There is a small, positive correlation between age of subjects and effect size.
- Attitudinal pencil and paper outcome measures are associated with larger effect sizes than behavioral outcome measures.
- Experiments and surveys were roughly equivalent with survey research associated with slightly greater mean effect sizes.
- Experiments using no-game controls resulted in slightly more aggressive outcomes than experiments with nonviolent video game controls.

ASSESSMENT OF THEORIES

Which theory or theories best explain video game effects? One way to approach this question is to state what each theory would predict, then evaluate these hypotheses relative to the meta-analysis findings. Results of the analysis are presented a matrix (Table 15.1).

TABLE 15.1
Matrix of Findings by Theories[a]

Finding	SLT	Arousal	Priming	Catharsis
Violence type	x	√	x	x
Playing time	x	√	x	√
Subject age	x	n/a	√	n/a
Outcome measure	√	n/a	n/a	n/a
Control type	p	√	p	p

[a] √, consistent with theory; x, not consistent with theory; p, possibly consistent with theory; n/a, not applicable because the theory does not specify an expected outcome.

Social Learning Theory

The most frequently cited mechanism by which the games can result in aggressive behavior is social learning theory (Alman, 1992; Brusa, 1988; Chambers & Ascione, 1987; Graybill, et al., 1985; Hoffman, 1995; Irwin & Gross, 1995; Schutte et al., 1988; Silvern, Lang, & Williamson, 1987; Winkel et al., 1987). Social learning theory (SLT) provides a complex explanation of behavioral learning embedded in a social context. Essentially, SLT posits that behavior is learned through imitation of attractive, rewarded models (Bandura, 1994). These behaviors become a relatively enduring part of the learner's behavioral repertoire. The conditions under which this learning can take place are highly complex. Bandura (1994) proposes four processes governing observational learning: attention, retention, production, and motivation. Attentional processes determine which models are observed and what information is retained. Proponents of SLT for video games argue that video games should have particularly powerful effects due to the high attention levels of players and the active identification of players with characters on the screen. For example, in *Mortal Kombat,* the player chooses from among a group of combatant characters, each possessing different fighting skills. The player then *becomes* the character, fighting other characters to the death. Retention processes deal with committing observed behaviors to memory. In many ways, retention is central to the video game experience. To win a video game, the player must memorize a sequence of moves and procedures. Because of the limits of computer memory, challenges placed before the player are rarely random, but occur in the same sequence each time. Retention of these sequences and strategies allows players to move to higher levels, and mastery is so common that many games allow players to start at higher levels to avoid the monotony of running through well-memorized sequences that offer no challenge.

Production processes deal with the ability of the individual to replicate the observed behavior. At this stage, the individual attempts to enact the behavior in real life. Early games presented highly abstracted violence that was impossible to replicate in the real world (e.g., destruction of asteroids or shooting down spaceships). Recent games offer more realistic violence, although even the most realistic fighting games offer moves that cannot be performed in the real world (e.g., jumping 6 feet vertically to kick someone, ripping a brain and spinal column out of another person). Still, these games offer easily replicated punches, kicks, and elbow strikes. Finally, motivational processes address incentives to exhibit modeled behavior including direct and vicarious rewards. Violent games reward players most highly skilled at meting out aggression with higher points and longer playing times. Further, peers often award status to players who reach the highest scores and levels. Some video game researchers argue that game players are rewarded directly for enacting symbolic violence, and therefore may transfer the learned aggression to the outside world.

Predictions

SLT would predict that games with human violence content will produce greater imitation effects than other game types because the human-like characters provide a more realistic model for the player. Therefore, human violence games (e.g., *Mortal Kombat*) and violent sports games that feature human characters (e.g., *Boxing*) should have greater effects than games that do not provide a human model (e.g., *Asteroids* or *Dactyl Nightmare*). The greatest amount of aggression should be associated with socially sanctioned human violence games due to greater motivational reinforcement. Second, SLT would predict that longer playing times should result in stronger effects because there is greater learning and reinforcement of the modeled behavior. Next, SLT would predict that children would be more vulnerable to the effects of video games because they possess fewer social sanctions against aggressive behavior and are less able to cognitively distinguish between the video game world and the real world. Fourth, according to SLT the presence of social sanctions would result in measured behavioral aggression being less than measured attitudinal aggression. That is, players may cognitively process and rehearse the violent action, but some will be unwilling to perform the action because of social sanctions against aggressive behavior. These social sanctions are part of the motivational processes that affect adoption of behaviors. Finally, SLT would predict no difference between experiments that use a nonviolent game control and studies that use a no-game control because neither of the control conditions contains models of aggressive behavior.

Assessment

The findings of this meta-analysis offer little support for SLT learning as an explanation of video game effects. Of the five major findings, one is consistent with

SLT, three are not consistent with SLT, and one provides indeterminable support. Games that had human characters were not associated with more aggression than nonhuman violent games. Additionally, games that displayed nonhuman destructive violence were more likely to result in greater aggression than games that displayed socially sanctioned human violence. The main difference between game types that was associated with greater amounts of subsequent aggression was whether the games showed destructive violence or socially sanctioned violence. This is opposite of what would be expected by SLT.

The findings of the meta-analysis differ from SLT predictions in two additional ways. First, playing time is negatively related to aggressive effects. This is opposite of what would be expected from SLT because longer game play would allow for more reinforcement of aggressive behaviors. Second, the meta-analysis shows a small positive correlation between age and aggressive effects. SLT would predict that younger children would be more vulnerable to effects, not older subjects. Consistent with SLT, behavioral outcome measures of aggression were associated with weaker mean effect sizes than attitudinal outcomes.

Support is unclear for the fifth major finding, that there should be no difference between experiments using different types of controls. Instead, the meta-analysis shows a small difference, suggesting that there is a greater effect when a no-game control is used than when a violent game is used as the control. However, the magnitude of the difference is not great, making it difficult to take a strong position either way.

Excitation Transfer

Another explanation offered for effects of violent video games is the excitation transfer model (Ballard & Wiest, 1995; Brusa, 1988; Calvert & Tan, 1994; Winkel et al., 1987). The role of media arousal in the facilitation of aggression has been examined most thoroughly by Zillmann and Tannenbaum, and their associates. Tannenbaum and Zillmann's (1975) first model, the elementary arousal model, was an attempt to explain the role of emotional arousal from film in facilitating aggression. This model states that arousal is a heightened, nonspecific drive state. As such, arousal from media communication (e.g., film or television) will heighten or amplify the response that an individual already has. That is, "presented with a need or opportunity to respond in some manner to a particular environmental situation, *the individual will do as he would ordinarily—but with increased energy and intensity due to the available residual arousal*" (Tannenbaum & Zillmann, 1975, p. 161, emphasis added). Experiments testing this model with film and television stimuli consisted of three phases: the subject was angered by a confederate; the subject was exposed to an arousing or a neutral film; and the subject was then allowed to administer shocks to the confederate who had previously angered the subject (e.g., Zillmann, 1971; Zillmann, Katcher, & Milavsky, 1972). Subjects in the condition with the most arousing stimulus administered significantly greater shocks to the confederate. However, there was no difference when the subject was not angered before arousal. A later modification, the two-factor formulation, states that aggression only results from the interaction of cognitive and emotional components. Therefore, both "... an aggressive disposition and arousal have to be present to obtain a significant increase in subsequent aggression" (Tannenbaum & Zillmann, 1975, p. 177). Supporters of the excitation transfer model for video games suggest that highly violent video games provide the arousal that is necessary to heighten aggressive responses. When coupled with a predisposition to act aggressively, the subject becomes more likely to act aggressively than the subject normally would be.

Predictions

Arousal theory suggests that subject's predisposition to act aggressively will be heightened by the arousing effects of media. All but one of the video game studies did not have a prior anger manipulation, meaning that the arousal theory was not directly tested in the meta-analysis. The one study in which subjects were angered before playing video games (Walker, 1985) showed an insignificant effect size of $r = .06$ with 60 subjects either playing a fantasy violence content game (*Space Invaders*) or a neutral film.

Assessment

Although the excitation transfer theory, as stated by Zillmann and Tannenbaum, is not directly tested, the results of the meta-analysis are consistent with the concept of an arousal effect. To the extent that destructive violence may be more arousing than socially sanctioned violence (or that there may be a greater absolute amount of violence in later games), the findings of the meta-analysis support the idea of differential arousal effects. It is also reasonable to hypothesize that arousal due to violent images will be reduced after 75 minutes of playing. Whereas the initial experience of the game might be highly stimulating, after 75 minutes arousal may be replaced by fatigue or boredom from repeating programmed sequences, thus blunting the aggressive reaction. The results of the control-type analysis also support an arousal component to the effects of video games. Because nonviolent video games are still somewhat arousing, we would expect a greater difference between violent games and the no-game control than between violent games and the nonviolent games. The difference may be small because the nonviolent games may not be as arousing as the violent games. Unfortunately, the final two findings cannot be examined because arousal theory does not address differences by age or differences in expectations of outcome measures.

Neo-Associative Networks/Priming Effects

Several studies offered the neo-associative networks or priming effects mechanism as an explanation of hypothesized effects of video games on aggression (Anderson & Ford, 1986; Anderson & Morrow, 1995; Hoffman, 1995). Berkowitz's priming effects theory of media influence is based on a large volume of literature on the associative networks metaphor for memory storage (see Fiske & Taylor, 1991, pp. 296–306, for a review) and suggests that cues from violent content may lead to aggression or hostility because of the priming of semantically related informational nodes (see Berkowitz & Rogers, 1986). The associative networks theory states that memory is organized as an interrelated network of informational nodes. When one of these nodes is primed or activated by a stimulus, nodes that are semantically associated with the primed node are also activated. This is the hypothesized process when we recall related ideas at the same time. This effect has been demonstrated with a wide variety of stimuli as simple as a list of words (Wyer & Hartwick, 1980; Wyer & Srull, 1981) or an audio stimulus (Berkowitz, 1970) or as complex as a film or television program (Turner & Berkowitz, 1972; Berkowitz & Geen, 1967). The effect is widely believed to be short term in duration, but linkages between nodes are believed to be strengthened through repeated associations (Collins & Loftus, 1975). In the case of video games, associative network theory would suggest that exposure to violent games will prime a series of nodes associated with violence/aggression. The priming of these violence-related nodes presents the opportunity for transfer of aggressive thoughts into action (Jo and Berkowitz, 1994). Additionally, the theory would suggest that repeated violent video game play will strengthen connections between aggression-related nodes. The stronger the linkages are, the longer the duration of the effect (Collins & Loftus, 1975).

Predictions

Adherents of the priming effects theory would predict no differences in aggression by video game content type because human violence, fantasy violence, and socially sanctioned sports violence should all be linked to aggression nodes. The theory would also predict greater effects from longer playing sessions because nodes would fire more times, strengthening linkages in the associative network. Further, because adults have more aggression-related nodes than children, it would be expected that there should be a greater priming effect of video games for adults than for children. Whereas the priming effects theory suggests that primed aggressive nodes can transfer into aggressive behavior, the theory does not specify the inevitability of this transfer, making it impossible to hypothesize a difference between attitudinal measures and behavioral measures. Finally, priming effects theory would predict no difference based on experimental control type used because aggressive primes should only be carried in the violent video game not in the nonviolent game or the no-game condition.

Assessment

Priming effects theory also receives mixed support from the meta-analysis. The idea of differential effects by type of game violence is inconsistent with priming effects in that more sports violence was associated with a lower mean effect size than was found in human and fantasy violence. Consistent with the theory is a finding of a positive correlation between age and strength of effect. Older subjects should have more violence-related nodes than younger subjects. As with SLT, we would not expect to see a difference due to type of control group used because only the violent games contained messages that could prime semantic nodes. The small difference found in the meta-analysis makes it difficult to strongly argue for or against the theory. The negative correlation between playing time and effect size is opposite to what would be predicted by the theory. Finally, the priming effects theory does not provide a prediction of differences between attitudinal and behavioral outcome measures.

Catharsis

Six studies addressed the issue of catharsis effects, in which violent content media are used as a safe outlet for aggressive thoughts and feelings (Calvert & Tan, 1994; Dominick, 1984; Graybill et al., 1985, 1987; Silvern et al., 1987; Silvern & Williamson, 1987). The expectation is that an angered individual may use violent media instead of engaging in aggressive behavior. Catharsis effects have long been held to be an unlikely explanation of television effects (Gunter, 1994), largely due to the positive overall effect size found in television aggression studies and the discrediting of the few experiments that tested a catharsis effect. However, in a study by Kestenbaum and Weinstein (1985), adolescent boys reported that they used violent content video games to discharge aggression and manage developmental conflicts. The authors argued that this is because games allow players to take an aggressive role that is not allowed in the real world. Because the study was a self-report survey, it is not possible to draw a causal behavioral conclusion about video game effects.

A more accepted theoretical approach that predicts the same effects as catharsis is found in drive reduction theories. Drive reduction theories contend that people struggle to maintain physical, emotional, and psychological equilibrium. This is a plausible explanation because individuals have reported use of video games to manage arousal (Sherry & Lucas, 2003). Consistent with the Kestenbaum and Weinstein study (1985), it is possible that highly stressed or frustrated individuals may choose to use violent video games to manage aggression in order to move toward equilibrium through arousal or relaxation.

Predictions

Catharsis theory suggests that individuals use media to manage feelings of aggression—to reduce an aggressive drive. Therefore, to properly test catharsis theory, a subject would have to be placed in an aggressive drive state and then offered the opportunity to discharge that aggressive drive through use of media. The expectation would be that an individual's level of aggression will be lower after playing a violent video game than it was before playing the game. Any game that allowed the individual to act out aggression should result in the same effect, so there should be no difference by game genre. The longer an individual played, the more aggression would be discharged. Therefore, we would expect a negative relationship between effect size and playing time. The theory does not specify difference by age or between behavioral and attitudinal effects, so predictions cannot be made relative to these variables. Finally, the control condition should not matter because neither the game nor nongame control allows for the discharge of aggression.

Assessment

At first look, it would seem that catharsis is not supported by the findings of this meta-analysis because of the overall positive effect size between game play and aggression. Unfortunately, none of the studies made a legitimate attempt to determine whether there was a catharsis effect. That is, none of the studies began with subjects who had an aggressive drive state. Nonetheless, there are some indications of support for the catharsis hypothesis. First, the overall effect size is small despite concerted attempts to produce an effect. The negative relationship between playing time and effect size is consistent with the catharsis hypothesis. The lack of strong differences by control type may also support the catharsis argument.

A NEW MODEL—PRIMED AROUSAL

The results of the meta-analysis suggest that theories designed to explain and predict the social influence of television are not adequate to account for video game effects. SLT receives almost no support in the video game literature, whereas priming effects, excitation transfer theory, and catharsis have mixed support. Inspired by the meta-analytic findings, we conducted further research to clear up some of the issues raised. First, and most important, we wanted to know the orientation of game players to the gaming experience. That is, do they use games for the same reason that people watch television? As we suspected, players have a much different orientation to playing video games (Sherry & Lucas, 2003). We conducted a series of focus groups followed by a survey of individuals in four age groups to understand the main reasons people play video games. Unlike television, video game players report that the main reason they play is for the challenge of getting to the next level and beating the game. Respondents also reported that playing was a reason to get together with friends and to compete with them to be the best game player.

We have also been interested in the role of arousal in the violent video game–aggression equation. Is the aggression that researchers are finding simply a reflection of greater arousal by game players? We conducted an experiment in which we tracked physiological arousal as subjects played either a violent or nonviolent video game (Sherry, Curtis, & Sparks, 2001). As we expected, there was much greater physiological arousal associated with playing the violent video game. Within 8 minutes of playing the games, however, mean arousal levels were the same between conditions, as were our measures of state aggression. Without arousal, there was no aggression.

Taking the results of the meta-analysis and subsequent research, we can begin theorizing about the influence of video games. Arousal would appear to play a central role in the stimulation of aggression via video games. But how long will that arousal last? Would it decrease with prolonged play as suggested in the meta-analysis? What about players who come to the experience in an aggressive drive state? Excitation transfer and priming effects theories together account for the major findings of the meta-analysis. The theories complement one another; arousal explains the playing time effect that priming cannot, whereas priming provides the aggression stimulus missing in the experiments and accounts for differences by subject age. Both theories account for differences due to type of video game violence and, to some extent, differences by control type.

Perhaps a better question to ask at this point in the history of video game research is why researchers have not been able to produce dramatic effects demonstrating that violent video games do indeed drive aggression. Further, why do some researchers (e.g., Gentile & Anderson, 2003) continue to argue that video games are dangerous despite evidence to the contrary? If video games are the threat that these researchers claim they are, the popularity of violent video games would dictate that we would see an increase in violent crime. However, the U.S. Department of Justice reports that violent crime rates have decreased 50% during the past decade and are at the lowest levels that have been since the department began tracking crime in 1973 (U.S. Department of Justice, 2002). If these games are having the dramatic effects that some claim, it is not being realized in the streets of America.

It is likely that the small effects we are seeing result from an integration of arousal and priming theories. Whereas excitation transfer theory provided an explanation for three of the major effects found in the meta-analysis, the experiments lacked the aggressive stimuli used in the Tannenbaum and Zillmann experiments to predispose subjects to aggressive behavior. Without such an aggressive stimulus, the theory does not hold up. Priming provides the aggressive predisposition lacking in the video game experiments by priming (or not) aggressive nodes that are semantically related to the violent content of the video games. Once these nodes are primed, arousal provides an intensification of the aggressive thoughts and feelings. The combination of initial strong arousal and the violent primes results in greater aggression effects in the short term, but as arousal lessens during long playing sessions or briefly after game play, the effects of initial arousal wear off, weakening the overall aggressive effects. Additionally, the priming effects mechanism explains the age effect found. Because older subjects have more aggressive links and nodes, the effects are slightly greater for older subjects than for younger subjects. The two mechanisms work in unison to explain the findings of the meta-analysis.

Still, it would be unwise to rule out a catharsis effect of violent video games at this time. Not only are the meta-analytic findings generally consistent with a catharsis effect, but the larger social data coming from the Justice Department are also consistent with catharsis. A general decrease in violence in America is certainly a complex phenomenon, and video games probably do not likely account for the entire effect. However, traditional markers of social level violence are present without an accompanying increase in violence. For example, class differences have become exacerbated during the past decade, and more people are living at the poverty level than at any time since the Great Depression. However, we do not see the increase in crime that has marked such eras in the past. Are people working out their aggressions in the fantasy world of violent video games? This possibility is as plausible as the powerful effects claims that are being made by some researchers.

CONCLUSIONS AND DIRECTIONS FOR NEW RESEARCH

Although meta-analysis is a useful tool for estimating true population effect sizes and isolating trends in the literature, it did not indicate causal relationships between the variables under study here. In addition, the small number of studies and the use of subanalyses presented here enhance the possibility of capitalization on chance. Nevertheless, this analysis sheds light on important relationships and suggests paths for future, more programmatic, research.

New research is needed to explore the catharsis hypothesis more closely. Tests need to be designed that allow fair evaluation of the theory; that is, subjects must be first placed in aggressive drive states before they play violent video games. Relationships requiring further exploration include treatment strength of the violent video game induction, with a closer analysis of the effects of different game attributes (e.g. action, graphicness, difficulty, and human qualities) and a more complete range of game exposure times to account for changes in arousal during play. An experiment using a broad range of games and varying on theoretically salient dimensions will reveal game characteristics that best predict aggressive or cathartic outcomes. Information gained from such a study can be applied to an additional experiment in which the most important dimensions are examined with various playing times.

To understand the social significance of video games, we must first be honest as to whether the effects really exist. Only then can we understand the mechanisms by which the aggressive behavior may be caused. If observed aggression after playing video games is due to arousal and priming of associative networks, the effects of violent video games are limited in temporal duration and are of greatest concern primarily where the game playing takes place (home or arcades). Parents can expect their children to be aroused in the short term after game playing and can make rules accordingly. Arcade owners may be confronted with patrons who are primed to act aggressively, thus exacerbating some of the social problems traditionally associated with arcades. New research needs to be done to probe the mechanisms of these theories, not simply demonstrate behavioral effects.

Overall, it is clear that video games cause a small increase in aggression after short-term exposure. The factors underlying this increase are not clearly discernible from current research. Promising areas for future research include more targeted theory testing, as well as examinations of content differences and playing durations. The implications of this research are important to both parents trying to deal with a multimedia environment and politicians grappling with the social and legal significance of new media.

REFERENCES

Alman, R. E. (1992). *Video games: Interaction vs. observation as sources of social learning.* Unpublished master's thesis, Michigan State University, East Lansing.

Anderson, C. A., & Ford, C. M. (1986). Affect of the game player: Short-term effects of highly and mildly aggressive video game. *Personality and Social Psychology Bulletin, 12,* 390–402.

Anderson, C. A., & Morrow, M. (1995). Competitive aggression without interaction: Effects of competitive versus cooperative instructions on aggressive behavior in video games. *Personality and Social Psychology Bulletin, 21,* 1020–1030.

Atkin, C. (1983). Effects of realistic TV violence vs. fictional violence on aggression. *Journalism Quarterly, 60,* 615–621.

Ballard, M. E., & Wiest, J. R. (1995, March). *Mortal Kombat: The effects of violent video technology on males' hostility and cardiovascular responding.* Paper presented at the Biennial Meeting of the Society for Research in Child Development, Indianapolis, IN.

Bandura, A. (1994). The social cognitive theory of mass communication. In J. Bryant & D. Zillmann (Eds.), *Media effects: Advances in theory and research.* Hillsdale, NJ: Lawrence Erlbaum Associates.

Berkowitz, L. (1970). Aggressive humor as a stimulus to aggressive responses. *Journal of Personality and Social Psychology, 16,* 710–717.

Berkowitz, L., & Alioto, J. (1973). The meaning of an observed event as a determinant of its aggressive consequences. *Journal of Personality and Social Psychology, 28,* 206–217.

Berkowitz, L., & Geen, R. (1967). Stimulus qualities of the target of aggression: A further study. *Journal of Personality and Social Psychology, 5,* 364–368.

Berkowitz, L., & Rogers, K. H. (1986). A priming effect analysis of media influences. In J. Bryant & D. Zillmann (Eds.), *Perspectives on media effects.* Hillsdale, NJ: Lawrence Erlbaum Associates.

Blumer, H. (1933). *The movies and conduct.* New York: Macmillan.

Brusa, J. A. (1988). Effects of video game playing on children's social behavior (aggression, cooperation) (Doctoral dissertation, DePaul University, 1987). *Dissertation Abstracts International-B, 48/10,* 3127.

Calvert, S., & Tan, S. L. (1994). Impact of virtual reality on young adult's physiological arousal and aggressive thoughts: Interaction versus observation. *Journal of Applied Developmental Psychology, 15,* 125–139.

Carlson, M., Marcus-Newhall, A., & Miller, N. (1990). Effects of situational aggression cues: A quantitative review. *Journal of Personality and Social Psychology, 58,* 622–633.

Chambers, J. H., & Ascione, F. R. (1987). The effects of prosocial and aggressive video games on children's donating and helping. *Journal of Genetic Psychology, 148,* 499–505.

Cohen, J. (1988). *Statistical power analysis for the behavioral sciences* (2nd ed.). Hillsdale, NJ: Lawrence Erlbaum Associates.

Collins, A., & Loftus, E. (1975). A spreading-activation theory of semantic memory. *Psychological Review, 82,* 407–428.

Cooper, J., & Mackie, D. (1986). Video games and aggression in children. *Journal of Applied Social Psychology, 16,* 726–744.

Dominick, J. R. (1984). Videogames, television violence, and aggression in teenagers. *Journal of Communication, 34*(2), 136–147.

Fiske, S. T., & Taylor, S. E. (1991). *Social cognition.* New York: McGraw-Hill.

Funk, J. (1993). Reevaluating the impact of video games. *Clinical Pediatrics, 32*(2), 86–90.

Gentile, D. A., & Anderson, C. A. (2003). Violent video games: The newest media violence hazard. In D. Gentile (Ed.). *Media violence and children.* Westport, CT: Praeger.

Graybill, D., Kirsch, J., & Esselman, E. (1985). Effects of playing violent versus nonviolent video games on the aggressive ideation of aggressive and nonaggressive children. *Child Study Journal, 15,* 199–205.

Graybill, D., Strawniak, M., Hunter, T., & O'Leary, M. (1987). Effects of playing versus observing violent versus nonviolent video games on children's aggression. *Psychology: A Quarterly Journal of Human Behavior, 24*(3), 1–8.

Greenberg, B. S. (1974). Gratifications of television viewing and their correlates for British children. In J. Blumler & E. Katz (Eds.), *The uses of mass communication: Current perspectives on gratifications research* (pp. 71–92). Beverly Hills, CA: Sage.

Gunter, B. (1994). The question of media violence. In J. Bryant & D. Zillmann (Eds.), *Media effects: Advances in theory and research.* Hillsdale, NJ: Lawrence Erlbaum Associates.

Hoffman, K. (1995). Effects of playing versus witnessing video game violence on attitudes toward aggression and acceptance of violence as a means of conflict resolution (Doctoral dissertation, University of Alabama, 1994). *Dissertation Abstracts International, 56/03,* 747.

Irwin, A. R., & Gross, A. M. (1995). Cognitive tempo, violent video games, and aggressive behavior in young boys. *Journal of Family Violence 10,* 337–350.

Jo, E., & Berkowitz, L. (1994). A priming effect analysis of media influences: An update. In J. Bryant & D. Zillmann (Eds.), *Media effects: Advances in theory and research.* Hillsdale, NJ: Lawrence Erlbaum Associates.

Kestenbaum, G. I., & Weinstein, L. (1985). Personality, psychopathology and developmental issues in male adolescent video game use. *Journal of the American Academy of Child Psychiatry, 24,* 329–337.

Paik, H., & Comstock, G. (1994). The effects of television violence on antisocial behavior: A meta-analysis. *Communication Research, 21,* 516–546.

Rubin, A. M. (1994). Media uses and effects: A uses-and-gratifications perspective. In J. Bryant & D. Zillmann (Eds.), *Media effects: Advances in theory and research.* Hillsdale, NJ: Lawrence Erlbaum Associates.

Schutte, N., Malouff, J., Post-Gordon, J., & Rodasta, A. (1988). Effects of playing video games on children's aggressive and other behaviors. *Journal of Applied Social Psychology, 18,* 451–456.

Scott, D. (1995). The effect of video games on feelings of aggression. *Journal of Psychology, 129,* 121–132.

Sherry, J. L. (2001). The effects of violent video games on aggression: A meta-analysis. *Human Communication Research, 27,* 409–431.

Sherry, J. L., Curtis, J., and Sparks, G. (2001, May). *Arousal transfer or priming? Individual differences in physiological reactivity to violent and non-violent video games.* Theme session paper presented at the annual convention of the International Communication Association, Washington, DC.

Sherry, J. L., & Lucas, K. (2003, May). *Video game uses and gratifications as predictors of use and game preference.* Paper presented at the annual meeting of the International Communication Association, San Diego, CA.

Silvern, S. B., Lang, M. K., & Williamson, P. A. (1987). Social impact of video game play. In *Meaningful Play, Playful Meaning. Proceedings of the 11th Annual Meeting of the Association for the Anthropological Study of Play.* Champaign, IL: Human Kinetics Publishers.

Silvern, S., & Williamson, P. (1987). The effects of video game play on young children's aggression, fantasy, and prosocial behavior. *Journal of Developmental Psychology, 8,* 449–458.

Tannenbaum, P. H., & Zillmann, D. (1975). Emotional arousal in the facilitation of aggression through communication. In L. Berkowitz (Ed.), *Advances in experimental social psychology (Vol. 8).* New York: Academic Press.

Turner, C., & Berkowitz, L. (1972). Identification with film aggressor (covert role taking) and reactions to film violence. *Journal of Personality and Social Psychology, 33,* 755–763.

U.S. Department of Justice. (2002). *Bureau of Justice statistics: National crime victimization survey.* Retrieved July 30, 2003, from http://www.ojp.usdoj.gov/bjs/abstract/cv01.htm.

Walker, M. R. (1985). The effects of video games and TV/film violence on subsequent aggression in male adolescents (Doctoral Dissertation, University of Southern Mississippi, 1985). *Dissertation Abstracts International, 46,* 2082.

Winkel, M., Novak, D., & Hopson, H. (1987). Personality factors, subject gender and the effects of aggressive video games on aggression in adolescents. *Journal of Research in Personality, 21,* 211–223.

Wyer, R., & Hartwick, J. (1980). The role of information retrieval and conditional inference processes in belief formation and change. In L. Berkowitz (Ed.), *Advances in experimental social psychology (Vol. 13).* New York: Academic Press.

Wyer, R., & Srull, T. (1981). Category accessibility: Some theoretical and empirical issues concerning the processing of information. In E. Higgins, C. Herman, & M. Zanna (Eds.), *Social cognition (Vol. 1).* Hillsdale, NJ: Lawrence Erlbaum Associates.

Zillmann, D. (1971). Excitation transfer in communication mediated aggressive behavior. *Journal of Experimental Social Psychology, 7,* 419–434.

Zillmann, D., Katcher, A. H., & Milavsky, B. (1972). Excitation transfer from physical exercise to subsequent aggressive behavior. *Journal of Experimental Social Psychology, 8,* 247–259.

16

Effects of Music

Mike Allen
*University of Wisconsin–
Milwaukee*

Jennifer Herrett-
Skjellum
*Mississippi State
University*

Jill Jorgenson
Daniel J. Ryan
*University of Wisconsin–
Milwaukee*

Michael R. Kramer
St. Mary's College

Lindsay Timmerman
*University of Wisconsin–
Milwaukee*

Claims for the positive effects of popular music abound. For example, we often hear that "music soothes the savage beast" or "music has powerful healing powers." On the other hand, social critics commonly lambast popular music for its alleged negative effects, claiming that the "savage jungle beat" creates unrest among the teenage natives or that "music takes control of your body" or "makes you lose your mind." For each generation, a new iteration of popular music creates new allegations of antisocial effects. Jazz, ragtime, swing, rock and roll, punk, rap, and grunge are examples of types of music that appealed to the young and offended the more conservative or older members of the society. In this chapter we consider whether particular outcomes are associated with the preference for, or exposure to, various forms of music. The critical question guiding this synthesis of the literature becomes what the available literature, when properly synthesized, demonstrates about the impact of music on various social outcomes. For the purpose of this chapter the term *social behaviors and attitudes* refers to academic success, attitudes toward violence, aggression, sexual intercourse, use of illegal drugs, delinquency, and vandalism as well as beliefs about issues such as Satanism, the occult, racism, date rape, and rebellion against social rules. An antisocial behavior or attitude occurs when the individual accepts, endorses, or engages in action that is illegal, self-destructive, or destructive to property or another person or fails to accept, endorse, or engage in a action that would be considered prosocial (e.g., succeeding in school and avoiding situations involving risk). The definition carries a strong sense of conventionality and some outcomes (such as violence against persons) are more clearly antisocial and less acceptable than other outcomes considered undesirable (endorsing voodoo as a desirable practice). Any definition of this type introduces an evaluative sense for the attitudes and behaviors that endorses conventional or mainstream elements of social judgments made about adolescents and defines the parameters of acceptable behavior.

With the advent of music television (MTV) the combination of video and audio became available in a more exciting and potentially explicit manner (Gow, 1994, argues that the effect is larger than that of traditional television). Televised music links the audio sounds to a particular visual representation that may involve abstract images for denotative words or concrete depictions of euphemisms that may provide many alternative interpretations. An alleged result of MTV is the sense of community and commonality of interpretive experience for the music (Wells, 1984). The concerns of parents and others about the potential impact of music increased as the popularity of the forum increased, particularly with the addition of new TV channels (VH-1 and VH-2). Music operates as part of the social system, and, especially for adolescents, the sounds of growing up are often the sounds of popular music. Music serves as a background noise for many activities (studying, working, playing, talking, and eating). Songs of the day represent feelings, politics, emotions, rebellion alienation, religion, and philosophy for the consumer. Adolescents identify themselves and with each other on the basis of a common cultural shared experience through the music in the environment.

Understanding the impact of music on the actions and attitudes of consumers provides an interesting set of theoretical problems. Extant sets of meta-analyses indicate a correlation between the content of different media and various possible outcomes (Allen, D'Alessio, & Brezgel, 1995; Allen, Emmers, Gebhardt, & Giery, 1995; Elasmar & Hunter, 1997; Hearold, 1979, 1986; Herrett-Skjellum & Allen, 1996; Hogben, 1998; Huesmann, Moise, Podolski, & Eron, 1999; Morgan & Shanahan, 1997; Paik & Comstock, 1994). A legitimate question exists about the connection between the exposure to various media images and the personal and social actions of consumers. The nature of the relationship deserves definition and continued exploration as evidence accumulates and alternative theoretical models develop and are empirically tested. Current syntheses consistently demonstrate that a relationship between media content and various outcomes. Disagreement and uncertainty center on generating a satisfactory explanation for this relationship. In addition, legislative, judicial, or policy implications of this relationship remain important areas of development.

The fundamental issue of interpretation involves the problem of trying to separate the impact of the media as a possible cause versus simply a marker of some self-selection feature that makes the consumption of media an outcome of an underlying cause that predicts both media consumption patterns and the social/ personal behavior of interest. The argument for a noncausal relationship between media content and outcome assumes some underlying condition (perhaps a personality trait) that predicts both media consumption and social outcome. The observed correlation in any meta-analysis between social outcome and media content reflects the outcome of an underlying causal process with a common cause generating two outcomes. The size of the correlation between media content and social outcome should reflect the multiplication of the paths between the underlying cause and each variable. So far, no particular variable has been identified and tested in a consistent manner with a fully developed theoretical rationale to provide support for this conclusion. At this point, the support for this position remains more a theoretical possibility than an empirically supported conclusion.

A second interpretation argues for a causal relationship such that media content contributes to an outcome. In this model the media content is somehow creating the outcome by providing content that the consumer accepts and acts on. The argument takes the form that the viewer or consumer of the material ultimately uses the content as the basis for making decisions. In this chapter we develop the most common explanation, social learning theory (SLT), which argues that the media provide information that serves as a basis for learning about the environment, which, in turn, creates the basis for action.

One method of assessing this issue is a comparison between survey outcomes and experimental investigations. Survey research often includes an estimate of the frequency of viewing particular media content. Level of exposure should correlate with some measure of social behavior, and, as the quantity of viewing increases, so should the corresponding attitude or behavior. This design permits self-selection of the material. Individuals indicate the degree to which they voluntarily watch, read, or listen to a particular media content. Of course, causality is impossible to determine when one is deciding whether the exposure causes the social behavior or is simply an additional outcome of some underlying process. Surveys fail to provide the potential to determine media causality because the level of media exposure relies exclusively on self-selection.

Experimental investigations, on the other hand, involve random assignment of research participants to the various exposure conditions. Any outcome or difference observed between the groups, all else being equal, stems from exposure to different media. The benefits of this method come from the ability of the investigator to control the experience of the participants and to compare the outcome on the basis of that difference in experience. The normal arguments against the utility of such *laboratory communication* experiments include a consideration of the lack of generalizability of findings to anything other than the laboratory conditions of exposure and dependent measurement. The additional control over experience sacrifices the *naturalness* or the realism that surveys may tend to capture in representing the actual associations.

Comparing results from the experiments and surveys provides one method of establishing whether the impact of a particular media content is the outcome of a self-selection bias. In their meta-analysis, Herrett-Skjellum & Allen (1996) compared whether exposure to material containing sexual stereotypes would generate higher levels of acceptance of sexual stereotypes among consumers. The results demonstrated that for both groups (experiments and surveys), exposure was correlated with increased acceptance of sexual stereotypes. The meta-analysis provided some evidence against the arguments that associations are caused by a self-selection bias. If the self-selection bias argument were correct, the observed effect for experimental studies should be zero or very small, because the randomly assigned groups should be equivalent before exposure.

SOCIAL LEARNING THEORY

The primary approach to understanding the effect of media on the lives of individuals has involved the application of some form of SLT (Bandura, 1973, 1977). The primary tenets of SLT suggest that the media represent a form of social information that people use as a basis for making decisions about their personal lives. The assumption is that the person consuming the material finds that the actions depicted would, if performed by the consumer, generate the same rewards or punishments. This process, *identification,* assumes that the person exposed to media material views the circumstances in the song as similar. The learning comes not from direct experience but instead is vicarious: The exhibited behavior as well as the rewards and punishments associated with the action in the fictional account serve as a model for the consumer. The information in the media account functions as a source of information that the consumer uses as a basis for comparison.

The audience should not be considered passive, because the audience members act on the media content (Lull, 1980, 1982). The media provide information in the sense of displaying rewards and punishments for particular behaviors. This information becomes part of the understanding about the world. The content of the media is analyzed by the consumer to establish which behaviors are rewarded and which are punished. Consumers identify with characters become identified and learn vicariously to associate behavior with particular outcomes.

The question about musical content is whether the content of music is positive or negative, that is, prosocial or antisocial. Although the particular content and representation of particular actions obviously vary a great deal across all forms of music, some musical genres represent general attitudes toward various actions. Numerous content analyses have established that the material in the music has consistently over the decades contained material considered antisocial (Cole, 1971; Huffman & Huffman, 1987; Kalis & Neuendorf, 1989; Kurtz, 1981; McKee

& Pardun, 1996; Sherman & Dominick, 1986; Vincent, 1989). The question is not whether popular music contains the themes associated with antisocial behavior but whether exposure to the mass entertainment culture with those themes generates any negative consequences.

The case is particularly relevant when one is dealing with relatively inexperienced populations, such as adolescents. People considered to be leading rewarding and desirable lifestyles portray the images in music. The entertainers serve as a potential source of influence for the viewer. This argument becomes heightened for adolescents, who lack direct experience with the content because such images become the source of information for evaluating the experience. The adolescent's information base comes from vicarious experiences as well as direct experience. For example, several studies have illustrated how sexually explicit materials (pornography) serve as a source of information about sexual behavior (Bryant & Brown, 1989; Duncan, 1990, Duncan & Donnelly, 1991). The images portrayed in the lyrics of songs or displayed on MTV may function as more than entertainment for an audience trying to develop appropriate behavioral responses. This learning could be increased if the musical stars are identified as desirable role models.

SLT can be applied to both antisocial and prosocial message content. The effect of consuming music occurs regardless of prosocial or antisocial media content. According to the simplest interpretation of SLT, media content that portrays positive images should generate prosocial impacts on consumers. The problem with SLT remains the sense of passivity and determinism seemingly attributed to media content. Media really are only one source of influence out of many for the behaviors and attitudes of an individual. One extension of SLT is the confluence model offered by Malamuth and Billings (1986). This model accepts media influence as a determinant of behaviors for the individual, but views it as one cause among many. According to this model, the impact of media is not the sole determinant or even perhaps the major factor in forming behavior. Moreover, music messages are interpreted within the confluence of a system of judgment developed in conjunction with other sources of influence. However, media preferences may serve as a basis for affiliation or identification with peer groups or other individuals. The social function of media that serves as a basis for reinforcing the values of a social peer group may serve as an uniting or bonding agent as adolescents share media experiences such as music. Thus, media, and particularly music, should serve to assist in defining a person and the peer group values experienced as that person matures.

In this meta-analysis, we examine to some degree not simply the influence of music but in addition how music combines with other influences to generate particular outcomes. The evidence could be interpreted as demonstrating how music does or does not combine with other possible experiences in providing a basis for particular justifications for actions or attitudes of individuals.

METHODS

Literature Search

The literature search was conducted using a variety of electronic databases deemed relevant for this investigation (ComIndex, ERIC, PsycLIT, and SocInfo). Studies for inclusion had to contain some measure of music exposure (either experimentally controlled or by self-report survey) and some measure of effect (e.g., attitudes or knowledge about violence, sexuality, or criminal actions). The effect of music had to contain either an explicit stipulation of the type of music or depend on some form of popular music (the genre or type varies with the decade). Table 16.1 contains a list of the studies included in this analysis.[1]

Studies were excluded if the investigations dealt with issues about the content of the media or dealt with whether or not the respondents liked the media, understood the message of the music, or examined motivations for consumption. Studies that dealt with issues such as "mood effects" or what activities the person was engaged in while consuming were not considered a part of this analysis. A complete list of studies considered and reasons for exclusion is available from the first author, as well as a complete bibliography.

Coding for Moderating Effects

A variety of potential moderating conditions exist that could change the observed relationships.[2] Each moderator variable was coded and tested for in this analysis to determine whether the overall observed effect differed, based on an examination of the moderator. The goal was to examination potential sources of variability that may differentiate between effects both in terms of direction (positive and negative) and magnitude. We required a minimum of three studies in the moderator type before it was used as a basis for analysis (this justification lies in the ability to generate a meaningful test of homogeneity, which requires some degree of variability).

Age of the respondents/participants was considered as a potential moderating influence. Media content, particularly music, might be more influential on the young and less influential on the older consumer. Conversely, it could be argued

---

[1]The complete bibliography relied on is available from the first author as well as the complete justifications for inclusion/exclusion of individual manuscripts as well as statistical calculations for particular effects.

[2]One potential moderator, arousal (either physiological or psychological), was not coded for because of the low number of times this variable appeared in designs. Excitation-transfer theory (see Zillmann, 1971; Zillmann, Bryant, Comisky, & Medoff, 1981; Zillmann, Hoyt, & Day, 1974; Zillmann & Sapolsky, 1977) requires both a prior provocation and subsequent arousal to evaluate the theoretical tenets. As such, the unavailability of on point evidence for the requirements of this approach in the existing data makes evaluation of this theory impossible.

TABLE 16.1
List of Effects

Study Author	Date	r	N	Design	Age
Arnett	1991a, 1991b	.188	245	Nonexperimental	17
Bleich, Zillmann, & Weaver	1991	.384	82	Experiment	17
Brown & O'Leary	1971	.120	547	Nonexperimental	15
Burke & Grinder	1966	.160	271	Nonexperimental	13
Dixon & Linz	1997	.300	172	Experimental	20
Gan, Zillmann, & Mitrook	1996	.403	55	Experimental	20
Hansen & Hansen	1991	.202	82	Nonexperimental	20
Hansen & Hansen Study I	1990	.350	366	Experimental	20
Hanse & Hansen Study II	1990	.195	387	Experimental	20
Johnson, Jackson, & Gatto	1995	.478	46	Experimental	14
Lakkaraju	1985	.026	230	Nonexperimental	13
Larson & Kubey	1983	.310	75	Nonexperimental	16
Lewis	1980	.275	2,950	Nonexperimental	16
Moore	1989	.000	193	Experimental	21
Peterson & Pfost	1989	.057	144	Experimental	21
St. Lawrence & Joyner	1991	.451	75	Experimental	21
Strouse, Buerkel-Rothfuss, & Long	1995	.068	214	Nonexperimental	21
Sun	1986	.195	587	Nonexperimental	Unknown
Tanner	1986	.024	452	Nonexperimental	16
Trostle	1986	.763	66	Nonexperimental	16
Waite, Hillbrand, & Foster	1992	.327	52	Experimental	29
Wanamaker & Reznikoff	1989	.364	10	Experimental	24
Zillmann et al.	1995	.104	154	Experimental	17

that for survey research the expectation would be that the findings should be largest for older samples if the effect is cumulative. If media function to effect attitude, the repetition of the message over the course of years would be expected to continue to change attitude over time, so that the persons exhibiting the largest impact should be the oldest consumers.

The type of investigation was considered as a source of potential variability. The two broad classes of investigations dealt with experimental and nonexperimental analyses. The question is one of control over the stimulus that the person is responding to; that is, does the investigator or the participant control the selection of particular materials? The type of methodology is important because the impact of self-selection artifacts can be evaluated on the basis of whether the two classes of research produced consistent findings.

Type of music was considered because some content is considered more antisocial than other content. This consideration involves an assessment of whether particular forms of music are more influential in producing outcomes than others. Unfortunately, this variable could not be considered as a potential source of moderation. No form had three studies or was identified specifically enough to permit analysis.

The last moderator to receive consideration was the type of dependent outcome used to assess the relationship between music and social behavior/attitude. A variety of methods exist to assess the outcomes that music may be associated with: (a) antiwoman attitudes as exhibited by acceptance of rape myths or violence in sexual relationships, (b) academic success or willingness to study, (c) use of drugs, (d) aggressive behavior, and (e) general indexes of delinquency or combined indicators of social behavior (e.g., vandalism, drinking, or sexual behavior).

Statistical Analysis

The statistical analysis involves three basic sets: (a) conversion to a common metric, (b) averaging the estimates, and (c) examining the degree of variability in the data set. In this meta-analysis, we used the metric of the correlation coefficient owing to the ease of statistical manipulation and interpretation of information. Each estimate was corrected for appropriate statistical artifacts (attenuation and dichotomization) as appropriate (other corrections such as restriction in range or regression to the mean did not exist in this data pool). The individual effects were averaged using a procedure that weighted the study by the size of the sample. The procedures used in this analysis are outlined by Hunter and Schmidt (1990) and by Rosenthal (1984).

A completely successful analysis of the variability produces an average that when compared with other averages is significantly different but that for each separate estimate will be based on a homogeneous set of data. The equivalent rules are similar to analysis of variance, for which the expectation is that there will be homogeneity of variance within a cell, but that the between-cell mean differences will indicate a source of variability that is significant (Hall & Rosenthal, 1991).

RESULTS

Overall, the results indicate that exposure to music increases antisocial actions and beliefs (average $r = .228, k = 23, N = 7,003$). An analysis of the variability demonstrates that the observed average effect is based on a sample of correlations that is heterogeneous ($\chi^2 2, N = 7,003 = 141.42, p < .05$). This result, while indicating a positive association, does indicate the probable existence of a moderator variable, and further analysis is needed to examine the potential sources of variability.

Design of Investigation

The first set of designs examined were the nonexperimental research studies The average effect was slightly smaller than the overall effect (average $r = .216, k = 11, N = 5,267$), but the average estimate was heterogeneous ($\chi^2 10, N = 5,267$,

$p < .05$). Two investigators reported particularly large effects (Lewis, 1980; Trostle, 1986). The larger effects for both studies are perhaps illuminating because they are efforts to match particular content of music to related outcomes. Trostle's survey dealt with comparing self-identified heavy metal "stoners" and their beliefs in various occult practices (belief in witches, voodoo, and black magic). The argument Trostle made is that the content of the music contains these themes, and persons with a strong preference for this music would be more likely to believe or accept the content as true compared with adolescents not listening to this form of music. Lewis examined the preference for particular kinds of music (e.g., heavy metal, rock, and country) and the self-reported use of drugs. The Lewis database is also extremely large ($N = 2,950$), and the analysis should be conducted with and without this particular large study; this examination is necessary to determine whether one study with a very large sample size is "drowning out" the rest of the investigations. Excluding both studies produces a smaller average effect (average $r = .123$, $k = 9$, $N = 2,251$) with the sample of effects now being homogeneous (χ^2 8, $N = 2,251 = 7.37$, $p > .05$).

Findings for the experimental investigations were similar: The effect was slightly larger than the overall (average $r = .236$, $k = 12$, $N = 1,736$) and highly variable effects (χ^2 11, $N = 1736 = 33.33$, $p < .05$). The overall effects demonstrate that the use of a type of method as a single moderator did not successfully account for the level of variability found among the data sets. However, one data set deserves special consideration in the examination of the effects. Moore (1989) conducted an experimental investigation in which participants were, as part of a "learning" investigation, asked to give electric shocks to another person. Moore was the only investigator who required a person to actually perform some action with consequences. Deleting this data set produces a higher average correlation (average $r = .265$, $k = 11$, $N = 1,543$) based on a homogeneous set of data points (χ^2 10, $N = 1,543 = 19.77$, $p > .05$).

Age

The average age of the participants was correlated with the size of the effect observed in the investigation. If age is related to the size of the effect, a correlation will exist between the effect and the age of the participants. Examining all 22 studies (Sun and Lull, 1982, did not provide any method of estimating age) with 6,416 participants, we found a correlation between age and size of the effect ($r = .31$). This indicates that as age increased, so did the effect size. Taking the 11 nonexperimental designs, we found that the correlation between age and size of effect was positive ($r = .38$, $k = 11$, $N = 5,267$), indicating that as age increased so did the size of the effect. The experimental studies showed virtually no correlation between age and effect size ($r = -.02$, $k = 12$, $N = 1,736$).

This finding suggests that the effect of media on outcome may be cumulative. That is, the association grows stronger over time as exposure to content increases. The lack of a correlation for experimental studies indicates that the only difference in exposure is based on the experimental manipulation (assuming that with random assignment the groups are equivalent before exposure). This finding does not resolve the controversy over causality, because the self-selection bias may be cumulative as the participants get older as well.

Type of Measure

Only two types of measures had the minimum of three studies necessary for conducting this analysis: antisocial behavior indexes and measures of academic success and attitude. The relationship between music and antisocial behavior was examined in 11 studies. The studies indicated a positive relationship (average $r = .186$, $k = 11$, $N = 2,281$) that came from a heterogeneous sample of effects [χ^2 (10, $N = 2,281$) = 44.25, $p < .05$]. The results demonstrate a relationship between exposure to music and various antisocial outcomes.

The measures of academic success and attitude were examined in six studies. The average effect was a positive relationship (average $r = -.113$, $k = 6$, $N = 2,086$) and found a homogeneous set of effects [χ^2 (5, $N = 2,086$) = 8.34, $p < .05$]. The finding indicates that exposure to popular music is associated with diminished levels of academic success. However, this finding does not provide complete information necessary for a causal explanation but should provide a sense of the consistency of the various findings generated in this report.

CONCLUSIONS

This meta-analysis demonstrates some connections between the consumption of various types of music and the social actions and beliefs of the consumer. The important finding involves the consistency of the information reported in Table 16.1. All studies show antisocial effects; that is, exposure to music is positively correlated with negative social outcomes (all effects were reversed scored as appropriate to provide consistent polarity for the results). Also, the findings indicate a justification for appropriate concern. This effect is consistent with an existing meta-analysis in which the positive association between preference for violent video games and various negative outcomes was examined (Sherry, 1997). The importance of arguing that media provide more than an entertainment function serves as a basis for understanding how this vicarious experience is interpreted and processed. The consistency of media effects, including those reported in this chapter, start to establish a case for possible causality. This analysis, however, provides no mechanism to differentiate between competing explanations about causality.

Some divergence in results occurs between the nonexperimental and the experimental data sets. The observed effect for the experimental data sets is larger than that for the nonexperimental designs. The methodological difference illustrates several important possible issues that deserve consideration. Survey research permits a person to respond to a stimulus word, and the word may mean many things to the individual. In contrast, experimental designs use an abstract conceptual idea and create a concrete, operationalized example of the stimulus to which all participants respond. Asking the question, "Do you listen to rock?" may indicate a group of musical possibilities that may differ widely from each other. The difference within the genre of music may be very great and may be important in understanding the "message" of the form. The difference between a generalized or abstract set of musical choices might just indicate a difference in how different persons define a musical genre (which is highly variable between persons), whereas experimental research removes this requirement by providing the stimulus.

The distribution of persons in an experiment means that not everyone is exposed to music with which they are familiar. The net effect is that a person exposed to a particular form of music for the first time may demonstrate larger effects; moreover, habituation may reduce the level of effect for any one particular song or genre of music. However, the correlation with age in survey research may indicate that the effect over the longer term is cumulative and may result in permanent attitude and/or behavioral change on the part of the consumer. That is, the first exposure produces the largest impact, and each subsequent exposure adds to that effect but in ever decreasing amounts. We are unable to evaluate this argument with the current analysis, other than to offer this as a possible explanation for the observed effects.

SLT is predicated on the viewer or listener mirroring what is seen or heard. SLT takes a "monkey see, monkey do" or, in this instance, "monkey hears, monkey does" approach. In the case of music's correlation to antisocial behavior, individuals may be listening to crude song lyrics and mimicking or acting out scenarios that they have heard. Fans of artists that sing about illegal actions or violent behavior may view these people as promoting or condoning the activity. Therefore, adolescents believe the music provides a permission or justification (from an admired source) to engage in similar types of conduct with evidence of the benefits for the action. If SLT is correct, then song lyrics constitute a primary influence on adolescent behavior. If the confluence argument made by Malamuth and Billings (1986) is correct, then music, like any media content, presents a social force that shapes the person along with other forces (e.g., peer, family, school, or). The influence of the media is in proportion to the ability of the material to work consistently with other perceptions of those other forces.

Not only may adolescents believe that content grants permission for these behaviors, but also these activities may become a method to emulate their heroes. The artists that perform songs with antisocial lyrics are linked to this type of behavior. These individuals become idolized, respected, admired, and worshipped by adolescents. Frequently, musicians are portrayed as wealthy individuals who possess everything in life and serve as role models for youths. Role models who advocate drugs, sex, alcohol, and deviant and criminal behaviors create a social danger potential. Listeners may try to imitate the role models by dressing like them, wearing their hair in a similar style, adopting the same tattoos and jewelry, and ultimately trying to act like their perceptions of the star. Through music videos and pictures people see how the stars dress, and wear their hair, but the one real way to gain insight into how the artist acts and thinks is to listen to his or her music. Therefore, to identify with a hero or idol, adolescents behave like the people their role models sing about or engage in activities that the songs describe. The songs become themes for behaviors and rebellions, as well as inspirations for other actions.

SLT theorists would argue that song lyrics could promote more appropriate and responsible behavior on the part of the adolescents. Increasing the amount of music advocating proper social conduct and promoting responsible behavior would be expected to help to lower the level of antisocial behavior. If adolescents replicate the conduct of antisocial songs through learning, a change in content alters the direction of the behavior. Mandating artists to change or rework lyrics so society could be improved may cause musicians and others to feel that their First Amendment right to free speech is being infringed on. Persuading artists to improve lyrics may be more difficult than persuading adolescents to stop antisocial behavior. The real solution involving any issue dealing with lyrics is going to require that adolescents simply stop listening to the message contained in the music as well as reducing the motivation that led to the desire to listen.

As in most media effects discussions, the threshold question is "Does the media content under study have an antisocial or otherwise negative effect?" As presented earlier, the answer to that question is clearly yes. That threshold being satisfied, the next question is: "What should we do about it?" Many individuals and groups will treat these findings as a class for action, particularly legislative action followed by judicial enforcement. Groups such as the National Parent Teachers' Association and the Parents' Music Resource Center, as well as prominent individuals such as former Vice President Gore and his wife Tipper (Mary Elizabeth) have sought to label, restrict, or in some way regulate the music industry (Clark, 1990–1991).

The finding of a positive association between certain types of music and antisocial behavior raises interesting legislative policy issues. The conclusions provide a justification for restrictions on content or access relative to rock, heavy metal, rap, or other music genres that are associated with violence, drug use, poor school performance or attendance, negative attitudes toward women, or other antisocial impacts. But what form those restrictions should take and how they should be administered require a difficult balancing of remedial action and First Amendment liberty. A complete ban on such music clearly would be overkill; other violent, sexually explicit, or otherwise deleterious media content exists and should be permitted to exist under the First Amendment. Holt (1990) concludes that any restrictive law would probably not meet the judicial standards necessary to demonstrate a compelling governmental interest that would permit serious constraints, particularly because the lyrics are more offensive than inciting. Therefore, the answer lies somewhere between total legislative prohibition and unfettered access.

Labeling and ratings provide one option for taking action. Films and television are obvious examples of this tactic. Informing the music consumer of the product's content and potential negative effects provides discriminating listeners and vigilant parents with opportunities to make knowledgeable purchasing choices. The music industry already has agreed to label certain music under limited circumstances. Recording companies and distributors could go farther in providing more information on advisory labels and making such labels more prominent on packages and at the point of purchase. Some people, however, believe that labeling only attracts undue attention to controversial content and renders such content more attractive—particularly to children and adolescents (although one available research study on the impact of parental advisory labels disputes this, Christensen, 1992). Labeling and ratings require vigilance on the part of parents in monitoring a child's entertainment activities. Such vigilance necessarily involves time that many adults are unable to provide. Because of the relatively large positive correlation found in this study and the reasons discussed above, a more severe restriction beyond labeling and rating may be warranted.

If further research indicates that the antisocial effects of music are most pronounced in children and adolescents, prohibiting minors from obtaining certain types of music may provide a more effective restriction. Such an approach exists for tobacco, alcohol, and adult entertainment industries. This approach obviously does nothing to address music's negative impact on adults, but it would eliminate many people's main concern regarding more extreme forms of music and the harm these pose for young people. Another restriction applicable to adults might make prohibition of certain types of music a condition of probation or parole for individuals convicted of offenses such as sexual assault, violent crimes. or other delinquent acts. The problem is that television may produce similar harm and that medium (as well as radio) is currently unrestricted.

Any legislative prohibition provokes serious debate about which "type" of music content to include. Classification and enforcement probably will vary from community to community based on different standards of tolerance. As a result, courts—in dealing with violating purchasers and merchants—will render post hoc interpretations as those community standards and the current research dictate. At a practical level, the ability to implement any restrictions and to provide assurance that a set of restrictions could be justified or defended appears dubious, if not outright impossible. The current level of scientific knowledge as perceived by the courts and legislators would constitute insufficient information to meet the standards necessary to provide "a degree of scientific certainty" that causality can be accepted as a proven explanation.

The database for these effects, although fairly substantial, is not exhaustive and does not provide sufficient information to fully document the range of possible responses to music. Whereas the potential variable effect from particular music forms exists, all the effects are positive (demonstrating a relationship between exposure to music content and outcome). Any proposed moderating variable should be expected to distinguish between larger and smaller positive effects rather than between positive and negative effects. The ability, however, to represent the relationship in a consistent direction represents a significant advance in understanding the issues.

An option to ban or restrict content in other ways involves media education. Current research on the effects of sexually explicit materials indicates that the negative consequences of exposure on attitudes vanish if proper education is provided (Allen, D'Alessio, Emmers, & Gebhardt, 1996). In this model not only may restrictions be avoided, but also more socially beneficial options exist. Moreover, comprehensive media education would avoid a great deal of the potential negative effects of exposure (by accident or to illegal) materials. A limitation to this solution is that the people most likely to suffer negative consequences (those with personality problems or a strong predisposition for antisocial behavior) are probably less susceptible to educational efforts.

In contrast, a superior case for media education can be made for more active consumers of material. Arguments for some type of cognitive filtering or assignment of value become more relevant. With active, informed consumers the content of the media material becomes a less potent predictor of negative outcomes because interpretive filters are used to process whatever content is represented in the media. This would explain the impact of educational materials for sexual materials (Allen, D'Alessio, Emmers, & Gebhardt, 1996). The educational materials used in investigations of sexually explicit materials are, for the most part, arguments about the content representing a fictional sexual fantasy. Educational materials remind the consumer that the depiction has little representation or correspondence to real world behavior or actions. An argument made by social cognitive models is that failure to develop the interpretive context creates the perception that the material becomes associated with real-life actions. For adolescents, the experience necessary to develop that interpretive defense mechanism may not exist, and the material becomes a source of learning or information rather than being contextualized as a source of entertainment or fantasy.

The next level of research on media effects should involve issues of education and a sustained effort to determine mechanisms to reduce the size of the observed relationships. Media messages are products consumed by persons. Just as medicines may produce undesirable side effects, entertainment material may produce unintentional and even unpredictable outcomes. Efforts to address issues such as media literacy or education may prove far more productive for handling the potential issues of undesirable media effects than trying to rely on media content restrictions. Although censorship has an inherent attraction, the effectiveness of such a control method appears dubious when considered in historical terms.

This analysis demonstrates that consumption of popular musical forms is related consistently to various outcomes. The problem is that the implications for this finding are not immediately apparent. There exist a variety of social alternatives and possibilities for handling, interpreting, or responding to the findings of this investigation. As additional meta-analyses on media effects begin to demonstrate outcomes associated with potential exposure to media content, the issues become more important in the legislative and social arena.

REFERENCES

References marked with an asterisk indicate studies included in the meta-analysis.

Allen, M., D'Alessio, D., & Brezgel, K. (1995). A meta-analysis summarizing the effects of pornography II. *Human Communication Research, 22,* 258–283.

Allen, M., D'Alessio, D., Emmers, T., & Gebhardt, L. (1996). The role of educational briefings in mitigating effects of experimental exposure to violent sexually explicit material: A meta-analysis. *Journal of Sex Research, 33,* 135–141.

Allen, M., Emmers, T., Gebhardt, L., & Giery, M. (1995). Exposure to pornography and acceptance of the rape myth. *Journal of Communication, 45,* 5–27.

*Arnett, J. (1991a). Adolescents and heavy metal music: From the mouths of metalheads. *Youth & Society, 23,* 76–98.

*Arnett, J. (1991b). Heavy metal music and reckless behavior among adolescents. *Journal of Youth and Adolescence, 20,* 573–592.

Bandura, A. (1973). *Aggression: A social learning analysis.* Englewood Cliffs, NJ: Prentice-Hall.

Bandura, A. (1977). *Social learning theory.* Englewood Cliffs, NJ: Prentice-Hall.

*Bleich, S., Zillmann, D., & Weaver, J. (1991). Enjoyment and consumption of defiant rock music as a function of adolescent rebelliousness. *Journal of Broadcasting and Electronic Media, 35,* 351–366.

*Brown, R., & O'Leary, M. (1971). Pop music in an English secondary school system. *American Behavioral Scientist, 14,* 401–413.

Bryant, J., & Brown, D. (1989). Uses of pornography. In D. Zillmann & J. Bryant (Eds.). *Pornography: Research advances & policy considerations* (pp. 25–56). Hillsdale, NJ: Lawrence Erlbaum Associates.

*Burke, R., & Grinder, R. (1966). Personality-oriented themes and listening patterns in teen-age music and their relation to certain academic and peer variables. *School Review, 74,* 196–211.

Christensen, P. (1992, Winter). The effects of parental advisory labels on adolescent music preferences. *Journal of Communication, 42,* 106–113.

Clark, A. (1990–1991). "As nasty as they wanna be": Popular music on trial. *New York University Law Review, 65,* 1481–1531.

Cole, R. (1971). Top songs in the sixties: A content analysis of popular lyrics. *American Behavioral Scientist, 14,* 389–400.

*Dixon, T., & Linz, D. (1997). Obscenity law and sexually explicit rap music: Understanding the effect of sex, attitudes, and beliefs. *Journal of Applied Communication Research, 25,* 217–241.

Duncan, D. (1990). Pornography as a source of sex information for university students. *Psychological Reports, 66,* 442.

Duncan, D., & Donnelly, J. (1991). Pornography as a source of sex information for students at a Southeastern university. *Psychological Reports, 68,* 802.

Elasmar, M., & Hunter, J. (1997). The impact of foreign TV on a domestic audience: A meta-analysis. *Communication Yearbook, 20,* 47–69.

*Gan, S., Zillmann, D., & Mitrook, M. (1996, May). *The stereotyping effect of African-American women's sexual rap on white audiences.* Paper presented at the International Communication Association Convention, Montreal, Canada.

Gow, J. (1994). Mood and meaning in music video: The dynamics of audiovisual synergy. *Southern Communication Journal, 59,* 255–261.

Hall, J., & Rosenthal, R. (1991). Testing for moderator variables in meta-analysis: Issues and methods. *Communication Monographs, 58,* 437–448.

Hansen, C., & Hansen, R. (1990). The influence of sex and violence on the appeal of rock music videos. *Communication Research, 17,* 212–234.

*Hansen, C., & Hansen, R. (1991). Rock music videos and social reality through music: Individual differences among fans of punk and heavy metal music. *Journal of Broadcasting and Electronic Media, 35,* 335–350.

Hearold, S. (1979). *Meta-analysis of the effects of television on social behavior.* Unpublished doctoral dissertation, University of Colorado, Boulder, CO.

Hearold, S. (1986). A synthesis of 1043 effects of television on social behavior. In G. Comstock (Ed.), *Public communication and behavior* (Vol. 1, pp. 65–133). Orlando, FL: Academic Press.

Herrett-Skjellum, J., & Allen, M. (1996). Television programming and sex stereotyping: A meta-analysis. *Communication Yearbook, 19,* 159–185.

Hogben, M. (1998). Factors moderating the effect of televised aggression on viewer behavior. *Communication Research, 25,* 220–247.

Holt, J. (1990). Protecting America's youth: Can rock music lyrics be constitutionally regulated? *Journal of Contemporary Law, 16,* 53–75.

Huesmann, R., Moise, J., Podolski, C., & Eron, L. (1998, July). *Longitudinal relations between children's exposure to television violence and their later aggressive and violent behavior in young adulthood: 1977–1992.* Paper presented at the International Communication Association Convention, Jerusalem, Israel.

Huffman, J., & Huffman, J. (1987). Sexism and cultural lag: The rise of the jailbait song, 1955–1985. *Journal of Popular Culture, 21,* 65–83.

Hunter, J. E., & Schmidt, F. L. (1990). *Methods of meta-analysis: Correcting error and bias in research findings.* Newbury Park, CA: Sage.

*Johnson, J., Jackson, L., & Gatto, L. (1995). Violent attitudes and deferred academic aspirations: Deleterious effects of exposure to rap music. *Basic and Applied Social Psychology, 16,* 27–41.

Kalis, P., & Neuendorf, K. (1989). Aggressive cue prominence and gender participation in MTV. *Journalism Quarterly, 66,* 148–154.

Kurtz, H. (1981). Differences in themes in popular music and their relationship to deviance. *Popular Music and Society, 8,* 84–88.

*Lakkaraju, L. (1985). *Music television and cultivation analysis.* Unpublished master's thesis, University of Georgia, Athens.

*Larson, R., & Kubey, R. (1983). Television and music: Contrasting media in adolescent life. *Youth and Society, 15,* 13–31.

*Lewis, G. (1980). Popular music, musical preference and drug use among youth. *Popular Music and Society, 7,* 176–181.

Lull, J. (1980). The social uses of television. *Human Communication Research, 6,* 197–209.

Lull, J. (1982). A rules approach to the study of television and society. *Human Communication Research, 9,* 3–16.

Malamuth, N., & Billings, V. (1986). The functions and effects of pornography: Sexual communications versus feminist models in light of research findings. In J. Bryant and D. Zillmann (Eds.), *Perspectives on media effects* (pp. 83–108). Hillsdale, NJ: Lawrence Erlbaum Associates.

McKee, K., & Pardun, C. (1996). Mixed messages: The relationship between sexual and religious imagery in rock, country, and Christian video. *Communication Reports, 9,* 163–171.

*Moore, J. (1989). *Music and mayhem: An examination of the influence of music videos on interpersonal aggression.* Unpublished doctoral dissertation, Ohio University, Athens.

Morgan, M., & Shanahan, J. (1997). Two decades of cultivation research: An appraisal and meta-analysis. *Communication Yearbook, 20,* 1–46.

Paik, H., & Comstock, G. (1994). The effects of television violence on anti-social behavior. *Communication Research, 21,* 516–546.

*Peterson, D., & Pfost, K. (1989). Influence of rock videos on attitudes of violence against women. *Psychological Reports, 64,* 319–322.

Rosenthal, R. (1984). *Meta-analytic procedures for social research.* Beverly Hills, CA: Sage.

Sherman, B., & Dominick, J. (1986, Winter). Violence and sex in music videos: TV and rock 'n' roll. *Journal of Communication, 36,* 79–93.

Sherry, J. (1997, May). *Do violent video games cause aggression? A meta-analytic review.* Paper presented at the International Communication Convention, Montreal, Ontario, Canada.

*St. Lawrence, J., & Joyner, D. (1991). The effects of sexually violent rock music on males' acceptance of violence against women. *Psychology of Women Quarterly, 15,* 49–63.

*Strouse, J., Buerkel-Rothfuss, N., & Long, E. (1996). Gender and family as moderators of the relationship between music video exposure and adolescent sexual permissiveness. *Adolescence, 30,* 505–517.

*Sun, S., & Lull, J. (1986, Winter). The adolescent audience for music videos and why they watch. *Journal of Communication, 36,* 115–125.

*Tanner, J. (1981). Pop music and peer groups: A study of Canadian high school students' responses to pop music. *Canadian Review of Sociology and Anthropology, 18,* 1–13.

*Trostle, L. (1986). Nihilistic adolescents, heavy metal rock music, and paranormal beliefs. *Psychological Reports, 59,* 610.

Vincent, R. (1989). Clio's consciousness raised? Portrayal of women in rock videos re-examined. *Journalism Quarterly, 66,* 155–160.

*Waite, B., Hillbrand, M., & Foster, H. (1992). Reduction of aggressive behavior after removal of music television. *Hospital and Community Psychiatry, 43,* 173–175.

*Wanamaker, C., & Reznikoff, M. (1989). Effects of aggressive and nonaggressive rock songs on projective and structured tests. *Journal of Psychology, 123,* 561–570.

Wells, J. (1984). Music television video and the capacity to experience life. *Journal of Popular Music and Society, 9*(4), 1–6.

*Zillmann, D., Aust, C., Hoffman, K., Love, C., Ordman, V., Pope, J., Seigler, P., & Gibson, R. (1995). Radical rap: Does it further ethnic division? *Basic and Applied Social Psychology, 16,* 1–25.

17

Positive Effects of Television on Children's Social Interaction: A Meta-Analysis

Marie-Louise Mares
University of Wisconsin–Madison

Emory H. Woodard, IV
Villanova University

It is a commonly held belief that television viewing does more harm than good, especially to young audiences. Particular attention has been focused on the negative effects of watching violent programming on social behavior. Over ten years ago, Paik and Comstock (1994) reviewed 217 studies on the link between viewing and aggression. In this chapter we review the effects of exposure to prosocial audiovisual content on children's social interactions. The goals are to update an earlier meta-analysis of prosocial effects conducted by Hearold (1986), to identify the conditions under which prosocial effects are strongest, and to compare effect sizes for prosocial content with the effect sizes for violent content reported by Paik and Comstock.

WHY EXPECT POSITIVE EFFECTS OF VIEWING?

Content analyses continue to find high levels of violence and criminal activity on television. Researchers for the National Television Violence Study (1996, 1997,

1998) reported that about 60% of programming broadcast between 6:00 A.M. and 11:00 P.M. contained violence. Moreover, children's shows were more violent than many other types of programming—66% of the children's programs sampled contained violence. Violence was often performed by heroic figures in the pursuit of justice, without causing realistic pain or suffering to the victim, and was frequently depicted as humorous.

What do we know about the prevalence of prosocial content? Early content analyses conducted during the 1970s found considerable variability in the frequency of various types of prosocial behavior. Liebert and Poulos (1975) analyzed broadcast programming for 1974 and reported that although an average of 11 altruistic acts and 6 sympathetic behaviors per hour of programming occurred, resistance to temptation and control of aggressive impulses occurred less than once per hour (see also Poulos, Harvey, & Liebert, 1976). Liebert and Sprafkin (1989) concluded that children watching during the 1970s (when a number of the studies analyzed in this chapter were conducted) were exposed to a fair number of prosocial interpersonal behaviors, but few instances of self-control behaviors.

Early content analyses also indicated that prosocial acts often appeared in the context of aggression. Greenberg, Atkin, Edison, and Korzenny (1980) analyzed the favorite programs of a sample of fourth, sixth, and eighth graders. They found that these programs contained an average of 42.2 acts of antisocial behavior and 44.2 acts of prosocial behavior in an average hour. The prosocial behavior included displays of altruism, empathy, and discussion of feelings. Liss and Reinhard (1980) analyzed prosocial cartoons (those with moral messages apparent to the adult researchers) and standard cartoons. They found that both types of cartoons contained equal amounts of aggression.

The flip side of this is a somewhat more recent finding reported by the National Television Violence Study (1998) that fewer than 4% of the violent programs shown on television contained an antiviolence theme. When prosocial content occurred, there was often violence mixed in; when violence occurred, there was seldom an anti-violence message attached.

The Annenberg Public Policy Center conducted annual content analyses of all children's programs aired over the course of a composite week in Philadelphia, a large urban media market. Woodard (1999) examined the frequency with which programs contained social lessons about interpersonal skills such as acceptance of diversity, altruism, and cooperation. In the 1998/1999 sample, 25% of all children's shows contained at least one such social lesson, though most appeared in programming for preschool children. How much prosocial content do children actually see? Woodard (1999) reported that out of the 20 shows with highest Nielsen ratings for children between the ages of 2 and 17, only two contained prosocial lessons as defined in this study, and only one of those was designed for children.

Given this discrepancy—high levels of glamorized or humorous violence in children's programming, and relatively low levels of specific prosocial messages—what does media effects research indicate? What are the effects of enforced exposure to prosocial content (as in the experimental setting) and what are the effects of self-selected exposure? Can prosocial messages have positive effects? Do they do so in "real life?"

Rushton (1979) suggested that prosocial content could potentially have stronger effects upon viewers than antisocial content, because prosocial behaviors are more in accord with established social norms. For example, there is a norm to help another person.

> If we asked a stranger in the street for directions, we would expect him or her to provide the information if possible and to apologize if not. If the stranger were instead to turn to us and say "Yes, I do know where that place is but I can't be bothered to tell you," we would be rather surprised. (Rushton, 1979, p. 324)

Of course, individuals vary in the extent to which these norms are internalized. Despite this variation, it seems plausible that prosocial depictions are more consistent with social norms than violent depictions, and that imitation of prosocial acts on television is more likely to be received positively than imitation of antisocial acts. (For instance, Grusec, 1991, reported that spontaneous altruism in young children is typically responded to with some form of social reinforcement such as thanks, hugs, or smiles.) Therefore, the argument is that exposure to positive content will be at least as powerful as exposure to antisocial content, other things (such as attractiveness of the models) being equal.

An alternative argument is that prosocial effects should be weaker than antisocial effects because prosocial acts often involve acting against one's self-interest, whereas antisocial acts often involve acting out desires. Prosocial depictions, then, may have to encourage people to act against their preexisting motives (should I help this person or should I get to my appointment on time?). Antisocial depictions may encourage people to act in accordance with desires that are present but are normally suppressed (I'd love to yell at that person who cut in front of me in line....). We might expect the weakest prosocial effects for attempts to bring about altruistic, self-sacrificing behavior (rather than positive acts that are easily accomplished and are rewarded), and the strongest antisocial effects for content that disinhibits preexisting antisocial desires. Another alternative argument is that the greater explicitness of violent acts leads to greater retention of those acts and the greater likelihood of subsequent reenactment (Abelman, 1991). Finally, it could be that conflict is integral to dramatic presentations (Zillmann, 1991) and thus is more engaging than prosocial depictions devoid of conflict and concomitant violence.

A meta-analysis of the early research on the effects of television found support for the powerful prosocial effects argument. Hearold (1986) reviewed 230 studies on television and social behavior published before 1978. She concluded that prosocial effects were stronger and more enduring than antisocial effects, both in the laboratory and in more natural conditions. Hearold reported an effect (d) of .63 for prosocial content on prosocial behavior, compared with an effect (d) of .30 for antisocial content on antisocial behavior. (Effect sizes reported as r would be approximately half of those reported as d.)

Hearold's work on antisocial effects was partially updated in Paik and Comstock's (1994) meta-analysis of violence effects. They reported an overall effect (d) of violent television content of .65, which was approximately double the antisocial effect found by Hearold. Our chapter provides a partial update of the prosocial effects component of her work. It is only a partial update because Hearold included a much wider range of positive outcomes than are considered here (e.g., imagination, buying books, library use, safety activism, and "conversation activism").

THE CURRENT STUDY

What does a prosocial effect size mean? In the experiments reviewed here, the effect size is often the difference between a control group and a group exposed to prosocial content or between a group that sees some negative content and a group that sees some positive content. These differences are standardized by dividing by the pooled standard deviation, so they can be compared across measures and studies. In surveys, the effect size is often the correlation between how much prosocial television content children watch and how positively they behave; it can be thought of as the difference between heavy and light viewers of prosocial television content.

Two other notions need explanation: television viewing and positive/prosocial. Television viewing is construed in its broadest sense here. That is, studies were included whether they measured number of hours of daily viewing or involved exposing subjects to specially constructed 5-minute videotapes of a model carrying out some particular behavior. In some of the early studies, "television viewing" really means watching a film. One of the questions to be answered is whether the effect size depends on the way television exposure was measured and conceived.

The notion of *prosocial* content is more difficult; it is not as easy as it first seems to sort out which behaviors are positive and which are negative. This is more than a hazy moral relativism. It is naive to assume that all groups in society place equal value on cooperation (rather than rugged individualism), tolerance of others (rather than willingness to stick up for one's own group), nonviolent conflict resolution (rather than heroism), or ability to resist temptation (rather than ability to seize the moment). Nonetheless, all of these have been used as prosocial outcomes in research.

There are two responses to this problem. The best would be to look at the interplay between the individual's perceptions of social norms and that individual's reactions to specific types of content. After all, groups that value machismo will probably react differently to a "prosocial" portrayal of two men deciding not to fight than will groups who value rational discussion as a solution to social conflict. This idea is not new to research on persuasion, but it generally has not informed the research on prosocial effects of television viewing. At most, a few researchers have compared children of high versus low socioeconomic status or children who were initially high in aggression with those who were less aggressive. So, unfortunately, this chapter investigates whether television has an influence on specific behaviors, with little regard for probable subgroup differences in responses.

Given this limitation, it was necessary to make a pragmatic decision about what would be included as positive effects for the purpose of this chapter. In this review, four clusters of outcomes related to social interactions were considered. For more details about selection procedures see Mares and Woodard (2005).

Defining the Dependent Measures

The first dependent measure was labeled *positive interaction.* This was a broad variable used to capture measures such as "friendly play" or "peaceful conflict resolution." Studies that simply gave a measure of "prosocial behavior" were coded in this category. In a typical study, (e.g., Friedrich-Cofer et al., 1979) children were assigned to watch *Mister Rogers' Neighborhood* or some neutral content. Afterwards, observers rated the children's play behavior, counting the number of aggressive acts, friendly behaviors, expressions of affection.

The second category was aggression. Although it was possible to think of this as the other end of the positive interaction continuum (and simply reverse the sign for effects of prosocial content on aggression), we decided to treat this as a separate, though related, variable. Both physical and verbal aggression were included. Unfortunately, studies often ran the two together, so we were not able to analyze them separately. To be consistent with the direction of other variables, we reversed the sign of effects on aggression so that a positive prosocial effect meant a reduction in aggression.

The third category was altruism, which included sharing, donating, offering help, and comforting. In a typical study of altruism (e.g., Bryan & Walbek, 1970), children were brought into the laboratory and told that they would learn how to play a new game by watching a video. The children watched one of several versions of the video, in which the model played the game, was rewarded by tokens that could be used to win a prize, and then immediately decided whether to behave altruistically (giving some of the tokens to charity or another child) or selfishly (cashing in all the tokens for a big prize). The children then played the game, won a fixed number of tokens, and were given the opportunity to donate some tokens. The measure of altruism was the number of tokens given.

The final outcome was stereotype reduction: the effects of counterstereotypical portrayals of gender and ethnicity on attitudes, beliefs, and behaviors. Most research has focused on simple short-term effects. For example, Gorn, Goldberg, & Kanungo (1976) showed children 12 minutes of *Sesame Street* programming with multicultural themes. They found strong effects on interest in playing with nonwhite hypothetical playmates but, not surprisingly, these effects tended to be very short lived. Goldberg and Gorn (1979) found that the effects had disappeared by the next day.

METHODS

Sample of Studies

We searched three databases: PsycLIT/PsychAbstracts, Social Sciences Index, and *Communication Abstracts*. The same strategy was used in all three computerized searches. First, we searched for the combination of telev* and prosocial, altruism, helping, sharing, empathy, friend*, cooperation, counterstereotyp*, nontrad*, charity, generosity, and moral*. Second, because some studies used videotaped or filmed models of prosocial behavior but were not described as studies of television, we substituted "model*" for "television" in combination with all other terms. In addition, studies were culled from the reference list for Hearold's (1986) meta-analysis and from an expanding search of the reference lists of all studies found on the topic.

Studies were included if they (a) involved exposure to audiovisual content deemed prosocial or positive by the researchers, (b) measured one or more of our four dependent variables, (c) were published in academic journals and (d) contained enough statistical information to allow for calculation of effect sizes. The final criterion proved to be a major factor: Many early studies included minimal (or no) statistical information.

Comparisons

It is only possible to judge the effect of prosocial content by comparing groups who watch prosocial material with those who watch less of it or who watch other content. Thus, there is no pure "prosocial effect." Rather the size of the effect depends on what forms the comparison group. We examined the following contrasts: prosocial content versus control (no content); prosocial versus neutral television content; prosocial versus antisocial television content; and correlations between prosocial viewing and prosocial outcomes. In addition, we looked at the comparison between aggressive prosocial content versus nonaggressive prosocial content. Finally, we also looked at the effect of augmenting prosocial television content with additional materials or instruction: prosocial plus supplements versus control; prosocial plus supplements versus neutral; and prosocial plus supplements versus antisocial.

Deciding on Number of Effect Sizes per Study

In calculating effect sizes, the goal was to divide the study's research participants into homogenous samples in order to make as fine-grained comparisons as possible. Different age groups and different sexes were treated as separate samples and an effect size was calculated for each sample within the study.

In addition, studies sometimes reported on more than one variable of interest, for example, both altruism and friendly play. A separate effect size was calculated for each of these variables for all the samples within a study. However, when the study reported on multiple measures of the same variable, those measures were averaged to form one effect size for that variable. The result was 34 usable sources and 108 effect sizes. This represented testing 5,473 children.

Moderator Variables

A number of moderator variables were coded, many of which subsequently proved to have too few cases to provide meaningful comparisons. The list of variables and coding decisions are summarized in Table 17.1.

Statistical Analysis

The effect size computed was r (Hunter & Schmidt, 1990). This r was weighted by sample size and converted to Z_{Fisher} to solve the skewness of r at the extreme ends of the distribution (Paik & Comstock, 1994) and as suggested by Hedges and Olkin (1985).[1] In this analysis, positive correlation coefficients reflect a greater increase in prosocial outcomes in the prosocial condition than in the comparison condition (whether this was antisocial, neutral, control, or pretest) or higher prosocial scores among heavy viewers of prosocial content than among light viewers. Positive values for r for the aggressive outcome reflect the prosocial content being associated with *less* aggression than in other conditions.

---

[1]The authors state that "Several approaches can be used to estimate ρ (overall effect size) via weighted linear combinations of estimators. A central issue is whether we should weight the product-moment correlations $r_1,...,r_k$, the unbiased estimators $G(r_1),...,G(r_k)$, the z-transformed versions, $z_1,...,z_k$, Kraemer's t-transforms $t_1,...,t_k$, or perhaps some other functions of the rs. The most direct approach, that of calculating a linear combination of $r_1,...,r_k$, has little to recommend it unless the sample sizes of all k studies are very, very large. An alternative is to estimate ρ from a linear combination of the unbiased estimators $G(r_1),...,G(r_k)$. Some simulation studies suggest that this approach is superior to the approach of using linear combinations of $r_1,...,r_k$, but differs very little from the more standard approach based on linear combinations of z-transformed correlations."

TABLE 17.1
Variables Coded for Each Effect Size

Publication information
  Number of effect sizes for this reference
  Year of publication
  Country (United States, Canada, Europe, Australia/New Zealand, Asia, other)
Subject information
  Number of subjects
  Age range, mean age
  Socioeconomic status (1 = low to 3 = high)
  IQ/ability: (1 = low, 2 = mixed, 3 = high)
  Ethnicity (1 = Anglo, 2 = black, 3 = Hispanic, 4 = other, 5 = mixed)
  Sex (0 = male, 1 = female, 2 = both)
  Institutionalized (0 = no, 1 = yes)
  Note. only use "mixed" code if authors report it as mixed. If no specific mention, code as 9.
Comparison information
Treatment comparison:
  pretest/control vs. prosocial; neutral vs. prosocial; neutral vs. aggressive prosocial; antisocial vs.
    prosocial; antisocial vs. aggressive prosocial; neutral vs. prosocial + materials; neutral vs.
    prosocial + elaboration; correlation prosocial TV with prosocial outcome; correlation prosocial
    TV with antisocial outcome
Treatment information
Prosocial treatment
  Mister Rogers' Neighborhood, Sesame Street, other educational programming, comedy, drama,
    mixed TV/films, modeled behavior
  Prosocial behavior rewarded: no, yes, don't say
  Production of prosocial content: live, animated, mix
  Realism of prosocial treatment: self-selected prosocial content, whole TV programs/films, edited
    programs/films, content produced by researchers
  Viewing time for prosocial content (minutes)
  Duration of prosocial treatment (days)
Antisocial treatment
  cartoon, comedy, drama, western, advertising, mixed TV/films, advertising, modeled behavior
Neutral treatment
  cartoon, comedy, drama, nonprosocial educational program, mixed TV/films
Outcome information
Type of outcome behavior: positive interaction (friendliness, cooperation, positive affect, general
    prosocial play and interaction, includes increased social play by former "isolates"); altruism
    (self-sacrificing kindness, generosity, helping at cost to self); reduced stereotyping—either
    attitudes or behavior; physical and mixed aggression; verbal aggression. *Note.* When there are
    multiple measures of the outcome choose the most reliable if reliability is given. If reliability is
    not given, but one measure is behavioral and one is attitudinal, use the behavioral measure. If
    neither of the above, average across the measures.
Choice of measure: only measure; most reliable measure/behavioral; averaged across measures
How outcome was measured: researcher observation of natural behavior; teacher/parent report of
    natural behavior; child self-report of natural behavior: what they habitually do; peer reports of
    children's behavior; researcher designed behavioral task (includes donating tokens/lollipops in
    experimental situation; push-pull marble game, pressing help button); child's reports of
    attitudes and hypothetical behavior; mix of natural measures; mix of measures

(Continued)

TABLE 17.1 (Continued)
Variables Coded for Each Effect Size

Time till tested: less than a day; number of days between treatment and measure
Design information
Similarity of treatment and task: behavior is same as that modeled in film; same type of thing: altruism is shown in treatment and a (different) altruistic outcome is measured; general/mixed effects: either general prosocial content was used, or researcher studied effects of one type of prosocial content on another type of prosocial outcome (showing altruism on levels of aggression)
Assignment to treatment: random; prepost; matched (either by individual or by matching classes); uncontrolled/self-selected
Significance of statistics used for effect size: no; yes; opposite direction to that predicted; mixed (some measures are significant, some are not)
Components of effect size
Effect size

RESULTS

If we look across dependent variables, comparisons, and research designs, the average effect size (Z_{Fisher}) for prosocial content on social interaction is .27. This measure is of only marginal interest given how many different issues are lumped together in this number. Nonetheless, it is a starting point for assessing our rival hypotheses about the relative ease or difficulty of persuading people to "be nice" as opposed to acting out mean desires. Paik and Comstock (1994) reported an overall Z_{fisher} of .32 for violence effects. Thus, at the aggregate level, the two types of content are quite similar in effectiveness.

How should the numbers be interpreted? Qualitative descriptions of effects sizes are controversial. A small change in behavior may be of critical importance or it may be trivial. The rule of thumb suggested by Cohen and Cohen (1983) is that an effect size of .20 or less should be considered small, an effect between .30 and .40 is medium, and an effect of .50 or greater is large.

Design Effects

Prosocial Content Compared to Other Content

Table 17.2 lists all the effects. Table 17.3 shows the effect sizes for each comparison, both across and within the four dependent variables (altruism, social interaction, aggression, and stereotype reduction). As the top part of Table 17.3 indicates, across dependent variables, children who saw prosocial content received higher prosocial scores than any of the comparison groups. The remainder of

TABLE 17.2
List of Effects

Author	Year	N^a	Age^b	Design	Effect Size^c
Abelman	1985	286	120	Correlational	0.4200*
Ahammer & Murray	1979	30	58	Experimental	−0.0770*
Ahammer & Murray	1979	24	53	Experimental	0.2520*
Bankart & Anderson	1979	22	54	Quasi-experimental	0.9500*
Baran, Chase, & Courtright	1979	81	96	Experimental	0.3170*
Baran et al.	1979	81	96	Experimental	0.3170*
Baran et al.	1979	81	96	Experimental	0.4310*
Bryan & Walbeck	1970	72	108	Experimental	0.2170
Collins & Getz	1976	54	158	Experimental	0.4760*
Collins & Getz	1976	54	158	Experimental	0.3050*
Collins & Getz	1976	54	158	Experimental	0.4650*
Collins & Getz	1976	54	158	Experimental	0.3990*
Davidson, Yasuna, & Tower	1979	36	66	Experimental	0.7090*
Davidson et al.	1979	36	66	Experimental	0.6330*
Drabman & Thomas	1977	40	60	Experimental	0.3980*
Drabman& Thomas	1977	40	60	Experimental	0.3380*
Durkin & Hutchins	1984	99	150	Experimental	0.1860
Durkin & Hutchins	1984	99	150	Experimental	−0.1170
Durkin & Hutchins	1984	99	150	Experimental	−0.0190
Durkin & Hutchins	1984	99	150	Experimental	−0.1690
Durkin & Hutchins	1984	99	150	Experimental	0.1200
Durkin & Hutchins	1984	99	150	Experimental	−0.1370
Durkin & Hutchins	1984	99	150	Experimental	0.2070
Durkin & Hutchins	1984	99	150	Experimental	0.1730
Elias	1983	109	132	Experimental	0.2920*
Elliott & Vasta	1970	48	72	Experimental	0.7550*
Elliott & Vasta	1970	48	72	Experimental	0.7550*
Elliott & Vasta	1970	48	72	Experimental	0.8570*
Forge & Phemister	1987	40	50	Experimental	0.4020*
Friedrich-Cofer, Huston-Stein, Kipnis, Susman, & Clewett	1979	141	50	Experimental	0.0000
Friedrich-Cofer et al.	1979	141	50	Experimental	0.2880*
Friedrich-Cofer et al.	1979	141	50	Experimental	0.2310*
Friedrich-Cofer et al.	1979	141	50	Experimental	−0.0620
Friedrich-Cofer et al.	1979	141	50	Experimental	0.3980*
Friedrich-Cofer et al.	1979	141	50	Experimental	−0.1600
Friedrich-Cofer et al.	1979	141	50	Experimental	0.2490*
Friedrich-Cofer et al.	1979	141	50	Experimental	−0.2990*
Friedrich-Cofer	1979	141	50	Experimental	−0.1360*
Geller & Scheirer	1978	24	57	Experimental	0.5670*
Goldberg & Gorn	1979	167	48	Experimental	0.2260*
Goldberg & Gorn	1979	167	48	Experimental	0.0000*
Gorn, Goldberg, & Kanungo	1976	205	54	Experimental	0.2390
Houser	1978	156	88	Experimental	0.6630*
Houser	1978	156	88	Experimental	0.7040*

(*Continued*)

TABLE 17.2 (Continued)
List of Effects

Author	Year	N^a	Age^b	Design	Effect Size^c
Keller & Carlson	1974	19	46	Experimental	0.4900*
Keller & Carlson	1974	19	46	Experimental	0.3240*
Liss & Reinhardt	1983	60	67	Experimental	0.9611*
Liss & Reinhardt	1983	60	67	Experimental	0.9753*
Liss & Reinhardt	1983	60	67	Experimental	0.9765*
Liss & Reinhardt	1983	120	91	Experimental	0.2693*
Liss & Reinhardt	1983	120	91	Experimental	0.1049*
McArthur & Eisen	1976	20	49	Experimental	0.4630*
McArthur & Eisen	1976	20	49	Experimental	0.4670*
O'Bryant & Corder-Bolz	1978	67	87	Experimental	0.2160*
O'Bryant & Corder-Bolz	1978	67	87	Experimental	0.4060*
O'Bryant & Corder-Bolz	1978	67	87	Experimental	0.3830*
O'Bryant & Corder-Bolz	1978	67	87	Experimental	−0.1020*
O'Connor	1969	13	42	Experimental	0.6300*
O'Connor	1972	31	42	Experimental	0.6010*
Pingree	1978	227	132	Experimental	−0.2760
Pingree	1978	227	132	Experimental	−0.0610
Pingree	1978	227	132	Experimental	0.2780*
Rao, Moely, & Lockman	1987	16	56	Experimental	0.5620*
Rao et al.	1987	16	56	Experimental	0.4850*
Rao et al.	1987	16	56	Experimental	0.4830*
Rosenwasser, Lingerfelter, & Harrington	1989	114	66	Correlational	−0.0250
Rosenwasser et al.	1989	114	66	Correlational	−0.0400
Rosenwasser et al.	1989	114	90	Correlational	0.4750*
Rosenwasser et al.	1989	114	90	Correlational	0.1650
Rosenwasser et al.	1989	114	66	Correlational	0.2300*
Rosenwasser et al.	1989	114	66	Correlational	0.0650
Rosenwasser et al.	1989	114	90	Correlational	−0.0200
Rosenwasser et al.	1989	114	90	Correlational	0.3150*
Rosenwasser et al.	1989	114	66	Correlational	0.0100
Rosenwasser et al.	1989	114	66	Correlational	0.2530*
Rosenwasser et al.	1989	114	90	Correlational	0.3950*
Rosenwasser et al.	1989	114	90	Correlational	0.1050
Rushton & Owen	1975	72	108	Experimental	0.2870*
Rushton & Owen	1975	72	108	Experimental	0.1970*
Silverman & Sprafkin	1980	90	60	Experimental	0.1070*
Silverman & Sprafkin	1980	90	60	Experimental	0.4350*
Silverman & Sprafkin	1980	90	60	Experimental	−0.3520*
Silverman & Sprafkin	1980	24	36	Experimental	−0.5090*
Silverman & Sprafkin	1980	24	36	Experimental	−0.4790*
Silverman & Sprafkin	1980	24	36	Experimental	0.3670*
Silverman & Sprafkin	1980	24	36	Experimental	0.5880*
Sprafkin, Liebert, & Poulos	1975	30	78	Experimental	0.8560*
Sprafkin et al.	1975	30	78	Experimental	0.1360

(Continued)

TABLE 17.2 (Continued)
List of Effects

Author	Year	N^a	Age^b	Design	Effect Size^c
Sprafkin & Rubinstein	1979	393	102	Correlational	0.0800
Teachman & Orme	1981	120	108	Experimental	0.1450*
Teachman & Orme	1981	120	108	Experimental	−0.0080
Teachman & Orme	1981	120	108	Experimental	0.4270*
Teachman & Orme	1981	120	108	Experimental	0.0850
Toeplitz-Winiewska	1977	152	200	Experimental	−0.2490*
Toeplitz-Winiewska	1977	152	200	Experimental	−0.1440*
Toeplitz-Winiewska	1977	152	200	Experimental	−0.3300*
Toeplitz-Winiewska	1977	152	202	Experimental	0.2300*
Toeplitz-Winiewska	1977	152	202	Experimental	0.0200
Toeplitz-Winiewska	1977	152	202	Experimental	0.2800*
Tower, Singer, Singer, & Biggs	1979	58	50	Experimental	−0.0440
Tower et al.	1979	58	50	Experimental	−0.2000*
Tower et al.	1979	58	50	Experimental	0.1290*
Tower et al.	1979	58	50	Experimental	0.2510*
Tower et al.	1979	58	50	Experimental	0.2900*
Tower et al.	1979	58	50	Experimental	0.3160*
Tower et al.	1979	58	50	Experimental	0.4190*
Tower et al.	1979	58	50	Experimental	0.3870*
Zimmerman & Brody	1975	37	132	Experimental	0.3080*

^{a}Total number of subjects in the referenced study. ^{b}The average age of subjects in months. ^{c}An asterisk denotes that the effect size was significant at the .05 level.

Table 17.3 shows that this pattern was consistent within each of the four dependent variables: Of 19 comparisons, 18 showed a significant positive effect of prosocial content. The only exception was for aggression, where children who saw prosocial content were not significantly less aggressive than those who did not watch any television.

Effects of Research Settings

A one-way analysis of variance found a marginally significant effect of comparison type on effect size across the four dependent variables $F(5, 103) = 2.07$, $p = .08$. That is, there were small-to-medium improvements in prosocial behavior for those who saw prosocial content in an experimental setting compared to control groups ($r = .31$), or compared to those who saw antisocial content (.26). The effects were smaller for the (few) studies that measured the correlation between self-selected exposure and behavior (.19). How do these findings compare with violence effects reported by Paik and Comstock (1994) and where do they leave our hypotheses? Paik and Comstock reported an effect of .37 for experimental

TABLE 17.3

Effect Sizes by Outcome and Comparison Type

Outcome Behavior	Comparison	r	Z_{Fisher}	k	N	95% CI
All Outcomes	All comparisons	.23	.27	108	5,473	(.25, .30)
	Prosocial vs. control	.31	.36	16	807	(.30, .42)
	Prosocial vs. neutral	.18	.21	43	2,072	(.16, .25)
	Prosocial vs. antisocial	.26	.31	29	1,133	(.25, .36)
	Correlation with prosocial TV	.19	.20	14	1,021	(.14, .26)
	Aggressive prosocial vs. neutral	−.35	−.37	1	60	(−.56, −.11)
	Aggressive prosocial vs. prosocial	.39	.56	5	380	(.49, .63)
Altruism	All comparisons	.37	.47	20	856	(.42, .52)
	Prosocial vs. control	.50	.57	5	154	(.45, .67)
	Prosocial vs. neutral	.23	.26	6	170	(.11, .40)
	Prosocial vs. antisocial	.35	.45	7	372	(.37, .53)
	Correlation with prosocial TV	—	—	0	0	—
	Aggressive prosocial vs. neutral	—	—	0	0	—
	Aggressive prosocial vs. prosocial	.44	.60	2	160	(.49, .69)
Social interaction	All comparisons	.24	.22	36	2,056	(.21, .30)
	Prosocial vs. control	.30	.30	2	161	(.15, .44)
	Prosocial vs. neutral	.20	.21	26	980	(.15, .27)
	Prosocial vs. antisocial	.36	.36	4	116	(.18, .52)
	Correlation with prosocial TV	.22	.23	2	679	(.16, .30)
	Aggressive prosocial vs. neutral	−.35	−.37	1	60	(−.56, −.11)
	Aggressive prosocial vs. prosocial	.44	.47	1	60	(.20, .62)
Aggression	All comparisons	.16	.27	15	747	(.20, .34)
	Prosocial vs. control	−.01	−.01	2	76	(−.24, .22)
	Prosocial vs. neutral	.09	.20	7	359	(.09, .30)
	Prosocial vs. antisocial	.20	.22	4	152	(.05, .37)
	Correlation with prosocial TV	—	—	0	0	—
	Aggressive prosocial vs. neutral	—	—	0	0	—
	Aggressive prosocial vs. prosocial	.32	.56	2	160	(.44, .66)
Reducing stereotypes	All comparisons	.20	.22	37	1,814	(.18, .27)
	Prosocial vs. control	.30	.36	7	416	(.27, .44)
	Prosocial vs. neutral	.18	.19	4	563	(.11, .27)
	Prosocial vs. antisocial	.19	.20	14	493	(.11, .28)
	Correlation with prosocial TV	.13	.13	12	342	(.02, .24)
	Aggressive prosocial vs. neutral	—	—	0	0	—
	Aggressive prosocial vs. prosocial	—	—	0	0	—

Note. r = the weighted effect size computed by the Hunter and Schmidt (1990) method; k = number of effect sizes averaged; N = total number of subjects used to compute effect size; confidence intervals are about the Z_{Fisher} value.

designs and an effect of .19 for surveys. So, according to these data, it is as easy to persuade viewers to be pleasant as it is to persuade them to be violent.

Across variables, two further questions were examined. First, we looked at the effect of enhancing viewing of prosocial content with supplementary classroom materials or activities. Despite reports within individual studies that children responded more positively when supplements were used, overall we found no such effect. The average effect size for prosocial content without supplements was .25 (number of effects = 100); for prosocial content with supplements (number of effects = 8), the average effect size was .24 (p = .812).

The second question concerned the effect of aggressive prosocial content (i.e., depicted physical or verbal aggression resolved in a prosocial manner). Despite the tiny sample size (number of effects = 11), there was evidence of pernicious effects of aggressive prosocial content. For all three of the variables for which it was measured, the contrast between prosocial content and aggressive prosocial content was larger than the contrast between pure antisocial and prosocial content. This is particularly alarming given the findings of content analyses that "positive" messages are often combined with plenty of preceding action and violence.

Differences by Dependent Measure

One-way analysis of variance showed a marginally significant effect of dependent measure on effect size [$F(3,104)$ = 2.55; p = .06]. Examination of the confidence intervals suggests that the strongest effects of prosocial content were on altruism. Effect sizes for positive interaction, aggression reduction, and stereotype reduction were remarkably similar to one another.

The strong effect on altruism runs counter to the argument posed earlier in this chapter that it should be hardest for prosocial messages to persuade people to make altruistic sacrifices (rather than to simply make them interact in a friendly manner). Why is this effect somewhat stronger? One explanation is that altruism was only investigated experimentally rather than in surveys (see Table 3), and effect sizes tend to be larger in experimental settings. We also considered various treatment effects (discussed below) as possible explanations.

Length of Delay in Testing

Are prosocial effects short-lived? Do studies with delayed testing show smaller effects? The correlation between time until testing (measured in days) and effect size is not significant (r = .064, p = .512). This correlation must be interpreted with caution given that 103 of the 108 effect sizes were measured with less than a day's delay.

There were no differences in time until testing between the dependent measures, $F(3, 104)$ = 1.28, p = .28. That is altruism was no more likely to be measured immediately than positive social interaction, aggression, or stereotype reduction; hence, this was not a possible explanation for the relatively strong effect of prosocial depictions on altruistic behaviors.

Similarity of Treatment and Outcome/Realism of Treatment

We coded the similarity of treatment and outcome: identical, similar, and general/mixed (see Table 17.1). One-way analysis of variance indicated significant differences in effect sizes [$F(2, 105) = 5.78; p < .01$]. The mean effect size for identical treatment was .44 [95% confidence interval (CI) (.36, .51)], for similar treatment it was .27 [95% CI (.19, .35)], and for general messages it was .26 [95% CI (.23, .29)]. Not surprisingly, prosocial effects were strongest when the prosocial treatment involved explicit modeling of the prosocial behavior to be imitated. Efforts to promote altruistic behavior were more likely to model behaviors identical to the observed outcome whereas efforts to promote other prosocial behaviors were less likely to have identical treatments and tasks [$\chi^2(6)$ $N = 108 = 21.35; p = .002$].

Effects of external validity. We also coded the realism (external validity) of the stimulus: self-selected content, whole television programs, edited programs, and content produced by the researchers. One-way analysis of variance found no significant differences in mean effect size.

Effects of rewards. There were no significant effects of depicting a model being rewarded for prosocial behavior. Children were no more likely to imitate a rewarded model than one who was not rewarded. This is consistent with Paik and Comstock's (1994) finding that reward had no significant effect on the tendency to imitate violence. Nonetheless, it is worth noting that there are only 10 comparisons testing the effects of reward on prosocial behavior.

Participant Effects

We examined the effects of gender, ethnicity, and socioeconomic status on the relation between prosocial exposure and behavior (see Table 17.4). Paik and Comstock (1994) reported that males were more strongly affected than females by TV violence in experimental settings (although not as a result of self-selected exposure as reported in surveys). We found no such differences: Males and females were equally positively affected by exposure to prosocial content. There were also no significant differences between ethnic or racial groups. Only socioeconomic status showed significant differences, such that prosocial television had a greater effect on participants from middle to upper class settings than on participants from lower class settings.

Age was a significant predictor of effect size [$r(108) = -.22; p < .05$]. Age ranged from 3 years to 16 years 10 months with a mean of 7 years 3 2/3 months ($SD = 44.33$). A curve fit analysis, displayed in Fig. 17.1, suggests that a cubic function best described the relationship between age and effect size. It appears that the effect of prosocial content increased sharply between the ages of 3 and 7,

TABLE 17.4
Effect Sizes by Demographic Group

Demographic	Group	r	Z_{Fisher}	k	N	95% CI
Gender	Male	.13	.13	27	1,229	(.07, .19)
	Female	.20	.22	16	474	(.13, .31)
Ethnicity	White	.20	.27	44	2,131	(.23, .31)
	Black	.37	.37	2	80	(.16, .55)
Socioeconomic Status	Low	.14	.16	22	1,175	(.10, .22)
	High	.25	.32	47	2,620	(.32, .39)

Note. r = the weighted effect size computed by the Hunter and Schmidt (1990) method; k = number of effect sizes averaged; N = total number of subjects used to compute effect size; confidence intervals are about the Z_{Fisher} value.

peaked at age 7, declined steeply until age 12, and then declined more gradually after that. This age pattern is inconsistent with Paik and Comstock's (1994) report that the youngest viewers were the most strongly negatively affected by exposure to violence. Perhaps the difference may lie in the visual salience and excitement of violent actions compared to the somewhat less striking acts of cooperation or kindness (see Abelman, 1991). The peak at age 7 suggests that younger children may lack the cognitive ability to fully grasp the nature of prosocial acts and the contexts that require them, when presented within a television program.

DISCUSSION

Both in experimental settings and at home, children who watched prosocial content behaved significantly more positively or held significantly more positive attitudes than others. This is striking news.

In addition, the results suggest that television is no more prone to fostering violence than it is to fostering prosocial behavior. Probably the most interesting comparison is of the effect sizes for self-selected exposure to violence versus prosocial content (as measured by surveys). In the "real world" of viewing at home, violence and prosocial content had small but identical effects. Unfortunately, the strength of the relationship says nothing about "real world" typical levels of viewing violence versus prosocial content or about the relative availability of TV violence versus prosocial content.

Taken as a whole, the results point to the critical combination of having seen a behavior modeled explicitly and perceiving a similar situation in which one could act that way. The more apparent the connection between the situation shown

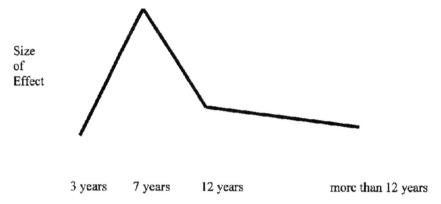

FIG. 17.1   Curve-fit analysis of the effect of age on effect size.

and viewers' own situations, the more likely it was that they used the modeled behaviors. In this study, effect sizes for altruism were marginally larger than for other dependent variables primarily because participants in studies of altruism were more likely to be placed in situations that were identical with the film they had just seen. Is this at all useful beyond the realm of academics? It suggests that producers of prosocial content should pay attention not only to the explicitness with which they model the desired behaviors, but also to making the contexts of the behaviors seem relevant and realistic to viewers.

In any event, the conclusion is that television has the potential to foster positive social interactions, reduce aggression, and encourage viewers to be more tolerant and helpful. Surely this is good news. Why, then, does the research on violence continue apace, whereas the number of studies on prosocial effects dwindles from year to year? We found 34 studies (108 hypothesis tests) that could be analyzed compared to the 217 studies (1,142 hypothesis tests) analyzed by Paik and Comstock (1994). The range of methodologies and of populations studied is much broader for the violence literature than the prosocial literature. Consider Table 17.3: Numerous cells remain empty or are filled by one or two studies. In particular, we have little sense of the everyday effects of television viewed at home: There are far fewer studies of self-selected exposure to prosocial content than of self-selected exposure to violent content. We know less about how to make prosocial programming effective than we know about how to make violence maximally effective. We have little sense of the individual and interactive effects of demographics such as ethnicity and socioeconomic status. This is problematic, given that television has been conceived of as a tool for eradicating subgroup differences in readiness for school.

Ideally, meta-analysis is the answer to the customary call for "more research to clarify the issue" that plagues media effects research. In this case, our hope is that it serves as a wake-up call to researchers that the question of prosocial effects should not languish as the topic of the 1970s, but should be the focus of more sophisticated attempts to use television as a tool for positive social change.

NOTE

This chapter is a somewhat abbreviated version of a previously published journal article (Mares & Woodward, 2005).

ACKNOWLEDGMENTS

This study was funded, in part, by a grant to Marie-Louise Mares from the Annenberg Public Policy Center, University of Pennsylvania.

REFERENCES

References marked with an asterisk indicate studies included in the meta-analysis.
*Abelman, R. (1985). Styles of parental disciplinary practices as a mediator of children's learning from prosocial television portrayals. *Child Study Journal, 15,* 131–145.
Abelman, R. (1991). TV Literacy III—Gifted and learning disabled children: Amplifying prosocial learning through curriculum intervention. *Journal of Research and Development in Education, 24,* 51–60.
*Ahammer, I. M., & Murray, J. P. (1979). Kindness in the kindergarten: The relative influence of role-playing and prosocial television in facilitating altruism. *International Journal of Behavioral Development, 2,* 133–157.
*Bankart, C. P., & Anderson, C. C. (1979). Short-term effects of prosocial television viewing on play of preschool boys and girls. *Psychological Reports, 44,* 935–941.
*Baran, S. J., Chase, L. J., & Courtright, J. A. (1979). Television drama as a facilitator of prosocial behavior: "The Waltons." *Journal of Broadcasting, 23,* 277–284.
*Bryan, J. H., & Walbek, N. H. (1970). The impact of words and deeds concerning altruism upon children. *Child Development, 41,* 747–757.
Cohen, J. & Cohen, P. (1983). *Applied multiple regression/correlation analysis for the behavioral sciences.* Hillsdale, NJ: Lawrence Erlbaum Associates.
*Collins, W. A., & Getz, S. K. (1976). Children's social responses following modeled reactions to provocation: Prosocial effects of television drama. *Journal of Personality, 44,* 488–500.
*Davidson, E.S., Yasuna, A., & Tower, A. (1979). The effects of television cartoons on sex-role stereotyping in young girls. *Child Development, 50,* 597–600.
*Drabman, R. S., & Thomas, M. H. (1977). Children's imitation of aggressive and prosocial behavior when viewing alone and in pairs. *Journal of Communication, 27*(3), 199–205.
*Durkin, K. & Hutchins, G. (1984). Challenging traditional sex-role stereotypes via careers education broadcasts: The reactions of young secondary school pupils. *Journal of Educational Television, 10,* 25–33.
*Elias, M. J. (1983). Improving coping skills of emotionally disturbed boys through television-based social problem solving. *American Journal of Orthopsychiatry, 53,* 61–72.
*Elliott, R. & Vasta, R. (1970). The modeling of sharing: Effects associated with vicarious reinforcement, symbolization, age, and generalization. *Journal of Experimental Child Psychology, 10,* 8–15.

*Forge, L. S. & Phemister, S. (1987). The effect of prosocial cartoons on preschool children. *Child Study Journal, 17,* 83–87.

*Friedrich-Cofer, L. K., Huston-Stein, A., Kipnis, D. M., Susman, E. J., & Clewett, A. S. (1979). Environmental enhancement of prosocial television content: Effect on interpersonal behavior, imaginative play, and self-regulation in a natural setting. *Developmental Psychology, 15,* 637–646.

*Geller, M. I., & Scheirer, C. J. (1978). The effect of filmed modeling on cooperative play in disadvantaged preschoolers. *Journal of Abnormal Child Psychology, 6,* 71–87.

*Goldberg, M. E., & Gorn, G. J. (1979). Television's impact on preferences of non-white playmates: Canadian "Sesame Street" inserts. *Journal of Broadcasting, 23,* 27–32.

*Gorn, G. J., Goldberg, M. E., & Kanungo, R. N. (1976). The role of educational television in changing the intergroup attitudes of children. *Child Development, 42,* 277–280.

Greenberg, B. S., Atkin, C. K., Edison, N. G., & Korzenny, F. (1980). Antisocial and prosocial behaviors on television. In B. S. Greenberg (Ed.), *Life on television: Content analysis of U.S. TV drama.* Norwood, NJ: Ablex.

Grusec, J. E. (1991). The socialization of altruism. In M. S. Clark (Ed.), *Prosocial Behavior* (pp. 9–33). Beverly Hills: Sage.

Hearold, S. (1986). A synthesis of 1043 effects of television on social behavior. In G. Comstock (Ed.), *Public communication and behavior* (Vol. 1, pp. 65–133). New York: Academic Press.

Hedges, L. V., & Olkin, I. (1985). *Statistical methods for meta-analysis.* New York: Academic Press.

*Houser, B. B. (1978). An examination of the use of audiovisual media in reducing prejudice. *Psychology in the School, 15,* 116–122.

Hunter, J. E., & Schmidt, F. L. (1990). *Methods of meta-analysis: Correcting error and bias in research findings.* Newbury Park, CA: Sage.

*Keller, M. F., & Carlson, P. M. (1974). The use of symbolic modeling to promote social skills in preschool children with low levels of social responsiveness. *Child Development, 45,* 912–919.

Kunkel, D., Wilson, B. J., Linz, D., Potter, J., Donnerstein, E., Smith, S. L., Blumenthal, E., & Gray, T. (1996). *National television violence study.* Studio City, CA: Mediascope.

Liebert, R. M. & Poulos, R. W. (1975). Television and personality development: The socializing effects of an entertainment medium. In A. Davids (Ed.), *Child personality and psychopathology: Current topics* (Vol. 2, pp. 61–97). New York: Wiley.

Liebert, R. M.,& Sprafkin, J. (1988). *The early window: Effects of television on children and youth.* New York: Pergamon Press.

*Liss, M. B., & Reinhardt, L. C. (1980). Aggression on prosocial television programs. *Psychological Reports, 46,* 1065–1066.

Mares, M. L., & Woodard, E. (2005). Positive effects of television on children's social interactions: A meta-analysis. *Media Psychology, 7,* 301–322.

*McArthur, L. Z., & Eisen, S. V. (1976). Television and sex-role stereotyping. *Journal of Applied Social Psychology, 6,* 329–351.

*O'Bryant, S. L., & Corder-Bolz, C. R. (1978). The effects of television on children's stereotyping of women's work roles. *Journal of Vocational Behavior, 12,* 233–244.

*O'Connor, R. D. (1969). Modification of social withdrawal through symbolic modeling. *Journal of Applied Behavior Analysis, 2,* 15–22.

*O'Connor, R. D. (1972). Relative efficacy of modeling, shaping, and the combined procedures for modification of social withdrawal. *Journal of Abnormal Psychology, 79,* 327–334.

Paik, H., & Comstock, G. (1994). The effects of television violence on antisocial behavior: A meta-analysis. *Communication Research, 21,* 516–546.

*Pingree, S. (1978). The effects of nonsexist television commercials and perceptions of reality on children's attitudes about women. *Psychology of Women Quarterly, 2,* 262–277.

Poulos, R. W., Harvey, S. E., & Liebert, R. M. (1976). Saturday morning television: A profile of the 1974–75 children's season. *Psychological Reports, 39,* 1047–1057.

*Rao, N., Moely, B. E., & Lockman, J. J. (1987). Increasing participation in preschool social isolates. *Journal of Clinical Child Psychology, 16,* 178–183.

*Rosenwasser, S. M., Lingenfelter, M., & Harrington, A. F. (1989). Nontraditional gender role portrayals on television and children's gender role perceptions. *Journal of Applied Developmental Psychology, 10,* 97–105.

Rushton, J. P. (1979). Effects of prosocial television and film material on the behavior of viewers. In L. Berkowitz (Ed.), *Advances in experimental social psychology* (pp. 321–351). New York: Academic Press.

*Rushton, J. P., & Owen, D. (1975). Immediate and delayed effects of TV modelling and preaching on children's generosity. *British Journal of Social and Clinical Psychology, 14,* 309–310.

*Silverman, L. T., & Sprafkin, J. N. (1980). The effects of Sesame Street's prosocial spots on cooperative play between young children. *Journal of Broadcasting, 24,* 135–147.

*Sprafkin, J. N., Liebert, R. M., & Poulos, R. W. (1975). Effects of a prosocial televised example on children's helping. *Journal of Experimental Child Psychology, 20,* 119–126.

*Sprafkin, J. N., & Rubinstein, E. A. (1979). Children's television viewing habits and prosocial behavior: A field correlational study. *Journal of Broadcasting, 23,* 265–276.

*Teachman, G., & Orme, M. (1981). Effects of aggressive and prosocial film material on altruistic behavior of children. *Psychological Reports, 48,* 699–702.

*Toeplitz-Winiewska, M. (1977). Influence of various models on aggressive behavior in individuals with different socialization experience. *Polish Psychological Bulletin, 8,* 215–222.

*Tower, R. B., Singer, D. G., Singer, J. L. & Biggs, A. (1979). Differential effects of television programming on preschoolers' cognition, imagination, and social play. *American Journal of Orthopsychiatry, 49,* 265–281.

Woodard, E. H. (1999). The 1999 State of Children's Television Report: Programming for Children over Broadcast and Cable Television. *Annenberg Public Policy Center Report No. 28,* University of Pennsylvania.

Zillmann, D. (1991). The logic of suspense and mystery. In J. Bryant & D. Zillmann (Eds.), *Responding to the screen: Reception and reaction processes* (pp. 281–303). Hillsdale, NJ: Lawrence Erlbaum Associates.

*Zimmerman, B. J., & Brody, G. H. (1975). Race and modeling influences on the play pattern of boys. *Journal of Educational Psychology, 67, 5,* 591–598.

18

Parasocial Relationships and Television: A Meta-Analysis of the Effects

Edward Schiappa
University of Minnesota

Mike Allen
University of Wisconsin–Milwaukee

Peter B. Gregg
University of Minnesota

The normal definition used by scholars for what constitutes an interpersonal relationship is usually some version of the developmental perspective (Miller & Steinberg, 1970) that requires some exchange of information with the expectation of a continued exchange or self-disclosure of information. This definition is an extension or application of what constitutes a small group for small group communication and is an attempt to avoid a definition of a group that would include a collection of individuals at a stop waiting for the bus.

The problem with defining a relationship with a media celebrity or character in a program as a relationship is that the relationship is unidirectional. Although opportunities for feedback exist, the ability for that direct connection of person to person generally is not possible. The perception by the audience member of a kind of relationship existing remains, however.

Although conceptualized and operationalized in a number of ways, *parasocial interaction* can be thought of simply as any communicative interaction taking place parasocially rather than interpersonally. Just as all communicative interaction does not lead to interpersonal relationships, not all television, radio, or film viewing leads to parasocial *relationships*. For the purposes of this meta-analysis, a parasocial relationship is the perception of a television viewer of a relationship with someone known through the media. The relationship is obviously not a "real" interpersonal relationship because there is no corresponding self-disclosure from the viewer to the person on the screen. However, the person on the screen may make what would appear to be self-disclosure to the audience and therefore undergoes the start of the process of forming an interpersonal relationship.

Horton and Wohl (1956) first described the idea of a kind of face-to-face interaction between the performer and the audience member as parasocial interaction. They borrowed Kenneth Burke's (1937) phrase "coaching of attitudes" to explain that through various televisual techniques, television audiences are encouraged to feel as if they are a part of the world taking place on their television screens. The television persona is relatively consistent and stable from episode to episode, and audiences quickly form attitudes about particular television personalities via a form of Burke's (1950) "collaborative expectancy" (p. 58). The audience must accept the explicit and implicit terms of the program and must be able to "play the part" that those terms require. Such interaction has been extended to television because the brain tends to process media experiences as though the interactions were with real people (Kanazawa, 2002; Reeves & Nass, 1996).

Perse and R. Rubin (1989) noted that mediated and face-to-face interpersonal interactions may satisfy similar communication and gratification needs, with increased feelings of intimacy and self-disclosure arising from increased and consistent interaction. Many studies already mentioned have linked perceived realism of television and attraction to the media figure to parasocial interaction (A. Rubin, Perse, & Powell, 1985; A. Rubin & Perse, 1987; R. Rubin & McHugh, 1987), indicating that the interpretation of media figures occurs along the same lines as evaluation of people in face-to-face contact. R. Rubin and McHugh (1987) found that social and task attraction to television celebrities better predicted parasocial interaction than physical attraction, and they argued that parasocial interaction is correlated positively with feelings of relationship importance and not to time of exposure. Perse and R. Rubin (1989) discovered that decreased uncertainty about characters' behavior and parasocial interaction were correlated and that parasocial interactions are akin to interpersonal friendships in three important ways: they are entered into voluntarily, they provide companionship, and they arise from social attractiveness. Clearly, the argument is not that the two are interchangeable; instead the argument is that both can be viewed (perhaps by different kinds of people) as interactions that fulfill the need for human contact.

Parasocial relationships may be formed with persons on talk shows such as hosts or guests. The persons are portraying or representing themselves as individuals. This is a different category then a person perceiving a relationship with a fictional character on a drama or comedy. The fictional character is portrayed by a performer, but the character does not exist outside of the particular program (or fictional venue). When a person believes a relationship exists with a person on television who is involved in a role, the basis for the relationship (a real person) at least exists.

A central question is why such relationships are formed and what the viewer as well as the media representative obtains from the formation of such relations. The media professional clearly would like the formation of regular relationships because the ability to attract and maintain viewers to an ongoing series enhances the ability to gain revenue from advertising. The more persons can become "hooked" on the viewing the program, the greater the sense of loyalty and repetition that comes every week or season with the particular program.

The portrayals on television often show groups like the family (e.g., *Sopranos, Frazier, Six Feet Under, Charmed Ones, Little House on the Prairie*, and *Malcolm in the Middle*), a group of friends (e.g., *Buffy the Vampire Slayer, Friends, Will & Grace*, and *Seinfeld*), a husband/wife or a person in a committed relationship/searching for such a relationship (e.g., *Mad about You* and *Sex in the City*), or a workplace (e.g., *CSI, Law and Order*, and *MASH*). These various portrayals take a set of characters and develop relationships among the characters. The interaction observed permits the audience to develop a "relationship" in the sense that the interactions "reveal" information about the character to the audience.

A consideration is whether television programs in particular can promote the development of these relationships. With celebrities the existence or belief in the existence of these relationships is well established. A central question is the description of the relationship of the audience to the celebrity. Parasocial relations with fictional characters start with an actor, who then creates a false person interacting with others. The goal, from a commercial view, is the development of characters and plots that the audience wishes to see continued, thus supporting continuation of the character and stories associated with that particular character.

MOTIVES FOR FORMING
PARASOCIAL RELATIONSHIPS

The question of why persons perceive the formation of parasocial relationships involves a number of interesting psychological and communication contingencies. Persons may form parasocial relationships because of a deficiency in their own set of interpersonal contacts. Persons could form such relationships simply because they enjoy television and find the relationships or characters satisfying. Indeed, the motivations for forming parasocial relationships are likely to be as varied as the motivations for forming interpersonal relationships.

One argument is that shyness and loneliness in a person's life create a void that the development or the perception of the development of this relationship fills. Much parasocial interaction research indicates it does not *require* loneliness, although it can be facilitated by and replace it; instead parasocial interaction is a normal consequence of television viewing. The anxiety felt about potential relationships and social situations can be avoided because the relationship is entirely one-sided and can be ended unilaterally. Additionally, should the television character portray a flaw in the personality or turn out to be antisocial or evil, the person can easily terminate the relationship by not watching the program. This control reduces the risk of getting involved or devoting time to the development of such relationships.

Choice is always important, because the viewer can form a relationship with someone of similar values and tastes. Alternatively, the viewer can form a relationship with a character whose values and tastes are those that the viewer desires to have in himself or herself or any potential live partner. The element of choice involves a kind of video personality (as well as possession) inventory that is developed in the program and can be used the compare to the desired characteristics in another person as well as to the self.

A final consideration is the degree to which the person experiencing parasocial interaction forms a parasocial relationship. Perse (1990) found that parasocial interaction occurred with local television news under particular conditions, but it was not the sole predictor of audience involvement. The higher the perceived realism of the news, the less recognition of news, and the happier the feelings during news viewing generally lead to parasocial interaction, but both parasocial interaction and information holding together predicted audience involvement more accurately than those variables taken separately. A person forming this relationship should have an affinity for viewing television and view television stories as more realistic. This element is important because the viewing of the character as more real indicates a more realistic element to the relationship, something not present in a complete fantasy relationship. Many studies already mentioned have linked perceived realism of television and attraction to the media figure to parasocial interaction (A. Rubin et al., 1985; A. Rubin and Perse, 1987; R. Rubin & McHugh, 1987), indicating that the interpretation of media figures occurs along the same lines as evaluation of people in face-to-face contact. This realism does not have to play at the level of the story or the setting; many television characters exist in worlds that bear little relationship to the "real" world (e.g., Hercules, Xena, Buffy, or Angel). The element of realism referred to in this sense is that the person acts realistically in terms of emotional and psychological reactions to the situations that the main character confronts. Such realism permits identification with the character by the viewer as someone to be understood and considered as a person.

METHODS

Literature Search

Literature was searched using the word *parasocial* to find various manuscripts that could be considered relevant.

To be included in this review, a manuscript had to have the following characteristics: (a) a report of original data presented in a manner so that the data were recoverable for the estimation of an effect size; (b) some measure of parasocial interaction with a television character(s); and (c) some measure of outcome or predictor with the development of a parasocial relationship.

Some manuscript reports were presented in a manner that did not permit the estimation of an effect and the data are unrecoverable (Cole & Leets, 1999; Conway & Rubin, 1991; Perse & A. Rubin, 1990; Perse & R. Rubin, 1989), and some presented conceptual or nonquantitative data (Nordlund, 1978). A complete bibliography of manuscripts examined, reasons for inclusion/noninclusion, as well as statistical conversion procedures is available from the first author.

Coding of Manuscripts

Amount of Television Viewing

The variable name describes accurately the content of this outcome. The variable constitutes some measure of television viewing, either in general or specific to the particular genre under consideration. The assumptions are that a person watching more television is likely to perceive parasocial relationships with television personalities.

Affinity for Watching Television.

This measure provides a sense of emotional reaction or desire to watch television. The person is asked to indicate the degree that watching television is found to be enjoyable and desirable. Not surprisingly, persons who view television as rewarding and pleasurable should find it more rewarding to form or report the formation of parasocial relationships. A necessary condition for such formation should be that the kind of "interaction" with the character is restricted to a means of presentation and that that means be viewed as something desirable.

Perceive Television Programs and Characters as Real

This set of measures indicates the degree that television content for fictional programs is perceived to represent real life actions and persons. The question is whether the reduced suspension of disbelief would translate into an increased level of parasocial relationships. Studies that only used stimuli involving fictional programs are included, when studies examined televangelists, news reporters, or other celebrities who are "real," this measure was not included. No study using such real persons did include this measure so no data were excluded on this basis from the current meta-analysis.

Perception of Television Characters as Attractive

This measure reveals to what extent the characters are considered attractive (physically, socially, or relationally). The expectation is that persons would be more likely to report a parasocial relationship with characters who are considered attractive. The function of the relationship that a person established would be to a character who has some aspect of the features of the person that are found to be desirable. One should note that the perception of attraction can be based not on some objective likeability issues but instead can reflect characteristics that the particular viewer would find attractive.

Perception of Homophily with Television Characters

This measure is conceptualized as the degree to which a viewer of a television program views a character as similar to himself or herself. For example, a character who shares the same taste in clothing, religion, or health issues could be viewed as more similar to the viewer. The expected relationship is that audience members will be more likely to report a parasocial relationship with characters who are perceived to be more similar to themselves.

Parasocialability

This measure considers the willingness or the belief of the viewer that there is a possibility of forming a relationship with the character on television. The measure indicates the sense that the habit of viewing the character constitutes a bond or form of relationship.

Gender

This classification shows whether respondents indicated the biological gender of the individual. When estimates were provided for each group, the estimates are compared, and a positive correlation indicates that women rate themselves higher in terms of parasocial interaction with the characters. The expectation is that women will be more likely to report the formation of parasocial relationships.

Age

Age was measured in terms of chronological years since birth. The estimate provided is an estimate for the effect of each separate sample. Samples varied in the range of the available participants, and, therefore, the findings should be treated cautiously because the distribution of typical convenience samples of college students may not include large groups of older persons.

Shyness/Loneliness/Communication Apprehension

This is a set of measures that reflect an anxiety or avoidance by a person for communication with others as well as an unhappiness with the amount of communication or support the person receives. The expectation is that persons with higher degrees of communication apprehension, higher levels of anxiety, and greater amounts of shyness will report a greater probability of forming parasocial relationships with persons appearing on television. The question of the desire to have a relationship should be increased when the current live relationships fail to provide the outcomes that the person seeks. The function of the parasocial relationship then is a provisional or temporary relationship that can be enjoyed.

Internal Locus of Control

These measures examine whether the person believes that the motive or basis for actions is found within the person (internal) or exists within the environment (external). The expectation is that persons with an internal locus of control would report a higher level of parasocial relationship formation. The decision to view a particular character or program and then continue this behavior should reflect a belief by the individual of a sense of control. Despite the claim of one network of "must see TV," the fact that choice exists and that viewers can select the programs means that the formation of the relationship should be viewed as voluntary.

Statistical Procedures

A variance-centered form of meta-analysis was used in this study. The procedure requires that the statistical information from each data set be transformed into a common metric (in this case the correlation coefficient) and then averaged using a procedure that weights each effect by the size of the sample. The sample of correlations is then assessed to determine whether the average effect generated comes from a homogeneous or heterogeneous set of estimates.

RESULTS

Table 18.1 presents a summary of the average effects found in this study.

Amount of Television Viewing

The results for the amount of television viewing provide 15 studies indicating that persons with parasocial relationships watch more television, $r = .217, k = 15, N = 4,945$. The set of samples provided a series of estimates that were homogeneous, $\chi^2 = 25.98 (14, N = 4,945), p > .05$. The findings show that persons indicating higher levels of parasocial relationships are watching more television. The fact that the chi-square test for homogeneity was nonsignificant indicates evidence for the robustness of the finding and the lack of any moderator variable.

TABLE 18.1
Summary of Average Effects

Outcome	Average r	k	N	χ^2
Amount TV viewing	.217	15	4,945	25.98*
Affinity for TV viewing	.273	12	5,370	261.05*
TV perceived as real	.476	7	1,843	88.74*
TV characters attractive	.599	7	879	43.43*
Homophily with TV Characters	.483	5	614	24.80*
Parasocialability	.340	4	1,356	36.53*
Gender (females +)	.181	8	2,126	13.49
Age	.037	5	1,839	18.40*
Shyness/loneliness/communication apprehension	.139	10	2,239	8.86
Locus of control (internal)	.260	4	959	0.68

Affinity for Watching Television

The more a person had a desire to watch television, the greater the prediction that a person would form a parasocial relationship, $r = .273$, $k = 12$, $N = 5,370$. However, this relationship was based on a sample of correlations that were heterogeneous, $\chi^2 = 261.05$, $(11, N = 5370)$, $p < .05$. Although a great deal of variability exists in the observed sizes of the correlations (ranging from .103 to .791), all of the observed effects were positive. The identification of any source for the variability would be examining a change in the degree or size of the relationship, not the direction of the relationship. The conclusion that a positive relationship exists remains warranted.

Perceive Television Programs Characters as Real

Seven studies examined the relationship between parasocial relationships and the degree to which a person perceives television programs and characters as real. The average effect was positive, $r = .476$, $k = 7$, $N = 1,843$, based on a heterogeneous set of correlations, $\chi^2 = 88.74$ $(6, N = 1843)$, $p < .05$.

Perception of Television Characters as Attractive

The association between the development of a parasocial relationship and the degree to which the characters were perceived as attractive was positive, $r = .599$, $k = 7$, $N = 879$. The variability found among the observed effects was large, $\chi^2 =$

43.43 (6, $N = 879$), $p < .05$, indicating the probable existence of a moderator variable. The findings are consistent with expectations; audience members are more likely to form relationships with characters whom they find attractive.

Perception of Homophily with Television Characters

The association between the perception of homophily with the television character and the development of a parasocial relationship was positive, $r = .483$, $k = 5$, $N = 614$, but represented a heterogeneous set of effects, $\chi^2 = 24.80$ (4, $N = 614$), $p < .05$. The effects were all positive, ranging from $r = .300$ to $r = .690$. The observed correlations are all positive, indicating that any moderator would distinguish between larger and smaller positive associations; however, directionally the valence is consistently positive. The conclusion is that the five studies all indicate a positive association between character homophily and parasocial relations. This conclusion is consistent with expectations that the choice to form a relationship would be preferred when the character portrays attributes that are shared with the viewer.

Parasocialability

Four studies examined whether a person who has a predisposition to a parasocial relationship would in fact establish such a relationship. Not surprisingly, the average correlation is positive, $r = .340$, $k = 4$, $N = 1,356$, but the average effect was based on a heterogeneous set of estimates, $\chi^2 = 36.53$ (3, $N = 1356$), $p < .05$.

Gender

A comparison of whether men or women are more likely to have developed the perception of a parasocial relationship indicates an average positive correlation, $r = .181$, $k = 8$, $N = 2,126$. This average was coded so that positive indicates consistency with expectations that women would be more likely to report forming such a relationship. The set of correlations indicated a homogeneous sample, $\chi^2 = 13.49$ (7, $N = 2,126$), $p > .05$, which indicates that the sample can be said to represent a single distribution with no evidence of a moderator variable present. The average effect, therefore, supports a consistent expectation that women are more likely to form parasocial relationships than men.

Age

Five studies showed the relationship between age and the report of parasocial interaction with television. The average across the five investigations was positive, $r = .037$, $k = 5$, $N = 1,839$, but relatively small. The sample demonstrated heterogeneity when tested, $\chi^2 = 18.30$ (4, $N = 1,839$), $p < .05$. The distribution of the effects had three positive and two negative correlations, indicating that the low correlation did not evidence a relationship with consistent valence. For the purposes of this review, the correlation will be considered zero, and there might exist a potential moderator variable. However, with only five studies in this particular analysis follow-up analyses were impossible to conduct with such a small data pool.

Shyness/Loneliness/Communication Apprehension

The 10 studies in this cluster demonstrated a positive relationship, $r = .139$, $k = 10$, $N = 2,230$, based on a homogeneous set of correlations, $\chi^2 = 8.86$ (9, $N = 2,230$), $p > .05$. The overall average correlation indicates that persons reporting higher degrees of loneliness and shyness also are more likely to engage in parasocial interactions and relationships with television characters. The projected explanation that parasocial relationships serve as an alternative form of relationship receives support.

Internal Locus of Control

Four studies showed the relationship between internal locus of control and parasocial relationships and the average correlation was positive, $r = .260$, $k = 4$, $N = 959$, and based on a sample of correlations that was homogeneous, $\chi^2 = 0.68$ (3, $N = 959$), $p > .05$. What the effect indicates is that persons with a greater feeling of internal control will report a higher probability of feeling as though a parasocial relationship exists to a television character.

CONCLUSIONS

The perception that persons have relationships with television personalities represents one functional move that consumers of the media create. The relationships are not "real" relationships in the sense that ongoing interaction exists between the person broadcast on television and the viewer of the program. However, the ability to form attachments and the perception of that relationship existing is something that is real persists. In this meta-analysis we examine the characteristics associated with the development of those types of relationships.

In our research we consider two aspects of such relationships. First, how such relationships are formed; that is, what elements of a televised character are perceived that would create the feeling that a relationship exists. Second, the characteristics of the person can contribute to the formation of such relationships. The dual questions pose an interaction between the perception of media content that combines with personality features of the person that contribute to the formation of such relationships.

Persons who consume a lot of media are more likely to form such relationships. Not surprisingly, the more time a person spends watching television, the more the person gains a sense of an understanding of the characters portrayed on television. This understanding begins to translate into a sense that there exists a kind of relationship with the character. The relationship is a regular one; it occurs every week (in some cases every day) and can be relived in reruns or copied and owned. The ownership aspect of the media represents a homology (Brummett, 1988); the person controls or owns the relationship. Such relationships are more likely to occur when a person perceives the TV character as real and attractive. Think of the promotional comments for television programs as real: "ripped from the headlines" and "based on a real case." The characters are portrayed in similar fashion, "a time we all remember" and "a man trying to find his way."

One aspect is that cancellation or loss of a television series is the loss of a relationship. However, the good thing about television is that another person is out there waiting to form an attachment with an audience. A consideration of the parasocial relationship is that there is always a replacement available, either in the next season or on another channel. Also, some series have endings that reflect the resolution of some crisis or long-term plot line. For example, the old series *The Fugitive* ended when the title character was exonerated, and *MASH* ended when the war in Korea was over and the characters were sent home. Some series simply end without any real sense of resolution or conclusion that ties together or resolves issues.

An area of future research could be the issue of reruns and the function of relationships for which outcomes are already known and the material is well established. The question of relational change is always an important one. In addition, the modification or switching from one series to another when the run is over provides an interesting set of questions with regard to loyalty, particularly in a relational sense.

Consider the distinction between whether one can reasonably expect to meet the character (celebrity) or not. In professional wrestling, the focus is on a live event for which the audience can go and meet the person or at least witness the person face to face. Although the televised events are important, the goal is an audience involved in the fortunes (both good and bad) of the wrestlers as they engage in combat. But there will not be a chance to meet most fictional characters or view them live; the characters exist only when portrayed in a box.

Our treatment in this chapter has done little to distinguish the types of or the divergent contexts in which parasocial relationships operate and flourish. The question of what kind of expectations or lack of expectations persons have for the potential for live interactions remains an issue requiring exploration. The ability to distinguish between the celebrity playing a part and the actual role played by the actor remains unresolved.

The impact of parasocial relationships in terms of the function served was not addressed in this chapter. The most important aspect of the formation of this kind of relationship is the purpose that the television viewer perceives this relationship serves. The issue of whether the relationship generates a kind of substitution for existing relationships, a curb in the desire to seek and form relationships, a perspective on the current relationships (a basis to evaluate), or simply an entertaining escape from the current life issues is not clear.

Another area of research could focus on production techniques or televisual approaches. The influence of chiaroscuro or flat lighting, the strategic placement of close-ups or establishing shots, deductive or inductive shot sequences, hip-hop editing, or desaturation have long been theorized to have some effect on audiences, but their influence on the formation of parasocial relationships is currently unexplored. One set of studies might examine how relationships formed toward a given program are altered by using close-ups on key moments instead of wide shots; another might focus on the differences between a bright, open set and a dark and gloomy set given the same narrative.

The next major theoretical step in the research agenda requires a comprehensive analysis of the literature to develop a causal model that attempts to contextualize the functions of parasocial relationships (cf. Giles, 2002). Such a process or causal model would begin to answer the issues associated with the development of the relationship and the function such a relationship serves for the television viewer. Once the function of the relationship is understood, then the examination of the value of such a function can be considered. Rather than such relationships being necessarily dysfunctional, parasocial relationships may serve very important purposes and consideration of such functions could guide an analysis of what impact television programs are having on individuals.

REFERENCES

References marked with an asterisk *indicates studies included in contributing data to the meta-analysis.

*Ashe, D., & McCutcheon, L. (2001). Shyness, loneliness, and attitude toward celebrities. *Current Research in Social Psychology, 6*. Retrieved November 2003 from http://www.uiowa.edu/~grp-proc/crisp/crisp.6.9.htm.

*Auter, P. (1992). *Development of parasocial interaction as a function of repeated viewing of a television program*. Unpublished doctoral dissertation, University of Kentucky, Lexington, KY.

*Auter, P. (1992). TV that talks back: An experimental validation of a parasocial interaction scale. *Journal of Broadcasting & Electronic Media, 36*, 173–181.

*Auter, P., & Lane, R. (1999). Locus of control, parasocial interaction and usage of radio and TV ministry programs. *Journal of Communication and Religion, 22*, 93–120.

*Auter, P., & Palmgreen, P. (2000). Development and validation of a parasocial interaction measure: The audience-persona interaction scale. *Communication Research Reports, 17*, 79–89.

*Babb, V. (1994). *The influence of psychological, sociological, and communication predictors on adolescents' development of parasocial relationships and their television uses and gratifications*. Unpublished doctoral dissertation, Regent University, Virginia Beach, VA.

Brummett, B. (1988). The homology hypothesis: Pornography on the VCR. *Critical Studies in Mass Communication, 5,* 202–216.

Burke, K. (1937) *Attitudes toward History, Vol. 1.* New York: New Republic.

Burke, K. (1950) *A Rhetoric of Motives.* New York: Prentice-Hall.

*Cohen, J. (1995). *Media consumption and mental models of attachment.* Unpublished doctoral dissertation, University of Southern California, Los Angeles, CA.

*Cohen, J. (1997). Parasocial relations and romantic attraction: Gender and dating status differences. *Journal of Broadcasting & Electronic Media, 41,* 516–529.

Cole, T., & Leets, L. (1999). Attachment styles and intimate television viewing: Insecurely forming relationships in a parasocial way. *Journal of Social and Personal Relationships, 16,* 495–511.

Conway, J., & Rubin, A. (1991). Psychological predictors of television viewing motivation. *Communication Research, 18,* 443–463.

*Corison, C. (1982). *Communication avoidance, media uses and gratifications, and parasocial interaction: A path analysis.* Unpublished doctoral dissertation, University of Oregon, Eugene, OR.

*Cortez, C. (1991). *Mediated interpersonal communication: The role of attraction and perceived homophily in the development of parasocial relationships.* Unpublished doctoral dissertation, University of Iowa, Iowa City, IA.

*Crouch, J. (2001). *The effect of physical, social, and task attraction and homophily on parasocial interaction within the scope of "reality" television.* Unpublished paper, Regent University, Virginia Beach, VA.

*Crouch, J. (2002). *The role of relational maintenance and equity in parasocial relationships.* Paper presented at the National Communication Association Convention, New Orleans, LA.

*Crouch, J. (2002). *The role of relational maintenance and equity in parasocial relationships within the scope of science fiction/fantasy television programming.* Unpublished doctoral dissertation, Regent University, Virginia Beach, VA.

*Eyal, K., & Rubin, A. (2003). Viewer aggression and homophily, identification, and parasocial relationships with television characters. *Journal of Broadcasting and Electronic Media, 47,* 77–98.

Giles, D. C. (2002). Parasocial interaction: A review of the literature and a model for future research. *Media Psychology, 4,* 279–305.

*Grant, A., Guthrie, K., & Ball-Rokeach, S. J. (1991). Television shopping: Media system dependency perspective. *Communication Research, 18,* 773–798.

*Gregg, P. (1971). *Television viewing as parasocial interaction for persons aged 60 years or older.* Unpublished master's thesis, University of Oregon, Eugene.

*Grubbs, J. (1997). *Real world, real conversations: Communication in an increasingly parasocial and pararealistic environment.* Unpublished doctoral dissertation, Indiana University, Bloomington.

*Hoffner, C. (1996). Children's wishful identification and parasocial interaction with favorite television characters. *Journal of Broadcasting & Electronic Media, 60,* 389–402.

Horton, D., & Wohl, R. R. (1956). Mass communication and parasocial interaction: Observations on intimacy at a distance. *Psychiatry, 19,* 215–219.

Kanazawa, S. (2002). Bowling with our imaginary friends. *Evolution and Human Behavior, 23,* 167–171.

*Levy, M. (1979). Watching TV news as para-social interaction. *Journal of Broadcasting, 23*(1), 69–80.

*Lewis, F. D. (1994). *Getting by: Race and parasocial interaction in a television situation comedy.* Unpublished doctoral dissertation, University of Kentucky, Lexington.

Miller, G., & Steinberg, G. (1970). *Between people: A new analysis of interpersonal communication.* Chicago: SRA Associates.

Nordlund, J. (1978). Media interaction. *Communication Research, 5,* 150–175.

*Perse, E. M. (1990). Media involvement and local news effects. *Journal of Broadcasting & Electronic Media, 34,* 17–36.

Perse, E. M., & Rubin, A. M. (1990). Chronic loneliness and television use. *Journal of Broadcasting & Electronic Media, 34,* 37–53.

Perse, E. M., & Rubin, R. B. (1989). Attribution in social and parasocial relationships. *Communication Research, 16,* 59–77.

Reeves, B, & Nass, C. (1996). *The media equation: How people treat computers, television, and new media like real people and places.* Cambridge, MA: Cambridge University Press.

*Rubin, A., & Perse, E. (1987). Audience activity and soap opera involvement: A uses and effects approach. *Human Communication Research, 14,* 246–268.

*Rubin, A., Perse, E., & Powell, R. (1985). Loneliness, parasocial interaction, and local television viewing. *Human Communication Research, 12,* 155–180.

*Rubin, R. & McHugh, M. (1987). Development of parasocial interaction relationships. *Journal of Broadcasting & Electronic Media, 31,* 279–292.

*Schiappa, E., Gregg, P., & Hewes, D. (2003). *Can one TV show make a difference? Will & Grace and college students' attitudes towards gay men.* Unpublished paper, University of Minnesota, Minneapolis.

*Step, M. (1998). *An emotional appraisal model of media involvement, uses, and effects.* Unpublished doctoral dissertation, Kent State University, Kent, OH.

*Tsao, J. (1991). *A multidimensional study of audience parasocial involvement.* Unpublished doctoral dissertation, Southern Illinois University, Carbondale.

*Tsao, J. (1996). Compensatory media use: An exploration of two paradigms. *Communication Studies, 47,* 89–109.

*Westmeyers, S. (1997). *The function of communication in interpersonal and parasocial friendships.* Unpublished doctoral dissertation, Kent State University, Kent, OH.

*Yanof, D. (1990). *The para-social and interpersonal relationships of heavy, light, and nonviewers of daytime television serials.* Unpublished doctoral dissertation, California School of Professional Psychology, Berkeley/Alameda.

19

Many Faces of
Media Effects

Tae-Seop Lim
University of Wisconsin-Milwaukee

Sang Yeon Kim
Michigan State University

The study of media effects has a relatively long history, tracking back to the end of the nineteenth century. The hypodermic needle theory or the bullet theory, the earliest conceptualization of the media effects, articulated the awe about the newly emergent mass media, claiming that the effects of mass media were immediate, direct, and immense. This perspective was largely influenced by the mass society theory, in which the view of the audience was extremely pessimistic (Lowery & DeFleur, 1988; McQuail, 1987). The theory posited that industrialization and urbanization resulted in destruction of communities and replacement of the public by the *mass,* the isolated, atomized, and mutually anonymous group of people whose behaviors were mainly motivated by self-interests (Arendt, 1951; Bell, 1960; Fromm, 1941; Kornhauser, 1959; C. W. Mills, 1956; Riesman, 1953). The audience of mass media, mostly ill informed, inevitably succumb to the power of the media.

The emergence of motion pictures and radio broadcasting, in the earlier part of the twentieth century, strengthened the belief that mass media overpowered the audience. This belief was supported more by real life events than by scientific research. On Halloween evening in 1938, the United States experienced mass hysteria that was prompted by a radio broadcast put on by Orson Welles through his *Mercury Theater of the Air*. People thought the nation was actually under attack by creatures from Mars. On September 21, 1943, Kate Smith made an appeal on CBS radio for the public to buy war bonds issued by the U.S. government and sold $39 million worth in 1 hour.

The myth of uniform and direct media effects began to shatter when Lazarsfeld and his colleagues published their study on people's voting behavior in the 1940 presidential election (Lazarsfeld, Berelson, & Gaudet, 1944). In their book entitled *The People's Choice,* they reported that media did not have direct effects on people's voting decisions and that opinion leaders exerted more influences on voters through interpersonal communication. They went further to propose a two-step flow model in which the influence comes from media to opinion leaders and then to the generic public.

After World War II, with the emergence of television, the research interests and perspectives of media researchers became diverse. Some researchers (Berelson, Lazarsfeld, & McPhee, 1954; Katz, 1959; Klapper, 1963) focused more on the functions of media and argued that media had limited effects or minimal effects. Some others who were interested in behavioral learning through media argued that media effects were still strong and direct (Bandura, 1977; Bandura, Ross, & Ross, 1961, 1963; Gerbner, 1969, 1970, 1973, 1977a, 1977b; McQuail, 1977); others who researched the process of adopting new ideas or innovations argued that media effects were often mediated by interpersonal communication as posited by the two-step flow model. The effects of mass media, then, are no longer considered uniform. They can be direct or indirect (or mediated), strong or weak, immediate or delayed, short-term or long-term, and universal or particular, depending upon the aspect of media that is studied.

The aspects of media that have been studied the most in relation to its effects include news, campaign, cultivation, and uses. News refers to everyday reports of the events or issues in the society. Most studies of news have been done in the domain of politics. A campaign is an organized set of communication activities intended to generate specific effects in a relatively large number of people within a prescribed period of time (Rogers & Storey, 1987). Political campaigns, the diffusion of innovation campaigns, and health communication campaigns are the ones that have been studied the most. Cultivation refers to the process in which media mold audience's perception of reality. Cultivation comprises simple mimicries, modeling on media personalities, and the adoption of the reality reflected in the messages of mass communication. Uses refer to the functions media serve to satisfy the needs of audience. People use media for a variety of reasons.

Different aspects of media research focus on different roles that media perform. For news, the media are considered a gatekeeper. Media professionals surveil the outside world and bring the information that they think is important to the audience. In campaigns, mass media professionals become persuaders or facilitators for a persuasive effort. They try to change or modify the behavior of the audience. For cultivation, media professionals perform the function of an educator. They tell the audience how to view the world and how to behave. In studying uses, media professionals are regarded as service providers. They satisfy certain needs of the audience.

NEWS, POLITICS, AND MEDIA EFFECTS

One of the oldest domains of media research is politics. Researchers have shown strong interests in the relationship between media and politics since the dawn of media research. In earlier stages, the effects of mass media on politics were believed to be profound. But, since the publication of *The People's Choice* (Lazarsfeld, Berelson & Gaudet, 1944), the minimal effects model began to gain ground.

The minimal effects model portrays the audience very strongly and claims that media alone do not cause people to change beliefs and behaviors. The best media can do is just to reinforce the preexisting attitudes of the audience. The minimal effects model obtained strong empirical support from selectivity research (Lazarsfeld, Berelson, & Gaudet, 1944; Lipset, Lazarsfeld, Barton, & Linz, 1954). Lipset et al. observed that people generally tend to expose themselves more readily and more often to communicative messages expressing views compatible with their own attitudes than to messages espousing incompatible views (McCroskey & Prichard, 1967). In other words, people selectively expose themselves to media. The selective-exposure hypothesis has been repeatedly confirmed by a number of empirical studies (e.g., Brodbeck, 1956; Cartwright, 1949; Ehrlich, Guttman, Schonbach, & Mills, 1951; McCroskey, & Prichard, 1967; J. Mills, Aronson, & Robinson, 1959; Rosen, 1961; Star, & Hughes, 1950).

In the 1960s and 1970s, Cohen (1963) and McCombs and Shaw (1972) challenged the minimal effects model. Cohen claimed that the news "may not be successful in telling people what to think, but it is stunningly successful in telling its readers what to think about." McCombs and Shaw found a remarkable similarity between the media's issue focus and the issue agenda of undecided voters, prompting them to propose the agenda-setting theory. The theory claims that the media are enforcing upon people what news is "important" and what news is "nonimportant," therefore, making decisions in a way for the public (Ott, 2001).

The recent discoveries of the priming and the framing effects of media have revealed that the media tell people not only what to think about but also how to think. Priming refers to the media calling attention to some particular issues or particular aspects of national life while ignoring others (Iyengar & Kinder, 1986). The dominant focus of media attention sets up the criteria for evaluating political leaders. Framing steers the audience to adopt the media's portrayal of the issue or event. Framing involves selection and salience (Entman, 1993). The media professional selects particular aspects of reality and makes them more noticeable, leading the audience to interpret, perceive, and evaluate in a particular way.

D'Alessio and Allen (chap. 26, this volume) propose four characteristics of news media that lead them to use priming and framing to influence audience: a journalistic entity, a commercial entity, property, and a political actor. As a journalistic entity, media are influenced by the journalists; as a commercial entity, media are influenced by the advertisers; as a property, media are influenced by the owner; and as a political actor, media are influenced by the company as a whole. Of the four parties related to the news business, the owner exerts the greatest influence on the ways in which news is presented.

D'Alessio and Allen also report the finding that a significant agreement exists between a newspaper's political preference, typically made by owners, and its coverage of a campaign. More specifically, at an aggregate level, news coverage is slightly biased toward Republican presidential campaigns.

Although it is evident that media influence people through agenda setting, priming, and framing, the impact seems to be neither strong nor consistent (Chaffee, 1992). Chaffee argued that because people are exposed to a variety of stories with conflicting frames and explanations, they get more confused than influenced.

In accordance with Chaffee, D'Alessio and Allen point out that a wide variety of political biases exist in the newspaper industry (pro-Republican vs. pro-Democratic) and especially that those preferences are all different in degree (extreme vs. mild). A comparison of renowned newspapers with those less regarded shows a diverse degree of political preferences. For example, newspapers that are national opinion leaders including the *New York Times,* the *Washington Post,* and the *Los Angeles Times* tend to be less conservative in their reporting compared with other newspapers.

In sum, the media seem to influence people in the political domain. The influence, however, is not very strong or lasting. Moreover, it is mediated by other factors such as the characteristics of the audience, the targeted component of attitudes, the type of media, and the nature of message.

THE EFFECTS OF MEDIATED CAMPAIGNS

Although news and campaigns are different in nature of occurrence, the ways they influence people are not substantially different. In the earlier stages of media research, mass mediated campaigns were thought to be as powerful as other messages of mass media. But, after the discoveries of opinion leaders and selective exposure (Lazarsfeld, Berelson, & Gaudet, 1944), the effects were believed to be indirect. The research of developmental communication campaigns or diffusion of innovation campaigns also showed the importance of opinion leaders and interpersonal communication in adopting new technologies (Rogers, 1983).

Recent research, however, has shown that mediated campaigns are not unsuccessful. Whether they are direct or indirect, mass media have significant political effects during election campaigns (McLeod et al., 1996). In particular, the media seem to have strong cognitive effects, being very successful in passing on political information and creating political images (Jeffres, 1997). Mediated health campaigns also exert significant influences on the audience. As with political campaigns, health campaigns are particularly "successful in affecting people's cognitions—the thoughts, images, beliefs, frameworks, information, and knowledge" (Jeffres, 1997).

However, the ultimate goal of campaigns is to change or reinforce people's external behavior. Turning the audience's knowledge into an actual behavior is not an easy task. Campaigners often assume that individuals are in total control of their behavior. However, people's behaviors are "complex phenomena with multiple motivations and uses" (Jeffres, 1997, p. 73). The adoption of a new behavior is often hindered by the motivations associated with older behaviors.

To be successful, campaigns need correct formulas, that is, the sophisticated strategies that are grounded in valid theories. Parcell and Bryant (chap. 21, this volume) recommend four "input theories" that can be incorporated into health campaigns: Hovland, Janis, and Kelley's (1953) instrumental learning perspective, Bandura's (1977) social learning theory, Ajzen and Fishbein's (1980) theory of reasoned action, and Petty and Cacioppo's (1981) cognitive response perspective. Parcell and Bryant also propose 11 tactics that can produce behavioral changes, based on the theories in marketing and social psychology.

In an attempt to assess the effectiveness of health campaigns, Parcell and Bryant meta-analyzed 12 studies on the relationship between the exposure to mediated health campaigns and behavioral changes for children and adolescents, with the issues ranging from anti-smoking, infant care, and safety, to AIDS. The results indicated that media health campaigns for our next generation have a small but significant effect. For a given campaign to succeed, Parcell and Bryant argue, cumulative and persistent efforts should be made over a long period of time with a clear purpose.

The effects of mediated health campaigns do not seem to be uniform for all types of behavioral change. For some campaigns that are aimed at modifying habitual behaviors the difficulties are great, because the changes involve abandonment of the motivations associated with the old habits. To conform to the message of these campaigns requires great determination on the part of the followers. In contrast, inducing a new behavior that does not contradict the lifestyles of the followers causes less distress, and, thus, has a higher probability of succeeding.

Snyder (chap 20, this volume) examines the effectiveness of health campaigns for three different types of behavioral change: adoption of a new behavior, cessation of an old one, and prevention of a new undesirable behavior. The results indicate that campaigns pursuing the adoption of new and desired behaviors yield the biggest average effect size, whereas those pursuing the other two types of behavioral change show meager effect sizes.

CULTIVATING EFFECTS OF MEDIA

In 1969, Gerbner proposed the strongest media effects model since the hypodermic needle theory, namely, cultivation theory. The theory claims that media mold society and shape how people view the world by presenting consistent and compelling versions of social reality. In other words, media play a great role in the process of socialization and enculturation of audience.

Cultivation refers to the process in which entire groups are affected by the contents of mass media. Gerbner uses *cultivation* as a theoretical term to represent his concerns in the effects on people's perception that are shaped over a long period of exposure to media messages (Potter, 1993). *Cultivation* occurs over time as media users repeatedly expose themselves to and incorporate into their beliefs the consistent messages transmitted through mass media channels.

Although media cultivation is a grand theory embracing a wide range of phenomena (Jeffres, 1997), Gerbner's research has focused on one particular medium, i.e., television, and its negative influence on people's perception of reality. Gerbner argued that television has surpassed religion as the key storyteller in our culture, and its stories (presented in dramas) are loaded with violence and crime. The repeated and intense exposure to these deviant definitions of reality leads the audience to perceive the reality as normal. The result is a social legitimization of the reality depicted in the mass media, which can influence people's behavior (Gerbner, 1973, 1977a, 1977b; Gerbner & Gross, 1976; Gerbner, Gross, Morgan, & Signorielli, 1980).

The discussion of media cultivation does not have to be limited to television or television dramas Other media such as newspapers and magazines and other television program genres such as news, talk shows, game shows, reality shows, and sitcoms also can cultivate audience. All they need to do is to present their audience with consistent and compelling versions of social reality for a prolonged period of time.

Although cultivation theory is focused on its negative side, media cultivation is not always negative. Sometimes media cultivation makes positive contributions to social integration and the advancement of human conditions. For example, American mass media altogether have created the reality that homosexuality is one of the legitimate sexual orientations.

Positive media cultivation is inevitably related to the educator's function of mass media. In the earlier stages of the AIDS outbreak, people thought that the disease was the problem of and the heavenly punishment to homosexuals. For the last decade or so, however, media professionals have educated themselves as well as the public to understand AIDS more accurately. A critical moment in redefining the reality related to AIDS was Earvin "Magic" Johnson's announcement in 1991 that he had tested positive for HIV (Casey et al., chap. 22, this volume).

Casey et al. meta-analyzed the influence of the disclosure that Magic was HIV positive. Results showed that the announcement affected a wide variety of public health issues ranging from an increased sense of vulnerability and more accurate knowledge about the disease to more people stating intentions to reduce risky behaviors, increased numbers of persons being tested for HIV infection, and more favorable attitudes toward those who were HIV positive. Broadly speaking, the announcement was effective in improving the public's level of knowledge, behavior, and perception.

Casey et al. argue that three key persuasive elements have worked for this cultivation: the salience of the issue, audience identification with Johnson, and the use of a variety of narratives generated by Johnson and those publicly discussing the disclosure. Issue saliency and identification alone, however, were not sufficient to lead to cognitive, affective, or behavioral change. Casey et al state the narrative form is what brings the "person" and his or her story to the audience. When an abundance of narratives, told by a variety of media characters, convey basically the same message over an extended period of time, media cultivation occurs. After Johnson's disclosure and subsequent prolonged media coverage, the combination of issue transformation and saliency, identification, and use of narrative created a potent and favorable environment within which individuals should be prompted to consider their personal risk, feelings of vulnerability and information adequacy, and general attitudes regarding HIV and those infected and affected.

MEDIA USES AND MEDIA EFFECTS

While other researchers were debating over how formidable media were, some researchers (Horton & Wohl, 1956; Katz, 1959, 1980; Katz & Lazarsfeld, 1966; Mendelsohn, 1963; Pearlin, 1959; Stephenson, 1967; Wright, 1960) showed more interest in the functions media served. Instead of questioning "What do media do to people?", these researchers asked "What do people do with media?" Katz (1959) named this approach *uses and gratifications* research. Katz, Blumler, and Gurevitch (1974) described the objectives of uses and gratifications as follows: to explain how people use media, to understand motives for media behavior, and to identify functions that follow from audience needs, motives, and behaviors. Katz, Gurevitch, and Hass (1973) proposed five categories of human needs that are gratified by the uses of media: cognitive, affective, personal integrative, social integrative, and tension release.

The uses and gratifications theory is grounded in five assumptions. "First, people are motivated and purposive in their communication behavior. Second, people take the initiative to select and use communication media and messages to satisfy felt needs or wants. Third, individuals are influenced by social and psychological factors when seeking to communicate and selecting among communication alternatives. Fourth, the media compete with other forms of communication for attention, selection, and use. Fifth, individuals are able to articulate their reasons for using media" (Rubin, 1989, p. 182).

As the media system becomes more complex owing to the emergence of new media such as Internet, uses and gratifications researchers show a great interest in the different uses of different media. They often question, "What kinds of people use what kinds of media more frequently?" and "Do different uses of media lead to differential social behavior?"

Hollander (chap. 23, this volume) meta-analyzed past research on the relationship between media uses and political involvement and reports that whereas exposure to newspapers is highly correlated with political involvement, the connection with television news shows is relatively loose. Miron and Bryant (chap. 24, this volume) report similar results. Although a significantly positive correlation exists between newspaper reading and voter turnout, the relationship between television viewing and voter turnout is uncertain. Past studies on television viewing yielded inconsistent results, with some reporting positive effects and others reporting negative effects.

These results in no way reflect differences in the degree of political influence between newspaper and television. What is reported here is that those who read newspapers more participate in politics more actively. As the uses and gratifications paradigm explains, those who watch television more and those who read newspapers more are different types of audiences with different kinds of needs. The observed difference in political participation between television viewers and newspaper readers should be attributed more to the difference in their needs than to the difference in the media effects.

SUMMARY

In this section, six chapters present the effects of mass media through meta-analysis. D'Alessio and Allen (chap. 26, this volume) analyze whether the political propensity of newspaper owners influences the coverage of the presidential campaign. They analyze 22 studies of the news contents of 209 presidential campaign coverages.

Hollander (chap. 23, this volume) and Miron and Bryant (chap. 24, this volume) examine the relationship between media exposure or media use and political involvement. Hollander meta-analyze 18 studies that passed the three stages of filtering. Miron and Bryant meta-analyze a very diverse (heterogeneous) data set composed of 40 studies.

Parcell and Bryant (chap. 21, this volume) examine the effect of mass communication health campaigns on children and adolescents. They meta-analyze 11 studies of various health-related issues including eight anti-smoking campaigns, three infant-care campaigns, two safety campaigns, and one campaign each for AIDS and family planning. These campaigns extended over a period of 26 years. Snyder (chap 20, this volume) estimates the effectiveness of media campaigns in bringing about health behavior change. They are particularly interested in the differences in media effects on three different types of behaviors: the adoption of a new behavior, the prevention of an undesirable behavior, and the cessation of an existing undesirable behavior. The chapter reports the results based on the meta-analysis of 48 health campaigns.

Casey et al. (chap. 22, this volume) attempt to assess the effects of a "celebrity disclosure" of a health-related condition or disease on people's knowledge and awareness of the condition or disease. Their study particularly focuses on the case of Magic Johnson's disclosure that he was HIV positive. Thirteen studies are meta-analyzed.

The results work to reaffirm and explain various issues in media effects. As with all summaries of research, the conclusions are important, but the unanswered questions and future possibilities offer fruitful ground for future research.

REFERENCES

Ajzen, I., & Fishbein, M. (1980). *Understanding attitudes and predicting social behavior.* Englewood Cliffs, NJ: Prentice-Hall.

Arendt, H. (1951). *The origins of totalitarianism.* New York: Harcourt Brace.

Bandura, A. (1977). *Social learning theory.* Englewood Cliffs, NJ: Prentice-Hall.

Bandura, A., Ross, D., & Ross, S. A. (1961). Transmission of aggression through imitation of aggressive models. *Journal of Abnormal and Social Psychology, 63,* 575–582.

Bandura, A., Ross, D., & Ross, S. A. (1963). Imitation of film-mediated aggressive models. *Journal of Abnormal and Social Psychology, 66,* 3–11.

Bell, D. (1960). *The End of Ideology.* New York: Free Press.

Berelson, B. R., Lazarsfeld, P. F., & McPhee, W. N. (1954). *Voting.* Chicago: University of Chicago Press.

Brodbeck, M. (1956). The role of small groups in mediating the effects of propaganda. *Journal of Abnormal and Social Psychology, 52,* 166–170.

Cartwright, D. (1949). Some principles of mass persuasion: Selected findings of research on the sale of United States war bonds. *Human Relations, 2,* 253–267.

Chaffee, S. H. (1992). Review of Shanto Iyengar: Is anyone responsible? How television frames political issues. *Journal of Broadcasting & Electronic Media, 36,* 239–241.

Cohen, B. (1963). *The press and foreign policy.* Princeton, NJ: Princeton University Press.

Ehrlich, D., Guttman, I., Schonbach, P., & Mills, J. (1951). Postdecision exposure to relevant information. *Journal of Abnormal and Social Psychology, 54,* 98–102.

Entman, R. (1993). Framing: Toward clarification of a fractured paradigm. *Journal of Communication* 43(3),51–58.

Fromm, E. (1941). *Escape from freedom.* New York: Farrar & Rinehart.

Gerbner, G. (1969). Toward 'cultural indicators': The analysis of mass mediated message systems. *AV Communication Review, 17*(2), 137–148.

Gerbner, G. (1970). Cultural indicators: The case of violence in television drama. *The Annals of the American Academy of Political and Social Science, 388,* 69–81.

Gerbner, G. (1973). Cultural indicators: The third voice. In G. Gerbner, L. Gross, & W. H. Melody (Eds.), *Communications technology and social policy* (pp. 555–573). New York: Wiley.

Gerbner, G. (1977a). The real threat of television violence. In J. Fireman (Ed.), *TV book: The ultimate television book* (pp. 358–359). New York: Workman Publishing Company.

Gerbner, G. (1977b). Television: The new state religion? *Et Cetera, 34*(2), 145–150.

Gerbner, G., & Gross, L. (1976). Living with television: The violence profile. *Journal of Communication, 26*(2), 173–199.

Gerbner, G., Gross, L., Morgan, M., & Signorielli, N. (1980). The "mainstreaming" of America: Violence profile no. 11. *Journal of Communication, 30*(3), 10–29.

Horton, D., & Wohl, R. R. (1956). Mass communication and para-social interaction: Observations on intimacy at a distance? *Psychiatry, 19,* 215–229.

Hovland, C., Janis, I., & Kelley, H. (1953). *Communication and persuasion.* New Haven, CT: Yale University Press.

Iyengar, S., & Kinder, D. R. (1986). More than meets the eye: TV news, priming, and public evaluations of the president. In G. Comstock (Ed.), *Public communication and behavior* (Vol. 1, pp. 135–171). Orlando, FL: Academic Press.

Jeffres, L. W. (1997). *Mass media effects* (2nd ed.). Prospect Heights, IL: Waveland Press.

Katz, E. (1959). Mass communication research and the study of daily serial listeners. An editorial note on a possible future for this journal. *Studies in Public Communication, 2,* 1–6.

Katz, E. (1980). On conceptualizing media effects. *Studies in Communication, 1,* 119–141.

Katz, E., Blumler, J. G., & Gurevitch, M. (1974). Utilization of mass communication by the individual. In J. G. Blumler & E. Katz (Eds.), *The uses of mass communications: Current perspectives on gratification research* (pp. 19–32). Beverly Hills, CA: Sage.

Katz, E., Gurevitch, M., & Hass, H. (1973). On the use of mass media for important things. *American Sociological Review, 38,* 164–181.

Klapper, J. T. (1963). Mass communication research: An old road resurveyed. *Public Opinion Quarterly, 27,* 515–527.

Kornhauser, W. (1959). *The politics of mass society.* New York: Free Press.

Lazarsfeld, P. F., Berelson, B., & Gaudet, H. (1944). *The people's choice: How the voter makes up his mind in a presidential campaign.* New York: Columbia University Press.

Lipset, S. M., Lazarsfeld, P. F., Barton, A. H., & Linz, J. (1954). The psychology of voting: An analysis of political behavior. In G. Lindzey (Ed.), *Handbook of social psychology* (Vol. 2). Cambridge, MA: Addison-Wesley.

Lowery, S., & DeFleur, M. L. (1988). *Milestones in mass communication.* New York: Longman, 1988.

McCombs, M. E., & Shaw, D. L. (1972). The agenda-setting function of mass media. *Public Opinion Quarterly, 36,* 176–187.

McCroskey, J. C., & Prichard, S. V. O. (1967). Selective-exposure and Lyndon B. Johnson's 1966 "State of the Union" address. *Journal of Broadcasting, 11,* 331–337.

McLeod, D. M., Guo, Z., Daily, K., Steele, C. A., Huang, H., Horowitz, E., et al. (1996). The impact of traditional and nontraditional media forms in the 1992 presidential election. *Journalism and Mass Communication Quarterly, 73,* 401–416.

McQuail, D. (1987). *Mass communication theory: An introduction* (2nd ed.). London: Sage.

Mendelsohn, H. (1963). Socio-psychological perspectives on the mass media and public anxiety. *Journalism Quarterly, 40,* 511–516.

Mills, C. W. (1956) *The power elite.* New York: Oxford University Press.

Mills, J., Aronson, E., & Robinson, H. (1959). Selectivity in exposure to information. *Journal of Abnormal and Social Psychology, 58,* 250–253.

Ott, B. (2001). Theory of agenda-setting. Retrieved March 2, 2004, from Colorado State University, Resource Center for Communication Studies Web Site: http://www.colostate.edu/Depts/Speech/rccs/rccs.html

Pearlin, L. I. (1959). Social and personal stress and escape television viewing. *Public Opinion Quarterly, 23,* 255–259.

Petty, R., & Cacioppo, J. (1981). *Attitudes and persuasion: Classic and contemporary approaches.* Dubuque, IA: Brown.

Potter, W. J. (1993). Cultivation theory and research: A conceptual critique. *Human communication research, 19,* 564–601.

Riesman, D. (1953). *The lonely crowd.* Garden City, NY: Doubleday.

Rogers, E. M. (1983). *Diffusion of innovations* (3rd ed.). New York: Free Press.

Rogers, E. M. & Storey, D. (1987). Communication campaigns. In C. Berger & S. Chaffee (Eds.), *Handbook of communication science* (pp. 817–846). Newbury Park, CA: Sage.

Rosen, S. (1961). Postdecision affinity for incompatible information. *Journal of Abnormal and Social Psychology, 63,* 188–190.

Rubin, A. M. (1989). Uses and gratifications of video cassette recorders. In J. L. Salvaggio & J. Bryant (Eds.), *Media use in the information age* (pp. 181–195). Hillsdale, NJ: Lawrence Erlbaum Associates.

Star, S., & Hughes, H. (1950). Report on an education campaign: The Cincinnati plan for the United Nations. *American Journal of Sociology, 55,* 389–400.

Stephenson, W. (1967). *The play theory of mass communication.* Chicago: University of Chicago Press.

Wright, C. R. (1960). Functional analysis and mass communication. *Public Opinion Quarterly, 24,* 605–620.

20

Meta-Analyses of Mediated Health Campaigns

Leslie B. Snyder
University of Connecticut

This is your brain. This is your brain on drugs.
　　—Ad Council TV Public Service Announcement, known as the frying pan ad

Be SunSmart—Slip on a shirt. Slop on sunscreen. Slap on a hat.
　　—The Cancer Council, Australia, Slip, Slop, Slap Campaign, since 1981

For people who believe in the power of the mass media, a mediated communication campaign is a logical tool for spreading a health message. A wide range of health issues have been addressed in mediated campaigns, including substance abuse prevention, mammography screening, dental care, skin cancer prevention, and bicycle helmet use. Campaigns are often created to battle the actual causes of death—the lifestyle and behaviors that contribute to the leading diseases, such as heart disease and cancer. Many of the most common actual causes of death—tobacco use, poor diet, physical inactivity, alcohol consumption, microbial agents, toxic agents, and motor vehicles (National Center for Chronic Disease Prevention and Health Promotion, 2004)—can be battled through health campaigns.

Given the societal need to communicate with large numbers of people about health recommendations, it is important to understand the efficacy of communication campaigns. The present chapter reviews the synthesized evidence on mediated health campaign effects.

DEFINITION

Communication campaigns are organized communication activity, directed at a particular audience for a particular period of time, to achieve a particular goal. The communication activity may include traditional mass media, new media such as video games, small media such as brochures, interpersonal communication such as talking with a health professional or volunteer, and communication within organizations. The concept of addressing the campaign to a target audience is very important, as is specifying detailed goals and objectives. Another campaign may target a different audience or alter the goals. The language has its roots in war—a communication campaign is analogous to a military campaign, waged to achieve a specific objective but not necessarily expected to win the whole war.

A BRIEF HISTORY

In the United States, communication campaigns have existed since Cotton Mather sought to inoculate the citizens of Boston against smallpox at the beginning of an epidemic in 1721; he used interpersonal communication and pamphlets (Paisley, 1981). Campaigns topics in the 1800s and early 1900s included the abolition of slavery, alcohol control, and child labor. Sanitation and antituberculosis campaigns by government agencies and nonprofit health organizations used mass media, promotions, pamphlets, and home visits. For example, the first Easter Seals stamps were sold to support services for the disabled. The Ad Council, a voluntary organization of professional advertising companies begun in 1942 to support the U.S. government in World War II with slogans like "A slip of the lip will sink a ship," expanded to other projects, such as creating Smokey Bear to help us prevent forest fires in 1944 and urging us to join the American Red Cross beginning in 1945. The U.S. government sponsored campaigns in the 1950s promoting dental hygiene domestically and modern agricultural practices in poorer nations. Campaigns began promoting family planning overseas in the 1960s with mixed results. The well-documented success of a heart disease prevention campaign in the 1970s (Fortmann, Williams, Hulley, Haskell, & Farquhar, 1981) inspired more campaigns aimed at individual lifestyle behaviors. Nongovernmental organizations such as the March of Dimes and the American Cancer Society increased their campaign activities, and national AIDS/HIV campaigns began in 1987. State governments such as California and Massachusetts began antitobacco campaigns in 1990 and 1993, respectively, following ballot initiatives that linked increased tobacco taxes to funding for antismoking campaigns and other control measures.

Campaigns were so accepted as having positive effects that Congress directly mandated the creation of two large campaigns—the $1 billion national youth antidrug media campaign run by the Office of National Drug Control Policy (ONDCP), and the Youth Physical Activity Campaign (now known as the Verb Campaign) run by the Centers for Disease Control. Court settlements mandated the national antitobacco "Truth" campaign run by the Legacy Foundation, a group created with the tobacco industry money, and an SUV safety campaign with money from the Ford Corporation.

Approaches to campaigns have become more sophisticated over time. Persuasion, information processing, and behavior change theories inform campaign message design. Campaign goals, target populations, and channel choices are based on formative research. Messages are pretested with members of the target group. Evaluation is strongly urged, in order to assess which aspects of the campaign work. Learning from techniques practiced in the marketing of commercial goods, campaign organizers now include promotions and pricing strategies in their arsenal of tools. Community organizing and public relations techniques may also be incorporated into campaigns.

Indeed, there has been some debate about the differences between communication campaigns, social marketing, and health education approaches (e.g., Maibach, 2002). Each approach has developed from a different academic discipline, and a good campaign practitioner today draws from all traditions.

THE NEED FOR META-ANALYSES

There seems to be a lay perception that media campaigns must work because advertising is powerful; otherwise commercial companies would not continue to use it to promote their goods. Similarly, successful politicians use the media in their campaigns (as do most unsuccessful candidates) and therefore may generalize from their own success to campaigns on other topics.

Despite a number of well-publicized successes, the evidence concerning the success of communication campaigns has been mixed. Researchers have debated their efficacy while pointing to successful case studies (e.g., Douglas, Westley, and Chaffee, 1970; Hornik, 2002; Hyman & Shetsley, 1947). It is also possible that campaigns said to be unsuccessful may have actually been successful, in that they may have caused effects not detectable by evaluations with too little "power" (Flay and Cook, 1989).

Syntheses of the research evidence on communication campaigns are useful for a number of reasons. First, media campaigns evaluations provide evidence of media effects in field settings, and can inform our understanding of media effects in general. Second, while there is currently a belief by legislative bodies, courts, and some health officials that campaigns can be successful, a research synthesis may better inform public policies. Third, campaign practitioners can use the results of meta-analyses to set realistic goals for their campaigns. Fourth, campaign funding agencies and evaluators can use information about average effects to compare to the effectiveness of a particular campaign. Fifth, evaluators can use information about average effects when designing evaluations.

The present chapter reviews what we have learned from research syntheses of health campaign evaluations. We focus on the following questions:

What are the average effects of mediated campaigns on health topics?
What are the impacts on intermediate outcomes?
When are the effects larger or smaller?
How do mediated campaigns compare with other types of interventions?

META-ANALYSIS DATA SETS

To answer the questions, we draw on a number of studies. Each is briefly described below. A few additional meta-analyses are mentioned only once in the analysis and are detailed within the text. When it was necessary to compute effect sizes or convert them to the average correlation ($\bar{r}$), the computer program *DSTAT* was used (Johnson, 1995).

U.S. Mediated Health Campaigns

A meta-analysis was made of 48 health campaigns that used at least one form of mass media (Snyder, 2001; Snyder & Hamilton, 2002; Snyder, Hamilton, Mitchell, Kiwanuka-Tondo, Fleming-Milici, & Proctor, 2004). The total N was 168,362. The campaign evaluations dated from 1974 to 1997. The other criteria for inclusion were publication in a book or academic journal, adequate statistics to compute the effect of the campaign on behavior, and being aimed at a "mass" audience, excluding school-based or workplace-based interventions. The outcome measure was short-term behavior change, measured at the end of or immediately after the campaign.

Family Planning Campaigns in Developing Countries

Snyder, Badiane, Kalnova, & Diop-Sidibé (2003) synthesized research from 58 campaigns in developing countries that promoted some form of family planning or reproductive health. The total N was 129,424 for 29 studies measuring behavior change, 92,729 for 21 studies measuring knowledge, and 24,965 for 10 studies measuring attitude toward family planning. The criteria for inclusion were the ability of the research team to obtain a copy of an evaluation report or published article about the campaign, the presence of outcome data for the intervention group, a design that allowed the effect of the intervention on the outcomes to be assessed, inclusion of at least one form of mass communication, and outreach that was not exclusively school-, clinic-, or workplace-based.

Youth Substance Abuse Prevention

A meta-analysis of mediated youth substance abuse prevention interventions was conducted by Derzon and Lipsey (2002). They coded information on a total of 72 campaigns, 48 reporting information on substance use, 39 on attitudes, and 24 on knowledge. The criteria for inclusion were media campaigns designed to address youth substance use (even if they targeted parents or other adults); aimed at general or specific audiences (including school-based programs); reporting pre- to postintervention change for knowledge, attitudes, or behaviors; reported in English; and carried out in a Western country. The effect size was reported in terms of a d-statistic, which was converted for the present analysis to $\bar{r}$. (For cases in which $-.41 < d < .41$, the formula $\bar{r} = .5d$ provides a very close approximation (Hunter and Schmidt, 1990).)

Ugandan AIDS Campaigns

Original data were collected on 100 HIV/AIDS campaigns in Uganda (Kiwanuka-Tondo & Snyder, 2002). The criteria for inclusion were appearance on the Uganda AIDS Commission's list of organizations doing AIDS work and having run at least one communication campaign or educational intervention. Sixty-seven percent of the organizations on the list participated in the study. The study reported information about organizational characteristics and attributes of the most recent AIDS intervention conducted by the organization, but very few campaigns assessed behavior change. The presence of a media component was not a requirement for inclusion in the analysis, and although campaigns used nine mediated channels on average, some campaigns relied only on interpersonal outreach.

RESULTS

Average Effects of Campaigns on Behavior

The average effect of mediated health communication campaigns in the United States on behavior was $\bar{r} = .09$, with a 95% confidence interval of .07 to .10 (Snyder et al., 2004). However, the campaigns were heterogeneous, meaning that there were substantial differences between campaigns (Snyder et al., 2004). Therefore, it was critical to look for patterns that could help explain some of the differences in campaign effectiveness.

Topic Differences

Campaigns for some health topics have been more effective than campaigns for other topics. Figure 20.1 shows the average campaign effect on behavior across a range of health domains. Seatbelt campaigns were the most effective, and youth substance abuse prevention campaigns were the least effective.

A meta-analysis of 17 mostly European media campaigns for HIV tests, myocardial infarction admissions, immunizations, and cancer screenings also found a positive effect of campaigns (Grilli, Freemantle, Minozzi, Domenighetti, & Finer, 1999). Unfortunately, it was not possible to directly compare the effect size in that study with the other meta-analyses (Snyder, 2000a). In developing countries, vaccination, breastfeeding, and vitamin A distribution appeared to have greater success than campaigns for some other topics, according to data reported in a review of 10 child survival campaigns sponsored by the Agency for International Development (Hornik, Contreras-Budge, McDivitt, McDowell, Yoder, Zimicki, & Rasmuson, 1992). Immunization campaigns, found to be relatively successful in both a meta-analysis by Grilli et al. (1999) and a review by Hornik et al. (1992) may have an advantage because of the relative simplicity, specificity, and time urgency of the message and the fact that the behavior (seeking a particular immunization) occurs only a handful of times at most.

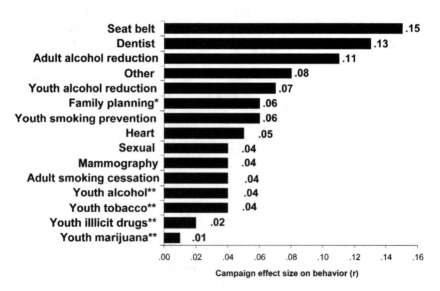

Note: Based on Snyder et al. (2004); Snyder, Diop-Sidibe, & Badiane (2003c) (*); and Derzon & Lipsey (2002) (**).

Figure 20.1.   Average campaign effect on behavior.

Health topics can also be grouped by whether the goal of the campaign is to promote a new behavior or substitute a new behavior for an old one, discourage an old behavior, or prevent a new behavior that is undesirable from the standpoint of public health. The grouping can be helpful when one is attempting to estimate potential campaign effects for new topics. Snyder et al. (2004) found that promotion or substitution of a new behavior is easier to achieve than cessation or prevention ($\bar{r} = .12$, vs. $\bar{r} = .05$ and $\bar{r} = .06$, respectively).

Effects Among Diverse Populations

Within the public health community, there is renewed interest in making sure that interventions reach diverse audiences. After reviewing the literature to date, a committee of the National Academy of Sciences stated, "There is an urgent need for evidence about differential effectiveness of campaigns in the context of particular diversity strategies" (Institute of Medicine, 2002, p. 122). Reanalysis of the U.S. mediated health campaign data suggested that campaigns targeting particular groups—such as youth, women, gays, poorer people, and ethnic minorities—have been at least as effective in changing behavior as those that have been more broadly targeted, although the conclusions for any one group are tentative, given the small number of relevant campaigns in the data set (Snyder, 2000b). Youth substance abuse campaigns have had greater success changing behaviors for girls than for boys (Derzon & Lipsey, 2002), perhaps reflecting a cultural tendency for boys in the United States to engage in more socially unacceptable behaviors. In contrast, family planning campaigns that specifically target men are, on average, more successful than campaigns targeting either women or both genders (Snyder et al., 2003), perhaps because of the special care taken when messages for men are deliberately included.

Studies of AIDS intervention organizations have found that, in the United States, community-based organizations targeted more precisely than educational and governmental organizations (Dearing et al., 1996). The most common criteria for targeting were age, ethnicity, sexual orientation, and gender, followed by behavior (e.g. drug use, prostitution), primary language, homelessness, education, and socioeconomic status (Dearing et al., 1996). In Ugandan AIDS interventions, specifying narrow targets led to better-quality message executions (Kiwanuka-Tondo & Snyder, 2002).

Campaign Effects of Intermediate Outcomes

Knowledge

Campaign effects on knowledge have been reported for only a few types of campaigns. The data, summarized in Figure 20.2, show that knowledge increased

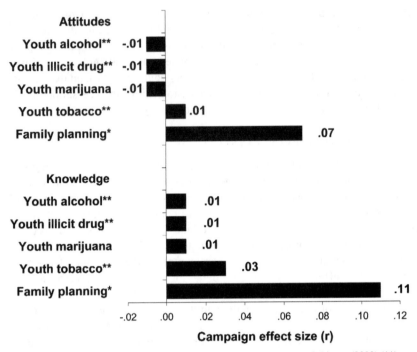

Note: Based on Snyder, Diop-Sidibe, & Badiane (2003c) (*) and Derzon & Lipsey (2002) (**).

Figure 20.2.   Average campaign effects on knowledge and attitudes.

on average for family planning campaigns and increased slightly for tobacco campaigns. Campaigns did not have an effect on average on knowledge of alcohol, marijuana, and other illicit drugs. (The effect sizes from Derzon and Lipsey (2002) were computed from data on their page 247, and they compare gains in campaigns that addressed the knowledge issue to control communities.)

Family planning campaigns had a greater effect on knowledge than on behavior (Snyder et al., 2003), but the same was not true of youth substance abuse campaigns. Both family planning and youth substance abuse prevention campaigns seem to increase knowledge more effectively among females than among males.

Importantly, at-risk youth did not learn as much from substance abuse campaigns as did other youth, which suggests that campaigns targeting at-risk youth may want to set more modest goals (Derzon & Lipsey, 2002). (Behavior change was also in the direction of lower effects for at-risk youth, although the difference was small (Derzon & Lipsey, 2002).) On the other hand, it is possible for campaigns designed to appeal specifically to high-risk and high-sensation-seeking youth to be successful (Palmgreen, Donohew, Lorch, Hoyle, & Stephenson, 2002).

Attitudes

As with knowledge, there are synthesized results on attitude change for only a few campaign topics (Fig. 20.2). There was an average improvement in approval of family planning, but not youth substance abuse prevention campaigns. That there was some behavior but no attitude change for youth substance abuse campaigns suggests that attitude change does not need to happen during the course of a campaign to enable behavior change.

Intervention Characteristics Related to Campaign Effects

Unfortunately, campaign write-ups in journals rarely contain detailed information about the intervention, making it difficult to compare the effectiveness of different strategies across campaigns. Meta-analyses have been able to glean some insights about campaign characteristics from the information that is reported (see Fig. 20.3).

Enforcement Component

Campaigns that contain messages about legal enforcement of the target behavior are much more successful than campaigns without an enforcement angle (Snyder & Hamilton, 2002). Enforcement messages have been used with campaigns about seatbelt use and alcohol sales to minors. For example, the seatbelt campaigns broadcast information about the increasing likelihood of police checkpoints. However, many topics do not lend themselves to coupling of a communication campaign with legal or regulatory enforcement.

New Information

Sharing information that is new to the target audience is associated with increased effectiveness (Snyder & Hamilton, 2002). The alternative—repackaging information that people already have had many opportunities to learn—does not seem to provide as much of an incentive for behavior change. New information may include the existence of new services or revised behavioral recommendations based on new research.

Services

Campaigns can successfully promote the use of health services (Snyder & Hamilton, 2002). Visiting a doctor or clinic is necessary for screening campaigns (such as AIDS/HIV, mammography, cervical cancer, and diabetes) and campaigns promoting ongoing health care (such as dental care, blood pressure regulation, and some family planning methods).

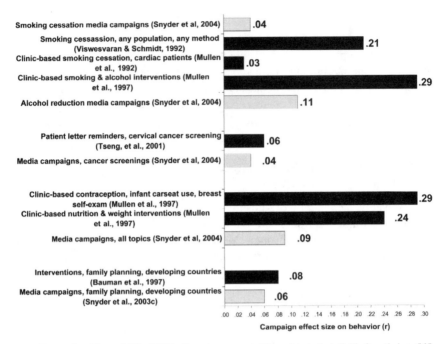

Note: Tseng, Cox, Plane, & Hla (2001) effect size computed from data in their Table 2 on their p. 565. Viswesvaran & Schmidt (1992) reported an average quit rate of 18.6% across 633 studies, which was here converted to $\bar{r}$.

Figure 20.3.   Comparison of the effectiveness of mediated campaigns, clinic-based interventions, and service reminder letters, for adult populations.

Family Communication

Campaigns may be able to promote increased communication with family members on campaign topics. There is evidence from campaigns on two types of health topics. Among family planning campaigns in developing countries, media campaigns were able to increase communication with spouse ($\bar{r} = .05$) and friends ($\bar{r} = .08$) about family planning and reproductive health, despite the fact that not all campaigns had messages about interpersonal communication (Snyder et al., 2003). Youth substance abuse prevention campaigns resulted in greater behavior change on average than in control communities when they had messages for parents to get them to talk to their children about substance abuse or when they had messages about what to say to others about use, and these campaigns were more successful than other types of substance abuse campaigns (Derzon & Lipsey, 2002). The campaigns aimed at parents also resulted in more knowledge change than in control communities (Derzon & Lipsey, 2002). It should be noted, however, that the apparent ability of substance abuse campaigns to promote parent-child communication may depend on who is doing the reporting; the current ONDCP antidrug campaign found parents reporting an increase in conversations with their children about drugs during the campaign, while their children reported a decrease in conversations with their parents (Hornik et al., 2002).

Other Messages

Other areas of message content that resulted in greater substance abuse behavior prevention on average in intervention communities than in control communities were messages about alternatives to substance use, positive attitudes to non-use, and consequences of use (Derzon & Lipsey, 2002). Campaigns that featured messages about resistance skills resulted in greater substance use than in control communities, and it appeared that campaigns about normative use had little effect compared with control communities (Derzon & Lipsey, 2002).

Campaign Reach and Communication Channels

Campaigns that reach a higher proportion of the target audience have a greater rate of success than campaigns reaching a smaller proportion (Snyder & Hamilton, 2002). Across mediated campaigns in the United States, on average only 40% of the target audience in intervention sites could recall exposure to the campaign (Snyder & Hamilton, 2002). The figure is higher in family planning campaigns in developing countries, at 56% (Snyder et al., 2003). Still, both figures are low, when we consider that the typical aim in most campaigns is to reach nearly everyone in the target audience.

Inappropriate or limited channel choice, inadequate number of message repetitions or executions, message clutter, and poor timing of messages may all contribute to the failure of a campaign to reach many people in the target audience. People may also fail to remember exposure if the campaign's messages did not command sufficient attention or were not fully encoded in memory. Campaigns resulted in greater youth substance abuse prevention if they had greater repetition of messages and were widely broadcast (Derzon & Lipsey, 2002). Campaigns utilizing a greater number of media channels resulted in greater exposure to family planning campaigns in developing countries (Snyder et al., 2003). The number of audio and video media also mattered to the effectiveness of clinic-based interventions (Mullen, Simons-Morton, Ramirez, Frankowski, Green, & Mains, 1997).

Budgetary limits may account for some compromises made in the planning of channels and messages. There are several ongoing youth campaigns reporting much higher levels of exposure, which are probably related to their very high media budgets. The $1 billion ONDCP national antidrug media campaign reached 80% of targeted youth and 73% of their parents by strategically purchasing air time formulated to achieve an average of 2.5 ad exposures per week for youth and 2.1 exposures per week for parents over 46 months (Hornik et al., 2002).

Seventy-five percent of youth reported exposure to the first year of the truth campaign, which spent $100 million in 2002 (Farrelly, Healton, Davis, Messeri, Hersey, & Haviland, 2002). In addition, campaign spending in Ugandan AIDS campaigns was positively related to the number of channels used and to the quality of the media executions (Kiwanuka-Tondo & Snyder, 2002).

Many campaigns combine the use of interpersonal and mediated channels. Youth substance abuse prevention campaigns in which the media campaign was supplemented by other types of outreach (such as group discussions or interpersonal counseling) had a greater effect of behavior compared with control communities and those that relied only on media campaigns (Derzon & Lipsey, 2002). Campaigns combining media and interpersonal communication are also more effective than clinic-based interventions on some topics. Clinic-based interventions on smoking, alcohol, nutrition, and weight were more successful when they used a greater number of audio or visual media than interventions using fewer channels or no media (Mullen et al., 1997). Note, too, that involving outreach workers in campaign design resulted in higher-quality messages in Ugandan AIDS campaigns (Kiwanuka-Tondo & Snyder, 2002).

Campaigns that utilized television, radio, and video were better than print channels at changing youth substance abuse behaviors, although video appeared to be the best media channel for attitude and knowledge change (Derzon & Lipsey, 2002).

Media Campaigns Compared with Clinic- and School-Based Interventions

In order to best allocate limited public health resources, it is important to know whether mediated campaigns are more or less effective and efficient than other types of interventions. Figure 20.3 compares the results of meta-analyses on the average effect of media campaigns and clinic-based interventions across a number of health domains aimed at adults. Adult smoking cessation, nutrition improvement, weight reduction, and other topics (contraception promotion, infant car seat use, breast self-exam, and stress reduction) have been promoted more effectively in clinical settings than in mediated campaigns. Mailed reminders for cervical cancer screenings are slightly more effective than media campaigns.

In developing countries, family planning interventions are only slightly more effective than mediated campaigns, and the apparent difference may be due to evaluation design. The 16 programs in the Bauman (1997) meta-analysis were evaluated with the use of true experimental designs and promoted by mailings, home visits, outreach workers, improved counseling, and group education.

Although there is not enough available data at present to meta-analyze the cost-effectiveness and efficiency of media campaigns, some tentative conclusions can be drawn. Cervical cancer screening letters are probably more cost-efficient than media campaigns, given the relatively low costs of mailings. However, it is likely that the ability of the media to reach larger numbers of people with only an incremental increase in cost is an important advantage over the costs associated with face-to-face clinic-based interventions on many health topics (Hornik, 1989). Without cost data, however, it is impossible to know the conditions under which the cost per person affected is lower for media campaigns.

The meta-analytic data for youth present a slightly different picture. Figure 20.4 shows the average effect of media campaigns and in-school interventions on substance use. In-school programs vary quite widely in choice of the communication channels (teachers or peers in classes, small groups, or one-to-one communication and use of supportive media), number of sessions, and content. The impacts on youth by media campaigns and interventions in schools are remarkably similar, with the mean effect of the intervention on behavior ranging between .02 and .07. It also appears that illicit drug use is slightly harder to affect than alcohol use, perhaps because alcohol use is more widespread.

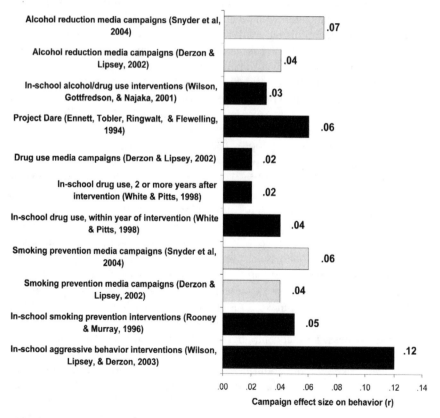

Figure 20.4. Comparison of media campaigns and in-school interventions for youth smoking, alcohol, drug abuse, and aggressive behavior prevention.

In-school interventions designed to decrease youth aggressive behaviors had a greater impact than youth substance use interventions. It may be that the perceived positive effects of substance use on the part of some youth make it a more difficult topic to deal with than aggression.

DISCUSSION

The meta-analytic record to date shows that media campaigns can have a positive impact on a wide variety of health issues. Campaigns are more successful when they reach a greater proportion of the target audience, promote the adoption of a new behavior, include an enforcement component, and share new information. Substance use campaigns in particular are more successful when they contain messages about alternatives to substance use, positive non-use attitudes, consequences of use, and resistance skills. Campaigns can promote the use of services and communication with others. Mediated campaigns are as effective as school-based interventions on youth substance use. Clinic-based interventions are more effective than media campaigns on most topics, but more studies are needed to know whether media campaigns are more cost-efficient.

Initial findings from recent national youth campaigns appear to be largely consistent with prior meta-analytic findings. During the first two years of the truth anti-smoking campaign, tobacco use declined nationally for middle and high school students by two percentage points more than the predicted trend without the campaign (Farrelly, et al., 2005). The national youth physical activity campaign found an increase in behavior in the first year (Huhman, Potter, Wong, Banspach, Duke, & Heitzler, 2005). The large ONDCP antidrug campaign findings to date are mixed, with some positive effects on parents but weak positive, null, or negative effects on youth behavior (Hornik et al., 2003).

As the campaign record grows, so does the opportunity to examine additional aspects of campaign effectiveness. There is an ever-changing media landscape, and channel-message combinations that have worked in past campaigns will need to be reevaluated. The fragmentation of the audience in the present media environment can be beneficial for a campaign if the target audience is attracted to a specific channel, or it can make it more difficult to reach the audience if it has few channels in common. There is even greater potential now for the audience to be exposed to messages that contradict a campaign via less regulated media, such as the internet, cable, and satellite television.

We need to know more about the effectiveness of different campaign techniques. What is the added value of supplementing a media campaign with community and interpersonal components, such as community coalitions, youth activist groups (like Florida's antitobacco truth campaign), events, group discussions, peer counseling, snowball counseling, one-to-one communication with an expert? What are the effects of advocacy campaigns and empowerment strategies (Kar, Pascual, & Chickering, 1999; Wallack, Dorfman, Jernigan, & Themba, 1993)?

As campaigns and other types of interventions begin to tackle new health problems—including drug treatment adherence, West Nile Virus prevention, SARS, and youth obesity—a better understanding may emerge as to which types of behaviors lend themselves to media campaigns versus other types of interventions.

Campaign designers could also benefit from more meta-analyses on issues related to campaign design. Campaigns often draw on theory to inform choices about message content—such as industry attack ads (e.g., tobacco campaigns), social norms, negative and positive consequences, resistance skills, and communication skills—but many theories have not been adequately tested in evaluated campaigns. We need to know more about matching message themes and emotional appeals with production features to maximize the effect on particular audiences (Farrelly et al., 2003). For example, a recent campaign showed that fast-paced and intense ads appeal can successfully alter the behavior of youth at risk of drug use (Palmgreen et al., 2002). The effects of intermediate outcomes for a campaign can also be used to assess the adequacy of a theory model. As detailed above, we only have information about knowledge and attitude effects for a few types of campaigns, despite the widespread use of theories that build on a stepped model of effects (e.g., McGuire, 1981; Rogers, 1995). We can also use more research on diversity strategies and the effects of branding in communication campaigns.

Attention has been focused recently on the possibility that the ONDCP antidrug campaign has boomeranged, making drug use appear to be more normative than it was earlier in the campaign (Hornik et al., 2003). Although additional waves of data need to be analyzed before that conclusion is warranted, the controversy highlights the special responsibility of prosocial campaigns to "do no harm." We need more research into the conditions under which campaigns boomerang and how to avoid them.

We still have gaps in our understanding of the decay of media campaign effects over time. What is the rate of decay for different types of behaviors, and how is it affected by campaign design factors? What is a reasonable amount of time to wait between campaigns on a given topic, before too much progress is lost?

Perhaps most importantly, we recommend that campaign evaluations move toward more uniform reporting of campaign effects. Across meta-analytic studies, authors detail the small percentage of studies that meet the methodological design and full reporting requirements for inclusion in a meta-analysis. Evaluations should have some form of control, at a minimum a control group or baseline measurements, and preferably both. The calculation of effect sizes depends on the extent of statistical information reported. If a campaign is not calculating effect sizes, then it should at least report results for all relevant comparisons (and not just those for statistically significant groups), standard deviations to go along with means, and sampling information, including response rates, attrition, and sample size. Cost data should also be given, so that we can begin to estimate the cost-effectiveness of campaigns.

ACKNOWLEDGMENTS

The author acknowledges and thanks those who enabled the present review by contributing directly to the meta-analyses on which this paper is based: Elizabeth Mitchell, James Kiwanuka-Tondo, Fran Fleming-Milici, Dwayne Proctor, Mark Hamilton, Louise Badiane, Nafisatou Diop-Sidibé, and Svetlana Kalnova. Special thanks to James Derzon for discussions about how to compare our findings.

REFERENCES

Bauman, K. E. (1997). The effectiveness of family planning programs evaluated with true experimental designs. *Public Health Briefs, 87,* 666–669.

Dearing, J. W., Rogers, E. M., Meyer, G., Casey, M. K., Rao, N., Campo, S., & Henderson, G. M. (1996). Social marketing and diffusion-based strategies for communication with unique populations: HIV prevention in San Francisco. *Journal of Health Communication, 1,* 343–363.

Derzon, J. H., & Lipsey, M. W. (2002). A meta-analysis of the effectiveness of mass-communication for changing substance-use knowledge, attitudes, and behavior. In W. D. Crano & M. Burgoon (Eds.), *Mass media and drug prevention: Classic and contemporary theories and research* (pp. 231–258). Mahwah, NJ: Lawrence Erlbaum Associates.

Douglas, D. F., Westley, B. H., and Chaffee, S. H. (1970). An Information campaign that changed community attitudes. *Journalism Quarterly, 47,* 479–490.

Ennett, S. T., Tobler, N. S., Ringwalt, C. L., Flewelling, R. L. (1994). How effective is drug abuse resistance education? A meta-analysis of project DARE outcome evaluations. *American Journal of Public Health, 84*(9), 1394–1401.

Farrelly, M. C., Healton, C. G., Davis, K. C., Messeri, P., Hersey, J. C., & Haviland, M. L., (2002). Getting to the Truth: Evaluating national tobacco countermarketing campaigns. *American Journal of Public Health, 92*(6), 901–908.

Farrelly, M. C., Niederdeppe, J., & Yarsevich, J. (2003). Youth tobacco prevention mass media campaigns: Past, present, and future directions. *Tobacco Control, 12*(Suppl. 1), i35–i47.

Farrelly, M. C., Hersey, K. C., Haviland, M. L., Messeri, P., & Healton, C. G. (2005). Evidence of a dose-response relationship between "truth" antismoking ads and youth smoking prevalence. *American Journal of Public Health, 95*(3), 425–431.

Flay, B. R., & Cook, T. D. (1989). Three models for summative evaluation of prevention campaigns with a mass media component. In R. E. Rice and C. K. Atkin (Eds.), *Public Communication Campaigns,* 2nd ed. (pp. 175–195). Newbury Park, CA: Sage.

Fortmann, S. P., Williams, P. T., Hulley, S. B., Haskell, W. L., & Farquhar, J. W. (1981). Effect of health education on dietary behavior: The Stanford Three Community study. *American Journal of Clinical Nutrition, 34,* 2030–2038.

Grilli, R., Freemantle, N., Minozzi, S., Domenighetti, G., & Finer, D. (1999). Mass media interventions: Effects on health services utilization (Cochrane Review). *The Cochrane Library, 4.* Oxford: Update Software.

Hornik, C. (1989). Channel effectiveness in development communication programs. In R. E. Rice and C. K. Atkin (Eds.), *Public Communication Campaigns,* 2nd ed. (pp. 309–330). Newbury Park, CA: Sage.

Hornik, R. C. (Ed.) (2002). *Public health communication: Evidence for behavior change.* Hillsdale, NJ: Lawrence Erlbaum Associates.

Hornik, R., Contreras-Budge, E., McDivitt, J., McDowell, J., Yoder, P. S., Zimicki, S., & Rasmuson, M. (1992). Communication for child survival: Evaluation of "Healthcom" Projects in ten countries. Unpublished manuscript.

Hornik, R., et al. (2002). *Evaluation of the National Youth Anti-Drug Media Campaigns: 2003 Report of Findings.* Report prepared for the national Institute on Drug Abuse (contract NO. N01DA-8-5063). Retrieved on March 26, 2004, from http://www.drugabuse.gov/PDF/DESPR/1203report.pdf.

Huhman, M., Potter, L. D., Wong, F. L., Banspach, S. W., Duke, J. C., & Heitzler, C. D. (2005). Effects of a Mass Media Campaign to Increase Physical Activity Among Children: Year-1 Results of the VERB Campaign. *Pediatrics, 116*(2), 277–84.

Hunter, J. E., & Schmidt, F. L. (1990). *Methods of meta-analysis: Correcting error and bias in research findings.* Newbury Park, CA: Sage.

Hyman, H. H., & Shetsley, P. B. (1947). Some reasons why information campaigns fail. *Public Opinion Quarterly, 11*(4), 412–423.

Institute of Medicine. (2002). *Speaking of health: Assessing health communication strategies for diverse populations.* Washington, DC: The National Academies Press.

Johnson, B. T. (1995). DSTAT, Version 1.11. Computer software. Hillsdale, NJ: Lawrence Erlbaum Associates.

Kar, S. B., Pascual, C. A., & Chickering, K. L. (1999). Empowerment of women for health promotion: A meta-analysis. *Social Science and Medicine, 49,* 1431–1460.

Kiwanuka-Tondo, J., & Snyder, L. B. (2002). The influence of organizational characteristics and campaign design elements on communication campaign quality: Evidence from 91 Ugandan AIDS Campaigns. *Journal of Health Communication, 7,* 1–20.

Maibach, E. (2002). Explicating social marketing: What is it and what isn't it? *Social Marketing Quarterly, 8* (4), 7–13.

McGuire, W. J. (1981). Public communication campaigns: The American experience. In R.E. Rice & W.J. Paisley (Eds.), *Public Communication Campaigns* (pp. 15–40). Beverly Hills, CA: Sage.

Mullen, P. D., Simons-Morton, D. G., Ramirez, G., Frankowski, F., Green, L. W., and Mains, D. A. (1997). A meta-analysis of trials evaluating patient education and counceling for three groups of preventive health behaviors. *Patient Education and Counseling, 32,* 157–173.

Mullen, D. P., Mains, D. A., and Velez, R. (1992). A meta-analysis of controlled trials of cardiac patient education. A meta-analysis of controlled trials of cardiac patient education. *Patient Education and Counseling, 19,* 143–162.

National Center for Chronic Disease Prevention and Health Promotion. (2004). *Fact Sheet: Actual Causes of Death in the United States.* Retrieved March 26, 2004, from http://www.cdc.gov/nccdphp/factsheets/death_causes2000.htm.

Paisley, W. J. (1981). Public communication campaigns: The American experience. In R.E. Rice & W. J. Paisley (Eds.), *Public Communication Campaigns* (pp. 15–40). Beverly Hills, CA: Sage.

Palmgreen, P., Donohew, L., Lorch, E.P., Hoyle, R.H., & Stephenson, M.T. (2002). Television campaigns and sensation seeking targeting of adolescent marijuana use: A controlled time series approach. In R. Hornik (Ed.), *Public health communication: Evidence for behavior change* (pp. 35–56). Hillsdale, NJ: Lawrence Erlbaum Associates.

Rogers, E. M. (1962, 1995). *Diffusion of innovations.* New York: Free Press.

Rooney, B. L., & Murray, D. M. (1996). A meta-analysis of smoking prevention programs after adjustment for errors in the unit of analysis. *Health Education Quarterly, 23*(11), 48–64.

Snyder, L. (2000a). Commentary: Mass media interventions may influence health services use. *Journal of Evidence-based Healthcare, 4*(1), 2.

Snyder, L. (2000b). *Evidence of the effectiveness of communication interventions across diverse populations.* Report submitted to the Committee on Communication for Behavior Change in the 21st Century: Improving the Health of Diverse Populations. Washington, DC: Institute of Medicine, National Academy of Sciences.

Snyder, L. B. (2001). How effective are mediated health campaigns? In R. Rice & C. Atkin (Eds.), *Public information campaigns,* 3rd ed. (pp. 181–190). Thousand Oaks, CA: Sage.

Snyder, L., Badiane, L., Kalnova, S., & Diop- Sidibé, N. (2003). *Meta-analysis of family planning campaigns advised by the Center for Communication Programs at Johns Hopkins University compared to campaigns conducted and advised by other organizations.* Submitted to

Johns Hopkins Bloomberg School of Public Health and the U.S. Agency for International Development.

Snyder, L. B., & Hamilton, M. A. (2002). Meta-analysis of U.S. health campaign effects on behavior: Emphasize enforcement, exposure, and new information, and beware the secular trend. In R. Hornik (Ed.), *Public health communication: Evidence for behavior change* (pp. 357–383). Hillsdale, NJ: Lawrence Erlbaum Associates.

Snyder, L. B., Hamilton, M. A., Mitchell, E. W., Kiwanuka-Tondo, J., Fleming-Milici, F., & Proctor, D. (2004). A meta-analysis of the effect of mediated health communication campaigns on behavior change in the United States. *Journal of Health Communication, 9*(1), 71–96.

Tseng, D. S., Cox, E., Plane, M. B., & Hla, K. M. (2001). Efficacy of patient letter reminders on cervical cancer screening. *Journal of General Internal Medicine, 16,* 563–568.

Viswesvaran, C., & Schmidt, F. L. (1992). A meta-analytic comparison of the effectiveness of smoking cessation methods. *Journal of Applied Psychology, 77*(4), 554–561.

Wallack, L., Dorfman, L., Jernigan, D., & Themba, M. (1993). *Media advocacy and public health: Power for prevention.* Newbury Park, CA: Sage.

White, D., & Pitts, M. (1998). Educating young people about drugs: A systematic review. *Addiction, 93*(10), 1475–1487.

Wilson, D. B., Gottfredson, D. C., & Najaka, S. S. (2001). School-based prevention of problem behaviors: A meta-analysis. *Journal of Quantitative Criminology, 17*(3), 247–272.

Wilson, S. J., Lipsey, M. W., & Derzon, J. H. (2003). The effects of school-based intervention programs on aggressive behavior: A meta-analysis. *Journal of Consulting and Clinical Psychology, 71*(1), 126–149.

21

An Analysis of Media Health Campaigns for Children and Adolescents: Do They Work?

Lisa Mullikin Parcell
Wichita State University

Jae Kwon
Dorina Miron
Jennings Bryant
University of Alabama

INTEREST IN THE TOPIC

Mass media health campaigns have gradually increased in number, rising to a flurry of activity in the 1990s. Unfortunately for communication scholars, most of these campaigns were and still are privately funded, and little or no evaluative research typically is presented to the public. A seminal spark for research in this arena was a national conference held at the Annenberg Center for Health Sciences in Rancho Mirage, California. The conference explored how the mass media could be used more effectively to improve public health. Believing that the information-dissemination function was key to improving public health, the conference organizers focused discussions on improving health campaigns and adding health information into news and entertainment programming. The conference included experts in journalism, advertising, entertainment, communication science, public policy, medical science, and public health who approached the subject from the standpoint of practitioners, academic scholars, members of government agencies, and advocacy groups. Sponsors of the conference included federal agencies such as the Office of Disease Prevention and Health Promotion, Office for Substance Abuse Prevention, and National Cancer Institute.

Atkin and Wallack's (1990) *Mass Communication and Public Health* includes the revised conference papers. In the first chapter, Atkin and Arkin (1990) noted that "with few exceptions, very little research has been conducted to assess the impact of health-related content on the public" (p. 34). They called for research on the comparative effectiveness of different sources, channels, message styles, formats, and appeals. Atkin and Arkin also pointed out that few attempts have been made to develop research-based guidelines for campaigns targeting specific populations, such as children or low-income minorities. They stressed the usefulness of such information for campaign planners.

BRIEF EXCURSION INTO COMMUNICATION CAMPAIGN HISTORY AND RESEARCH

Back in early American colonial times, a dispute over the effectiveness and use of the smallpox vaccine led to a newspaper campaign designed to convince the public of the need for the vaccine. Eventually, the smallpox vaccine became so prevalent that the disease was wiped out, historically marking that early health campaign a success.

In World War I, both the United States and the European nations used massive media campaigns to influence public opinion and participation in the war. The effectiveness of those propaganda efforts led many communication scholars to believe that the media were extremely powerful: All the media had to do was feed the public a message, and the public would respond. But that enthusiasm gradually faded as researchers started finding limited effects or no effects in communication-campaign research.

A classic example of the "limited effects" research is Lazarsfeld, Berelson, and Gaudet's (1948) study on voter decision-making in the presidential election of 1940 in Erie County, Ohio. The researchers found that once people had made their decisions on how to vote, they rarely changed their minds. Lazarsfeld and his colleagues also found that interpersonal influence was strong. Based on that discovery, they launched the two-step flow model of persuasion, which they tested in a study on female consumers' decisions in Decatur, Illinois (Katz & Lazarasfeld, 1955). The results confirmed that information gained from other consumers was more influential than were campaign messages.

Other authors provided additional support for the limited effects theory of campaign effects. Hyman & Sheatsley's (1947) article, "Some Reasons Why Information Campaigns Fail," analyzed various campaigns aimed at increasing public affairs knowledge. They noted that when conducting a campaign, simply increasing the number of messages does not ensure success. Hyman and Sheatsley concluded that the media audience was composed of "know-nothings" who selectively exposed themselves to, perceived, and retained media messages that generally conformed to their previous knowledge and attitudes.

Another study by Star and Hughes (1950), who examined a Cincinnati campaign to garner support for the United Nations, showed that information is functional only when the issue is presented as personally relevant to the target audience.

Cartwright (1949, 1954) offered several reasons for campaign failure in two articles designed to help campaign planners. He suggested that campaign planners take a receiver-centered, psychologically centered approach. Cartwright believed that in order for campaigns to actually influence behavior, they had to develop and convey a cognitive, motivational, and behavioral structure that was conducive to the desired action.

In 1960, Klapper synthesized research findings about limited effects. He concluded that the model was generalizable to all mass media campaigns.

But that conservative view of campaign effects was subject to further change in the 1960s and 1970s, when the major efforts in campaign research were directed toward the identification of communication strategies that enhanced the effectiveness of media campaigns. Mendelsohn's (1973) article, "Some Reasons Why Information Campaigns Can Succeed," held that successful campaigns needed formative evaluation, reasonable campaign goals, established audience segmentation, and an understanding of interpersonal channels. The greater emphasis on formative research changed the way failed campaigns were evaluated: No longer was it the apathetic audience's fault that they did not get the message; now researchers tried to determine what aspect of the message, channel, or formative research failed. Researchers also began to recognize the importance of multiple channels of communication, in particular interpersonal communication. Rogers and Storey (1987), for example, found that changes in audience members' behaviors are greater than the sum of the effects of each separate channel.

More recent research has examined campaign failures and successes from various perspectives: identifying target audiences, evaluating messages, determining effects, studying sources, choosing proper channels, and so forth. Researchers have found that media are useful in influencing people cumulatively, through repeated exposure over long periods of time (Katz, 1980; Maccoby & Roberts, 1985). Failed campaigns are now believed to be the result of poor conceptualization, insufficient formative research, and/or poor planning, preparation, production, and dissemination (Atkin, 1979, 1981a, 1981b; Blane & Hewitt, 1980; Flay, 1981; Novelli, 1982; O'Keefe, 1985; Palmer, 1981; Solomon, 1984; Wallack, 1981).

DIFFICULTIES ASSOCIATED WITH THE
INTEGRATION OF RESEARCH FINDINGS

Conceptualization

Unfortunately, scholars do not even agree on one definition of health communication campaign. Rogers and Storey (1987) held that a communication campaign
"intends to generate specific outcomes or effects in a relatively large number of
individuals, usually within a specified period of time and through an organized set
of communication activities" (p. 821). Paisley (1981) said that public communication campaigns can be defined in two ways: Considering their objectives, they
are strategies of social control in which one group attempts to affect the beliefs
or behavior of another group; considering their methods, public communication
campaigns are noncommercial advertising, and the way the message is sent makes
a great difference. Flay and Burton (1990) defined public health communication
campaigns as "an integrated series of communication activities, using multiple
operations and channels, aimed at populations or large target audiences, usually of
long duration, with a clear purpose" (p. 130). This definition also incorporates all
the aspects of definitions used by other communication scholars (Atkin, 1981a;
Paisley, 1981; Rogers & Storey, 1987; Solomon, 1982). In our study, we utilized
Flay and Burton's (1990) definition, with the exception that we also incorporated
campaigns using one or more forms of media.

Methodological Diversity
Due to Interdisciplinarity

Because mass communication health-campaign research is not firmly rooted in
one discipline, but incorporates aspects of many fields (e.g., communication, psychology, health, sociology), research methods differ across studies, which makes
comparisons between campaigns rather difficult.

One problem is associated with the different approach from the communication
and medical perspectives. Communication scholars tend to look at the micro level
of change. Typically they are concerned with changes in the attitudes and beliefs
of individual people. Medical scholars, on the other hand, are more concerned
with the macro level. They conduct epidemiological studies to trace large changes
or trends over time. They use much larger samples, and their results are usually
reported as fluctuations in national or citywide health indices, disease or inocula-
tion statistics, or total numbers of something sold (e.g., bicycle helmets, cigarette
packages). As the two approaches collect and report different types of data, their
comparability is questionable.

The second problem is associated with the strong influence of marketing
research. The practical interest in finding the correct formula for a successful
health campaign eventually led to the formation of best-practice models. Many

models drew on prior advances in persuasion registered in other sciences. The business areas of advertising and marketing contributed theory about how the campaign is "marketed" to the public. Solomon (1989), for example, argued that many of the design and implementation aspects of communication campaigns are similar to those of social marketing. For example, the four P's of marketing—product, price, place, and promotion—are also applied to social marketing. The marketing approach leaves much to be desired in terms of systematicity and has low explanatory and predictive power.

The third problem is associated with the theoretical inspiration and import from cognitive and social psychology. Campaign researchers have imported theories about message processing as well as value, attitude, and behavior changes. For example, Flay and Burton (1990, p. 141) offered a list of recipes for behavior change based primarily on Bandura's (1977, 1986) social learning theory and Becker's (1974) health belief model:

1. Demonstrating or modeling the desired behavior.
2. Presenting the behavior as effective in achieving desirable objectives, particularly immediate ones such as feeling and looking better.
3. Presenting the behavior as related to real-life circumstances, rather than in the abstract. Stressing the incentive or value of freedom from risk.
4. Instilling the belief that a particular act or pattern of behavior will preclude or ameliorate a specific risk. Nurturing the motivation to avoid harm or improve well-being in the longer term.
5. Presenting the behavior as enjoying the approval and support of the community.
6. Mobilizing public support for the desired changes.
7. Providing specific guidance for the self-management of behavior change.
8. Providing specific guidance for the self-management of relapses by recycling and trying again.
9. Encouraging the development of interpersonal social support for change attempts and changed behavior.
10. Providing the infrastructures to support change attempts and changed behavior, encouraging the use of existing infrastructures, or encouraging proactive behavior by the target audience in the form of pressure on government or other responsible agencies to provide such infrastructures.
11. Encouraging activism against any part of the social system that tends to undermine the desired behavior changes.

Such efforts to import theory from other social and health sciences and to synthesize extant knowledge have created at least two problems: On the one hand, they resulted in unsystematic lists of things to do or focus on in persuasion campaigns. On the other hand, theory importation was accompanied by the importation of research methodologies. Consequently, the diverse variables and measures for campaign characteristics and effects make it difficult to compare findings about campaign effectiveness.

Tension Between Micro-Research and Theoretical Integration

Disappointment with the magic recipe style of "theorizing" motivated some researchers to become more systematic. McGuire (1989) designed an input/output matrix in an attempt to explain how the construction of a campaign message system is related to information-processing, which involves a sequence of steps that have to be taken in order for persuasion to occur. McGuire's matrix helps detect missteps or breakdowns in the sequence, so that campaign strategy and procedures can be adjusted.

Other researchers focused on inputs or outputs. Among the input models was Hovland, Janis, and Kelley's (1953) instrumental learning theory, which addressed source credibility, the incentives in the message appeal, and repetition. Bandura's (1977b) social learning theory stressed the importance of the source role models, the exact portrayal of desired behaviors, and the demonstration of different positive and negative reinforcements. Ajzen and Fishbein's (1980) theory of reasoned action maintained that people's attitudes and decisions for action are based on expected consequences and the positive or negative nature of such consequences. People also take into consideration the perceived orientations of certain groups or persons toward that action or attitude. Petty and Cacioppo's (1981) cognitive response theory proposed that a message receiver compares new information to already acquired knowledge and experience, and forms new connections and beliefs.

Output theories generally provide sequences of audience responses that are necessary for persuasion to occur. Among the authors who tried to synthesize and adapt existing persuasion models for health campaigns are Albert (1981), Atkin (1981a), and Flay (1981). Flay proposed a model that included four intermediate processes and seven dependent variable outcomes. Rogers' (1983) diffusion-of-innovation model included a sequence of knowledge gain, persuasion, decision, and confirmation. Atkin and Freimuth (1989) proposed that receivers of a persuasive message move through five basic steps (exposure/attention; information processing; gaining knowledge and skills; forming or changing beliefs, values, attitudes, and behavioral intentions; and changing behavior). Each step in Atkin and Freimuth's model has several substeps. For example, information processing includes comprehension of the content, selective perception of source and appeals, and evaluative reactions, such as liking, agreeing, and counterarguing.

Overall, researchers' need to learn about persuasion phenomena in more detail and rely in their micro-issue investigations on relevant theory imported from other fields made cause-effect findings increasingly harder to articulate into mid-level theories that could provide general frames for the development of successful campaigns.

CAMPAIGN EFFECTIVENESS ASSESSMENT

As theorizing in the area of health campaigns is still volatile and offers campaign designers little firm ground to build on, campaign assessment has been used as an alternative way of gaining knowledge about campaign effectiveness.

Models for Evaluating Campaign Effectiveness

Studies conducted to assess the effectiveness of specific campaigns typically use one of three general models: The *advertising model* utilizes audience surveys to determine the reach of message, message recall, appeal of message, self-reported estimation of action in response to new knowledge and attitudes, and the "whys" of the above (e.g., Popham, Muthen, Potter, Duerr, Hetrick, & Johnson, 1994). The *impact-monitoring model* uses data that are routinely collected from a management information system or other archival source to track the effects of a campaign over a long period of time (e.g., Bruerd, Kinney, & Bothwell, 1989; Pierce, Macaskill, & Hill, 1990). The *experimental model* compares effects of communication campaigns on treatment and control groups. This final method is the most common for mass media health campaigns aimed at children (e.g., Dannenberg, Gielen, Beilenson, Wilson, & Joffe, 1993; Flynn, Worden, Secker-Walker, Badger, Geller, & Costanza, 1992; Hafstad & Aaro, 1997; Hafstad, Aaro, & Langmark, 1996; Kline, Miller, & Morrison, 1974; Murray, Prokhorov, & Harty, 1994).

Recent Findings

Logan and Longo (1999) reviewed the past three generations of antismoking campaigns aimed at adolescents and adults. They found that the most effective campaigns combined strategies from multiple models. They concluded that in order to overcome the still strong resistance to media messages, campaign planners would have to use even more complex campaign strategies.

In a meta-analysis, Sowden, Arblaster, and Stead (2003) compared studies that assessed the effectiveness of multicomponent community interventions versus single-component or school-based programs that targeted young people under the age of 25. They found some limited support for the effectiveness of community interventions in helping to prevent the uptake of smoking in young people. Wakefield and Chaloupka (2000) analyzed journal articles, publicly released reports, and working papers that evaluated the effectiveness of comprehensive statewide tobacco control programs in reducing teenage smoking in five states. They found that such programs resulted in high levels of advertising recall and produced generally positive improvements in smoking-related beliefs and attitudes among teenagers.

The Purpose of Our Study

Given the small number of integrative studies on the effectiveness of health campaigns and the limited scope of those investigations, campaign sponsors and underwriters are still unsure if their efforts are worthwhile, and if their time and money are wisely invested for protecting the safety and well-being of children and adolescents.

In response to Atkin and Wallack's (1990) call for general assessments of health campaigns, this chapter provides a meta-analysis of studies about the effectiveness of health campaigns aimed at children and adolescents. Our purpose is to determine whether this particular type of campaign is effective in changing health-related attitudes and/or behaviors of health related practices.

META-ANALYSIS

Method

Search Procedure

We identified the studies for our meta-analysis utilizing the ERIC, Medline, PSYCHINFO, and EAI data bases, as well as card catalogs for the older publications. We also used the references in the articles we found. In addition, we perused every issue of the scholarly journals *Health Communication* and the *Journal of Health Communication,* looking for pertinent articles that might not have been referenced in the sources we consulted. Finally, we ran another computer database search (using the same databases) on the names of the authors whose works we had located, to see if they had published any other related articles.

Selection Criteria for Inclusion of Studies: Studies Not Included

The studies selected for this meta-analysis had to meet several criteria. First, we limited this study to refereed journal articles or chapters in edited scholarly books. We recognized that this decision would eliminate a great number of privately or federally sponsored campaigns that yielded research reports, but it helped control for biased studies in order to protect the integrity of the research as a whole. This criterion eliminated a number of privately funded alcohol and tobacco studies that had issued press releases and widely circulated private reports.

Second, the campaigns had to address or benefit youth no older than 18.

Third, the studies had to present effects of campaign exposure on behavioral change in the direction suggested by the campaign. This criterion eliminated a study by Stephenson, Morgan, Lorch, Palmgreen, Donohew, and Hoyle (2001) that examined the impact of several audience features (traditionally considered mediating factors of campaign effects: drug-use attitudes, intentions, behavior/

marijuana use, sensation-seeking, risk and protective factors, normative factors) on exposure to an antimarijuana campaign.

Fourth, the reported data had to include measures of exposure to the media campaign and measures of effects due to that exposure. That requirement was particularly important in studies of complex campaigns that included media and other forms of education and persuasion, where we had to distinguish between media effects and effects of other campaign components. This criterion eliminated a number of otherwise interesting studies: O'Keefe (1971) found that only those who were already inclined to give up smoking were affected by antismoking commercials, but the author did not report any media measures. Bruerd, Kinney, and Bothwell (1989) found that a combination of training and media campaign (print) for caretakers of young children reduced the incidence of BBTD (baby bottle tooth decay), but the effect of the media campaign was not assessed separately from that of group training sessions. DiGiuseppi, Rivara, Koepsell, and Polissar (1989) found that a community-wide bicycle-helmet campaign including school intervention and a media campaign had a positive impact on the number of children using bicycle helmets, when compared to helmet usage in a similar city that did not receive the communication campaign. But the authors did not report separately the effects of the school and media components. Penz, Dwyer, MacKinnon, Flay, Hansen, Wang, and Johnson (1989) found that their entire campaign using a combination of school intervention, parental involvement in homework, and mass media affected the prevalence rates of drug use for youths, but effects of media were not reported separately. Crawford, Jason, Riordan, Kaufman, Salina, Sawalski, Ho, and Zolik (1990) found that children who were prompted to watch mass media telecasts on AIDS prevention were more knowledgeable about the disease than children who were not prompted to watch the campaign, but the authors did not report any exposure measure. Soumerai, Ross-Degnan, and Kahn (1992) found that the professional and lay media were important means of providing information to health professionals and parents about the relationship between aspirin and Reye's syndrome, but the authors did not provide exposure details. Dannenberg, Gielen, Beilenson, Wilson, and Joffe (1993) examined the impact of a bicycle helmet campaign that included legislation, school-based education, and a media campaign. The authors found that the campaign changed helmet use from 8% to 18% at a high level of campaign exposure and from 7% to 11% at a minimal level. Unfortunately campaign exposure was assessed as number of sources, without discriminating between media and interpersonal sources. Flynn et al. (1994) found that a combination of school instruction and media campaign was more effective than school intervention alone, but media effects could not be determined from the report. Murray, Prohorov, and Harty (1994) found insignificant net effects of a complex 5-year smoking prevention intervention in Minnesota (using Wisconsin as a control). The campaign included legislation, smoking prevention curriculum, and a media campaign whose effects could not be separated from those of the other two components, and the authors argued that a media campaign might be insufficient to generate significant reductions in adolescent tobacco use without school-based tobacco prevention measures. Rouzier and Alto (1995) evaluated a bicycle helmet campaign whose effect was measured as children observed wearing a helmet before and after the campaign. No media exposure measures were involved in the study. McPhee, Ngyuen, Euler, Mock, Wong, et al. (2003) reported that a media-led information and education campaign aimed at Vietnamese-American parents increased those parents' knowledge of hepatitis B vaccinations and the number of "catch-up" vaccinations among their children, but the researchers did not report actual individual exposure to that campaign.

The fifth criterion for selecting meta-analyzable studies was the availability of comparable data (correlations between media exposure and effects, or variance change in measures of campaign effects caused by exposure to a media-delivered campaign, or other measures that could be transformed into correlation r). This requirement eliminated Popham, Potter, and Hetrick's (1994) study on an antismoking campaign that reduced smoking prevalence and nonsmokers' thinking about starting to smoke, and enhanced antismoking attitudes. Another study that did not report meta-analyzable data was McDivitt, Zimicki, and Hornik's (1997) evaluation of a vaccination campaign in the Philippines. The authors found significant campaign exposure to be a significant predictor of vaccination knowledge, but they did not report the variance change attributable to campaign exposure only. Siegel and Biener (2000) examined progression to established smoking after an antismoking campaign and found that exposure to TV ads made children aged 12–13 less likely to progress to established smoking, but the campaign had no significant effect on youths aged 14–15. Unfortunately, the authors reported odds ratios without the corresponding probability data. The last study that we regretfully had to drop from our pool for lack of meta-analyzable data was Hecht, Marsiglia, Elek, Wagstaff, Kulis, Dustman, and Miller-Day's (2003) assessment of a culturally grounded substance use prevention campaign (*Keep It R.E.A.L.*). The authors found statistically significant effects on gateway drug use as well as norms, attitudes, and resistance strategies (reported only as mean differences).

Included Studies

The studies that satisfied all criteria and were included in our meta-analysis are listed in chronological order in Table 21.1.

The studies included in our meta-analysis examined campaigns for various health-related issues: antiaddiction (six antismoking, one for burn injuries, one for oral health, and one for family planning). Five studies were conducted in the United States, two in Norway, one in Australia, and one in Ireland.

These studies were conducted over a period of 30 years, with a noticeable increase in the second half of the time interval: One study was conducted in the 1970s, one in the 1980s, four in the 1990s, and three between 2000 and 2003.

TABLE 21.1

Studies Included in the Meta Analysis

#	Authors	Subject	r	N
1	Kline, F. K., Miller, P. V., & Morrison, A. J. (1974)	Family planning	.25	535
2	Bauman, K. E., Brown, J. D., Bryan, E. S., Fisher, L. A., Padgett, C.A., & Sweeney, J. M. (1988)	Smoking	.13	917
3	Pierce, J. P., Macaskiill, P., AppStat, M., & Hill, D. (1990)	Smoking	.04	69,385
4	Flynn, B. S., Worden, J. K., Secker-Walker, R. H., Badger, G. J., Geller, B. M., & Costanza, M. C. (1992)	Smoking	.12	2,540
5	Hafstad, A., Aaro, L. E., & Langmark, F. (1996)	Smoking	.02	3,670
6	Hafstad, A., & Aaro (1997)	Smoking	.05	1,832
7	Sly, D. F., Hopkins, R. S., Trapido, E., & Ray, S. (2001)	Smoking	.02	1,820
8	Friel, S., Hope, A., Kelleher, C., Comer, S., & Sadlier, D. (2002)	Oral health	.16	689
9	MacArthur, C. (2003)	Burn injuries	.08	504

Variables and Measures

In this meta-analysis we were interested in the effect of exposure to media campaigns on behavior change. We used sample size and zero-order correlation data. Wherever possible, we transformed other measures into correlation r.

Findings

Analysis 1

We started by conducting a meta-analysis of all nine studies and found the following:

Mean of the study correlations:	0.045
Variance across studies:	7.125×10^{-4}
Sampling error variance:	1.094×10^{-4}
Variance of population correlations:	6.031×10^{-4}
Corrected population standard deviation:	$1.832 < 1.96$

As the corrected population standard deviation is lower than the 1.96 threshold of significance, we cannot conclude from the nine studies considered together that exposure to health-related media campaigns addressed to or designed to benefit children and youth under 18 are generally effective.

The fact that the corrected population standard deviation is close to significance justifies further investigation of possible reasons why some campaigns were less effective than expected.

Analysis 2

Our first concern was that one of the nine campaigns we retained in our pool (Macarthur, 2003) was actually addressed to parents of young children. As campaign effects on parents may be different from campaign effects on children, whose processing skills and motivations are different, we decided to conduct a separate meta-analysis on the eight campaigns to which children where directly exposed. Our findings were the following:

Mean of the study correlations:	0.045
Variance across studies:	7.064×10^{-4}
Sampling error variance:	0.979×10^{-4}
Variance of population correlations:	6.085×10^{-4}
Corrected population standard deviation:	$1.815 < 1.96$

Excluding the study that targeted parents slightly lowered the corrected population standard deviation, so we cannot conclude from the eight studies we meta-analyzed that campaigns addressed directly to children are generally effective. The lower value of the corrected population standard deviation when the campaign to parents was excluded suggests that parents of young children may have better understanding of the campaign information and higher motivation to follow advice that benefits their children. Consequently, we recommend that campaigns designed to benefit children but are targeted to their parents should be meta-analyzed separately from campaigns targeted directly to children.

Analysis 3

The pool of studies retained for our meta-analysis included four foreign campaigns. Suspecting differential effects of culture on campaign results, we conducted a separate meta-analysis on the five American studies. Here are our findings:

Mean of the study correlations:	0.101
Variance across studies:	40.72×10^{-4}
Sampling error variance:	7.763×10^{-4}
Variance of population correlations:	32.961×10^{-4}
Corrected population standard deviation:	$1.751 < 1.96$

As the corrected population standard deviation again failed to reach significance, we cannot conclude from the five U.S. studies we meta-analyzed that campaigns for children's health are generally effective within the boundaries of the American culture. Because the corrected population standard deviation for the American studies is also close to significance, we addressed one more possible reason why some campaigns were not effective.

Analysis 4

Six of the studies in our meta-analysis pool evaluated antismoking campaigns. Hypothesizing that campaigns on different topics may have a different impact on the target audience, we meta-analyzed separately the six antismoking campaign studies and found the following:

Mean of the study correlations:	0.042
Variance across studies:	3.320×10^{-4}
Sampling error variance:	74.583×10^{-6}
Variance of population correlations:	2.574×10^{-4}
Corrected population standard deviation:	$2.650 > 1.96$

As the corrected population standard deviation is above the significance level, we conclude that antismoking media campaigns directed to youth under 18 are generally effective in preventing or reducing smoking.

Analysis 5

Finally, we checked the possibility that campaign topic and culture together may affect campaign significance. The meta-analysis we conducted on the three U.S. antismoking campaign studies had the following results

Mean of the study correlations:	0.087
Variance across studies:	23.934×10^{-4}
Sampling error variance:	5.601×10^{-4}
Variance of population correlations:	18.334×10^{-4}
Corrected population standard deviation:	$2.039 > 1.96$

The significant corrected population standard deviation allows us to conclude that antismoking campaigns in the United States are effective. The fact that the corrected population standard deviation was slightly lower when we considered only U.S. antismoking campaigns indicates that the effectiveness of such campaigns may be higher abroad. It is possible that foreign antismoking campaigns have better design, the target populations in other countries are more receptive, the target population abroad is more receptive than in the United States, or the American culture is more permissive to smoking, which undercuts antismoking educational efforts.

DISCUSSION

Our meta-analysis conducted on a limited number of studies that evaluated health campaigns addressed to or designed to benefit youth under 18 shows that anti-smoking campaigns are generally effective in preventing or reducing smoking. Our findings suggest that the topic of health campaigns targeting youth under 18 can significantly affect campaign effectiveness.

From a technical point of view, we encountered difficulties in constructing a data pool because a large number of studies on health campaign for children did not include or report measures of media exposure and/or measures of campaign effects that could be attributed to the media component of the campaign. In addition to this problem, some studies reported the findings using incomplete information (e.g., missing probability values) or measures that we could not convert to correlation r. Therefore, we recommend that researchers make an effort to standardize as much a possible the campaign evaluation methodologies, statistical analysis, and the style of reporting results. Such standardization would facilitate further attempts to integrate findings through meta-analysis.

Because most groups historically associated with media health campaigns for children have limited resources, it is imperative for campaign managers to assess and publicize the positive results of their campaigns on a regular basis. Conducting and publishing comparable evaluations would pay off in the long run by gradually revealing effective campaign strategies for others to use in the future rather than rely on hunches and guesswork.

REFERENCES

Ajzen, I., & Fishbein, M. (1980). *Understanding attitudes and predicting social behavior*. Engle-wood Cliffs, NJ: Prentice-Hall.

Albert, W. (1981). General models of persuasive influence for health education. In D. Leathar, G. Hastings, & J. Davies (Eds.), *Health education and the media* (pp. 169–185). Oxford: Pergamon.

Atkin, C. K. (1979). Research evidence on mass mediated health communication campaigns. In D. Nimmo (Ed.), *Communication yearbook 3* (pp. 655–669). New Brunswick, NJ: Transaction.

Atkin, C. K. (1981a). Mass communication research principles for health education. In M. Meyer (Ed.), *Health education by television and radio* (pp. 41–55). Munich: Saur.

Atkin, C. K. (1981b). Mass media information campaign effectiveness. In R. E. Rice & W. J. Paisley (Eds.), *Public communication campaigns* (pp. 265–280). Beverly Hills, CA: Sage.

Atkin, C. K., & Arkin, E. B. (1990). Issues and initiatives in communication health information. In C. K. Atkin, & L. Wallack (Eds.), *Mass communication and public health: Complexities and conflicts* (pp. 13–40). Newbury Park, CA: Sage.

Atkin, C. K., & Freimuth, V. (1989). Formative evaluation research in campaign design. In R. E. Rice & C. K. Atkin (Eds.), *Public communication campaign* (2nd ed., pp. 131–150). Newbury Park, CA: Sage.

Atkin, C. K., & Wallack, L. (Eds.). (1990). *Mass communication and public health: Complexities and conflicts*. Newbury Park, CA: Sage.

Bandura, A. (1977). *Social learning theory*. Englewood Cliffs, NJ: Prentice-Hall. Bandura, A. (1986). *Social functions of thought and action: A social cognitive theory*. Englewood Cliffs, NJ: Prentice-Hall.

Bauman, K. E., Brown, J. D., Bryan, E. S., Fisher, L. A., Padgett, C. A., & Sweeney, J. M. (1988). Three mass media campaigns to prevent adolescent cigarette smoking. *Preventive Medicine, 17*, 510–530.

Becker, M. H. (1974). *The health belief model and personal health behavior*. Thorofare, NJ: Slack.

Blane, H., & Hewitt, L. (1980). Alcohol, public education, and mass media: An overview. *Alcohol Health and Research World, 5*, 2–16.

Bruerd, B., Kinney, M.B., Bothwell, E. (1989). Preventing baby tooth decay in American Indian and Alaska Native communities: A model for planning. *Public Health Reports, 104*, 631–640.

Cartwright, D. (1949). Some principles of mass persuasion: Selected findings of research on the sale of United States War Bonds. *Human Relations, 2*, 253–267.

Cartwright, D. (1954). Achieving change in people: Some applications of group dynamics theory. *Human Relations, 4*, 381–392.

Crawford, I., Jason, L. A., Riordan, N., Kaufman, J., Salina, D., Sawalski, L., Ho, F. C., & Zolik, E. (1990). A multimedia-based approach to increasing communication and the level of AIDS knowledge within families. *Journal of Community Psychology, 18*, 361–373.

Dannenberg, A. L., Gielen, A. C., Beilenson, P. L., Wilson, M. H., & Joffe, A. (1993). Bicycle helmet laws and educational campaigns: An evaluation of strategies to increase children's helmet use. *American Journal of Public Health, 83*, 667–674.

DiGiuseppi, C. G., Rivara, F. P., Koepsell, T. D., & Polissar, L. (1989). Bicycle helmet use by children. *Journal of the American Medical Association, 262*, 2256–2261.

Flay, B. R. (1981). On improving the chances of mass media health promotion programs causing meaningful changes in behavior. In M. Meyer (Ed.), *Health education by television and radio* (pp. 56–91). Munich: Saur.

Flay, B. R., & Burton, D. (1990). Effective mass communication strategies for health campaigns. In C. K. Atkin & L. Wallack (Eds.), *Mass communication and public health: Complexities and conflicts* (pp. 129–146). Newbury Park, CA: Sage.

Flynn, B. S., Worden, J. K., Secker-Walker, R. H., Badger, G. J., Geller, B. M., & Costanza, M. C. (1992). Prevention of cigarette smoking through mass media intervention and school programs. *American Journal of Public Health, 82*, 827–834.

Flynn, B. S., Worden, J. K., Secker-Walker, R. H., Pirie, P. L., Badger, G. J., Carpenter, J. H., & Geller, B. M. (1994). Mass media and school interventions for cigarette smoking prevention: Effects 2 years after completion. *American Journal of Public Health, 84*, 1148–1150.

Friel, S., Hope, A., Kelleher, C., Comer, S., & Sadlier, D. (2002). Impact evaluation of an oral health intervention amongst primary school children in Ireland. *Health Promotion International, 17*, 119–126.

Hafstad, A., & Aaro, L. E. (1997). Activating interpersonal influence through provocative appeals: Evaluation of a mass media-based antismoking campaign targeting adolescents. *Health Communication, 9*, 253–272.

Hafstad, A., Aaro, L. E., & Langmark, F. (1996). Evaluation of an antismoking mass media campaign targeting adolescents: The role of affective responses and interpersonal communication. *Health Education Research, 11*, 29–38.

Hecht, M. L., Marsiglia, F. F., Elek, E., Wagstaff, D. A., Kulis, S., Dustman, P., & Miller-Day, M. (2003). Culturally grounded substance use prevention: An evaluation of the *Keepin' it R.E.A.L.* curriculum. *Prevention Science, 4*, 233–248.

Hovland, C., Janis, I., & Kelley, H. (1953). *Communication and persuasion*. New Haven, CT: Yale University Press.

Hyman, H., & Sheatsley, P. (1947). Some reasons why information campaigns fail. *Public Opinion Quarterly, 11*, 412–423.

Katz, E. (1980). On conceptualizing media effects. *Studies in Communication, 1,* 119–141.

Katz, E., & Lazarsfeld, P. (1955). *Personal Influence.* New York: Free Press.

Klapper, J. (1960). *The effects of mass communication.* Glencoe, IL: Free Press.

Kline, F. K., Miller, P. V., & Morrison, A. J. (1974). Adolescents and family planning information: An exploration of audience needs and media effects. In J. Blumler & E. Katz (Eds.), *The uses of mass communication: Current perspectives on gratifications research* (pp. 112–136). Newbury Park, CA: Sage.

Lazarsfeld, P., Berelson, B., & Gaudet, H. (1948). *The people's choice.* New York: Columbia University Press.

Logan, R. A., & Longo, D. R., (1999). Rethinking antismoking media campaigns: Two generations of research and issues for the next. *Journal of Health Care Finance, 25*(4), 77–90.

MacArthur, C. (2003). Evaluation of Safe Kids Week 2001: Prevention of scald and burn injuries in young children. *Injury Prevention, 9,* 112–116.

Maccoby, N., & Roberts, D. (1985). Effects of mass communication. In G. Lindzey & E. Aronson (Eds.), *Handbook of social psychology* (Vol. 2, 3rd ed., pp. 183–207). New York: Random House.

McDivitt, J. A., Zimicki, S., & Hornik, R. C. (1997). Explaining the impact of a communication campaign to change vaccination knowledge and coverage in the Philippines. *Health Communications, 9*(2), 95–118.

McGuire, W. J., (1989). Theoretical foundations of campaigns. In R. E. Rice & C. K. Atkin (Eds.), *Public communication campaigns* (2nd ed., pp. 42–65). Newbury Park, CA: Sage.

McPhee, S. J., Nguyen, T., Euler, G. L., Mock, J., Wong, C., Lam, T., Nguyen, W., Nguyen, S., Huynh, M. Q., Do, S. T., & Buu, C. (2003). Successful promotion of hepatitis B vaccinations among Vietnamese-American children ages 3 to 18: Results of a controlled trial. *Pediatrics, 111,* 1278–1288.

Mendelsohn, H. (1973). Some reasons why information campaigns can succeed. *Public Opinion Quarterly, 37,* 50–61.

Murray, D. M., Prokhorov, A.V., & Harty, K. C. (1994). Effects of a statewide antismoking campaign on mass media messages and smoking beliefs. *Preventative Medicine, 23,* 54–60.

Novelli, W. (1982). You can produce effective PSAs. *Public Relations Journal, 16,* 30–32.

O'Keefe, G. J. (1985). "Taking a bite out of crime": The impact of a public relations campaign. *Communication Research, 12,* 147–178.

O'Keefe, T. (1971). The antismoking commercials: A study of television's impact on behavior. *Public Opinion Quarterly, 35,* 242–248.

Paisley, W. J. (1981). Public communication campaigns: The American experience: In R. E. Rice & W. J. Paisley (Eds.), *Public communication campaigns* (pp. 15–20). Beverly Hills, CA: Sage.

Palmer, E. (1981). Shaping persuasive messages with formative research. In R. E. Rice & W. J. Paisley (Eds.), *Public communication campaigns.* Beverly Hills, CA: Sage.

Penz, M. A., Dwyer, J. H., MacKinnon, D. P., Flay, B. R., Hansen, W. B., Wang, E. Y. I., & Johnson, C. A. (1989). A multicommunity trial for primary prevention of adolescent drug abuse. *Journal of the American Medical Association, 261,* 3259–3266.

Petty, R., & Cacioppo, J. (1981). *Attitudes and persuasion: Classic and contemporary approaches.* Dubuque, IA: Wm. C. Brown.

Pierce, J. P., Macaskill, P., & Hill, D. (1990). Long-term effectiveness of mass media led antismoking campaigns in Australia. *American Journal of Public Health, 80,* 565–569.

Pierce, J. P., Macaskill, P., Appstat, M., & Hill, D. (1990). Long-term effectiveness of mass media led Antismoking Campaigns in Australia. *American Journal of Public Health, 80*(5), 565–569.

Popham, W. J., Muthen, L. K, Potter, L. D., Duerr, J. M., Hetrick, M. A., & Johnson, M. D. (1994). Effectiveness of the California 1990–1991 tobacco education media campaign. *American Journal of Preventative Medicine, 10,* 319–326.

Popham, W. J., Potter, L. D., & Hetrick, M. A. (1994). Effectiveness of the California 1990–1991 Tobacco Education Media Campaign. *American Journal of Preventive Medicine, 10*(6), 319–326.

Rogers, E. M. (1983). *Diffusion of innovations* (3rd ed.). New York: Free Press.

Rogers, E. M., & Storey, D. (1987). Communication campaigns. In C. Berger & S. Chaffee (Eds.), *Handbook of communication science* (pp. 817–846). Newbury Park, CA: Sage.

Rouzier, P., & Alto, W. A. (1995). Evolution of a successful community bicycle helmet campaign. *Journal of the American Board of Family Practice, 8*, 283–287.

Siegel, M., & Biener, L. (2000). The impact of an antismoking media campaign on progression to established smoking: Results of a longitudinal youth study. *American Journal of Public Health, 90*, 380–386.

Sly, D. F., Hopkins, R. S., Trapido, E., & Ray, S. (2001). Influence of a counteradvertising media campaign on initiation of smoking: The Florida "truth" campaign. *American Journal of Public Health, 91*, 233–238.

Solomon, D. S. (1982). Health campaigns on television. In D. Pearl, L. Bouthilet, & J. Lazar (Eds.), *Television and behavior* (pp. 308–321). Rockville, MD: National Institute of Mental Health.

Solomon, D. S. (1984). Social marketing and community health promotion: The Stanford heart disease prevention program. In L. Frederiksen, L. Solomon, & K. Brehony (Eds.), *Marketing health behavior* (pp. 115–135). New York: Plenum.

Solomon, D. S. (1989). A social marketing perspective on communication campaigns. In R. E. Rice & C. K. Atkin (Eds.), *Public communication campaigns* (2nd ed., pp. 87–104). Newbury Park, CA: Sage.

Soumerai, S. B., Ross-Degnan, D., & Kahn, J. S., (1992). Effects of professional and media warnings about the association between apirin use in children and Reye's Syndrome. *The Milbank Quarterly, 70*, 155–182.

Sowden, A., Arblaster, L, & Stead, L. (2003). Community interventions for preventing smoking in young people. *Cochrane Database of Systematic Reviews, 1*, CD001291.

Star, S., & Hughes, H. (1950). Report on an education campaign: The Cincinnati plan for the United Nations. *American Journal of Sociology, 55*, 389–400.

Stephenson, M. T., Morgan, S. E., Lorch, E. P., Palmgreen P., Donohew, L., & Hoyle, R. H. (2001). Predictors of exposure from an anti-marijuana media campaign: Outcome research assessing sensation seeking targeting. *Health Communication, 14*, 23–43.

Wakefield, M., & Chaloupka, F. (2000). Effectiveness of comprehensive tobacco control programmes in reducing teenage smoking in the USA. *Tobacco Control, 9*, 177–186.

Wallack, L. (1981). Mass media campaigns: The odds against finding behavior change. *Health Education Quarterly, 8*, 209–260.

22

The Impact of Earvin "Magic" Johnson's HIV-Positive Announcement[*][1]

Mary K. Casey
Michigan State University

Mike Allen
University of Wisconsin–Milwaukee

Tara Emmers-Sommer
University of Arizona

Erin Sahlstein
University of Richmond

Dan DeGooyer
University of North Carolina–Greensboro

Alaina M. Winters
Amy Elisabeth Wagner
Tim Dun
University of Iowa

Americans embrace the renowned and the notorious, and many a celebrity has harvested this admiration to champion social causes, oftentimes supporting organizations concerned with disease eradication. For example, Jerry Lewis has become inextricably associated with the Muscular Dystrophy Association, and Michael J. Fox has become recognized as an advocate for Parkinson's disease. Similar to celebrity advocacy, celebrity disclosure of a disease is likely to focus attention on a particular affliction, perhaps more so than advocacy because the

[*]Drs. Allen and Emmers-Sommer received support for this research from the Central States Communication Association Federation Prize.

[1]For a more complete and thorough presentation of the results as well as additional information, an earlier version of the material in this chapter appears in Casey et al. (2003).

363

social issue has become "personal" to the celebrity, and he or she is considered a credible source on the issue, given direct experience.

Earvin "Magic" Johnson's announcement that he had tested positive for HIV in 1991 contributed to a changed image of the disease. Payne and Mercuri (1993) argued that the new image of an African American heterosexual athlete with the disease stood in stark contrast to the image of a "gay" disease. Johnson's disclosure should stimulate a change to reflect increased accuracy in personal perceptions of risk for HIV infection. Magic's story should increase the motivation of individuals to learn about the disease and increase feelings of vulnerability that should contribute to an increased desire for protection (Kalichman, 1998).

Three elements of persuasion deserve attention in considering the impact of Magic's announcement: (a) issue salience, (b) identification, and (c) the use of narrative. Each element provides a basic ingredient to understanding the influence of the announcement and the consequent impact on the knowledge, attitude, and subsequent behavior by the population. As each element transforms as a result of his public confession, public perception of HIV infection was notably changed.

AIDS (caused by HIV infection) was symbolically a disease or condition associated with homosexuals or intravenous drug users. The infection was the result of a kind of transgression of the expectations for social behavior. In addition, the disease was portrayed by images of white male patients looking like victims of starvation and abuse or neglect. The impact of these characterizations made the disease one that most of the public viewed with low salience. In a meta-analysis of fear appeals (Witte & Allen, 2000) demonstrated that a predictor of the effectiveness of any fear appeal (particularly in a public health message) is whether an audience member views the content of the message as having personal efficacy. Essentially, do audience members perceive the threat contained in the message to apply to them? Work by Pollack (Pollack, 1994; Pollack, Lilie, & Vittes, 1993) and others illustrated the power of Magic and the ethnic, social, cultural and behavioral characteristics he put forth with his messages (Flora, Schooler, Mays, & Cochran, 1996). Magic Johnson's admission of infection shortens that distance between the image of those contracting the disease and the audience member.

Kelman's (1961) conceptualization of identification posited the idea that a message from a desirable source provides a means for a person to create a positive self-image by demonstrating consistency with that source. For example, "be like Mike," represents a method for the person viewing a commercial message to demonstrate identification with Michael Jordan by purchasing a particular product. In the commercial, a model behavior and acceptance of attitudes displayed by the message source provides a means for the target to demonstrate that identification. This process takes a variety of forms and exists in various theories of persuasion such as behavioral modeling in social cognitive theory (Bandura, 1986), homophily in diffusion of innovations (Rogers, 1983), and congruity theories (Tannenbaum, 1968).

The identification process as the influential mechanism generally relies on particular endorsement of an action. Usually, the source endorses or models an action or behavior that the message receiver associates with the source. Therefore, it is important to distinguish the example of Magic Johnson's admission as a celebrity "disclosure" as opposed to a celebrity "endorsement." The effectiveness of an endorsement is probably contingent on the association with the professional or celebrity's reason for notoriety (e.g., athlete, film star, rock star, or politician) and the object of endorsement. Persona, not person, is a persuasive aspect of the endorsement (McCracken, 1989). In Johnson's case, both his persona and personal story contribute to any impact of his confession. In particular, in this case the admission becomes a warning to not perform the behaviors of the celebrity and to reject the values endorsed or enacted by the messenger.

Identification is the process via which personal salience or concern may be heightened; however, it is the narrative form that brings the "person" and his or her story to the audience (Basil & Brown, 1997). Narration or the narrative form is the fundamental structure of human communication, a structure learned in infancy and that underlies the development of seemingly more sophisticated discourse and formal argument (Fisher, 1989). Through narrative persons learn about and make sense of the world; reify history, values, and traditions; reveal attitudes and emotions; and create communities. Beck (2001) asserted that public presentations of personal narratives, such as the celebrity disclosure of a health issue, spur public dialogues that function in a number of ways to (a) establish a connection with similar others by communicating that "IT could happen to you" (p. 240) or by influencing perceived susceptibility to a disease and (b) reach out to offer assistance or support those similarly affected or to appeal for legislation, accountability, research, or preventive efforts. Beck clarified the relationship between identification and narrative as such (p. 241):

> For individuals or organizations who ultimately want to step beyond the public sharing of personal traumas or to promote some sort of awareness or prevention outreach ..., a critical mid-step involves identification, illustrating a clear connection between the stricken person/people and others and their respective behaviors, in order to construct a coherent and consistent narrative.

The process of perception represents an ongoing, emergent, and dynamic process with constant evaluation and reevaluation. For example, a recent challenge to prevention efforts has been the development of more effective antiviral treatments for HIV infection that diminish the perception that it is deadly and a terminal illness (Allen et al., 2002; Catz, Meredith, & Mundy, 2001). The key to any effect of Magic Johnson's admission lies in the combination of issue transformation and saliency, identification, and use of narrative. Whether the message generates a fundamental change in the perception of the application of the risk to self and whether the response is one that is perceived as efficacious and possible is the focus herein.

The publicity surrounding the announcement, by its very nature, set the media agenda on HIV infection and AIDS for a period of time. This spotlight on Johnson and the disease should minimally result in heightened public awareness and also a likely increase in knowledge of this disease. The effect of Johnson's announcement may not have been uniform for all possible outcomes. One expectation for knowledge acquisition is that salient knowledge gains are permanent. The long-term implication of this knowledge gain is unclear, however, in an environment of a disease such as HIV infection for which knowledge changes relatively rapidly. Learning may occur, but the knowledge may become obsolete as newer and better information emerges.

Engaging in risk-reduction behaviors or seeking out an HIV test involves a more complex set of factors that may be influenced by Johnson's disclosure. Risk reduction behaviors must be undertaken not once, but replicated on each occasion to protect against infection. For example, a risk-reducing behavior, such as using a condom during sex, requires ongoing support for the individual and reinforcement and repetition of the behavior. Permanent changes in knowledge must be reflected in permanent changes in practice for knowledge to be considered useful.

In 1991, Johnson's face was a novel one to associate with HIV/AIDS. As a professional basketball player much admired for his athletic ability, an African American, an affluent individual, and a married heterosexual, Johnson represented an individual who had achieved the "American dream" and a population of individuals who may not have previously considered themselves at risk for HIV infection. The research dealing with the impact of his disclosure provided a unique opportunity to examine the influence of a contemporary celebrity's story of contracting a disease. Our meta-analysis examines the persuasive impact, if any, of Magic Johnson's announcement.

METHODS

Literature Search Method

A full description of the method is available elsewhere (Casey et al., 2003), including a complete list of inclusions and exclusions. Essentially, the search involved examination of a variety of online indexes and examination of literature reviews and references of materials found. To be included in this review a study had to

1. Provide a means of analyzing the impact of the Magic Johnson announcement by either using awareness of Johnson's HIV status or through a pre- and posttest design.
2. Use a quantitative analysis that permitted estimation of an effect size.

3. Analyze some measure of knowledge about HIV transmission, perception of vulnerability, perception of persons testing positive, the desire to obtain more information about HIV infection, intentions to or a report of diminished risk behaviors, and/or taking an HIV test.

Potential Sources of Variability

In the literature review we considered several potential sources of variation: (a) vulnerability felt toward infection with HIV, (b) knowledge of HIV, (c) attitudes toward persons with AIDS, (d) intentions to get tested or diminish risk behaviors, (e) reports of actual diminished risk behaviors, (f) changes reported in the number of persons being tested for HIV, and (g) a desire to find out more about HIV/AIDS. The results might differ based on the particular dependent variable considered, so separate analyses are provided. Whenever sufficient demographic information (e.g., race, gender, or age) existed, these separate factors were considered in the analysis.

The impact of time is important when one considers the effect of any single event. Time of the data collection may serve as a potential moderator that could indicate the existence of an outcome that covaries with time. The impact of a celebrity announcement may be permanent for some features (such as knowledge) but generate less permanent effects for other outcomes (intentions to diminish risk behavior, number of HIV tests, and attitudes toward persons with HIV/AIDS). Once "learned," medical information about HIV would probably not be forgotten; however, actions that require constant practice (safer sex practices such as the use of a condom, diminished number of sexual partners, or regular HIV testing) may be larger immediately after the event and then diminish over time. Therefore, the length of time between the announcement and the measurement of the dependent variable was assessed.

Description of Statistical Analysis

This meta-analysis uses the variance-centered analysis procedures as outlined by Hunter and Schmidt (1990). The statistical method involves essentially four steps: (a) conversion of estimates to a common metric, (b) correction of effects for various sources of artifact and bias, (c) averaging of the available effects, and (d) assessment of variability among the estimates for the associations. This last step requires at least three studies to provide the minimum number of estimates for the test to be valuable.

The conversion to a common metric (in this case the correlation) is accomplished using standard formulas. The polarity (positive or negative) of the correlation was coded in terms of the desirability of the announcement producing a positive impact. For the dependent variables considered, the impact of the announcement should (a) increase perceptions of vulnerability, (b) increase knowledge, (c) diminish negative perceptions of persons testing positive for HIV, (d) increase intentions to diminish risky behaviors, (e) diminish risk behaviors, (f) increase the number of persons testing for HIV, and (g) generate a desire for persons to get more information about HIV. A positive correlation indicates that the outcomes were in the expected direction.

The assessment of variability is conducted using a chi-square test that compares the observed variability in the observed data to a theoretical amount of variability that would exist due to random sampling error. A significant chi-square result indicates that the level of variability is more than would be expected due to random chance and the average effect should be interpreted cautiously.

RESULTS

Type of Outcome Measured

Vulnerability to HIV Infection

Thirteen studies examined the impact of the announcement of Magic Johnson on perceptions of vulnerability to HIV infection. The average effect was essentially zero (average $r = -.017$, $k = 13$, $N = 3,460$, variance $r = .022$), but based on a heterogeneous sample of observed correlations, $\chi^2 = 76.88$ (12, $N = 3,460$), $p < .05$. The existence of heterogeneity indicates the probable existence of a moderator variable and prompted the following examination.

The sample of 13 estimates was split on the basis of age into 7 studies that included adult (older than 18) samples and 6 studies dealing with children (adolescents and younger). The 7 studies using adult samples demonstrated a positive relationship (average $r = .130$, $k = 7$, $N = 2,002$, var. $r = .001$) that was homogeneous $\chi^2 = 2.81$ (6, $N = 2,002$), $p > .05$. This finding indicates that for adults, the announcement consistently demonstrate an increased perception of vulnerability to HIV infection.

The data for adolescents and children demonstrates a different outcome. The six studies examining the effect of the announcement provide a negative association (average $r = -.120$, $k = 6$, $N = 1,458$, var. $r = .013$) based on a heterogeneous set of outcomes $\chi^2 = 19.33$ (5, $N = 1,458$), $p < .05$. The results, although requiring some caution in interpretation because of the inconsistency among effects, demonstrate a direction of average effects inconsistent with the data dealing with adults.

A comparison of the mean effect for adults and children demonstrates that the two effects are statistically different ($z = 7.23$, $p < .05$), indicating a difference between the studies that examined the effect of the Magic Johnson announcement on adults and the studies that looked at the impact on children. For adults, the announcement increased the level of vulnerability felt, whereas adolescents and children experienced a diminished sense of vulnerability to HIV infection. This should not be surprising, because one of the comments Magic provided constantly in television interviews was information about the means of transmission of the disease. Magic emphasized that behaviors children engage in (e.g., hugging or holding hands) would not transmit the virus. If this argument is true, then children should show a large increase in knowledge as a result of the announcement. Similarly, adults should show an increase in knowledge, but this increase would emphasize the vulnerability of the sexually active heterosexual (including African Americans, athletic or not) to contracting HIV infection. Essentially, accurate information for one audience would diminish anxiety, but the same message for a different audience would increase anxiety or vulnerability to the disease.

Knowledge about HIV/AIDS

Six studies examined the impact of the announcement of Magic Johnson on changes in the accuracy of knowledge about HIV. The average effect was positive (average $r = .194$, $k = 6$, $N = 1,919$, var. $r = .014$), but based on a heterogeneous sample of observed correlations, $\chi^2 = 26.62$, $(5, N = 1,919) p < .05$. Again, the significant chi-square result provides evidence for the possible existence of a moderator variable.

The impact of age on the outcomes was considered. Three of the six studies incorporated adult samples, and the average effect is positive (average $r = .144$, $k = 3$, $N = 558$, var. $r = .010$), which was significantly less than ($z = 2.71$, $p < .05$) the association demonstrated by children (average $r = .280$, $k = 3$, $N = 1,041$, var. $r = .006$). These findings indicate that whereas accuracy of the level of knowledge of HIV infection improved in adults after the announcement, the gain was less than the gain in knowledge accuracy for children and adolescents. The knowledge gain provides the connection between the issues of knowledge and vulnerability based on age. Both adults and children gain in knowledge, but the application of the knowledge to the individual differs; essentially adults interpret the knowledge as increasing the efficacy of the threat whereas for children the efficacy of the threat diminishes.

Attitudes Toward Persons with HIV/AIDS

Six studies examined the impact of the announcement on changes in participant's attitudes toward people testing positive for HIV or persons with AIDS. The average effect was positive (average $r = .092$, $k = 6$, $N = 2,767$, var. $r = .002$). The examination of variability indicates a homogenous sample of observed correlations, $\chi^2 = 4.33$, $(5, N = 2,767) p > .05$. The nonsignificant chi-square result indicates that the average across the six studies is based on a sample of effects that differ individually on the basis of sampling error. The announcement of Magic Johnson's HIV infection indicated a reduced hostility toward or an improved image of those infected with the disease. The image of the person infected with HIV changed to a less negative view.

Intention to Reduce Risk Behaviors

Two studies examined the impact of Magic Johnson's announcement on changes in the intention of a person to either reduce risk behaviors or get an HIV test. The average effect was positive (average $r = .176$, $k = 2$, $N = 484$). The existence of only two estimates prevents an examination of the variability. The limited results indicate a pattern consistent with the other findings.

Reduction of Risk Behaviors

Four studies examined the impact of the announcement of Magic Johnson on changes in the report of subsequent risk behavior (e.g., sharing needles, number of sexual partners, and unprotected sexual encounters). The average effect was positive but small (average $r = .044$, $k = 4$, $N = 1,040$, var. $r = .005$). The examination of variability indicates a homogenous sample of observed correlations, $\chi^2 = 5.21$, $(3, N = 1,040)$ $p > .05$. The nonsignificant chi-square result indicates that the average across the four studies is based on a sample of effects that differ individually on the basis of sampling error.

Number of Tests for HIV

The impact of Magic Johnson's announcement on the number of persons seeking HIV tests was examined in two studies. The average effect was positive and large (average $r = .522$, $k = 2$, $N = 2,194$). The existence of only two estimates prevents the use of an examination of the variability for a test of homogeneity. Given the small number of studies this should be interpreted with some caution; however, the effect is in the expected direction and large. These two studies demonstrate a large increase in the number of persons going to clinics for an HIV test.

Desire to Obtain More Information about HIV

Two studies examined the impact of the announcement of Magic Johnson on changes in the desire to obtain more information about the HIV virus. The average effect was positive (average $r = .171$, $k = 2$, $N = 637$). The existence of only two estimates prevents the use of an examination of the variability for a test of homogeneity. Given the small number of studies this should be interpreted with some caution; however, the effect is in the expected direction. Both effects demonstrated an increase in the desire of persons to learn more about the HIV virus.

Analysis Considering the Impact of Time

The impact of the delay of measurement was assessed for three of the dependent variables: (a) vulnerability, (b) knowledge, and (c) attitudes toward persons testing positive for HIV. The analysis considers whether the length of time after the announcement demonstrates changes in the size of the effect. A positive correlation indicates that the size of the effect is becoming larger, whereas a negative correlation indicates that the size of the effect is diminishing.

The studies dealing with vulnerability have to consider the data generated from adults and adolescents/children separately because the direction for the two estimates differ. The impact of the announcement for children/adolescents was to diminish the perception of vulnerability whereas for adults the impact of the announcement was to increase the perception of vulnerability. The adult data demonstrate a negative correlation or slope ($r = -.380$) as does the adolescent/ children data ($r = -.434$). What the two data sets indicate is that as the time from the announcement lengthens, the size of the effect diminishes. This is not surprising because the feeling of vulnerability is something that can change over time as confidence grows or wanes about the probability of becoming infected with the disease.

The data examining the impact of time on knowledge demonstrates a larger effect as the time interval after the announcement increases. Adults ($r = .257$) and children/adolescents ($r = .639$) both demonstrate positive effects for knowledge as time passes. This should not be surprising because the celebrity announcement may have created a desire to obtain more knowledge about the disease. Alternatively, the effect may also include the impact of simple maturation because, in addition to the Magic Johnson announcement, other sources of information and learning existed in the environment. The knowledge in these investigations reflects the level of understanding about the means of transmission for HIV. Once learned, one would not expect that this information would be forgotten or that the information would itself change. This finding may not generalize to other sets of knowledge that change over time or with circumstance (e.g., treatment techniques and effectiveness of treatment) or knowledge of a very technical nature.

The final dependent variable was attitudes toward person testing positive for HIV. The effect for time is negative ($r = -.422$), the original attitude of tolerance gained by the announcement shows signs of decay. The result of the announcement on this attitude is transitory rather than permanent. The decay indicates that the image of the athlete provides a temporary diversion or replacement from the dominant image. Whether repetition of the new image would prevent the decay is unknown.

DISCUSSION

The disclosure by Magic Johnson that he was now living with HIV infection contributed to some changes. The impact of a celebrity disclosure of a disease or condition remains something believed to be important. Similarly, the use of fictional programs to illustrate and educate, particularly about HIV (Svenkerud, Rao, & Rogers, 1999) provides important revelations about the image of disease. The results point to the need not simply to provide information but also to develop and create images productive in assisting public health efforts. Creating conditions for accurate dissemination of information should assist in meeting the goals of public health campaigns, and celebrity assistance may provide one means of improving effectiveness.

A limitation exists in our analysis regarding sample size for both the number of participants and the number of studies. The problem of examining a "real-world" and "real-time" set of circumstances that are unpredictable means that the number of studies are small. The impact of the various limitations has been discussed elsewhere (Hale & Dillard, 1991; O'Keefe, 1991). The fact remains that the amount of data is relatively small and limited to a single historical incident. However, the importance of single events (as demonstrated on September 11, 2001, in New York City) can generate both immediate and long-term repercussions. This historical incident, when compared with data from other events can serve to evaluate various theoretical approaches.

The results of the analysis demonstrate knowledge increases in the samples hearing the announcement. Age functioned as a moderator variable, children and adolescents learned more after the announcement than did adults (although adults demonstrate increases in knowledge). However, the knowledge gain is accompanied by a corresponding change in the perception of vulnerability to HIV infection. The valence of the changes however, is different for adults and children. Adults demonstrate increases in the perception of vulnerability while children and adolescents report a decline in the perception of vulnerability to the disease. The differentiation provides evidence that the information served different functions for two separate audiences. One audience learned material that increased the application to themselves while another audience learned information that reduced application of the disease to self.

Messages designed to weigh the impact of health threats often consider the combination of (a) severity of the threat and (b) the probability of the threat applying to the person (see Witte & Allen, 2000, for a meta-analytic summary of research on these issues). In this case, the threat of HIV/AIDS represents an outcome with severe consequences, but the receiver must determine the level of risk for contracting the virus. Within that determination the person must have an understanding of the means of transmission of infection and the degree to which the audience member believes she or he to be at risk. Knowledge about disease transmission constitutes a necessary condition for accurately understanding risk. Persons believing that only homosexuals or intravenous drug users are at risk would accept the severity of the threat but not believe that the threat applied to them (assuming they are not homosexual or intravenous drug users). The image of the disease represents a belief about the nature of the disease and the level of risk the individual faces. A celebrity with the disease or other prominent illustration of the disease may change that image and the corresponding beliefs in vulnerability.

The reaction (similar to dissonance) can, of course, be avoided if the status of the celebrity (or the action) represents something the audience can use to distance themselves from the celebrity. For example, a celebrity contracting HIV infection but also claiming to have slept with 10,000 partners would provide a means of avoidance (most persons do not have 10,000 sexual partners). Or if the celebrity has a reputation for engaging in an alternative lifestyle (consider Liberace), the necessary application to the individual can be avoided. The question is how the announcement of the celebrity is viewed as applicable to the persons hearing the disclosure. If the celebrity explains or educates about the disease (as Magic did), then improved knowledge can provide a basis for new evaluation.

The net effect of Magic's disclosure was most marked by a sharp increase in the number individuals obtaining HIV tests immediately after the announcement as well as an improved image of those persons living with HIV/AIDS. The impact of the disclosure was a kind of immediate reaction or image shifting with the corresponding behavioral and attitudinal changes. But the shock to the system of such an announcement was followed by a reassertion of the old attitudes. However, knowledge change should represent a more permanent outcome: Knowledge about the disease should not be forgotten (however, such knowledge is subject to change). The valence or emotional reaction may not be constant, and the initial reaction may change as additional information becomes available (in this case whether other celebrities are infected and the continued imagery of those persons infected with HIV). Johnson's disclosure becomes an episode in the drama and not the event as other persons become infected and represented in the media. The balance of images may simply provide for a renewal of the original attitudes.

Sexual conduct may not be subject to change, regardless of the celebrity announcement. This feature perhaps represents the most important element addressed herein. Does the long-term risk behavior for the individuals change, particularly for heterosexuals? Condom use, on a consistent and long-term basis (as well as a decreased number of sexual partners), represents the real target for prevention. Sexual behavior, even when well intentioned, is subject to a number of issues that require consideration (Allen, Emmers-Sommer, & Crowell, 2002; Bradford, Allen, Casey, & Emmers-Sommer, 2002). A central difficulty of sexual behavior change is that most sex involves at least two people and provides a forum for a kind of negotiation in which the intentions of one person must interact with the intentions of another person.

Perceptions of a disease exert more influence on relevant attitudes and behavior than the actual scientific and medical information available. Disclosure by a positively regarded public figure about an issue perceived as unfamiliar, stigmatized, and or frightening may help to personalize the issue. HIV may no longer be conceived to be about "them" but rather as about "all of us." The research led by Pollack (Pollack, 1994; Pollack et al., 1993) clearly illustrates the shift in "value-coloration" of HIV/AIDS issues given Johnson's disclosure. Magic Johnson, like Patty Duke (mental illness) and Betty Ford (alcoholism) before him, sparked public discourse, enabling individuals to communicate with others about a socially tainted, perhaps personal, issue without prohibitive embarrassment or shame. Research by Flora et al. (1996) based on McCracken's (1989) concept of meaning transfer, revealed that African-American men differed in their perceptions of Magic as a credible source on a number of messages in association with their own level of sociocultural identity. Thus, to be maximally influential, the attributes of the celebrity persona should confer desirable and consonant attributes toward the behavior advocated.

The impact of the announcement of Earvin "Magic" Johnson illustrates the potential of a celebrity to have an impact on public health discourse by revealing a diagnosis. The impact takes on relevant affective, cognitive, or behavioral forms, sometimes with long-lasting effects and other times generating outcomes that are transient. The impact of celebrities on the perception of a disease and the need to seek treatment remains an important part of public health campaigns that continues to require attention. The use of the mass media by celebrities to disclose health conditions provides a potential for effective communication that contributes to positive public health outcomes.

REFERENCES

Allen, M., Casey, M. K., Carson, E., Chopski, K., Considine, J., Donlin, M., et al. (2002, April). *Changing circumstances: The impact of marketing HIV treatment on AIDS education and prevention.* Paper presented at the Central States Communication Association Convention, Milwaukee, WI.

Allen, M., Emmers-Sommer, T., & Crowell, T. (2002). Couples negotiating safer sex behaviors: A meta-analysis of the impact of conversation and gender. In M. Allen, R. Preiss, B. Gayle, & N. Burrell (Eds.), *Interpersonal communication research: Advances through meta-analysis* (pp. 263–280). Mahwah, NJ: Lawrence Erlbaum Associates.

Bandura, A. (1986). *Social foundations of thought and action: A cognitive social theory.* Englewood Cliffs, NJ: Prentice Hall.

Basil, M., & Brown, W. (1997). Marketing AIDS prevention: The differential impact hypothesis versus identification effects. *Journal of Consumer Psychology, 6,* 389–411.

Beck, C. (2001). *Communicating for better health: A guide through the medical mazes.* Needham Heights, MA: Allyn & Bacon.

Bradford, L., Allen, M., Casey, M., & Emmers-Sommer, T. (2002). A meta-analysis examining the relationship between Latino acculturation levels and HIV/AIDS risk behaviors, condom use, and HIV/AIDS knowledge. *Journal of Intercultural Communication Research, 31,* 167–180.

Casey, M., Allen, M., Emmers-Sommer, T., Sahlstein, E., DeGooyer, D., Winters, A., et al. (2003). When a celebrity contracts a disease: The example of Earvin "Magic" Johnson's announcement that he was HIV positive. *Journal of Health Communication, 8,* 249–266.

Catz, S., Meredith, K., & Mundy, L. (2001). Women's HIV transmission risk perceptions and behaviors in the era of potent antiretroviral therapies. *AIDS Education and Prevention, 13,* 239–251.

Fisher, W. (1989). *Human communication as narration: Towards a philosophy of reason, value, and action.* Columbia, SC: University of South Carolina Press.

Flora, J., Schooler, C., Mays, V., & Cochran, S. (1996). Exploring a model of symbolic social communication: The case of 'Magic' Johnson. *Journal of Health Psychology, 1,* 353–366.

Hale, J., & Dillard, J. (1991). The uses of meta-analysis: Making knowledge claims and setting research agendas. *Communication Monographs, 58,* 463–471.

Hunter, J., & Schmidt, F. (1990). *Methods of meta-analysis: Correcting for artifact and bias in research findings*. Thousand Oaks, CA: Sage.

Kalichman, S. (1998). *Preventing AIDS: A sourcebook for behavioral intentions*. Mahwah, NJ: Lawrence Erlbaum Associates.

Kelman, H. (1961). Processes of opinion change. *Public Opinion Quarterly, 25*, 57–78.

McCracken, G. (1989). Who is the celebrity endorser? Cultural foundation of the endorsement process. *Journal of Consumer Research, 16*, 310–321.

O'Keefe, D. (1991). Extracting dependable generalizations form the persuasion effects literature: Some issues in meta-analytic reviews. *Communication Monographs, 58*, 471–481.

Payne, J., & Mercuri, K. (1993). Crisis in communication: Coverage of Magic Johnson's AIDS disclosure. In S. Ratzan (Ed.), *AIDS: Effective communication for the 90s* (pp. 151–172). Washington, DC: Taylor & Francis.

Pollack, P. (1994). Issues, values, and critical moments: Did 'Magic' Johnson transform public opinion on AIDS? *American Journal of Political Science, 38*, 426–446.

Pollack, P., Lilie, S., & Vittes, M. E. (1993). On the nature and dynamics of social construction: The case of AIDS. *Social Science Quarterly, 74*(1),123–135.

Rogers, E. (1983). *Diffusion of innovations* (3rd ed.). New York: Free Press.

Svenkerud, P., Rao, N., & Rogers, E. (1999). Mass media effects through interpersonal communication: The role of "Twende na Wakati" on adoption of HIV/AIDS prevention in Tanzania. In W. Elwood (Ed.), *Power in the blood: A handbook on AIDS, politics, and communication* (pp. 243–256). Mahwah, NJ: Lawrence Erlbaum Associates.

Tannenbaum, P. (1968). The congruity principle: Retrospective reflections and recent research. In R. Abelson, E. Aronson, W. McGuire, T. Newcomb, M. Rosenberg, & P. Tannenbaum (Eds.), *Theories of cognitive consistency: A sourcebook* (pp. 52–71). Chicago: Rand McNally.

Witte, K., & Allen, M. (2000). A meta-analysis of fear appeals: Implications for effective health campaigns. *Health Education & Behavior, 27*, 591–615.

23

Media Use and
Political Involvement

Barry A. Hollander
University of Georgia

> The democratic citizen is supposed to be interested in public affairs, but even during a presidential campaign—presumably the high point of political intensity—not every citizen is interested.
>
> *—Berelson, Lazarsfeld, & McPhee* (1954, p. 24)

This classic quote describes the 1948 presidential election but applies just as well to today's electorate. The most dramatic of U.S. political events, the presidential campaign, draws relatively little interest until the final months and that interest, as indicated by public opinion polls and voter turnout, falls short of what some theorists suggest is necessary for a healthy democracy. For most people, contact with the political world comes from the mass media, traditionally mainstream sources such as newspapers, television, radio, and magazines, and a large number of studies have attempted to explore the link between exposure to these sources of information and the involvement people have with public officials and the major political institutions. This is not a trivial question, for involvement in its many forms can have dramatic effects on whether and how people think about politics and its actors. In studies of persuasion, for example, involvement affects not only whether attitude change takes place but how and when the process takes place. Indeed, the dominant models within social psychology view involvement or personal relevance as a cornerstone in how or whether people deal with new information and communication. Other fields and traditions treat involvement differently. Political scientists tend to use involvement as a control variable, something to be held constant through multivariate techniques to test the influence of large sets of independent variables on their dependent variables of interest. Depending on their training, mass communication scholars often follow one of the two approaches discussed earlier. However, unlike the political science and social psychology traditions, mass communication scholars investigate the impact of media use on political involvement, hoping to discover what role the media play in how people view the political world.

In this chapter we focuses on these concepts—political involvement and media use—two broad terms rife with conceptual and methodological difficulties. Involvement has a number of theoretical cousins: relevance, interest, knowledge, expertise, and sophistication to name a few. These terms appear to tap the same concept regardless of the academic discipline, generally suggesting that an attitudinal object can be of varying personal relevance to different individuals and that this degree of relevance can have dramatic effects on how people attend to, process, and incorporate messages into their beliefs or opinions. Media use, although lacking the academic pedigree of involvement, also provides a wide range of related concepts and scholarly disagreements over important questions such as what the concept truly means and the best way to measure it. Further discussion of both follow, but it is important to note here that in any review of political involvement and media use researchers must make difficult choices as to which concepts best apply and should be pursued when considering which studies to use in a meta-analysis.

THE PROBLEM OF INVOLVEMENT

It is difficult to imagine a political concept broader than *involvement*. Ripe with meaning in cognitive, affective, and behavioral terms, use of the concept fluctuates, depending on the theoretical and methodological preference. For those working from a social psychological perspective, specifically in studies of persuasion, involvement is best summed up as personal relevance, although as we will see later even this simple definition has come under intense criticism by some researchers. To say that someone is "involved" with an issue or object means that the person sees it as bearing directly on his or her life. Even in this psychological perspective, which has strongly influenced the meaning of involvement in other fields such as mass communication and political science, ample disagreement exists on how to conceptualize and operationalize the construct. A brief list, for example, includes ego involvement (Sherif, 1980; Sherif & Hovland, 1961), issue involvement (Kiesler, Collins, & Miller, 1969), and personal involvement (Apsler & Sears, 1968), all variables with subtle but, to some, very real differences.

The social judgment theory studies of Sherif and Hovland (1961) are perhaps the earliest and clearest attempt to explicate involvement, again primarily from an attitude change-persuasion paradigm. In this perspective, individuals are high in involvement when an issue has intrinsic importance or significant consequences in their own lives (Apsler & Sears, 1968). This avenue of research resulted in the well-known *latitudes of rejection* and *latitudes of acceptance* studies. Sherif and Sherif (1967) argued that involvement would cause people to be less susceptible to persuasive messages and that involvement would interact in important ways with other key variables, an observation later to come under attack by cognitive response models of persuasion.

The modern debate focuses on message involvement, the relationship between the individual and some form of communication. At odds are those who prefer a single, parsimonious definition of involvement that attempts to capture most types of involvement under one tent versus those who argue that involvement is best understood by viewing it in three different ways. For Petty and Cacioppo (1990), involvement is best understood as to whether a message is "important to the self" (p. 368). This seemingly straightforward definition was in response to Johnson and Eagly's (1989) meta-analysis of the effects of involvement on persuasion, a study challenging the single definition and one in which they propose that scholars distinguish among three types of involvement. *Outcome-relevant involvement* would incorporate what is typically considered personal relevance or issue involvement. Of the three, this one best sums up the type of involvement most explored by mass communication scholars. *Value-relevant involvement* refers to a psychological state that is generated in ego-involved situations or value-expressive goals (Katz, 1960). Finally, *impression-relevant involvement,* which is similar to the "response involvement" work of Leippe and Elkin (1987) and others, has to do with objectives designed to please potential evaluators. Although this continuing debate goes beyond the scope of this chapter, it raises a cautionary flag about the disagreement over exactly what constitutes involvement and whether the term is too broad, as Johnson and Eagly (1989) suggest, or the most useful concept presently available (Petty and Cacioppo, 1990).

Cognitive response models of persuasion, which have dominated the attitude change field for some two decades, conceptualize involvement as a factor in the likelihood to engage in issue-relevant thinking. The greater the involvement, the greater is the likelihood that a receiver will be motivated to engage in thoughtful consideration of some message, which in turn may lead to persuasion or counter-arguing against the message. This basic tenet of models such as the elaboration likelihood model (Petty & Cacioppo, 1979a, 1979b, see also 1981) generally manipulated involvement in laboratory settings to explore its relationship with cognitive responses to a persuasive message. These approaches also differ greatly from the social judgment theory approach to involvement in that the modern models allow for persuasion even among those with high involvement with the message topic.

These models of persuasion hold that both ability and motivation must be present for respondents to engage in extensive elaboration. A long series of studies support this view (Petty & Cacioppo, 1979b, 1981, 1984; Petty, Cacioppo, & Goldman, 1981). The elaboration of information relevant to the message does not necessarily that mean persuasion has taken place. Indeed, in high-involvement circumstances, it is more likely that no persuasion takes place, that those who find some topic to be of high personal relevance will counterargue by drawing on their own knowledge or interest in the topic. The Petty et al., (1981) study is a prototype of this perspective in which respondents in a high-involvement group were more convinced by high-quality arguments (the central route to persuasion) whereas respondents in a low-involvement group were more persuaded by the perceived expertise of the source (the peripheral route to persuasion).

Political involvement appears, on the surface, to be more specific and thus simpler. However, relevance is too confining, and a brief examination of the literature quickly reveals that in the political sphere the range of related terms expands rather than contracts. How broad is political involvement? Perhaps Zaller (1992) extended the concept to its limit by suggesting that *awareness* is a more useful construct, one that "denotes intellectual or cognitive engagement with public affairs" (p. 21). Certainly this definition touches on the relevance the political world has for an individual and smacks of the cognitive response approach to involvement having a powerful influence on how people think about an issue. Zaller (1992) noted that a wide assortment of similar concepts are available, ranging from political expertise to political involvement. Choices of these terms may have to do with taste or disciplinary tradition, he notes, and indeed this is often the case. Political scientists generally prefer political interest, primarily because of its availability in data sets such as the National Election Study. Zaller's awareness captured, in his terms, "what has actually gotten into people's minds, which, in turn, is critical for intellectual engagement with politics" (p. 21). This approach places strong emphasis on political knowledge, which he argued is a influential tool in demonstrating an individual's interest and involvement in the political sphere.

MEDIA USE

Media use is not as broad as involvement, yet conceptual difficulties do exist. *Media use* is a two-pronged problem. *Media* in the mass communication tradition often involves pitting various forms of communication against each other in an intramural squabble to see which concept best predicts or is most strongly associated with some dependent variable. Television news use and newspaper use have long competed in this scholarly battle for supremacy, although the use of radio, magazines, and, of late, so-called new media such as talk radio and the Internet make occasional appearances. These new media do not have enough of a scholarly track record with which to conduct a meta-analysis and are therefore excluded from further discussion.

Whereas *media* is a fairly simple term to deal with, *use* provides a whole new set of challenges. Exactly what does *use* mean? Here the vagaries of conceptualization often become intertwined with the vagaries and the necessities of operationalization. In the majority of early studies and even today, *use* simply means exposure—most often measured by asking respondents how many times, usually during a week, they made use of a specific medium. Early studies generally supported newspaper exposure's superiority over other media, particularly television news, leading some scholars to suggest that television news impedes political learning (Clarke & Fredin, 1978).

However, in the 1980s a number of alternatives began to emerge, some of them offered on conceptual grounds and others brought forth due to methodological variations in question wording or in the secondary analysis of other data. One well-known example is *attention* versus *exposure* to television. Scholars questioned whether exposure to television news, which can often be haphazard and inadvertent, was a powerful enough variable to capture the way in which many people view such programming. Indeed, attention to television news has been found to account for substantially more variation in various studies compared with the effects of simple exposure (Chaffee & Schleuder, 1986; McLeod & McDonald, 1985; Semetko, Brzinski, Weaver & Wilnat, 1992), although other studies have uncovered few if any differences between the two concepts (Weaver & Drew, 1993; Chaffee, Zhao, & Leshner, 1994).

Other concepts that have received varying degrees of scholarly attention include reliance (McLeod, Glynn, & McDonald, 1983) and dependence (Miller & Reese, 1982; McLeod & McDonald, 1985). This is an interesting attack on the problem, an approach that seems to have its roots in viewing the media as one would a drug that one comes to "rely" or "depend" on. These two concepts share in common the notion that people vary in the extent to which they rely or depend on that medium for some purpose and that, to a certain extent, these media will have differing effects on those people most reliant or dependent on them. In other words, the more you need a medium, the greater its influence.

After enjoying a brief burst of popularity in the late 1970s and 1980s, the work on reliance and dependence dwindled, and most scholars returned to exposure or, in fewer instances, a consideration of attention as alternate concepts. Reliance, dependence, and related concepts seem to have fallen from favor for a number of reasons. First, there was little agreement among scholars studying in this area about which of the concepts was superior, the result being a host of similar sounding studies that differed only in which term was used. Second, the various concepts never gained acceptance outside the small circle of mass communication scholars working in this area, and the concepts died from a lack of academic attention. For example, the National Election Study, the dominant data collection tool for political scientists, continued to measure media exposure and, later, media attention, but never accepted or tested such alternatives as reliance. Finally, the handful of scholars devoted to these alternative measures soon found other avenues of research. Without their attention and academic production, interest in reliance and dependence soon disappeared.

METHODOLOGY

Because the traditional approach to studying media use is to explore differences based on the medium, newspapers and television news are separated for study as the two primary sources of information and of scholarly research. As discussed earlier, media use variables generally fall into one of two categories: exposure versus some measure of attention, reliance, or dependence. Therefore, four meta-analyses are conducted in the following: newspaper exposure, television news exposure, newspaper attention, and television news attention. Studies that use reliance, dependence, attention, or some measure other than mere exposure to a medium are collapsed for the sake of simplicity.

Only published studies were considered for the analysis. The literature search was conducted in two ways. First, a computer-based search of *Current Contents,* PsycINFO, and SocioAbs was used to find the mention of any of the key terms and those with similar conceptual meaning in the titles or abstracts. In addition, major journals such as *Journalism and Mass Communication Quarterly* and *Communication Research* were reviewed for any studies that may have been missed due to the keyword search. Studies included in the analysis pool were checked for references that may include useful studies missed in the two previous methods. Thus, a search was conducted for involvement and its various possible synonyms in the literature: interest, relevance, and the like. The same was conducted for media use but, in this case, individual media as well as the conceptual differences of exposure, attention, reliance, and the like were sought. To meet the criteria for inclusion, a published article had to

1. Include media use (exposure, attention, reliance, etc.) and political involvement (interest, relevance, etc.) as part of the overall study.
2. Analyze the association between media use and political involvement. Manuscripts that did not include a test of the relationship between these two concepts were excluded from further analysis.
3. Include the necessary bivariate statistical details to permit a meta-analysis estimate of the association between the two key concepts. Manuscripts that survived the first two steps but did not meet the third step were excluded from further analysis.

ANALYSIS

A broad number of studies survived the first two stages of seeking work that includes both some measure of political involvement and media use. However, a large number of these studies relied on multivariate analyses and did not include in footnotes or some other form the bivariate relationships among the key concepts. Indeed, one of the early criticisms of studies pitting newspaper exposure against television news exposure was a reliance on bivariate analysis without controlling for important demographic factors such as education. This well-founded criticism also resulted in many studies relying on multiple regression but without also reporting the raw zero-order Pearson correlations, a failure that seriously impairs a meta-analysis.

Nonetheless, 18 studies survived the three stages discussed previously and are included in the analysis in this chapter. Table 23.1 provides a brief description of the studies. As Table 23.2 shows, the mean correlations with involvement are strongest for newspaper exposure (.33) and newspaper attention (.22) and weakest for television news exposure (.13) and television news attention ($-.05$). However, this frequency-weighted correlation can give greater weight to studies with larger sample sizes compared with studies with small sample sizes, so additional analysis is required. By adjusting the analysis with the sample error variance and then determining a 95% confidence interval for the mean correlations, the result is a clear picture of newspaper use being much more strongly associated with political involvement whereas television news use enjoys a weaker relationship.

The correlation for newspaper exposure of .33 has a 95% confidence interval of .07, meaning it could range from .26 to .40. Attention to newspapers (.22) has the same .07 confidence interval and therefore a range of .15 to .29. Television news exposure (.13) has a .08 confidence interval and thus ranges from .05 to .21 while attention to television news ($-.05$) has a .07 confidence interval and could range from $-.12$ to .02. Taken together, the studies support the generally accepted wisdom that television news use is weakly associated to political involvement compared with the relationship between newspaper use and involvement.

MULTIVARIATE STUDIES

Whereas our meta-analyses reinforce the generally accepted wisdom concerning use of newspapers versus use of television news, the truth is more complex. Unfortunately, a large number of studies did not qualify for the analyses in this chapter because they failed to provide bivariate tests of the relationships between involvement and media. Without controls for important demographic characteristics such as education or socioeconomic status, we cannot be sure that the bivariate results are indeed valid or instead are due to the influences of underlying demographic

TABLE 23.1

Summary and Descriptive Information for Studies Included in the Analysis

Atkin, Galloway, & Nayman, 1976. A secondary analysis of a national survey of 846 respondents found that exposure to newspapers, magazines, television news, and radio news are all significantly associated with both political interest and political knowledge.

Becker & Dunwoody, 1982. A survey of 550 Columbus, Ohio, respondents revealed that newspaper and radio exposure were both positively associated with candidate knowledge whereas television news exposure was unrelated to such knowledge.

Becker, Sobowale, & Casey, 1979. A survey of 460 Syracuse, New York, adults found that knowledge of city public affairs was positively associated with newspaper dependency but was negatively associated with television news dependency.

Choi & Becker, 1987. A panel survey of 170 potential voters during the 1982 Iowa gubernatorial campaign found newspaper exposure to be positively associated with information motivation and television exposure to be unrelated to information motivation.

Culbertson & Stempel, 1986. A survey of 450 Ohioans during that state's 1983 election found that newspaper exposure was positively associated with the number of arguments respondents could produce about the campaign whereas television exposure was unrelated to such an ability to generate thoughts. Newspaper reliance was unrelated to argument production whereas television reliance was negatively associated with it. Finally, both focused newspaper reading and television news viewing (similar to attention) were positively associated with argument production.

Faber, Tims, & Schmitt, 1993. Two hundred and eighty-six Minnesota voters were surveyed with analysis revealing that newspaper attention and television news attention are positively associated with political involvement.

Fiske, Lau, & Smith, 1990. A survey of 232 Pittsburgh-area voters over a 1-year period found that print media use (largely newspaper) was positively associated with political knowledge whereas electronic media use (largely television news) was negatively associated with political knowledge.

Gandy & Waylly, 1985. A survey of 218 Washington, DC, metropolitan area respondents found that political knowledge was positively associated with both newspaper and magazine exposure but unrelated to television news exposure.

Hofstetter, Zukin, & Buss, 1978. A national survey of 1,034 respondents during the 1972 campaign found that newspaper exposure and television news exposure both were positively associated with political involvement.

Hollander, 1995. A secondary analysis of data drawn from a 1992 survey of 844 respondents to a North Carolina survey showed that campaign knowledge was positively related to newspaper exposure and television news exposure.

Jackson-Beeck, 1979. A panel study of 191 6th, 7th, and 8th grade students at a suburban public middle school found that newspaper exposure was positively associated with political interest but that television news exposure was negatively associated with such interest.

Kennamer, 1987. A telephone survey of 388 respondents in the Richmond, Virginia., area found both newspaper and television news attention to be positively related to political interest.

Kennamer, 1990. Telephone survey of 500 respondents of the Richmond, Virginia, area during the 1988 campaign found campaign cognition was positively associated with both newspaper and television news exposure.

Kent & Rush, 1976. Three groups of older citizens in the Gainesville, Florida, area were surveyed in 1974. Analysis of the approximately 140 responses showed that public affairs knowledge was positively associated with newspaper exposure and magazine exposure but was unrelated to television news and radio news exposure.

(Continued)

TABLE 23.1 (Continued)
Summary and Descriptive Information for Studies Included in the Analysis

Martinelli & Chaffee, 1995. A mail survey with approximately 200 respondents who had recently become naturalized in the United States central California region found that knowledge of the candidates was positively associated with newspaper exposure, newspaper attention, and television news attention but was unrelated to television news exposure.

Miller & Reese, 1982. Secondary analysis of data from a 1976 national survey with 2,402 respondents found newspaper exposure and reliance to be positively associated with an index of several political factors. Television exposure was positively associated and television reliance negatively associated with the same index.

Pettey, 1988. Telephone interviews with 737 adults in Dane County, Wisconsin., during the 1984 presidential campaign found that newspaper exposure was positively associated with political knowledge while television exposure was negatively associated with such knowledge.

Tan & Vaughn, 1976. A survey of 61 African-Americans in a Texas city found that public affairs knowledge was positively related to both newspaper and magazine exposure but was unrelated to television news exposure.

factors. This makes a brief review of studies that include such multivariate tests a useful exercise.

Most multivariate studies, however, do not treat political involvement in its many forms as a dependent variable. One exception is public affairs knowledge, viewed here as a cognitive measure of involvement. The results are mixed. For example, a series of studies showed that many of the differences between the explanatory power of television news use variables and newspaper use variables disappear (Weaver & Drew, 1995, Drew & Weaver, 1991). The 1995 study is particularly illuminating because it uses political interest as the dependent variable. After a host of demographic controls and the entry of a wide range of media variables, only television news attention and radio news attention retain statistical significance. Although the large number of media variables may cause some problems in the regression analysis, the results suggest that with controls television news attention can outperform either exposure or attention to newspapers in predicting political interest. Researchers utilizing multivariate techniques have found support for no significant difference between use of the two media (i.e., Atkin, Galloway, & Nayman, 1976), whereas others point to a continuing difference even after demographic controls are utilized (Kennamer, 1987, 1990; Pettey, 1988; Martinelli & Chaffee, 1995).

CONCLUSIONS AND DISCUSSION

Meta-analysis of 18 studies that include some bivariate test of the relationship between newspaper or television news use and political involvement supports the general wisdom that newspaper use is superior to television news in terms of

TABLE 23.2

Correlations of Media Use and Political Involvement

		Newspaper		Television News	
Study Authors	N	Exposure	Attention[a]	Exposure	Attention[a]
Atkin, Galloway, & Nayman, 1976	846	.41		.36	
Becker & Dunwoody, 1982	550	.22		.03	
Becker, Sobowale, & Casey, 1979	460		.20		−.19
Choi & Becker, 1987	170	.21		−.03	
Culbertson & Stempel, 1986	450	.26	.07	.05	−.23
Faber, Tims, & Schmitt, 1993	286		.46		.25
Fiske, Lau, & Smith, 1990	232	.52		−.21	
Gandy & Waylly, 1985	218	.26		.05	
Hofstetter, Zukin, & Buss, 1978	1,034	.30		.12	
Hollander, 1995	844	.14		.08	
Jackson-Beeck, 1979	191	.14		−.28	
Kennamer, 1987	500	.32		.25	
Kennamer, 1990	388		.55		.52
Kent & Rush, 1976	144	.37		.02	
Martinelli & Chaffee, 1995	200	.24	.36	.02	.33
Miller & Reese, 1982	2,402	.48	.15	.27	−.15
Pettey, 1988	737	.23		−.17	
Tan & Vaughn, 1976	61	.34		.05	
Mean correlation		.33	.22	.13	−.05

[a]For the sake of simplicity, reliance and dependence are considered the same as attention in the analyses above.

Note. Entries are zero-order correlation coefficients. Studies differed in the type of media use variable used, so some cells are blank. Motivation-based involvement (political interest, involvement, etc.) and cognitive-based involvement (political knowledge) are collapsed into a single involvement measure here.

association with political involvement. This is hardly surprising because these studies rely solely on bivariate tests of association. However, even a brief review of multivariate tests demonstrates that in many cases this finding retains significance even after controlling for powerful predictors of involvement such as education and income.

Rather than focusing on the differences between newspaper and television news use in relation to political involvement, we should perhaps consider the relatively weak overall associations between media use and involvement, particularly because the media act as the primary provider of political information for most people. These weak associations become even more interesting when one considers that some scholars perceive media use as simply another measure of involvement itself. A number of factors may be at work here. For example, the media may be poor transmitters of information and the content does little to actually inform or motivate users to care about public affairs. Political involvement as measured by political interest seems to be in decline as scholars turn to behavioral measures, such as participation in voting or nonvoting political activities or in affective attachments to candidates and political institutions, so it may be that any media relationship will remain a weak one.

Studies included in the analyses in this chapter and published before 1985 differ little from those published after 1985 in terms of the relationship between newspaper exposure and political involvement. However, for television news exposure, the more recent studies reveal a much stronger negative relationship between use of that medium and involvement. Although this finding may be an artifact of the individual studies, it also suggests that the growing reliance on electronic news may be associated with the general downward trend in overall political interest among the public or that the two are moving hand-in-hand as the public becomes disenchanted with the political process.

Is low involvement itself necessarily a bad thing? Again we return to *Voting,* the classic publication in politics by Berelson et al. (1954):

> How could a mass democracy work if all the people were deeply involved in politics? Lack of interest by some people is not without its benefits, too. True, the highly interested voters vote more, and know more about the campaign, and read and listen more, and participate more; however, they are also less open to persuasion and less likely to change. Extreme interest goes with extreme partisanship and might culminate in rigid fanaticism that could destroy democratic processes if generalized throughout the community. Low affect toward the election—not caring much—underlies the resolution of many political problems.... (p. 314)

If low-involvement individuals did not participate in the ultimate of political acts, participation at the ballot box, then the earlier observation might be more comforting. However, persuasion research suggests that involvement holds a key place in not just whether persuasion takes place but also in what kinds of methods will be the most effective. Among the less involved, peripheral cues such as source expertise and likeability can have enormous impact. The generally weak relationship between media use and political involvement, particularly between television news use and involvement, suggest that such cues will have even greater impact in the future.

Another related aspect of the media not discussed previously is the so-called new media such as talk radio, which although not a new medium has taken on a new and powerful political role, and the Internet, which includes thousands of discussion groups and the World Wide Web. Relatively few studies have been conducted so far, far too few for meta-analysis, and yet there is some suggestion that the use of these media have a greater mobilizing impact on users (see, for example, Hollander, 1997). The format of media presentations combined with the political self-efficacy of users may play an important role in their involvement with the political process. For average users, public affairs information is relatively uninvolving, especially as presented by mainstream news organizations striving for balance and fairness and following standard journalistic practices. With new media such as talk radio and sites on the World Wide Web often an obligation to follow these traditions is not felt, and, indeed, they are often scoffed at, and yet there seems to be a stronger relationship emerging between use of these new media and political involvement. More research must be conducted, obviously, but the style of presentation combined with how much of an impact users believe they have on the political process may shed light on the relationships seen previously between television news and newspaper use and on the changes now occurring with the new media.

REFERENCES

Apsler, R., & Sears, D. O. (1968). Warning, personal involvement, and attitude change. *Journal of Personality and Social Psychology, 9,* 162–166.

Atkin, C. K., Galloway, J., & Nayman, O. B. (1976). News media exposure, political knowledge and campaign interest. *Journalism Quarterly, 53,* 231–237.

Becker, L. B., & Dunwoody, S. (1982). Media use, public affairs knowledge and voting in a local election. *Journalism Quarterly, 59,* 212–218.

Becker, L. B., Sobowale, I. A., & Casey, W. E. (1979). Newspaper and television dependencies: Effects on evaluations of public officials. *Journal of Broadcasting, 23,* 465–473.

Berelson, B. R., Lazarsfeld, P. F., & McPhee, W. N. (1954). *Voting.* Chicago: University of Chicago Press.

Chaffee, S. H., & Schleuder, J. (1986). Measurement and effects of attention to media news. *Communication Research, 13,* 76–107.

Chaffee, S. H., Zhao, X., & Leshner, G. (1994). Political knowledge and the campaign media of 1992. *Communication Research, 21,* 305–324.

Choi, H. C., & Becker, S. L. (1987). Media use, issue/image discriminations, and voting. *Communication Research, 14,* 267–291.

Culbertson, H. M. & Stempel, G. H. (1986). How media use and reliance affect knowledge level. *Communication Research, 13,* 579–602.

Clarke, P., & Fredin, E. (1978). Newspapers, television and political reasoning. *Public Opinion Quarterly, 42,* 143–160.

Drew, D., & Weaver, D. (1991). Voter learning in the 1988 presidential election: Did the debates and the media matter? *Journalism Quarterly, 68,* 27–37.

Faber, R. J., Tims, A. R., & Schmitt, K. G. (1993). Negative political advertising and voting intent: The role of involvement and alternative information sources. *Journal of Advertising, 22,* 67–76.

Fiske, S. T., Lau, R. R., & Smith, R. A. (1990). On the varieties and utilities of political expertise. *Social Cognition, 8,* 31–48.

Gandy, O. H., & Waylly, M. E. (1985). The knowledge gap and foreign affairs: The Palestinian-Israeli conflict. *Journalism Quarterly, 62,* 777–782.

Hofstetter, C. R., Zukin, C., & Buss, T. F. (1978). Political imagery and information in an age of television. *Journalism Quarterly, 55,* 562–569.

Hollander, B. A. (1995). The new news and the 1992 presidential campaign: Perceived vs. actual campaign knowledge. *Journalism and Mass Communication Quarterly, 72,* 786–798.

Hollander, B. A. (1997). Fuel to the fire: Talk radio and the Gamson hypothesis. *Political Communication, 14*, 355–370.

Jackson-Beeck, M. (1979). Interpersonal and mass communication in children's political socialization. *Journalism Quarterly, 56*, 48–53.

Johnson, B., & Eagly, A. H. (1989). Effects of involvement on persuasion: A meta-analysis. *Psychological Bulletin, 106*, 290–314.

Katz, D. (1960). The functional approach to the study of attitudes. *Public Opinion Quarterly, 24*, 163–204.

Kennamer, J. D. (1987). How media use during campaign affects the intent to vote. *Journalism Quarterly, 64*, 291–300.

Kennamer, J. D. (1990). Political discussion and cognition: A 1988 look. *Journalism Quarterly, 67*, 348–352.

Kent, K. E., & Rush, R. R. (1976). How communication behavior of older persons affects their public affairs knowledge. *Journalism Quarterly, 53*, 40–46.

Kiesler, C. A., Collins, B. E., & Miller, N. (1969). *Attitude change: A critical analysis of theoretical approaches*. New York: Wiley.

Leippe, M. R., & Elkin, R. A. (1987). When motives clash: Issue involvement and response involvement as determinants of persuasion. *Journal of Personality and Social Psychology, 52*, 269–278.

Martinelli, K. A., & Chaffee, S. H. (1995). Measuring new-voter learning via three channels of political information. *Journalism and Mass Communication Quarterly, 72*, 18–32.

McLeod, J., & McDonald, D. (1985). Beyond simple exposure: Media orientations and their impact on political processes. *Communication Research, 12*, 3–34.

McLeod, J. M., Glynn, C. J., & McDonald, D. G. (1983). Issues and images: The influence of media reliance in voting decisions. *Communication Research, 10*, 37–58.

Miller, M. M., & Reese, S. D. (1982). Media dependency as interaction: Effects of exposure and reliance on political activity and efficacy. *Communication Research, 9*, 227–248.

Pettey, G. R. (1988). The interaction of the individual's social environment, attention and interest, and public affairs media use on political knowledge holding. *Communication Research, 15*, 265–281.

Petty, R. E., & Cacioppo, J. T. (1984). The effects of involvement on responses to argument quantity and quality: Central and peripheral routes to persuasion. *Journal of Personality and Social Psychology, 46*, 69–81.

Petty, R. E., & Cacioppo, J. T. (1979a). Effects of forewarning of persuasive intent and involvement on cognitive responses and persuasion. *Personality and Social Psychology Bulletin, 5*, 173–176.

Petty, R. E., & Cacioppo, J. T. (1979b). Issue involvement can increase or decrease persuasion by enhancing message-relevant cognitive responses. *Journal of Personality and Social Psychology, 37*, 1915–1926.

Petty, R. E., & Cacioppo, J. T. (1990). Involvement and persuasion: Tradition versus integration. *Psychological Bulletin, 107*, 367–374.

Petty, R. E., & Cacioppo, J. T. (1981). *Attitudes and persuasion: Classic and contemporary approaches*. Dubuque, IA: Brown.

Petty, R. E., Cacioppo, J. T., & Goldman, R. (1981). Personal involvement as a determinant of alignment-based persuasion. *Journal of Personality and Social Psychology, 41*, 847–855.

Semetko, H. A., Brzinski, J. B., Weaver, D., & Wilnat, L. (1992). TV news and U.S. public opinion about foreign countries: The impact of exposure and attention. *International Journal of Public Opinion Research, 4*, 20–36.

Sherif, C. W. (1980). Social values, attitudes, and involvement of the self. In M. M. Page (Ed.), *Nebraska Symposium on Motivation 1979: Beliefs, attitudes, and values* (pp. 1–64). Lincoln: University of Nebraska Press.

Sherif, M., & Hovland, C. I. (1961). *Social judgment: Assimilation and contrast effects in communication and attitude change*. New Haven, CT: Yale University Press.

Sheriff, M., & Sherif, C. W. (1967). Attitude as the individual's own categories: The social judgment-involvement approach to attitude and attitude change. In C. W. Sherif & M. Sherif (Eds.), *Attitude, ego-involvement, and change* (pp. 105–139). New York: Wiley.

Tan. A., & Vaughn, P. (1976). Mass media exposure, public affairs knowledge, and black militancy. *Journalism Quarterly, 53,* 271–279.

Weaver, D., & Drew, D. (1993). Voter learning in the 1990 off-year election: Did the media matter? *Journalism Quarterly, 70,* 356–368.

Weaver, D., & Drew, D. (1995). Voter learning in the 1992 presidential election: Did the "nontraditional" media and debates matter? *Journalism and Mass Communication Quarterly, 72,* 7–17.

Zaller, J. (1992). *The Nature and Origins of Mass Opinion.* Cambridge: Cambridge University Press.

24

Mass Media and Voter Turnout

Dorina Miron
Jennings Bryant
University of Alabama

The purpose of this chapter is to synthesize research on the relationship between mass media and voter turnout. To identify the research relevant to the topic, we consulted the following databases:

ABC Political Science on Disc, 1984–1997
America: History and Life, 1982–1997
Dissertation Abstracts International, 1994–1997
ERIC, 1966–Present
PsycINFO Database, 1967–Present
PsycINFO Bookchapters, 1987–1997
Expanded Academic ASAP, 1995–1997
Expanded Academic Index Backfile, 1980–1994

After this bibliographical search, we also resorted to authors' references to provide a more comprehensive coverage of the topic.

In this study we reviewed 40 research reports presented in various formats: 4 books, 3 book chapters, 1 governmental study, 1 dissertation, and 31 articles that have undergone peer review.

From these materials we extracted key information relative to the variables employed; theories and concepts tested; methods, samples, and statistical procedures utilized; and the relevant findings. This information is summarized in the Appendix to this chapter available from the authors.

CONCEPTUALIZATIONS AND OVERVIEW

Voting is a major form of political participation in a democracy. Because only approximately one in three Americans of voting age have voted in post-Watergate elections (Boylan, 1991), the turnout problem has serious political implications. According to pollster Peter Hart, low participation of the population in the electoral process threatens to turn the United States into a "miniocracy" (Zaccheo, 1976, p. 16). Hart further noted that the situation is alarming because the largest group of nonvoters is formed by the young, which means that the United States may end up with a "lost generation" of voters (Zaccheo, 1976, p. 16). As Ansolabehere, Behr, and Iyengar (1991) pointed out, the danger is aggravated by the fact that "electoral success in the United States is, for better or worse, increasingly contingent upon candidates' media strategies and media treatment of political events" (p. 109).

Researchers have addressed the causes of low turnout as well as the possibility that some members of the so-called "party of nonvoters" may not be irreversibly apathetic. The question, "What makes people apathetic?," brought into discussion a wide range of factors, one of which is the mass media, which provide most of the contact people have with candidates for major offices (Boylan, 1991). One frequent complaint against the mass media in connection with political coverage is the "gotcha mentality" of news people (Porter, quoted in Gordon, 1995, p. 9), which is a distortion of the watchdog function of the press into an adversarial disposition towards politicians, combining negativism, sensationalism and scapegoating, and propagating the professional cynicism of most journalists into the public (Gordon, 1995). Observed Rieder (1996): "Accentuating the positive is almost a violation of the macho code. It's a sign of terminal naivete" (p. 6)—a rationale and a tactic that may serve the journalists, but whose side effect may be the transfer of a negative perceptual frame on the electorate, prejudicing the population against politicians and disengaging them from the political process.

If we consider the effects of mass media content on turnout, the attitudes that filter and frame the information appear to have a stronger effect on turnout than information pure and simple, and information is never pure and simple. Upon endorsing the alienation explanation of decreasing turnout, Wolfinger, Glass, and Squire (1990) emphasized the emotional aspects of the public's estrangement from politics: "disaffection," "malaise," "distrust" coming from a perception of failure of the political system, a feeling that it "is rotten or at least unresponsive" (p. 554). But Weaver (1994) observed that voters are also sensitive to and resent the joint efforts of politicians and the media to impose their own agendas on the electorate, so instead of involvement, the outcome of such efforts is more likely to be voter alienation.

In addition to concerns about media content influencing turnout through gate-keeping, framing, agenda setting, editorializing, persuasion, priming, and so on—along with the more positive effects of informing and socializing—researchers have manifested interest in the differentiated effects of the various media. The conventional wisdom is that print media have a positive effect on turnout, whereas broadcast media, especially television, have a negative impact (e.g., Feldman & Kawakami, 1991; O'Keefe, 1980; Reagan, 1981). Gans (1990) cast a heavy, though overgeneralizing, blame on television, claiming (with no empirical support) that

> It has served to atomize our society; weaken our institutions; reduce participation by making people spectators and consumers rather than involved participants; decrease reading, comprehension and conversation; and increase public confusion. It gives information in undifferentiated blips and by highlights of the most visually exciting. It has, in addition, established unreal expectations for our political system by creating heroes and as quickly destroying them and by offering in its advertising panaceas that give the society a belief it can have equally rapid panaceas. (p. 536)

In the case of television, the negative aspects of coverage related to journalists and mentioned previously are aggravated by medium-specific problems: the priority of the visual, the potential of contrasts and emotionality to arrest and hold attention, the speedy pacing and the kaleidoscopic structure of content, and the lowest-common-denominator orientation. Gans (1990) listed among the consequences of television-specific constraints (both technical and economic): television's inability to focus on more than two candidates at a time, its disinterest in substance and issues and its preference for drama, its arrogance in predicting outcomes of political processes by polling and controlling campaigns, its low sensitivity to both politicians and the public, and its destruction of the sense of history and political process. To these, Hart (1996) added the fragmentary, juxtaposed, kaleidoscopic presentation resulting in "cameo politics" (p. 109). Gitlin (1996) described television's coverage of the political process as "an extended 'horizontal' cacophony," in which "significance bleeds from one story into another" (pp. 83–84). Politicians are willing to put up with all these because television has the advantage of instant and massive penetration. As could only be expected from politicians, they have adapted the political process to fit the medium. The question is "to what gains or costs to the public?" Herein we will only address the effects in terms of voter turnout.

As early as 1962, Campbell raised the question of whether television has reshaped politics. He observed that radio had produced a revolution before the advent of television. Radio broadcasts of campaign events were put on the air in 1924, but full coverage of the electorate was not achieved until after the 1932 election. Between the elections of 1932 and 1940, the turnout records jumped more than 8 percentage points, and the off-year congressional vote increased even more markedly, from 33.7% in 1930 to 44.1% in 1938. Campbell's (1962) explanations were that, on the one hand, radio reached the less educated and the less involved sections of the population, and, on the other hand, the "radio age" was a time of depression and political urgency. When television was introduced in the late 1940s, it was expected to stimulate political interest and participation. Indeed, said Campbell,

> in the presidential elections of 1952, 1956, and 1960 the turnouts were considerably higher than in the elections of 1944 and 1948, but if we drop back to the period just before the war, we find that turnouts in 1936 and 1940 were almost as high as they have been in the most recent elections. There has been a small proportionate increase in the presidential vote during the television era, although it has fluctuated and at its lowest point in 1956 [relative to 1962, the year when the article was written] (60.6%) exceeded by only a percentage point the high of the pre-television period. (p. 11)

The small and inconsistent impact of the then new medium on turnout prompted Campbell (1962) to ask three key questions: "Was there a virgin area of the population not being reached by the mass media when television came on the scene? Was television as effectively different from existing media as radio had been a generation earlier? Was there an unsatisfied demand for political communication in the electorate when television appeared?" (p. 13) The answer to the first question is "no." The answers to the other two questions seem to be "yes." Television is different (its specificity was briefly presented earlier), and very likely television meets higher and/or different needs from a uses and gratifications perspective. First and foremost, television has the spectacular capacity to accommodate politicians as actors, and the electorate as a willing-to-be-entertained audience, which results in the "showbiz" aspects of today's politics, meaning staging on the politicians' side and passivity and vicarious experience on the electorate's side. Hart (1996) argued that television "produces an overwhelming passivity in viewers even when making them feel politically involved" (p. 109). Television has the potential to project the electorate into a virtual reality, while the real political game may be played off-stage, in an invisible and inaccessible reality. According to Hart (1996), "by making politics easy, television has made citizenship easy, and that is a dangerous thing," because "people are at their most arrogant when they are being ocular: 'I've seen it, so it must be true'" (p. 110). This view is not new; we can trace it back to the 1940s concept of the "narcotizing dysfunction" of the media (Lazarsfeld & Merton, 1948). In the television era, people "drift lazily across the political landscape" and "pay less and less attention"; watching becomes more and more habitual and functions as a surrogate of direct political participation (Hart, 1996, p. 118).

Contemporary viewers may be lazy and superficial, but they are increasingly better educated, more familiar with statistics, and therefore more inclined to trust numbers, for example, polls, rather than immaterial political discourse. On the other hand, the politically relevant data available to the public have more and more predictive power. For example, in 1952, when sampling estimations were first announced at 8:30 EST, three million returns (out of a final total of 61 million) were showing 100 to 1 chances that Eisenhower would win. By 1980, estimations had become very accurate, and a projection in a very close race, based on returns from 22 states, was made public at 8:15 EST when NBC News pronounced Ronald Reagan the winner. In the early 1990s, the chance that a projection could be wrong dropped below 1 in 200 (St. Thomas, 1993).

Considering the growing reliance of an increasingly better educated public on the power, neutrality, and "infallibility" of statistics, what can a reasonable voter be expected to do when confronted not only with election night projections, but even with pre-election estimations that tell people who will win before anybody had a chance to cast a vote? Those voters who are satisfied with the projection will very likely say "Why bother voting, if my candidate is going to win anyway," whereas the disgruntled voters will probably shrug their shoulders and choose not to fight a lost battle. Both categories of potential voters are susceptible to developing a belief that voting is a mere ritual, and an individual vote cannot change anything anymore. Added to the already mentioned general disappointment with politicians, this feeling of technical powerlessness and individual insignificance can only aggravate alienation and decrease turnout.

Some scholars claim that the effect of knowing the outcomes before polls' closing times is greatest among people marginally inclined to vote, that is, casual voters who are less partisan and less ideological, and among the undecided who make up their minds at the last minute and are more likely to react impulsively to the latest news (Schneider, 1984). Within the context of a dwindling interested and highly involved electorate, this category of voters has become proportionately more important, often decisively so. Indeed, such potential voters are the primary target of campaigns, especially in close races in which the candidates tend to converge toward the electorate's ideal and in which the distinction among or between front runners is a matter of peripheral features, emphasized through last-minute issue manipulations and *coups-de-theatre*. Given the nature of such campaigns, in which impression, speed, and penetration count, politicians rightly choose television as a means of reaching the electorate. And polls are the preferred instrument for bringing issues and candidate features to the front stage. Both politicians and the media use polls and flood the audience with data. But even efforts made by the media in good faith to promote citizens' interests seem to be doomed to fail:

Since 1992, some news organizations have attempted to intervene directly in the agenda-setting process during campaigns [...]. Citizens were polled for their sense of the important questions that the candidates should address in the party primaries. The questions were put to the principal gubernatorial candidates. The answers appeared in the newspaper and over the radio. But the answers were brief and frequently evasive. Moreover, many of the issues designated as "important" by the public ... were the products of a positive feedback loop, in which the public embraces those issues defined by the media to be the burning questions of the moment. (Gitlin, 1996, p. 81)

Most polling conducted or sponsored by the media is not issue centered but rather is outcome focused, and it promotes a horse-race style of coverage and of campaigning (Barber, 1992; Dinkin, 1989; Patterson & McClure, 1976). According to Patterson and McClure (1976),

a presidential election is surely a super contest with all the elements that are associated with spectacular sports events: huge crowds, rabid followers, dramatic do-or-die battles, winners and losers. It is this part of the election that the networks emphasize. ... In its own way, a presidential election has all the pageantry, color, glamour, and decisiveness of the Kentucky Derby ... The opinion polls are cited frequently, indicating the candidates' positions on the track. The strengths and weaknesses of all the participants are constantly probed, providing an explanation for their position and creating drama about how the race might change as they head down the home stretch. The feverish activity that accompanies the campaign provides the back-barn setting that lends color and "inside-dope" to the coverage. ... Crowds are ... testimony to the drawing power of the candidates and certain proof of what is at stake as they near the finish line. (pp. 40–42)

The image of the electoral process created by television coverage is not one of dignity but rather one of gambling. Some voters may not like horse race/gambling politics and may not wish to be involved in it.

The disclosures, exposures, or confessions about the polling techniques used to create statistical pictures that match candidates' campaign goals are conveying to the public an additional discouraging message that "In practice, American politics has come to be run by full-time insiders" (Boylan, 1991, p. 35). Hitchens (1992) provided a list of classical types of polling manipulations, going from piss-them-off, rush-them, confound-them-tactics, to sampling, interview timing, suggestive or confusing question phrasing, and answer option design. Of course, we could go further and add choice of statistical procedures, choice and use of control variables, and other "technicalities." But the essence is the same, as highlighted by Hitchens (1992, p. 50): "A good pollster is like a good attorney, and fights for the result that the commissioning party expects or needs." A poll is successful to the extent it shapes "fluidity," that is, the "chaos and ignorance" that pollsters (and the politicians behind them) seek to control, to shape into a pattern, build up as "momentum." Hitchens (1992) bitterly but humorously argued that "money and press coverage follow the polls as doggedly as trade follows the flag, speed is of the first importance" (p. 51). This new reality of poll campaigning on the one hand dazzles voters with a huge array of "hard data," most of which are irrelevant to people, and on the other hand elicits bandwagon (Lazarsfeld, Berelson, & Gaudet, 1944) or spiral-of-silence (Noelle-Neumann, 1984) effects, depending on whether estimations and projections match the voters' own expectations and/or wishes or not. Information overload diverts voters' attention from analyzing the meanings of the data to measuring themselves against the data: if they "fit," they may be stimulated to go along, to bandwagon; if they don't, they will either abstain from voting or adjust to fit the trend and avoid social marginalization (Noelle-Neumann, 1984). Research by Goidel and Shields (1994) and Schmitt-Beck (1996) added empirical support to the notion of a media-induced bandwagon effect. Goidel and Shields (1994) found that exposure to the mass media increased the likelihood of voting for the incumbent, and the bandwagon effect resulted in vanishing preferences for minor candidates. But our concern here is limited to voter abstention and does not encompass displacements, so we will not enlarge on those findings.

One other issue that has just started to kindle researchers' interest is the development of new media technologies. Given their potential for interactive political communication, they are generally expected to increase participation in political decision making. Critics such as Gitlin (1996) are nevertheless skeptical about new media's potential for strengthening democracy. Gitlin argued that the Internet and other linkages based on affinity and selectivity are conducive to "public sphericules" rather than a large forum for public debate (p. 81), and, at the same time, they will deepen the "gulf" between the information-saturated and the information-deprived, aggravating the class division between the politocracy and the rest of the population (p. 82). Although the new forms of political participation made possible by new technologies (e.g., computer-based political communication, teleconferencing, and televoting) may revolutionize politics and ultimately replace the current system of voting (thus substantially reducing abstention), such forms of political communications have not reached the mass level yet, so they are not a legitimate object for our investigation.

The 40 research reports that constitute the potential data pool for the present study deal with the relationship between exposure to traditional media (i.e., television, radio, newspapers, and magazines) and voter turnout behavior. The assessment of these studies will follow the order of the information categories selected for comparison: variables, theoretical framework, research methods, samples, and statistical procedures. In the discussion we will emphasize those aspects that raise problems from a meta-analytical perspective. Finally, instead of commenting on the reported findings, we will attempt to perform meta-analyses based on the results presented in the reports under consideration.

VARIABLES

A first glance at the distinction between independent and dependent variables tells us that mass media have not always been treated as a predictor of turnout. Some researchers posited a relationship in the opposite direction, with media consumption as a dependent variable (Lazarsfeld et al., 1944; Tan, 1981).

Most studies addressed this relationship in a larger context, including many other variables. The focus of some researchers was on other aspects of the political process or of political communication, and findings relevant to our topic were secondary. Few authors spent time defining the concepts, probably considering that exposure to mass media and voter turnout were self-explanatory. This lack of conceptual clarification resulted in a variety of operationalizations across studies.

The distinctions made in connection with the mass media factor were in terms of (a) forms of media (with broad classifications as traditional/nontraditional, mass/quasi-mass—including church and professional media, or television alone, or various combinations of several media), (b) content categories (ranging from campaign communication and early projections to news and public affairs, to detailed classifications of genres), and (c) geographical coverage (from local to international). Other researchers developed voter-related variables such as (d) exposure (measured as self-reported time of viewing early projections, self-assessed duration/intensity of exposure, frequency, regularity, diversity/number of channels followed, whether or not the viewer was exposed to specific campaigns), (e) use (in terms of purpose), (f) preference or reliance (in general and/or for political decision making), and (g) interest/attention level. These traditional variables were supplemented by ingenious, less orthodox ones such as (h) cross-pressure on a potential voter caused by a combination of media with different political biases, (i) negativism, that is, perceptions that the media control or are controlled by politicians, and perceptions of advertising as being predominantly negative, (j) third-person perceptions, that is, potential voters' perceptions of other people believing and being influenced by polls and advertisements, (k) set ownership in the case of radio and television, and (l) density of TV sets in the area (supposed to reflect the level of local exposure). The last two variables were used as surrogates of exposure to mass media in secondary data analyses for which no direct media exposure information was available.

The dependent variable, that is, the voter turnout factor was studied in two ways, directly and indirectly. The direct sources were (a) self-reported voting in a particular election and/or in several elections within a specific interval of time, (b) official turnout statistics, (c) validated vote (i.e., self-reported checked against official turnout records), and (d) voting patterns (with ordinal categories such as regular voter, late decider, contingent voter, and persistent nonvoter). The indirect measures used as surrogates for turnout were (e) intention to vote, (f) likelihood of voting, (g) perceived importance of voting, (h) perceived efficacy of voting, and (i) general political efficacy. Voting (intention) information was sometimes collected closely before or after the elections or weeks and even months and years after the elections. Indices were sometimes constructed, combining information about several elections and/or information about both intentions and actual voting or both self-reported information and validated data. When secondary sources were used and aggregate data were available, the analysis was conducted across elections and/or geographic regions. To further complicate the picture, turnout surrogates were sometimes treated as mediators of voting.

The inclusion of mediating variables and controls dramatically complicate the picture. Some of the controls used in the studies under review were voter related. Many of these can be classified as objective features, such as demographics (gender, age, marital status, education, level of income, social class, ethnicity or race, and religion), parental and/or family characteristics (parents' education, un/employment [white-collar vs. blue-collar], and union membership of respondent and/or spouse), geographic location (urban/rural, South/non-South or Northeast/South/Midwest/West, time zones, length of residence or geographic mobility, and community size), community integration (church attendance and membership in clubs, in ethnic organizations, and/or interest groups); and use of interpersonal media.

Certain objective voter-related variables used as controls were closely associated with the political process, as, for example, direct contact with campaign staff, party members/politicians, and candidates; public affairs information and political knowledge/understanding; knowledge of campaign issues; and interpersonal political communication.

Many voter-related controls involved some degree of subjectivity, as, for example: perceived occupational prestige; leisure time; perceptions of the current and future state of the economy (worse/better); economic, political, and cultural attitudes; personal effectiveness or feeling of citizen duty; interest in politics; self-interest in the election; political efficacy, political self-confidence, or voting efficacy; interest in the campaign; trust in government/politicians; partisan orientation (measured directly as preference or support or affiliation and indirectly as level of satisfaction with the election results); and partisanship strength/intensity/loyalty.

Other mediating variables were objective characteristics of the system, such as: state voting age population; level of education in the state (percentage of high school graduates); unemployment rate in the state; legal restrictions (e.g., requirement to register, registration procedures, and interval between registration closing date and election); time of early projections, time of polls closing, and time between projections and closing; state total number of polling hours; race closeness; and senate and gubernatorial races on the ballot.

The inconvenience of all these mediating variables from a meta-analytical perspective is that in regression-based analyses they eat away turnout variance attributable to media exposure, leaving the media impotent, insignificant (e.g., Dennis, 1991; Tannenbaum & Kostrich, 1983). Moreover, different authors choose to look at certain intervening variables and ignore others. If in zero-order correlations such choices make no difference, in regressions they are crucial for the meta-analyzability of reported findings, and we will elaborate on this issue in the section devoted to statistical procedures.

Another critical aspect is the combination of variables into factors, which in some cases is intuitive and idiosyncratic and in other cases is based on factor analysis, with reliability coefficients ranging from barely acceptable (.40) upward.

Some of the studies we looked at used as independent variables aggregate measures of media exposure (e.g., Blumler & McLeod, 1974; Wald, 1985), the underlying assumption being that all media affect voting in the same direction. The danger in such situations is that effects in opposite directions, if any, cancel out one another, and the overall effect appears to be smaller and simpler than it really is. Moreover, composite media exposure measures, once aggregated, cease to reflect the different levels of intensity with which different media impact voting.

Other studies in our data pool made distinctions among exposure and/or attention to and/or interest in and/or preference for and/or reliance on individual media and/or different types of content. Such approaches assume that different media and genres may affect turnout in opposite directions (e.g., Reagan, 1981) or with different intensities (e.g., Glaser, 1965) or they affect different aspects of political participation (e.g., Bybee, McLeod, Luetscher, & Garramone, 1981). Such assumptions are associated with the researchers' belief that it would be more useful to understand and be able to control individual effects of various media and genres rather then learn about the overall effect of general media exposure, which has less potential for control by political campaigners or people otherwise interested in voter turnout.

Faced with a database reflecting these conflicting assumptions, we had to make a decision of principle, and we chose the conservative approach of conducting (if possible) separate meta-analyses on findings about exposure to mass media in general and on findings about exposure to specific types of media.

But that decision did not solve the genre dilemma: Which genres deserve individual attention? Our database reveals little agreement among researchers in that respect. Should campaign coverage, news, public affairs, political advertising, entertainment, features, and documentaries be treated as separate categories? Should we make a distinction between coverage in own-party media and opposite-party media? Should we look at media usage in general and/or for political information purposes and more precisely for monitoring the election campaign? Such questions of detail posed at the theoretical level remained unanswered in this study because our decisions as to which reports to include in the meta-analysis were based on higher-order criteria such as medium and statistical procedure, and genres just happened not to be an issue in the selected studies.

Another problem we faced when we examined the variable sets in the 40 studies under review was that some authors who relied on secondary data sometimes resorted to doubtful surrogates of exposure to mass media, such as set ownership or county density of television sets or campaign expenditures, or—in the case of early-call election studies—the amount of time polls remained open after the first network projection. Similarly, when direct dependent measures of voting behavior (i.e., self-reported voting or official turnout data) were not available, indirect measures were used (e.g., intention to vote, likelihood of voting, political self-efficacy, or perceived importance of voting). The question that emerged at the theoretical level was to what extent surrogate measures could be aggregated with direct measures of media exposure. The decision remained to be made on a case-by-case basis, but, again, higher-order criteria prevailed in the selection of studies for meta-analysis, and they reduced the pool of 40 to small subsets in which the surrogate issue did not materialize.

The purpose of mentioning these unanswered questions is to sensitize other researchers to meta-analytic difficulties, in the hope that we can all work toward variable standardization, which would render more of our findings about the media–voting relationship suitable for aggregation procedures such as meta-analysis.

The fuzzy picture of variables related to the problem under investigation here may have left the impression that research to date has been dominated by arbitrary or idiosyncratic choices. We hope to mitigate this impression in the next section in which we refer to the theoretical grounds on which the authors based their research design.

THEORETICAL FRAMEWORK

Not all studies under review were grounded in theory. Actually 9 of 40 (22.55%) research reports had neither an explicit nor implicit theoretical framework. Some authors developed their design based on or in response to previous research and did not offer a discussion at the conceptual level. Other authors included a literature review that at least outlined the theoretical frameworks of previous projects. The types of approaches in the remaining 31 studies were diverse, including political, sociological, and psychological perspectives.

Despite the impressive theoretical arsenal deployed in the studies under investigation, the effects of mass media on political participation in general and voting in particular have not yet been captured by any general theory. The most valuable attempt to synthesize and articulate existing knowledge into a comprehensive model of voting turnout that includes the media among other factors is that of Dennis (1991). He classified explanations of turnout into three groups: atheoretical, based mostly on electorate demographics; alienationist theories, including the media as a cause of political cynicism and abstention; and rationalist or economic theories that assume voters' evaluation of the costs and return of voting. Dennis tested the alienationist and rationalist models for predictive power and noticed that they are significantly correlated ($\phi = .486$), which suggests a substantive overlap in the two theories. Together with "atheoretical" demographics, the alienationist and rationalist variables accounted in Dennis's study for as much 54% of total turnout variance, which indicates that a three-pronged approach is highly effective. But the more complex the system of turnout variables, the lower the significance of each variable. In Dennis's three-pronged model, for example, the media factor ("information motivation") lost significance, although it predicted political alienation at $\beta = .14$, $p = .02$, and the alienation block of variables entered first in the regression equation accounted for 35% of total turnout variance ($N = 275$).

Authors' choices of theories and/or concepts as a basis for their research may indirectly affect the meta-analyzability of their findings. The theoretical framework of a study determines the choice for independent variables, the way they are grouped, and the order in which they are entered in regression or their sequencing in path analysis models. Thus, theoretical preference ultimately affects quantitative findings. Consequently, comparing studies with different theoretical frameworks, different sets of variables, or differently structured variables becomes a highly problematic enterprise.

Further aggravating the situation is the diversity of research methods used to investigate the problem under study, that is, the relationship between mass media and voter behavior. This issue will be addressed in the next section.

RESEARCH METHODS

The studies reviewed for this project made almost equal use of primary and secondary data (21 and 23 cases, respectively, with four studies using both types of sources). Five data sets came from panel studies, four of which were original. Thirty-two reports (80%) presented or discussed survey data, which came from 17 original studies and 15 secondary sources. Twelve studies (30%) used election data collected by the Center for Political Studies at the University of Michigan. Ten studies used official election statistics, and two discussed data originating in media diaries (secondary sources in both cases). Five reports failed to provide complete or any description of secondary sources. As an extreme case, Simon and Stern (1955) used the 1952 temporary "FCC Freeze" on the construction of new television stations as an opportunity to study the effect of television penetration in a sort of "natural experiment," although their analysis was based on secondary data.

The variety of methods for collecting data is not important in itself, but it indicates the varying levels of accuracy, reliability, and validity we can expect. Generally, the quality of the data is higher for official statistics and research based on national probability samples, but lower and uneven in the rest of the studies, depending on instruments, sample structure and size, and data collection instruments and methods.

The overall preference of researchers seems to go in the direction of survey data, either primary or secondary. One explanation is that surveys can collect a wide range of information about many variables that can be regressed on the variable of interest. Moreover, surveys can be conducted on large samples of respondents, which is important when external validity is an issue. In a meta-analysis, the sample sizes in the studies under consideration determine the relative weights of those studies.

The following section will enlarge upon the samples used in the studies that make up our data pool.

SAMPLES

Thirty-five studies (87.5%) were conducted in the United States, four (10%) in Europe—three on English samples (two local and one national), and one comparative study used national samples from six European countries—and another study was conducted in Japan on convenience samples. Thirteen studies (32.5%) reported findings about local samples, 8 (20%) presented regional findings in the United States, 17 (42.5%) referred to national phenomena (16 relative to the United States and 1 relative to England), and only 1 study compared several European states.

Only two reports presented findings on convenience samples (Austin & Pinkleton, 1995; Feldman & Kawakami, 1991). Seven analyses (17.5%) used census data and official election statistics. Thirty-one studies (77.5%) relied on data obtained from random/probability/systematic samples, but at least 11 (12.5%) samples had some kind of implicitly or explicitly stated bias in terms of regional, urban/rural, racial, or age representation. If we endorse Shaffer's (1981) observation that the samples used by the Center for Political Studies at the University of Michigan excluded peripheral groups less likely to vote, then 8 more studies would be affected by this kind of sample bias.

The 37 noncensus studies (92.5%) had samples ranging in size from 257 (Austin & Pinkleton, 1995) to 14,405 (Morgan & Shanahan, 1992). Three studies (7.5%) specified units of analysis other than individuals (Carter, 1984; Delli Carpini, 1984; Simon & Stern, 1955). Two authors mentioned the use of control samples.

The diversity in sampling procedures across studies results in a varying degree of representativeness. This poses an additional threat to the comparability and potential for meta-analysis of the reports under consideration.

The last, but not least critical issue when studies are considered for meta-analysis is the diversity of statistical methods used to process the data.

STATISTICAL PROCEDURES

The oldest studies on the media–voting relationship that we could access were conducted in the 1940s. They made use of frequencies, which some authors continued to rely on even in the 1980s and 1990s. Frequencies were an exclusive method in nine (22.5%) of the studies analyzed here, and another seven (17.5%) studies used them in combination with other methods. *t* tests were present in the

1950s studies. Correlations appeared in the 1960s reports. Regression analysis, path analysis, and discriminant analysis began to be applied in the 1970s.

The preferred method by far was regression, used in 22 studies (55%), 3 of which used the probit model of regression, and 1 used Silberman and Durden's (1975) model. The major statistical problem with regression studies that undermines their meta-analyzability is the composition and structure of the variable set. In the context of this investigation, for example, the critical aspects are whether exposure to the media was treated as one variable or a block of variables, whether there were any other variables entered in the same block with media exposure, and whether media exposure was entered first or was preceded by other variables. Studies in which media exposure was not entered first and/or variance findings were not reported did not qualify as candidates for this meta-analysis.

The second most popular class of statistical methods in the studies under review were correlations and associations (phi, gamma, and Kendall's tau coefficients), used in 14 studies (30%). The next most frequent method was path analysis, used in 5 studies (12.5%). Following in order of preference were the *t* test, factor analysis, discriminant analysis, and LISREL (linear structural relations)—each mentioned in 2 reports and analysis of variance (ANOVA), ECTA (log-linear contingency table analysis), and categorical analysis of variance (Flanigan & Zingale's, 1974 method)—each mentioned in 1 report.

The general preference for multivariate methods reflects researchers' perception that mass media effects cannot be examined in isolation from other turnout predictors and also that the mass media affect other political communication variables beside turnout. Nevertheless, there was little agreement among researchers as to which variables need to be considered as turnout predictors, and this situation affected the comparability of the relatively numerous regression studies, in which different authors used different controls, grouped differently in blocks, and entered in the regression equations in different order.

The diversity of statistical procedures applied in the studies under review raised the problem of convertibility of results reached through different methods. The questions to ask in such situations are which findings can be aggregated as such, which are convertible to comparable measures, what transformation formulae are available, and what restrictions or limitations apply.

The following section will provide procedural details about our selection of meta-analyzable findings, thus illustrating the difficulties usually encountered by researchers who attempt meta-analyses.

META-ANALYSIS

The possibility of conducting a meta-analysis on the relationship between mass media and voter turnout was suggested by the considerable number of extant studies on or related to the topic ($N = 40$). Our first move was to separate studies that could be meta-analyzed from those that for technical reasons could not be used.

Nine reports were based exclusively on frequencies, which cannot be compared with correlation or regression results. Two studies considered media use as a dependent of political participation. Three other studies used unique, unorthodox independent variables (i.e., TV set density in the area, campaign expenditures, and voter negativism including media-related attitudes). Another report came from a dissertation. So, we were left with 26 candidates for meta-analysis. Because our pool was shrinking alarmingly, we decided to retain books and book chapters by reputable authors.

The second move was to see whether the remaining reports were addressing exactly the same issue, with comparable statistical procedures, or had to be grouped into separate units for the meta-analysis.

Five of the 26 studies included a particular media effect on turnout, namely the impact of early network projections on voting in post-call districts in the West. Five other studies on the same topic (Dubois, 1983; Epstein & Strom, 1981, 1984; Fuchs, 1965, 1966) had already been discarded because they relied exclusively on frequencies, so we were able to examine only five reports as potential sources for a separate meta-analysis on this special topic. Tuchman and Coffin (1971) looked at the change in voting turnout plans between exposed and unexposed voters in the West, and the t test they ran showed an insignificant difference ($t = .70, p = .48, N = 1,972$). Jackson (1983) used the probit model of regression to predict likelihood of voting based on individual exposure to early network projections. Tannenbaum and Kostrich (1983) performed regressions on earlier data sets and found contradictory results depending on whether turnout was regressed only on exposure to early projections (exposure $\beta = .14, p > .05$) or exposure was entered in the equation together with other well-known predictors of turnout (exposure $\beta = .03$, $p < .05$). Carter (1984) used Silberman and Durden's (1975) regression model to compute the media impact on turnout based on the number of post-projection polling hours in each state. Delli Carpini (1984) used in regression an interaction term as the independent variable (i.e., socioeconomic status $\times$ post-call polling time). In conclusion, the whole subset of early-projection studies was too heterogeneous to be meta-analyzed, as only two reports (Tannenbaum & Kostrich, 1983; Tuchman & Coffin, 1971) included comparable t test and regression findings about media exposure effects on turnout. So, the whole subset of early-call studies had to be abandoned, which left us with 21 candidates for meta-analysis.

Correlational findings were considered to be the core of our data pool, but three more studies of this type had to be rejected because they did not report any correlation coefficients relevant to the media–turnout relationship. The correlation-based data pool was thus reduced to 6 studies. The 12 remaining non-correlational studies were examined in terms of their comparability, that is, convertibility of findings, which depended on the statistical methods used to process the data.

The most promising source for supplementing the correlation subset was the group of regression studies. But Blumler and McLeod (1974) compared young with older and Conservative with Labour voters in Britain. Bybee et al. (1981) compared young Americans (younger than 27) with older people and found that only newspaper reading frequency predicted vote abstention with young people ($\beta = -.16, p < .05$). St. George and Robinson-Weber (1983) compared whites and blacks. The distinctions made by these authors rendered their findings unique and not comparable.

Blumler (1983) and Wober (1987) used regressions to analyze data relative to the European Parliament elections. Wober (1987) looked at the media effects on Londoners' voting in the European election and found significant effects of exposure to television cultural programming, which suggested that culture might be a significant mediating variable of participation in European elections. That possibility may account for the intercountry differences identified by Blumler (1983), who compared the effects of exposure to television, newspapers, and campaign upon turnout in six countries (only betas reported, no variance information available). In addition, we suspected that the motivations to vote in the European Parliament elections and in the national elections differed in intensity and probably in nature too. Consequently, we discarded the two aforementioned regression studies.

In Weaver and Drew's (1995) and Knack's (1997) regression analyses the media variables were preceded in the equation by other variables, and media R^2s were not reported, so those studies were also dropped.

All three probit studies were eliminated earlier for other reasons (two belonged to the early-call group and the third used unorthodox independent variables).

Shaffer's (1981) report did not provide sufficient regression data to be meta-analyzed (incremental variance information was missing). It also presented discriminant analysis findings that were not convertible, so the study was dropped together with Reiter's (1979) discriminant analysis report, which included whites only.

From the path analysis subset, three studies were previously discarded for various other reasons, which left only Shaffer's (1981) model and Wald's (1985) two models to be considered. Shaffer (1981) calculated the average of 1960 to 1976 path coefficients (not presented individually), and Wald (1985) compared two different models (using ordinary least squares and logit coefficients). So, the whole set of path analysis studies could not be utilized in the meta-analysis.

Walker (1988) was the only researcher who used ANOVA. But it was a two-way ANOVA (TV/newspapers $\times$ image/issue information), so no conversion to r was possible, and the study was abandoned.

Rust, Bajaj, and Haley (1984) conducted a log-linear contingency table analysis, the results of which were also impossible to convert to r, so their report had to be ignored.

The media variables used by Glaser (1965) were set ownership for broadcast media (which is not comparable with exposure) and regular reading for newspapers. Newspaper exposure could have been useful if the author had not chosen an association measure (phi coefficient) for which no conversion formula is available. So, that study had to be discarded.

Zimmer (1981) also used associations. He examined the relationship between media exposure and public involvement (including voting) as mediated by perception of race closeness. No direct media–voting relationship findings were reported, so that study was also eliminated. In conclusion, none of the 12 candidate noncorrelational studies could be used to supplement the correlational data pool. The six potentially meta-analyzable correlational studies are presented in Table 24.1.

TABLE 24.1
Meta-Analyzable Correlational Studies

Author(s)	Independent Variables	Dependent Variables	Subjects
O'Keefe (1980)	Reliance on television and newspapers for political decision making	(Indirect) Efficacy of voting	$N = 1,966$ Multistage area probability sample (Summit, OH)
Miller & Reese (1982)	(Newspapers + television) × (exposure + reliance)	(Indirect) Political efficacy	$N = 2,402$ U.S. national probability sample
McLeod & McDonald (1985)	(Newspapers + television) × (exposure + public affairs content use + attention to public affairs content); reliance: primary source for political information	Political participation within the past year (4-item index, components not reported)	$N = 589$ Random sample (Dane County, OH)
Dennis (1991)	Political information processing motivation (special efforts and attention to newspaper, radio and TV campaign information)	Self-reported voting in 1984 and previous elections	$N = 275$ (Subset of the U.S. NES sample)
Morgan & Shanahan (1992)	Overall television viewing	Voting	$N = 14,405$ U.S. NES samples for the 1972–1988 presidential elections
Wober, Brosius, & Weinmann (1996)[*]	Exposure to press and TV coverage of election; exposure to news & current affairs; exposure to documentary and features	Intention to vote; self-reported voting	$N = 1,685$ U.K. BARB quota sample

[*]Study concerning elections for the European Parliament.

The group of studies listed in Table 24.1 prompts the question whether national elections can be assimilated with elections for the European Parliament. As already discussed in connection with regression studies, a conservative approach considering culture, prior knowledge, level of interest, and personal involvement as strong mediators of turnout would require separate treatment of national and "transnational" elections. If we eliminate the European study, we are left with an American subset of five studies. Here we are faced with an independent variable problem. Dennis (1991) used a general media-independent variable, whereas the other authors considered the various media separately. Consequently, Dennis's results cannot be compared with the other findings. On the other hand, the dependent variables used in the remaining four studies are different. Morgan and Shanahan (1992) were the only authors who used voting. O'Keefe (1980) used voting efficacy, whereas Miller and Reese (1982) used political efficacy, which some authors consider close enough substitutes for turnout. McLeod and McDonald (1985) used a four-item index of political participation, but they failed to specify whether turnout was a component. So, by very conservative standards, we should not venture to run any meta-analysis on the subset of correlational studies.

If we choose a moderate approach and consider the dependent variables equivalent, then we can meta-analyze separately the American studies (top four in Table 24.2) that use exposure to television as an independent variable of voting or of

TABLE 24.2
Correlational Studies Used for Meta-Analyses on the Effect
of Television Exposure on Voter Turnout

Authors	Independent Variable	Dependent Variable	Correlation Coefficient	Sample
O'Keefe (1980)	Reliance on television for political decision making	Efficacy of voting	$r = .07$	$N = 1,966$
Miller & Reese (1982)	Television exposure	Political efficacy	$r = .10$	$N = 2,402$
McLeod & McDonald (1985)	Television watching	Political participation	$r = -.19$	$N = 589$
Morgan & Shanahan (1992)	Television viewing	Voting	$r = -.14$	$N = 14,405$
Wober, Brosius, & Weinmann (1996)[*]	Exposure to TV coverage of election	Intention to vote	$r = -.17$	$N = 4,000$

[*]Study concerning elections for the European Parliament

turnout surrogates. We can also run a meta-analysis on the three American studies (top three in Table 24.3) that use exposure to newspapers as an antecedent of voting.

The meta-analysis on the top four studies in Table 24.2 yielded the following results:

Mean of the study correlations:	$-.09$
Variance across studies:	9.24×10^{-3}
Sampling error variance:	$.21 \times 10^{-3}$
Variance of population correlations:	9.04×10^{-3}
Corrected population standard deviation:	$-.9465$

Because the absolute value of the corrected population standard deviation is smaller than 1.96, we cannot draw conclusions about the impact of television on turnout based on these four studies.

If we take a liberal approach in terms of both geographic considerations and variables and include the European parliamentary election study in our pool, the meta-analysis results are as follows:

Mean of the study correlations:	$-.104$
Variance across studies:	8.4×10^{-3}
Sampling error variance:	$.21 \times 10^{-3}$
Variance of population correlations:	8.2×10^{-3}
Corrected population standard deviation:	-1.15

TABLE 24.3

Correlational Studies Used in the Meta-Analysis on the Effect of Newspaper
Exposure on Voter Turnout

Authors	Independent Variable	Dependent Variable	Correlation Coefficient	Sample
O'Keefe (1980)	Reliance on newspapers for political decision making	Efficacy of voting	$r = .09$	$N = 1,966$
Miller & Reese (1982)	Newspaper exposure	Political efficacy	$r = .29$	$N = 2,402$
McLeod & McDonald (1985)	Newspaper reading	Political participation	$r = .14$	$N = 589$
Wober, Brosius, & Weinmann (1996)[*]	Exposure to press coverage of election	Intention to vote	$r = -.14$	$N = 4,000$

[*]Study concerning elections for the European Parliament.

As we can see, the mean of the study correlations, the variance across studies, and the variance of population correlations went down, the sampling error variance remained the same, but the corrected population standard deviation, although higher in absolute value, is still smaller than 1.96, which means that the results continue to be inconclusive despite adding one study to our data pool.

The studies on the effect of newspaper exposure on voter turnout that we retained as possible candidates for meta-analysis are presented in Table 24.3. The results of a moderate meta-analysis performed on the top three studies in Table 24.3 yielded the following results:

Mean of the study correlations:	.193
Variance across studies:	9.1×10^{-3}
Sampling error variance:	$.56 \times 10^{-3}$
Variance of population correlations:	8.5×10^{-3}
Corrected population standard deviation:	2.08

As the corrected population standard deviation is higher than 1.96, based on these three studies, we can predict that correlation coefficients between exposure to newspapers and voting will fall within the .147 and .239 interval with a probability of 95%.

If we add the European election study, the meta-analysis results worsen:

Mean of the study correlations:	.044
Variance across studies:	32.4×10^{-3}
Sampling error variance:	$.44 \times 10^{3}$
Variance of population correlations:	31.95×10^{-3}
Corrected population standard deviation:	.2461

The inconclusiveness of these findings supports our hypothesis that transnational elections, such as those for the European Parliament, are essentially different from national elections, and therefore transnational and national election findings should not be aggregated.

The findings of the meta-analyzed studies about television effects on voter turnout are more controversial than those regarding newspaper effects. This is reflected in higher variance of television-related results across studies (in the moderate approach). Our meta-analysis results appear to support the general belief that exposure to television has different effects on the electorate than newspaper reading.

This tentative meta-analysis of the currently available studies that deal with the impact of mass media on voter turnout indicates that the problem is complex, that is, it involves a large number of mediating factors and so far the research designs and statistical methods in this area have been too heterogeneous to allow for a comprehensive assessment of findings across studies. It seems that more time is needed for research on this topic to accumulate and to mature. A maturity feature would be the homogeneity of studies in terms of variable definition, selection, operationalization and measurement; research methods; and statistical procedures. What we expect to happen in research on the media–voter turnout is not a reduction of variable inventories and data-processing methods, but a convergence toward a system of variables and a system of statistical procedures that have produced significant results. More thorough approaches in terms of data collection, data analysis, and findings reporting would automatically result in a higher proportion of meta-analyzable findings.

REFERENCES

Ansolabehere, S., Behr, R., & Iyengar, S. (1991). Mass media and elections: An overview. *American Politics Quarterly, 19,* 109–139.

Austin, E. W., & Pinkleton, B. E. (1995). Positive and negative effects of political disaffection on the less experienced voter. *Journal of Broadcasting & Electronic Media, 3,* 215–235.

Barber, J. D. (1992). *The pulse of politics: Electing presidents in the media age.* New Brunswick, NJ: Transaction.

Blumler, J. G. (1983). Communication and turnout. In G. Blumler (Ed.), *Communicating to voters* (pp. 181–209). Beverly Hills, CA: Sage.

Blumler, J. G., & McLeod, J. M. (1974). Communication and voter turnout in Britain. In T. Leggatt (Ed.), *Sociological theory and survey research: Institutional change and social policy in Great Britain* (pp. 265–312). Beverly Hills, CA: Sage.

Boylan, J. (1991). Where have all the people gone? Reflections on voter alienation and the challenge it poses to the press. *Columbia Journalism Review, 30,* 30–35.

Bybee, C. R., McLeod, J. M., Luetscher, W. D., & Garramone, G. (1981). Mass communication and voter volatility. *Public Opinion Quarterly, 45,* 69–90.

Campbell, A. (1962). Has television reshaped politics? *Columbia Journalism Review, 1,* 10–13.

Carter, J. R. (1984). Early projections and voter turnout in the 1980 presidential election. *Public Choice, 43,* 195–202.

Delli Carpini, M. X. (1984). Scooping the voters? The consequences of the networks' early call of the 1980 presidential race. *Journal of Politics, 46,* 866–885.

Dennis, J. (1991). In W. Crotty (Ed.), *Political participation and American democracy* (pp. 23–65). Westport, CT: Greenwood.

Dinkin, R. J. (1989). *Campaigning in America: A history of election practices.* New York: Greenwood.

Dubois, P. L. (1983). Election night projections and voter turnout in the West: A note on the hazards of aggregate data analysis. *American Politics Quarterly, 11,* 349–364.

Epstein, L., & Strom, G. (1981). Election night projections and West Coast turnout. *American Politics Quarterly, 9,* 479–491.

Epstein, L., & Strom, G. (1984). Survey research and election night projections. *Public Opinion, 7,* 48–50.

Feldman, O., & Kawakami, K. (1991). Media use as predictors of political behavior: The case of Japan. *Political Psychology, 12,* 65–80.

Flanigan, W., & Zingale, N. (1974). The measurement of electoral change. *Political Methodology, 1,* 49–82.

Fuchs, D. A. (1965). Election day newscasts and their effects on Western voter turnout. *Journalism Quarterly, 42,* 22–28.

Fuchs, D. A. (1966). Election-day radio-television and Western voting. *Public Opinion Quarterly, 30,* 226–236.

Gans, C. (1990). Remobilizing the American voter. *Policy Studies Review, 9,* 527–538.

Gitlin, T. (1996). Television's anti-politics: Surveying the wasteland. *Dissent, 43,* 78–85.

Glaser, W. A. (1965). Television and voting turnout. *Public Opinion Quarterly, 29,* 71–86.

Goidel, R. K., & Shields, T. G. (1994). The vanishing marginals, the bandwagon, and the mass media. *The Journal of Politics, 56,* 802–810.

Gordon, C. (1995). The real threat to Canada's future. *Maclean's, 108,* 9.

Hart, R. P. (1996). Easy citizenship: Television's curious legacy. *Annals of the American Academy of Political and Social Science, 546,* 109–119.

Hitchens, C. (1992). Voting in the passive voice: What polling has done to American democracy. *Harper's Magazine, 284(1703),* 45(8).

Jackson, J. E. (1983). Election night reporting and voter turnout. *American Journal of Political Science, 27,* 615–635.

Knack, S. (1997). The reappearing American voter: Why did turnout rise in '92? *Electoral Studies, 16,* 17–32.

Lazarsfeld, P. F., Berelson, B., & Gaudet, H. (1944). The people's choice: How the voter makes up his mind in a presidential campaign. New York: Duell, Sloan and Pearce.

Lazarsfeld, P. F., & Merton, R. (1948). Mass communication, popular taste, and organized social action. In W. Schramm (Ed.), *Mass communications* (pp. 429–503). Urbana: University of Illinois Press.

McLeod, J. M., & McDonald, D. G. (1985). Beyond simple exposure: Media orientations and their impact on political processes. *Communication Research, 12,* 3–33.

Miller, M. M., & Reese, S. D. (1982). Media dependency as interaction: Effects of exposure and reliance on political activity and efficacy. *Communication Research, 9,* 227–248.

Morgan, M., & Shanahan, J. (1992). Television and voting 1972–1989. *Electoral Studies, 11,* 3–20.

Noelle-Neumann, E. (1984). *The spiral of silence: Public opinion, our social skin.* Chicago: University of Chicago Press.

O'Keefe, G. J. (1980). Political malaise and reliance on media. *Journalism Quarterly, 57,* 227–248.

Patterson, T. E., & McClure, R. D. (1976). *The unseeing eye: The myth of television power in national politics.* New York: Putnam.

Reagan, J. (1981). *Media exposure and community integration as predictors of political activity.* Unpublished doctoral dissertation, Michigan State University, East Lansing.

Reiter, H. L. (1979). Why is turnout down? *Public Opinion Quarterly, 43,* 297–311.

Rieder, R. (1996). A skeptical view of the cynicism epidemic. *American Journalism Review, 18,* 6.

Rust, R. T., Bajaj, M., & Haley, G. (1984). Efficient and inefficient media for political campaign advertising. *Journal of Advertising, 13,* 45–49.

Schmitt-Beck, R. (1996). Mass media, the electorate, and the bandwagon: A study of communication effects on vote choice in Germany. *American Journal of Political Science, 25,* 68–95.

Schneider, W. (1984). Early returns: Is the real effect paradoxical? *The New Republic, 190,* 7(2).

Shaffer, S. D. (1981). A multivariate explanation of decreasing turnout in presidential elections, 1960–1976. *American Journal of Political Science, 25,* 68–95.

Silberman, J., & Durden, G. (1975). The rational behavior theory of voter participation: The evidence from Congressional elections. *Public Choice, 23,* 101–108.

Simon, H. A., & Stern, F. (1955). The effect of television upon voting behavior in Iowa in the 1952 presidential election. *American Political Science Review, 49,* 470–477.

St. George, A., & Robinson-Weber, S. (1983). The mass media, political attitudes, and behavior. *Communication Research, 10,* 487–508.

St. Thomas, L. (1993). The media and exit polls and predictions. *St. Louis Journalism Review, 22(153),* 2–3.

Tan, A. S. (1981). Political participation, diffuse support and perceptions of political efficacy as predictors of mass media use. *Communication Monographs, 48,* 133–145.

Tannenbaum, P. H., & Kostrich, L. J. (1983). *Turned-on TV/turned-off voters: Policy options for election projections.* Beverly Hills, CA: Sage.

Tuchman, S., & Coffin, T. E. (1971). The influence of election night television broadcasts in a close election. *Public Opinion Quarterly, 35,* 315–326.

Wald, K. D. (1985). The closeness-turnout hypothesis: A reconsideration. *American Politics Quarterly, 13,* 273–296.

Walker, J. R. (1988). How media reliance affects political efficacy in the South. *Journalism Quarterly, 65,* 746–750.

Weaver, D. (1994). Media agenda setting and elections: Voter involvement or alienation? *Political Communication, 11,* 347–356.

Weaver, D., & Drew, D. (1995). Voter learning in the 1992 presidential election: Did the "nontraditional" media and debates matter? *Journalism & Mass Communication Quarterly, 72,* 7–17.

Wober, J. M. (1987). Voting in Europe: Television and viewers' involvement in the 1984 European parliamentary election. *European Journal of Communication, 2,* 473–448.

Wober, J. M., Brosius, H., & Weinmann, G. (1996). The European election of 1989: British television viewers' knowledge, attitudes and voting behavior. *British Journal of Social Psychology, 35,* 233–244.

Wolfinger, R. E., Glass, D. P., & Squire, P. (1990). Predictors of electoral turnout: An international comparison. *Policy Studies Review, 9,* 551–574.

Zaccheo, M. (1976, September 13). The turned-off voter. *Newsweek, 88,* 16.

Zimmer, T. A. (1981). Media exposure to campaigns: Public anticipation and involvement in elections. *Communication Research, 8,* 189–204.

25

The Spiral of Silence:
A Meta-Analysis
and Its Impact

James Shanahan
Cornell University

Carroll Glynn
Andrew Hayes
Ohio State University

This chapter presents a summary of research on the theory known as the "spiral of silence." It includes a discussion of the results of a meta-analysis we conducted (Glynn, Hayes, & Shanahan, 1997), along with a summary of results that have accumulated since that time. The spiral of silence is a theoretical contribution developed by Elisabeth Noelle-Neumann (1984, 1993) to explain aspects of public opinion that, in her opinion, had been underexamined. According to Noelle-Neumann, it was important to emphasize that public opinion should be considered in terms of how people view others around them (public opinion as social control) as well as how individuals actually feel about the issues (public opinion as *raisonnement*). Many public opinion studies had essentially cumulated people's individual views about certain issues to arrive at conclusions about the whole, emphasizing the rational/individual aspect of public opinion. Noelle-Neumann felt it was equally important to study how people make judgments about the opinions of those around them, as well as to determine how these judgments affect the likelihood of people expressing their own opinions on issues.

Noelle-Neumann refocused attention on the socially normative aspects of public opinion. These dimensions of public opinion clearly reveal that more than just individuals' opinions need to be taken into account in any explanation of public opinion dynamics; an account should also be offered of how we express our opinions based on our perceptions of the views of others. In addition, the dynamics involved in how these perceptions are created also should be considered. Thus, Noelle-Neumann's theory, at its broadest level, is focused on the following question: "How does the sum of individual opinions as determined by public opinion research translate into the awesome political power known as 'public opinion'?" (1993, p. 198).

Noelle-Neumann originally set forth the spiral of silence as a comprehensive theory of social control through public opinion and included both micro-psychological and macro-sociological approaches. Noelle-Neumann's theory, in its most complete version, asks investigators to answer five questions: 1) what is the current climate of opinion on a given issue (i.e., what is the distribution of public opinion), 2) how does the public perceive the trend for the issue climate in the future, 3) how willing are individuals to speak out on a given issue, 4) is there a strong moral component to the issue and 5) what is the media position on the issue; that is, what is the media "tenor"?

However, as with many comprehensive theories of media effects and public opinion, most empirical investigations have not been ambitious enough to tackle the whole theory. Glynn and McLeod (1985), for instance, suggested deleting examinations of the media tenor to simplify the theory. Though Noelle-Neumann herself has not approved of such attempts, the majority of empirical investigations to date have actually focused only on the relation of one's perceptions of majority opinion to one's willingness to speak out. It was these investigations that we examined in our 1997 meta-analysis of the spiral of silence.

META-ANALYZING THE SPIRAL
OF SILENCE

In this section we review our meta-analysis of the spiral of silence. As with other meta-analyses conducted around this period (see, for instance, Morgan and Shanahan, 1997), our meta-analysis was intended to summarize one of the important public opinion/media effects theories that had cumulated enough similar studies to permit a meta-analysis to take place. Initially it appeared that the spiral of silence was perhaps a marginal candidate for such an analysis. Compared with broader-based communication theories, such as cultivation or agenda setting, where dozens of studies had been conducted, we found that actual studies of the spiral of silence could be reduced to only a couple dozen combined findings.

All meta-analysts are limited by the data available to them, and so we focused on only two specific aspects of the theory:

1. Are people who perceive less support for their own beliefs or opinions less willing to express those opinions than people who perceive more support for their opinions? and

2. Are people who perceive that their own opinions are losing popularity less willing to express those opinions than people who perceive their opinions are gaining popularity?

That is, we focused on questions of *current* majority support for an individual's opinion and *future/trend* support. In doing so, we narrowed Noelle-Neumann's questions down to 1–3 of those listed above. The media question was left out because, even though Noelle-Neumann's work has been presented as often in a media theory context as in a pure public opinion context, most of the studies simply have not tested the spiral of silence as a media theory. Questions of whether the issue was morally loaded or not had not been operationalized in any of the studies we looked at. Scholars appeared to have assumed that all of the studies contained some morally interesting aspect that would make them worth studying. Thus, our meta-analysis says nothing about the importance of the moral aspect of the issue as it relates to the spiral of silence process.

The method we followed in the analysis was straightforward. Using sources such as *PsychLit, ISI Web of Science, Sociological Abstracts,* and *Dissertation Abstracts International,* we found 17 separate studies. Although the number of individual studies that met our criteria for inclusion in the meta-analysis was relatively small, taken together they produced 123 tests of the relationship between willingness to speak out and perceptions of majority opinion. In addition to searches of the standard sources, we made every effort to locate more difficult-to-find sources, including contacting investigators with a history of work in this area for their own unpublished research or any unpublished research they were aware of.

As with any meta-analysis, we needed to focus on specific types of findings to ensure comparability across studies. For this reason, we analyzed only studies where an individual was presented with a hypothetical situation and was then asked whether he or she would be willing to enter a conversation or express his or her opinion. While this left out some interesting and important studies, it allowed us to accumulate data that came closest to Noelle-Neumann's original idea of relating perception of opinion climate to hypothetical willingness to speak out.

Noelle-Neumann had originally proposed the "train test" as a measure of spiral of silence. This test asks the respondent to imagine himself in a train compartment with someone who held an opinion divergent from his own (1993, pp. 17–18). The respondent would be asked about his likelihood to express his divergent opinion in that situation. Noelle-Neumann often focused on hypothetical situations in order to measure willingness to express opinions. She argued that "many people have the imagination to experience situations described in an interview so vividly that they react to them as if they were reality" (1993, p. 47). To come closest to the original intent of the theory, we worked only with studies that were limited to this type of operationalization of the influence of public opinion climate on willingness to speak out.

We excluded results from studies where individuals stated which opinion was likely to become more or less popular rather than whether their own opinion was gaining or losing ground (e.g., Matera and Salwen 1989). Furthermore, we used only survey-based results in our study; although there have been some experimental tests, there are not very many, and survey tests are closer to the spirit of the theory developed by Noelle-Neumann. In addition, we excluded studies in which willingness to speak out was compared between individuals that were "objectively" in the majority versus the minority in reference to current public opinion polls or the data itself (e.g., Katz and Baldassare 1992; Tokinoya 1996) to reflect our focus on perceptions of the climate of opinion rather than the actual opinion climate.

As with any meta-analysis, our goal was to report on the collected studies' effects sizes in order to yield an overall, average effect size that would be more valid as an indicator than any individual study. In this regard, we transformed all effect sizes that were finally analyzed with Fisher's r-to-Z transformation.

We included a number of indicators that we thought might act as moderator variables, that is, as variables that might specify the overall relationship given their absence or presence. Table 25.1 summarizes the moderator variables that we used.

Beginning with the 123 different effect size reports found in the various studies, we boiled down our analysis to results that were statistically independent of each other. In studies where more than one result was reported, these were collapsed into weighted averages to represent the single study's overall contribution to our analysis (see Glynn, Hayes, & Shanahan, 1997 for more details on the pro-

TABLE 25.1
Moderators (adapted from Glynn, Hayes, & Shanahan, 1997)

Express opinion to a member of the media (TO MEDIA). In some studies, respondents were asked if they would express their opinion to a member of the media (e.g., TV interviewer, radio station host). In other studies, the person was not a member of the media (e.g., a person on a bus).

Converse or speak opinion (STATE OPINION). This moderator denotes whether the respondents were asked if they would be willing to "speak about" a particular opinion or simply "engage in a conversation" with a person about the topic.

Presumed beliefs of target of expression (DISAGREE). In some studies, it was left unspecified what the target person would think about the opinion to be expressed. In contrast, in some studies the wording of the questions made it clear that the target audience contained only people who would disagree with the respondent.

Target toward whom expression is directed (STRANGER). This moderator reflects whether the audience of the opinion expression was a stranger or a member of the local community.

Measurement of response variables (DICHOTOMIZATION). A study was coded as "dichotomous" if either the independent (perceived support) or dependent (willingness to express) variable was coded dichotomously. If neither was measured dichotomously, the study was coded as non-dichotomous.

Source of effect size (PUBLISHED). We also coded the studies with respect to whether the results were published (in professional journals or book chapters) or unpublished (conference presentations, unpublished theses, and other unpublished results).

---

cedures used). After these procedures, we ended up with 24 independent correlations dealing with "current opinion" and 11 for "future opinion."

Looking at all of the studies taken together, we found an average effect size of .05 (Pearson r). The result was statistically significant, although there was evidence of heterogeneity in the effect sizes, suggesting that there might be a moderator. We found minimal differences between current and future reports. Using a test of combined probability, it was also determined that we would have needed to find 221 studies with zero effect size to negate our conclusion that there is at least one statistically positive effect in the literature. In sum, the results of our meta-analysis showed that there is a small but statistically significant relationship between perception of opinion climate and willingness to speak out. As a point of comparison, Richard et al. (2003) found that social psychological studies in general, based on a summary of meta-analyses, have revealed an average effect size of .21. By virtually any standard, then, our average effect size was small and not especially supportive of the much-discussed theory. It also was lower than that seen in meta-analyses of other media theories such as cultivation (Morgan and Shanahan, 1997, found an average effect size of about .09)

Despite the heterogeneity of effect sizes in the literature, our moderator analyses did not turn up convincing evidence that explained this study-to-study variation. There was weak evidence that the magnitude of the correlation might be related to whether or not the target of opinion expression is a member of the media, but the differences were only marginally significant.

Overall, we concluded that the survey-based literature on the spiral of silence was not very convincing. At that time, we argued that research should look more at actual willingness to speak out, as opposed to a hypothetical willingness to speak out. We speculated that hypothetical questions do not generate enough expectation of actual social isolation to generate the fear that is hypothesized by Noelle-Neumann. We further argued that experimental studies could better answer the questions posed originally by Noelle-Neumann.

RESEARCH IMPACTS OF
THE META-ANALYSIS

When scholars conduct a meta-analysis the intent is to provide a statistical summary of the corpus of literature on the topic. However, good meta-analyses can also be a springboard for new research directions (Wolf, 1986). Meta-analyses that have been conducted on communication and media effects studies have rarely proved conclusive in terms of affecting acceptance or rejection of the theory in question. This has certainly been the case with examinations of the spiral of silence. New studies on the spiral of silence have been conducted since our 1997 analyses. In this section we summarize the results of several of these new studies, particularly in light of the original study's findings.

There is no doubt that a well-done meta-analysis yields a very citable paper. As of the publication of this book, our meta-analysis article has been cited 25 times in the Web of Science database, indicative of a frequently cited paper. Whether new authors are critics or adherents or are developing novel applications of the theory, the meta-analysis provides a quickly referenced credential that the theory is legitimate and time-tested (see, e.g., Niven, 2002; Petric & Pinter, 2002).

The first thing that can be pointed out is that a meta-analysis exposes the theory in question to possible comparisons with other theories. As Shanahan (1999) pointed out,

> ... meta-analytic results need to be interpreted in light of theory, not simply as "small" "moderate" or "large" effect sizes. Thus, for instance, in the cultivation example, theory does not predict large effect sizes. An average effect size of about .10 was seen as consistent with theory. On the other hand, in Glynn et al.'s. meta-analysis of spiral of silence, an average effect size of .05 or less was seen as inconsistent with a theory which predicted large relationships between beliefs about majority opinion and willingness to express one's own opinion.

Most theories in mass communication that have been meta-analyzed have yielded average effect sizes less than .20, with the whole perhaps averaging around .10. By this standard, the results of the meta-analysis are not flattering to the theory. Not surprisingly, some studies used our analysis as a quick reference for criticism of the spiral of silence. Kim et al. (1999) presented the study in this way. But this was by no means a leitmotif in the response to the meta-analysis. For a variety of reasons, the theory maintains its own energy to support continued studies, and some of these have been informed by the results of the meta-analysis.

Further Studies

Several studies followed our meta-analysis that were inspired at least in part by the findings of the meta-analysis. Hayes, Shanahan, and Glynn (2001) attempted to look at willingness to express opinions in a more "real" setting. In this study we found that people reported a greater willingness to engage in a discussion with others on topics that they had previously ranked relatively higher in terms of perceptions of greater consensus between their own opinions and the public. The realism of the situation was introduced by bringing people into a laboratory environment and leading them to believe that they were selecting a topic to be discussed right then and there with a group in the laboratory with them. The resulting effect size was a bit larger than what we had seen in the meta-analysis. Although the analytical method used was somewhat different from that used in most of the studies in the meta-analysis, and this by itself could account for the stronger effect we observed, we can see here the effect of the meta-analysis project moving the research toward measures of willingness to express an opinion that are sensitive to at least the potential of actual discussion rather clearly being hypothetical.

Our suggestions were also picked up by Scheufele, Shanahan, and Lee (2001), who investigated whether a more realistic measure could better capture spiral of silence effects. They found that students' willingness to volunteer for actual participation in a discussion was more related to perceptions about opinion climate than were the perceptions of students who were asked about hypothetical willingness. This was in response to the direct comparison approach suggested by the meta-analysis. The authors argued that the results were "consistent with the suggestions noted earlier that spiral of silence research should include more realistic measures of expression. Indeed, the simplest explanation seems to be that respondents' willingness to speak is better captured by the more realistic measure" (p. 320). This study also built on another of the suggestions from the meta-analysis, that experimental designs be used (this study was a survey, but used a split-ballot technique).

Both of the aforementioned studies suffer from the weakness that no actual discussion ever occurred. Although the situations themselves were presented as real, because no discussion occurred, it is impossible to determine what participants would have actually said if the opportunity to express their opinion had presented itself. McDevitt, Kiousis, & Wahl-Jorgensen (2003) is the only study we are aware of since the publication of our meta-analysis to overcome this limitation. They experimentally manipulated the climate of opinion in a face-to-face or computer-mediated communication context and observed the consistency between the participant's pre-test beliefs about abortion and the perceptions the participant's interaction partners had of the participant's opinion after an actual discussion about abortion. They also analyzed the content of conversation to see if the manipulation of the climate of opinion affected actual opinion expression. Neither outcome variable was affected by the manipulation of the climate of opinion. Instead, they observed generalized moderation, in that the participants were perceived by their interaction partners to hold less extreme opinions than they actually held, and more so in the CMC condition. The only other noteworthy finding was that people assigned to the minority condition tended to speak *more than* those in the majority condition. However, they did not speak more about their own opinions specifically.

Perry and Gonzenbach (2000) picked up on two suggestions resulting from our discussion. First, they used an experimental design to determine whether the number of exemplars in a newscast could affect a person's willingness to express opinion. They found no effect of such exemplars, tending to confirm the lack of an effect in the meta-analysis, although focusing on a somewhat different question. They also used our suggestion to use multiple forms of expression when measuring willingness to express opinions, though it's not very clear from their discussion whether they considered this to be a benefit in the final analysis.

Moreno-Riaño (2002) also pursued an experimental study of the spiral of silence by manipulating the climate of opinion in a survey context. Respondents to the survey were presented with information or no such information about public support for affirmative action policies at the respondents' university before responding to a set of questions assessing a person's opinion about their support for preferential hiring and promotion of minorities and quotas for student admission. Their data are substantially underanalyzed, but from information they provide in the article, our own analysis of the results indicates that those who were told the majority of the public (defined as students at the respondents' university) supported affirmative action policies on campus were more likely to report that they supported preferential hiring and promotion of minorities than those provided no information about the distribution of public opinion. They also included questions more consistent with the operationalization of willingness to speak out that was employed in studies included in our meta-analysis. However, Moreno-Riaño's analyses did not precisely examine the effects of the match between the manipulated climate of public opinion and the respondent's own opinions on willingness to speak out, and insufficient information is provided in their manuscript to conduct such an analysis without further information.

Another Review

Another way of approaching a theoretical review of the spiral of silence literature was at least partially inspired by the meta-analysis. Scheufele and Moy (2000) produced a conceptual review of the spiral of silence. They noted that the differences and weakness of results found in our meta-analysis could be explained by differences in the conceptualization of the studies, measurement differences in key variables, and insufficient attention to "macroscopic" variables (such as cross-cultural differences in the appropriateness of being outspoken). Although they did not discount the value of the meta-analysis, their suggestions for future research were based strictly on theoretically driven observations. For them the small effect sizes did not count as a rejection of the theory; they were just an index of the need for stricter control over the operationalization of its measures and perhaps a refinement of the procedural details of the study itself.

Focusing on Individual Differences

Another recent major tendency in research on the spiral of silence is to look at the role of individual differences in the process. In line with Noelle-Neumann's explanation that self-censorship is driven by a fear of social isolation, numerous investigators have tried to determine whether dispositional fear of isolation predicts willingness to express an opinion in a train-test-like hypothetical scenario (Moy, Domke, & Stamm, 2001; Petric & Pinter, 2002; Scheufele, Shanahan, & Lee, 2001; Wilnat, Lee, & Detenber, 2002). The results of these studies have been mixed—some studies have shown the expected negative relationship between fear of isolation and willingness to express an opinion, and others have shown no relationship or conflicting findings within the same study. The lack of consistency in the literature can probably be attributed in part to the use of ad hoc measures of fear of isolation that are either low in face validity or low in reliability, or whose validity has not been empirically established. If this line of research is to bear fruit, researchers need to settle on an operationalization of fear of social isolation and use it consistently. In our judgment, the measure by Willnat et al. shows the most promise, in that the items in their measure focus specifically on fears of social rejection and worries about how a person is perceived in general rather than in specific opinion expression contexts.

Although research on the fear of isolation mechanism is needed, there is some debate over just how relevant existing studies are to this question. It should come as no surprise if it can be established that people who fear social isolation are less willing to express their opinion, because fear of social isolation is undoubtedly correlated with other individual differences associated with opinion expression, such as shyness and willingness to argue. Indeed, several of the measures of fear of isolation include items that can easily be interpreted as indicators of shyness or argumentativeness rather than fear of social isolation specifically. If fear of isolation is the mechanism leading people to withhold their opinion expression in a hostile environment, then we should see that people who score relatively higher on measures of fear of social isolation are more affected by perceptions of the climate of opinion than are people who have no such fear (or relatively less fear). In short, fear of isolation and perceptions of the climate of opinion should interact in explaining individual variation in willingness to express an opinion. If there is no interaction between fear of social isolation and perceptions of the climate of opinion, then the relationship between fear of isolation and opinion expression is probably just an epiphenomenon of other individual differences that such fears are correlated with.

To our knowledge there is only one existing study that has looked for a differential impact of perceived climate of opinion on opinion expression as a function of individual differences in fear of social isolation. Hayes, Glynn, Shanahan, Scheufele, Moy, Domke, & Stamm (2002) reanalyzed data from some of their respective spiral of silence studies that included both a perceived opinion climate and a fear of social isolation measure in search of this interaction. In 28 tests for such an interaction, none were statistically significant. Of course, a failure to reject a null hypothesis is always ambiguous. In this case, our failure to find such an interaction can as easily be attributed to previously mentioned problems with the existing fear of social isolation measures as it can be to a failure of the theory itself.

We have recently taken a different perspective on individual differences in the spiral of silence process, based on the results of our meta-analysis. Rather than construing willingness to express an opinion as being affected by a specific individual difference such as "fear of social isolation," perhaps it is more helpful to conceptualize people as differing in their sensitivity to the climate of opinion when choosing whether or not to speak an opinion publicly. Some people might be especially sensitive, *for any number of reasons,* to the distribution of public opinion and the consequences of expressing an unpopular position, whereas others do not care not about the consequences of stating their opinion in a hostile climate. The former people are "facilitators" of a spiral of silence, in that their decisions to speak or not are dictated in part by perceptions of the climate of opinion. The latter, by contrast, are "inhibitors" of silence spirals because their choices to speak out or not are not influenced by the climate of opinion. The small effect size seen in the literature and reflected in our meta-analysis may be the result, in part, of lumping into one group people who differ in their susceptibility to the influence of the climate of opinion, treating them as if they were all affected equally (or not) by perceptions of the distribution of opinion.

To distinguish between facilitators and inhibitors (groups that lie on opposite ends of a continuum), we have developed the "Willingness to Self-Censor" scale, an eight-item self-report measure that includes such statements as "There have been many times when I thought others around me were wrong but I didn't let them know" and "I'd feel uncomfortable if someone asked my opinion and I knew he or she wouldn't agree with me" (Hayes, Glynn, & Shanahan, 2005a; Hayes, Glynn, Shanahan, & Uldall, 2003). The measure has been studied in several populations and shows good reliability as well as evidence of convergent and discriminant validity. This research paints the self-censor as a person with a mosaic of related and theoretically relevant characteristics. Compared with people low in willingness to self-censor, those who score high tend to be more anxious about social interaction, more concerned about how others evaluate them, more likely to use the behavior of others for guidance on how to act, more shy, less argumentative, and lower in self-esteem and experience fewer good feelings and more bad feelings in the course of their day-to-day lives.

The research on this measure is ongoing, but a recent experimental validation study (Hayes, Glynn, & Shanahan, 2005b) indicates that the effect of the climate of opinion on a person's stated willingness to express his or her opinion does in fact vary as a function of his or her willingness to self-censor. Participants were administered the willingness to self-censor scale as well as a measure of shyness and political interest in a pre-test. Four weeks later, long after the participants could remember they even responded to the scale, the participants were given a hypothetical opinion expression scenario and were asked how willing they would be in this context to express their opinion about one of three political topics, with the topic randomly assigned to each participant. Within the scenarios was an experimental manipulation of the climate of opinion, with half of the participants told that the climate of opinion was hostile to their own opinion and the other half told the climate of opinion was friendly. As expected, the participants who scored relatively high on the willingness to self-censor scale were more affected by manipulation of the climate of opinion than were those who scored relatively low, even after controlling for dispositional shyness, interest in politics, and gender. These results not only serve as a validation of the willingness to self-censor scale; they also illustrate that people can be identified with respect to their susceptibility to the climate of opinion and that they actually do respond at least to hypothetical opinion expression scenarios accordingly.

Noelle-Neumann's Response

Noelle-Neumann herself has not remained silent on recent work conducted on the spiral of silence theory. As is common with the developers of theories, she takes the role of noting how and where studies diverge from the research template that she laid out originally. Perhaps her major objection to the entire body of research, including those in our meta-analysis, was the idea that people could somehow perceive and report on their perceptions of opinion climate. In a commentary in the *International Journal of Public Opinion Research* reacting to two studies (Hayes, Shanahan and Glynn, 2001; Scheufele & Eveland, 2001), she noted:

> By far the most common misunderstanding—a misunderstanding on which the two studies presented in this issue are also implicitly founded—is the assumption that observing one's environment, the "quasi-statistical sense," assessing majority and minority opinions and observing the upsurge and decline of various opinions are conscious processes which respondents or test subjects can easily talk about. This assumption is not, however, in keeping with the spiral of silence theory. Studies that ask respondents to assess whether they hold the majority view, to rank various opinions or to estimate what percentage of the population holds a particular view seldom obtain satisfactory findings, and to a certain extent also fail to grasp the essence of the spiral of silence theory. When an opinion is losing ground in public, those who hold this opinion unconsciously perceive this process and fall silent—even if they claim, in response to direct questions, that everyone else thinks exactly the same way they do. For this reason, investigative approaches that focus solely on whether respondents feel they share the majority opinion or not—regardless of which position they actually take on a concrete issue—generally do not yield any particularly valuable results. The question of which view is in fact gaining or losing ground among the population is decisive here, not whether the individual also consciously perceives this process. (Noelle-Neumann, 2001, pp. 59–60)

This observation, if taken literally, would mean that our meta-analysis is an analysis of something other than spiral of silence theory, but most observers have not taken such a strict view of how the theory should be operationalized. Whether a meta-analysis of a theory operationalized in the way Noelle-Neumann prefers is even possible is not something we will attempt to assess here. However, this statement by Noelle-Neumann does point out that future studies need to deal with Noelle-Neumann's more macroscopic conception of public opinion in relation to the cognitively focused survey and experimental studies that are still being pursued.

CONCLUSIONS

Even without the orthodox protestations of Noelle-Neumann, there is plenty of room left to explore the ideas she has raised. The media aspect of the spiral of silence has not been widely explored in relation to directly measured perceptions of opinion climate. Direct measures of variables such as fear of isolation are likely to receive further attention. Individual differences of other types will need to be folded into the studies. The assertion by Scheufele and Moy that cultural variables should be included is also of value. It seems that the greatest issue is the coordination of these complex issues across levels, ranging from individual perceptions to the macrosocial context.

Comparing the results of our study with those that have been done since, and assessing the directions perceived in new research, we can reach one definitive conclusion: Individuals do not *simply* base their willingness to speak out on perception of majority opinion, or they do so only very slightly. Whether this result means that the vast majority of researchers have misinterpreted the spiral of silence theory or that the theory had some inherent weaknesses is now beside the point. Researchers have agreed that newer and more complex models have to be proposed. A future meta-analyst will be confronted with the difficult task of figuring out how to reconcile and assess the wave of studies that is sure to come.

REFERENCES

Glynn, C. J., Hayes, A. F., & Shanahan, J. (1997). Perceived support for one's opinion and willingness to speak out: A meta-analysis of survey studies of the "spiral of silence." *Public Opinion Quarterly, 61,* 452–463.

Glynn, C. J., & McLeod, J. (1985). Implications of the spiral of silence theory for communication and public opinion research. In K. Sanders, L. Kaid, & D. Nimoo (Eds.), *Political communication yearbook, 1984* (pp. 43–65). Carbondale, IL: Southern Illinois University Press.

Hayes, A. F., Shanahan, J., & Glynn, C. J. (2001). Willingness to express one's opinion in a realistic situation as a function of perceived support for that opinion. *International Journal of Public Opinion Research, 13,* 45–58.

Hayes, A. F., Glynn, C. J., Shanahan, J., Scheufele, D. A., Moy, P., Domke, D., & Stamm, K. (2002). *Fear of isolation and the climate of opinion: Moderating the spiral of silence?* Paper presented at the annual meeting of the Association for Education in Journalism and Mass Communication, Miami Beach, FL.

Hayes, A. F., Glynn, C. J., Shanahan, J., & Uldall, B. (2003). *Individual differences in willingness to self-censor.* Paper presented at the annual meeting of the American Association for Public Opinion Research, Nashville, TN.

Hayes, A. F., Glynn, C. J., & Shanahan, J. (2005a). Willingness to self-censor: A construct and measurement tool for public opinion research. *International Journal of Public Opinion Research, 17,* 298–323.

Hayes, A. F., Glynn, C. J., & Shanahan, J. (2005b). Validating the willingness to self-censor scale: Individual differences in the effect of the climate of opinion on opinion expression. *International Journal of Public Opinion Research 17,* 443–455.

Katz, C., & Baldassare, M. (1992). Using the "L-word" in public: A test of the spiral of silence in conservative Orange County. *Public Opinion Quarterly 56,* 232–235.

Kim, J., Wyatt, R. O., & Katz, E. (1999). News, talk, opinion, participation: The part played by conversation in deliberative democracy. *Political Communication, 16*(4), 361–385.

Matera, F., & Salwen, M. (1989). *"Speaking up" for one's views: Support for Radio Marti among Miami's Cubans and non-Cubans.* Paper presented at the annual meeting of the Association for Education in Journalism and Mass Communication, Washington, D.C.

McDevitt, M., Kiousis, S., and Wahl-Jorgensen, K. (2003). Spiral of moderation: Opinion expression in computer-mediated discussion. *International Journal of Public Opinion Research, 15*(4), 454–470.

Moreno-Riaño, G. (2002). Experimental implications for the spiral of silence. *The Social Science Journal, 39,* 65–81.

Morgan, M., & Shanahan, J. (1997). Two decades of cultivation research: An appraisal and a meta-analysis. In B. Burleson (Ed.), *Communication yearbook 20* (pp. 1–45). Thousand Oaks, CA: Sage.

Moy, P., Domke, D., & Stamm, K. (2001). The spiral of silence and public opinion on affirmative action. *Journalism and Mass Communication Quarterly, 78*(1), 7–25.

Niven, D. (2002). Bolstering an illusory majority: The effects of the media's portrayal of death penalty support. *Social Science Quarterly, 83*(3), 671–689.

Noelle-Neumann, E. (1984, 1993). *The spiral of silence: Public opinion, our social skin.* Chicago: University of Chicago Press.

Noelle-Neumann, E. (2001). Commentary. *International Journal of Public Opinion Research, 13,* 59–60.

Perry, S., & Gonzenbach, W. (2000). Inhibiting speech through exemplar distribution: Can we predict a spiral of silence? *Journal of Broadcasting and Electronic Media, 44*(2), 268–281.

Petric, G., & Pinter, A. (2002). From social perception to public expression of opinion: A structural equation modeling approach to the spiral of silence. *International Journal of Public Opinion Research 14*(1), 37–53.

Richard, F., Bond C., & Stokes-Zoota, J. (2003). One hundred years of social psychology quantitatively described. *Review of General Psychology, 7*(4), 331–363.

Scheufele, D. A., & Moy, P. (2000). Twenty five years of the spiral of silence: A conceptual review and empirical outlook. *International Journal of Public Opinion Research, 12,* 3–28.

Scheufele, D., Shanahan, J., & Lee, E. (2001). Real talk: Manipulating the dependent variable in spiral of silence research. *Communication Research, 28,* 304–324

Scheufele, D., & Eveland, W. (2001). Perceptions of "Public Opinion" and "Public" Opinion Expression. *International Journal of Public Opinion Research, 13,* 25–44.

Shanahan, J. (1999). Meta-analysis and mass communication criticism. *Critical Studies in Mass Communication, 16*(3), 370–373.

Tokinoya, H. (1996). A study of the spiral of silence theory in Japan. *KEIO Communication Review 18,* 1–13.

Willnat, L., Lee, W., & Detenber, B. (2002). Individual-level predictors of public outspokenness: A test of the spiral of silence theory in Singapore. *International Journal of Public Opinion Research, 14*(4), 391–412.

Wolf, F. (1986). *Meta-analysis: Quantitative methods for research synthesis.* Newbury Park, CA: Sage.

26

On the Role of Newspaper Ownership on Bias in Presidential Campaign Coverage by Newspapers

Dave D'Alessio
University of Connecticut–Stamford

Mike Allen
University of Wisconsin–Milwaukee

Concerns about media bias and its potential consequences date roughly to the invention of mass media (Schramm, 1988). Not long after the invention of the printing press governmental efforts to control the content of printed materials started. For instance, Stevens (1982) quoted an (unnamed) colonial governor of Virginia claiming in 1671 "printing ... libels against the government. ..." (p. 29); because there was no printing press in Virginia in 1671, this may have been the first preemptive claim of media bias.

Subsequently, questions about media content, the role it should play in the political process and the role it actually does play have become commonplace. Presidents Jefferson and Jackson were vocal about their concerns with the press; in this century we see these concerns tied directly to electoral processes, with prominent political figures such as Jim Farley (Franklin Roosevelt's campaign manager), presidential candidates Adlai Stevenson and Bob Dole, and vice president Spiro Agnew all registering complaints that the media were interfering with the electoral process by, in essence, taking sides.

Their concerns, although possibly unfounded, are not unreasonable. One of the capabilities of the media is status conferral, that is, the ability to transform an unknown person into a mediated image (Lazarsfeld & Merton, 1948/1971), and this is clearly a critical element of the process of being elected president. But most politicians prefer to exert control over the image and placing that process in the hands of sometimes recalcitrant reporters and editors means yielding part of that control. Voters' beliefs about political figures, as is generally the case with beliefs about things with which people have little direct contact, are created largely from mediated images, and the common reasoning is that to the extent that media present biased images of the candidate and campaign, the voters' belief structure will be biased as well, with electoral consequences.

This reasoning is simple and compelling, but at the same time it is overly simplistic. It is based on the concept of a monolithic media speaking with one voice to a completely passive audience; however, these conditions generally do not exist. Competition among media assures that they cannot speak monolithically, and it has been demonstrated that people are not readily susceptible to messages that they disagree with (Klapper, 1960). Finally, a great proportion of the electoral populace is not even listening (Lazarsfeld, Berelson, & Gaudet, 1944).

However, as we have recently seen, the election of a president and so the direction of the nation can hinge on a relatively small number of voters. A media effect size that would in social science terms be regarded as unmeasurably small could have changed the outcome of the Florida vote in 2000—or perhaps did so. Someone may determine whether the Florida media were biased and in whose favor if so; some people may draw conclusions based on that information. No one will be able to prove that media bias altered the outcome, but the possibility may exist, and so media bias needs to be considered seriously. For instance, Shaw (1999) detected influences on voters by campaign coverage that would have been sufficient in magnitude to turn the 2000 election.

NATURE OF NEWS MEDIA

Discussion of media bias tends to be fairly direct and to focus largely on only one element, partisan bias or the enacted preference of the media for one political party over the other. But the fact is that, sociologically speaking, the news media are complex entities that possess a wide variety of characteristics, any of which could lead to systematic variations in content. A news outlet, say, in this case, a given newspaper, is simultaneously (a) a journalistic entity, staffed by a number of people with formal or ad hoc training in journalism. These people share to a degree a certain ethical code and perspective on the world and a newspaper's role in it, but also have a sense for the nature of news and the need to tell a "good" story. A newspaper is also (b) a commercial entity that is in the business of making money and doing so by attracting advertisers who in turn have the expectation of having the newspaper supply readers for the advertisements. But even from this commercial perspective it also has to be remembered that a newspaper is (c) property. It is owned by somebody or something (generally a corporation if not a person), and the owner has the capability and authority to override the newspaper's attempts to achieve the goals required in servicing its other needs. Readers are referred to the great film *Citizen Kane,* particularly the scenes representing the early days of Kane's career, when he takes over a newspaper and bends its agenda to his will simply because he is the owner and he can. And finally, a newspaper is also (d) a political actor. People refer to the media as the "fourth branch of government" for the reason that the media are both the conduit for the political dialog that allows the nation to be governed but are also, via editorial materials, a voice in that dialog.

Each of these natures has some impact in shaping the content, both reportage and editorial, of a newspaper. In many cases the needs of one nature directly contradict those of another, and a complex set of processes are deployed to resolve these contradictions. Or maybe not—maybe the boss just comes in and tells everyone what to do.

Each of these natures introduces one or more biases into reportage.

DEFINING BIAS

It is pointless to continue a discussion of bias without offering a definition. This area, so often debated, is based on a concept that is so frequently ill defined. Of course, the importance of media bias is essentially a political question and for political purposes it is often best to allow the topic to remain undefined: one can simply point at whatever one pleases and say "See? Bias!" without fear of contradiction.

But the definitional inadequacy is also manifest in the scientific literature. Williams (1975), for instance, who critically reviewed four books on bias and questions related to it, pointed out that each had failed to define it—but also offered no formal definition himself! He did, however, argue that media bias, as opposed to "unfairness" or "saying something we don't like" or "statistical accident," is characterized by at least four elements. Specifically, to be defined as "biased," regular trends in media content must be

1. volitional. Media content must be deliberately skewed as opposed to accidentally. "Accidental bias" constitutes nothing more than an honest mistake;
2. influential, although Williams may have meant to say "teleological." Media bias is done for a reason and is not pointless. One presumes that media are biased to whatever extent to advance one or more of the media outlet's goals associated with one or more of its natures;
3. threatening to conventional values. Radical and reactionary viewpoints from radical or reactionary sources are simply too extreme to lead to much consequential persuasion, and most such sources are simply ignored.

Finally, bias must be

4. sustained. It is nonsense to describe one story as "biased." A single report may be unfair or unbalanced or inaccurate, but the nature of bias is that it is consistent and persistent across time. A useful definition of media bias should incorporate these four elements.

Another problem is that a bias is also a divergence; that is, it is observed as some relative divergence from a standard of some sort. A simplistic construction would be to require that bias be measured against some form of "truth," but were it possible for people to have direct access to truth, there would be no need for media, persuasion, or in fact most communicative activities (at least those associated with factual goals). There would be no need for beliefs or belief structures; there would simply be the known and the unknown.

In the absence of direct access to truth, a set of standards, perhaps arbitrary but necessarily well defined, needs to be constructed. Westerstahl (1983), who was tasked with overseeing reporting in Scandinavia where state-run news media are expected to be objective as part of their requirements, approached objectivity as a hierarchical, four-part structure. Two of the elements of objectivity, truth and relevance, constitute factuality; news media are expected to have their facts right.

More important to our discussion is the idea that Westerstahl terms *impartiality*. Impartiality is composed of a neutral presentation and also the requirement of balance or nonpartisanship; that is, that the reporter does not take sides. Although he does not define balance, his discussion refers to the relative amounts of coverage each side of a story gets.

Other journalistic researchers, (e.g., Fico & Cote, 1999; Lacy, Fico, & Simon, 1991) have worked routinely with the concepts of fairness and balance. Fairness is the basic idea that in a story about an issue on which there is more than one significant orientation, all major viewpoints should be represented in reportage. Balance is the far more stringent requirement that all viewpoints must be treated with equal respect, with respect generally being operationalized to mean with "space" (the raw amount of coverage) and/or "play" (the prominence of coverage in terms of headline size, placement on the page, location in the paper, and so on).

McQuail (1992) described media bias as "a systematic tendency to favour (in outcome) one side or position over another" (p. 191). However, we prefer to define media bias as "a systematic, persistent unbalance in mainstream news coverage for the purpose of influencing opinion on key issues." To us, *systematic* means consistent in valence, that is, consistently promoting the same position, *persistent* is intended to apply to the short or middle terms of a period of weeks, months, or years rather than either days or decades and the nature of the opinion to be influenced is unspecified—it could be the public, elite groups, government officials, or any other audience. It should also be noted that biases can change because they are teleological: If the goals of the media entity change, so may the biases.

(It is the ideas of persistence and teleology, taken from Williams, that we are adding to McQuail's formulation.)

Types of Bias

As we have seen, the complex sociological nature of media implies a wide variety of possible biases that may meet the needs of any of the essential natures of the media outlet. Between them, Page and Shapiro (1992) and Patterson (1993) identified a number of them. For instance, Patterson has pointed out that news media tend to have journalistic biases. Journalists are in the business of telling stories, and certain types of story are inherently more interesting or engaging to users than others. For instance, there is an overabundance of "bad" news, for example, reports of killer earthquakes, train wrecks, hurricanes, and so on. These are newsworthy in part because they are unusual; the vast majority of the time the earth does not quake, the train does not wreck, and the wind does not reach hurricane force. Patterson is more specifically concerned, however, with the idea that these journalistic biases in favor of the new or unusual turns the coverage of political campaigns away from the discussion of issues and toward the consideration of a campaign in terms of the new, for example, the latest poll results. Issue positions are stable and so are rarely new, but the latest poll result is always new and frequently treated as news. (This is called *horse-race journalism.*)

Similarly, Page and Shapiro pointed out that in the commercial desire to attract audience, media act in ways that reflect the cherished beliefs of audiences. For instance, they identify nationalistic, anticommunist and procapitalist biases in U.S. media. Commercially this is eminently sensible, because U.S. readers generally prefer news of the United States and overwhelmingly prefer capitalism to communism. Even apart from the fact that most members of media organizations also hold these positions, it would be commercial suicide for the mainstream media to fail to account for these audience preferences.

As property, Page and Shapiro pointed out that, like many businesses, media organizations prefer minimal government interference with their ability to engage in whatever activities that they please and routinely oppose the imposition of taxes or regulation on the press. They term this a *minimal government bias,* although a better term would be *libertarian.*

Not all departures from fair or balanced coverage can be described as "bias". A procapitalist leaning may occur, not as a deliberate attempt to promote capitalism but accidentally: Capitalism so permeates our social institutions that it may not generally occur to reader, reporter, editor, or publisher to question it. This may or may not be a good thing: Although challenging one's assumptions is generally regarded as valuable, it is probably not useful to constantly challenge every assumption all of the time. And this may or may not constitute bias; the point is arguable.

However, for the political actors, media bias is a concern often expressed. The central nature of the U.S. political system with regard to both corporate and personal realms means that a great many entities are encouraged by ideals or self-interest to attempt to influence that system, often by influencing the outcome of elections. This is particularly true in the media, through which different actors attempt to influence the political system by influencing the flow of discourse (e.g., debate or campaigns) central to the system.

Most observers of media are concerned with the possibility of ideological biases in this flow of discourse that are created by the media outlets, that is, the extent to which media entities are actors in the system as well as being the channel of communication. In particular, there is the concern over whether the media have an ideological bias reflecting one or another political philosophy. For instance, Patterson and Donsbach (1996) discussed an activist bias in news reporting, in which news reports have a tendency to favor progressive social change over the status quo. As in the comment attributed to media critic H. L. Mencken, one of the functions of the media is to "afflict the comfortable and comfort the afflicted." Progressive reform of this sort is associated with liberal ideology (T. W. Smith, 1990).

Ideological biases are sometimes associated, positively or negatively, with biases derived from a nature of the media other than their political nature, as explicated earlier. For instance, anticommunist biases (such as those described by Bernhard, 1999) are arguably both commercial and ideological (conservative) in origin. Similarly, the same can be said of antifeminist biases such as those examined by Davis (1982; K. B. Smith, 1997, suggested that antifeminist bias is abating): It is difficult to tell whether the origin is structural or ideological or some combination of the two. The multiple essences of commercial news media in the United States makes them subject to many masters, and each has its preference in content and some means of enforcing that preference.

Partisan Bias

In the present two-party electoral system, ideological biases map as partisan biases; that is, a preference for certain positions on issues translates into a preference for the political party that supports those positions. For instance, because the Democrat party is associated with liberal ideology (at least to a greater extent than the Republican party), the essentially liberal activist bias is expected to translate into support for the Democrat party's candidates. This is consequential to this discussion because of the importance of electoral politics to everyday life. The different policies of different parties can lead into or out of war, raise or lower taxes, or increase or reduce educational financial aid. Thus, a great deal of public discourse is expended on considering the nature and amount of partisan bias.

The mechanisms surrounding accusations of partisan media bias are generally expected to be simple and straightforward. One school of thought, generally espoused by the ideological right (e.g. Bozell & Baker, 1990; Ephron, 1971), holds essentially that (a) it is demonstrably true that news reporters and editors are ideologically more liberal than the mainstream. (For instance, Dautrich & Hartley,

1999, reported that 89% of Washington news reporters voted for Clinton in 1992; 50% self-described as Democrats and 61% as liberal. The figures for the general public are 43.3% (53.5% excluding Perot voters), 34%, and 20%, respectively); (b) this ideology is manifested in the news reports that reporters prepare (whether the manifestation is deliberate or not is in dispute and for the purposes of this report irrelevant), and, consequently, (c) media show preference for candidates espousing liberal views, which is to say the Democrats.

This view of potential media bias is not universal. Liebling (1961/1975) pointed out that although reporters may be liberal as a group, the owners and publishers of media outlets are conservative. This is still the case: Almost 77% of publishers supported Bob Dole over Bill Clinton in 1996 (Giobbe, 1996) and more than 73% expressed a preference for George W. Bush over Al Gore in 2000 (Mitchell, 2000).

In the power relationship that is the employer/employee balance, it is the employer who has the upper hand; workers cannot fire their bosses in the news industry. Thus, Liebling (1961/1975) argued that media take on the viewpoints of the owners and those viewpoints tend to be conservative and consequently pro-Republican. Note that this viewpoint grows out of the idea that media are property.

As an example, Kahn and Kenney (2002) discovered an association between editorial endorsement and valence of coverage in Senate races. They looked at a total of 79 Senate races between 1998 and 1992, and for each content analyzed the coverage of the race in the state's highest circulation (and so potentially most influential) newspaper. After coding a number of structural variables for each race (such as the seniority of candidates, campaign spending, challenger quality, and the competitiveness of the race), they found that the newspaper's endorsement had a significant effect on the tone of coverage of incumbent senatorial candidates. Whether this is a generalized partisan bias or a pro-incumbent bias is not known.

As media outlets increasingly become the property of large, publicly held corporations (Straubhaar & LaRose, 2002), there is reason to believe that the conservative influence of management will decline. Whereas a corporation has a preference for an amicable business climate, publicly held corporations are expected by shareholders to grow profits. This would lead to a centrist, or middle-of-the-road, bias, as the middle of the road reflects the location of the largest and most profitable audiences (e.g., Gerbner, Gross, Morgan, & Signiorelli, 1982).

More recently, liberal critics (e.g., Cooper & Soley, 1990; T. Lieberman, 2000a) tried to document the attempt by right-wing organizations to co-opt public opinion by the promotion of specific, amicable voices as experts. Lieberman pointed, for instance, to the efforts made to make viewpoints provided by organizations such as the American Enterprise Institute, the Heritage Foundation, and the Cato Institute available to the media and subsequent representation of their conservative, pro-business (and presumably pro-Republican) views into media discourse on subjects such as benefits for the elderly and the role of the Food and Drug Administration.

RESEARCH QUESTION

In this chapter we consider partisan bias in the media coverage of presidential campaigns in the United States and in particular consider the role of largely conservative owners and publishers in controlling the newspaper coverage consumed by potential voters. This question represents something answerable using existing research methodology. The process should raise the awareness of fellow social scientists of the problems faced when one tries to objectively examine the question of media bias and should encourage the development of more sophisticated models of media content and biases, more sensitive methodologies for measuring them, and increasingly objective discussion of the genesis, magnitude, and consequences of media bias.

As noted earlier, bias is a relativistic notion, not unlike the notion of speed. Einstein (1916/1961) pointed out that the idea of the speed of an object, without reference to any external standard, is meaningless, because in the absence of an outside standard there is nothing against which to measure the object's speed. The same is true of bias. A news media outlet cannot just be biased; it must be biased for or against something by measurement against some standard that represents an unbiased state.

Bias in Presidential Campaigns

Presidential campaigns between major party candidates provide a unique situation for the examination of partisan bias (and through it, ideological bias), allowing that it is not unreasonable to stipulate a priori that balanced reporting constitutes unbiased reporting. The major political parties in the United States have attracted remarkably similar popular support since the World War II era, and each routinely nominates a figure who appears to be adequately of national stature for each presidential campaign. It is not unreasonable to operationalize unbiased coverage as balanced coverage in this particular application.

Previously, we (D'Alessio & Allen, 2000) considered the aggregate bias in three major news media (newspapers, TV, and magazines) as total systems. Our meta-analysis of 69 research reports found that in the presidential campaigns from 1948 to 1996 there was basically no evidence of consistent media bias as measured against the standard of balanced reporting. That was a very specific conclusion designed to consider simply the idea of an all-pervasive, industry-wide preference for one party or another that would be indicative of a similar ideological bias.

Niven (2002) suggested that the standard of balanced reporting may be unreasonable. He (Niven also cited Kobre, 1953, and Westerstahl, 1983, raised the same point) pointed out that not all campaigns are equally newsworthy and therefore providing balanced coverage would require the news outlets to either ignore items for the more active campaign or manufacture them for the less active. This is manifestly true. Niven cited the McGovern campaign as being short of news, and arguably the same is true of Jimmy Carter's 1980 campaign: Beset by foreign and domestic disaster, Carter attempted a "Rose Garden" strategy, trying to emphasize his leadership task as president over active campaigning. But in the aggregate it is unlikely that there would be systematic differences between political parties with regard to the activity of campaigns; instead, one would expect inefficient campaigners to be distributed randomly across candidates and parties and so differences would cancel out in the aggregate. This is consistent with our findings, as our overall data set was homogeneous, meaning that differences from campaign to campaign were simply random noise. In short, different campaigners may generate more or less news, but on the whole they even out across parties.

This discussion points up the difficulty of finding and enforcing external standards in the attempt to measure media bias. One campaign is more newsworthy than another, but how is that determined? News ultimately is that which ends up reported in the news media, and to achieve that status it is a necessary condition that one or more members of the news media must have decided that an act or event was newsworthy. If there is a possibility that members of the news media act in biased ways, then it necessarily follows that this news judgment is a biased standard against which to measure bias. (News judgment is certainly subject to the journalistic bias discussed previously!)

The process of selecting certain events from a universe of events and describing that subset as "news" is called *gatekeeping*. Bagdikian (1971) pointed out the magnitude of this effect: In one night the editor Bagdikian observed threw out more than 79% of the material he was given to choose from by the wire services he was using—without noticing that the material he was culling came from an already reduced larger pool of information selected and provided by the various wire service workers. Gatekeeping decisions are based on a wide variety of criteria, including the ideological: When White (1950) discussed one evening's worth of choice decisions with the editor making them, almost 10% of the rejections were explicitly for reasons of the editor's personal politics (and it is unknown how many of the numerous stories he rejected as being uninteresting were deemed as such due to the editor's ideological beliefs).

Because we have no access to the universe of all stories, it is impossible to try to measure bias against any measurement of the extent of the news hole against some internally constructed zero point: It is clear that a constructed zero point is as subject to bias as any measurement made against it. Instead, we have chosen, as discussed earlier, to measure bias against the theoretical idea of "balance," at least in the case of political campaigns between political parties of roughly equal potential. Niven's (and Kobre's, and Westerstahl's) point that not all campaigns are equally newsworthy is well taken, but it must be noted that balance is first of all an ideal or goal state and so is not always easy to obtain and also that balance, along with fairness, is one of the goal states that the journalism industry has adopted for itself (Society of Professional Journalists, 1996).

Measuring Partisan Bias

Having established that we will be measuring media content about the major party candidates in presidential campaign against the theoretical and philosophical idea of balance, we are left with the question of what exactly can be measured. Media content, particularly campaign reportage published in newspapers, possesses a number of characteristics that are measurable in a variety of ways.

The first is what we (D'Alessio & Allen, 2000) have called *volumetric* measurements. Volumetric measurements are concerned with simple, nonevaluative, counting-type characteristics: the number of stories about one campaign or another or their length, measured in words or column-inches (the column-inch is the amount of text in a newspaper article 1 inch high and the width of one of the columns used by the newspaper for layout purposes). Researchers have also counted paragraphs, sentences, and the number and size of photographs in newspapers and other print media; for television and voice-based media volumetric measurements include the length of a report in time (e.g., so many seconds of air time) or words. In the volumetric measures the critical identification is simply which campaign the story is about. No attempt is made to evaluate the content qualitatively; that is, there is no evaluation of whether the content is supportive of or destructive to the campaign.

Content analytic procedures are often used to attempt to reach some type of agreement as to what we have come to call the *valence* of each report. Valenced measures are designed to have coders or judges consider a content unit of a predetermined size and arrive at a consensus as to whether the content is helpful to the campaign of a given candidate or hurtful to it. In measuring valence-based bias it is generally assumed that items that are hurtful to one campaign are helpful to the other, and thus indices are constructed based on the sum of the number of items that are pro to one side plus anti to the other. Valence bias measures at the level of the story and also at the level of individual statements, and a small number of researchers have even considered whether there are elements of commentary in the placement of stories in a newspaper (e.g., page 1 vs. pages inside the paper) or the relative attractive elements of photos selected.

A third approach to the measurement of bias is to consider whether stories were being disproportionately selected from the universe of stories, which we have termed *selection* bias. As we have seen, this bias is problematic in that the universe of stories has already been subject to at least one potentially biased culling before it becomes the universe of stories, but as long as we recognize that we are not attempting to measure bias against an unknown news hole but instead against the ideal of balance, we can produce results that are consistent with the examination of bias as we have been considering it herein.

To illustrate the difference between the three types of bias, let us assume a universe of exactly two stories of the same length, one about each campaign. Story A describes candidate A as having been arrested for drunk driving years before;

story B describes candidate B as having volunteered to serve in a war zone as a journalist. If a newspaper runs both stories, then the newspaper's coverage is balanced volumetrically.

To consider valence bias, we have a series of coders judge the two articles; they judge the first to be negative for candidate A (and so presumably positive for B) and the second story to be positive for B. If the newspaper runs both, or either by itself, then a lack of balance favorable to B is shown. (Recall that this decision in and of itself is not bias and does not rise to the level of bias unless the newspaper makes a habit of such selection, but a series of decisions of this sort across the length of the campaign is regarded as valence bias.)

To measure selection bias, we would consider the universe of one story about each side. Selecting both or selecting neither would show equal selection for both sides; selecting only one would be considered a lack of balance favoring the selected side.

Editorial Endorsements

Having laid a groundwork for measuring bias, our final consideration in examining the control over coverage as suggested by Liebling (1961/1975) and also by Kahn and Kenney's (2002) research is attempting to determine the preferences of owners and publishers in partisan elections. Fortunately, this is relatively simpler than the measurement of bias: St. Dizier (1985) demonstrated that the endorsement of presidential candidates is one of the few editorial decisions that owners and publishers reserve for themselves. This would not be a useful means of distinguishing the attitudes of reporters from those of publishers if those opinions were distributed evenly, but it is clear that they are not: Newspaper editorials, dominated by publishers and owners, showed preference for Republican presidential candidates in 1940, 1944, 1948, 1952, 1956, 1960, 1968, 1972, 1976, 1980, 1984, 1988, and 1996 ("Newspaper endorsements," 1996). For the 1972 election about 14 newspapers endorsed Republican Richard Nixon for every one newspaper that endorsed Democrat George McGovern, and ratios favorable to the Republican candidate of 4 and 5 to 1 are not uncommon.

Although the decline in personal ownership of newspapers has led to decreasing trends in both endorsements of presidential candidates generally and in the proportion of endorsements made by owners and publishers specifically, Giobbe (1996) has found that as late as 1996, 42% of endorsements were still being made by publishers without input from the editorial staff. In previous elections, the proportion of endorsements made by the publishers was substantially higher—St. Dizier (1985), for instance, found that publishers made 81% of the endorsements in 1984. In view of this, we felt that it was reasonable to make an imputation of the partisan preference of owners and publishers by examining the editorial endorsements that the newspapers made for the presidential campaign.

Obviously, this fails to allow us to consider the interjection of conservative bias by the provision of conservative experts as sources, as is T. Lieberman's (2000) concern. However, the other two models make specific predictions about the relationship between a newspaper's news content and its editorial policies. If reporters are biased and that bias manifests in news content, then unbalance in the content of the news hole should be unrelated to the newspaper's endorsement, as the reporters have no means of control over the publisher's endorsement. That is, each element (coverage and editorial) could show systematic favoritism without regard for the favoritism of the other. (We will not be explicitly considering this model, because, given the nature of statistical testing, tests of it would also constitute tests of the null hypothesis.)

However, if it is true that the political desires of owners and publishers manifest themselves not only in the newspaper's endorsement but also by the mechanism of employment power described by Liebling (1961/1975), then there should be an association between a newspaper's endorsement policy and its preferential treatment of one candidate over another. Specifically, newspapers endorsing Republican candidates will show preferential coverage favoring Republicans, and newspapers endorsing Democrats should show the same for Democratic candidates. This is our primary hypothesis.

Ancillary Questions

General knowledge of the data set we are dealing with and historical conditions that change across the time of this study suggest consideration of the impact of two additional variables: the impact of sampling effects and time. Starting in 1961, Stempel conducted a series of content analyses focusing on the 16 newspapers designated by *Editor and Publisher* as being "prestige" papers. (The designation was peer-nominated; that is, *Editor and Publisher* was reporting the results of a poll of newspaper editors conducted by *Practical English* magazine, "Nation's editors pick," 1960.) Later, other writers followed Stempel's lead, and examined the activities of the *prestige press* (e.g., King, 1995; Lacy et al., 1991). The list of prestige press papers consists of a number of large, well-known papers with at least one known sampling flaw (papers in the Midwest and East are overrepresented), and selection of those papers is clearly nonrandom. Our second research question asks whether the distributions of unbalance and endorsement are similar for the prestige press and the other papers researched.

Also, as previously mentioned, it is a general trend for newspapers to increasingly belong to large, publicly held corporations. As commercial entities, it is distinctly likely that they are increasingly unwilling to alienate their audience by taking strong political stands. *Editor and Publisher* has repeatedly indicated that the number of papers making endorsements for president has decreased with almost every recent election, and as time continues it could be that the remaining editorials are increasingly written by editors rather than publishers, so the direct influence of the employer on news reporting may be reduced over time. Consequently, our third task will be to examine the influence of time on the relationship between endorsement and coverage.

METHOD

We started by returning to the collection of research reports we had previously assembled. The details of how we found those articles are reported in D'Alessio and Allen (2000). From that collection we selected all of the articles that met the following characteristics:

1. An article had to provide any measurement of volume, valence, or selection (as discussed previously) for any individual newspaper's news coverage of a presidential campaign for.
2. Any newspaper that was either named specifically or whose editorial preference was reported in the article.

If editorial preference was not reported in the article, the preference was obtained, if possible, from the quadrennial polls of editorial preference published in *Editor and Publisher.*

We also searched a number of online indexes (for instance, the Social Science Citation Index and PsycINFO) and recent issues of *Journalism Quarterly, Political Communication,* and the *Newspaper Research Journal* for additional reports.

Articles were excluded if they reported only the content of TV or news magazines. They were also excluded if they failed to publish individual data for individual newspapers separately or if they failed to publish both the identity of the newspaper in question and its editorial preference. Finally, we excluded studies that reported insufficient data as to allow calculation of our effect size statistic.

We limited our database to studies of the news content of newspapers. We feel that the expectations regarding fairness and balance do not necessarily apply to material that is clearly labeled as opinion. Additionally, we used materials that are able to examine the entire campaign. When possible, that is, for reports giving month-by-month data, we stuck to the traditional Labor Day to Election Day campaign length to avoid confounding with reporting on primary campaigns or nominating conventions and did not include the reports devoted to analysis of just presidential debates.

Eventually we located 22 books and articles that reported some kind of content measurement of campaign coverage for anywhere from 1 to 34 newspapers. Ultimately, a total of 209 campaign coverages were located, although some newspapers were represented multiple times across campaign years and a small number were represented twice or more for the same campaign. (Although this violates the assumption of independence of cases, we felt that the variation of methodologies employed by different researchers would preclude statistical difficulties in this regard.)

For each, we recorded quantities for as many of the following variables as data were presented: volumetric measurements including number of stories, column inches, number of paragraphs, number of sentences, number of photos, and column inches of photos; valenced measurements including valenced number of stories (where anti one side is counted as pro the other), valenced column inches, and valenced photographic tone; and any measure of selection. We recorded as many of these variables for each article as were reported. We omitted measures of play or potential bias in layout issues (such as size of headline or placement of story on the page) as most formulations of play tend to be highly idiosyncratic from researcher to researcher. Thus, we ended up with anywhere from one to four estimates of bias for each newspaper's coverage. (Because we are talking about aggregate coverage across the entire campaign, we feel that this is a sufficiently persistent unit of analysis to justify use of the term *bias*.)

Accumulating Effects

Although in most cases the Pearson product-moment correlation is regarded as the best means of estimating effect sizes for meta-analytic purposes (Hunter, Schmidt, & Jackson, 1982), in this case, as we did in 2000, we chose to use the d' statistic (Rosenthal, 1991). r is frequently preferred because it is common, easily comprehended, and not affected by sample size, but d' possesses each of these characteristics as well, because it is simply the difference between two proportions; that is, if 55% of the coverage were Democratic and 45% Republican, $d' = .55 - .45 = .10$. Being a proportion, it is also both readily interpretable and unaffected by sample size.

Unbalance in favor of the Democratic candidate was arbitrarily coded as positive, and so any $d' > 0$ refers to a Democratic bias. $d' < 0$ indicates a Republican unbalance; $d' = 0$ indicates perfectly balanced coverage. d' can range in magnitude from 0 to 1, with 1 indicating that the coverage was entirely one-sided. We actually did observe one d' of -1: In the 1952 campaign the *Idaho Daily Statesman* ran three photographs of Dwight Eisenhower (R) and none of Adlai Stevenson (D). This was the only instance of a d' of 1 magnitude observed.

Although it is a common practice in meta-analysis (Hunter & Schmidt, 1990), we chose not to conduct tests of homogeneity. The large number of units of analysis—for instance, the *New York Times* routinely supplies more than 1,000 column inches of campaign coverage per campaign—virtually ensures that tests of homogeneity will fail. As a consequence, moderator variables were examined using analysis of variance (ANOVA) and contingency tables, employing the chi-square test statistic to examine the distributions.

It should be noted that late in our research we discovered an archive of coverage data that was made available electronically. Unfortunately, the machine-readable data did not provide anything useful for the purposes of this report. Because each of the reports (Alvarez, 2003; Beck, Dalton, & Huckfeldt, 1992) discusses only one election, it is unlikely that that either one would influence any of our overall results; however, future efforts may prove fruitful in adding these data.

RESULTS

Across the 209 campaign reports we were able to find sufficient data to calculate 409 d' statistics. These data are available from the authors on request. The sources from which the d' information was calculated are numbered in the reference section of this paper. In all cases only Republican and Democratic content was used in the calculation of d'. Neutral coverage and coverage of third-party candidates were omitted from the calculations.

Of the d's calculated, 194 were positive, 199 were negative, and 16 instances of completely balanced coverage were found. Considering only the set of $|d'| > 0$ (that is, omitting the 16 instances of balanced coverage), 49.4% of the coverages examined favored the Democrats and 50.6% the Republicans.

Of the 209 newspapers, 87 endorsed Republican candidates and 68 Democrats. In the remaining 54 cases either the newspaper did not endorse a candidate (30 cases) or we were unable to determine which candidate they had endorsed (24 cases). Reducing the number of cases wherein we are unable to determine the endorsement is another area for which we intend to continue amassing data for the future.

The total set of 409 tests yielded an unweighted mean d' of $-.054$. Although this is statistically significantly ($SE = .011$, $t(408) = 4.91$, $p < .001$) different from perfect balance in coverage ($d' = 0$), we have to conclude that this quantity of bias is insubstantial. If we translate a d' of $-.054$ into content, it means that 52.7% of content was Republican and 47.3% Democratic, or a bias amounting to a change in valence in about one-fortieth of the total news content.

Also of interest is the fact that the distribution of d' is leptokurtic (kurtosis = 2.36), or "skinnier" than the standard normal distribution. This could be characteristic of at least some of the newspapers considering balanced coverage to be a goal state; if they were not attempting to arrive at relatively balanced coverage, the distribution should have displayed normal kurtosis.

To examine our first research question, we considered that if publishers and owners were to be using their organizational power to influence news coverage, we would observe two characteristics in the data: (a) the mean d' for papers endorsing Republicans should be less than that for newspapers endorsing Democrats, with neutral papers in between; and (b) the combinations of endorsement preference and content preference should be distributed nonrandomly, with cases of agreement between endorsement and content overrepresented and cases for which they disagree underrepresented.

To examine the first characteristic, we conducted a one-way ANOVA with d' score as the dependent variable and the endorsement (Democratic, none, or Republican) as the independent variable. We found an overall main effect of $F(2, 406) = 29.7$, $p < .0001$, indicating some relationship between endorsement and coverage. The mean d' for Democratically endorsing papers was $+.054$, for nonendorsing papers it was $-.057$, and for Republican endorsing papers $d' = -.124$. These means differed significantly when tested with Fisher's least significant difference test (and, in fact, using any post hoc test of means).

The distribution of newspapers across the various combinations of endorsement and coverage unbalance is shown as Table 26.1. It should be noted that the "other" column in Table 26.1 includes any condition in which the newspaper did not endorse a candidate or we could not find the endorsement plus the small number of coverage tests that were completely balanced.

As is clear in the first line of Table 26.1 (the row associated with this research question), combinations of agreeing coverage unbalance and endorsement are overrepresented in the distribution, and this overrepresentation is statistically significant at the $p < .0001$ level.

Together these findings suggest that there is a fairly substantial agreement between a newspaper's endorsement of a candidate and the valence of that newspaper's coverage of the campaign, and specifically that coverage is valenced to favor the endorsed candidate.

TABLE 26.1
Distribution of Newspaper Content Tests by the
Combination of Endorsement and Valence of d'

	Endorsement-Content Combination					
	D-D	R-R	R-D	D-R	Other	$\chi^2(1)$
Overall	92	124	64	32	97	48.2***
Prestige papers	78	49	41	29	58	15.4***
Nonprestige	14	75	23	3	39	22.8***
Prestige papers only						
Pre-1976	55	42	30	5	32	35.9***
1976+	23	7	11	24	26	0.8 (ns)

***$p < .001$.
Note. D, Democrat; R, Republican. The first letter refers to endorsement and the second to coverage ($d' > 0 =>$D; $d' < 0 = >$R). "Other" is all other combinations (no or unknown endorsement and/or $d' = 0$).

Prestige Papers

The second research question deals with the role that the known oversampling of the prestige press papers may play in the previous finding. As a consequence of the long-term program of research on the same 15 (originally) newspapers, 250 of the 409 tests we located were performed on the content of prestige press papers. This would constitute a random sample if there were only about 28 papers in the nation; because there are clearly more than 28 daily newspapers, it follows that the prestige press papers are overrepresented.

This is of particular importance because of the nature of the papers selected as being prestigious. Since the original survey reported in *Editor and Publisher* ("Nation's editors pick," 1960) makes no note that the editors voting on the nation's top papers were provided with any objective criteria on which to base their votes, it follows that the vote was based on the papers' gestalt reputation. It is distinctly likely that the veteran newsmen doing the voting would have taken into account issues such as the degree to which the publisher interferes with the reporting process. Newsmen like to be free to pursue their journalistic tasks in the same way that publishers prefer the freedom to pursue profits! Thus, it is possible that the balance between ideological biases between publishers and reporters in the content of the paper may be different in the prestige press than in other papers.

As examples, the prestige press papers include national opinion leaders such as the *New York Times,* the *Washington Post,* and the *Los Angeles Times.* It also includes unique papers such as the *Wall Street Journal,* whose business orientation is virtually unique among newspapers, the *Christian Science Monitor,* a national newspaper founded by a religious group devoted to the power of knowledge, and the *Milwaukee Journal,* the largest media entity in the United States that is wholly owned by its employees. (As such, the *Journal* is the only paper on which the reporters actually DO have power over the publishers!)

For the record, the remaining prestige press papers are the *Atlanta Constitution* (now the *Journal-Constitution*), the *Baltimore Sun,* both the *Chicago Daily News* and the *Tribune,* the *Des Moines Register,* the *Kansas City Star,* the *Louisville Courier-Journal,* the *Miami Herald* and the *St. Louis Post-Dispatch.* The *Chicago Daily News* ceased operations in the 1970s. Tribune Media Services, the multimedia conglomerate that also owns the Chicago Cubs, owns the *Tribune,* the *Sun,* and the *Los Angeles Times.* Seven of the others are also owned by large multimedia conglomerates (Gannett: *Courier-Journal* and *Register*; Knight-Ridder: *Herald* and *Star*; Cox: *Journal-Constitution*). The *New York Times,* the *Post,* and the *Post-Dispatch* are basically independent companies.

In a manner similar to the tests performed to answer the first research question, we also tested this research question in two ways. First, we constructed a one-way ANOVA that tested the average d' for prestige press papers against that of the nonprestige papers. Then, we constructed contingency tables comparing the distribution of d's by editorial endorsement. These data are presented as lines 2 (prestige papers) and 3 (nonprestige) in Table 26.1.

The ANOVA showed that the mean d' for prestige press papers was significantly higher (that is, less negative) than that for the other papers. The mean for each group differs significantly from zero, and each is negative in valence: for the prestige press papers, the average d' was $-.021$ ($n = 250$, $SE = .011$, $t(249) = 1.91$, $p < .05$); for the others, $d' = -.106$ ($n = 159$, $SE = .021$, $t(158) = 5.05$, $p < .0001$). The overall test of difference between the two means yielded $F(1, 407) = 15.465$, $p < .0001$. The prestige press papers differed from the others by being less conservative in their reporting.

Each subset of papers showed a significant relationship between the editorial endorsement made by the paper and valence of coverage, and in both cases the relationship was one of association: Democratic endorsements associated with Democratic coverage and Republican with Republican. It should be noted that this association is substantially less for the prestige press papers than for the others as the overall chi-square test statistic was lower (about two-thirds the magnitude) for the prestige papers. (It should be noted that differences in chi-square statistics are themselves distributed as a chi-square statistic and that any difference between chi-square statistics with the same number of degrees of freedom is automatically statistically significant. It is more important to our point that the difference in chi-square test statistics between the two is substantively different.)

From this we conclude that the Prestige Press papers are not representative of the population of papers. Their coverage was more balanced and showed less influence that can be attributed to the publisher. Despite this, there is a measurable association between endorsements and coverage in both prestige and nonprestige papers.

Time

To consider our time-based research question, we decided to break our study into two time intervals: elections in 1972 and earlier and the 1976 and later election campaigns. We chose to break the data at that point because it is roughly in the middle of the study and because the Watergate scandal, which arguably changed way that the politics is conducted in the United States, occurred between the 1972 and 1976 elections (Pournelle, 1992).

This division is unfortunate in that to make our time-based tests we will have to rely on using the prestige press papers. The continuing research program by Stempel and his colleagues means that we have information on the performance of the prestige press throughout most of the time period that this research covers. Data on the vast majority of nonprestige papers was gathered before 1976, in three major studies: Blumberg (1954), Graber (1971), and Graber (1976). If one looks at the distribution of d's on a two-by-two contingency table with prestige/nonprestige on one dimension and pre- and post-Watergate on the other, there are almost no tests in the post-Watergate/nonprestige cell. Because we have already demonstrated that prestige papers and the others are not completely comparable, we would not want to have an overrepresentation of the other papers in the pre-Watergate sample. Consequently, we chose to examine our time-based research question using only tests calculated on prestige press papers.

In the earlier time period, the aggregate d' for the prestige press differs significantly from zero ($d' = -.031$, $n = 155$, $SE = .015$, $t(154) = 2.05$, $p < .05$), but the mean drops essentially and statistically to zero for reportage of elections starting in 1976 ($d' = < -.004$, $n = 95$, $SE = .015$, $t(94) = 0.27$ ns). The difference between epochs does not differ significantly ($F(1,248) = 1.374$ ns), nor does it differ substantively.

Examination of the contingency table (see Table 26.1, final two data rows) is far more informative. There is clearly a significant relationship between editorial endorsement and direction of coverage in the pre-1976 prestige press, but this literally disappears starting after the Watergate era. (Whether the Watergate scandal itself is contributory to finding this is unknown.)

Part of this finding may be due to the increasing trend of newspapers to not endorse candidates at all, removing the publisher's desires from the coverage equation at those papers. This is observable in the prestige press and also in more representative samplings of newspapers. Another critical trend across the time period of this study is the increasing concentration of ownership of newspapers into corporate hands, with the presumed search for higher profits by finding the middle ground on matters of opinion that we have already discussed. In fact, even several of the prestige papers are now the flagships of corporate media empires, including the *New York Times,* the *Washington Post,* and the *Chicago Tribune.* (Readers are referred to the corporate Web sites of The New York Times Company, the Washington Post Company, and Tribune Media Services.) To the extent that the prestige papers are subject to the same trends in the industry at large and so demonstrate the consequences of those trends, we are able to conclude that the influence of publishers over the news content of newspapers has declined since the mid-1970s.

DISCUSSION

Although we have discussed a number of types of potential media bias to attempt to contextualize discussion of this controversial topic, we eventually set out to examine the influence of newspaper proprietors on the news coverage their newspapers provide on presidential elections. Although—like reporters and editors—publishers and owners vary in their ideologies from person to person, as a class they tend to be white, male, upscale, and conservative. The influence of the first three on newspaper content is unknown, but we have established that a substantive and substantial correspondence exists between the preferences of publishers and the coverage their newspapers provide.

In contradiction of our previously reported finding that unbalance in newspaper coverage of presidential campaigns does not significantly differ from zero, we found a statistically significant pro-Republican bias in this study. There are a number of reason why this might be: We have added several manuscripts to our data set in the last 2 years, and, more importantly, because we are examining the activity of individual newspapers in this study, as opposed to the last, in which we were interested in "the media" more broadly, the unit of analysis has moved from the aggregate findings of each study to the individually coded content unit in each newspaper. This move has the effect of increasing the number of observations, thus making statistical tests more sensitive.

As an aside, the data show that the use and deployment of photographs appears to be substantially more subject to unbalance and is more closely related to editorial position than are the written elements of news reports. A study is presently underway to examine this phenomenon. But the preponderance of studies of photographic bias date to the 1950s, when biases were larger generally, and so they may have had some effect on the mean d'. But the far more important conclusion about the magnitude of aggregate bias is that on the whole it amounts to essentially nothing. These data appear earlier but bear repeating: the mean d' of $-.054$ means that news content was 52.7% Republican and 47.3% Democratic. The result is significant but not substantive.

We have also established that the correspondence between editorial endorsement of a presidential candidate, typically made by a publisher, and the newspaper's unbalance in coverage is larger among less regarded newspapers. This finding is not insignificant: the *New York Times* may be a member of the prestige press, but far more New Yorkers read the *New York Post* or the *New York Daily News*. In the future we plan to consider the consequences of this fact, as we plan to examine data with regard to ownership and circulation as they relate (if they do) to biases in coverage.

Finally, we have established that to the extent that the prestige papers are representative of the newspaper industry as a whole, the influence of publishers over content is declining. However, it is equally clear that there are still publishers who regard newspapers as merely their own playthings. B. Lieberman (2000) reported that R. Mellon Scaife, publisher of the Pittsburgh-area *Tribune-Review* (and owner of its corporate parent) ordered his editors to essentially bury the Gore campaign: No pictures of the candidate were to appear and Associated Press copy was rewritten to benefit Bush. Scaife did not comment for Lieberman, but his intentions are clear: He might as well have been saying "It's my newspaper and I'll do what I want with it."

This case points up one of the many themes of this report, which is to attempt to start to lay a broadly based groundwork for the extensive study of the sources of media bias. We were explicitly and directly examining partisan bias, but partisan biases in a complex sociological organism, just as in a newspaper, are necessarily the consequence of a wide variety of competing processes. For instance, we can presume that impacts created by the notion of a newspaper as property ought to be very different depending on whether the paper is privately or publicly owned (or owned, like the *Milwaukee Journal,* by the people who work on it). A private owner who is independently wealthy—R. Mellon Scaife comes to mind—can treat his newspaper like a plaything, without regard to profit. A newspaper that is part of a publicly owned corporation such as Gannett must be run in the manner of a business, and if it is not run well, it will go the way of badly run businesses. In this day of media competition, one need not look further than the travails of the U.S. airline industry to see what can happen to businesses when they are run badly. Each of these ways of approaching the newspaper industry may have consequences that may assert themselves in the news content.

The finding of insubstantial aggregate amounts of bias also does not mean that individual papers all attempt to hew to a middle row. One of the papers examined in Blumberg's (1954) book was the *Chicago Tribune,* which in 1952 was still the personal property of the formidable Col. Robert McCormick. The *Tribune* reflected the Colonel's view of politics: the four tests of the *Tribune* yielded a mean d' of $-.421$ (and, yes, the Colonel did endorse Eisenhower, the Republican). This is not necessarily a record: Kenney and Simpson's (1993) data show the *Washington Times* at mean d' of $-.693$ in 1988. But it is important to remember that in 1952 Chicago readers could also choose the *Chicago Daily News* (which was also nominated to be one of the prestige press papers) and Washingtonians had the *Washington Post* as an alternative.

Increasingly, though, there are few reliable news alternatives. The number of newspapers in the nation and their readership as well is declining and has been since the mid-1980s. Increasingly, there is only one local newspaper in town, wherever the town is. Television news coverage of political campaigns continues to decline in quantity and quality (Center for Media and Public Affairs, 2000; Lichter, 2001), and Internet sources range from the unreliable (e.g., the Drudge Report) to those accessible by fees only (e.g., the *New York Times Online*) to those wholly controlled by the candidates and consequently filled only with those things the candidates want you to see (Stromer-Galley, 2000). We are a long way from being able to evaluate the electoral consequences of biased campaign reporting, but at least we are starting to take the first steps toward being able to evaluate bias. Once we have the tools and techniques to measure the causes, we can get to work on measuring the effects.

But even as we develop these analytic techniques, the raw data needed as input for them is beginning to dry up in the mainstream communications and journalism literature. We found only one study, which yielded only five tests of content, for the 1996 campaign. (Kern, 2001, did examine news stories provided by the online services of various newspapers, but did not break her results down by paper/Web site.) For 2000, we did not find any useful studies of newspaper content, although Pritchard (2001, 2002) looked at newspaper content as part of his research agenda examining the consequences of media cross-ownership. (Unfortunately, he only reported a summary statistic of his own invention called *slant,* which is valence-based but not convertible to d'. In the absence of raw data, we are unable to accommodate his findings in this report.) There is additional data out there, but as the journals in our field increasingly show preference for theoretically driven work, the content analytic work needed for meta-analytic work in this area is being pushed out of the refereed journals and into computer archives (where it may become unreadable) or master's theses (where it may never be found).

And finally, as meta-theoretic positions start to dominate a field, constructions outside of those positions start to disappear. For instance, Gerald Pomper quadrennially provides a survey of communication processes surrounding each election, with one chapter in each book devoted to media coverage. To Marion Just (1997), who wrote for the volume on 1996, the only coverage of the campaign was on TV: She reported data on network coverage but none on newspaper reports. In contrast, the report on the 2000 campaign (Hershey, 2001) not only focuses only on TV, but it is also an analysis of the candidates' attempts to frame issues in the media. Media activity independent of the actions of the Bush and Gore campaigns is not considered.

We have demonstrated herein that the nature of bias is dynamic and that it can change based on a number of influences and is changing over time. There continues to be a need for content analysis, and this need will continue until all the questions are answered. And this need is fundamental. Although theory-driven research is presently on an upswing, the purpose of a theory is to explain a set of facts. With the exception of certain impacts attributed solely to the nature of a medium (vide McLuhan, 1964), the effects of media are driven by the content of the media. The examination of content is a necessary precondition to the meaningful examination of effects or the formulation of useful theory.

REFERENCES

Studies represented in the meta-analysis are indicated by numbers in parentheses.

Alvarez, R. M. (2003). Media Content Coding Analysis, 1980 Presidential Campaign, Los Angeles Times [Computer file].

Bagdikian, B. H. (1971). *The information machines.* New York: Harper and Row.

(19) Batlin, R. (1954). San Francisco newspapers' campaign coverage: 1896, 1952. *Journalism Quarterly, 31,* 297–303.

Beck, P., Dalton, R. J., & Huckfeldt, R. (1992). Cross-National Election Studies: United States Study [Computer file].

(18) Berelson, B. R., Lazarsfeld, P. F., & McPhee, W. N. (1954). *Voting: A study of opinion formation in a presidential campaign.* Chicago: University of Chicago Press.

Bernhard, N. E. (1999). *US television news and Cold War propaganda: 1947–1960.* New York: Cambridge University Press.

(4) Blumberg, N. B. (1954). *One party press?* Lincoln, NB: University of Nebraska Press.

Bozell, L. B., & Baker, B. (1990). *And that's the way it isn't.* Alexandria, VA: Media Research Center.

(20) Cavanaugh, J. W. (1995). *Media effects on voters: A panel study of the 1992 presidential election.* Lanham, MD: University Press of America.

Center for Media and Public Affairs (CMPA). (2000). Campaign 2000 final: How TV news covered the general election campaign. *Media Monitor, 14.* Retrieved December 5, 2005 from http://www.cmpa.com/mediaMonitor/documents/novdec00.pdf.

Cooper, M., & Soley, L. C. (1990). All the right sources. *Mother Jones, 15,* 20–27, 45–48.

D'Alessio, D., & Allen, M. (2000). Media bias in presidential elections: a meta-analysis. *Journal of Communication, 50,* 133–156.

Dautrich, K., & Hartley, T. H. (1999). *How the news media fail American voters: Causes, consequences and remedies.* New York: Columbia University Press.

Davis, J. (1982). Sexist bias in eight newspapers. *Journalism Quarterly, 59,* 456–460.

Ephron, E. (1971). *The news twisters.* Los Angeles: Nash.

Einstein, A. (1916/1961). *Relativity: The special and the general theory.* New York: Crown.

(10) Evarts, D., & Stempel, G. H. (1974). Coverage of the 1972 campaign by TV, news magazines and major newspapers. *Journalism Quarterly, 51,* 645–648, 676.

Fico, F., & Cote, W. (1999). Fairness and balance in the structural characteristics of newspaper stories on the 1996 presidential election. *Journalism and Mass Communication Quarterly, 76,* 124–137.

Gerbner, G., Gross, L., Morgan, M., & Signiorelli, N. (1982). Charting the mainstream: Television's contributions to political orientations. *Journal of Communication, 32,* 100–127.

Giobbe, D. (1996, October 26). Dole wins ... in endorsements. *Editor and Publisher,* pp. 7–11.

(14) Graber, D. A. (1971). Press coverage patterns of campaign news: The 1968 presidential race. *Journalism Quarterly, 48,* 502–512.

(13) Graber, D. A. (1976). Effect of incumbency on coverage patterns in 1972 presidential campaign. *Journalism Quarterly, 53,* 499–508.

Hershey, M. R. (2001). The campaign and the media. In Pomper, G. R. (Ed.), *The Election of 2000: Reports and interpretations.* New York: Chatham House.

(11) Hofstetter, C. R. (1978). News bias in the 1972 campaign: A cross-media comparison. *Journalism Monographs, 58,* 1–30.

Hunter, J. E., & Schmidt, F. L. (1990). *Methods of meta-analysis: Correcting error and bias in research findings.* Newbury Park, CA: Sage.

Hunter, J. E., Schmidt, F. L., & Jackson, G. B. (1982). *Meta-analysis: Cumulating research findings across studies.* Beverly Hills, CA: Sage.

Just, M. R. (1997). Candidate strategies and the media campaign. In Pomper, G. R. (ed.), *The election of 1996: Reports and interpretations.* Chatham, NJ: Chatham House.

Kahn, K. F., & Kenney, P. J. (2002). The slant of the news: How editorial endorsements influence campaign coverage and citizens' views of candidates. *American Political Science Review, 96,* 381–394.

(1) Kenney, K., & Simpson, C. (1993). Was coverage of the 1988 presidential race by Washington's two major dailies biased? *Journalism Quarterly, 70,* 345–355.

Kern, M. (2001). Disadvantage Al Gore in election 2000. *American Behavioral Scientist, 44,* 2125–2139.

(21) King, E. G. (1995). The flawed characters in the campaign: Prestige newspaper assessments of the 1992 presidential candidates' integrity and competence. *Journalism and Mass Communication Quarterly, 72,* 84–97.

Klapper, J. (1960). *The effects of mass communication.* New York: Free Press.

Kobre, S. (1953). How Florida dailies handled the 1952 presidential campaign. *Journalism Quarterly, 30,* 163–169.

Lacy, S., Fico, F., & Simon, T. (1991) Fairness and balance in the prestige press. *Journalism Quarterly, 68,* 363–370.

Lazarsfeld, P. F., Berelson, B., & Gaudet, H. (1944). *The people's choice: How the voter makes up his mind in a presidential campaign.* New York: Columbia University Press.

Lazarsfeld, P. F., & Merton, R. K. (1948/1971). Mass communication, popular taste, and organized social action. In W. Schramm & D. F. Roberts (Eds.). *The process and effects of mass communication.* Urbana: University of Illinois Press.

Lichter, S. R. (1991). A plague on both parties: Substance and fairness in TV election news. *Press/Politics, 6,* 8–30.

Lieberman, T. (2000a). *Slanting the story: The forces that shape the news.* New York: New Press.

Lieberman, B. (2000b, November 13). 'Tribune-Review' covers half a campaign. *Editor and Publisher,* pp. 9, 12.

Liebling, A. J. (1961/1975). *The press.* New York: Pantheon.

(9) Mantler, G., & Whiteman, D. (1995). Attention to candidates and issues in newspaper coverage of 1992 presidential campaign. *Newspaper Research Journal, 16,* 14–28.

McLuhan, M. (1964). *Understanding media: The extensions of man.* New York: Signet.

McQuail, D. (1992). *Media performance: Mass communication and the public interest.* Newbury Park, CA: Sage.

(5) Meadow, R. G. (1973). Cross-media comparison of coverage of the 1972 presidential campaign. *Journalism Quarterly, 50,* 482–488.

(17) Millspaugh, M. (1949). Baltimore newspapers and the presidential elections. *Public Opinion Quarterly, 13,* 122–123.

Mitchell, G. (2000, November 6). Bird in the hand for Bush? *Editor and Publisher,,* pp. 24–27.

Nation's editors pick 15 'superior' papers (1960, April 2), *Editor and Publisher,* p. 12.

Newspaper endorsements for president since 1940 (1996, October 26), *Editor and Publisher,* p. 13.

Niven, D. (2002). *Tilt? The search for media bias.* Westport, CT: Praeger.

(16) Nollet, M. A. (1968). The *Boston Globe* in four presidential elections. *Journalism Quarterly, 45,* 531–532.

Page, B. I., & Shapiro, R. Y. (1992). *The rational public: Fifty years of trends in Americans' policy preferences.* Chicago: University of Chicago Press.

Patterson, T. E. (1993) *Out of order.* New York: Knopf.

Patterson, T. E., & Donsbach, W. (1996). News decisions: Journalists as partisan actors. *Political Communication, 13,* 455–468.

Pournelle, J. (1992). Introduction. In R. A. Heinlein, *Take back your government! A practical handbook for the private citizen who wants democracy to work.* Riverdale, NY: Baen.

Pritchard, D. (2001). A tale of three cities: "Diverse and antagonistic" information in situations of local newspaper/broadcast cross-ownership. *Federal Communications Law Journal, 54,* 31–52.

Pritchard, D. (2002) *Viewpoint diversity in cross-owned newspapers and television stations: A study of the news coverage of the 2000 presidential campaign.* Retrieved August 22, 2005 from http://hraufoss.fcc.gov/edocs_public/attachmatch/DOC-226838A7.doc.

Rosenthal, R. (1991). *Meta-analytic procedures for social research* (rev. ed.). Newbury Park, CA: Sage.

Schramm, W. (1988). *The story of human communication: Cave painting to microchip.* New York: HarperCollins.

Shaw, D. R. (1999). The impact of news media favorability and candidates' events in presidential campaigns. *Political Communication, 16,* 183–202.

Smith, K. B. (1997). When all's fair: Signs of parity in media coverage of female candidates. *Political Communication, 14,* 71–82.

Smith, T. W. (1990). Liberal and conservative trends in the United States since World War II. *Public Opinion Quarterly, 54,* 479–507.

Society of Professional Journalists. (1996). Society of Professional Journalists' Code of Ethics. Retrieved August 22, 2005, from http://www.spj.org/ethics_code.asp.

St. Dizier, B. (1985). Republican endorsements, Democratic positions: An editorial page contradiction. *Journalism Quarterly, 62,* 581–586.

(15) Staten, C. L., & Sloss, G. S. (1993). The media and politics: A content analysis of the *Louisville Courier-Journal* during the 1992 presidential election. *Journal of Political Science, 21,* 90–98.

(8) Stempel, G. H. (1961). The prestige press covers the 1960 presidential campaigns. *Journalism Quarterly, 38,* 157–163.

(7) Stempel, G. H. (1965). The prestige press in two presidential elections. *Journalism Quarterly, 42,* 15–21.

(2) Stempel, G. H. (1969). The prestige press meets the third party challenge. *Journalism Quarterly, 46,* 699–706.

(3) Stempel, G. H., & Windhauser, J. W. (1984). The prestige press revisited: Coverage of the 1980 presidential campaign. *Journalism Quarterly, 61,* 49–55.

(6) Stempel, G. H., & Windhauser, J. W. (1989). Coverage of the prestige press of the 1988 presidential campaign. *Journalism Quarterly, 66,* 894–896, 919.

(12) Stempel, G. H., & Windhauser, J. W. (1991). Newspaper coverage of the 1984 and 1988 campaigns. In G. H. Stempel and J. W. Windhauser (Eds.). *The media in the 1984 and 1988 campaigns.* New York: Greenwood.

Stevens, J. D. (1982). *Shaping the First Amendment.* Beverly Hills, CA: Sage.

Straubhaar, J., & LaRose, R. (2002). *Media now: Communications media in the information age.* Belmont, CA: Wadsworth/Thompson Learning.

Stromer-Galley, J. (2000). On-line interaction and why candidates avoid it. *Journal of Communication, 50,* 111–132.

(22) Waldman, P., & Devitt, J. (1988). Newspaper photographs and the 1996 presidential election: The question of bias. *Journalism and Mass Communication Quarterly, 75,* 302–311.

Westerstahl, J. (1983). Objective news reporting: General premises. *Communication Research, 10,* 403–424.

White, D. M. (1950). The gate-keeper: A case study in the selection of news. *Journalism Quarterly, 27,* 383–390.

Williams, A. (1975). Unbiased study of television news bias. *Journal of Communication, 25,* 190–199.

27

What's in a Meta-Analysis[*]

Michael Pfau
University of Oklahoma

This book offers a systematic application of meta-analysis in the realm of mass media effects. Meta-analysis involves "the quantitative cumulation and analysis of descriptive statistics across studies" (Hunter, Schmidt, & Jackson, 1982, p. 137). Its value is most pronounced in extensive literature domains, where "the information-processing task becomes too taxing for the human mind" (1982, p. 129).

Thus, meta-analysis is an appropriate tool for synthesizing research about many media effects' contexts. The study of media effects is the oldest and most established quantitative research tradition in communication. There are decades of research about the effects of exposure to media violence or pornography across various venues (movies, comic books, television, and the Internet), the influence of mediated political and social action campaigns, and other issues. In many of these contexts, "the need ... is not additional empirical data but some means of making sense of the vast amounts of data that have been accumulated" (1982, pp. 26–27). I am an enthusiastic proponent of the use of meta-analysis in these circumstances.

The authors of the various chapters in this book include many leading experts in specific media effects' contexts. The book's title suggests that meta-analysis provides "advances" in mass media research. In most respects, this volume

*The author thanks Dr. Amy Johnson, University of Oklahoma, for her feedback about this chapter.

achieves this objective, but not in all effects' contexts. The unevenness is, in large part, a function of sometimes satisfactory—and sometimes unsatisfactory—answers to a fundamental question that should be asked about all meta-analytic studies, namely: What's *in* a meta-analysis?

Roskos-Ewoldsen, Klinger, and Roskos-Ewoldsen (chap. 5, this volume) argue that the goals of meta-analysis are, first, identifying the "strength or confidence" with which various knowledge claims in a content domain can be made and, second, advancing theory. In this chapter, I will use these as overarching criteria for the purpose of assessing chapters of this book. I will organize my comments in three parts: first, examining the contributions of specific chapters to advances in media effects' theory; second, assessing the extent to which individual chapters contribute either to the strengthening of existing knowledge claims or the generation of new knowledge; and third, arguing that there are circumstances in which meta-analysis may not *advance* theory or knowledge claims.

As an overview, I believe that the book, on balance, makes a valuable contribution to mass media research. As a scholar who has conducted a fair amount of research on media effects and as a teacher who has taught media effects' courses on and off for nearly 30 years, I found most of the chapters of this book to be extremely useful.

ADVANCES IN THEORY

A number of chapters in this book advance theory, either by sorting out conflicting claims, or in one instance, by causing me to revisit a theory, which I had assumed was grounded on a solid foundation of research. However, most of the chapters in this book do not advance theory. This is not the fault of the authors per se but rather the nature of meta-analysis, which is a tool to assess theoretically based knowledge claims. The logic underpinning such claims would have been posited previously by scholars initially responsible for formulating a theory or subsequently responsible for tweaking it.

Meta-analysis is an excellent tool to sort out conflicting claims about theory. Chapter 14 by Hoffner and Levine, "Enjoyment of Mediated Horror and Violence: A Meta-Analysis," provides an excellent example. The results supported Zillmann's model of excitation transfer. The viewers of horror films, especially males, experience suspense, enjoyment, and negative affect. However, there was no link between viewing and arousal. Examination of personality characteristics associated with viewing, especially empathy, was revealing about the underlying process at work in Zillmann's model. Based on the results, the authors speculated that "The self-oriented focus of personal distress, for example, suggests that this component may be associated with less enjoyment of horror, regardless of the outcome," while "empathetic concern reflects an other-oriented focus of concern and caring for others." The authors argued that, "this type of response [empathetic concern] may enhance enjoyment of horror, but only if threatened characters successfully escape or triumph."

In addition, the results revealed significant correlations between sensation-seeking and enjoyment of horror and violence and, for males, between aggressiveness and enjoyment of horror and violence. Finally, results indicated that viewers' enjoyment of horror follows a curvilinear relationship with age, peaking during adolescence. Based on the results of this meta-analysis, the authors called for further research and theorizing designed to integrate "separate lines of inquiry into a unified approach to understanding of entertainment." This is an example of meta-analysis providing insights that lead to theoretical advances.

Chapter 15 by Sherry, "Violent Video Games and Aggression: Why Can't We Find Effects?," is another example of meta-analysis sorting out conflicting theoretical claims. The results revealed that video game effects are consistent with Zillmann's excitation transfer theory and, to a lesser degree, with Berkowitz's priming effects theory. By contrast, results were at odds with Bandura's social learning theory, "the most frequently cited mechanism by which the games can result in aggressive behavior." The results were not consistent with catharsis theory, although "none of the studies made a legitimate attempt to determine whether there was a catharsis effect." Sherry did an effective job of integrating results and theory. He concluded that the theories of excitation and priming "work in unison to explain the findings of the meta-analysis," whereas the results are at odds with social learning theory and catharsis. This chapter provides an excellent exemplar in using meta-analysis to "narrow the range of possible theories" (Hale & Dillard, 1991, p. 470), thereby advancing understanding of, in this case, the effects of video games on children.

One chapter in this book caused me to rethink a theory that makes intuitive sense and which struck me as grounded on a solid foundation of research (I have read most of the original studies of third-person effects). Chapter 6 by Paul, Salwen, and Dupagne, "The Third-Person Effect: A Meta-Analysis of the Perceptual Hypothesis," indicated a significant overall effect in third-person effect research but revealed no effects for most of the relevant moderator variables, including source, method (survey vs. experiment), medium, country, and desirability. So far, so good.

However, the authors reported, what is to me, a cautionary result with two moderator variables. The results indicated that third-person effects were much greater with nonrandom samples as opposed to random samples and with college student samples versus noncollege student samples. The authors concluded: "The findings that nonrandom samples and student samples yielded greater third-person perception than random samples and nonstudent samples are intriguing and perhaps disturbing." A question must be resolved as to whether third-person effects are an artifact of the samples employed in this research. As the authors concluded, it is not the method, "but the use of student samples in the experiments and surveys that causes generalization problems." This chapter raises doubts about the external validity of third-person effects, and, until this issue can be resolved, we should exercise caution in positing claims about third-person effects. This is a theory that I had accepted on the basis of a consistent pattern of support across many studies. However, the meta-analysis revealed a macro flaw across studies that I had missed in my seriatim reading of individual studies.

KNOWLEDGE CLAIMS

The value of meta-analysis lies in its ability to assess theoretically based knowledge claims. Rosenthal (1984) maintained that "meta-analytic reviews ... are more systematic, more explicit, more exhaustive, and more quantitative" than traditional literature reviews and, as a result, "are more likely to lead to summary statements of greater thoroughness, greater precision, and greater ... objectivity" (p. 17). Meta-analysis contributes to accurate and stable knowledge claims (Allen & Preiss, 1998), which, in turn, enhances communication science (Cappella, 1991).

This is precisely what the chapters in this book do best. They contribute to what Hale and Dillard (1991) characterize as, "the promise of cumulation" (p. 469). In most instances, chapters in this book confirmed knowledge claims. However, in some cases, they disconfirmed knowledge claims, some of which had achieved the status of conventional wisdom. Finally, in one instance, a chapter clarified or nuanced what had been rather blunt findings.

Not surprisingly, given the bias in published studies for findings as opposed to null outcomes [This is characterized as the "publication bias" (Jackson, 1984), but it does not seem to exert much impact on meta-analytic findings (Hunter & Hamilton, 1998, pp. 42–43; Rosenthal, 1984, p. 30).], most of the chapters in this book tended to confirm theoretically grounded knowledge claims. In this way, they contribute to "durable knowledge claims that result from cumulation" (Hale & Dillard, 1991, p. 469).

In chapter 10, "Effects of Media Violence on Viewers' Aggression in Unconstrained Social Interaction," Christensen and Wood reported significant effects for young viewers' exposure to media violence and their interpersonal aggressiveness. These effects were larger in laboratory than in field studies, and they were larger for preadolescents than for either very young children or adolescents. The authors cautioned that manipulations employed in laboratory studies were typically "unlike real-world exposure settings." Findings were consistent with past meta-analyses examining television viewing and aggressiveness.

In chapter 13, "Effects of Gender Stereotyping on Socialization," Oppliger found significant effects for viewing of gender stereotypes and sex-type attitudes and behaviors. Anticipated moderator variables (e.g., method, gender, or age) were not significant. This is one of the few chapters in this book in which meta-analytic results were consistent with Bandura's social learning theory. Oppliger concluded that social learning theory offered "a more plausible explanation" for the results than the cognitive developmental approach. In chapter 23, "Media Use and Political Involvement," Hollander found that newspaper use and exposure was more strongly associated with people's political involvement than television use and exposure. In addition, he reported that, in more recent studies, television use has shown a more negative relationship with political involvement, suggesting "that the growing reliance on electronic news may be associated with the general downward trend in overall political interest among the public or that the two are moving hand-in-hand as the public becomes disenchanted with the political process." In chapter 26, "On the Role of Newspaper Ownership on Bias in Presidential Campaign Coverage by Newspapers," D'Alessio and Allen reported that more newspapers endorsed Republican than Democratic candidates and, when there was an endorsement, the volume of coverage favored the endorsed candidate. They also found that prestige newspapers exhibited less bias.

In other chapters findings that bolstered a variety of knowledge claims were reported: mass media health campaigns (most antismoking campaigns) achieve effects that average 2% to 3% (chap. 21, Parcell & Bryant); newspaper use is related to voting (chap. 24, Miron & Bryant); prosocial television, particularly programs that stress altruism, exert moderate effects, with the greatest impact on children between 3 and 7 years of age (chap. 17, Mares & Woodard); children's exposure to music (type of music was not specified) is associated with antisocial beliefs and actions, an association that increases with age and is negatively related to academic performance (chap. 16, Allen, Herrett-Skjellum, Jorgenson, Kramer, Ryan, & Timmerman); the news media exerts an agenda-setting influence, an effect that is impervious to number of issues, unit of analysis, or other methodological considerations (chap. 4, Wanta & Ghanem); and mass media exposure primes, but effects are small, with experimental studies revealing greater effects than surveys and, as a result, violence studies generating more impact than political studies (the latter feature a heavy proportion of surveys as opposed to experiments) (chap. 5, Roskos-Ewoldsen, Klinger, & Roskos-Ewoldsen).

Whereas the results reported in the chapters above tended to confirm knowledge claims, results of other meta-analyses in this book questioned accepted knowledge claims and, therefore, make an important contribution to extant knowledge of media effects. The results reported in chapter 7, "The Selective Exposure Hypothesis and Media Choice Processes," by D'Alessio and Allen confirmed the results of past meta-analyses that supported selective exposure. This finding is at odds with what became conventional wisdom on the basis of earlier reviews: namely, the absence of support for selective exposure.

Selective exposure posits that people are drawn to content consistent with attitudes and away from content that is at odds with attitudes. Following extensive literature reviews conducted by Freedman and Sears in the 1960s (see Freedman & Sears, 1965, for a synopsis), scholars questioned selective exposure, which was an axiom of cognitive dissonance theory and, a "cornerstone" of Klapper's minimal effects paradigm (D'Alessio & Allen). Lack of support for selective exposure became the conventional wisdom. D'Alessio and Allen, using 22 studies, most published after Freedman and Sears' last review, but including only 5 of the 18 studies reviewed by Freedman and Sears, found that "people routinely selectively expose themselves to messages in accord with their existing attitudinal structures and avoid incongruent messages," also supporting selective exposure within the context of dissonance theory.

This finding is interesting because it is at odds with what became conventional wisdom. D'Alessio and Allen do not claim that their results challenge the accuracy of Freedman and Sears' conclusion, drawn nearly four decades earlier. The studies used in D'Alessio and Allen's meta-analysis differ significantly from those employed in Freedman and Sears' reviews. This raises an important point about knowledge claims, one that I will return to shortly: namely, that the quality of the conclusions drawn in both meta-analytic and narrative reviews ultimately depends on the sample of studies employed, both its thoroughness and, to the extent that some studies are excluded, its representativeness.

Another chapter, whose results challenged extant knowledge claims, is chapter 12, "Effects of Sexually Explicit Media," by Mundorf, Allen, D'Alessio, and Emmers-Sommer. Most of the findings reported in this chapter confirm knowledge claims based on traditional reviews and are consistent with social learning and/or excitation transfer theories, such as exposure to sexually explicit materials is modestly related to acceptance of the rape myth; exposure to nudity, in itself, actually diminishes sexual aggression; and educational materials can eradicate harmful effects of people's exposure to pornography. These authors also found a negative relationship between sexual arousal and behavioral aggression.

Results of the meta-analysis also indicated that exposure to both violent and nonviolent sexual material is associated with aggressive behavior. The former finding was predicted and is grounded in social learning and excitation transfer theory. The latter finding about nonviolent sexual material is at odds with social learning theory and what has become conventional wisdom. The authors concluded that the latter finding "contradicts ... social learning theory because the aggression occurs in the absence of cues in the material that link sexual gratification to violent behavior," in other words, it "run[s] contrary to an argument the violence in sexual materials causes increases in aggression and not the sexually explicit content." This is, to say the least, an important finding with implications for research and policy.

WHEN DOES META-ANALYSIS NOT ADVANCE KNOWLEDGE CLAIMS?

I return to the first goal of meta-analysis, as articulated in chapter 5 by Roskos-Ewoldsen, Klinger, and Roskos-Ewoldsen, that meta-analysis should enhance the "strength or confidence" with which various knowledge claims in a content domain can be made. Proponents of meta-analysis (e.g., Hunter et al., 1982) maintain that meta-analysis is superior to narrative reviews in this respect. My position is that the superiority of meta-analysis depends on what is in, or more to the point, not in, a meta-analysis. There are circumstances in which meta-analysis does not enhance confidence of knowledge claims over narrative reviews, and some of them are illustrated in chapters of this book.

Circumstances in Which Meta-Analysis Is Not Appropriate

Sometimes, meta-analysis is simply not needed or warranted. This is particularly true when few studies have been conducted. After all, the main value of meta-analysis is to resolve the "problem of poor cumulation" (Rosenthal, 1984, p. 9), which stems from the problems associated with traditional reviews of vast literature domains (Hunter et al., 1982; Rosenthal, 1984). As Hunter et al. (1982) advised: "Ideally, cumulation of results works best if it is based on a large number of studies acquired by exhaustive search procedures" (p. 29). Hale and Dillard (1991) added that, "meta-analytic claims ... based on ... undesirably small numbers of studies ..." reduce confidence in knowledge claims and, thus, require replication (p. 466).

Two chapters in this volume are based on so few studies that meta-analysis was not useful. One of these, chapter 8, "Meta-Analysis of Television's Impact on Special Populations," by Abelman, Lin, and Atkin, is based on results of five studies, after excluding more than twice that many. In this instance, a through, well-executed, narrative literature review would have sufficed.

The other, chapter 22, "The Impact of Earvin 'Magic' Johnson's HIV-Positive Announcement," by Casey et al., features 13 studies about, what I would characterize as, a micro domain within the media effects' literature. The authors found no overall effect, but when divided by age, the results revealed that adults were more inclined—and children less inclined—to accept their vulnerability to HIV infection because children did not experience the knowledge gains that adults did after exposure to Johnson's announcement. A combination of the small number of studies, coupled with the very narrow content niche, limits the value of this meta-analytic review.

Still another chapter cannot provide needed nuance to make the meta-analysis worthwhile. In chapter 16, "Effects of Music," Allen, Herrett-Skjellum, Jorgenson, Kramer, Ryan, and Timmerman reported that exposure to music reduces academic performance and enhances antisocial beliefs and actions, effects that increase with age. The conclusion is blunt, but undoubtedly premature. Obviously, type of music matters a great deal. There are enormous differences in musical genres. It would be critical to know what kind of music exerts these effects, but, because of the insufficient number of studies in different musical genres, type of music "could not be considered as a potential source of moderation." This is not the fault of the authors, but of available studies. However, if the results of this study found their way to jurists or politicians, who failed to understand their nuance, it might fuel a call for a broad-based censorship of popular music which, in addition to First Amendment considerations, is not warranted based on the overly broad findings of this meta-analysis.

The Problem of Excluding Studies on Statistical Grounds

At other times, the sample of studies employed calls into question the results. I view thoroughness and, when studies are excluded, representativeness of the sample of studies used in a traditional or meta-analytic review as a precondition to the quality of the knowledge claims advanced. The starting point in either form of review is an exhaustive search for all relevant studies.

However, there is one aspect of meta-analysis that is not usually done in narrative reviews. Once all studies are collected, meta-analytic researchers often consciously exclude relevant published studies. The most common rationale for the exclusion of, what are otherwise, perfectly good studies is meta-analysis' need for data that can be converted into standardized scores (Hunter & Hamilton, 2002) and the fact that such data are not available in many published studies. As a consequence, many (sometimes most) sophisticated studies that feature either multivariate analyses or multiple regression are excluded in meta-analysis studies. Such exclusion is not the fault of the person conducting the meta-analytic review or of the author(s) of excluded studies who, when writing their results, were not thinking about future cumulation.

Nonetheless, if a goal of meta-analysis is to enhance the confidence of knowledge claims, then the final sample of studies employed in the review must be representative of the population of studies from which it is drawn. When existing studies are excluded from meta-analytic reviews, their findings *may* misrepresent extant knowledge. As Hunter and Hamilton (1998) admonish: "If available studies are unrepresentative ..., this creates a disaster for any approach to science, not just meta-analysis" (p. 43).

I am frankly amazed at the lack of attention to this issue in meta-analytic essays. Hunter et al. (1982) caution about "*systematically*" excluding studies, warning that, "Reliance on a convenience sample always involves some risk" (p. 29), but they do so in the context of potential bias in published studies, the so-called "file-drawer problem." I maintain that, if meta-analytic reviews exclude a large proportion of studies, even if exclusion is justified, then reported results have the potential to misrepresent extant knowledge *more* than would be the case with a thorough, careful narrative review.

A number of chapters in this volume excluded a great many published studies. As noted previously, in chapter 7 on selective exposure, D'Alessio and Allen excluded 13 of the 18 studies used in the Freedman and Sears' review. To their credit, D'Alessio and Allen provided a thorough explanation of the reasons why these studies were excluded. In chapter 10 on the effects of media violence on interpersonal aggression, described previously, Christensen and Wood excluded 11 of 24 studies, although they provided a rationale for the exclusions.

More problematic were the chapters that excluded studies, but failed to list them, thus preventing a reader from making a judgment about the impact of their exclusion. For example, the in chapter 23, "Media Use and Political Involvement," Hollander used 18 studies that met the following criteria: measuring media use, analyzing the association between media use and involvement, and providing requisite bivariate statistical details. The author acknowledged that, "a large number of these studies [those that met the first two criteria] relied on multivariate analyses and did not include ... the bivariate relationships among key concepts..." or employed multiple regression "but without also reporting the raw zero-order Pearson correlations." In short, a large number of studies were excluded, but we do not know which ones.

I am a coauthor of some of the excluded studies, the results of which supported Hollander's claim about newspaper use enhancing involvement, but which found the relationship between television use and involvement to be more nuanced than Hollander suggests (e.g., see Pfau, Cho, & Chong, 2001).

Even more problematic is chapter 24, "Mass Media and Voter Turnout" by Miron and Bryant. The authors started with 40 studies, but subsequently based their meta-analytic findings on from 3 to 6 studies. The authors aptly characterized their effort as a "tentative meta-analysis." I would have more confidence in the knowledge claims about mass media use and voting based on a narrative review of 40 studies than a meta-analytic review of a small subset of those studies.

Given the problem of excluding relevant published studies, the methodology of meta-analytic reviews takes on added import. Authors must provide clear criteria for inclusion/exclusion, a list of studies included and excluded, and a full justification for studies excluded. However, "excluded studies are rarely mentioned [in meta-analytic reviews], and this is unfortunate" (O'Keefe, 1991, p. 474). "Not specifying excluded studies has the effect of needlessly reducing the credibility of the review (O'Keefe, 1991, p. 473). Allen and Preiss (1998) emphasized the importance of thoroughness in both narrative and meta-analytic reviews. They acknowledge "the nature of the original data" as an "important limitation" (p. 248). They advised: "The limitations and definitions of existing data ... should be read with extreme interest. The conclusions of the meta-analysis are bounded by these definitions and limitations" (p. 248).

The authors of some chapters in this volume could have done a better job of describing criteria for inclusion/exclusion, listing the studies excluded, and/or providing adequate justification for these decisions. For example, Mundorf, Allen, D'Alessio, and Emmers-Sommer in chapter 12, "Effects of Sexually Explicit

Media," were sketchy as to the criteria for inclusion/exclusion and failed to list the studies excluded. Allen, Herrett-Skjellum, Jorgenson, Kramer, Ryan, and Timmerman in chapter 16, "Effects of Music," clearly indicated criteria for inclusion/exclusion but failed to list the studies excluded. Mares and Woodard in chapter 17, "Positive Effects of Television on Children's Social Interaction: A Meta-Analysis," retained 34 studies in the analysis, excluding 17 studies. However, more information was warranted about studies excluded from the analysis. Finally, Sherry in chapter 15, "Violent Video Games and Aggression," offered no specific details about the criteria for inclusion/exclusion and provided no information about studies excluded from the meta-analysis.

CONCLUSION

The title of this book suggests that meta-analysis provides "advances" in mass media research. On balance, the book does so, providing both a useful and important contribution to mass media research. However, some chapters of this volume do not strengthen confidence in knowledge claims beyond what can be attained in a traditional narrative review. Why? Sometimes meta-analysis was not needed or warranted. Other times, too many studies were excluded from the meta-analysis and/or authors failed to list the studies excluded or to adequately justify decisions to exclude. The conundrum of exclusion stems from the intrinsic nature of meta-analysis, which requires data that may not be contained in published studies. In these circumstances, an uncomfortable proportion of studies may be excluded, which *can* render samples of studies unrepresentative of the population from which they are drawn. In these instances, meta-analytic conclusions can be compromised.

I am not skeptical about use of meta-analysis in reviews. It is a useful tool. I am simply calling for perspective about the benefits of meta-analysis. Meta-analytic reviews are often more useful than narrative reviews, but sometimes they are not.

Nonetheless, we can learn things about media effects from all of the reviews featured in this volume. Why? Let us remember that meta-analysis provides starting points and not "definitive pieces of research" (Hale & Dillard, 1991, p. 469; Dillard, 1998). Meta-analysis is "a tool to clarify existing research for the conduct of future research." As such, meta-analytic reviews provide "a beginning point of departure for the scholar, not a destination" (Allen & Preiss, 1998, p. 253). The domain of mass media research is richer for the contributions of each of the chapters of this volume, even though some claims must be viewed as tentative. Some chapters advance theory and/or knowledge, whereas other chapters offer useful starting points for further research on mass media effects. All of them, therefore, advance knowledge.

REFERENCES

Allen, M., & Preiss, R. W. (1998). Evaluating the advice offered by the tool users. In M. Allen & R. W. Press (Eds.), *Persuasion: Advances through meta-analysis* (pp. 243–255). Cresskill, NJ: Hampton Press.

Cappella, J. (1991). The biological origins of automated patterns of human interaction. *Communication Theory, 1,* 4–35.

Dillard, J. P. (1998). Debating and using meta-analytic knowledge claims. In M. Allen & R. W. Press (Eds.), *Persuasion: Advances through meta-analysis* (pp. 257–270). Cresskill, NJ: Hampton Press.

Freedman, J. L., & Sears, D. O. (1965), Selective exposure. *Advances in Experimental Social Psychology, 2,* 57–97.

Hale, J. K., & Dillard, J. P. (1991). The uses of meta-analysis: Making knowledge claims and setting research agendas. *Communication Monographs, 58,* 463–471.

Hunter, J. E., & Hamilton, M. A. (2002). The advantages of using standardized scores in causal analysis. *Human Communication Research, 28,* 552–561.

Hunter, J. E., & Hamilton, M. A. (1998). Meta-analysis of controlled message designs. In M. Allen & R. W. Press (Eds.), *Persuasion: Advances through meta-analysis* (pp. 29–52). Cresskill, NJ: Hampton Press.

Hunter, J. E., Schmidt, F. L., & Jackson, G. B. (1982). *Meta-analysis: Cumulating research findings across studies.* Beverly Hills, CA: Sage.

Jackson, S. (1984). *Meta-analysis and generalization in communication research.* Paper presented at the annual meeting of the Central States Speech Association, Chicago, IL.

O'Keefe, D. J. (1991). Extracting dependable generalizations from the persuasion effects literature: Some issues in meta-analytic reviews. *Communication Monographs, 58,* 472–481.

Pfau, M., Cho, J., & Chong, K. (2001). The impact of communication forms presidential campaigns: Influences on candidate perceptions and democratic process. *The Harvard International Journal of Press/Politics, 6,* 88–105.

Rosenthal, R. (1984). *Meta-analytic procedures for social research.* Beverly Hills, CA: Sage.

28

Meta-Analysis: Demonstrating the Power of Mass Communication

Elizabeth Perse
University of Delaware

Mass communication has always drawn scrutiny, comment, and controversy. Over the years, concerns about the penny press, dime novels, movies, and even comic books have drawn the interest of educators, parents, and politicians. These concerns reflect the central and public role that mass communication plays in our society. Although most scholars agree that mass communication is functional for society (e.g., Wright, 1986), the open and commercial nature of media content often drives a "legacy of fear" about the impact of mass communication on culture, society, adults, and children.

There are several reasons for these concerns. First, mass communication, more than any other form of communication, operates in the public sphere. Television, radio, film, newspapers, the World Wide Web (WWW), and recorded music are available to just about anyone to view, read, or listen to. In addition, the content of the mass media often transcends its primary location in time and space. There are real concerns about the amount of violence in the movies, not only for those who watch them in the theaters or at home, but also for those who "accidentally" see previews and snippets as they are promoted and discussed across other media. The Parents Television Council (http://www.parentstv.org/), for example, reported that 23% of the ads for movies aired during television's "family hour" (8:00–9:00 p.m.)

were for R-rated movies. Even television programs with mid-sized audiences are given wider exposure because of cross-media coverage of creativity and sensationalism. At the time this chapter was being written, for example, the television program *The Swan* (which deals with issues related to plastic surgery and self-esteem) is the topic of public comment and several newspaper articles, even though the program itself has only a modest audience size. The public nature of mass communication draws attention well beyond its audience.

The public nature of mass communication draws the attention of politicians and other advocates. Shortly after the Columbine High School shooting, politicians turned their focus to violent video games and movies as a contribution to adolescent crime. A concern for sexual exploration by young people is driving concern about broadcast indecency (e.g., Thompson, 2004). Over the years, media content has often become the scapegoat for societal problems. Politicians have turned to regulating media content as an easy way to fix problems with complex causes. And, although much of the public feel that they are immune to media's negative effects, they often support restrictions on media content because of a "third-person effect," by which they expect that others will be negatively affected by the media (e.g., Perloff, 2002).

A second reason for the concerns about the impact of mass communication grows out of disagreements about its role in society. Scholars and educators are optimistic about the potential for mass communication to deliver knowledge, raise awareness of public affairs and health issues, open remote worlds to our children, improve the quality of life in developing nations, and deliver culture to society. We have ample evidence that *Sesame Street* has more than achieved its original educational goals of teaching simple concepts, letters, and numbers to preschool children. Public service announcements are effective in increasing awareness of and compliance with safer health practices such as using seat belts and designating nondrinking drivers. An earlier meta-analysis (Hearold, 1986) indicated that the prosocial effects of television are more common and stronger than the negative effects. She concluded that "the potential for prosocial effects overrides the smaller but persistent negative effects of antisocial [television] programs" (p. 116). This optimism drives many of publically funded health and public service campaigns.

Political communication scholars recognize the privileged position the mass media have in society and point out that with privilege comes responsibility. For them, the role of mass communication is to enhance the democratic process by monitoring the environment for relevant events, by scrutinizing the activities of public officials and institutions, by highlighting key issues for the public, by providing a platform for advocacy by different political groups, by facilitating discussion between those in power and diverse groups, and by providing information to allow people to become active and informed participants in their governance (Gurevitch & Blumler, 1990; McLeod, Kosicki, & McLeod, 2002).

The realities of mass communication, however, are that it exists as the profitable business venture of large conglomerate corporations (Bagdikian, 2000). Its prime purpose for its owners is to generate profits. The need for profits often conflicts with the prosocial potential of media content. All too often, prosocial media content is expensive and attracts smaller audiences. Media producers often argue that they create violent movies because violence drives U.S. and international box office receipts. News organizations, in a search for large audiences, have turned to giving people "what they want," which results in increased crime news coverage and less focus on international events and issues. Coverage of the final episodes of situation comedies such as *Friends* and *Frasier* leads news producers to set aside their responsibilities to democracy. The need for profits also drives a focus on advertising over prosocial content. Advertisements for fast foods, sodas, and sugared cereals drown out the nutritional messages of public service announcements (e.g., Signorielli &Lears, 1992). Reliance on tobacco advertising can diminish discussion of tobacco's health risks (Kessler, 1989).

A prime reason for a scholarly focus on the study of media effects is that we recognize that the stakes are so high. Mass communication is pervasive in our society. When I chat with my colleagues who do research on interpersonal communication, I often hear about the need to create several different messages to represent a category of messages (e.g., persuasive or comforting) to ensure that message effects are not due to idiosyncratic aspects of a single message (Jackson & Jacobs, 1983). This is not an issue for mass communication scholars. A single television program, newspaper headline, political ad, public service announcement, film, or piece of music will be watched, read, or listened to by hundreds of thousands (if not millions) of people. The idiosyncracies of a single message can have profound effects.

WHAT DO WE KNOW ABOUT
MEDIA EFFECTS?

Our field is based on the assumption that the mass media have effects. This assumption underlies research on pro- and antisocial effects. It undergirds the focus on the responsibilities of the mass media in society (e.g., Gurevitch & Blumler, 1990; Minow & LaMay, 1995); public service programming is assumed to change the thoughts, attitudes, and behaviors of its audience. The assumption of effects also drives advertising; advertisers believe that carefully constructed messages can shift perceptions about products, practices, and politicians, as well as influence consumers' purchasing and voting behavior.

There was an era in the study of media effects where some scholars advocated that the media have only "limited effects." That is, scholars believed that, for the most part, media content only reinforced existing cognition, affect, and behavior (e.g., Chaffee & Hockheimer, 1982; Klapper, 1960). Certainly reinforcement is an important (and understudied) effect of the mass media, but the limited effects view downplayed the conditions under which mass media had noticeable short- and long-term as well as ongoing, cumulative effects on their audience.

Now arguments about the evidence for media effects are becoming rare (Perse, 2001; cf., Fowles, 1999; Freedman, 2002). So much evidence has accumulated to convince us that the media can be useful tools to educate and socialize as well as forces that can disrupt and displace. Now, our field has moved to more sophisticated research and analysis to understand the *strength* and *process* of media effects.

How Large Are Media Effects?

Prior meta-analyses have shown us that media effects can best be described as *moderate*. Hearold (1986), for example, found that television's negative impact was moderate (about .3 of a standard deviation). Paik and Comstock's (1994) update indicated a somewhat stronger impact (about .65 of a standard deviation, which reflected the stronger impact of laboratory experiments). Wood, Wong, and Chachere (1991) found that effects of more ecologically valid experiments to be a bit weaker (about .27 of a standard deviation). Herrett-Skjellum and Allen (1996) noted that television had an impact on sex-role stereotyping ($r = .10$ for nonexperimental studies; $r = .21$ for experimental studies). Allen, Emmers, Gebhardt, and Giery (1995) found that pornography had an impact on rape-myth acceptance ($r = .15$ for experiments; $r = .02$ for surveys). Morgan and Shanahan (1997) identified a significant cultivation effect across 52 samples ($r = .09$).

I have argued elsewhere that media effects are most likely stronger than the evidence suggests (Perse, 2001). Observation of media effects might be limited by methodological imprecision and conflicting theoretical forces. For ethical reasons, our research on media's negative effects is limited to research designs, manipulations, and observations that cannot harm participants. So, we create hypothetical situations rather than real situations. In some pornography research, for example, men have been asked how they would act in a rape scenario rather than placing them in a situation in which they could commit actual sexual violence (e.g., Malamuth, Haber, & Feshback, 1980). Or, media violence researchers look for the impact of television violence on aggressive play, rather than provide situations in which participants could commit actual violence (e.g., Josephson, 1987; Joy, Kimball, & Zabrack, 1986).

Our ability to measure important variables is also limited because of the often private nature of media use. In-home media use is so common and inattentive that people do not remember how much or what they have watched or read (e.g., Ferguson, 1994; Webster & Wakshlag, 1985), so measurement of exposure to media content is certainly filled with random error.

Most studies of media effects assume a linear relationship between exposure and impact. That is, we expect that as participants read, view, or listen more, the effects will be stronger. Our field depends on statistical techniques that are based on linear relationships, such as correlation and regression. If the true impact of the mass media is nonlinear, our research will underestimate effects (Eveland, 1997). There is some strong evidence that media's impact can be nonlinear. McGuire (1986) summarized research that argued for a threshold model of media effects, in which media content does not have an impact until a certain level of exposure has been reached. Conversely, there might be ceiling effects, at which media exposure begins to have diminishing levels of impact (Ettema & Kline, 1977). Persuasion research has identified a curvilinear relationship between message exposure and impact. Exposure is related to impact up to a point; as messages are repeated, impact decreases. Continued repetition can eventually lead to lower levels of persuasion (e.g., Cacioppo & Petty, 1979).

Greenberg (1988) proposed that some media effects might result from a "drench" effect. Although a linear approach to media effects assumes that media content has a cumulative "drip, drip" effect, there might be times that a single media image, personality, program, or event might command so much attention that it has a strong immediate impact—a drench effect. A single news story about a famine in Ethiopia in 1984, for example, activated the public's concern and generosity when more than 100 newspaper articles in the *New York Times* did not. More recently, exposure of a woman's breast during the *Superbowl* energized the public when years of sexual themes on mainstream radio and television did not. It is clear that a focus on linear assumptions and methods underestimates media effects.

How Do Media Effects Happen?

Our field has ample evidence that the mass media have effects but less understanding of how these effects occur. Understanding the process of media effects is important because if we understand how effects occur, we can take steps to enhance positive effects and to mitigate the negative ones. Already we know that we can limit negative effects through education. Linz, Arluk, and Donnerstein (1990), for example, found that discussions about rape myths limited the negative effects of slasher films. Media literacy activities have been found to help children understand how television works and have made them less susceptible to its effects (e.g., Potter, 2001; Van Evra, 2004). There is also evidence that when people are reminded that television might be the source for their views of reality, cultivation effects are limited (e.g., Morgan & Shanahan, 1997; Shrum, Wyer, & O'Guinn, 1998).

Various theories, processes, and models have been proposed as explanations for media effects (Perse, 2001). Selectivity processes, such as selective exposure, attention, perception, and recall (e.g., Zillmann & Bryant, 1985) are seen as prime causes for reinforcement effects because people seek out and interpret media content that is consistent with already existing beliefs and attitudes. Different types of mental processing of messages (e.g., systematic vs. heuristic or central vs. peripheral) are seen as the explanation for different types of message effects (e.g., Petty, Priester, & Brizol, 2002; Shrum, 2002). Bandura's (2002) social learning theory explains how and when audiences might model media content. The framing and salience of media messages can evoke short-term media effects based on priming (e.g., Roskos-Ewoldsen, Roskos-Ewoldsen, & Carpentier, 2002).

The sophistication of our theoretical explanations allows a greater understanding of how media effects occur. This understanding allows us to use that knowledge to enhance positive effects and limit negative ones. The study of mass communication has progressed over the past half-century. It has become less important to research *whether* media effects occur; it is more important to uncover *how large* they are and *how* they occur.

META-ANALYSIS AND MEDIA EFFECTS

The centrality of the study of media effects demands regular analysis of our research so that we can answer the important questions about the strength and process of media effects. As a social science, our field is especially reliant on meta-analysis for summarizing and evaluating our research. Because we focus on humans, we can rarely have a random sample, so the impact of a single study limits our abilities to generalize, and we need to rely on cumulative findings to advance our understanding of media effects. The chapters in this volume reinforce an important tenet of our field: Mass media have effects, and those effects are probably stronger than one single study can demonstrate.

Because theory in our field is cumulative, we build knowledge on the aggregate results of our research. A strength of the chapters in this book is that they contribute directly to our understanding of important mass media effects and processes. Some of these studies are updates of earlier studies that have informed our field. Christenson and Wood (chap. 10, this volume), for example, updated the Wood et al. (1991) study of the effects of media violence on aggressive behavior in naturalistic settings. Mares and Woodard (chap. 17, this volume) built on Hearold's (1986) meta-analysis of the prosocial effects of television content. Mundorf, Allen, D'Alessio, and Emmers-Sommer (chap. 12, this volume) updated studies by Allen and his colleagues (Allen, D'Alessio, & Brezgel, 1995; Allen, Emmers et al., 1995). D'Alessio and Allen (chap. 7, this volume) reanalyzed the widely cited study by Sears and Freedman (1967/1971). In all, these chapters also give us additional insight into the strength of media effects as well as our understanding of how media effects occur.

THE STRENGTH AND PROCESS
OF MEDIA EFFECTS

Agenda-Setting Effects

Agenda setting is one of the most widely recognized areas of mass communication's political effects research. It is important to remember that the original authors, McCombs and Shaw (1972), identified agenda setting as a "function," one of the useful aspects of mass media coverage. Initially, there was a great deal of discussion about agenda setting and questions arose about definitions of terms, different ways of measuring the public agenda (e.g., De George, 1981), the time involved in establishing the effect (e.g., Eyal, Winter, & De George, 1981), the direction of causality (e.g., Becker, 1982), and the influence of audience characteristics on the effects (e.g., McCombs & Weaver, 1985). Wanta and Ghanem's meta-analysis (chap. 4, this volume) of 90 studies demonstrates what has been apparent for years: Agenda setting is a common and noticeable effect of the mass media that has been demonstrated over and over again. Wanta and Ghanem found that overall, there is a moderately strong (for our field) media influence on the audience agenda ($r = .529$). And, they provide evidence that the effect is robust. The statistical relationship does not significantly alter when single versus multiple issues are studied. Nor do the results differ based on individual-level or aggregate data. As Wanta and Ghanem noted, "methodological artifacts had little impact on the magnitude of effects found in agenda-setting research." That the news media influence what people think is a consistent, replicated media process.

Wanta and Ghanem's analyses also give some insight into the process of agenda setting. Researchers typically conduct one of two types of studies. The first, similar to the initial McCombs and Shaw (1972) study, includes a content analysis of the news to isolate the media agenda. Then, people's own listing of important issues is compared directly with the media agenda. The second holds that actual exposure to news, rather than the simple existence of content, is the important independent variable. In these studies, self-reported (or experimental) news exposure is compared with respondents' listing of important issues. Clearly, both find agenda-setting effects. Wanta and Ghanem, however, point out that the overall relationship between content and audience agenda is a bit stronger ($r = .531$) than the overall relationship between exposure and audience agenda ($r = .489$).

This finding deserves empirical exploration and theoretical discussion. Agenda setting demonstrates the power of the mass media to influence people without having to account for selective exposure to the news. As Wanta and Ghanem explain, some issues and events are "high threshold." That is, they command so much media attention (e.g., Clinton's impeachment or the World Trade Center attack) that they take over the media agenda. In such cases, no one needs to watch or read very much news to know that an issue is important. Wanta and Ghanem also note that interpersonal discussion of issues in the news can bring issue awareness without exposure to the news (e.g., Katz & Lazarsfeld, 1955). The results of their meta-analysis show that agenda setting remains a demonstration of the impact of mass media content that is not moderated much by aspects of the audience. Moreover, some of the studies included in Wanta and Ghanem's meta-analysis were published in the mid-1990s, with the beginning of the use of the Internet for news. Already, research has shown that media coverage is linked to online agendas (Roberts, Wanta, & Dzwo, 2002). Future researchers should explore whether agenda setting remains as consistent an effect with greater delivery of online news.

Third-Person Effects

Perloff (2002) noted that the third-person effect is a relatively new area of mass communication research that has drawn a good deal of scholarly attention. He reported that, when he wrote his chapter, there were already about 100 journal articles published exploring this topic. Third-person effects researchers examine how people respond to their own perceptions about others' reactions to the mass media. In general, this is a robust effect; for the most part, people believe that other people will be more affected by a wide range of negative media messages (see chap. 6 by Paul, Salwen, & Dupagne for a summary of those topics). Evidence of this effect is confirmed by the meta-analysis of Paul and colleagues. They found that, across 32 published studies, people saw that media content would affect others significantly more than they would be affected themselves: $r = .50$. As the authors note, although this is characterized as a moderate-sized effect, for our field, it is "rather substantial." Paul and colleagues found only a few factors moderated this effect. Effects were larger in studies that used nonrandom and college student samples. As the authors explain, college student samples might reflect the impact of "biased optimism" in the third-person effect. That is, college students, because they are more intelligent (and presumably drawn from mass communication classes and therefore educated about our research), might judge themselves as smarter and more resistant to media effects. Clearly, future researchers should continue to explore how third-person effects differ by sample.

This meta-analysis provides strong support for the existence of the perceptual component of third-person effects. But, because of limits in research reporting, Paul and colleagues were not able to conduct a meta-analysis of the behavioral component of third-person effects, that is, how perceptions of third-person effects leads to support for media censorship. Censorship is a complex concept influenced by a range of personal and situational variables (Lambe, 2002). Although the First Amendment mandates as little restriction on the media as possible, for certain types of media content (e.g., obscenity and indecency) and at certain times (e.g., during war or anticipated terrorist attacks), the public often endorses media censorship (e.g., McLeod, Perse, Signorielli, & Courtright, 1999). Examination of the behavioral component of third-person effects will add to our understanding of censorship.

Spiral of Silence

Noelle-Neumann's (1991) spiral of silence is a theory about the expression of public opinion that places a great deal of emphasis on the power of the mass media to establish dominant public opinion and reduce the number of divergent views. There are two important components to this theory: an individual's fear of isolation and the mass media. According to Noelle-Neumann, people are strongly motivated by a fear of being isolated from others in society. One way to avoid isolation is to not express views that would be rejected by the majority. So, people monitor their environment before expressing public views. The mass media cover public issues and become a major way to monitor public opinion. So, the mass media have the power to define for the public the dominant views about public issues.

Glynn, Hayes, and Shanahan conducted a meta-analysis of the central relationship of the spiral of silence: the connection between perceptions of opinion support and willingness to express opinion. In 17 studies conducted in 6 countries, the authors found a small positive correlation between perceptions of support for one's viewpoint and willingness ($r = .054$).

The spiral of silence has been widely scrutinized. Although its premises make sense, studies have found inconsistent support. Some scholars suggested that the spiral of silence operates differently in different societies with different cultures and media systems (e.g., Glynn & McLeod, 1985; Salmon & Kline, 1985). Moreover, a focus on people's willingness to speak out illuminates only one aspect of the theory. Noelle-Neumann assumes that people not only attend to media coverage of public opinion, but also accept that it represents a dominant view. There is evidence that, during times of crisis, the "rally" coverage of the media does lead to acceptance of views that might not be dominant (e.g., Eveland, McLeod, & Signorielli, 1995). Future researchers should explore how media coverage is linked to pluralistic ignorance.

Media's Effect on Voter Turnout

Miron and Bryant (chap. 24, this volume) summarized the strong case for exploring the link between media use and voter turnout. Television has been criticized for creating an apathetic voting public for several reasons, especially as voter turnout has declined in the decades following the adoption of television. First, because of an emphasis on visual images and a reliance on episodic framing, television simplifies political problems (e.g., Iyengar, 1991). Television also personalizes the news to focus on human interest, rather than issues, which might lead to less interest in politics (e.g., Price & Czilli, 1996). And, some scholars have found that the proliferation of negative campaigning has been linked to lower levels of political efficacy and voting intention (e.g., Ansolabehere & Iyengar, 1996). The 2000 election also reintroduced concerns about how television's election coverage can shape close elections (e.g., Tannenbaum, 1986).

Unfortunately, Miron and Bryant found that there were too few studies to draw substantive conclusions about the impact of the media on voter turn-out. They did find that, based on a small number of studies, the impact of newspaper use on voter turnout differs from the impact of television use. The results of the three studies of newspaper use suggest that newspaper use has a positive impact on voter turnout. Another useful finding of this meta-analysis is that, when one studies the impact of the media on voter turnout, it is not helpful to combine the results from different countries and political systems. Perhaps differences in media and political systems limit the generalizability of election studies across countries.

Prosocial Media Effects

Mass communication scholars often hold great optimism about the ability of the mass media to improve society. The example of *Sesame Street* showed that a television program could educate as well as entertain children. There are many other examples of how television has been used to create knowledge and instill prosocial attitudes (e.g., Singhal & Rogers, 1989). Four of the chapters in this book address the effectiveness of prosocial media content. It is clear that this is still an understudied area of media research. Mares and Woodard (chap. 17), for example, found only 39 studies exploring the positive effects of television on children's social interaction, compared to the 217 studies of television's antisocial effects identified by Paik and Comstock (1994). As they explain, this lack of research not only limits our understanding of the media's prosocial effects but also hinders our abilities to develop theoretical explains for *how* media content can work to promote prosocial effects.

Mares and Woodard found consistent small prosocial effects for television: $r = .23$. And, as expected, the effects were larger in the laboratory than when content is self-selected. Prosocial content had the largest effect on children's altruism. The authors explain that the strength of this effect might be due to meeting the conditions of social learning theory (Bandura, 2002); studies of altruism used dependent measures that more clearly modeled media content. Mares and Woodard identified an interesting age effect: The effects of prosocial television content were strongest between ages 3 and 7. Between the ages of 7 and 12 there is a steep decline in the effects. After age 12, the effects still diminish, but at a slower rate.

This chapter offers some new insights into the effects of prosocial content. Earlier meta-analyses (Hearold, 1986) had indicated that television's prosocial effects were stronger than its antisocial effects. Mares and Woodard point out that their meta-analysis suggests that prosocial and antisocial effects are equally as strong. But, they recognize that these results are based on far fewer studies and encourage scholars to study the prosocial impact of television.

Their finding about age mediating the prosocial effects of television is also notable. It seems that television's prosocial potential should be aimed at younger children, especially preschool age, when the effects might be the strongest.

Parcell and Bryant report a meta-analysis of 11 studies of health campaigns targeted to the health behaviors of children and adolescents (up to age 18). These studies dealt with a range of topics: smoking (8 studies), infant care, safety, AIDS, and family planning. They identified a small significant effect for health campaigns: $r = .026$. This small effect should not be dismissed. Their meta-analysis focused on actual behavior change (e.g., giving up smoking). Given that mass communication health campaigns can reach hundreds of thousands of people (or more), small effects can be very meaningful.

Snyder (chap. 20, this volume) also focused on the effectiveness of health campaigns and found that the mass media can be an effective tool, even in difficult situations. Overall, media health campaigns were effective ($r = .09$). Again, this small effect can be meaningful. The authors explain that their finding means that 8.9% of a community exposed to a health campaign would adopt the recommendations of the campaign, compared with a community not exposed. The authors also note that the effect sizes for media campaigns are smaller than for clinical intervention ($r = .27$ compared with $r = .09$), but point out that media campaigns can reach far more people and are much more cost effective.

Their analyses indicate that the effects of health campaigns are even stronger when different types of behaviors are targeted. Adoption campaigns (seat belts, mammograms, PAP screening, condom use, dental checkups, fruit and vegetable consumption, and crime prevention) are more successful ($r = .12$) than prevention ($r = .06$) or cessation campaigns ($r = .05$) (e.g, smoking, alcohol use, or unprotected sex).

The authors also found that when the campaign took place affected success. Consistent with diffusion of innovations (Rogers, 2003), adoption and cessation campaigns are more successful if they take place when about half the population has either adopted or ceased a health-related behavior. This is so because most people are in the majority (i.e., they are not innovators or early adopters). Moreover, when many people have already adopted a behavioral recommendation, there are many models for the behavior and interpersonal sources for influence.

The meta-analysis of Casey and colleagues (chap. 22, this volume) of the effects of Magic Johnson's 1991 announcement that he was HIV positive supported Greenberg's (1988) drench effect hypothesis. The researchers found that media coverage of that single event had a number of prosocial effects: an increase in knowledge about HIV and AIDS ($r = .194$), positive changes in attitudes toward people with HIV/AIDS ($r = .092$), and increased intention to reduce risk behaviors ($r = .044$), get tested for HIV ($r = .522$), and get more information about HIV ($r = .171$).

The number of studies also allowed the examination of the duration of the effect. The authors reported that personal vulnerability declined over time as well as the intention to get tested. Knowledge about HIV/AIDS, however, did not decline, and, in fact, increased with time. The authors suggest that Johnson's announcement was accompanied by several other sources of information in the media environment at the time that served as sources of knowledge.

Once again age was an important intervening variable in understanding the impact of Magic Johnson's announcement that he was HIV positive: participants older than 18 felt more personally vulnerable to HIV/AIDS after hearing Johnson's announcement ($r = .130$) whereas younger people felt less vulnerable ($r = -.120$).

Negative Effects of Media Content

The study of the mass media's negative effects traditionally gets the most visibility in our field. Overall, the range of the chapters in this book present a much more balanced view of our field, and four of the chapters present some new understanding of how the mass media are a negative force in society.

Christensen and Wood (chap. 10) updated a widely cited meta-analysis (Wood et al., 1991) and focused on the effects of media violence on aggression in unconstrained social interaction. Results were similar to the original study; the authors found that exposure to violent media content was linked to increased aggression: $d = .35$ (weighted mean, $d = .48$ for the unweighted mean, compared to Wood et al.'s $d = .27$ weighted and $d = .40$ unweighted). A notable finding of their analysis is a curvilinear relationship between age and effects. The largest effects of violent media content were seen in preadolescent children compared with very young children or teens. The authors suggest that young children are less likely to understand media content fully because of limits on their information-processing abilities, and older adolescents have greater understanding of societal rules and sanctions, so they are less likely to mimic the violent actions.

Oppliger (chap. 13, this volume) built on prior research that explored how stereotypical gender role portrayals in the media affect sex-role stereotyping. She found that media's effect was fairly direct, that is, not mediated by intervening variables. Across 31 studies, there was a relationship between media exposure and evidence of sex-role stereotyping: $r = .117$ (for nonexperimental studies) and $r = .235$ (experimental). Media exposure was linked to stereotypical behaviors ($r = .305$) as well as attitudes ($r = .156$). The effect was identified with U.S. samples ($r = .099$) as well as with international samples ($r = .211$). The effect was found with adults ($r = .096$), children ($r = .210$), males ($r = .157$), and females ($r = .170$). Note that none of these effects were significantly different from the others; media's impact clearly is consistent across groups.

Mundorf, Allen, D'Alessio, and Emmers-Sommer updated earlier meta-analyses that explored the negative impact of pornography (Allen, D'Alessio, et al., 1995; Allen, Emmers, et al., 1995). Consistent with earlier research, Mundorf and colleagues found antisocial effects associated with exposure to pornography. Pornography use was linked to more negative attitudes (typically rape myths): $r = .056$

(in nonexperimental settings) and $r = .145$ (in experimental settings). These effects hold for different types of pornography: nonviolent pornography $r = .125$ and violent pornography $r = .112$.

Researchers have been concerned that pornography increases violent behavior. Mundorf and colleagues found that violence was linked to different types of sexual content: violent sexual materials $r = .216$, nonviolent sexual materials $r = .171$, and nudity $r = -.137$.

This study offers two interesting conclusions. Although nudity in the mass media might offend some, nudity itself does not have the same kinds of negative effects as pornography. And interestingly, debriefing and other educational materials eradicate the negative effects of watching pornography: $r = .29$.

Music has often been seen as a positive influence in life. Allen, Herrett-Skjellum, Kramer, Ryan, and Timmerman (chap. 16, this volume), however, explored the antisocial effects of music. Studies examined by Allen and colleagues were probably motivated by some of the themes and phrases in some musical genres. Although the meta-analysis included studies of all types of music, an examination of the titles of the studies reveal that a number of studies were concerned with heavy metal, rap, and "deviant" rock music. Overall, exposure to music was significantly linked to antisocial actions and beliefs: $r = .228$. The researchers also found that music could be linked to antisocial attitudes ($r = .186$) and to lower levels of academic achievement ($r = -.113$). They also found that age was a significant moderator of effects: As participants got older, effects were stronger $r = .38$.

Sherry (chap. 15, this volume) pointed out that the study of video games has been marked by inconsistent results. Everything about this medium suggests that it should have strong effects: violent and realistic content played by gamers who devote a good deal of time and cognitive energy to the games. Gaming is not a passive activity; in fact, it is quite arousing. Gamers vicariously commit more acts of violence the longer than they play. The effects of game playing, however, are small; the connection between playing video games and aggression is $r = .15$. This effect is much smaller than the one connecting television and aggression. Moreover, the effect diminishes the longer the games are played. Sherry suggests that our traditional theories might not be broad enough in scope to translate to the video game context. The finding that length of time playing games is inversely related to aggression contradicts social learning theory and priming. Arousal-based theories, such as excitation transfer and catharsis, might be more useful when examining the effects of video games.

HOW MEDIA EFFECTS OCCUR

As a field, the study of mass communication has matured, and the study of media effects has grown beyond simply identifying the effects of media exposure. Several of the meta-analyses in this text explore the processes of media effects or provide explanations for how media effects occur.

Selective Exposure

Selective exposure is one of the "classic" concepts of our field. As D'Alessio and Allen (chap. 7, this volume) explained, many of the initial beliefs in limited media effects (e.g., Klapper, 1960) relied on evidence from dissonance theory and research (Festinger, 1957): People tend to avoid messages that contract their beliefs, attitudes, and typical actions. Sears and Freedman (1967/1971) conducted a widely cited study that called selective exposure based on dissonance into question.

D'Alessio and Allen conducted a meta-analysis of the same studies used by Sears and Freedman (1967/1971) and found contrary results. The meta-analysis reported in this book offered consistent support for selective exposure based on dissonance; people selected and avoided messages based on their desire to avoid dissonance: $r = .241$. Moreover, D'Alessio and Allen expand on this notable finding to explore a more up-to-date model of selective exposure. Because of increased channel choice offered by the newer media environment, D'Alessio and Allen suggest that people now do not make a single choice between a number of available messages. Instead, people are more likely to make sequential choices among various pairs of alternatives. They found that selective exposure based on this sequential model was even stronger: $r = .642$. Clearly, selective exposure is an important aspect of understanding selection and effects of media content.

Priming

Priming is a cognitive process that has been explored by social psychologists for about a quarter of a century. Priming occurs when a salient attribute of the environment activates or cues cognitive activity that influences subsequent perceptions, judgments, and actions (see chap. 5 in this volume by Roskos-Ewoldson, Klinger, & Roskos-Ewoldson for a more complete explanation). It has become a more widely held explanation for the impact of media exposure with the evidence that many media effects are not similar in character to media content (discounting modeling theories) as well as evidence that some media effects are relatively short-term (discounting learning theories). In their chapter, Roskos-Ewoldson and colleagues ask several important questions that allow us to see how priming can be an explanation for media effects.

First of all, the researchers found support for priming as the process of some media effects. Across all studies, media primes had significant, although small, effects on subsequent perceptions or behaviors: $r = .16$. As expected, the laboratory brings control; effects were larger in experiments ($r = .26$) than in surveys

($r = .12$). Roskos-Ewoldson and colleagues found that priming effects differed by domain. Effects of violent media primes ($r = .28$) were stronger than primes of political media messages ($r = .13$). More intense, longer exposure to priming media content had a stronger impact ($r = .28$) than exposure to shorter, less intense media primes ($r = .21$). In the studies available for meta-analysis, there was no impact on effect size due to time interval. From the evidence that we have, it is not possible to draw conclusions about how the impact of priming decays over time. Finally, the researchers also found that exposure to violent media primes interacts with trait aggressiveness. As the authors note: "People with high trait aggressiveness tended to show stronger media priming effects than did people who were low on trait aggressiveness."

Together, the results of this meta-analysis offer several insights into how salient media content can evoke priming effects, or effects on media users' perceptions, judgments, and actions. The authors conclude, however, that priming by media content might not be identical to priming phenomena typically studied by social and cognitive social psychologists, primarily because of the evidence that effects of media priming are of longer duration. This difference might be due to the nature of media exposure. Most people spend a good deal of time with the mass media, and personal preferences often mean that people are being exposed to similar types of content (e.g. Webster & Phalen, 1997). So, in the real world, priming can happen regularly. And, as Roskos-Ewoldson and colleagues explained, repeated exposure to the same primes can lead to chronic accessibility (e.g., Shrum & O'Guinn, 1993), so that certain ideas are always at top of mind and ready to influence judgments and behaviors.

Involvement

Involvement is another important concept in media effects. As Hollander (chap. 23, this volume) explained, it has many meanings, such as relevance and interest. Persuasion researchers have understood that involvement dictates how people respond to, process, and are affected by messages (e.g., Petty & Cacioppo, 1986). Hollander's meta-analysis explored the relationship between political involvement and media use. The results revealed that television use has a weaker relationship to political involvement than newspaper use. This finding is important, because it verifies the hypotheses of several studies and reinforces the consistent findings of prior research: Television is limited as a political resource because of its reliance on dramatic images, simple story-telling, and episodic framing (Perse, 2001).

News Gatekeeping

The media have often been damned for being biased toward either liberal (e.g., Lichter, Rothman, & Lichter, 1986) or conservative slants (e.g., Herman & Chomsky, 1988). Several sources exist for this bias, ranging from individual journalists, from the political slants of editors, or from policies enforced by corporate media owners (Shoemaker & Reeser, 1996). In their meta-analysis, D'Alessio and Allen (chap. 26, this volume) explored the impact of newspaper ownership on political bias. In this extension of their earlier study (D'Alessio & Allen, 2000), they noted that, as a reflection of the more conservative views of corporate owners, there was a small, but significant, pro-Republican bias in news reporting (52.7% of content was pro-Republican; 47.3% was pro-Democrat). This is a small relationship, but if there is a link between news coverage and voting decisions, this result must be placed in the context of the close races in some recent presidential elections. It is also interesting that the authors noted that the relationship between political party bias in political candidate coverage is becoming less linked to endorsement. The authors suggested that concentration of newspaper ownership might be limiting publisher/owner effects on endorsements.

MAJOR CONCLUSIONS ABOUT MEDIA EFFECTS

Media effects are significant and meaningful. The meta-analyses reported in this book support prior analyses. Media effects range from small to moderate. But, several authors have noted that effects might be larger than the effect sizes reveal. Christensen and Wood (chap. 10) noted that effects even in laboratory studies might be underestimated because of limits on the types of media content used as a stimulus. It is clear that with special technical and digital effects, audiences are exposed to more violent and more graphic media violence that in earlier decades. Effects might be stronger and more salient (see also Roskos-Ewoldson et al. [chap. 5] for information on the impact of stronger media primes). We also know that media content does not occur in isolated settings. People often are part of an audience, so media content that affects one person might lead to behavior that itself can stimulate others. Aggression as result of media content might have contagious effects. Moreover, Wanta and Ghanem's analysis shows how media content's impact can spread beyond those directly exposed to it. And, the results of meta-analyses of media campaign's prosocial effects point out that small effects can be quite meaningful; although media campaigns have only small effects on cessation of unhealthy behaviors, even small effects translate into positive changes for large numbers of people.

Draw conclusions from cross-national research with caution. Several of the meta-analyses reported in this book have included research conducted in other countries than the United States. We expect our theories to be broad in scope, that is, to work beyond national boundaries. When dealing with media content, however, it is important to remember that media content can vary by media system. Morgan and Shanahan (1997), for example, reported that cultivation effects were not consistently found outside the United States. Meta-analyses of political effects reveal that some media effects might not translate to other countries and that media effects can differ based on forms of government and election rules.

Age is an important intervening variable in understanding media effects. The results of these meta-analyses again reinforce a central tenet of our field: Children and adolescents are special audiences and the media might affect them differently. For some media effects, children are more affected; for other, they are less affected. Casey and colleagues (chap. 22), for example, found that adolescents younger than 18 were affected differently than adults by the news that Magic Johnson was HIV positive. Although children gained more knowledge about HIV/AIDS than adults, they felt a diminished sense of vulnerability to contracting the disease, compared with adults. This finding is unfortunate, as young adults might be especially vulnerable to the kinds of risky behaviors that can be associated with HIV.

Christensen and Wood's results suggest that the effects of violent media content are mediated by children's information-processing abilities and social context. In their meta-analysis, they found that the youngest children and older adolescents were less affected by media violence that younger adolescents. Young children might be less likely to understand the message, so they were less affected. Older adolescents have a greater understanding of societal rules and sanctions and so are less likely to accept the messages. Their findings suggest that there is an age at which children might be most susceptible to the effects of media violence.

Mares and Woodard (chap. 17), on the other hand, found that effects of prosocial television content were strongest between ages 3 and 7. This different effect might reflect the nature of media content. Perhaps violent content is more complex and less easily understood than prosocial media content. Hoffner and Levine (chap. 14, this volume) found that, although there were overall effects for age on liking violence and horror, young children did not like that content. For children in grades kindergarten though sixth, age was negatively related to liking this content. Together these findings suggest that targeting youngsters with prosocial education messages is appropriate and effective. But, future researchers need to explore how age intervenes in negative media effects.

New media technology might alter the process of media effects. D'Alessio and Allen's (chap. 7) meta-analysis indicated the value of modifying traditional concepts in a changed media environment. As they pointed out, when people surf the Web, listen to the radio, or watch television, they no longer are making simple choices from a few available alternatives. Thus, the authors tested a sequential model of selective exposure and found that the impact of dissonance is even stronger in the new media environment than it was in Sears and Freedman's era. It is clear that models of choice are changing, as the number of channels increases (e.g., Ferguson & Perse, 1993; Heeter, 1985).

Sherry's (chap. 15) discussion of the effects of playing aggressive video games and the various theories that would explain these effects indicated that video games should not be considered the same as television. The theories that we have used to explain the effects of television do not seem to explain the effects of video games. His prime finding, that effects of video games diminish with time spent playing, suggests that modeling and priming theories might not apply to gaming. Sherry suggested a focus on arousal-based theories, such as excitation transfer and catharsis, to understand this finding. Although catharsis has generally been rejected as a viable justification for media violence, it might have some applicability to understanding the appeal of and effects from video game playing. Comstock, Chaffee, Katzman, McCombs, and Roberts (1978) suggested that there were two types of catharsis. Vicarious behavior catharsis proposes that arousal and negative feelings can be displaced by watching drama. Overt behavior catharsis, on the other hand, proposes that arousal and negative feelings can be diminished by "acting out" feelings. There is evidence that overt behavior catharsis might be an effective release of aggression (Comstock et al., 1978). Future researchers need to apply new theories to new media.

Public policy concerns remain. This chapter began with the reminder that mass communication is subject to scrutiny because of public policy concerns. The results of these meta-analyses offer some insights into policy issues. Media violence, which is a common part of much media content, should continue to concern parents, educators, and policy makers. Attention should be particularly focused on younger adolescents, who appear to be most vulnerable to its effects.

Allen and colleagues (chap. 16) suggested that the results of their meta-analysis indicate that the effects of music are cumulative, because effects increase with age. Another interpretation might be linked to the curvilinear relationship between age and negative effects identified by Christensen and Wood (chap. 10). Perhaps younger music listeners do not fully understand the lyrics in some musical forms. There is much anecdotal evidence that young children misinterpret lyrics dealing with notions that are unfamiliar. Future researchers should explore how age interacts with comprehension of music. These studies could inform music labeling activities.

The results of the meta-analysis of Mundorf and colleagues (chap. 12) offer some hope to those concerned about the negative effects of pornography. Educational materials and debriefings can diminish negative effects. It also notable that most of the studies included in the meta-analysis were published more than a decade ago. Researchers should continue to explore the effects of pornography, especially as it has become widely available because of the WWW. Policy makers and educators should continue to implement educational programs to help mitigate negative effects. The finding that nudity is not linked to negative effects also has policy implications for those who are concerned with indecent media content. Although this content can offend, there is little evidence that it is harmful (see also Donnerstein, Wilson, & Linz, 1992).

Finally, it is clear that mass media have positive effects; mass communication can be a positive force in society. The results of the meta-analyses should encourage foundations and government agencies to continue to fund campaigns for prosocial aims. Even small effects can have meaningful impacts.

SUMMARY

We know a good deal more about the process and effects of mass communication as result of the work of the researchers who conducted these meta-analyses. These studies reinforce the importance of mass communication as both a positive and negative force in society. As our statistical methods become more sophisticated, we can draw stronger conclusions about the impact of mass communication. Several of these studies have not only served to organize and summarize knowledge, but the authors have also pointed out new insights and new directions for research. The range of topics covered in this book demonstrates that ours is a vibrant field and our students still have a lot of work to do.

REFERENCES

Allen, M., D'Alessio, D., & Brezgel, K. (1995). A meta-analysis summarizing the effects of pornography. II: Aggression after exposure. *Human Communication Research, 22,* 258–283.

Allen, M., Emmers, T., Gebhardt, L., & Giery, M. A. (1995). Exposure to pornography and acceptance of rape myths. *Journal of Communication, 45*(1), 5–26.

Ansolabehere, S., & Iyengar, S. (1996). The craft of political advertising: A progress report. In D. C. Mutz, P. M. Sniderman, & R. A. Brody (Eds.), *Political persuasion and attitude change* (pp. 101–122). Ann Arbor: University of Michigan.

Bagdikian, B. H. (2000). *The media monopoly* (6th ed.). Boston: Beacon Press.

Bandura, A. (2002). Social cognitive theory of mass communication. In J. Bryant & D. Zillmann (Eds.), *Media effects: Advances in theory and research* (2nd ed., pp. 121–153). Mahwah, NJ: Lawrence Erlbaum Associates.

Becker, L. B. (1982). The mass media and citizen assessment of issue importance: A reflection on agenda-setting research. In D. C. Whitney, E. Wartella, & S. Windahl (Eds.), *Mass communication review yearbook* (Vol. 3, pp. 521–536). Beverly Hills: Sage.

Cacioppo, J. T., & Petty, R. E. (1979). Effects of message repetition and position on cognitive response, recall, and persuasion. *Journal of Personal and Social Psychology, 37,* 97–109.

Chaffee, S. H., & Hockheimer, J. L. (1982). The beginnings of political communication research in the United States: Origins in the "limited effects" model. In E. Rogers & F. Balle (Eds.), *The media revolution in America and Western Europe* (pp. 262–283). Norwood, NJ: Ablex.

Comstock, G., Chaffee, S., Katzman, N., McCombs, M., & Roberts, D. (1978). *Television and human behavior.* New York: Columbia University Press.

D'Alessio, D., & Allen, M. (2000). Media bias in presidential elections: A meta-analysis. *Journal of Communication, 50*(4), 133–156.

DeGeorge, W. F. (1981). Conceptualization and measurement of audience agenda. In G. C. Wilhoit & H. De Bock (Eds.), *Mass communication review yearbook* (Vol. 2, pp. 219–224). Beverly Hills: Sage.

Donnerstein, E., Wilson, B., & Linz, D. (1992). On the regulation of broadcast indecency to protect children. *Journal of Broadcasting & Electronic Media, 36,* 111–117.

Ettema, J. S., & Kline, F. G. (1977). Deficits, differences, and ceilings: Contingent conditions for understanding the knowledge gap. *Communication Research, 4,* 179–202.

Eveland, W. P., Jr. (1997). Interactions and nonlinearity in mass communication: Connecting theory and methodology. *Journalism and Mass Communication Quarterly, 74,* 400–416.

Eveland, W. P., McLeod, D. M., & Signorielli, N. (1995). Actual and perceived U.S. public opinion: The spiral of silence during the Persian Gulf War. *International Journal of Public Opinion Research, 7,* 91–109.

Eyal, C. H., Winter, J. P., & DeGeorge, W. G. (1981). The concept of time frame in agenda setting. In G. C. Wilhoit & H. De Bock (Eds.), *Mass communication review yearbook* (Vol. 2, pp. 212–218). Beverly Hills: Sage.

Ferguson, D. A. (1994). Measurement of mundane TV behaviors: Remote control device flipping frequency. *Journal of Broadcasting & Electronic Media, 38,* 35–47.

Ferguson, D. A., & Perse, E. M. (1993). Media and audience influences on channel repertoire. *Journal of Broadcasting & Electronic Media, 37,* 31–47.

Festinger, L. (1957). *A theory of cognitive dissonance.* Stanford, CA: Stanford University.

Fowles, J. (1999). *The case for television violence.* Thousand Oaks, CA: Sage.

Freedman, J. L (2002). *Media violence and its effect on aggression: Assessing the scientific evidence.* Toronto, Ontario, Canada: University of Toronto Press.

Glynn, C. J., & McLeod, J. M. (1985). Implications of the spiral of silence theory of communication and public opinion research. In K. R. Sanders, L. L. Kaid, & D. Nimmo (Eds.), *Political communication yearbook 1984* (pp. 43–65). Carbondale: Southern Illinois University Press.

Greenberg, B. S. (1988). Some uncommon television images and the drench hypothesis. In S. Oskamp (Ed.), *Applied social psychology annual. Vol. 8: Television as a social issue* (pp. 88–102). Newbury Park, CA: Sage.

Gurevitch, M., & Blumler, J. G. (1990). Political communication systems and democratic values. In J. Lichtenberg (Ed.), *Democracy and the mass media: A collection of essays* (pp. 269–289). Cambridge, England: Cambridge University Press.

Hearold, S. (1986). A synthesis of 1043 effects of television on social behavior. In G. Comstock (Ed.), *Public communication and behavior* (Vol. 1, pp. 65–133). Orlando, FL: Academic Press.

Heeter, C. (1985). Program selection and the abundance of choice: A process model. *Human Communication Research, 12,* 126–152.

Herman, E. S., & Chomsky, N. (1988). *Manufacturing consent: The political economy of the mass media.* New York: Pantheon Books.

Herrett-Skjellum, J., & Allen, M. (1996). Television programming and sex stereotyping: A meta-analysis. In B. R. Burleson (Ed.), *Communication yearbook* (Vol. 19, pp. 157–185). Thousand Oaks, CA: Sage.

Iyengar, S. (1991). *Is anyone responsible: How television frames political issues.* Chicago: University of Chicago Press.

Jackson, S., & Jacobs, S. (1983). Generalizing about messages: Suggestions for design and analysis of experiments. *Human Communication Research, 9,* 169–191.

Josephson, W. L. (1987). Television violence and children's aggression: Testing the priming, social script, and disinhibition predictions. *Journal of Personality and Social Psychology, 53,* 882–890.

Joy, L. A., Kimball, M. M., & Zabrack, M. L. (1986). Television and children's aggressive behavior. In T. M. Williams (Ed.), *The impact of television: A natural experiment in three communities* (pp. 303–360). Orlando, FL: Academic Press.

Katz, E., & Lazarsfeld, P. F. (1955). *Personal influence: The part played by people in the flow of mass communications.* New York: Free Press.

Kessler, M. (1989). Women's magazines' coverage of smoking related health hazards. *Journalism Quarterly, 66,* 316–322, 445.

Klapper, J. T. (1960). *The effects of mass communication.* New York: Free Press.

Lambe, J. L. (2002). Dimensions of censorship: Reconceptualizing public willingness to censor. *Communication Law & Policy, 7,* 187–235.

Lichter, S. R., Rothman, S., & Lichter, L. S. (1986). *The media elite.* Bethesda, MD: Adler & Adler.

Linz, D., Arluk, I. H., & Donnerstein, E. (1990). Mitigating the negative effects of sexually violence mass communications through preexposure briefings. *Communication Research, 17,* 641–674.

Malamuth, N. M., Haber, S., & Feshbach, S. (1980). Testing hypotheses regarding rape: Exposure to sexual violence, sex differences, and the "normality" of rapists. *Journal of Research in Personality, 14,* 121–137.

McCombs, M. E., & Shaw, D. L. (1972). The agenda-setting function of mass media. *Public Opinion Quarterly, 36,* 176–187.

McCombs, M. E., & Weaver, D. H. (1985). Toward a merger of gratifications and agenda-setting research. In K. E. Rosengren, L. A. Wenner, & P. Palmgreen (Eds.), *Media gratifications research: Current perspectives* (pp. 95–108). Beverly Hills: Sage.

McGuire, W. J. (1986). The myth of massive media impact: Savagings and salvagings. In G. Comstock (Ed.), *Public communication and behavior* (Vol. 1, pp. 173–257). Orlando, FL: Academic Press.

McLeod, D. M., Kosicki, G. M., & McLeod, J. M. (2002). Resurveying the boundaries of political communication effects. In J. Bryant & D. Zillmann (Eds.), *Media effects: Advances in theory and research* (2nd ed., pp. 215–267). Mahwah. NJ: Lawrence Erlbaum Associates.

McLeod, D. M., Perse, E. M., Signorielli, N., & Courtright, J. A. (1999). Public hostility toward freedom of expression during international conflicts: A case study of public opinion during the Persian Gulf War. *Free Speech Yearbook, 36,* 104–117.

Minow, N. N., & LaMay, C. L. (1995). *Abandoned in the wasteland: Children, television, and the First Amendment.* New York: Hill and Wang.

Morgan, M., & Shanahan, J. (1997). Two decades of cultivation research: An appraisal and meta-analysis. In B. R. Burleson (Ed.), *Communication yearbook* (Vol. 20, pp. 1–45). Thousand Oaks, CA: Sage.

Noelle-Neumann, E. (1991). The theory of public opinion: The concept of the spiral of silence. In J. A. Anderson (Ed.), *Communication yearbook* (Vol. 14, pp. 256–287). Newbury Park, CA: Sage.

Paik, H., & Comstock, G. (1994). The effects of television violence in antisocial behavior. *Communication Research, 21,* 516–546.

Perloff, R. M. (2002). The third-person effect. In J. Bryant & D. Zillmann (Eds.), *Media effects: Advances in theory and research* (2nd ed., pp. 489–506). Mahwah. NJ: Lawrence Erlbaum Associates.

Perse, E. M. (2001). *Media effects and society.* Mahwah, NJ: Lawrence Erlbaum Associates.

Petty, R. E., & Cacioppo, J. T. (1986). *Communication and persuasion: Central and peripheral routes to attitude change.* New York: Springer-Verlag.

Petty, R. E., Priester, J. R., & Brizol, P. (2002). Mass media attitude change: Implications of the elaboration likelihood model of persuasion. In J. Bryant & D. Zillmann (Eds.), *Media effects: Advances in theory and research* (2nd ed., pp. 155–198). Mahwah, NJ: Lawrence Erlbaum Associates.

Potter, W. J. (2001). *Media literacy.* Thousand Oaks, CA: Sage.

Price, V., & Czilli, E. J. (1996). Modeling patterns of news recognition and recall. *Journal of Communication, 46*(2), 55–78.

Roberts, M., Wanta, W., & Dzwo, T.-H. (2002). Agenda setting and issue salience online. *Communication Research, 29,* 452–465.

Rogers, W. M. (2003). *Diffusion of innovations* (5th ed.). New York: Free Press.

Roskos-Ewoldsen, D. R., Roskos-Ewoldsen, B., & Carpentier, F. R. D. (2002). Media priming: A synthesis. In J. Bryant & D. Zillmann (Eds.), *Media effects: Advances in theory and research* (2nd ed., pp. 97–120). Mahwah, NJ: Lawrence Erlbaum Associates.

Salmon, C. T., & Kline, F. G. (1985). The spiral of silence ten years later. In K. R. Sanders, L. L. Kaid, & D. Nimmo (Eds.), *Political communication yearbook 1984* (pp. 3–30). Carbondale: Southern Illinois University Press.

Sears, D. O., & Freedman, J. L. (1967/1971). Selective exposure to information: A critical review. In W. Schramm & D. F. Roberts (Eds.), *The process and effects of mass communication* (rev. ed., pp. 209–235). Urbana: University of Illinois.

Shoemaker, P. J., & Reese, S. D. (1996). *Mediating the message: Theories of influences on mass media content* (2nd ed.). White Plains, NY: Longman.

Shrum, L. J. (2002). Media consumption and perceptions of social reality: Effects and underlying processes. In J. Bryant & D. Zillmann (Eds.), *Media effects: Advances in theory and research* (2nd ed., pp. 69–95). Mahwah, NJ: Lawrence Erlbaum Associates.

Shrum, L. J., & O'Guinn, T. C. (1993). Processes and effects in the construction of social reality. *Communication Research, 20,* 436–471.

Shrum, L. J., Wyer, R. S., Jr., & O'Guinn, T. C. (1998). The effects of television consumption on social perceptions: The use of priming procedure to investigate psychological processes. *Journal of Consumer Research, 24,* 447–458.

Singhal, A., & Rogers, E. M. (1989). Prosocial television for development in India. In R. E. Rice & C. K. Atkin (Eds.), *Public communication campaigns* (2nd. ed., pp. 331–350). Newbury Park, CA: Sage.

Signorielli, N., & Lears, M. (1992). Television and children's conceptions of nutrition: Unhealthy messages. *Health Communication, 4,* 245–257.

Tannenbaum, P. H. (1986). Policy options for early election projections. In J. Bryant & D. Zillmann (Eds.), *Perspectives on media effects* (pp. 189–203). Hillsdale, NJ: Lawrence Erlbaum Associates.

Thompson, J. (2004, April 26). Why I complain about indecency. *Broadcasting & Cable,* p. 48.

Van Evra, J. (2004). *Television and child development* (3rd ed.). Mahwah, NJ: Lawrence Erlbaum Associates.

Webster, J. G., & Phalen, P. F. (1997). *The mass audience: Rediscovering the dominant model.* Mahwah, NJ: Lawrence Erlbaum Associates.

Webster, J. G., & Wakshlag, J. (1985). Measuring exposure to television. In D. Zillmann & J. Bryant (Eds.), *Selective exposure to communication* (pp. 35–62). Hillsdale, NJ: Lawrence Erlbaum Associates.

Wright, C. R. (1986). *Mass communication: A sociological perspective* (3rd ed.). New York: Random House.

Wood, W., Wong, F. Y., & Chachere, J. G. (1991). Effects of media violence on viewers' aggression in unconstrained social interaction. *Psychological Bulletin, 109,* 371–383.

Zillmann, D., & Bryant, J. (Eds.). (1985). Selective exposure to communication. Hillsdale, NJ: Lawrence Erlbaum Associates.

29

The Challenge of Media Effects for Teaching and Policy

Mike Allen
Nancy A. Burrell
University of Wisconsin–Milwaukee

Raymond G. Preiss
University of Puget Sound

The application and implication of the revolution that meta-analysis has created continues to have an impact on the social sciences community. Meta-analysis continues to generate interest and implications for a variety of social and scientific issues (Allen, 1998; Cooper & Hedges, 1994; Fitzpatrick, 2002). Meta-analysis serves the role of summarizing existing data to provide sense of what is often a confusing set of empirical findings. The conclusions of any particular meta-analysis require replication and extension to achieve authoritative empirical and theoretical formulations. However, when a body of meta-analyses creates an interlocking web of conclusions, to not accept the scientific claims flies in the face of empirical reality. The impact of not accepting a huge body of scientific data is simply practicing a form of cognitive denial. At the current time, meta-analyses provide a consistent finding: Media content produces predictable and demonstrable effects on those consuming that material. Acceptance of that conclusion will probably prove difficult for a variety of reasons, and acceptance of this claim fails to warrant any particular policy action (the most probable is censorship). Despite the fears and warnings that are entailed by the findings, as Mr. Spock would say, "There are always alternatives." The questions facing the next generation of scholarly researchers require the consideration and evaluation of various alternatives to simple censorship. In addition, the value or outcomes of censorship or any restriction need to be considered and addressed to determine whether even that alternative produces the kinds of outcomes sought by the advocates.

The purpose of this chapter, besides the discussion of a few alternatives, is predominantly pedagogical. The goals are the evaluation of the content of textbooks that provide knowledge to students in courses across the country. Scientific knowledge is empirical, and textbooks should incorporate and reflect the current empirical findings (the state of the art). The belief of the authors is that eventually the acceptance of empirical facts begins to standardize and unify the content of the material in mass media courses. This move becomes inevitable for scientists; once a fact becomes established (on the basis of repeated empirical demonstrations) then the facts should be taught. Kuhn (1970) pointed out that the nature of scientific advancement by acceptance and ultimately consensus involves a process not purely rational but largely inevitable. Challenges to traditional models of science (Harding, 1986, 1991) still require acceptance by the scientific mob to gain legitimacy. Although the process of generating consensus may take a variety of forms, the scientific process of collecting and analyzing data (with numerous replications) eventually generates a consensus in the community about the state of empirical data that propels the next theoretical formulation and defines the next search for information.

THE BASIS OF KNOWLEDGE

Meta-analysis is simply, at the heart, a means of combining data sets (Allen & Preiss, 2002). The goal is the reduction of Type II errors (false negatives), the identification of Type I errors (false positives), and the consideration of various sources of variability/moderation in the observed set of relationships. The result of a meta-analysis should provide a much clearer picture of the issues about the conditions under which a relationship is observed as well as the consistency of observed that relationship. When combined with the correction for statistical and methodological artifacts (Hunter & Schmidt, 1990), the emerging empirical picture should provide useful and clear information.

The knowledge of any relationship in a scientific sense only generates partial understanding of the issues. The problem with scientific knowledge is that empirical knowledge often serves as the basis for various actions. However, the existence of a particular fact, or set of facts, does not necessarily imply or require a particular set of actions or policies. Scientific facts can serve as justifications for various actions that expect or require a set of empirical circumstances to be true to justify the action. There exist a variety of different methods for generating understanding. Figure 29.1 provides a view of the authors on the issues about elements of knowledge claims. The argument by the authors is that a full picture of knowledge will combine the four methods depicted (qualitative, quantitative, rhetori-

Horizontal axis—Purpose/Type of Conclusion
Vertical axis—Level of Decision-making Methodology

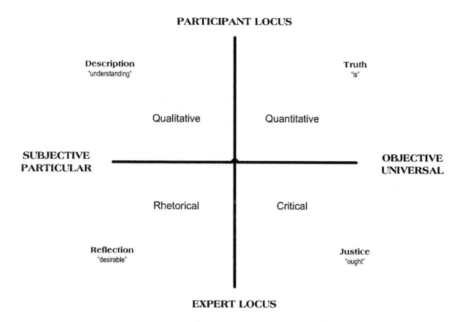

FIG. 29.1   Elements of knowledge.

cal, and critical). Such a method requires the integration of claims that sometimes are antagonistic to each other. However, full knowledge that permits a basis for action will combine scientific universal truth (quantitative), ethnographic understanding (qualitative), a moral and ethical view (critical), and a means for reflective understanding of the desirable (rhetorical). The challenge of finding a means of collaboration between the methods is difficult but necessary (Allen, 1999). A problem emerges when any particular method of claim making tries to assume ascendancy or control over another or assert privilege and deny access to other methods (for an example see Frey, Pearce, Pollock, Artz, & Murphy, 1996). The point is that scientific findings only point to a set of facts; the interpretation and application of those facts require knowledge that science cannot provide. The cultural knowledge necessary for application and understanding cannot be found in the meta-analysis. The facts provided by meta-analysis should be used by policymakers, but any fact can imply a large number of varying policies.

In the case of media effects, science can provide evidence for the existence of those effects or not. But the existence of any particular set of associations does not inherently mandate any particular action. The problem is that empirical facts should guide actions, but which alternative should be pursued is not always entirely clear in the findings. The goal of this book is scientific: the articulation of observed associations and the theoretical implications of those empirical observations. The implications that the particular facts have for the formulation of policy and pedagogy remain a question yet to be answered. In the process of answering one must consider that any particular set of facts permits multiple answers consistent with the facts. In other words, the facts do not, "speak for themselves"; facts require interpretation and application before the implementation of any action consistent with that sense of empirical reality.

Actions require moral and ethical decisions in addition to accurate knowledge. For example, the fact that scientists can clone does not mean that scientists should clone. Even if the effect of exposure to particular media content is a set of antisocial or prosocial actions, this result does not require controls on the media. Questions about the value of a media free from governmental intrusion require decisions of a legal, moral, and ethical nature that no meta-analysis can answer.

THE IMPLICATIONS OF KNOWLEDGE

Some scientific claims, when accepted as true, require appropriate incorporation into decision making and other bodies involved in public discourse. The impact of improved knowledge (particularly more accurate understanding of empirical relations) should improve decision making. Scientific knowledge clarifies the various impacts of the media and can help in the evaluation of the outcomes of various policy choices. Although the knowledge does not provide certainty (knowledge in the sciences is based on probability—although the probability of being wrong may be very small in some circumstances), understanding the various outcomes and the probabilities associated with them provides a distinct advantage over trying to sort out the implications or desires for an action with less known consequences.

When a discourse makes reference to some fact about the impact of media, then scientific knowledge can be invoked to evaluate whether that fact is true or not. The implication of establishing a fact is that some policy or other action may assume the existence of some truth as a basis for the conclusion offered. Goodnight (1982) pointed out that the issues of argumentation are often divided into the public, personal, and technical spheres. One of the unfortunate possible consequences of meta-analysis may be the rise of the technocracy in social issues such as media effects. The ability of science to authoritatively provide facts on social issues in this century can make issues previously considered matters of opinion change to questions that are empirical. The consequences of this shift and the need to redefine public address requires some effort.

Consider a person wishing to ban, censor, restrict, or modify the level of violence in music. One argument is that the violence in the music produces some sort of antisocial outcome, such as more violent behavior among the consumers of the material. This assumption is an empirical fact that can be considered and either affirmed or denied. If the meta-analysis confirms that existence of an effect (and the data pool is large enough, variable enough, and externally and internally valid) then the basis for consideration of the implication of the fact may carry serious consequences. However, science should be neutral to the fact in the sense that scientific data should be capable of affirming or denying any such empirical relationship. If policy reflects the existence or depends on the existence of a particular association, then a changing understanding of the facts would necessitate a change in policy to be consistent with those facts. Whether mass media policymakers can simply surrender decision making to the body of scientists engaged in such research is probably not only impossible but for many reasons also undesirable.

The argument about the effect of the media on some demonstrable outcome is a different argument than a person saying, "We should ban this music because it offends me." An argument that a particular type of music is offensive and therefore subject to restriction does not rely on scientific evidence and cannot be accessed or empirically verified on the basis of scientific method. But when the advocate says that the impact of the music is to promote violence that kills people and scientific evidence proves this, the advocate now argues to save lives. The argument shifts from one of a moral position based on views of appropriateness to one of the necessity to save lives.

Although scientific knowledge provides the basis for a large number of potential claims, many claims or standards for evaluation are not relevant to the existence of particular empirical facts. The challenge of the First Amendment to any scientific position is that the First Amendment is the expression of a set of values, and values as such are not empirically based but rooted in a valence of desires, independent of any particular set of facts. Much like religious belief or any other moral belief, the assumptions are grounded not in the empirical but in the desirable. The challenge facing policymakers becomes finding a means of resolving the clash over the arguments about public policy when different sets of facts emerge.

First Amendment considerations can be expressed in a number of ways. For example, critical legal scholars (Delgado & Stefancic, 2004) might view the normal interpretations of the First amendment as outdated and argue for an updating of the mechanical view of First Amendment freedoms. Such a view would be more likely to perceive the First Amendment's freedom as needing to serve a social purpose and therefore the protection in the Bill of Rights afforded the media would be subject to more social evaluation. Under that logic, the impact of media content (such as that of hate speech) could be evaluated and justifying a lack of restrictions on content could become difficult. The view of the First Amendment may change as the understanding of media effects begins to change.

The authors are not arguing that a critical legal theory is the most appropriate approach to First Amendment issues. Instead the authors are suggesting that under a critical view of "freedom of the media", the justification for regulation can be more readily accepted on the basis of what kinds of empirical effects exist. The development of knowledge creates an understanding of the implications of social action (or inaction). The challenge for those engaged in setting policy will be maintaining freedom in an environment in which the effects of media are not always benign.

ASSESSING REPRESENTATIONS OF KNOWLEDGE

Textbooks offer to the beginning, intermediate, and advanced student efforts to summarize and represent a broad base of research. The goal is to permit the person to examine the book and gain an overall understanding of the level of knowledge that exists about any general media outcome. The representation of empirical literature should be conducted in a manner that over the longer term standardizes the treatment of various material. If one accepts a scientific statement about an association between two variables as possible, then empirical research should seek to resolve the status of the "truth" about statements that are empirically based. For example, it would be difficult for someone to state that the world is flat and a boat that sails too far into the horizon will fall off the edge.

This section offers a kind of review of the claims made by general texts about the state of knowledge for media effects. The sample of textbooks is not random or scientific; as such, it may not be representative. The goal of this exercise is to illustrate the variability and divergence in the level of knowledge that exist when one considers various issues of media outcomes. Several of the books represent textbooks that the authors used as students and provide a kind of retrospective on the education of the authors. Some of the textbooks are considered classics and been used over a number of years. The impact of the choice is less a report card on the state of the art in the discipline but instead provides a simple basis example of how to evaluate various textbook representations.

Ultimately, the representations should become more uniform. The goal of the scientific enterprise is the generation of more uniform statements of the consensus about knowledge. Science operates to present a form of knowledge that represents a consensus about the state of the empirical world. However, such statements denote representations that are the "best" representations of what is considered true and reflect theories that are accepted as "probably" true. The representations are subject to change as more information is gathered, estimates are revised, and more accurate theories are generated. The process only works if data can accumulate in such a manner that the accuracy of any particular claim can be subject to improvement as the result of additional data collection. If data cannot be accumulated to permit increased accuracy (including generalizability, validity, reliability, measurement, and so on) than the entire process starts to break down. The fundamental challenge to the social sciences was whether such a process could be said to exist and an explanation made about how such a process would be represented (Hunter & Schmidt, 1990).

The questions that are being considered are basic: Is there a relationship? The implications of answering the very simple question of whether the media have any effect at all are important. Any discussion of the control of media content (e.g., censorship, standards, or v-chips) assumes either that (a) specific media content is generating particular outcomes on audience members (e.g., violent media content viewed by children promotes violent behavior or sexually explicit material viewed by men increases probability of rape), or (b) particular media content is offensive and should be banned (moral standards, profane, obscene, and so on). The first standard is relevant to the outcomes of meta-analysis because the argument assumes that media content produces a particular outcome, and the society would want to minimize sources of negative influence. Such a position assumes an empirical fact (media content generates outcomes) and can be evaluated on an empirical or scientific basis. Meta-analysis, particularly a lot of meta-analyses, can establish whether or not a general pattern (indicating the potential validity of a theoretical argument) exists. If such a pattern exists, then one necessary condition for the censorship, restriction, or regulation of the media exists. The lack of any such consistent effect would indicate that one may be concerned about the effect of the media, but no evidence (empirical) exists for such a conclusion. Table 29.1 provides a quick summary of the main points of each chapter in this book.

When examining the textbook assessments in Table 29.2, the first noticeable feature is the exclusion of meta-analyses. Many of the textbooks considered in this analysis deal with relatively few issues of media effects as defined by the assembled meta-analyses. The content of many texts deal less with the issues of media effects and more with issues that explain the structure and history of the media.

The second issue is the mixed sense of accuracy. By and large, there were no negative (inconsistent) representations, but a number of $+/-$ representations, which indicate a kind of partial accuracy. The issue for representations was that the books indicated either the existence of moderator variables or addressed the nature of the inconsistency as a methodological or additional artifact rather than considering sampling error as the basis for the inconsistency. Textbook authors seem reluctant to simply accept the fact that a relationship exists between the content of material and various outcomes. This reluctance provides a less accurate view of the impact of the media on consumers.

One problematic feature found in the textbooks is the problem of journalism or media ethics when scientific practice is confronted. Consider the fact that "good" media practice includes the expectation that any issue will have more than one side and that the goal of representation should be the inclusion of many sides. The problem is that for scientists there comes a time for debate and after appropriate empirical evaluation the findings (when consistent) represent facts.

TABLE 29.1
Summary of Media Effects Chapters

1. Media Priming (Roskos-Ewoldsen, Klinger, & Roskos-Ewoldsen, chap. 5). Media priming effects were observed and some decay occurred with the effect.

2. Agenda Setting (Wanta & Ghanem, chap. 4). The results provide evidence that media coverage results in agenda setting, particularly news, in establishing a sense of agenda among the consumers.

3. Gender Sexual Stereotypes (Oppliger, chap. 13). The results demonstrate that media influence the development of sexual stereotypes.

4. Health Campaigns (Snyder, chap. 20). The results indicate that public health campaigns conducted via the use of media are effective in producing behavioral and attitudinal changes.

5. Magic Johnson Announcement on HIV (Casey, Allen, Emmers-Sommer, Sahlstein, DeGooyer, Winters, Wagner, & Dun, chap. 22). The research demonstrates that the impact of Earvin "Magic" Johnson's announcement that he was HIV positive increased knowledge, increased the number of persons getting tests for HIV, and increased anxiety about HIV for adults but diminished anxiety about HIV for children.

6. Media Campaigns for Adolescents and Children (Parcell, Kwon, Miron, & Bryant, chap. 21). Although there is an impact on adolescents and children, the effect is small ($r = .02$).

7. Mediated Horror and Violence Impact (Hoffner and Levine, chap. 14). Results indicate that persons with higher levels of aggression and sensation seeking show more affinity for horror and persons with higher levels of empathy show less enjoyment.

8. Music (Allen, Herrett-Skjellum, Jorgenson, Kramer, Ryan, & Timmerman, chap. 16). The results indicate that preferences for musical content are consonant with the values and behaviors of the viewers.

9. Newspaper Ownership Bias Impact on Presidential Coverage (D'Alessio & Allen, chap. 26) The findings indicate that the coverage of presidential candidates across elections remains essentially fair when Republican or Democrat candidates are compared.

10. Parasocial Impact of Television (Schiappa, Allen, & Gregg, chap. 18). The development of a parasocial relationship with television characters is associated with increases in television watching, affinity for television, perceptions of television as real, attractiveness and homophily with television characters, loneliness, and an internal locus of control; females exhibit higher levels of parasocial effects.

11. Political Participation (Hollander, chap. 23) Newspapers have a stronger predictor for political involvement than television, and the relationship remains even after controlling for income and education.

12. Third-Person Effect (Paul, Salwen, & Dupagne, chap. 6). Results demonstrate that persons perceive the media generating larger effects on others than on self.

13. Selective Exposure (D'Alessio & Allen, chap. 7). Persons generally expose themselves to materials with congruent messages.

14. Sexually Explicit Media (Mundorf, Allen, D'Alessio, & Emmers-Sommer, chap. 12). Meta-analyses establish that consumption is associated with rape myths and increased aggressive behavior, but these effects are removed when appropriate media education is provided.

15. Social Interaction Effects on Children (Mares & Woodward, chap. 17). The results demonstrate that the media generates both prosocial as well as antisocial effects for social interaction on children.

16. Special Children Populations (Abelman, Lin, & Atkin, chap. 8). Children in these groups demonstrate a high correlation between the perceived realism of television and the perceived realism of commercials.

17. Video Game Effects (Sherry, chap. 15). There is a small association between video game violence and attitudinal and behavioral measures.

18. Violence Impacts on Social Aggression (Christenson & Wood, chap. 10). Violent media are correlated with increases in social aggression.

TABLE 29.2
Evaluation of Media Textbooks

Meta-analyses*	Textbooks[a]									
	Agee	Berger	Black	Gunter	Hamelink	Hiebert	Jawitz	McQuail	Schramm	Tan
1				+		+				+
2				+		+				+
3						+/−				+
4										+
5										
6										+
7										
8										
9										
10										
11										
12										
13						+/−				+
14						=/−				
15										
16										
17										
18				+	+	+	+/−			+

[a]See References for complete citation, first author listed only here
*See Table 29.1 for description and conclusion

Textbooks often provide a kind of point/counterpoint discussion of the findings and/or causality. However, such an approach is not warranted or honest when scientific facts are established. The problem is that many can and will dispute the existence of a fact. For example, some scientists and persons still would not admit that HIV causes AIDS. Although there may be two sides to a particular issue (in the sense that some dissenter exists), if the dissent is so bizarre, and its proponents represent such a small group, is the public (or students) served by the representation of a controversy when none really exists? This issue represents a challenge for the workings of the media because the media's orientation to controversy in this case ill serves the student.

The results of the analysis indicate that much of the focus of media textbooks is not centered on the effects of the media. When the effects of the media are considered, the textbooks have done a reasonable job at representing the results. When compared with interpersonal communication textbooks (Allen & Preiss, 2002) or persuasion textbooks (Allen & Preiss, 1998), the mass media textbooks have done an exceptional job of providing accurate representations of the literature. This may indicate or reflect an advanced state of the knowledge and/or application when one considers the relationship of understanding of the media in the discipline of communication compared with other disciplinary areas.

The better representations may reflect the relatively straightforward and simple questions that are asked about the media. The focus of this question crosses many different domains (e.g., sexual, music, violence, and health) but remains essentially the same, "Does media content generate influence in the consumer?" What this focus provides is the ability of various content areas to generate information that can be synthesized or compared with that of other areas with a more direct sense of comparison.

THE APPLICATION OF KNOWLEDGE

Many implications for practical action stem from an understanding of the effects on persons that view particular media content. The acceptance of particular facts or relationships as items that should be accepted as real begins the next step of the debate about how to handle or incorporate these outcomes within the ongoing debates over censorship and media control. The difficulty with a fact is that many persons will take that representation and draw divergent implications about what the fact indicates for possible actions or policies. Such a position is inevitable and necessary as indicated in the diagram about the elements of knowledge. The movement from a fact to action represents both a rational and necessary step in translating what is believed to be true into something that provides useful implications for society. Society should use knowledge as a basis for action, but any knowledge should never be viewed as indicating a justification for a specific and particular action. However, to deny the scientific fact because the implication is unpleasant also indicates a denial of what is true and the potential implications of what the facts reveal.

The position of the chapter authors is that suggesting that content be banned or restricted may appear inviting and desirable, but that such restrictions may not produce the outcome sought. Although clearly limitations on material (for adults only, in private, not involving the commission of a crime in the making of the material) can be justified, the outright censorship of the material is not necessarily warranted. For example, pornography seems to have a negative impact on male sexual offenders but does not have the same negative consequences on other males (Allen, D'Alessio, & Emmers-Sommer, 1999). Educational efforts seem to remove the consequences of the effects as well (Allen, D'Alessio, Emmers, & Gebhardt, 1996).

Censorship ultimately reflects a particular set of values. Clearly, the First Amendment to the Constitution of the United States provides a statement of unambiguous commitment to the need and advantages of free speech (and the media). Restrictions on the content of the media are permitted only under a few conditions, and are usually narrowly drawn. Using scientific data may prove difficult because scientific definitions for media content are often functional rather than structural. For example, pornography for scientists is often defined as material that has the effect or intent of sexual arousal. For most, explicit depictions of sexual behavior between persons would qualify; however, for pedophiles the pajama ads in a catalog would serve as sexually arousing as would footwear ads for persons with a foot fetish. For the scientist this variability represents no problem; however, for policy formulation the lack of an identifiable structure (or specific content) makes censorship or restriction difficult.

Mandating content and using the media to produce socially desirable outcomes through education may be more fruitful, but even then the impact of various educational efforts may be less than desired. Media content is selected, and the impact of media content reflects a voluntary choice to consume and then internalize the material. Scientific findings may provide evidence for the positive impact of celebrities, but the translation of that abstract information into effective application requires ethnographic understanding of the culture that no meta-analysis can provide.

THE FUTURE OF KNOWLEDGE

Any scientific endeavor requires at the beginning an admission of a lack of knowledge. The lack of knowing is what ultimately inspires the scientific enterprise, because the scientific method has the purpose of proposing and evaluating the veracity or empirical accuracy of various knowledge claims. The meta-analyses in this book are not the final word for knowledge; instead they offer a place to pause and examine the state of the knowledge.

The chapters in this book do not spell an end to research about mass media effects. The meta-analyses viewed as a body, however, should begin to change the nature of the questions asked about media effects. The first issue is that media content does have an effect on the persons consuming that media. That fundamental empirical fact should be accepted. Every meta-analysis in this book shows a relationship between media content and various behaviors and attitudes of the individuals consuming that material. Once that statement is accepted (and that statement makes no claim about the size or potential moderators), then the next step in the research process begins.

Probably no impact of meta-analysis should be greater than its impact on the development of future research (Eagly & Wood, 1994) and theoretical development (Miller & Pollock, 1994). One goal of meta-analysis should be the examination of implications at a theoretical level. Every finding of a meta-analysis should advance theoretical thinking (regardless of whether the meta-analysis itself is fundamentally theoretical). The contribution of the meta-analysis to the weaving of a web of interrelated meta-analyses permits either the evaluation or formation of theoretical arguments. The more well developed the theoretical position is and the more articulated (specific), the more capable it is of empirical evaluation. A useful theory makes clear and consistent predictions that can be compared with the empirical data. A theory can be consistent or inconsistent with a well-defined theoretical system.

A real impact is the change on the nature of archiving or scientific progression. The next generation of theoretical thinking must not simply be consistent with a few empirical studies. The next generation of theoretical thinking must now be consistent with data that are 100 years old in some cases. Data accumulate and theoretical thinking must provide explanative consistency with older data sets. What statement this implies is that the era of reinventing the wheel whenever a new theory becomes espoused no longer is necessary. Theoretical thinking becomes more difficult but more fruitful.

Many other meta-analyses exist that consider the various impacts of media in a variety of settings and issues. The impact of negative political advertising (Allen & Burrell, 2002; Lau, Sigelman, Heldman, & Babbitt, 2001), the effects of pretrial publicity (Steblay, Besirevic, Fulero, & Jimenez-Lorente, 1999), and the impact of presidential debates (Benoit, Hansen, & Verser, 2003) are examples that provide additional examinations of the impact of the media in various settings. The basis of potential claims and the web of empirical findings continue to escalate and grow. The impact of meta-analysis, rather than providing a simple or final answer, must be viewed as contributing to a growing picture of findings. The findings of any meta-analysis then require a consideration of what other summaries generate and a comparison of the direction and magnitude of the effect. When placed within a theoretical context, the synthesis provides an ability to interpret a broad array of findings.

Meta-analysis does permit the testing of more sophisticated theoretical models and combinations of variables, even if not all the variables exist in the same study (Emmers-Sommer & Allen, 1999). This aspect means that older data sets still provide utility for future theoretical tests, even if the theory did not exist at the time the data were collected. This practice reflects the reality of physics, chemistry, medicine, and astronomy (as well as political science) and makes the social sciences more consistent in actual practice with other sciences.

One aspect is, "If there are effects for the media, why and what can be done about it?" That question begins the important process of shifting the debate in a slightly different but important direction. Future research can be planned to take advantage of this set of findings, and conducting the research becomes more urgent and the responsibility for consideration of alternatives becomes greater. The questions that arise out of assuming a set of empirical facts makes for an interesting debate that will grow in the rest of this century about the formulation of First Amendment principles. Delgado and Stefancic's (2004) arguments about a critical legal theory reassessment of fundamental First Amendment doctrines will continue to receive consideration.

The findings not only provide a basis for content control but also can also be utilized to promote and justify the use of particular content or approaches to media. Media can and do generate prosocial outcomes in a variety of venues. The question facing the community should never be whether media structure and/or content is good or bad. Rather, the question should be the extent to which government wants to be involved in regulation that shapes and uses that content.

Ultimately, solutions require attention to the use of media education. The outcomes of exposure to media content are probably not inevitable and unstoppable. The easy path is that of censorship, simply concluding that what is required is a ban on the materials. If the materials are considered dangerous or offensive, the solution of simply removing those materials from the public provides an attractive solution because of the simplicity of the act. The action, however, is not simple, because defining the offensive material and making clear what constitutes material to be restricted is difficult, and often impossible.

An example of the power of educational efforts in the context of media effects is found in the meta-analysis examining the impact of pre- and debriefing efforts when considering sexually explicit materials (Allen et al., 1996). The results demonstrate that both preexposure and postexposure educational materials eliminated the attitudinal effects of exposure to the materials. Unlike persons not exposed to educational materials, the persons exposed to educational materials about sexuality were not affected by exposure to pornography. Exposure to pornography results in the objectification of women and greater acceptance of rape myths (e.g., women can resist a rapist if they want to or rape victims are "asking" for it). The exposure to pornography is generally associated with acceptance of these claims (see Mundorf, Allen, D'Alessio, Emmers-Sommer, chap. 12, this volume, as well as Allen, D'Alessio, & Brezgel, 1995; Allen, Emmers, Gebhardt, & Giery, 1995). The work of Wilson (1987) and Nathanson (Nathanson, 2004, Nathanson & Cantor, 2000; Nathanson, Wilson, McGee, & Sebastian, 2002; Nathanson & Yang, 2003) dealing with mediation of media effects for children demonstrates that with parental intervention, the negative consequences of exposure to violence/horror films can be reduced. The impact of this finding for both theory and practice need to be explored because the fact that the relationship can be altered on the basis of education indicates that a fundamental reconsideration of causality of the media is required.

THE FUTURE OF THE MEDIA

Media experience continues to change. The growth of the Web and the Internet, the use of DVD, and interactive possibilities create a fundamentally different media environment for the 21st century. The ability of consumers to find and select material to satisfy the most individual and unique appetites represents a change to a consumer-controlled media model. Rather than a limited set of networks and stations controlling access, the availability of the cable and the Internet allow consumers to choose a great deal of diverse content that can be stored from broadcast 24 hours a day and watched as often as desired.

Rather than arguing for a re-creation of every empirical finding that exists in the new media environment, a more reasonable argument can be made. The underlying goal should be a theoretical model that provides an explanatory device in accounting for the observed set of relationships. If the model is accurate, the underlying conceptual scheme should provide a generative function that when applied to the changing media environment should continue to provide hypotheses that receive empirical support. A theoretical model should not simply be accurate with existing data but should make predictions about future findings that remain consistent. Such a theoretical model proves very useful for both practitioners and those engaged in scientific research.

The formulation of valuable theories requires facts. Facts serve as the grist for the theory mill. An interplay exists between fact and theory, because one postulates theory on the basis of existing facts, and accurate theory predicts or expects particular facts. The dynamic interplay permits both elements to advance and increase in accuracy and utility. The publication of these "facts" will cause a reevaluation and ultimately a new energy for those interested in theoretical development. From this continued scholarship will emerge improved practical application.

REFERENCES

Agee, W. K., Ault, P. H., & Emery, E. (1982). *Perspectives on mass communications.* New York: Harper & Row.

Allen, M. (1998). Methodological considerations when examining a gendered world. In D. Canary and K. Dindia (Eds.), *Handbook of sex differences & similarities in communication: Critical essays and empirical investigations of sex and gender in interaction* (pp. 427–444). Mahwah, NJ: Lawrence Erlbaum Associates.

Allen, M. (1999). The role of meta-analysis for connecting critical and scientific approaches: The need to develop a sense of collaboration. *Critical Studies in Mass Communication, 16,* 373–379.

Allen, M., & Burrell, N. (2002). The negativity effect in political advertising: A meta-analysis. In J. Dillard and M. Pfau (Eds.), *The persuasion handbook: Developments in theory and practice* (pp. 83–98). Thousand Oaks, CA: Sage.

Allen, M., D'Alessio, D., & Brezgel, K. (1995). A meta-analysis summarizing the effects of pornography. II: Aggression after exposure. *Human Communication Research, 22,* 258–283.

Allen, M., D'Alessio, D., & Emmers-Sommer, T. (1999). Reactions of criminal sexual offenders to pornography: A meta-analytic summary. In M. Roloff (Ed.), *Communication Yearbook 22* (pp. 139–169). Thousand Oaks, CA: Sage Publications.

Allen, M., D'Alessio, D., Emmers, T., & Gebhardt, L. (1996). The role of educational briefings in mitigating effects of experimental exposure to violent sexually explicit material: A meta-analysis. *Journal of Sex Research, 33,* 135–141.

Allen, M., Emmers, T., Gebhardt, L., & Giery, M. (1995, Winter). Pornography and rape myth acceptance. *Journal of Communication, 45,* 5–26.

Allen, M., & Preiss, R. (1998). Evaluating the advice offered by the tool users. In M. Allen and R. Preiss (Eds.), *Persuasion: Advances through meta-analysis* (pp. 243–256). Cresskill, NJ: Hampton Press.

Allen, M., & Preiss, R. (2002). Meta-analysis and interpersonal communication: Function and applicability. In M. Allen, R. Preiss, B. Gayle, & N. Burrell (Eds.), *Interpersonal communication research: Advances through meta-analysis* (pp. 3–12). Mahwah, NJ: Lawrence Erlbaum Associates.

Benoit, W. L., Hansen, G. J., & Verser, R. M. (2003). A meta-analysis of the effects of viewing U. S. Presidential debates. *Communication Monographs, 70,* 335–350.

Berger, C. (2002). A prototype theory for interpersonal communication. In M. Allen, R. Preiss, B. Gayle, & N. Burrell (Eds.), *Interpersonal communication research: Advances through meta-analysis* (pp. 451–479). Hillsdale, NJ: Lawrence Erlbaum.

Black, J., & Whitney, F. C. (1983). *Introduction to mass communication.* Dubuque, IA: Brown.

Cooper, H., & Hedges, L. V. (1994). Research synthesis as a scientific enterprise. In H. Cooper and L. Hedges (Eds.), *Handbook of research synthesis* (pp. 3–14). New York: Russell Sage Foundation.

Delgado, R., & Stefancic, J. (2004). *Understanding words that wound.* Boulder, CO: Westview.

Eagly, A. H., & Wood, W. (1994). Using research syntheses to plan future research. In H. Cooper and L. Hedges (Eds.), *Handbook of research synthesis* (pp. 485–502). New York: Russell Sage Foundation.

Emmers-Sommer, T., & Allen, M. (1999). Variables related to sexual coercion: A path model. *Journal of Social and Personal Relationships, 16,* 659–678.

Fitzpatrick, M. A. (2002). Better living through science: Reflections on the future of interpersonal communication. In M. Allen, R. Preiss, B. Gayle, & N. Burrell (Eds.), *Interpersonal communication research: Advances through meta-analysis* (pp. 407–422). Mahwah, NJ: Lawrence Erlbaum Associates.

Frey, L. R., Pearce, W. B., Pollock, M. A., Artz, L., & Murphy, B. A. (1996). Looking for justice in all the wrong places: On a communication approach to social justice. *Communication Studies, 47,* 110–127.

Goodnight, T. (1982). The personal, technical, and public spheres of argument: A speculative inquiry into the art of public deliberation. *Journal of the American Forensic Association, 18,* 214–227.

Gunter, B. (2000). *Media research methods: Measuring audiences, reaction, and impact.* London: Sage.

Hamelink, C. J., & Linné, O. (1994). *Mass communication research: On problems and policies. The art of asking the right questions: In honor of James D. Halloran.* Norwood, NJ: Ablex.

Harding, S. (1986). *The science question in feminism.* Ithaca, NY: Cornell University Press.

Harding, S. (1991). *Whose science? Whose knowledge? Thinking from women's lives.* Ithaca, NY: Cornell University Press.

Hiebert, R. E., & Gibbons, S. J. (2000). *Exploring mass media for a changing world.* Mahwah, NJ: Lawrence Erlbaum Associates.

Hunter, J., & Schmidt, F. (1990). *Methods of meta-analysis: Correcting error and bias in research findings.* Newbury Park, CA: Sage.

Jawitz, W. (1996). *Understanding mass media* (5th ed.). Lincolnwood, IL: National Textbook.

Kuhn, T. (1970). *The structure of scientific revolutions* (2nd ed., enlarged). Chicago: University of Chicago Press.

Lau, R., Sigelman, L., Heldman, C., & Babbitt, R. (2001). The effects of negative political advertisements: A meta-analytic assessment. *American Political Science Review, 102,* 113–145.

McQuail, D. (1987). *Mass communication theory: An introduction* (2nd ed.). Newbury Park, CA: Sage.

Miller, N., & Pollock, V. E. (1994). Meta-analytic synthesis for theory development. In H. Cooper and L. Hedges (Eds.), *Handbook of research synthesis* (pp. 457–484). New York: Russell Sage Foundation.

Nathanson, A. (2004). Factual and evaluative approaches to modifying children's responses to violent television. *Journal of Communication, 54,* 321–336.

Nathanson, A. I., & Cantor, J. (2000). Reducing the aggression-promoting effect of violent cartoons by increasing children's fictional involvement with the victim: A study of active mediation. *Journal of Broadcasting and Electronic Media, 44,* 125–144.

Nathanson, A. I., Wilson, B. J., McGee, J., & Sebastian, M. (2002). Counteracting the effects of female stereotypes on television via active mediation. *Journal of Communication, 52,* 922–937.

Nathanson, A. I., & Yang, M. (2003). The effects of mediation content and form on children's responses to violent television. *Human Communication Research, 29,* 111–134.

Schramm, W. (1973). *Men, messages, and media: A look at human communication.* New York: Harper & Row.

Steblay, N., Besirevic, J., Fulero, S., & Jimenez-Lorente, B. (1999). The effects of pretrial publicity on juror verdicts: A meta-analytic review. *Law and Human Behavior, 23,* 219–235.

Tan, A. (1985). *Mass communication theories and research* (2nd ed.). New York: Wiley.

Wilson, B. J. (1987). Reducing children's emotional reactions to mass media through rehearsed explanation and exposure to a replica of a fear object. *Human Communication Research, 14,* 3–26.

Author Index

A

Aaro, L. E., 351, 355, 359
Abelman, R., 96, 98, 121, 122, 125, 126, 129, 130, 132, 134, 283, 290, 296, 298
Adams, J. S., 107, 110, 116
Adamski, L., 22, 30
Agahi, E., 224, 234, 242
Agee, W. K., 497, 502
Ahammer, I. M., 290, 298
Ahrens, M. G., 126, 130, 133
Albert, S. M., 110, 116
Albert, W., 350, 358
Albin, R., 187, 195
Alioto, J., 246, 260
Allen, M., 10, 12, 18, 20–22, 27, 29, 30, 32, 34, 36, 82, 92, 95, 98, 109, 117, 181, 184, 186, 193–195, 203, 206, 212, 224, 240, 264, 266, 276–278, 363–366, 372–375, 436, 438, 441, 451, 458, 463–465, 470, 472, 478, 482, 485, 486, 489, 490, 491, 497, 498, 500–503
Alman, R. E., 251, 260
Alto, W. A., 354, 361
Aluja-Fabregat, A., 226, 227, 235, 240
Alvarez, R. M., 443, 450
Ajzen, I., 319, 323, 350, 358
Amaral, J., 170, 177
Anasolabehere, S., 392, 411, 475, 485
Anderson, C. A., 54, 59, 68, 75, 146, 159–161, 164, 165, 245, 246, 254, 258, 260, 261
Anderson, C. C., 290, 298
Anderson, D. R., 119, 133, 204, 208, 213, 214
Anderson, J., 55, 75
Anderson, K. B., 54, 59, 68, 75, 161, 164
Anderson, L. I., 146, 168
Anderson, R. B., 44, 48

Andison, F. S., 146, 147, 148, 165
Ang, P. H., 89, 99
Apanovitch, A. M., 227, 240
Applefield, J. M., 156, 168
Apsler, R., 378, 379, 388
Arblaster, L., 351, 361
Arendt, H., 315, 323
Arkin, E. B., 346, 358
Arluk, I. H., 471, 487
Armfield, G. G., 69, 77
Arnett, J., 269, 277
Aronson, E., 107, 118, 151, 165, 317, 324
Artz, L., 491, 503
Ascione, F. R., 251, 261
Atkin, C. K., 220, 240, 246, 260, 282, 299, 346–348, 350, 352, 358, 384, 385, 386, 388
Atkin, D., 121, 124, 125, 131, 133, 134
Atwater, T., 44, 48
Atwood, E. L., 44, 48
Atwood, R. A., 204, 211
Ault, P. H., 497, 502
Aust, C. F., 218, 219, 221, 226, 228, 237, 244, 269, 279
Austin, E. W., 173–175, 177, 403, 411
Axsom, D., 154, 165

B

Babb, V., 312
Babbitt, R., 500, 503
Badger, G. J., 351, 353, 355, 359
Badiane, L., 330, 333, 334, 336, 337, 343
Bagdikian, B. H., 437, 450, 469, 485
Bahk, C. M., 227, 240
Bajaj, M., 406, 412

505

Bajpai, S., 171, 179
Baker, B., 434, 450
Balaban, T., 202, 209, 214
Baldassare, M., 418, 427
Baldwin, T., 124, 133
Ball-Rokeach, S. J., 313
Ballard, M. E., 245, 248, 253, 260
Bandura, A., 5, 12, 140, 144, 164, 165, 182,
    192, 195, 201, 211, 251, 260, 266, 277,
    316, 319, 323, 349, 350, 359, 364, 374,
    472, 476, 485
Bankart, C. P., 290, 298
Banspach, S. W., 340, 343
Baran, S. J., 123, 126, 129, 133, 290, 298
Barber, J. D., 396, 411
Barden, R. C., 221, 240
Bargh, J. A, 54, 57, 60, 61, 63, 66, 71, 72,
    76–79
Barkley, R. A., 120, 133
Baron, R. A., 149, 165, 189, 195
Barrett, G., 189, 195
Barrett, K. C., 221, 240
Bartholow, B. D., 59, 75
Barton, A. H., 317, 324
Barton, J. N., 122, 133
Basehart, J. R., 44, 50
Basil, M. D., 96, 98, 365, 374
Batlin, R., 450
Bates, M., 22, 30
Bauman, K. E., 336, 338, 342, 355, 359
Beauvais, F., 174, 179
Beaver, E. D., 54, 55, 59, 68, 76
Beck, C., 365, 374
Beck, P., 443, 450
Becker, L. A., 110, 116
Becker, L. B., 40, 44, 49, 384, 386, 388, 473,
    485
Becker, M. H., 349, 359
Becker, S. L., 384, 386, 388
Behr, R. L., 44, 48, 392, 411
Beilenson, P. L., 351, 353, 359
Bell, D., 204, 212, 315, 323
Bell, P., 189, 195
Bell, R., 189, 195
Bem, S. L., 205, 211
Benjamin, A. J. Jr., 59, 75, 160, 165
Benoit, W. L., 500, 503
Benson, P., 205, 211
Benton, M., 44, 48
Bereck, S. R., 90, 98

Berelson, B. R., 2, 12, 316, 317, 318, 323, 324,
    346, 360, 377, 387, 388, 396, 397, 412,
    430, 450, 451
Berger, C., 497, 503
Berkowitz, L., 53, 54, 58, 62, 63, 74, 76, 78,
    148, 153, 155, 165, 167, 188, 189, 191,
    195, 246, 255, 260–262
Berkowitz-Stafford, S., 22, 30
Berndt, T. J., 162–163, 165
Bernhagen, M., 22, 30
Bernhard, N. E., 434, 450
Berry, M., 223, 240
Besirevic, J., 500, 504
Betsch, T., 153, 165
Bettencourt, B. A., 160, 165
Beuf, A., 208, 211
Biblow, E., 154, 165
Biener, L., 354, 361
Biggs, A., 292, 300
Billings, V., 267, 273, 278
Bjorkqvist, K., 62, 71, 78, 227, 228, 234, 240
Black, J., 497, 503
Blanchard, D. C., 223, 240
Blanchard, R. J., 223, 240
Blane, H., 347, 359
Bleich, S., 269, 277
Blumberg, N. B., 446, 449, 450
Blumer, H., 246, 260
Blumler, J. G., 4, 12, 321, 324, 400, 406, 411,
    468, 469, 486
Blut, D., 191, 196
Bodenhausen, G. V., 55, 59, 68, 70, 80
Bollin, K. A., 58, 76
Bond, C. F., 159, 168, 419, 427
Bond, R. N., 60, 61, 66, 72, 76
Borre, O., 44, 50
Boster, F. J., 21, 30
Botha, M. P., 223, 240
Bothwell, E., 351, 353, 359
Boush, D., 173, 177
Boyanowsky, E. O., 108, 116
Boylan, J., 392, 396, 411
Bozell, L. B., 434, 450
Bradford, L., 373, 374
Bradley, S. D., x, xiii
Brand, J., 173, 177, 178
Brandenburg, J. D., 223, 226, 227, 235, 241
Brannon, L. A., 54, 60, 69, 78
Branscombe, N. R., 54, 59, 80
Bresolin, L. B., 146, 166

Brewer, M. B., 151, 165
Brezgel, K., 82, 92, 95, 98, 181, 186, 193, 195,
    264, 277, 472, 478, 485, 501, 502
Briere, J., 188, 195
Brinker, D. B., 209, 212
Brislin-Slutz, J., 188, 197
Brizol, P., 472, 487
Brock, T. C., 107, 110, 116
Brodbeck, M., 107, 110, 116, 317, 323
Brody, G. H., 292, 300
Bronfenbrenner, U., 123, 124, 131, 133
Brooks, S. C., 41, 49
Brooks, T., 216, 240
Brosius, H., 38, 43, 44, 47, 48, 83, 84, 85, 98,
    407–409, 413
Bross, M., 191, 196
Brotman, S. N., 123, 133
Brown, D., 182, 195, 267, 277
Brown, J. D., 85, 98, 202, 213, 355, 359
Brown, N., 44, 49
Brown, R., 119, 133, 269, 277
Brown, V., 200, 206, 208, 209, 212
Brown, W., 365, 374
Browne, L., 173, 175, 178
Bruerd, B., 351, 353, 359
Brummett, B., 311, 313
Brusa, J. A., 251, 253, 260
Bryan, E. S., 355, 359
Bryan, T., 120, 133
Bryant, J. H., 2–4, 7, 9–12, 108, 116, 119, 133,
    182, 184, 185, 188, 189, 195, 197, 198,
    217, 224, 238, 243, 244, 267, 277, 285,
    290, 298, 471, 488
Brzinski, J. B., 381, 389
Buchanan, M., 83, 89, 91, 99
Buck, E. B., 204, 206, 208, 213
Buerkel-Rothfuss, N., 269, 279
Buller, D., 27, 30
Burke, K., 302, 313
Burke, R., 173, 178, 269, 277
Burrell, N., 500, 503
Burt, M., 187, 188, 195
Burton, D., 348, 349, 359
Busby, L. J., 200, 211
Bushman, B. J., 54, 59, 61, 62, 64, 68, 76, 146,
    159, 160, 164, 165
Buss, T. F., 384, 386, 388
Butler, P. M., 204, 213
Butter, E., 174, 177
Buu, C., 354, 360

Buvinic, M. L., 58, 76
Bybee, C. R., 400, 406, 411
Byrne, D., 188, 197
Byrnes, J. E., 40, 44, 49

C

Cacioppo, J., 319, 324, 350, 360
Cacioppo, J. T., 115, 118, 379, 380, 389, 471,
    481, 485, 487
Cairns, R. B., 155, 166
Call, T., 120, 133
Callendar, A., 22, 30
Calvert, S., 253, 256, 261
Cameron, P., 152, 165
Cameron, G. T., 55, 70, 79
Camino, L., 155, 167
Campbell, A., 393, 394, 411
Campbell, D. T., 147, 165
Campo, S., 333, 342
Campos, J. J., 221, 240
Cantor, J., 108, 116, 189, 195, 216, 218,
    220–224, 226–228, 233, 234, 238–241,
    243, 501, 503
Cappella, J., 458, 465
Carlson, M., 248, 261
Carlson, P. M., 291, 299
Carnagey, N. L., 160, 165
Carpenter, J. H., 353, 359
Carpentier, F. R. D., 472, 487
Carson, E., 365, 374
Carter, J. R., 403, 405, 411
Cartwright, D., 317, 323, 347, 359
Carver, C. S., 54, 59, 68, 76
Carveth, R., 189, 198
Casey, M. K., 22, 30, 32, 36, 333, 342, 363,
    365, 366, 373, 374
Casey, W. E., 384, 386, 388
Caswell, S., 174, 175, 177
Catz, S., 365, 374
Cavanaugh, J. W., 451
Ceniti, J., 188, 189, 196
Center for Media and Public Affairs, 449, 451
Chachere, J. G., 145, 146, 150, 151, 158, 159,
    162, 168, 470, 472, 478, 488
Chaffee, S. H., 318, 323, 329, 342, 381, 385,
    386, 388, 389, 470, 484, 485
Chaiken, S., 115, 118
Chaloupka, F., 351, 361

Chambers, J. H., 251, 261
Chambers, W., 54, 59, 68, 76
Chapin, M., 191, 196
Chase, L. J., 290, 298
Check, J. V. P., 54, 59, 68, 78, 188, 191, 195, 196
Cherry, K. L., 69, 77
Chickering, K. L., 340, 343
Cho, J., 463, 465
Choi, H. C., 384, 386, 388
Choi, Y. H., 63, 76
Chomsky, N., 481, 486
Chong, K., 463, 465
Chopski, K., 365, 374
Christensen, P. N., 150, 168, 275, 277
Chung, Y., x, xiii
Clark, A., 274, 277
Clark, P., 44, 49
Clarke, P., 381, 388
Clewett, A. S., 285, 290, 299
Clifford, B. R., 119, 133
Climie, R. J., 58, 76
Cobb, N. J., 209, 211
Cochran, S., 364, 374
Coffin, T. E., 405, 413
Cohen, A. A., 206, 208, 214
Cohen, B., 317, 323
Cohen, J., 90, 99, 158, 165, 247, 261, 289, 298, 313
Cohen, P., 289, 298
Cohen, R. S., 201, 213
Cole, R., 266, 277
Cole, T., 304, 313
Collins, A., 255, 261
Collins, B. E., 378, 389
Collins, C., 174, 177
Collins, P. A., 204, 213
Collins, W. A., 162–163, 165, 207, 209, 213, 290, 298
Comer, S., 355, 359
Comisky, P., 184, 188, 198
Comstock, G., 82, 87, 88, 91, 92, 95, 100, 146–148, 162, 167, 181, 197, 247, 261, 264, 278, 281, 284, 287, 289, 292, 295–297, 300, 470, 476, 484, 485, 487
Condry, 177
Connolly, G., 174, 175, 177
Considine, J., 365, 374
Contreras-Budge, E., 332, 342
Conway, J., 305, 313
Cook, F. L., 81, 84, 85, 101

Cook, T. D., 106, 117, 146, 147, 165, 329, 342
Coombs, S. L., 41, 49
Cooper, H. M., 17, 30, 151, 160, 165, 489, 503
Cooper, J., 154, 165, 202, 209, 214, 245, 261
Cooper, M., 435, 451
Cooper, R., 2, 6, 8, 12, 89, 96, 100
Coover, G., 55, 70, 79
Corder-Bolz, C. R., 209, 213, 291, 299
Cordua, G., 202, 204, 212
Corey, D. M., 224, 240
Corison, C., 313
Cornish, I. M., 204, 213
Cortez, C., 313
Corty, E., 185, 197
Costanza, M. C., 351, 355, 359
Cote, W., 432, 451
Cotton, J. L., 109, 110, 117
Courtright, J. A., 96, 99, 290, 298, 474, 487
Cox, E., 336, 344
Coyle, J., 90, 91, 96, 100, 101
Craff, D., 44, 48, 63, 76
Craig, K. M., 54, 59, 68, 78, 227, 242
Crawford, I., 353, 359
Crouch, J., 313
Crowell, T., 373, 374
Culbertson, H. M., 85, 99, 384, 386, 388
Cunningham, C. E., 120, 133
Curtis, J., 258, 262
Cutbirth, C., 44, 51
Cutler, R. L., 120, 122, 134
Czilli, E. J., 475, 487

D

Daily, K., 318, 324
D'Alessio, D., 27, 30, 32, 34, 36, 82, 92, 95, 98, 109, 117, 181, 184, 186, 193–195, 264, 276, 277, 436, 438, 441, 451, 472, 478, 482, 485, 498, 501, 502
Dalton, R. J., 443, 450
Dambrot, F. H., 200, 201, 204, 206, 212, 213
Danielian, L., 37, 39, 49
Dannenberg, A. L., 351, 353, 359
Daulton, A. R., 69, 77
Dautrich, K., 434–435, 451
Davidson, E. M., 119, 134
Davidson, E. S., 204, 212, 290, 298
Davidson, J. E., 121, 135
Davis, D. M., 200, 212
Davis, G. A., 121, 133

Davis, J., 434, 451
Davis, K. C., 338, 342
Davis, M. H., 218, 219, 235, 241
Davison, W. P., 81, 83, 99
Dawson, B., 174, 177
Day, K., 183, 189, 198
Dean, W. W., 228, 242
Dearing, J. W., 333, 342
DeFleur, L., 44, 49
DeFleur, M. L., 3, 5, 11, 12, 44, 49
DeFour, G., 227, 232, 241
DeGeorge, W. F., 473, 485
DeGeorge, W. G., 473, 486
DeGooyer, D., 32, 36, 363, 366, 374
Deinzer, G., 174, 177
Delgado, R., 493, 500, 503
Delli Carpini, M. X., 403, 405, 411
Demare, D., 188, 195
Demers, D. P., 44, 48, 63, 76
DeNeve, K. M., 59, 75, 161, 164
Dennis, J., 399, 401, 407, 408, 411
Derzon, J. H., 331–334, 336–339, 342, 344
Deshpande, R., 55, 70, 77
Detenber, B., 422, 427
Deuser, W. E., 54, 59, 68, 75
Devitt, J., 453
Dickenberger, D., 153, 165
Diener, E., 223, 227, 232, 241
Difranza, J., 173, 178
DiGuseppi, C. G., 353, 359
Dillard, J. P., 73, 74, 76, 77, 217, 218, 234, 241,
    243, 372, 374, 457, 458, 461, 464, 465
Dillman, A., 170, 178
Dillman Carpentier, F., 53, 59, 60, 66, 79
Dindia, K., 21, 30
Dinkin, R. J., 396, 411
Diop-Sidibé, N., 330, 333, 334, 336, 337, 343
Dixon, T., 269, 277
Do, S. T., 354, 360
Dobbs, A. R., 59, 79
Dolan, L., 121, 133
Domenighetti, G., 332, 342
Dominick, J. R., 6, 8, 13, 246, 256, 26, 267, 2791
Domke, D., 54, 55, 60, 68, 70, 76, 422, 423,
    426, 427
Donlin, M., 365, 374
Donnelly, J., 182, 196, 267, 277
Donnerstein, E., 148, 165, 183, 188, 189, 191,
    195, 197, 223, 240, 471, 484, 487
Donnerstein, M., 189, 195
Donohew, L., 334, 341, 343, 352, 361

Donohue, T. R., 120, 125, 126, 129–131, 133,
    177, 178
Donohue, W. A., 22, 30, 125, 126, 129, 130–133
Donsbach, W., 434, 452
Doob, A. N., 58, 76
Dorfman, L., 340, 344
Dorr, A., 120, 121, 133
Dorr, N., 161, 164
Douglas, D. F., 329, 342
Dovidio, J. F., 70, 78
Downs, A., 43, 49
Dozier, D. M., 44, 51
Drabman, R. S., 154, 165, 202, 204, 212, 290, 298
Drew, D., 381, 385, 388, 390, 406, 413
Driscoll, P. D., 89, 95, 97, 99
Dubois, P. L., 405, 411
Duck, J. M., 85, 90, 99
Duerr, J. M., 351, 360
Duke, J. C., 340, 343
Dun, T., 32, 36
Dunand, M., 59, 68, 78
Duncan, D., 182, 196, 267, 277
Dunlap, W. P., 224, 240
Dunn, R., 121, 134
Dunwoody, S., 384, 386, 388
Dupagne, M., 2, 6, 8, 12, 81, 82, 83, 87–89, 96,
    100–102
Durden, G., 404, 405, 412
Durkin, K., 199, 203, 210–212, 290, 298
Dussault, M., 126, 127, 134
Dustman, P., 354, 359
Dwyer, J. H., 353, 360
Dzwo, T. -H., 474, 487

E

Eagly, A. H., 160, 165, 379, 389, 499, 503
Eaton, H. Jr., 44, 49
Eberl, 126
Edison, N. G., 282, 299
Edwards, E., 220, 235, 241
Ehrlich, D., 107, 112, 117, 317, 323
Einstein, A., 436, 451
Eisen, S. V., 209, 213, 291, 299
Eisenberg, N., 218, 237, 241
Einsiedel, E. F., 44, 49, 189, 195
Eisenstock, B., 204, 212
Elasmar, M., 264, 277
Elek, E., 354, 359
Elias, M. J., 290, 298

Elkin, R. A., 379, 389
Elliot, S. N., 38, 50
Elliott, R., 290, 299
Ellis, G. T., 154, 166
Emery, E., 497, 502
Emmers, T., 34, 36, 181, 184, 186, 195, 224, 240, 264, 267, 277, 470, 472, 478, 485, 498, 501, 502
Emmers-Sommer, T. M., 10, 12, 27, 30, 32, 36, 181, 194, 195, 363, 366, 373, 374, 498, 500–503
Engel, D., 83–85, 98
Engels, F., 5, 13
Ennett, S. T., 339, 342
Entman, R., 317, 323
Ephron, E., 434, 451
Epstein, L., 405, 411
Erbring, L., 42, 44, 49
Eron, L. D., 220, 242, 264, 278
Esselman, E., 245–246, 251, 256, 261
Ettema, J. S., 471, 486
Eubanks, J., 160, 165
Euler, G. L., 354, 360
Evans, R., 189, 195
Evarts, D., 451
Eveland, W. P. Jr., 36, 82, 100, 425, 427, 471,475, 486
Eyal, C. H., 37, 41, 43, 44, 46, 51, 473, 486
Eyal, K., 313
Eyman, R. K., 120, 133

F

Faber, R. J., 82, 89, 97, 99, 101, 102, 384, 386, 388
Fabes, R. A., 218, 237, 241
Farqhar, J. W., 328, 342
Farrelly, M. C., 338, 340, 341, 342
Fazio, R. H., 57, 60, 61, 63, 66, 76, 79
Feather, N. T., 107, 110, 117
Fechter, J. V., Jr., 125, 133, 154, 166
Federal Ruling overturning EPA report on environmental tobacco smoke should cause re-evaluation of smoking bans and restrictions, 171, 178
Feldman, O., 393, 403, 411
Felson, R. B., 146, 150, 166
Fenigstein, A., 216, 220, 224, 227, 232, 236, 241
Ferguson, D. A., 470, 483, 486

Feschbach, N., 170, 178
Feshbach, S., 130, 133, 148, 152, 166, 188, 196, 470, 487
Festinger, L., 103, 109, 111, 117, 480, 486
Ficarrotto, T. J., 127, 128, 129, 132, 133, 154, 166
Fico, F., 432, 440, 451
Fidler, D. S., 209, 212
Fields, J., 81, 99
Finer, D., 332, 342
Fink, A. H., 120, 122, 134
Fischer, M., 169, 174, 178
Fishbein, M., 319, 323, 350, 358
Fisher, G., 204, 212
Fisher, L. A., 355, 359
Fisher, W., 365, 374
Fiske, S. T., 255, 261, 384, 386, 388
Fitzpatrick, M. A., 489, 503
Flanagan, M., 160, 165
Flanigan, W., 404, 411
Flay, B. R., 329, 342, 347–350, 353, 359, 360
Fleming-Milici, F., 330–333, 336, 339, 344
Fletcher, C., 173, 178
Flewelling, R. L., 339, 342
Flex, V. C., 209, 212
Flora, J., 364, 374
Florsheim, R., 173, 178
Flynn, B. S., 351, 353, 355, 359
Folger, R., 148, 166
Ford, C. M., 245, 254, 260
Ford, M. E., 221, 240
Forehand, M. R., 55, 70, 77
Forge, L. S., 290, 299
Fortmann, S. P., 328, 342
Foster, H., 269, 279
Fowles, J., 470, 486
Fox, S., 155, 167
Franken, R. E., 219, 235, 241
Frankowski, F., 336–338, 343
Franks, B., 121, 133
Frazier, P. J., 44, 48
Fredin, E., 381, 388
Freedman, J. L., 81, 101, 105–107, 109–111, 117, 118, 145–147, 150, 151, 166, 459, 465, 470, 472, 480, 486, 488
Freeman, C., 173, 175, 177
Freemantle, N., 332, 342
Freimuth, V., 350, 358
Freitag, A., 2, 10, 13
Frey, D., 108, 110–113, 117, 118
Frey, L. R., 491, 503

Friederich, L. K., 154, 166
Friederich-Cofer, L. K., 146–148, 166
Friel, S., 355, 359
Friestad, M., 173, 177
Froming, W. J., 54, 59, 68, 76
Fromm, E., 315, 323
Fuchs, D. A., 405, 412
Frueh, T., 207, 208, 212, 213
Fulero, S., 500, 504
Funk, J., 246, 261
Funkhouser, G. R., 39, 44, 49
Fuson, I., 191, 196

G

Gadow, K. D., 120, 121, 125–129, 132–134,
    154, 156, 166, 168
Galloway, J., 384–386, 388
Gan, S., 269, 277
Gandy, O. H., 384, 386, 388
Ganellen, R. J., 54, 59, 68, 76
Gans, C., 393, 412
Garber, J., 221, 240
Garcia, L., 188, 196
Garramone, G., 400, 406, 411
Garry, S., 81, 100
Gaschke, Y. N., 239, 242
Gatignon, H., 173, 178
Gatto, L., 269, 278
Gaudet, H., 316–318, 324, 346, 360, 396, 397,
    412, 430, 451
Gebhardt, L., 34, 36, 181, 184, 186, 195, 224,
    240, 264, 276, 277, 470, 472, 478, 485,
    498, 501, 502
Geen, R. G., 54, 58, 59, 62, 68, 71, 76, 77, 146,
    149, 166, 255, 260
Geis, F. L., 200, 206, 208, 209, 212
Geller, B. M., 351, 353, 355, 359
Geller, M. I., 290, 299
Gentile, D. A., 246, 258, 261
Gentry, J., 173, 178
Genuis, M., 185, 197
Gerbner, G., 5, 12, 143, 144, 316, 319, 320, 323,
    435, 451
Gershoff, E. T., 160, 166
Getz, S. K., 290, 298
Ghanem, S., 39, 49
Gibbons, S. J., 497, 503
Gibson, K. J., 219, 235, 241
Gibson, R., 269, 279

Gielen, A. C., 351, 353, 359
Giery, M. A., 181, 186, 195, 224, 240, 264, 277,
    470, 472, 478, 485, 501, 502
Giles, D. C., 312, 313
Giobbe, D., 435, 439, 451
Gitlin, T., 393, 396, 397, 412
Glaser, W. A., 400, 406, 412
Glass, D. P., 392, 413
Glass, G. V., 105, 117
Glynn, C. J., 81, 82, 84, 87, 88, 90, 95, 98, 99,
    381, 389, 415, 416, 418, 420, 423,
    424–427, 475, 486
Goff, D. H., 204, 212
Goff, L. D., 204, 212
Goidel, R. K., 54, 68, 77, 397, 412
Gold, S. R., 54, 55, 59, 68, 76
Goldberg, M. E., 174, 178, 286, 290, 299
Goldenberg, E. N., 42, 44, 49
Goldman, R., 380, 389
Goldstein, A., 169, 174, 178
Goldstein, S., 209, 211
Goodnight, T., 492, 503
Gordon, C., 392, 412
Gordon, M. T., 41, 49
Gorman, T. F., 55, 59, 68, 70, 80
Gorn, G., 173, 178, 286, 290, 299
Gorney, R., 152, 167
Gottfredson, D. C., 339, 344
Gottfredson, M. R., 149, 166
Gow, J., 264, 277
Gozenbach, W. J., 44, 49, 421, 427
Graber, D. A., 446, 451
Graczyk, B., 223, 240
Grant, A., 313
Grant, S. C., 61, 66, 77
Gray, T., 223, 240
Graybill, D., 245, 246, 251, 256, 261
Grayson, P., 120, 126, 127, 129, 134, 156, 168
Green, L. W., 336, 337, 338, 343
Greenberg, B. S., 119, 122, 124, 133, 173, 177,
    178, 204, 214, 220, 240, 246, 261, 282,
    299, 471, 477, 486
Greenberg, J., 148, 166
Greer, D., 155, 167
Gregg, P., 313, 314
Griggs, S., 121, 134
Grilli, R., 332, 342
Grinder, R., 268, 277
Gross, A. M., 245, 251, 261
Gross, L. P., 5, 12, 320, 323, 435, 451
Grubbs, J., 313

Grube, J., 174, 178
Grusec, J. E., 209, 212, 283, 299
Guerrero, J. L., 110, 117
Guilford, J. P., 95, 99
Gunter, B., 58, 77, 119, 133, 146, 166, 201, 206, 208, 211, 212, 216, 220, 223, 241, 256, 261, 497, 503
Gunther, A. C., 82–85, 89–91, 96, 99
Guo, Z., 318, 324
Guralnick, E. A., 155, 166
Gurevitch, M., 5, 12, 321, 324, 468, 469, 486
Guthrie, K., 313
Guttmann, A., 222, 241
Guttmann, I., 107, 112, 117, 317, 323

H

Haber, S., 188, 196, 470, 487
Hafstad, A., 351, 355, 359
Hale, J. K., 4, 22, 30, 57, 372, 374, 458, 461, 464, 465
Hale, J. L., 73, 74, 77, 217, 234, 241
Hale, K., 44, 49
Haley, G., 406, 412
Hall, G., 181, 196
Hall, J., 27, 30, 270, 278
Hall, W. M., 155, 166
Hallahan, D. P., 120, 134
Hallam, J., 189, 196
Hamelink, C. J., 497, 503
Hamilton, M., 20, 30
Hamilton, M. A., 330–333, 335–337, 339, 344, 458, 462, 465
Hammer, D., 202, 204, 212
Hampson, S., 224, 234, 242
Haney, R. D., 44, 50
Hansen, C., 269, 278
Hansen, C. H., 54, 70, 77, 223, 224, 241
Hansen, G. J., 500, 503
Hansen, D. R., 223, 224, 241
Hansen, R. D., 54, 70, 77, 269, 278
Hansen, W. B., 353, 360
Hanson, C. A., 204, 213
Hanyoun, S., 89, 99, 101
Hapkiewicz, W. G., 152, 166
Harding, S., 490, 503
Haridakis, P. M., 3, 5, 13, 227, 241
Harmonay, M., 122, 134
Harrington, A. F., 204, 214, 291, 300
Harris, R. J., 223, 226, 227, 235, 241

Hart, R. P., 393, 394, 412
Hartley, T. H., 434–435, 451
Hartwick, J., 255, 262
Harty, K. C., 351, 353, 360
Harvey, S. E., 282, 300
Hass, H., 321, 324
Hassett, M. J., 207, 214
Haskell, W. L., 328, 342
Haviland, M. L., 338, 340, 342
Hay, T. A., 217, 224, 238, 244
Hayes, A. F., 82, 87, 88, 95, 98, 99, 415, 418, 420, 423–427
Hayes, C. D., 221, 244
Haynes, R. B., 6, 7, 8, 13
Healton, C. G., 338, 340, 342
Hearold, S., 146–148, 166, 203, 212, 264, 278, 281, 283, 299, 468, 470, 472, 476, 486
Heath, L., 146, 166
Hecht, M. L., 354, 359
Hedges, L. V., 17, 30, 153, 157, 159, 166, 287, 299, 489, 503
Heeter, C., 44, 49, 112, 117, 483, 486
Heidel, C., 219, 226, 231, 243
Heider, F., 83, 99
Heitzler, C. D., 340, 343
Heldman, C., 500, 503
Helmick, A. L., 223, 226, 227, 241
Henderson, G. M., 333, 342
Henry, K. L., 146, 168
Herman, E. S., 481, 486
Herr, P. M., 54, 77
Herrett, J., 188, 196
Herrett-Skjellum, J., 32, 36, 203, 206, 212, 264, 266, 278, 470, 486
Hersey, J. C., 338, 342
Hersey, K. C., 340, 342
Hershey, M. R., 450, 451
Hess, V. L., 162–163, 165
Hetherington, M. J., 54, 69, 77
Hetrick, M. A., 351, 360
Hewes, D., 239, 241, 314
Hewitt, L., 347, 359
Heyduk, R. G., 216, 220, 236, 241
Hiebert, R. E., 497, 503
Hieser, R. A., 109, 110, 117
Higgins, E. T., 54, 57, 60, 63, 71, 77, 78
Highton, B., 54, 69, 77
Hill, D. B., 38, 44, 49, 351, 360
Hillbrand, M., 269, 279
Himmelweit, H., 119, 134
Hirschi, T. A., 149, 166

Hirschman, E. C., 223, 226, 241
Hirschman, R., 181, 196
Hitchens, C., 396, 412
Hla, K. M., 336, 344
Ho, F. C., 353, 359
Hobfoll, S. E., 227, 240
Hockheimer, J. L., 470, 485
Hockett, A. B., 228, 242
Hodgson, K., 236, 243
Hoekstra, S. J., 223, 226, 227, 235, 241
Hoffman, K., 248, 251, 254, 261, 269, 279
Hoffner, C., 83, 89, 91, 99, 218, 221, 223, 224,
   226, 228, 233, 234, 238, 239, 241, 243, 313
Hofstetter, C. R., 384, 386, 388, 451
Hogben, M., 153, 167, 264, 278
Hogg, A. J., 84, 90, 99
Holbert, R. L., 69, 77
Hollander, B. A., 384, 386–389
Holsti, O. R., 88, 99
Holt, J., 274, 278
Hoorens, V., 85, 99
Hope, A., 355, 359
Hopkins, R. S., 355, 361
Hopson, H., 246, 251, 253, 262
Hornik, C., 339, 342
Hornik, R. C., 329, 332, 342, 354, 360
Horowitz, E., 318, 324
Horton, D., 302, 313, 321, 323
Houser, B. B., 290, 299
Hovland, C. I., 88, 100, 162, 167, 319, 324, 350,
   359, 378, 379, 389
Hoy, M., 173, 178
Hoyle, R. H., 334, 341, 343, 352, 361
Hoyt, J., 183, 189, 198
Hu, Y. W., 42, 44, 50, 91, 100
Huang, H., 318, 324
Huang, W., 174, 175, 179
Hubbard, J., 44, 49
Huckfeldt, R., 443, 450
Huesmann, L. R., 58, 77, 164, 167, 220, 242
Huesmann, R., 264, 278
Huff, C., 209, 214
Huffman, J., 266, 278
Hughes, C. E., 162, 167
Hughes, H., 317, 325, 347, 361
Huhman, M., 340, 343
Hulley, S. B., 328, 342
Hunter, J. E., 17, 18, 20, 22, 30, 65, 77, 82,
   86–88, 92, 100, 105, 106, 117, 173, 178,
   186, 196, 207, 208, 212, 224, 225, 242,
   264, 270, 277, 278, 287, 293, 296, 299,
   331, 343, 367, 375, 442, 451, 455, 458,
   461, 462, 465, 490, 495, 503
Hunter, P., 126, 134
Hunter, T., 246, 256, 261
Huston, A. C., 146–148, 155, 166, 168, 208,
   214
Huston-Stein, A., 155, 167, 285, 290, 299
Hutchins, G., 290, 298
Huynh, M. Q., 354, 360
Hyman, H. H., 104, 117, 329, 343, 346, 359

I

Imrich, D. J., 224, 243
Innes, J. M., 82, 85, 90, 100, 110, 117
Institute of Medicine, 333, 343
Intons-Peterson, M., 191, 196
Irwin, A. R., 245, 251, 261
Iyengar, S., 41, 42, 44, 48, 49, 53, 54, 59, 60,
   62–64, 69, 72, 73, 77, 317, 324, 392, 411,
   475, 485, 486

J

Jablonski, C. K., 223, 228, 242
Jablonski, P. M., 44, 49
Jaccard, J., 173, 178
Jackson, J. E., 405, 412
Jackson, G. B., 82, 86–88, 100, 224, 242, 442,
   451, 455, 461, 462, 465
Jackson, L., 269, 278
Jackson, S., 239, 242, 458, 465, 469, 486
Jackson-Beeck, M., 384, 386, 389
Jacobs, S., 239, 242, 469, 486
Jaffe, R., 173, 178
Janis, I. L., 162, 167, 319, 324, 350, 359
Janky, C., 152, 165
Janssen, S. C., 223, 228, 234, 243
Jarvie, G. J., 202, 204, 212
Jason, L. A., 353, 359
Jawitz, W., 497, 503
Jecker, J. D., 107, 109, 110, 112, 117
Jeffres, L. W., 90, 100, 318–320, 324
Jeffrey, D. B., 174, 177
Jennings-Walstedt, J., 200, 206, 208, 209, 212
Jernigan, D., 340, 344
Jimenez-Lorente, B., 500, 504
Jo, E., 62, 74, 78, 255, 261
Joffe, A., 351, 353, 359

Johnson, B. T., 64, 78, 153, 167, 330, 343, 379, 389
Johnson, C. A., 353, 360
Johnson, J. D., 70, 78, 269, 278
Johnson, K., 174, 177
Johnson, M. D., 351, 360
Johnston, D. D., 223, 226, 228, 231, 237, 242
Jonas, E., 110, 112, 113, 117
Jones, C. R., 57, 77
Jones, E. E., 83, 100
Jordan, T., 170, 178
Josephson, W. L., 54, 59, 62, 68, 78, 155, 167, 470, 486
Joy, L. A., 470, 486
Joyner, D., 268, 278
Just, M. R., 450, 451

K

Kahn, J. S., 353, 361
Kahn, K. F., 435, 439, 451
Kaid, L. L., 44, 49
Kalichman, S., 364, 375
Kalis, P., 266, 278
Kalnova, S., 330, 333, 334, 336, 337, 343
Kamahawi, R., 2, 6–8, 10, 12
Kanazawa, S., 302, 313
Kant, J., 127, 134
Kanungo, R. N., 286, 290, 299
Kar, S. B., 340, 343
Karafa, J. A., 223, 226, 227, 235, 241
Kardes, F. R., 57, 60, 63, 76
Katcher, A. H., 253, 262
Katz, C., 418, 427
Katz, D., 379, 389
Katz, E., 5, 12, 316, 321, 324, 346, 347, 360, 420, 427, 474, 486
Katz, H., 189, 197
Katz, P., 204, 212
Katzman, N., 484, 495
Kauffman, J. M., 120, 134, 353, 359
Kawakami, K., 393, 403, 411
Kelleher, C., 355, 359
Keller, M. F., 291, 299
Kelley, H., 319, 324, 350, 359
Kelly, E., 120, 126, 127, 129, 132–134
Kelly, H. H., 162, 167
Kelly, S., 174, 175, 179
Kelman, H., 364, 375
Kendzierski, D. A., 146, 165
Kennamer, J. D., 384–386, 389

Kennedy, P., 173, 178
Kenney, K., 449, 451
Kenney, P. J., 435, 439, 451
Kent, K. E., 384, 386, 389
Kepplinger, H., 38, 43, 44, 47, 48
Kern, M., 449, 451
Kessler, M., 469, 486
Kestenbaum, G. I., 256, 261
Kiesler, C. A., 378, 389
Kiesler, D. J., 160, 167
Kim, H., 218, 243
Kim, J., 420, 427
Kim, M. S., 82, 87, 100, 202, 207, 212
Kimball, M. M., 470, 486
Kinder, D. R., 41, 42, 49, 53, 54, 62–64, 69, 72, 73, 75–78, 317, 324
Kinder, K., 69, 77
King, C. M., 224, 238, 242
King, E. G., 440, 451
King, G. A., 60, 77
Kinney, M. B., 351, 353, 359
Kiousis, S., 421, 427
Kipnis, D. M., 285, 290, 299
Kirsch, J., 245–246, 251, 256, 261
Kiwanuka-Tondo, J., 330–333, 336, 338, 339, 343, 344
Klapper, J., 104, 117, 347, 360, 430, 451
Klapper, J. T., 316, 324, 470, 480, 487
Kleck, R. E., 110, 117
Klees, S., 173, 178
Klein, M., 209, 214
Klein, W. M., 85, 102
Kline, F. G., 471, 475, 486
Kline, F. K., 351, 355, 360
Knack, S., 406, 412
Kobre, S., 436, 451
Kohlberg, L., 201, 212
Kolbe, R. H., 204, 212
Kornhauser, W., 315, 324
Koepsell, T. D., 353, 359
Korzenny, F., 220, 240, 282, 299
Kosicki, G. M., 54, 60, 61, 69, 79, 468, 487
Kostrich, L. J., 399, 405, 413
Koukounas, E., 225, 228, 233, 242
Kovaric, P., 120, 133
Kowalczyk, L., 83, 89, 91, 99
Krafka, C., 188, 191, 196
Krebs, D. L., 149, 167
Krosnick, J. A., 54, 60, 62, 64, 69, 72, 75, 77, 78
Krygowski, W., 54, 70, 77
Kubey, R., 176, 178, 269, 278
Kuhn, T., 490, 503

Kulis, S., 354, 359
Kurtz, H., 266, 278

L

Lachendro, E., 84–85, 102
Lacy, S., 432, 440, 451
Lagerspetz, K. M. J., 62, 71, 78, 220, 227, 228, 234, 242
Lakkaraju, L., 269, 278
Lalumiere, M., 181, 196
Lam, T., 354, 360
LaMay, C. L., 469, 487
Lambe, J. L., 474, 487
Lane, R., 312
Lang, A., x, xiii, 96, 100
Lang, G. E., 41, 49
Lang, M. K., 41, 49, 251, 256, 262
Langefeld, C. D., 204, 212
Langley, T., 54, 59, 68, 78, 227, 242
Langmark, F., 351, 355, 359
Larsen, D. C., 44, 50
LaRose, R., 435, 453
Larson, R., 269, 278
Lasorsa, D. L., 44, 49, 81, 82, 89, 95, 100
Lau, R. R., 60, 78, 384, 386, 388, 500, 503
LaVoie, A. L., 110, 117
Lawrence, P. A., 216, 220, 235, 238, 242
Lazarsfeld, P. F., 316–318, 321, 323, 324, 346, 360, 377, 387, 388, 394, 396, 397, 412, 429, 430, 450–452, 474, 486
Lears, M., 208, 214, 469, 488
Leary, T., 160, 167
Lee, C., 81–82, 100
Lee, E., 173, 175, 178, 421, 422, 427
Lee, S., x, xiii,
Lee, W., 422, 427
Leets, L., 83, 101, 305, 313
Leff, D. R., 41, 49
Leggett, D, 38
Lehrer, S. K., 204, 212
Leiman, B., 221, 240
Leippe, M. R., 379, 389
Leonard, K., 185, 189, 196
Lepper, M. R., 83, 102
Leshner, G., 381, 388
Levi, S., 209, 214
Leviton, L., 106, 117
Levy, M., 313
Lewis, F. D., 313
Lewis, G., 269, 271, 278

Leyens, J., 59, 68, 78
Leyens, J. P., 153, 155, 167
Lichter, L. S., 481, 487
Lichter, S. R., 449, 452, 481, 487
Lieberman, B., 448, 452
Lieberman, T., 440, 452
Liebert, R. M., 119, 120, 134, 282, 291, 299, 300
Liebling, A. J., 435, 439, 440, 452
Light, R. J., 157, 167
Lilie, S., 364, 373, 375
Lin, C. A., 121, 134
Lindloff, T. R., 5, 12
Ling, C., 54, 69, 78
Ling, P. A., 152, 155, 167
Lingenfelter, M., 204, 214, 291, 300
Linné, O., 497, 503
Linz, D., 188, 191, 196, 269, 277, 471, 484, 486, 487
Linz, J., 317, 324
Lips, H., 188, 195
Lipset, S. M., 317, 324
Lipsey, M. W., 331–334, 336–339, 342, 344
Liss, M. B., 282, 291, 299
List, J. A., 207, 209, 213
Litle, P., 220, 244
Lockman, J. J., 291, 300
Loftus, E., 255, 261
Logan, G. D., 61, 66, 77
Logan, R. A., 351, 360
Lombardi, W. J., 54, 57, 60, 61, 63, 66, 71, 72, 76–78
Long, E., 268, 279
Longo, D. R., 351, 360
Lorch, E. P., 334, 341, 343, 352, 361
Love, C., 269, 279
Lowry, D. T, 1, 5, 9–11, 13
Lowery, S., 315, 324
Loye, D., 152, 167
Lucas, K., 246, 256, 257, 262
Luecke-Aleksa, D., 204, 213
Luetscher, W. D., 400, 406, 411
Lull, J. T., 204, 213, 266, 269, 271, 278
Luthgens, C., 110, 118
Lyle, J., 119, 134
Lynn, R., 224, 234, 242

M

MacArthur, C., 355, 356, 360
Macaskill, P., 351, 360
Maccoby, N., 146, 168, 347, 360

Mackie, D., 245, 261
MacKinnon, D. P., 353, 360
Macklin, M. C., 174, 178
MacKuen, M. B., 41, 49
Maibach, E., 329, 343
Mains, D. A., 336–338, 343
Malamuth, N. M., 54, 59, 68, 78, 188, 189, 191, 267, 273, 278, 470, 487
Malouff, J., 245, 251, 261
Mantler, G., 452
Marcus-Newhall, A., 248, 261
Mares, M. L., 285, 297, 299
Martin, M., 172, 173, 178
Martinelli, K. A., 385, 386, 389
Marsh, E., 216, 240
Marsiglia, F. F., 354, 359
Marx, K., 5, 13
Marx, M. J., 204, 213
Mason, L., 82, 100
Masters, J. C., 221, 240
Matera, F. R., 44, 50, 418, 427
Mavin, G. H., 60, 77
Mayer, J. D., 239, 242
Mayerson, S., 188, 197
Mayes, S. L., 204, 213
Mays, V., 364, 374
McAleer, J., 119, 133
McArthur, L. Z., 209, 213, 291, 299
McCabe, A. E., 155, 167
McCabe, M. P., 225, 228, 233, 242
McCauley, C., 208, 213, 222, 238, 242
McClure, R. D., 396, 412
McCombs, M. E., 5, 13, 37–39, 42–45, 47, 49, 50, 59, 60, 78, 222, 242, 317, 324, 473, 484,485, 487
McCoy, K., 55, 60, 70, 76
McCracken, G., 365, 374, 375
McCroskey, J. C., 110, 118, 317, 324
McCutcheon, L., 312
McDermott, S., 220, 240
McDevitt, M., 421, 427
McDivitt, J. A., 332, 342, 354, 360
McDonald, D. G., 81, 99, 381, 389, 407–409, 412
McDowell, J., 332, 342
McGee, J., 501, 504
McGhee, P. E., 207, 208, 212, 213
McGraw, K. M., 54, 78
McGuire, W. J., 141, 144–147, 160, 162, 167, 341, 343, 350, 360, 471, 487
McHugh, M., 302, 304, 314
McKee, K., 266, 278
McKoon, G., 63, 78

McLeod, D. M., 82, 100, 318, 324, 468, 474, 475, 486, 487
McLeod, J. M., 40, 44, 49, 381, 389, 400–409, 411, 412, 416, 426, 468, 475, 486, 487
McLuhan, M., 5, 13, 450, 452
McPhee, S. J., 354, 360
McPhee, W. N., 316, 323, 377, 387, 388, 450
McQuail, D., 315, 316, 324, 432, 452, 497, 503
Meadow, R. G., 452
Medoff, N., 184, 188, 198
Meeds, R., 90, 100
Meier, K., 173, 178
Meili, H., 173, 177
Melburg, V., 149, 167
Melville, D. J., 204, 213
Mendelberg, T., 54, 69, 78
Mendelsohn, H., 321, 324, 347, 360
Mendelsohn, M., 69, 78
Mercuri, K., 364, 375
Meredith, K., 365, 374
Merton, R. K., 394, 412, 429, 452
Messeri, P., 338, 340, 342
Meyer, B., 204, 213
Meyer, G., 333, 342
Meyer, T. P., 126, 129, 133, 189, 197
Meyers, D. E., 56, 78
Mikos, L., 217, 242
Milavsky, B., 253, 262
Miles, J., 209, 214
Milgram, S., 149, 152, 167
Miller, A. H., 42, 44, 49
Miller, D. T., 149, 159, 167, 168
Miller, G., 301, 313
Miller, J. M., 54, 69, 78
Miller, L. S., 58, 77
Miller, M. M., 202, 208, 213, 381, 385, 386, 389, 407, 408, 409, 412
Miller, N., 160, 165, 248, 261, 378, 389, 499, 503
Miller, P. A., 237, 241
Miller, P. V., 351, 355, 360
Miller, R. E., 37, 43, 44, 49
Miller-Day, M., 354, 359
Mills, C. W., 315, 324
Mills, J., 106, 107, 112, 117, 118, 317, 323, 324
Millspaugh, M., 452
Minow, N. N., 469, 487
Minozzi, S., 332, 342
Miron, D., 2–4, 10, 12
Mischel, W., 201, 213
Mitchell, E. W., 330–333, 336, 339, 344
Mitchell, G., 435, 452
Mitrook, M., 269, 277

Mock, J., 354, 360
Moely, B. E., 291, 300
Moffet, E. A., 6, 8, 13
Moise, J., 264, 278
Molitor, F., 216, 243
Mongeau, P., 21, 22, 30
Mook, D. G., 148, 167
Moore, J., 269, 271, 278
Moreno-Riaño, G., 421, 427
Morgan, M., 5, 12, 82, 87, 100, 200, 202, 203,
    208, 213, 264, 278, 320, 323, 403, 407,
    408, 412, 416, 419, 427, 435, 451, 470,
    471, 483, 487
Morgan, S. E., 352, 361
Moriarity, R. J., 155, 167
Morley, D. D., 227, 243
Morrison, A. J., 351, 355, 360
Morrow, M., 54, 59, 75, 254, 260
Morse, W. C., 120, 122, 134
Moscovici, S., 110, 118
Mosher, D., 188, 189, 197
Moy, P., 422, 423, 427
Mueller, C., 189, 197
Mullen, D. P., 336, 343
Mullen, P. D., 336, 337, 338, 343
Mundorf, N., 218, 219, 221, 224, 226, 228, 237,
    242, 244
Mundy, L., 365, 374
Mundy, P., 82, 83, 84, 85, 90, 99
Murphy, B. A., 491, 503
Murphy, S. T., 55, 70, 79
Murray, D. M., 173, 178, 339, 343, 351, 353, 360
Murray, J. P., 290, 298
Muthen, L. K., 351, 360
Mutz, D. C., 54, 69, 79, 81, 90, 99, 100

N

Najaka, S. S., 339, 344
Nass, C., 302, 314
Nathanson, A. I., 82, 100, 227, 228, 234, 240,
    501, 503, 504
National Center for Chronic Disease Prevention
    and Health Promotion, 327, 343
National Television Violence Study, 153, 164,
    167
Nation's editors pick 15 'superior' papers, 440,
    445, 452
Nayman, O. B., 384–386, 388
Neal, J., 188, 197
Neely, J. H., 58, 63, 79

Nelson, J. A., 122, 134
Nemeth, C., 110, 118
Neuendorf, K. A., 227, 228, 242, 266, 278
Newspaper endorsements for president since
    1940, 439, 452
Newton, B. J., 204, 206, 208, 213
Nguyen, S., 354, 360
Nguyen, T., 354, 360
Nguyen, W., 354, 360
Nicholson, T., 182, 196
Niedereppe, J., 341, 342
Nikken, P., 201, 213
Nisbett, R. E., 83, 100
Niven, D., 420, 427, 436, 452
Noelle-Neumann, E., 81, 100, 396, 397, 413,
    415–417, 425, 427, 475, 487
Nollet, M. A., 452
Nordlund, J., 305, 313
Novak, D., 246, 251, 253, 262
Novelli, W., 347, 360

O

O'Bryant, S. L., 209, 213, 291, 299
O'Connor, R. D., 291, 299
Oddone-Paolucci, E., 185, 197
Ognianova, E., 90, 100
O'Gorman, H., 81, 100
O'Guinn, T. C., 60, 66, 79, 471, 481, 488
O'Keefe, D. J., 22, 30, 372, 275, 463, 465
O'Keefe, G. J., 347, 360, 393, 407–409, 412
O'Keefe, T., 353, 360
O'Leary, M., 246, 256, 261, 269, 277
Oliver, M. B., 218, 220, 223, 228, 238, 239, 242
Olkin, I., 153, 157, 159, 166, 287, 299
O'Neal, E. C., 54, 59, 68, 78, 227, 242
Oppenheim, A. N., 119, 134
Ordman, V., 269, 279
Orford, J., 160, 167
Orlofsky, J. L., 201, 213
Orme, M., 292, 300
Ostman, R. E., 81, 84, 99
Ott, B., 317, 324
Ottati, V., 59, 77
Otto, V., 174, 177
Owen, D., 291, 300

P

Padgett, C. A., 355, 359
Padgett, V., 188, 197

Page, B. I., 433, 452
Paik, H., 82, 87, 88, 91, 92, 95, 100, 146–148, 162, 167, 181, 197, 247, 261, 264, 278, 281, 284, 287, 289, 292, 295–297, 300, 470, 476, 487
Paisley, W. J., 328, 343, 34, 3608
Palmer, E. L., 228, 242, 347, 360
Palmgreen, P. C., 44, 49, 216, 220, 235, 238, 242, 312, 334, 341, 343, 352, 361
Pan, Z., 54, 60, 61, 69, 79
Pardun, C., 267, 278
Parke, R. D., 153, 155, 167
Parker, E. B., 119, 134
Pascual, C. A., 340, 343
Pastorek, A., 83, 89, 91, 99
Patterson, J. N., 202, 204, 212
Patterson, T. E., 396, 412, 433, 434, 452
Paul, B., 81, 82, 88, 100, 101
Paulman, P., 173, 178
Pauly, J. J., 5, 13
Payne, J., 364, 375
Pearce, W. B., 491, 503
Pearlin, L. I., 321, 324
Pechmann, C., 173, 178
Peeters, A. L., 201, 213
Peevers, B. H., 204, 213
Peffly, M., 54, 68, 77
Peirce, K., 201, 213
Penz, M. A., 353, 360
Perloff, R. M., 6–8, 13, 81, 82, 83, 85, 100, 101, 202, 208, 213, 468, 474, 487
Perry, D. K., 58, 79
Perry, S., 421, 427
Perse, E., 302, 304, 314
Perse, E. M., 302, 304, 305, 313, 314, 470, 471, 474, 481, 483, 486, 487
Pessin, B. M., 44, 48, 63, 76
Peters, M. D., 53, 54, 62, 64, 69, 72, 73, 77
Peterson, D., 269, 279
Petric, G., 420, 422, 427
Pettey, G. R., 125, 132, 385, 386, 389
Petty, R. E., 115, 118, 319, 324, 350, 360, 379, 380, 389, 471, 472, 481, 485, 487
Pfau, M., 463, 465
Pfost, K., 269, 279
Phalen, P. F., 481, 488
Phelps, J., 173, 178
Phemister, S., 290, 299
Phillips, D. P., 58, 76
Pierce, J. P., 351, 360
Pillemer, D., x, xiii
Pillion, O., 69, 77

Pingree, S., 209, 213, 291, 300
Pinkleton, B. E., 403, 411
Pinney, N., 54, 69, 78
Pinter, A., 420, 422, 427
Pirie, P. L., 353, 359
Pitts, M., 339, 344
Plane, M. B., 336, 344
Plotkin, R. S., 83, 89, 91, 99
Podolski, C., 264, 278
Polissar, L., 353, 359
Pollack, P., 364, 373, 375
Pollock, M. A., 491, 503
Pollock, V. E., 499, 503
Pope, J., 269, 279
Popham, W. J., 351, 360
Popovich, P. M., 204, 213
Post-Gordon, J., 245, 251, 261
Potter, L. D., 340, 343, 351, 360
Potter, W. J., 2, 6, 8, 12, 89, 96, 101, 320, 324, 471, 487
Potts, C. R., 155, 168
Potts, R., 70, 79
Poulos, R. W., 120, 134, 282, 291, 299, 300
Pournelle, J., 446, 452
Powell, M. C., 57, 60, 63, 66, 76
Powell, R., 302, 304, 314
Power, J. G., 55, 70, 79
Prasad, V., 174, 178
Preiss, R., 18, 30, 490, 497, 502, 503
Prentice, D. A., 159, 168
Preiss, R. W., 458, 463–465
Price, V., 60, 62, 75, 79, 90, 99, 475, 487
Prichard, S. V. O., 110, 118, 317, 324
Priester, J. R., 472, 487
Prisco, A. G., 54, 55, 59, 68, 76
Pritchard, D., 449, 452
Proctor, D., 330–333, 336, 339, 344
Prokhorov, A. V., 351, 353, 360
Protess, D. L., 41, 49

Q

Quay, H. C., 120, 134
Quinsey, V., 181, 196

R

Ramirez, G., 336–338, 343
Ramirez, J., 189, 197
Ramsden, M. W., 201, 213

Raney, A. A., 223, 226, 231, 235, 238, 239, 242, 243
Rao, N., 291, 300, 333, 342, 371, 375
Rapaport, R., 191, 197
Rasmuson, M., 332, 342
Ratcliff, R., 63, 78
Ratneshwar, S., 173, 178
Raudy, J., 209, 214
Ray, S., 355, 361
Reagan, J., 393, 400 412
Reep, D. C., 200, 201, 204, 206, 212, 213
Reese, S. D., 10, 13, 381, 385, 386, 389, 407–409, 412, 482, 488
Reeves, B., 204, 208, 213, 214, 302, 314
Reilly, S., 223, 227, 228, 240
Reinhardt, L. C., 282, 291, 299
Reiter, H. L., 406, 412
Repetti, R. L., 202, 208, 214
Reynolds, A., 222, 242
Reznikoff, M., 269, 279
Rhine, R. J., 106, 107, 118
Rhodes, N. D., 162, 163, 168
Rholes, W. S., 57, 77
Ricciotti, L. A., 83, 89, 91, 99
Richard, F., 419, 427
Richard, F. D., 159, 168
Richards, J., 169, 173, 174, 178
Rieder, R., 392, 412
Riesman, D., 315, 324
Riffe, D., 2, 10, 13
Rimm, S. B., 121, 133
Rinaldi, R. C., 146, 166
Ringwalt, C. L., 339, 342
Riordan, N., 353, 359
Rivara, F. P., 353, 359
Roberts, D. F., 146, 168, 347, 360, 484, 485
Roberts, M., 474, 487
Robertson, S. J., 202, 204, 212
Robertson, T., 173, 178
Robinson, H., 107, 118, 317, 324
Robinson-Weber, S., 406, 412
Rodasta, A., 245, 251, 261
Roden, A. H., 152, 166
Roderiguez, M., 174, 179
Roger, R. W., 209, 212
Rogers, E., 364, 371, 375
Rogers, E. M., 4, 5, 11, 13, 53, 79, 316, 318, 325, 333, 341–343, 347, 348, 350, 361, 476, 488
Rogers, J., 110, 118
Rogers, W. M., 477, 487
Rogers, K. H., 255, 260

Rojas, H., 82, 89, 97, 99, 101
Rojas, T., 169, 174, 178
Rokeach, M., 81, 102
Rooney, B. L., 339, 343
Rosch, M., 110, 117
Rose, G., 173, 177
Rosen, S., 107, 118, 317, 325
Rosene, J., 189, 197
Rosenthal, R., 64, 65, 79, 86, 91, 92, 101, 105, 114, 118, 151, 153, 159, 165, 168, 270, 278, 279, 442, 452, 458, 461, 465
Rosenwasser, S. M., 204, 214, 291, 300
Roskos-Ewoldsen, B., 53, 59, 60, 66, 79, 191, 196, 472, 487
Roskos-Ewoldsen, D. R., 53, 59, 60, 66, 76, 79, 108, 116, 472, 487
Ross, A., 106, 107, 118
Ross, D., 316, 323
Ross, L. B., 83, 84, 101, 102, 156, 168, 208, 214
Ross, S. A., 316, 323
Ross-Degnan, D., 353, 361
Rossiter, T. S., 170, 178
Rothchild, N., 208, 213
Rothman, S., 481, 487
Rouner, D., 174, 179
Rouzier, P., 354, 361
Rowland, G. L., 219, 235, 241
Rozin, P., 208, 213
Ruble, D. N., 202, 209, 214
Rubin, A. M., 3, 5, 13, 115, 118, 246, 261, 302, 304, 305, 313, 314, 321, 325
Rubin, D. B., 159, 168
Rubin, R. B., 302, 305, 314
Rubinstein, E. A., 120, 135, 292, 300
Rucinski, D., 82, 83, 84, 101
Ruiter, S., 85, 99
Rule, B. G., 59, 79
Rush, R. R., 384, 386, 389
Rushton, J. P., 283, 291, 300
Rust, R. T., 406, 412
Rutter, M., 120, 134

S

Saarni, C., 221, 243
Sadlier, D., 355, 359
Sahlstein, E., 32, 36, 363, 366, 374
Salina, D., 353, 359
Salmon, C. T., 82–84, 101, 475, 488
Salomon, G., 121, 134
Salomone, K. L., 44, 49

Salovey, P., 227, 240
Salwen, M. B., 44, 48–50, 81, 82, 88–91, 95, 97, 99–101, 418, 427
Sanbonmatsu, D. M., 57, 60, 63, 76
Sanborn, F. W., 223, 226, 227, 235, 241
Sapolsky, B. S., 189, 197, 198, 216, 243
Sarnoff, R. W., 121, 134
Sawalski, L., 353, 359
Sawin, D. B., 156, 168
Schaller, M., 237, 241
Scharrer, E., 54, 59, 68, 79
Scheirer, C. J., 290, 299
Scheufele, D. A., 422, 423, 427
Schiappa, E., 314
Schleuder, J. D., 55, 70, 79, 381, 388
Schmidt, F. L., 17, 18, 30, 265, 77, 82, 86–88, 92, 100, 105, 106, 117, 173, 178, 186, 196, 207, 212, 224, 225, 242, 270, 278, 287, 293, 296, 299, 331, 336, 343, 344, 367, 375, 442, 451, 455, 461, 462, 465, 490, 495, 503
Schmitt, K. G., 384, 386, 388
Schmitt, K. L., 204, 213
Schmitt-Beck, R., 397, 413
Schneider, F. P., 44, 49
Schneider, W., 395, 412
Schneider, S., 83, 89, 91, 99
Schoenbach, K., 42, 49
Schonbach, P., 107, 112, 117, 317, 323
Schooler, C., 364, 374
Schramm, W., ix, x, xiii, 2, 5–9, 13, 53, 79, 119, 134, 429, 452, 497, 504
Schulz-Hardt, S., 110, 112, 113, 117, 118
Schuman, H., 81, 99
Schutte, N., 245, 251, 261
Schvaneveldt, R. W., 56, 78
Schwartz, P., 169, 174, 178
Schwarz, J. E., 208, 214
Scott, C. L., 223, 226, 227, 235, 241
Sears, D. O., 81, 101, 105, 106, 107, 109, 111, 117, 118, 246, 262, 378, 379, 388, 459, 465, 472, 480, 488
Sebastian, M., 501, 504
Sebastian, R. J., 153, 155, 167
Secker-Walker, R. H., 351, 353, 355, 359
Segrin, C., 217, 224, 243
Seigler, P., 269, 279
Sekyra, F. III, 154, 166
Semetko, H. A., 381, 389
Semlak, W., 44, 51
Shaffer, S. D., 403, 406, 412

Shah, D. V., 82, 97, 101, 102
Shanahan, J., 82, 87, 88, 95, 98–100, 264, 278, 403, 407, 408, 412, 415, 416, 418–427, 470, 471, 483, 487
Shanahan, W., 22, 30
Shapiro, M., 44, 51
Shapiro, R. Y., 433, 452
Shaw, D. L., 5, 13, 37, 39, 42, 44, 47, 49, 50, 59, 60, 78, 317, 324, 473, 487
Shaw, D. R., 430, 452
Shaw, D. V., 54, 60, 68, 76
Sheatsley, P., 346, 359
Sheatsley, P. B., 104, 117, 346, 359
Shetsley, P. B., 329, 343
Sherif, C. W., 378, 379, 389, 390
Sherif, M., 378, 379, 389, 390
Sherman, B., 267, 279
Sherman, S. J., 185, 197
Sherry, J. L., 246, 245, 256–258, 262, 272, 279
Shields, T. G., 54, 68, 77, 397, 412
Shirley, M., 191, 196
Shoemaker, P. J., 10, 13, 482, 488
Shondrick, D., 181, 196
Shotland, R. L., 149, 152, 167
Shrum, L. J., 60, 66, 79, 471, 472, 481, 488
Siegel, A. E., 156, 168
Siegel, M., 354, 361
Sigelman, L., 500, 503
Signorielli, N., 5, 12, 200, 203, 207, 208, 214, 320, 323, 435, 451, 469, 474, 475, 486–488
Silberg, K., 83, 89, 91, 99
Silberman, J., 404, 405, 412
Silverman, L. T., 291, 300
Silverman, W., 173, 178
Silverman-Watkins, L., 209, 214
Silvern, S. B., 251, 256, 262
Simon, A., 44, 49, 54, 60, 69, 77
Simon, H. A., 402, 403, 412
Simon, T., 432, 440, 451
Simons-Morton, D. G., 336, 337, 338, 343
Simonson, H. M., 156, 168
Simpson, C., 449, 451
Singer, D. G., 199, 204, 214, 292, 300
Singer, J. D., 157, 167
Singer, J. L., 199, 204, 214, 292, 300
Singer, R. D., 130, 133, 148, 152, 166
Singhal, A., 476, 488
Siune, K., 44, 50
Slater, M. D., 146, 168, 174, 179
Sleight, C., 218, 243
Sloss, G. S., 81, 100, 452

Sly, D. F., 355, 361
Smeaton, G., 188, 197
Smith, K. A., 44, 50
Smith, K. B., 434, 452
Smith, L., 174, 178
Smith, R. A., 156, 168, 384, 386, 388
Smith, T. W., 434, 452
Snyder, L. B., 330–339, 343, 344
Sobowale, I. A., 384, 386, 388
Society of Professional Journalists, 437, 452
Soffin, S., 44, 49
Sohn, A. B., 44, 48, 50
Sohn, H., 44, 48
Soley, L. C., 435, 451
Solomon, D. S., 347–349, 361
Somera, L., 218, 243
Soumerai, S. B., 353, 361
Sowden, A., 351, 361
Sparks, C. W., 216, 243
Sparks, G. G., 96, 101, 216, 218, 226–228, 236, 237, 242, 243, 258, 262
Spellman, C., 44, 50
Spirek, M. M., 226, 236, 243
Spitzberg, B. H., 217, 241
Sprafkin, I., 154, 166
Sprafkin, J. N., 119–121, 125–129, 132, 133–135, 154, 156, 166, 168, 282, 291, 292, 299, 3000
Squire, P., 392, 413
Srull, T., 255, 262
Srull, T. K., 57, 58, 71, 79, 255,
Stafford, S., 22, 30
Stamm, K., 422, 423, 427
Standley, T. C., 84, 101
Stanley, C., 44, 49
Stanley, T. L., 211, 214
Star, S., 317, 325, 347, 361
Starnes, W. T., 122, 133
Staten, C. L., 452
St. Dizier, B., 439, 452
Stead, L., 351, 361
Steblay, N., 500, 504
Steele, C. A., 318, 324
Steele, G., 152, 167
Stefancic, J., 493, 500, 503
Stein, A. H., 154, 166
Steinberg, G., 301, 313
Stempel, G. H., 85, 99, 384, 386, 388, 451, 453
Stenbjerre, M., 83, 101
Step, M., 314
Stephenson, M. A., 38, 43, 50

Stephenson, M. T., 334, 341, 343, 352, 361
Stephonson, W., 321, 325
Stern, F., 402, 403, 412
Sternberg, R., 121, 135
Steur, F. B., 156, 168
Stevens, J. D., 429, 453
Stevens-Long, J., 209, 211
St. George, A., 406, 412
Stiff, J. B., 218, 219, 224, 226–228, 231, 233, 235, 243
St. Lawrence, J., 268, 279
Stock, W., 188, 197
Stokes-Zoota, J. J., 159, 168, 419, 427
Stone, G. C., 44, 50
Stone, R. D., 152, 166
Storey, D., 316, 325, 347, 348, 361
Straubhaar, J., 435, 453
Strauss, M. A., 161, 165
Strawniak, M., 246, 256, 261
Striefel, S., 120, 126, 135
Strom, G., 405, 411
Stromer-Galley, J., 449, 453
Strouse, J., 268, 279
St. Thomas, L., 395, 413
Sun, S., 269, 271, 279
Surgeon General's Scientific Advisory Committee on Television and Social Beahvior, 120, 135
Susman, E. J., 285, 290, 299
Sutton, S., 21, 30
Svenkerud, P., 371, 375
Svenson, O., 85, 101
Swaim, R. C., 146, 168
Swanson, D. L., 44, 50
Swanson, L. L., 44, 50
Sweeney, J. M., 355, 359
Swisher, L., 70, 79

T

Tamoborini, R., 108, 118, 216, 218, 219, 224, 226–228, 231, 233, 235, 236, 243
Tan, A. S., 207, 209, 214, 385, 386, 390, 397, 413, 497, 504
Tan, S. L., 253, 256, 261
Tannenbaum, P. H., 123, 135, 189, 197, 253, 254, 258, 262, 364, 375, 399, 405, 413, 475, 488
Tanner, J., 269, 279
Tascher, D., 189, 197

Taylor, B. R., 59, 79
Taylor, D., 188, 197
Taylor, S. E., 185, 189, 196, 255, 261
Teachman, G., 292, 300
Tedeschi, J. T., 149, 167
Terry, D. J., 85, 89, 99
Tewksbury, D., 60, 62, 75, 79
Thangavelu, K., 208, 213
Thelen, N., 110, 112, 113, 117
Thomas, D. R., 152, 155, 167
Thomas, L., 191, 196
Thomas, M. H., 154, 165, 290, 298
Thomas, S. L., 58, 77
Thomas, S. V., 146, 165
Thompson, J., 468, 488
Thompson, S. K., 110, 117
Thorp, J., 169, 179
Thorson, E., 85, 90, 91, 96, 99–101
Tims, A. R., 384, 386, 388
Tipton, L., 44, 50
Tizard, J., 120, 134
Tobler, N. S., 339, 342
Todorov, A., 57, 60, 79
Toeplitz-Winiewska, M., 292, 300
Tokinoya, H., 418, 427
Torres, M., 55, 60, 70, 76
Torrubia-Beltri, R., 226, 227, 235, 240
Tota, M. E., 60, 61, 66, 72, 76
Tower, A., 204, 212, 290, 298
Tower, R. B., 292, 300
Tracz, S. M., 92, 101, 109, 113, 118
Trapido, E., 355, 361
Trawalter, S., 70, 78
Trostle, L., 269, 271, 279
Tsao, J., 314
Tschida, D. A., 69, 77
Tseng, D. S., 336, 344
Tuchman, G., 200, 214
Tuchman, S., 405, 413
Turk, J., 38, 43, 50
Turner, C., 255, 262
Twitchell, J. B., 221, 243
Tyler, T. R., 81, 84, 85, 101

U

Uldall, B., 424, 426
Unnikrishnan, N., 171, 179
U. S. Commission on Civil Rights, 199, 214
U. S. Department of Education, 122, 135

U. S. Department of Justice, 258, 262
U. S. Environmental Protection Agency, 171, 179
U. S. Office of Education, 120, 135

V

Valentine, J. C., 160, 165
Valentine, K. B., 204, 213
Valentino, N. A., 54, 69, 80
Vallone, R. P., 83, 102
Valkenburg, P. M., 223, 228, 234, 243
van den Berg, S., 44, 50
Van Evra, J., 119, 135, 170, 179, 471, 488
Van Leuven, J., 174, 179
van Vuuren, D. P., 223, 240
Vasta, R., 290, 299
Vaughn, P., 385, 386, 390
Velez, R., 336, 343
Verser, R. M., 500, 503
Vial, V., 108, 118, 226, 243
Vidmar, N., 81, 102
Vince, P., 119, 134
Vincent, R., 267, 279
Vincent, S., 205, 211
Violato, C., 185, 197
Viswesvaran, C., 336, 344
Vittes, M. E., 364, 373, 375
Volgy, T. J., 208, 214

W

Wackman, D. B., 54, 68, 76, 120, 135
Wagner, A., 32, 36
Wagstaff, D. A., 354, 359
Wahl-Jorgensen, K., 421, 427
Waite, B., 269, 279
Wakefield, M., 351, 361
Wakshlag, J., 108, 118, 228, 243, 470, 488
Walbek, N. H., 285, 290, 298
Wald, K. D., 400, 406, 413
Waldman, P., 453
Walker, J. R., 406, 413
Walker, K. B., 227, 243
Walker, M. R., 254, 262
Wallack, L. D., 174, 178, 340, 344, 346, 347, 352, 358, 361
Walsh, J., 174, 177
Walsh, P., 204, 212
Wanamaker, C., 269, 279

Wang, E. Y. I., 353, 360
Wann, D. L., 54, 80
Wanta, W., 37–39, 42–44, 46, 48–50, 474, 487
Ward, S., 120, 135, 173, 178
Ware, W., 82–83, 87, 89, 102
Wartella, E., 120, 135
Watkins, B. A., 155, 167
Watt, J. H. Jr., 44, 50
Waylly, M. E., 384, 386, 388
Weaver, D., 2, 6–8, 10, 12, 381, 385, 388, 389,
    390, 392, 406, 413
Weaver, D. H., 7, 9, 10, 13, 38, 39, 40–42, 44,
    50, 473, 487
Weaver, J., 216, 224, 242, 243, 269, 277
Weaver, J. B., 185, 197, 216, 218–221, 226,
    228, 237, 244
Webber, G., 204, 211
Webster, J. G., 470, 481, 488
Weikel, K., 174, 177
Weinmann, G., 407–409, 413
Weinstein, L., 256, 261
Weinstein, N., 84, 85, 102
Weinstein, N. D., 84–85, 102
Weiss, A. J., 34, 36, 174, 179, 224, 243
Weiss, N. A., 207, 214
Wells, J., 264, 279
Wells, W. D., 151, 168
West, S. G., 153, 155, 167
Westby, S., 207, 209, 213
Westerstahl, J., 432, 436, 453
Westley, B. H., 329, 342
Westmeyers, S., 314
Wheaton, J., 110, 117
While, D., 174, 175, 179
Whitaker, J., 155, 167
White, A. V., 55, 70, 79
White, D. M., 339, 344, 437, 453
White, H. A., 83, 102
White, L., 189, 197
Whiteman, D., 452
Whitley, B., 202, 214
Whitman, D., 85, 102
Whitmore, K., 120, 134
Whitney, F. C., 497, 503
Wiest, J. R., 245, 248, 253, 260
Wildmon, D. E., 121, 135
Willett, J. B., 157, 167
Williams, A., 431, 453
Williams, J., 44, 49
Williams, K. R., 161, 168
Williams, P. T., 328, 342

Williams, W. Jr., 44, 50, 51
Williamson, P. A., 251, 256, 262
Willnat, L., 54, 69, 80, 381, 389, 422, 427
Wilson, B. J., 34, 36, 174, 179, 224, 228, 243,
    484, 486, 501, 504
Wilson, D. B., 339, 344
Wilson, M. H., 351, 353, 359
Wilson, S. J., 339, 344
Wilson, T. D., 151, 165
Wimmer, R. D., 6–8, 13
Windhauser, J. W., 453
Winkel, M., 246, 251, 253, 262
Winn, M., 121, 135
Winter, J. P., 37, 41, 43, 44, 46, 51, 473, 486
Winters, A., 32, 36, 363, 366, 374
Wisocki, P. A., 208, 214
Witte, K., 21, 30, 364, 372, 375
Wober, J. M., 224, 244, 406–409, 413
Wober, M., 206, 208, 212, 216, 220, 243
Wohl, R. R., 302, 313, 321, 323
Wolf, F. M., 86, 87, 102, 419, 427
Wolf, T. M., 209, 214
Wolf-Gillespie, N., 173, 178
Wolfinger, R. E., 392, 413
Wood, W., 145, 146, 150, 151, 158–160, 162,
    163, 168, 470, 472, 478, 488, 499, 503
Woodward, E., 285, 297, 299
Woody, L. W., 223, 241
Wong, C., 354, 360
Wong, F. L., 340, 343
Wong, F. Y., 145, 146, 150, 151, 158, 159, 162,
    168, 470, 472, 478, 488
Worden, J. K., 351, 353, 355, 359
Wright, C. R., 321, 325, 467, 488
Wright, J. C., 155, 168
Wright, K., 174, 177
Wroblewski, R., 208, 214
Wu, Y. C., 42, 44, 50, 91, 100
Wyatt, R. O., 420, 427
Wyer, R. S., 55, 57–59, 68, 70, 71, 79, 80, 255,
    262, 471, 488
Wyllie, A., 173, 179

Y

Yagade, A., 44, 51
Yang, M. H., 9, 12, 501, 504
Yang, S., 81–82, 100
Yang-Ho, C., 44, 48
Yanof, D., 314

Yarsevich, J., 341, 342
Yasuna, A., 204, 212, 290, 298
Yi, Y., 55, 70, 80
Yoder, P. S., 332, 342
Yost, E. A., 54, 59, 68, 78, 227, 242
Youn, S., 89, 102
Young, B. M., 120, 135

Z

Zabrack, M. L., 470, 486
Zaccheo, M., 392, 413
Zahn, S. B., 204, 211
Zaller, J. R., 73, 80, 380,390
Zaslow, M. J., 221, 244
Zebrowitz, L. A., 84, 102
Zeitz, H., 82, 85, 90, 100

Zemach, T., 206, 208, 214
Zhang, G., 173, 179
Zhao, X., 381, 388
Zhu, J., 39, 44, 51, 54, 69, 80
Ziemke, D., 227, 240
Zillmann, D., 75, 80, 140, 144, 183–185, 188,
    189, 195, 197, 198, 216–228, 234, 235,
    237, 238, 242–244, 253, 254, 258, 262,
    268, 269, 277, 279, 283, 292, 300, 471, 488
Zimbardo, P., 84, 102
Zimicki, S., 332, 342, 354, 360
Zimmer, T. A., 407, 413
Zingale, N., 404, 411
Zolik, E., 353, 359
Zuckerman, D. M., 199, 204, 214
Zuckerman, M., 216, 219, 220, 235, 236, 238,
    239, 244
Zukin, C., 384, 386, 388

Subject Index

advertising, 56, 169, 170, 171, 174–177, 351, 430
agenda setting, 3, 5, 33, 37–40, 46, 47, 48, 473, 474
    agenda of attributes, 39
    automaton studies, 40
    Cognitive Portrait Studies, 41, 42
    Content versus exposure, 42
    mass persuasion studies, 39
    Natural History Studies, 41
aggression, 3, 128, 130, 145, 148, 149, 150, 158, 160, 161, 185, 245, 246, 274–276
bias, 426–435, 443–447
    bias in presidential elections, 436, 437
    defining bias, 431–433
    editorial endorsements, 439, 440
    partisan bias, 434, 435, 438, 439
    types of bias, 433, 434
Children and the media, 3, 119–132, 162–164, 169–171, 174–175, 201, 281–300
cognitive development, 184, 185, 201, 202
cognitive dissonance, 103–105, 108–111, 114–116
cultivation research, 3, 5, 319–321
    drip drip or frequent viewing effect, 200
distraction, 27
Ecologically embedded niches, 124, 125, 130–132
effect sizes, xiii, 17, 18
excitation transfer, 183, 184, 191, 192, 216, 253, 254, 456
framing, 3
gap hypothesis, 3
gender stereotyping, 199–202
health campaigns, 3, 327–344
hypodermic needle theory, 200
Involvement, 378–380, 415–425, 481

limited effects model, 200, 346–347
magic bullet hypothesis, 3
Media Campaigns, 327–344, 345–361, 459
    AIDS, 331
    aimed at children, 345–361
    behavior issues, 331–333
    evaluating messages, 347, 357
    family planning, 330–331
    health, 327–344
    intermediate outcomes, 333–335
    intervention characteristics, 335–340
    political, 59–61, 64, 317–318, 377–390, 392–413, 463, 475, 476
    substance abuse, 331
    target audience, 347
Media Celebrity Message Effects, 363–375, 461
Media Choice Processes, 112–114, 116
media effects, 27, 28, 31, 32, 35, 36, 104, 137–138, 142, 143, 146, 147, 163, 264–266, 271–273, 315–325, 459–461, 467–472, 482–485, 489, 492–494, 498–502
    active audience members, 139, 266
    drench or hip drip effect, 201, 202
    field research, 147–151, 159
    individual differences, 139, 265
    laboratory effects, 147–151, 159
    media consumption, 31, 32, 142
    media content, 3, 33, 265
    news and political effects, 317–318, 377–390, 392–413
    positive effects, 281–300, 476–478
    relationship with media, 33–35, 143, 265, 271–272
media ownership bias, 429–453

Media persuasion studies, 39, 363–375
  identification, 377–390, 392–413
  involvement, 364, 365, 369, 371
  issue salience, 364, 368, 369, 371
  risk-reduction behavior elicited, 365, 370, 371
  use of narrative, 364, 370, 371
Media Priming, 53–73, 254, 255, 256, 257, 480, 481
  intensity and recency, 57, 67, 71
  media violence, 58, 59, 66. 67, 71, 72
  political, 59, 60, 61, 64, 72, 73
  prime fade, 57, 58, 71
media types, 8
  broadcast, 8, 9
  print, 8
Media Use and Involvement, 363–375, 377–390, 392–413, 481
Media violence, 54, 58, 59, 71, 138, 145, 146, 149, 160–164, 215–240, 252, 478, 479
Mediated Fright, 215–240
Meta-analysis, 16–29, 36, 73–75, 98, 105, 106, 455–465, 467–488, 490–492
modeling theories, xi
music effects, 263–279, 461, 479
  MTV, 264
network models of memory, 56
news coverage, 54, 55, 56, 59–61, 317, 318, 481, 482
  campaigns, 318, 328–329
  political, 59–61, 64, 317–318
Para social Relationships, 301–312
  coaching of attitudes/affinity, 302, 305, 308
  communication apprehension, 306–307, 310
  expectancy of realism, 302,305, 306, 308
  gender/age differences, 306, 309–310
  internal locus of control, 307, 310
  interpersonal relationship formation, 303–304, 308–309
perceived realism, 127–129, 305
Pornography, 181,182
Primed Arousal, 257–260
Pro-social content and behavior, 281–285, 292, 294–298
  positive interaction, 285–286
public opinion, 328–329, 363– 375, 392–413, 415–425

Research Methodology, 3, 5–7, 10, 272, 294
  conceptualization, 348
  Cross sectional, 11, 12, 43, 46
  Integration of methods, 11
  Longitudinal, 12, 32, 43, 46, 249
  methodological diversity, 348
  Qualitative, 3, 5–7,10, 249
  Quantitative, 10, 11
Selective exposure, 104–108, 114–116, 480
sense-extension theory, 5
Sexually Explicit Media, 181–190, 193, 194, 478, 479
  attitudinal response, 186, 187
  behavioral response, 187–190
  educational possibilities, 190, 191, 193
socialization , 199, 200
Social learning theory, 3, 5, 182, 183, 191, 192, 201, 251–253, 266–267, 273–274, 458, 459
Social Scientific Enterprise , xi, 28, 29
Spiral of Silence, 415–427, 475
stereotyping, 199, 200
  sex stereotyping, 202
suspense enjoyment, 216–220, 225, 229, 234, 238, 239, 240
  age differences, 220, 233, 234, 237
  aggressive tendencies, 216, 217, 219, 231, 236
  emphatic response to characters, 216, 218, 219,229, 230, 235
  gender role socialization, 216, 220, 229, 232, 233, 237
  sensation seeking and arousal needs, 216, 217, 219, 229, 231, 235, 457
test of statistical significance, 7, 8
textbook knowledge, 494–498
theoretical issues, 3, 4, 9, 15, 140,141, 350, 456, 458
third person effect, 3, 81–86, 89, 90–98, 457, 474
  attribution theory, 83, 84
  biased optimism, 83–85
type I and type II errors, xi, 17, 247
unconstrained social interactions, 145, 150, 158
uses and gratifications research, 3, 5, 27, 34, 201, 246, 302, 321–322
violent video games, 245–262

Author Biographies

Robert Abelman (PhD, University of Texas) is Professor of Communication at Cleveland State University. His books include: *The Televiewing Audience: The Art & Science of Watching TV, Mass Communication: Issues & Perspective, Reclaiming the Wasteland: TV and Gifted Children, Television and the Exceptional Child* and *Religious Television: Controversies & Conclusions.* He has published in many journals including: *Journal of Broadcasting & Electronic Media, Critical Studies in Mass Communication, Roeper Review, Human Communication Research* and *Journal of Advertising Research.*

Mike Allen (PhD, Michigan State University) is Professor and Chair of the Department of Communication at Wisconsin-Milwaukie. His more than 150 published works deal with issues of HIV/AIDS education and prevention, drug use, persuasion, and other sources of social influence. His work has appeared in *Health Education and Behavior, Human Communication Research, Journal of Personal and Social Relationships, Law and Human Behavior,* and *Communication Education.* He is co-author of *Persuasion: Advances through Meta-analysis, Interpersonal Communication Research: Advances through Meta-analysis,* and *Classroom Communication and Instructional Processes: Advances through Meta-analysis.*

David J. Atkin (PhD, Michigan State) is a Professor of Communication at Cleveland State University and Professor in Residence in Communication at University of Connecticut. Atkin received the *Kreighbaum Under 40 Award,* recognizing the field's top junior journal scholar, in 1999 and a University of Connecticut Distinguished Scholar Award in 2000. Journalism Quarterly,

Jennings Bryant (PhD, Indiana University) is a Professor of Telecommunication and Film at the University of Alabama. He is an Associate Dean for Graduate Studies, the CIS Distinguished Research Professor and the Ronald Reagan chair of broadcasting. Author or editor of more than a dozen books, 60 book chapters, and 50 referred journal articles, Bryant's primary research interests are in entertainment theory, media effects, advanced communications technologies and systems, and media education. Bryant currently serves as co-editor of the *Journal Media Psychology*.

Nancy A. Burrell (PhD, Michigan State University) is a Professor at the University of Wisconsin-Milwaukee. Professor's Burrell's Research centers on managing conflict in family, workplace, and educational contexts. She is co-author of *Interpersonal Communication Research: Advances through Meta-analysis*, and *Classroom Communication and Instructional Processes: Advances through Meta-analysis*. She has published in *Human Communication Research, Communication Monographs*, and *Management Communication Quarterly*.

Rod Carveth (PhD, University of Massachusetts) is an Associate Professor and Chair of the Communication Arts Department at Marywood University. He is a co-author of *Media Economics: Theory and Practice*.

Mary K. Casey (PhD, Michigan State University) teaches for the University of Wisconsin-Milwaukee. Her research interest involves examination of institutional issues in health communication. Her work as appeared in *Communication Research, Journal of Health Communication*, and *Communication Research Reports*.

P. Niels Christensen (PhD, University of Texas A & M) is an Assistant Professor of Psychology at Radford University. He has published in *European Review of Social Psychology. Personality and Social Psychology Bulletin, Cognitive Behavior Therapy*, and *Psychological Science,*

R. Glenn Cummins (PhD, University of Alabama) is an Assistant Professor in the Department of Communication at Kennesaw State University. His book chapters appear in the *Encyclopedia of social issues, Encyclopedia of religion, communication and media, Handbook of sports and medicine*, and *Changing media cultures in Europe and abroad: Research on new ways of handling information and entertainment content.*

Dave D'Alessio (PhD, Michigan State University) is an Assistant Professor of Department of Communication at the University of Connecticut-Stamford. His research articles appear in *the Journal of Broadcasting and Electronic Media. Journal of Communication, Communication Yearbook, Human Communication Research, Journal of Sex Research*, and *Women and Language*.

Dan DeGooyer (PhD, University of Iowa) is an Assistant Professor in Communication at the University of North Carolina-Greensboro. His work has appeared in the *Southern Communication Journal, Small Group Research, Communication Yearbook*, and *the Journal of the Northwest Communication Association.*

Roger Desmond (PhD, The University of Iowa) is a Professor in and Director of the School of Communication at The University of Hartford. His research appeared in journals including *Human Communication Research, Applied Developmental Psychology*, and *Sex Roles.* He was awarded a fellowship in media literacy at The Annenberg School of Communication at The University of Pennsylvania and a one-year position at Eric Marder Associates in New York where he worked with C.B.S. soap operas "Guiding Light" and "As The World Turns". He has also served as a consultant to numerous media organizations regarding news, entertainment and public relations such as completing survey research for two P.B.S. TV programs for children ("Mundo Real" and "The New Voice"),

Tim Dun (PhD, University of Iowa) is an assistant professor at NE Illinois University. His work has appeared in *Journal of Social and Personal Relationships* and *Journal of Health Communication.*

Michel Dupagne (PhD, Indiana University) is an Associate Professor in Journalism at the University of Miami. His research has appeared in *Journalism and Mass Communication Quarterl y, Telecommunications Policy*, and *The Journal of Media Economics, and Feedback.* He co-authored *High-Definition Television: A Global Perspective.* He serves on the editorial board of the *Journal of Broadcasting & Electronic Media, Journalism and Mass Communication Quarterly*, and *The Journal of Media Economics.*

Tara M. Emmers-Sommer (PhD, Ohio University) is an Associate Professor and Graduate Studies Director of Communication at University of Arizona. Professor Emmers-Sommer's research is published in outlets such as the *Journal of Social and Personal Relationships, Personal Relationships, Journal of Communication, Human Communication Research, Communication Yearbook, Journal of Sex Research, Journal of Health Communication, Western Journal of Communication*, and *Communication Studies.* She is a co-author of two scholarly books, *Sex and gender differences in personal relationships: Toward an activity-based perspective* and *Safer sex in personal relationships: The role of sexual scripts in HIV infection and prevention.*

Barbara Mae Gayle (PhD, University of Oregon) is Professor and Vice President of Academic Affairs at Saint Martin's University. She is a 2001–2002 Carnegie Scholar and co-author of *Interpersonal Communication Research: Advances through Meta-analysis*, and *Classroom Communication and Instructional Processes: Advances through Meta-analysis.* She is published in *Women's*

Studies in Communication, Management Communication Quarterly, Journal of Applied Communication, and *Communication Education.*

Salma Ghanem (PhD, University of Texas at Austin) is an Associate Professor and Chair of the Department of Communication at the University of Texas-Pan American. She is an expert on media issues, political communication, and the Middle East. Her chapters are published in books such as: *Communication and Democracy,* ???

Peter B. Gregg (MA, University of Minnesota) is a lecturer in the Department of Communication Studies at the University of Minnesota. His work has been presented at the National Communication Association.

Cynthia Hoffner (PhD, University of Wisconsin, Madison) is an Associate Professor of Communication at the Georgia State University. Her research appears in *Media Psychology, Journal of Communication, Communication Research, Human Communication Research, Journal of Broadcasting and Electronic Media, Motivation and Emotion, Communication Research Reports, Communication Monographs, Journal of Career Development, Journal of Child Language, Child Development, Child Study Journal, Journal of Applied Developmental Psychology,* and *Developmental Psychology.*

Barry A. Hollander is a Professor in the Grady College at the University of Georgia.

Jill Jorgenson (MA, University of Wisconsin-Milwaukee) was a graduate student and instructor at UW-Milwaukee.

Sang Yeon Kim (MA, University of Wisconsin-Milwaukee) is a graduate student at the Michigan State University specializing in intercultural communication.

Mark R. Klinger (PhD, University of Washington) is an Associate Professor of Psychology at the University of Alabama. He has published in *American Journal of Psychology, Journal of Experimental Psychology: Learning, Memory, and Cognition, Journal of Autism and Developmental Disorders,* and *Contemporary Psychology.*

Michael R. Kramer (PhD, University of Minnesota) is an Assistant Professor at St. Mary's College.

Jae Kwon was a doctoral student at the University of Alabama.

Tae-Seop Lim (PhD, Michigan State University) is a Professor of Communication at the University of Wisconsin-Milwaukee. Dr Lim's research focuses on face and facework across cultures; characterization of culture as an explanatory scheme; speech and verbal behavior in Asia; intergenerational communication; media language. His research has appeared in the *Journal of Cross-cultural Gerontology, Human Communication Research*, the *Journal of Multilingual and Multicultural Development*, and the *Korean Journal of Communication Studies*.

Carolyn A. Lin (PhD, Michigan State University) is a Professor in the Department of Communication Science at University of Connecticut. She is a co-author of the forthcoming book: *Communication technology and social change: Theory, effects and applications. Her research appears in Health Communication, CyberPsychology and Behavior, Journal of Broadcasting & Electronic Media, Media Psychology*, and *Communication Theory*.

Kenneth J. Levine (PhD, Michigan State) is an Assistant Professor in the School of Communication Studies at the University of Tennessee.

Marie-Louise Mares (PhD, University of Wisconsin-Madison) is an Assistant Professor in the Department of Communication Arts at the University of Wisconsin-Madison. She is interested in life-span developmental changes in the effects of mass media content. Her research appears in the Journal of Communication, Communication Monographs

Dorina Miron (PhD, University of Alabama) is a Senior Research Fellow in the Institute for Communication and Information at the University of Alabama. Her work appears in the *Journal of Communication* and in the book *A Companion to Media Studies*.

Norbert Mundorf (PhD, Indiana University) is a Professor of Speech Communication at the University of Rhode Island. His research deals with the entertainment function of the media, factors influencing the recall of mediated messages, personality and media use, user acceptance of screen based information services as well as changes in European telecommunications systems. Dr. Mundorf's research has been published in various advertising journals, such as *Journal of Advertising, Journal of Personality and Social Psychology, Gazette (The Netherlands), Publizistik (Germany), The Gerontologist, Communication Research, Journal of Broadcasting and Electronic Media, Sex Roles* and *Humor*. His book chapters focus on information technology, international communication via the Internet, and Internet security, including an analysis of the Top 100 German industrial websites.

Robin I. Nabi (PhD, Annenberg School for Communication, University of Pennsylvania) is an Associate Professor of Communication at the University of California, Santa Barbara. Her work has appeared in several journals, including *Communication Theory, Communication Research, Communication Monographs,*

Journal of Communication, Media Psychology, and *Cognition and Emotion.* Prof. Nabi has also served or is serving on the editorial boards of several journals, including *Human Communication Research, Communication Monographs,* and *Journal of Communication.* She was a co-editor of a special issue of *Communication Theory* focused on conceptualizing media enjoyment.

Patrice A. Oppliger (PhD, University of Alabama) is an Assistant Professor of Communication at La Salle University. Her research interests lie in gender studies, humor, and media effects. She publishes in communication and humor journals, writes book chapters, and presents at national and international conferences. Dr. Oppliger recently published a book on the effects and appeal of professional wrestling titled *Wrestling and Hyper-Masculinity.*

Lisa Mullikin Parcell (PhD, University of Alabama) is an Assistant Professor in the Elliot School of Communication and the Associate Director of WSU-LINK at Wichita State University. Her publications include the book: *American Journalism: History, Principles, Practices* and several book chapters. Her main research interests include news writing style, newspaper history, civic journalism, and community engagement. As the Associate Director of WSU-LINK, she helps to form mutually beneficial partnerships between WSU and the community.

Bryant Paul teaches at Indiana University

Raymond W. Preiss (PhD, University of Oregon) is a Professor of Communication Studies at the University of Puget Sound. He is co-author of *Persuasion: Advances through Meta-analysis, Interpersonal Communication Research: Advances through Meta-analysis,* and *Classroom Communication and Instructional Processes: Advances through Meta-analysis.* His work has appeared in *Human Communication Research, Communication Quarterly, Management Communication Quarterly,* and *Communication Research Reports.*

Beverly Roskos-Ewoldsen (PhD, Indiana University) is an Associate Professor of Psychology at the University of Alabama. She has published chapters in such books as: *The psychology of entertainment media: Blurring the lines between entertainment and persuasion* and *Media effects in theory and research* and her research appears in journals such as the *American Journal on Mental Retardation, Brain and Cognition, Teaching of Psychology, Journal of Environmental Psychology, Psychological Research-Psychologische Forshung, Journal of Mental Imagery, Journal of Experimental Psychology,* and *Communications.*

David R. Roskos-Ewoldsen (PhD, Indiana University) is a Professor of Psychology at the University of Alabama. His research has appeared in journals such as *Communication Monographs, Communications, Journal of Experimental*

Social Psychology, Basic and Applied Social Psychology, Cognition and Emotion, and *Human Communication Research.* His book chapters have appeared in *Persuasion: Developments in theory and practice, Blurring the Lines Between Entertainment and Persuasion: The Psychology of Entertainment Media, Media effects in theory and research, Communication Yearbook,* and *Communication and emotion: Essays in honor of Dolf Zillmann.*

Daniel J. Ryan (PhD, Texas A&M University) is a trial jury consultant.

Erin Sahlstein (PhD, University of Iowa) is an Assistant Professor of Interpersonal Communication in the Department of Rhetoric and Communication Studies at the University of Richmond. Dr. Sahlstein's articles appear in *Communication Reports, Journal of Social and Personal Relationship,* and *Journal of Health Communication* and book chapters appear in *Interpersonal Communication Research: Advances through meta-analysis, Maintenance enhancement,* and *Handbook of Language and social behavior.*

Michael B. Salwen (PhD, Michigan State University) is a Professor of Journalism at University of Miami. Dr. Salwen is the author/co-author of more than 65 journal articles in many of the leading journalism and mass communication journals on mass communication effects, public opinion and international communication. He has also published several books such as: *Online News and the Public, An Integrated Approach to Communication Theory and Research,* and *Latin American Journalism.* He serves on the advisory board of *Communication Research* and as an associate editor of *Journalism & Mass Communication Quarterly,* the foremost academic journal in journalism and mass communication.

Edward Schiappa (PhD, Northwestern University) holds the Paul W. Frenzel Chair of Liberal Arts and is the Chair of the Department of Communication Studies at the University of Minnesota. His research has appeared in such journals as *Philosophy & Rhetoric, Quarterly Journal of Speech, Rhetoric Review, Argumentation, Communication Monographs,* and *Communication Theory.* Dr. Schiappa has published five books: *The Beginnings of Rhetorical Theory in Classical Greece, Protagoras and Logos, A Study in Greek Philosophy and Rhetoric, Squeeze Play: The Campaign for a New Twins Stadium, Landmark Essays on Classical Greek Rhetoric,* and *Warranting Assent: Case Studies in Argument Evaluation.*

John L. Sherry (PhD, Michigan State University) is an Assistant Professor of the Department of Communication at Michigan State University. His research appears in journals such as *Communication Reports, Communication Research, Media Psychology, Communication Theory, Communication Monographs, International Journal of Advertising, Journal of International Communication,* and *Journal of Broadcasting and Electronic Media.* He also has book chapters in *The*

Internet Encyclopedia. And *Talking Up a Storm: The Social Impact of Daytime Talk Shows.*

Leslie B. Snyder (PhD, Stanford University) is an Associate Professor in the Department of Communication Science at the University of Connecticut. Her research has appeared in books such as *Public health communication: Evidence for behavior change* and *Handbook of International and Intercultural Communication* and in journals such as *Journal of Health Communication, Journal of Alcohol Studies, Health Communication,* and *AIDS Education and Prevention: An International Journal.* Dr. Snyder has a large federal grant (NIAAA) to study the effect of advertising exposure on youth alcohol consumption and is studying the effectiveness of family planning and reproductive health campaigns in less developed countries, funded by Johns Hopkins University's Center for Communication Programs.

Lindsay Timmerman (PhD, University of Texas-Austin) is an Assistant Professor in Communication at the University of Wisconsin-Milwaukee. Her research has appeared in the *Handbook of communication and social interaction skills, Interpersonal Communication: Advances Through Meta-Analysis, Communication Monographs,* and *Communication Quarterly.*

Amy Elisabeth Wagner University of Iowa

Wayne Wanta (PhD, University of Texas) is a Professor of Journalism and Executive Director of the Center for the Digital Globe at the University of Missouri. He has been an active researcher in political communication, media effects, visual communication, sports journalism, Internet use and effects, and negative political advertising. He has authored one scholarly book, seven book chapters, more than 40 journal articles and more than 60 conference papers. He was elected vice president of AEJMC and will become president of the organization in 2007.

Alaina Winters was a doctoral student at the University of Iowa.

Wendy Wood (PhD, University of Massachusetts, Amherst) is a James B. Duke Professor in Psychology, Marketing, Director of Social Psychology and Co-Director, Social Science Research Institute at Duke University. Her research interests are in the areas of sex differences and attitudes and behavior. Her work has appeared in numerous books and journals such as the *Journal of Personality and Social Psychology, American Psychologist, Annual Review of Psychology,* and *Psychological Bulletin.* She is co-author of the book, *Group process and productivity: The Texas A&M Symposium on Group Dynamics.*